TEACHING THE LANGUAGE ARTS

EXPANDING THINKING THROUGH STUDENT-CENTERED INSTRUCTION

Third Edition

Cathy Collins Block

Texas Christian University

ALLYN AND BACON

Boston London Toronto Sydney Tokyo Singapore

Dedicated to my loving, devoted, and continually supportive husband, Stan Block; my wonderful family, JoAnn Zinke, Wanda Zinke, Michael Donegan, Donna and Jordan Cowman, Michelle, Regie, and Paige Goldsmith, Randy Block, Rosalyn and Maury Wolfson; and John Mangieri, whose faith, courage, and wisdom helps me help others.

Series Editor: Arnis E. Burvikovs
Editorial Assistant: Patrice Mailloux
Senior Marketing Manager: Brad Parkins
Cover Administrator: Linda Knowles
Production Editor: Christopher H. Rawlings

Editorial-Production Service: Omegatype Typography, Inc.
Photo Research: Marissa Falco and Katharine Cook
Composition and Prepress Buyer: Linda Cox
Manufacturing Buyer: Julie McNeill
Electronic Composition: Omegatype Typography, Inc.

Between the time Website information is gathered and published, some sites may have closed. Also, the transcription of URLs can result in typographical errors. The publisher would appreciate notification where these occur so that they may be corrected in subsequent editions. Thank you.

Many of the designations used by manufacturers and sellers to distinguish their products are claimed as trademarks. Where those designations appear in this book, and Allyn and Bacon was aware of a trademark claim, the designations have been printed in initial or all caps.

Library of Congress Cataloging-in-Publication Data
Block, Cathy Collins.
    Teaching the language arts: expanding thinking through student-centered instruction/ Cathy Collins Block.—3rd ed.
        p. cm.
    Including bibliographical references.
    ISBN 0-205-30924-0 (alk. paper)
        1. Language arts. I. Title.
LB1576 .B499 2001
428'.0071—dc21   00-059417

Photo Credits: Will Faller, pp. xii, 65, 68, 155, 286, 372, 380, 428, 436, 460; Robert Harbison, 46, 117; Will Hart, pp. 37, 74, 90, 138, 190, 240, 332, 414, 500, 546, 574; Stephen Marks, pp. 119, 600

Printed in the United States of America

10 9 8 7 6 5 4 3 2 1   05 04 03 02 01 00

CONTENTS

PREFACE

Teaching the Language Arts, Third Edition, is designed as the major textbook for teaching language arts methods and reading/language arts block courses at the undergraduate and graduate levels. The goal of the third edition is to provide research-based knowledge of educational philosophies and instructional strategies to preservice, inservice, and graduate students. This knowledge can then be used to create exemplary language arts and reading programs for students in preschool through eighth grade. This book constructs bridges between research and practice.

Both preservice and inservice teachers can find unique professional support in this textbook. Preservice teachers can discover how 14 exemplary language arts classrooms teach reading and language arts to preschool through middle school students. As these classroom programs unfold, they can discover the language development continuum, and learn instructional, technological, and assessment strategies that have proven to be highly effective in advancing students' language abilities. This textbook can enhance inservice teachers' language arts programs with the most recent research findings and innovative activities of award-winning educators.

ORGANIZATION OF THE THIRD EDITION

Each chapter is divided into three sections. **Section 1: Theoretical Foundations** describes the research and philosophies that guide developments in, and instruction of, the language arts. In every chapter, these sections open with a scenario taken from an award-winning classroom that represents the language arts curriculum at a particular grade level from daycare through middle school. The same four children, Juan, Michael, Allison, and Meisong, are present in every class so that the differences in their language arts development can be tracked throughout their preschool, elementary, and middle school years. In addition, Section 1 describes how numerous national standards from the International Reading Association, National Council of Teachers of English, and National Association for the Education of Young Children can become the foundation of language arts instruction.

Section 2: Putting Theory into Practice describes how the basic principles and research in Section 1 can be incorporated into a language arts, student-centered classroom. This section also illustrates how communication abilities can be developed through minilessons, workshops, learning centers, technological support, and thematic units. After presenting many learning experiences, Section 2 also highlights several needs in language arts programs with unique features such as the following:

- How to use children's literature to increase students' competencies in language arts. More than 5,000 of the most recently written and highly acclaimed selections of quality children's literature are featured in 40 separate Literature Cards that can advance students' language competencies in numerous, innovative ways

[handwritten margin notes: "4 children", "National Standards", "Applies sect 1"]

- How to add resources to the daily language arts program that address individual students' special language arts needs
- How to include and enhance student voices, choices, challenges, and cultures to advance every class member's learning
- How to use numerous assessment tools to discover student strengths and weaknesses
- How to obtain and implement award-winning technological teaching aids for speaking, listening, reading, writing, viewing, and thinking

Section 3: Teachers as Continual Learners contains several discussions that increase teaching competencies for the topic being discussed in that chapter. This section opens with a Professional Development Activity designed to develop your professional skill to increase students' language arts abilities. For Your Journal enables you to keep a professional journal as you read this textbook, and introduces 14 types of journals that can increase students' communication abilities. The entries you create can be used as examples when you introduce each type to your students. Connecting Classrooms, Parents, and Communities describes methods by which you can build strong bridges between home and school experiences for your students. Methods by which community agencies can add resources to your language arts program are also presented. How to Do It: Using What You've Learned enables you to assess how much you have learned in each chapter. Key Terms lists important concepts so you can assess whether you have learned these definitions in a first reading. For Future Reference concludes each chapter by providing books, articles, and teaching aids that can be used as reference materials for yourself, colleagues, students, parents, and community members.

NEW FEATURES IN THE THIRD EDITION

Teaching the Language Arts, Third Edition, has several new features to make learning more enjoyable and permanent. Among these are

- a new chapter and discussions within each chapter on reading and writing so that three full chapters address new research on reading instruction and three full chapters address new discoveries concerning writing development
- expanded coverage of instructional strategies for phonemic awareness, phonics, listening development, visual analysis, critical viewing abilities, and multicultural understanding
- more than 500 key terms introduced and assessed, and more than 80 end-of-chapter activities to increase your ability to apply what you learn
- scenarios of how language develops from age 1 through age 14 in the lives of children from four distinct multicultural perspectives
- numerous activities in each chapter that illustrate how to use specific selections of children's literature and leveled books in daily instruction (these activities are marked by special icons and are reproduced in scenarios that actually took place in award-winning language arts programs)

- two full chapters on how to integrate drama, viewing analysis skills, creativity, and higher-level thinking development activities into the language arts and content area disciplines
- a full chapter on most recent assessment practices, instruments, and performances that grade and evaluate students' language arts abilities
- seven thematic units prepared for instruction and seven discussions of recent technological advancements that can be implemented in your language arts program
- a website designed specifically to accompany this textbook that contains instructional forms, teaching aids, resources, and additional websites to add to your language arts program

INSTRUCTOR RESOURCES

Accompanying this textbook is an updated Instructors' Resource Manual/Test Bank and a multisite web-linked web page. The Instructors' Manual/Test Bank is a 120-page resource kit that includes 500 multiple-choice, true/false, fill-in-the-blank, and essay questions, and more than 50 pages of teaching aids, black lines, and overhead projector masters for classroom instruction. The web page contains more than 200 multilinked resources organized by chapters of the text and additional pages of information and resources to enhance your language arts program.

ACKNOWLEDGMENTS

Many people contributed to this book. My mother assisted me with many aspects of its publication. My students provided the inspiration and award-winning educators contributed numerous ideas. To each of these people, I extend my deepest gratitude.

I extend my sincere appreciation to the outstanding professionals at Allyn and Bacon. Arnis Burvikovs, my editor and friend, supported me in every way. Judy Fiske and the team at Omegatype Typography gave many hours and much expertise to increase the quality of this book. I am also grateful to the following reviewers who spent hours offering advice and suggestions that improved the book immensely: Dr. Elaine V. Batenhorst, University of Nebraska at Kearney; Richard C. Pearson, Idaho State University; and Rosemary F. Schiavi, Brescia University.

The curiosity to learn, and especially to learn the language arts, begins before age 3.
Students need their teachers' and parents' guidance to discover the power of language arts.

CHAPTER 1

LEARNING LANGUAGE
AND THE LANGUAGE ARTS

The curiosity to learn, and especially to learn the language arts, begins before age 3. At the daycare level, students need the guidance of their teachers and parents to discover the power of language arts. Ms. Johnson's daycare provides such guidance. One day, as school began, Juan stared at his mother's car as it pulled out of the parking lot. "Come back!" he cried as his eyes filled with tears. Ms. Johnson hugged Juan and asked why he was so sad. "Mommy forgot to kiss me goodbye." Ms. Johnson empathized, "I understand. Do you want to write a letter to tell her why you are sad, and to remind her to kiss you goodbye tomorrow?" "Yes," Juan said as his eyes filled with hope. He took Ms. Johnson's hand and walked to the Writing Center. He dictated as Ms. Johnson wrote his message: "Dear Mommy, I cried today when you left because you didn't kiss me goodbye. Please don't forget again. It makes me too sad. My head stays with you and not at my daycare. I love you." Next, Ms. Johnson guided his hand to sign his name and write "Mommy" on the envelope. Then, Juan took it to the plastic bags that hung on the chalkboard ledge. He looked carefully at each name to make sure he had the one that said "Juan" and not "Juanita." When he was certain, he confidently dropped the letter in his bag so he could take it home at the end of the day. With a smile on his face, he skipped outside to play with Meisong, Allison, Michael, and his other daycare friends.[1]

Throughout this book you will learn other ways to assist students from birth through middle school to master the language arts. In the process you will discover how language enables students to expand their world and unlock its mysteries.

Every chapter in this book is divided into three sections. The first section, Theoretical Foundations, describes the research-based theories, philosophies, and principles that guide language learning. You will develop competencies documented

---

[1]Adapted from an event that actually occurred at the University of Delaware Laboratory Preschool, as reported by Jane Davidson in *Emergent Literacy and Dramatic Play in Early Education* (1996).

in scientific studies cited in the National Council of Teachers of English and the International Reading Association's *Standards for the English Language Arts* (1996) and *Standards for Reading Professionals, Revised* (1998). You will also learn developmentally appropriate practices recommended by the National Association for the Education of Young Children (NAEYC) and numerous state and provincial curriculum guidelines. After reading all 14 chapters, you will have gained knowledge about 105 standards on which to base exemplary instruction for teaching language arts.

The second section of each chapter, Putting Theory into Practice, describes how theory can be put into practice in your classroom. These discussions can help you to (a) increase your knowledge about specific, exemplary instructional and assessment methods; (b) learn how to meet individual student needs; and (c) develop strategies that enhance the cultural richness in your classroom. The third section, Teachers as Continual Learners, provides information and methods that expand your teaching skills in specific areas of students' language arts development. In this section you can engage in professional development activities, journal writing experiences, opportunities to connect classrooms to parents and communities, and practices that develop your technological literacy.

By the end of the first chapter, you will have answers to the following questions about the standards for exemplary instruction established by the International Reading Association (IRA), the National Council of Teachers of English (NCTE), the National Association for the Education of Young Children (NAEYC), and Texas Essential Knowledge and Skills Curriculum (TEKS), as well as other statewide and provincially governed educational agencies:

1. How do children learn language and language arts?

2. What research-based practices and principles guide successful language arts programs?

3. What characterizes highly effective language arts teachers?

4. What are the physical, perceptual, emotional, social, cultural, environmental, and cognitive influences on learning language?

5. What is the interrelationship of language, the language arts, higher-level thinking, visual representation, and technological competencies?

6. Who are the past and present literacy researchers and what are their contributions to our understanding of how children read, write, speak, and listen?

7. Why do students need to read a wide range of literature from many genres to understand the philosophical, ethical, and aesthetic dimensions of our human experience?

8. How can students learn how to use many strategies to comprehend, evaluate, and appreciate language and literacy? How can you support their understanding of life as they draw on prior experiences, interactions with other readers and writers, and commonly shared responses to classical as well as contemporary children's and young adults' literature?

● ●

SECTION 1   THEORETICAL FOUNDATIONS

Learning the Language Arts

> *"The beginning is the most important part of the work."*   —Plato, THE REPUBLIC

You may have been apprehensive when you began to read this textbook. It is an enormous responsibility to help students communicate more effectively. How can you meet all students' needs? Should students choose what they want to learn? How can 25 students do so at once? How can you help those who can't express their needs well? What do you do when students do not make wise choices or don't learn from your lessons? Are the best language arts teachers charismatic leaders who rally their students? If so, how do they teach their students to motivate themselves if the charisma of others does not ignite their interests? Is your major responsibility to implement content objectives or to assist students to blossom into unique individuals, or both? Which assessments best indicate that students are achieving at their highest levels of capability?

Moreover, you may be confused by terms that are used in language arts instruction, such as student voice, phonemic awareness, KWLs, thinking guides, virtual learning realities, Venn diagrams, discovery discussions, writing workshops, and LEAs. These strategies may not have been used when you were in elementary schools. They have been created so that students can assume a more active role in planning, implementing, and assessing their own language arts learning. Such strategies are based on research that demonstrates the advantages of instruction that relates to students' immediate language needs and to the lives they live outside of school (Block, 1999; Piaget, 1966; Vygotsky, 1978; Bruner, 1995). To answer the questions raised previously and to master the strategies above, it is helpful to begin by learning the definitions of basic terms in language arts instruction.

BASIC TERMS

The term **language arts** consists of two equally important concepts. **Language** is a structured system of rules that enable two or more people to understand the meaning of words, phrases, and ideas. Arts refers to the acquired skills, talents, knowledge, and imagination needed to produce meaningful communications. **Language arts instruction** involves the study of the systems and structures of language and language conventions (including grammar, punctuation, spelling, and handwriting). According to the *Standards for the English Language Arts* (NCTE & IRA, 1996), language arts instruction should produce competency in speaking, listening, reading, writing, technology, visual representation, higher-level thinking processes, observing, viewing, and creative expression and should fulfill each individual's lifelong needs for (1) learning, (2) enjoyment, (3) persuasion, (4) creation, and (5) sharing new knowledge.

Oral language skills are effective when others can clearly understand and contemplate a person's thoughts when they are communicated through speech. **Listening**

(as opposed to hearing) is a conscious effort to hear, attend to, comprehend, and respond effectively to human and technological voices. **Reading** is interpreting the meaning of written language by analyzing the significance of the ideas in printed words and by incorporating them into one's life. **Writing** is the ability to compose thoughts in print so people can receive new ideas and information. **Higher-level thinking** is the ability to organize language; to explain ideas; to conceive, analyze, and infer meaning; and to resolve discrepancies in information. **Observing** or **viewing** is the ability to gain meaning from nonlanguage stimuli by interpreting body language, gestures, and movements; by interacting with technological media (such as films, multimedia disks, cinematography); and by appreciating many forms of artistic expression. **Technological literacy** is the ability to use technology to communicate effectively and to learn new technologically driven communication tools soon after they are created.

To use all of these language arts, students must learn to translate their thoughts into rules and conventions that govern a specific language, such as English. These systems can be assembled into four groups. The first is **phonology,** the study of speech sounds. For students to become highly effective speakers, they must make appropriate vocalization with the mouth, lips, and tongue so that individual phonemes can be distinguished by themselves and others. **Phonemes** are defined as a class or family of closely related speech sounds (phones) that signify single sounds. They are represented in phonetic transcription by one symbol within slashes, even though the sound of the phoneme (for example, /r/ in *bring, red,* and *route*) may be altered slightly by the modifying influences of the adjacent sounds in each word. Thus, /r/ is written as *r,* the letter that represents all the slight variations associated with one common sound that we hear when we say the printed words above. Discerning phonetic differences, or **phonemic awareness,** is an important skill for developing oral and written language ability. Starting to develop this ability at the preschool stage better ensures that students will not experience difficulties in acquiring effective oral and written language abilities when they enter school. To make distinctions between phonemes, children must recognize that /r/ and /b/ are different sounds, and that /r/ can sound slightly modified in individual words because of the influences of adjacent sounds in those words. These modifications, however, do not forfeit the place of /r/ as a distinct phone in the phonemic classification of sounds in the **International Phonetic Alphabet (IPA).** IPA is the alphabet that records every possible sound that is produced in human languages.

Hand in hand with phonemic awareness is the need to build students' phonic knowledge. **Phonics** is the study of rules that govern how spoken sounds are written. For example, in English it is necessary not only for children to learn that /r/ and /b/ are different sounds (that can be altered slightly through dialectical differences), but also for children to learn that /r/ can be written as the letter *r.* At a higher level, students must also learn the phonetic rule that *p* in *phone* is not /p/ and that both the *b*'s in *bomb* are not /b/. Instead, the phonics system that governs English allows *ph* to spell /f/ and *mb* at the end of words to spell /m/. Thus, when 2- and 3-year-old children begin to express interest in, and an aptitude for, learning language, it is important that you answer their questions about the phonemic and phonic rules of English. Such instruction is a necessary prerequisite to their future success and pleasure in learning to read. In addition, because English has such a complex rule-based system, many new words and ideas from other languages can become a part of our language. We are fortunate. If English were not built on such a comprehensive foundation, it could not accommodate the addition of new concepts every year, and our abilities to communicate vivid ideas would be curtailed.

At the same time that students learn phonemic and phonic systems, they must learn that English is guided by morphological rules. **Morphology** is the study of how words and word parts, such as prefixes, suffixes, and root/base words, convey meaning. For example, students need to learn that *thanksgiving* can be divided into three morphemes (i.e., *thanks, giv,* and *ing*) that convey three distinct meanings. When these meanings are combined, the word *thanksgiving* can be decoded to mean "in the process of giving thanks." Alternatively, students must realize that if they divide *thanksgiving* without attending to English morphological rules, it would not be profitable (e.g., *than + ksgiv + in + g*). Even though *than* and *in* are English words, they do not serve as morphemes in the word *thanksgiving* because they do not combine to make a meaning, but merely serve as single letters inside the larger morphemes, which are the meaning-bearing units of this word.

In addition, morphological rules apply to the order in which words can appear in print and are combined in coherent speech. The set of morphological principles that govern how words are ordered and combined to form sentences is called **syntax. Grammar** is the set of overarching principles that establish the structure of morphemes within words and the arrangement of words that occurs within spoken or written words, phrases, sentences, and paragraphs. **Semantics** is a branch of grammar concerned with how meaning is conveyed through spoken and written language. Knowledge of semantic rules is applied when students try to choose specific words (from a domain of synonyms) to create an exact image in readers' minds, or when they use other words in the context of a sentence to figure out the meaning of a word they do not know. Through effective instructional techniques, students can advance their abilities in all these rule-based language systems.

HOW CHILDREN LEARN LANGUAGE

It is an exciting time to be an educator. With 6,000 scientific reports published daily, our understanding of how students learn language is mushrooming. As these works accumulate, it becomes increasingly clear that students must *construct* their own meanings to comprehend (constructivist theory of language learning), must *integrate language systems* in multiple ways when immersed in language-rich classrooms (psycholinguistic theory), and must *interpret* language in the context of social interactions in classroom communities (sociolinguistic theory).

CONSTRUCTIVIST THEORY

Constructivist theory is based on research that has demonstrated that meaning is created through the unique interaction of print and speech with individual minds (Udall & Daniels, 1991; Dyson, 1999). As students try to understand language, their individual cognitive processes and personal feelings influence their interpretations of meaning. Thus, each printed and spoken message elicits different and special responses depending on how students choose to (or have been taught to) interpret that message. Moreover, through constructivist research, we now know that when curriculum studied in the classroom is tied to what students are learning outside of school (and the problems solved in school are those that students are likely to face after school), language development occurs more rapidly. Therefore, in classrooms that adhere to constructivist theory, students learn how to impose their prior knowledge of language systems to give meaning to new information. You can assist them by drawing analogies and suggesting metaphors based on what students know to help them connect to what they do not understand. For example, when Ms. Johnson read the book *Alpha Beta Chowder* (Steig, 1995), her daycare students asked whether the letter they saw on each consecutive page was the same letter that began their own names. Stopping to discuss these questions as she read assisted them in learning the meaning of letters. Learning the alphabet gained meaning for Ms. Johnson's students by being tied to a personally meaningful object in their lives, their own name.

Aristotle was the first to propose that the depth of students' thinking determined the types of language they could use (Anderson, 1985). This interdependence between thinking and language is made vivid by Helen Keller's words:

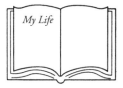

My Life

> As the cool stream gushed over my hand, Ann Sullivan finger spelled into my other hand the word "water," first slowly, then rapidly. I stood still, my whole attention fixed upon the motions of her fingers. Suddenly I felt a misty consciousness as of something forgotten——a thrill of returning thought; and somehow the mystery of language was revealed to me. I realized then that water meant the wonderful cool something that was flowing over my hand. That living word awakened my soul, gave it light, hope, joy, set it free . . . I left the well-house eager to learn. Everything had a name and each name gave birth to a new thought. (1955, p. 36)

Similarly, as students learn how to read, write, speak, and listen, they effectively transform ephemeral thoughts into principles that increase meaning and pleasure in their lives. This transformation occurs because single ideas enter the mind as cognitive entries. They seek to bond with collective categories of previous but similar thoughts. These categories of enmeshed thoughts are subsequently stored as a dense cognitive structure called **schema.** Each time learning occurs, schema expand the collection of knowledge, experiences, emotions, and values one has had about a topic. Exposed nerve endings of schema in the brain increase in length and breadth, and eventually more and more dendrites (branches from nerve endings) are forced to intertwine (Jensen, 1998; Smith, 1978).

These connections grow more efficiently if early childhood instruction incorporates real-world examples because schemata collections of topical knowledge are like file folders, which expand to create greater wisdom when new experiences are repeatedly deposited in them. Your class can enable students to experience a mountain through a book and again on a field trip so that the multiple emotions, thoughts, and images relative to that experience are stored in their mountain schema, which helps them learn that concept more completely. For example, in a moment I will ask you to read a word and to pay attention to the schema that word activates when it enters your mind. You will know which folder is opened by the visual images of the memories the word brings to mind. Ready? What image comes to mind when you read the word *crane*? If you have observed construction sites more frequently than water birds, you likely activated the more strongly reinforced memory of a piece of yellow construction equipment. Conversely, if you have experienced the graceful movements of long-necked water birds more frequently than construction sites, you likely imagined a white crane.

The importance of building all students' schema and background experiences cannot be overemphasized, as shown in the following example. Juan, Michael, Allison, and Meisong had never seen anything but small house pets for their schema of cats. Ms. Johnson wanted to enhance her daycare children's schemas, so she scheduled a field trip to the zoo. While they were there, Juan asked why the leopards, tigers, and lions were all together. Ms. Johnson used this opportunity to explain the connections between these larger felines and their smaller cousins, house cats. This experience expanded these children's schema of cats. Subsequently, whenever she read books about any feline, her students' minds ignited experiential and emotive responses to many types of cats in the cats schema folder so their understanding of the topic was more complete. Thus, if you do not consistently ignite students' thinking, writing, reading, speaking, and listening schemas, you repeatedly limit their knowledge (Collins, 1991). As Gardner and Hatcher (1990) state, we must assist students to "become adroit manipulators of language, logical forms, computer programs, and other symbol systems that, in effect, can serve as vehicles for thought" (p. 48).

Research has also demonstrated that even preschoolers come to school with well-established schema about life and language. Our job is to refine inaccurate ideas, embellish schema that are underdeveloped, and teach new concepts. Rigg and Allen (1989) report that learning

> is not simply a matter of having taken something in and mapping it onto our old self; [our] new thinking [about language and learning] is to relate [new learning] to everything else we have, in an individual way. Indeed, each aspect of learning is unique because of previous schema we possess; those schema predispose us to see the world in a certain way, and they also provide the boundaries, so to speak, of where [our] learning will fit.

Leaders in this research are Bruner (1986), Kozulin (1990), and Vygotsky (1978). Vygotsky theorized that thinking is shaped through the use of specific words. If you teach language arts from this perspective, you can develop thinking simultaneously with language. Such instruction assists students to translate ideas, feelings, and experiences into words. At the same time, the accuracy and specificity of this translation will increase the depth and precision of students' thinking. For example, when students are asked to state their thoughts aloud (or exercise a language art), they may realize that their thinking is not clear. As a result, they may add a novel example to state their point more clearly. In the process they will likely evolve a deeper sense of the concept for themselves as well as others. Similarly, when students have to write to convince their classmates, they often provide the reasons for their thinking, which is often not fully developed in their own minds until they are required to write it. Likewise, when classmates misunderstand a peer's argument, the peer may think through it again, which improves his or her thinking. In summary, Vygotsky's ideas on the origins of language and thought is that when students use both simultaneously, new ideas are more rapidly internalized and more truly become one's own (Forman & Cazden, 1995).

Also, according to constructivist theory, learning occurs most rapidly as a result of **disequilibrium** (a schema is absent, or a new event disrupts an existing schema—Piaget, 1969). When disequilibrium occurs, students **learn** (develop new knowledge, expand prior understandings, or apply learning tools) to reach a state of **equilibrium** (a sense of mastery is restored). Without a highly capable teacher, however, many students retreat from the confusion and frustration that disequilibrium produces. Many also resist language learning. Fortunately, when teaching relates new knowledge to previous schema, students can enter language situations with greater competence and more easily reach a state of equilibrium. Knowledge can be transmitted by speaking, listening, reading, writing, viewing, thinking, observing, and learning language, and deep understanding can be constructed through students' guided applications of language to their thoughts.

Moreover, contrary to the myth that thinking and reasoning abilities naturally escalate as people mature, critical and creative thinking abilities *do not* develop automatically. Adults who were not taught to think critically and creatively exhibit cognitive abilities that are no more advanced than the thinking processes they used when they were in sixth grade (Gardner & Hatch, 1989; Knapp, 1998).

Another reason to build students' cognitive and language competence is related to a deficiency in contemporary society. Prior to the twentieth century, after-school apprenticeships increased students' analytical reasoning abilities. Every day children worked with adults. They observed and questioned their mentors as they made decisions concerning work and world events, which they experienced side by side. In addition, students were active partners in conversations and asked questions about the stories their parents and grandparents told and read by the fireplace. These adults often explained the thought processes they used that led to their wisdom. Through the activities in this textbook, you can recreate such thinking and language opportunities for today's students (Block & Mangieri, 2000).

Third, knowledge in our world increases 15 percent per year; many jobs our students will hold in the near future have not yet been invented; and our present information about technology will represent less than 10 percent of that which today's preschoolers will need when they become adults (Duffy, 1992). Therefore, although much of the content in language arts can become obsolete, and the communication competencies students need will change in the future, the thinking strengths you develop will retain their utility and value (Jimenez, Moll, Rodriquez, & Berrera, 1999).

Finally, if students are to continue to rise to international leadership positions, we must teach them to think, use fair-minded flexibility in groups, create ideas cooperatively, generate multiple options, and select among equally attractive alternatives. Our instruction must shift from telling facts to teaching how to form ideas. Thus, if you now have a tendency to lecture, according to constructivist research, these habits should diminish.

In summary, constructivist theory posits that learning occurs as language and thought interact and as a result of disequilibrium. Without a highly capable teacher, however, many students retreat from the confusion and frustration that disequilibrium produces, resist learning language arts, and thus limit their world and their communication abilities. Fortunately, when teaching relates new knowledge to previous schema, students can enter language situations with greater confidence and learn with less pain. Your instruction must engage students' schema and establish a disequilibrium so students, with your assistance, can construct larger bodies of knowledge and eliminate their confusions.

PSYCHOLINGUISTIC THEORY

The **psycholinguistic theory** describes children's abilities to select meaning by combining different information sources (Rumelhart, 1976). These sources include the meaning they have derived from past living experiences and from engaging in language, including syntax, phonemic/phonic features of letters, and morphemic aspects of words. It examines how language users play an intentional role in learning language (Smith, 1971; Goodman, 1967). To learn language students must initiate and unite the constructions of human purpose, intention, and motivation with the cognitive processes of perception, attention, comprehension, learning, and memory. When students are immersed in a language-rich environment in which all forms of language are encouraged and enhanced, they more rapidly learn to use the redundancies in spoken and written messages (such as sentence pattern cues and rhyme and rhythm) to derive meanings (Spiegel, 1995).

According to psycholinguistic theory, language learning is often viewed as a "whole," with teachers having the responsibility of guiding students' learning. Important principles about English should be deduced by students themselves as a result of their interaction with materials provided by the teacher (Knapp, 1998). For example, instead of completing worksheets, students should interview, dramatically play, talk through puppets, journal write as if they are the main character, and have conversations about the feelings and events that have meaning in the experience of reading a book.

This theory is illustrated with Juan's solution to his problem concerning what to do with the letter that Ms. Johnson had written for him. He used all the psycholinguistic information he had in an interactive manner. He realized that the letter *J* was not enough of a label to distinguish his take-home bag from Juanita's, and he knew that his letter would be read by his mother and that writing down his thoughts enabled his mother to know how he felt.

The continuity between the classroom environment and life outside of school, proposed in psycholinguistic theory, is also important. It enables students to develop faith in themselves as constructors of knowledge (Davidson, 1996). When students are confident with their communication abilities in one setting, but meet criticism in another, they doubt their abilities and language. Students must feel comfortable with being daring, creative, and capable of acting on ideas, even if their initial attempts are unsuccessful (Jensen, 1998; Bruner, 1999). When children are told that the majority of their constructions are wrong, they become less willing to trust their ideas and subsequently to initiate their own learning about language.

Confidence in learning language arts is also enhanced when a classroom community is coconstructed and codesigned by students and teachers. Through this process, students can feel more in control and part of their learning experience.

Leaders in Psycholinguistic Theory.   Contemporary researchers such as Frank Smith, Kenneth Goodman, and Jerome Harste encourage teachers to focus classroom activities around making meaning and dissuade the practice of drilling on separate, discrete language skills by using worksheets and word flash-card games. As Smith (1985) reports, experiences and observations as well as direct instructions are powerful mediums of learning.

Having this sense of control and connection is becoming even more important in the twenty-first century. The rapid pace of daily life removes these senses necessary for maximum brain growth from young children (Jensen, 1998). For example, in 1960, the average 2-year-old spent an estimated 200 hours in a car. Today's 2-year-old will spend an estimated 700 hours strapped in a car seat! Although infant safety is vital, few parents ever compensate for these confined, strapped-in hours. We are beginning to understand the importance of developing self-control and its connection to reading, stress response, writing, attention, and memory development. As one example, brain-based research on the inner ear has shown that the vestibular area plays a key role in reading readiness. As Restak (1979) reports, "Infants who were given periodic vestibular stimulation by rocking gained weight faster and developed vision earlier, and, that by age four, a brain has essentially been designed and it is not going to change very much" (Kotulak 1966, p. 7). Although much learning happens after age 4, much of the brain's infrastructure will be already in place.

As another illustration, television is limiting control and sensory development because it is two-dimensional. A developing brain needs depth, says V. L. Ramachandran, a neuroscientist and vision specialist at the University of California at San Diego. Television moves fast and deals in abstractions that are often nonexistent in the child's environment. It does not allow the eyes any time to relax. This stress can create language learning difficulties. Moreover, television is a poor replacement for sensory–motor development time. The exposure to violence and a too-fast vocabulary also takes a toll on young children's language development (Healy, 1990; Strasburger, 1992). Many scientists and researchers say they would ban television for all children before age 8 (Hannaford, 1995). This would give the brain time to better develop language, social, and motor skills (Jensen, 1998).

Psycholinguistic researchers also discovered the value of using whole texts in language arts instruction. Because these materials use natural language patterns to introduce print to students, young and less mature readers can use their knowledge of oral language to predict words and meanings in selections of children's literature. The psycholinguistic perspective proposed that students' language errors are not negative. Instead, they are windows into the workings of individuals' schema, cognition, and present level of knowledge concerning the language arts.

Students learn language best when in an environment in which they can persist, despite challenges and obstacles, and delight in accomplishing their work. Therefore, students need options in learning activities to kindle their curiosity, to satisfy their natural drive to understand, and to increase their opportunities to express their ideas through various language modalities. Similarly, students won't self-initiate when they are punished or when their creative ideas become problems for the class.

For example, based on psycholinguistic theory, students in one preschool were asked to bring items from home to share for show and tell. A particular preschooler,

Sara, was so excited about the special surprise she had brought that she kept it hidden in a paper grocery sack. When it neared time for show and tell, Sara approached her teacher, clutching her sack tightly. She asked to leave the room, but the teacher became disturbed by the request because they didn't have enough time. When Sara's teacher asked why she wanted to leave and what was in the sack, Sara surrendered her secret. She whispered to the teacher that she had brought a new ballet tutu and that she had wanted to put it on so she could dance into the classroom just like a fairy godmother to surprise everyone by granting them their wishes.

The teacher replied in a gruff voice, "Oh, OK, but HURRY!! We don't have all day!" After rushing to change, Sara reentered the room not dancingly, but with her head down and tears in her eyes. She never mentioned to her classmates her original plan of becoming their wish-granter but merely reported that her grandmother had spent 4 weeks making this outfit by hand and that she had wanted her classmates to be the first to see it. At the end of that statement, Sara sat down. She never contributed her original ideas to class events again that year.

In addition to support for their initiative, students need to know that you have high expectations for their capabilities. If they are allowed to just drop in and out of activities and to show little or no loyalty to their own goals, their language abilities will not grow effectively. In summary, according to psycholinguistic theory, students need to set goals, and they will not sustain their self-initiation unless you provide them space, support, and encouragement to achieve purposes that mean something to them.

SOCIOLINGUISTIC THEORY

Although many claim that sociolinguistics began with Labov (1972) and Baratz and Shuy (1969), others point to Dewey (1938) for its roots. Eighty years ago, Dewey stated one of the main tenets of sociolinguistic theory: Language arts instruction should have a social component:

> Not only does social life demand teaching and learning for its own permanence, but the very process of living together educates. It enlightens experience; it stimulates and enriches imagination; it creates responsibility for accuracy and vividness of statement and thought. No number of object lessons, got up as object lessons [separate language drills] for the sake of [giving facts and drill on separate facts about language], can afford even the shadow of a substitute for [experiences] with plants and animals of the farm and garden acquired through actual living among them and caring for them. A certain discipline of memory can be acquired through lessons in [separate skills related to speaking, reading, and other language abilities]; but after all, this is somewhat remote and shadowy compared with the training of attention and of judgment that is acquired in doing things with a real motive behind and a real outcome ahead. (p. 7)

Sociolinguistic theory helps us appreciate the importance of context. Sociolinguists understand the importance of social activity, culture, and community in developing language abilities. As described above, Dewey reports that socialization is necessary for students to organize thought and refine meaning through language-sharing with others. Language, according to sociolinguistics, also serves a basic need because humans are social animals. Because language is shaped by cultures and home values, educators should take special care to encourage varied cultural experiences and appreciate cultural variations in language use as well as in attitudes toward learning and the language arts.

Bloome (1986a) captures the complex, interactive, multidimensional quality of sociolinguistic theory:

> Although members of a [classroom] community have a shared framework for the use of reading, writing, speaking, listening, viewing, and thinking, this does not mean that the use of these within any specific situation is static or predetermined. As people come together and interact, they must establish a shared communicative context. . . . Communicative contexts are established by how people act and react to each other's communicative efforts. . . . Literacy is not monolithic; rather, it depends on the community for its definition . . . people are continuously building and rebuilding literacy—On one hand, the nature of literacy has continuity across a community, while on the other, it is continuously evolving and situation-specific. (p. 72)

This theory is especially important in today's multicultural, mainstreamed classrooms where students are communicating with many social, emotional, physical, and cultural differences. As Unrau and Ruddell put it (1995):

> I think the reason why I understand the meaning of "The Laughing Man" now is because of our discussion in class. When I first read it, I didn't realize that the Laughing Man was the coach. By hearing what others thought of the story, they helped me realize the meaning of the story and the significance to life. (p. 20)

For example, at the daycare level, Ms. Johnson implemented sociolinguistic theory by putting signs in the block center. The children just ignored them until one day Michael built a large building. He watched other children driving their trucks around his blocks recklessly. He kept himself between them and his building, but he wanted to leave to get some more blocks. So he picked up a sign, put it in front of his building, and said, "This says stop, no crashing my building." Then, of course, everyone wanted to use language to satisfy their social needs. Soon there were not enough signs, so many wrote their own. Michael's social needs instantly taught the children to use writing in ways that Ms. Johnson had been trying to do, through suggestion and having available materials, for several weeks.

To sum up, although much is unknown about students' language development, at least four conclusions can be drawn from present research:

1. Students' language is systematic, interactive, and organized. At any age or point of development, students exhibit cognitive, constructivist rule-governed, coherent behavior that reflects their current understanding of how language works.

2. Students are active participants and constructors of their own language and communication competencies. They build their own theories; activate their own schemata; test their own hypotheses; and establish their own rules about speaking, reading, writing, listening, thinking, observing, and viewing.

3. Students' language development is influenced by their world knowledge, social interactions, and classroom environment. This includes the number of language models available to them and the number of opportunities they have to use their language in real-world contexts.

4. To develop confidence and self-initiation students must have home and school congruence, and know that teachers appreciate their attempts to learn. Valuing cultural routines, rituals, and understandings as well as children's own stories, fosters thinking and language development.

To further review the information in this section of the chapter, you can assess whether you have already developed a teaching style and philosophy that capture the principles of these theories by taking the test in Table 1.1. To evaluate your present level of constructivist, psycholinguistic, and sociolinguistic understanding, check "yes" or "no" to answer each of the 20 questions. After you have completed the test, turn to the Answer Key at the back of the book to learn about the predominant philosophy you employ and the degree to which each of these contemporary theories influence your present teaching philosophy.

LEARNING THE RULE SYSTEMS THAT GOVERN LANGUAGE

Language development requires a child to make new connections between brain regions that process oral, print, artistic, and body language. A Chinese proverb states: "A child's life is like a piece of paper on which every passerby leaves a mark." When passersby are language-related constructions, the continuous, effective interactions with oral, written, and visual stimuli over time increase the volume of connections in their brain. This maturity occurs across the four language systems defined on pages 13–17: the phonological, semantic or morphological, syntactical, and pragmatic systems. I describe each below in more depth so that you can guide individual students to employ each more effectively.

PHONOLOGICAL SYSTEM

The **phonological language system** is a set of principles that describe all the possible sounds in a language that combine to make meaning in that language. To obtain meaning, students must recognize and operate the **phonological clues** or sound to meaning and letter correlations in their language. Dialect determines how many sounds students learn and produce as various English dialects are comprised of 44 to 46 **phonemes** (individual sounds) that are spelled by 26 letters and 310 major and minor phonemic word patterns or letter combinations. Similarly, students use their knowledge of the relationship between phonemes and **graphemes** (letters and letter combinations) to read and spell. For example, young children often spell *was* as *wuz* because these letters represent the sounds they hear as they say the word to themselves. However, when these students are immersed in a rich classroom in which they hear adult and peer models' pronunciations closely approximating the correctly spelled sounds in the word, and when they read the word repeatedly in meaningful contexts, they more quickly assimilate a new schema for the spelling of *was*.

Research demonstrates that by the time most students enter first grade they have a high level of mastery over the phonological system, although it may not be at the conscious level (Cazden, 1992; Cunningham, 1995; Ruddell & Ruddell, 1995). For

TABLE 1.1 DO YOU EMPLOY PRINCIPLES FROM CONSTRUCTIVISTIC, PSYCHOLINGUISTIC, AND SOCIOLINGUISTIC THEORIES IN YOUR LANGUAGE ARTS PROGRAM?

	YES	NO
1. Do you (or will you) allow students to reflect during class time?	❑	❑
2. Do you make a daily commitment to present activities that stimulate multiple intelligences?	❑	❑
3. Can your students (or will your future students be able to) recall celebrative experiences from your class that involved literacy?	❑	❑
4. Do your students tell you that they have jumped passionately into projects and that they think about them at home?	❑	❑
5. Do you become frustrated with the routine side of teaching and all the paperwork?	❑	❑
6. Have you held (or will you hold) discussions with your students in which one group stated "pros" and another stated "cons"?	❑	❑
7. Do you (or will you) read books to students each week?	❑	❑
8. Do you (or will you) create quiet opportunities for your students to write every day about topics they select?	❑	❑
9. Have you studied other cultures?	❑	❑
10. Do you (or will you) ask students what they want to learn at the beginning of new units of study?	❑	❑
11. Do you every once in a while take (or yearn to take) a risk in class and laugh at yourself in front of your students?	❑	❑
12. Do you feel comfortable with disagreements in discussions?	❑	❑
13. Even though you want to ask good questions, do you prefer that your students ask good questions?	❑	❑
14. Do you appreciate the creative, if troublesome, child in a class?	❑	❑
15. Even though you want other teachers to ask what you are doing in your class so they can model you, do you prefer to close the door so your class can bond together as a group?	❑	❑
16. Do you find that some people label you "persistent"?	❑	❑
17. Do you wake up having solved a problem you toiled over the day before?	❑	❑
18. Do you believe that playing word games will be more beneficial than putting on plays students write or a play they select from published authors?	❑	❑
19. Do you want your students to show you that they are eager to learn by pulling a book off the shelf to read even if they rush through a paper-and-pencil activity to do so?	❑	❑
20. Have you taught (or will you teach) about the phonological, semantic, practical, and syntactical aspects of language through direct instruction?	❑	❑

example, in the scenario that opened the chapter, Juan demonstrated his knowledge that letters can be used to locate appropriate names and labels. Because of this development, he appears to be on track to expand his knowledge throughout his preschool and kindergarten years so all aspects of the phonological system described above will be mastered and operational by the time he enters first grade.

SEMANTIC OR MORPHOLOGICAL SYSTEM

The **semantic or morphological system** is the name given to characterize the meanings of individual words and how these words combine to determine the meanings that can be constructed in the total context. As defined earlier, **morphological clues** are a specialized type of meaning clue in that a **morpheme** is the smallest string of sounds that give meaning to what students say, hear, read, think, and write that contain a meaning in and of themselves. For example, *free* in the word *freedom* is a morpheme because it has a specific meaning; *dom* is not a morpheme because this combination of letters does not always portray a specific concept. Morphemes can be either **free morphemes** (having meaning in and of themselves, such as *help* in the word *helper*); or **bound morphemes** (having no meaning unless attached to a free morpheme, such as the *er* in *helper*). Morphological development is also generally well developed upon entry into preschool (Read, 1975; Ruddell & Ruddell, 1995; Truman, 1993). In addition, students usually acquire 3,000 to 5,000 words every year thereafter (Crawford, 1993). Through the development of listening, speaking, reading, and writing vocabularies, students learn shades of meaning, depth of expression, connotations, and more beautiful ways to communicate their newly evolving emotions and experiences. When students learn to appreciate this beauty of their words and the precision in their language, eloquence in communication can advance.

To illustrate, consider a field trip arranged for Juan, Meisong, Michael, and Allison's daycare, located in Secoma, Washington, 30 miles east of Mount St. Helens. Ms. Johnson began to prepare for the field trip to Mount St. Helens Park by reading selections from *Volcano: The Eruption and Healing of Mount St. Helens,* a Newbery Honor Book winner by Patricia Lauder (1986). After she had read the following paragraph, she stopped:

Volcano

> For well over a hundred years the volcano slept. Each spring, as winter snows melted, its slopes seemed to come alive. Wildflowers bloomed in meadows. Bees gathered pollen and nectar. Birds fed, found mates, and built nests. Bears lumbered out of their dens. Herds of elk and deer feasted on fresh green shoots. Thousands of people came to hike, picnic, camp, fish, paint, birdwatch, or just enjoy the scenery. Logging crews felled tall trees and planted seedlings. (p. 2)

Because she wanted to develop the students' morphological language system, she (1) reread each sentence individually, (2) asked students to act out the meanings they heard, and (3) wrote words from the passage on chart paper so students could explain their meanings. Then, students selected one sentence to draw, scribble, or write themselves. After this instructional enrichment of their morphological language system, Juan and his classmates astonished park guides during the field trip. These young children asked what types of "seedlings" were being planted; when "elk" and "green shoots" would be seen on the volcano; where "pollen" came from; and how much longer the volcano would "sleep."

SYNTACTICAL SYSTEM

The **syntactical system** is the set of rules that govern how words can be put together to make sentences. **Syntactical cluing** is how the order in which words appear in a sentence determine their meaning. Each language has its own syntactical system. For example, in Spanish, adjectives follow the noun they describe—for example *casa don Juan* means "house of Juan" and *casa blanca* means "the house of white." In English, adjectives generally precede the noun—for example, *Juan's house* or *white house.*

The components of the English syntactical system also govern how we communicate when events occur, the number of people and objects in that event, and the emphasis in the points a writer or speaker is making. Within each of these syntactical ordering systems, specific principles describe the order in which words appear, the endings that can be placed on nouns and verbs, and the placement of phrases in a sentence. For example, to describe a scene outside the window that occurred yesterday, emphasizing that the people were enjoying each other's company, an author could use the plural form of nouns, the past tense, and place the most important descriptive phrase at the beginning or end of the sentence, as in the following:

> *The group basked in the sun, ate plentifully, and frolicked with complete abandon in the pleasure of true friends.*

On the other hand, the author could modify the meaning conveyed by altering only the syntactical order of the above sentence, for example:

> *They are basking in the sun, frolicking with complete abandon in the pleasure of true friends, and eating plentifully.*

PRAGMATIC SYSTEM

Pragmatics, or the pragmatic system, includes the clues to meanings that arise from the social and cultural variations in language. Students are attending to the pragmatic system when they alter their speech, writing, and thinking to achieve a specific purpose for a particular audience. Within this cluing system are varied pronunciations and word choices known as **dialects,** which are the ways that language is modified among social classes, culture groups, geographic regions, and ethnic traditions. The language used in most schools is **Standard English,** the form that communicates in more formal, objective writings that can be found in newspapers and documents, which are designed to be understood by people who speak a variety of dialects.

Because Standard English is the language of business, government, the press, and other aspects of national activities, schools are expected to teach it. In doing so, students must not be taught that their own dialect is deficient or inferior, but shown how their language differs in vocabulary, syntax choices, and phonology. When students learn to use many forms of language, they become more effective users of different systems of language to communicate in specific situations. For example,

Michael, like most 3-year-olds, uses shorter sentences when he speaks with his day-care peers than when he communicates with adults. He usually says "Get" when he is asking students to move and locate an object that he or the group wants. When he speaks with adults the same request would be, "Can you give me the Crayola?" When Ms. Johnson explained how these two systems of language are used effectively, Michael became more sensitive to the advantages of using complete sentences when he spoke.

EMERGENT LANGUAGE ARTS ABILITIES FROM BIRTH TO AGE 3

In the past decade, studies of children's early literacy experiences have yielded profound insight into how children's literacy begins (IRA & NCTE, YCE, 1999; Neuman, 1999). Although Chapters 2 through 9 describe specific speaking, listening, reading, writing, and spelling competencies from ages 4 to 12, more global behaviors common to most children from preschool to grade 6 are described in Figure 1.1. As you read Figure 1.1, you will find that to be literate is not to have arrived at some predetermined destination, but to be able to use reading, writing, and speaking skills progressively to enlarge one's world (Davidson, 1996). Such emergent learning begins at home. To illustrate, 78 percent of children who read before they enter kindergarten have parents who frequently read and write at home. In contrast, only 22 percent of students who began preschool not knowing how to read had no such support available in the home (Durkin, 1966; Graves, 1982; Calkins, 1986).

For the past several years, researchers have established a close link between parent–child interaction and young children's development as competent language users. Such interactions are both direct and indirect (Heath, 1995; Davidson, 1995; Newell & Durst, 1993). Parents' direct contributions emanate from the quality of behaviors adults exhibit when speaking, writing, reading, thinking, and viewing with toddlers. When parents vary their tone of voice (speaking in whispers, overtones, or coos), ask their children to identify objects in storybooks, or encourage their children to hold the book and read along with them; children will associate such attentive, warm, and enjoyable experiences with language arts (Powell, 1995; Davidson, 1996).

To illustrate, consider Juan's experience with Ms. Johnson when he was 2 years old as she read books and they talked about the pictures. On one such day, while reading *Jill the Farmer and Her Friends* (Butterworth, 1986), Juan spent a long time looking at the picture of Dave the Builder, who drove the dump truck. Because Ms. Johnson had made the *BRRRRRMMM* noise for the dump truck in numerous previous reads, Juan suddenly did so ahead of her. When the reading was completed, he hurried to the block corner and put on a hard hat, which Ms. Johnson purposely placed in that center to actualize psycholinguistic, constructivistic, and socialistic research at her daycare. "I'm Dave, the Builder" he announced, as he drove the dump truck around in a circle, "BRRRMMM, BRRMMM, says the truck!" (Modified from Davidson, 1996). Juan blossomed in this enriched environment.

Alternatively, research demonstrates that when adults use language full of directives and control tactics in teaching and disciplinary situations, they can, unwittingly, depress students' language use (Hess & McDevitt, 1984). Investigators speculated

	Preschool	Kindergarten	First Grade	Second Grade
Speaking	Many preschoolers gradually obtain the ability to transform declarative sentences.  Ex. I want Sally to come. Is Sally coming?	Many kindergartners use language for a variety of purposes, such as to entertain. Ex. Humor I want to tell you a riddle. Why did the chicken cross the road?	With socialization, first-graders practice language in a wider variety of situations and functions. Ex. Marcy is excited. Why is Marcy so happy?	Many second-graders' oral language abilities increase to deeper discussions with peers. Ex. Do you have a pet? What is your pet's name?
Reading	Many preschoolers can identify the beginning and ending of books and stories and enjoy picture books and pattern books. Ex. 	Many kindergartners understand the orientation of print, pretend read, and read environmental print. Ex. 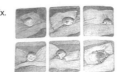	Most readers begin to construct meaning with print. Ex.	Most readers begin to read using predominantly print cues. Ex. 
Writing	The preschooler writes through scribbles, letter-like symbols, and scrawls. Ex.	Meaning is conveyed through drawing pictures and pre-phonetic and phonetic invented spelling. Ex. Dangrcepout Danger seeped out.	Many first-graders write a single letter for every sound they hear. Ex.	Many second-graders form sentences around familiar words, use repetitive phrases, and sentence starters they have read. Ex. My Teeth Last nit I pold out my tuth and I put it ondr my pelr. And when I wok up I fid a two dilr bel.

	Third Grade	Fourth Grade	Fifth Grade	Sixth Grade
Speaking	The third-grader takes turns in discussions and the average number of words in oral sentences increases to eight words. Ex. It's Julius's turn to talk.	Fourth-graders increase skill in participating in group discussions and include more relevant details. May I express my opinion on this subject?	The fifth-grade student acknowledges and responds thoughtfully to the ideas of others and the average number of words per sentence increases to ten. Ex. I never thought of it that way before, but I see what you mean.	The sixth-grader participates willingly in planned discussions to learn from others as well as make contributions. Ex. I like the way you wrote that story. It taught me how to write in first person. Would you help me make my story better?
Reading	Most third-graders make a transition from easy readers to chapter books. Ex.	Many fourth-grade students enjoy reading for pleasure, and construct meaning through interrelating text cues and experience. Ex.	As their maturity level increases, fifth-graders read books that are personally significant to them. Ex.	The sixth-grade student reads to learn so he/she may share information with others. Ex.
Writing	The third-grade child begins to focus his writing on a single topic. Ex. I was makking fun of the ducke and it started runing at me.	Writing includes simple characterization and the sense of story plot. Ex.	Written language becomes more complex, through the effective use of narrative and descriptive writing. Ex. Dear Mr. Taylor I want to know why the mothers in those books were different from other mothers. Where do you get your ideas? Where do you get your characters? Did you like learnin about lions for the book Sniper? Thank you for reading this. You are a good author. Sincerely	Writing is more fluent and is expressed from their own point of view (writer's voice). Ex.

FIGURE 1.1 CONTINUUM OF LANGUAGE ARTS DEVELOPMENT

	Preschool	Kindergarten	First Grade	Second Grade
Listening	Most preschoolers understand about 1,500 words. Ex. Preschoolers could understand "one," "two," and "three," but would not understand past, present, and future tenses.	Kindergartners' vocabulary increases to about 2,500 words and students begin to understand more adjectives, adverbs, and pronouns. Ex. Children can understand "Get it and put it here."	Most first-graders begin to understand language symbolically, but experience difficulty with phrases that begin with "before," "after," and "next." Ex. "Before you read your book, write in your journal."	Most second-graders can understand relative pronouns and clauses that begin with "that," "which," "when," and "because." Ex. Students can understand "I have a book that I read everyday."
Observing & Viewing	Most preschoolers can attend to many pictures and visually presented information and identify main idea. Ex. Charlotte's Web Videotape Main idea: friendship	The child learns rapidly from adult and audio-visual models. Ex. Manners—The child models "thank you" and "please."	Children develop prediction and sequential thinking abilities rapidly when they are asked to retell and predict what they saw. Ex. Field Trip to the Zoo	Most second-graders can separate extraneous noises in the environment to focus intently on an object or scene, and not be distracted. Ex. The child can focus on the subject even if someone drops a book.
Thinking	Preschoolers internalize common qualities of objects and connect these features to the objects name/label. Ex. A dog has four legs and barks.	Kindergartners' thinking is affected by individual firsthand experiences. Ex. Learning by doing.	First-graders begin to think and solve problems internally. Ex. How will my actions affect others?	Second-graders realize that they have feelings and can express their opinions. They benefit from the discovery of their individualities. Ex. "I disagree. I think it is an apple."

	Third Grade	Fourth Grade	Fifth Grade	Sixth Grade
Listening	Most third-graders can relate concepts to general ideas with use of words like "meanwhile" and "unless." Ex. "I don't want to go unless Suzy does."	Most fourth-graders can easily recognize when details are tangential, relevant, highly relevant, or irrelevant. Ex. "That's important."	Most fifth-graders can distinguish between past, past perfect, and perfect tenses of verbs, deeper nuances, and subtleties of meaning. Ex. "Skinny is not the same as thin."	The sixth-grader responds rapidly to instruction that assists them to condense, summarize, expand, and revise what they heard based on a specific purpose. Ex. "It's concisely stated."
Observing & Viewing	Most third-graders appreciate objects and scenes that are very different from familiar community and home events. Ex. "I want to do something new."	Most fourth-graders recognize and avoid the influence of propaganda devices when viewing and observing conversations. Ex. Knows "Everyone should" testimonials and emotional appeals are often used in advertisements.	Most fifth-graders can image mentally while reading and writing and recognize underlying structure in objects and complex plots that are viewed. Ex. "Romeo and Juliet could still happen today."	Most sixth-graders can select audio visual information that is of higher quality than other examples in the same category when criteria for "best" is established. Ex. "It was much better than last year's winner."
Thinking	Third-graders can understand that the same action can be interpreted from many points of view. They can define their own point of view. Ex. "I believe Georganna was correct because . . . "	Most fourth-graders can establish objective criteria for making personal decisions, but have difficulty anticipating probable consequences of alternative actions. Ex. "I believe this, this, and this."	Fifth-graders begin to use metacognitive thinking effectively to self-regulate, self-appraise, and increase self-knowledge. Ex. "I know how I figured out this word."	Most sixth-graders can respond thoughtfully to the ideas of others. Ex. "You made a good point because . . . "

Created by Cathy Collins Block and Susanna L. Douglas, 2000, principal and master of educational administration degree candidate at Texas Christian University, Fort Worth, TX. Used by permission.

that adults who too rigidly limit language play imply that the ability to solve problems and the exploration of language belong to adults. Subsequently, some children come to associate negative consequences with language use. Thus, the responsibility of building home, school, teacher, and community partnerships is not a frill.

Even if schools could successfully develop children's literacy by cloistering it within the school setting, only half the purpose of education would be fulfilled. Children might acquire the skills to use language successfully, but they would not have the desire to use these skills to best advantage in their lives outside of school (Davidson, 1996). To learn language, a four-way language system must be mastered, and a four-way partnership of parents, children, teachers, and community agencies should be nurtured. An exercise in partnership can be inviting parents to visit the classroom to model language-enriching actions; students will profit from interpreting what they are seeing. Parents can observe their children scribbling in the writing center and be given a brief description of this stage of writing development. They can also be informed of the value of asking their children to tell them what the children wrote; such "reading" and sharing of scribbles helps develop writing abilities.

In closing our discussion of research-based theories, it is important to emphasize that each student is unique yet passes through similar stages in language development (Brown & Campione, 1986; Sternberg, 1995; Wigfield, Eccles, & Rodriguez, 1999). In Chapters 3 through 12 detailed information about speaking, listening, reading, writing, spelling, viewing, creativity, and reflective thinking development is presented. Figure 1.1 summarizes the close relationship that exists for all communication processes. I encourage you first to read Figure 1.1 horizontally to discern the developmental stages from birth through grade 6 in each language art. Immediately following that, I encourage you next to read the information vertically to discover how similar and interconnected language development is at each stage in a child's life. You may also enjoy comparing your development (or that of a young child in your life) to this typical developmental continuum. You may come to better understand why acquiring one language function facilitates the ability to master a second one (Destefano, 1978; Zimmerman, 1999; Ruddell, 1995). Research also documents that students from classrooms that incorporate the demonstrations in Figure 1.1 can master a wider range of language functions than students from classrooms that limit the number of these demonstrations (Moll, 1992; 1999).

SECTION 2   PUTTING THEORY INTO PRACTICE

Principles of Language Arts Instruction

Now that you have read about the theories of language learning, you may wonder how you implement them in the classroom. How can you use many learning approaches simultaneously? Today's most successful language arts teachers make a difference in students' lives by putting theory into practice and adhering to high standards (Pressley, Allington, Morrow, & Block, 1999). When the standards described in this textbook are met, instruction has a balanced foundation, built on child-centered, challenging, but achievable, tasks that are guided by teachers who make effective decisions. As Gutierrez, Baquedano-Lopez, and Turner (1997) summarize, classrooms in the past tended to focus on instructional approaches, rather than on language and language learning, which may have contributed to current debates that deconstruct language arts into binary categories. "These categories, on the one hand, set up unresolvable tensions but on the other, help construct curricular materials and pedagogical practices that adhere to rigid ideological stances about language instruction. Debates in the current public discourse generally center on the merits of instructional approaches and strategies, such as phonics versus literature-based approaches, rather than debating how children actually learn language and acquire literacies" (p. 368).

Balance refers to equalizing attention in classrooms to both skill instruction, literary interpretation, higher-level reasoning and responses to communications, independent motivation and discovery in learning. To achieve balance, you can blend a variety of rich programs to emphasize multidimensionality. This will help curtail making only cursory excursions into research-based practices and theory. Research suggests that the principles stated below provide the strongest infrastructure for such a dynamic language arts program.

PRINCIPLES ON WHICH TO BUILD LANGUAGE LEARNING ACTIVITIES

Throughout this textbook, Section 2 in each chapter contains specific lessons, methods, and activities that apply the theory presented in Section 1 of the chapters, with the exception of this first chapter, which instead describes the basic guidelines that comprise these activities. The purpose in providing these principles is to explain why some lessons are more effective than others. As in Section 1 of this chapter, activities that subscribe to the theoretical tenets below will provide greater success for learning the language arts.

Principle 1. *Language arts classes must be positive, comfortable, and challenging environments, and classes in which students learn concepts that they value.* A student-centered classroom is one in which everyone shares their writing, life-stories, views, and culture with exercises in communication providing opportunities to learn from one another. In this community, cooperation is championed; competition is moderated (Johnson, 1995; Presslay, 1998).

Students are surrounded with good literature as well as many peers and adults who serve as role models (Morrow, 2000; Ruddell, 1997). Each person's contributions are celebrated, their limitations are braced, and their differences are welcomed. Students ask questions, admit confusion, and chance making mistakes. You grant them permission to do so through statements such as "I'm glad you took a chance," "What are you thinking?" and "Good question." With your leadership, students will begin to realize that they can produce meaningful ideas in the minds of others (Costa & Lowry, 1989).

You should also model that for students to be right most of the time, they have to risk being wrong some of the time. You do so by demonstrating that you are not afraid to leave the "safe harbors" of familiar knowledge and explore new ideas. Through this modeling, students learn that less successful efforts need not be final. By restructuring inadequate solutions, students also learn that "trying again" is an effective strategy for life. They must have your support, guidance, and encouragement in times of trial before they believe that they can reach greater levels of communication competence. Some must see how you may fail in communicating but get up undaunted and become successful again before they overcome their fear of communicating. As Harste, Woodward, and Burke (1984) state: "only when things go wrong, when the expected relationships or known rules do not hold, is a language user forced to develop new rules and new responses in order to cope. To live within existing rules and predictable patterns is not to grow. It is only under conditions in which all of the relationships are not known that language users must scamper to outgrow their current selves" (p. 136).

You can also provide your class with challenges students want to conquer, and sensory stimuli, materials, and vicarious experiences that push the limits of your students' language. Such classroom activities provide an environment as shown in Figure 1.2. As you read this figure, you will notice that many of these are student-led projects. When these activities comprise your language arts program, your students are likely to move beyond merely repeating what you tell them, memorizing information, moving their eyes across the page as their minds wander, copying from the board, and thinking what you want them to think. They will enact their own initiatives, speak up, listen actively, and read and write with purpose. Your students' successes and needs will become as important to you as they are to them.

Principle 2. *Students engage in authentic tasks.* **Authentic language arts tasks** touch on matters that extend into the community, mirror literacy as used in students' homes, and are important to students. For example, in authentic, meaning-based instruction, students write ideas that are uniquely their own, and engage in social collaborations to resolve important world, school, community, and classroom issues. Presently at least 80 percent of all students exert little or no effort to improve their language because school doesn't address these language arts needs. The old theory that " 'We can make 'em work; all we have to do is get tough' has never produced intellectual effort in the history of the world" (William Glaser, 2000). In your class, students can satisfy their needs for belonging, power, caring, and sharing, as well as creating and cooperating with others through language arts tasks that have meaning to them.

To illustrate, Juan's preschool class wanted to contribute something to the people and store owners who lived on the same block as their preschool. With this goal in mind, for 3 consecutive days these preschoolers walked into shops and knocked on doors to explain their goal to community members. Their teacher wrote on a large notebook every need expressed for which students felt they had the resources to contribute. After gathering this information, students developed a plan and scheduled time each week to work toward assisting community members. As individual projects were completed, students delivered them to the community and took

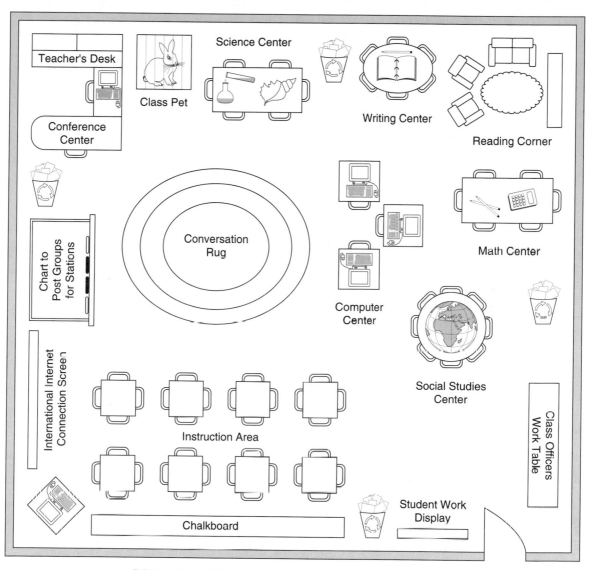

FIGURE 1.2 SAMPLE CLASSROOM ACTIVITY CENTERS

Created by Summer Heap, 2000, senior music education major at Texas Christian University, Fort Worth, TX. Used by permission.

pictures of the event for their classroom scrapbook. At the end of the year, the class presented their project, scrapbook, and individual stories concerning the importance of this project to the kindergarten class. This gave preschoolers an authentic experience in the kindergarten class that they would attend in the following year, which helped diminish their apprehension of moving to a new school.

In addition, your students should learn to read for their own purposes as well as to recognize books, thoughts, and discussions they value, which they will do as adults. For the rest of their lives students will read books; therefore, they should read children's literature at school. As Rigg and Allen (1989, p. 44) state:

> If you and I were in my car . . . and we got stuck in rush-hour traffic, and while sitting there I nudged the car forward a little so I could read the bumper sticker on the car in front of me . . . you'd think my behavior perfectly normal. But if as we sat there, I whipped a set of flash cards out of my purse and started reading each one in my announcement voice—*can, close, if, too, this*—you'd think me strange. (Stranger still if I started giving definitions for each one.)

If you are implementing Principle 2 effectively, your students will do assignments in class that reflect what they have to do in their lives outside of school.

Principle 3.   *Classroom instruction in speaking, writing, reading, listening, and viewing is integrated so that one can improve another.* In this sense, experiences in one language modality will reverberate throughout the other language systems. Thus, the more enriched and diverse linguistic experiences students have, the more meaning they can bring to new words that they hear and read. Although there are differences between language arts (e.g., writing is not simply speech written down), the similarities are more dominant.

Reading and listening are alike in that both require interpretations that lie beneath literal words (Clay, 1999; Dyson, 1999). Listening and speaking rely on rich language clues not available in print, such as pitch, pauses, tone, mood, pace, volume, dialect, spoken grammatical registers, body language, viewing, and the rhythms and melodies of spoken language. Similarly, oral language, listening, thinking, and viewing are akin. As Vygotsky stated (1962, p. 43): "when speech begins to serve intellect and thoughts begin to be spoken . . . the child's sudden, active curiosity about words, his questions about every new thing; and the resulting rapid, saccadic increases in vocabulary enable thoughts to become verbal and speech rational."

Reading and writing are also intricately intertwined. Reading and writing engage interchangeable, inseparable thought processes (Bruner, 1999; Vygotsky, 1979). For example, when readers prepare to comprehend, they establish a purpose for reading and elicit background knowledge. When writers compose, they establish a purpose for writing and must recall information to communicate. Moreover, when students become authors, they simultaneously enter the intimate circle of appreciative readers. Furthermore, when they become writers, they become more fascinated as they read by the new layers of meaning that can evolve through carefully crafted writing.

Principle 4.   *Language arts teachers know they are important forces in their students' lives. They continuously work to nurture characteristics that correlate with high student achievement.* As Ginott puts it (1992, p. 16): "I have come to a frightening conclusion. I am the decisive element in a classroom. It is my personal approach that creates the climate. It is my daily mood that makes the weather." The student who taught me this was a shy sixth-grader in Axle, Texas. Charles was barely passing from grade to grade before entering our sixth-grade classroom. When I asked him why he thought he was doing so much better this year than last, his sincere explanation astonished and warmed me: "It's because I like myself now that I'm here with you."

During the past 20 years, researchers have identified qualities that distinguish the most effective language arts teachers. Ruddell and Ruddell (1995) summarized the data into five categories: (1) personal characteristics, (2) understanding learners' potential, (3) attitude toward subject, (4) being concerned about learners' life, and (5) a quality-based instructional repertoire. Bruner (1986) also stated that effective educators do not present knowledge as a set of facts but allow students to draw their own conclusions; they "become one who helps students to *search* rather than *follow*" (Brooks & Brooks, 1993, p. 171). They do so by providing just enough guidance so that students do not give up in frustration and not so much as to deny students' personal satisfaction and growth because all the thinking was done for them by their teachers. In essence, "children who see their teacher getting excited about an activity or sharing a discovery have the gift of example" (Johnson, 1999, p. 54). Specific actions you can take to develop these competencies include the following:

- Give clear purposes and directions, explain why what you are teaching is important, and enable students to set their own language goals (Block, 1996; Good & Grouws, 1975; Porter & Brophy, 1988; Rosenshine & Furst, 1971; Ruddell, 1999).

- Develop students' positive attitudes toward language arts, and promote high self-esteem (Berliner & Tikunoff, 1976; Medly, 1977).

- Coconstruct class rules; share class responsibilities so your students can attend to their personal and learning needs without asking for approval and permission (Collins, 1987; Gage, 1978).

- Engage students' problem-solving abilities by posing possibilities, exploring students' questions, and talking about problem-solving strategies that you use (Johnson, 1995; Block & Mangieri, 1995a, 1995b, 1996).

- Scaffold (which will be described in more depth near the end of this chapter) to support students' initial attempts at new language arts tasks and tell students what you are thinking when you read, write, listen, speak, or view. You can do so by demonstrating processes and sample end products of speaking, reading, writing, reflecting, and viewing before students create their own and by engaging in the same activities that you assign students, such as reading in view of students (Block & Mangieri, 2000; Cazden, 1999; Porter & Brophy, 1988).

- Become a continuous learner yourself and frequently reflect on what, why, and how you are succeeding as a teacher (Berliner, 1994; Porter & Brophy, 1988; Sternberg & Horvath, 1995).

- Maintain high expectations of yourself and your students (Erickson, 1993; Block, 1995; Leibert, 1991; Ruddell, 1999).

- Become an advocate for your students. This advocacy is not only with adults but with students' classmates. For example, Ms. Johnson frequently advances students' language learning with comments such as: "Meisong, Allison, and Michael, Juan wants to learn to read words and sometimes it is difficult for him. You are helping by answering his questions about the words he sees in the classroom. I know this takes extra effort on your part, and I know he appreciates it as I do. With your help, Juan is reaching new goals. Thank you."

- Listen intently and actively, as if the next sentences that your students say are the most important that they have ever said (Block, 2000).

Pause for a moment to reflect about a specific teacher who increased your language arts abilities. Ask yourself: Did this teacher care deeply about you and other students? Did this teacher ensure that no student just dropped in and out of activities or became faceless? Did this teacher's classroom cause you to want to think and to learn more about language? If so, you are likely to have had a teacher who modeled the above effective teaching qualities for you.

In the future, to evaluate how well you use this principle, pause at the end of the day and recount how often you have employed the following actions in that day's events: How often did your students tell you what they wanted to learn next and why? How many times did you require students to pose their own questions? Did you ask questions for which you already knew the answer? Was the class a place where students really lived, where important, life-changing events occurred?

Principle 5. *Just as the printing press had a significant impact on oral traditions, technology is enhancing the role that books, magazines, and newspapers serve in students' language learning.* Developing students' technological competencies and desires to "retool" continually is an important language arts objective, especially when we consider technology's prevalence in the world in which children will live and work as adults. For example, approximately 95 percent of today's jobs already rely on computer literacy competencies. It is predicted that within a few years 95 percent will also require a high level of technology literacy (Johnson, 1993).

Using technology such as computers, audiovisual equipment, networking, and the Internet can also satisfy children's strong desire to understand and receive explanations. By using grade-level-appropriate representations and models too expensive to create in the average classroom without technology, computers can help students achieve more. Technology also demands higher language use than is possible without it (Calfee, 1994). "The ultimate criterion for curriculum and instruction offered disadvantaged students is whether it promises to impart the analytical and communicative skills and knowledge needed for their full participation in a technological society" (Mathews, 1988, p. 69).

To increase your knowledge of technology, Chapters 3 through 9 describe technological aids that enable you to provide such dynamic visual and interactive experiences to increase students' learning in each of the language arts.

Principle 6. *It is important to solicit students' voices and choices in the language arts. Such pursuit increases students' confidence and broadens their perspectives.* By affirming that there are multiple paths to meaning, you champion the worth of numerous points of view. These validations help students who come from different cultures to connect with each other. Their knowledge, skills, and cultural values can also become part of the language arts program. Furthermore, such a program can act as an agent for the formation of individual character traits that are compatible with societal norms; can transmit the cumulative knowledge and values of civilization; can develop social consciousness; and is the ultimate means of continual social progress (Gay, 1995, p. 7).

Culture has been defined as the people, objects, and events that impart meaning to our lives. All students come to school with a native language and a particular way of behaving in the world; being socialized into several cultures; and holding their parents' hopes, dreams, and values related to the future.

> *Culture* is that part of human interactions and experiences that determine how one feels, acts and thinks. It is through one's culture that one establishes standards to judge right from wrong, beauty and truth, and to make judgments about oneself as well as others. The things and ideas one values and cherishes, how one learns, believes, reacts, etc. are all immersed in and impacted by one's culture. (Nakagawa, 1986, p. 6)

Specifically, all cultural groups respond differently in their confrontational style; degree of cooperation in groups; response to competition; desire to work independently; and method of taking turns in conversation, meeting deadlines, and asking questions. Cultures change from generation to generation and locale to locale, and each student belongs to more than one group. They derive part of their identity by belonging to each one.

More than ever, an understanding and respect for human diversity is vital to your language arts classroom and to students' well-being. By learning about the lives of other people, students gain tolerance, different perspectives on how to live their lives, and new ways to deal with old problems. As a whole, a multicultural language arts curriculum increases the chances for a more peaceful, communicative world. Such a curriculum involves making visible students' cultural patterns, of which they may not even be aware. No longer should students' language alienate them from their classroom, classmates, school, or community as language use achieves similar purposes for all students (Gay, 1999). As Marie Clay (1999, p. 7) stated:

> Children accumulate experience over massive exposures, directing their attention to parts of the environment while ignoring others and integrating information in order to survive. Children change as a result of an individual history of interactions in their cultures, and yet they maintain quite similar learning paths despite their vastly different kinds of opportunities.

Each chapter in *Teaching the Language Arts* includes specific discussions about methods of integrating this principle into your language arts program. This discussion is titled "Inside Culturally Enriched Classrooms," and all of Chapter 13 discusses a multicultural curriculum in depth. As Suzuik stated, "Multicultural education basically amounts to sound educational practice coupled with a vision for a better society" (1979, p. 50).

Principle 7. *Language arts instruction should center on quality literature.* Literature has been defined as "the imaginative shaping of life and thought into the forms and structures of language . . . [through the subjects of] human conditions; feelings, thought, and insights" (Huck, 1992, p. 3). "Literature records the depths and heights of the human experience. It develops compassion by educating the heart as well as the mind. It helps children entertain new ideas, develop insights, stretch their imagination, create new experiences, and develop a sense of what is true and just and beautiful" (Cambourne, 1998, p. 317). When language arts instruction begins with quality literature, students are often transported to new understandings of reality that they might not have experienced without literature. As Newell and Durst (1993, p. 10) state: "Part of the satisfaction we obtain from reading literature is seeing our desires, concerns, and experiences take shape in a poem, play, or story."

Thus, a major objective of your language arts program is to help students develop an appreciation and enjoyment for literature and how living vicariously through literary characters can enrich their lives. Literature should become a powerful tool for understanding and fostering humanity; for transporting children to marvelous settings; for building a network by which social knowledge can be transmitted; and for expanding students' foresight, discernment, and insight. Such understandings are enhanced when language arts are integrated; then students can speak, listen, read, write, view, and reflect simultaneously about their goals. When children's literature is used throughout all subjects, students' cognitive and affective domains grow more rapidly. Such integration can be advanced by using this book in three ways: by implementing the strategies for using children's literature in the classroom, marked by the book icons in the margin; by selecting books to read from the literature cards; and by employing the thematic units at the end of even-numbered chapters. The strategies marked by the icons can also be adapted for use with specific literature selections in your language arts curriculum. Each chapter of *Teaching the Language Arts* discusses suggestions for interweaving literature and the language arts into your language arts program.

INTEGRATING THE LANGUAGE ARTS

Using Varied Genres

Defining what is quality literature has never been easy. Most definitions include originality, importance of ideas, imaginative use and beauty of language, as well as literary and artistic styles that enable work to remain fresh, interesting, and meaningful throughout time (Norton, 1995). To assist you and your students' parents to select quality books for children, *Teaching the Language Arts* provides Literature Cards. Literature Cards are the size of notecards so they can be copied, cut, and stored for your future reference for instruction. They are designed to copy and post in the classroom for student use when choosing books, and for parents' use when purchasing or borrowing books. Books listed in these resource cards possess the features of quality literature described above and have been recommended by exemplary teachers and their students. For example, Literature Cards 1 and 2 list the winners and honorary winners of the prestigious Newbery and Caldecott Awards for Children's Literature since they began in 1922 and 1938, respectively.

Studying many genres offers distinct benefits to students, as described in *Teaching the Language Arts*. Each subsequent chapter explains the value of exposure to a different genre. By the end of Chapter 13, you will have learned how to include these additional genres in your program: Caldecott and Newbery Award–winning books; picture books, wordless books, big books, predictable books, and alphabet books; folktales and fairytales; high-interest, low-vocabulary books, magazines, and newspapers; contemporary realistic fiction; modern fantasy and science fiction; fables, legends, and myths; historical fiction; informational books; poetry; plays; self-help, hobbies, biographies, and autobiographies; and multicultural books.

Literature Card 1

NEWBERY AWARD–WINNING BOOKS

1922	*The Story of Mankind* by H. Van Loon, Liveright
1923	*The Voyages of Doctor Doolittle* by H. Lofting, Lippincott
1924	*The Dark Frigate* by C. Hawes, Atlantic/Little Brown
1925	*Tales from Silver Lands* by C. Finger, Doubleday
1926	*Shen of the Sea* by A. Chrisman, Dutton
1927	*Smoky, the Cowhorse* by W. James, Scribner's
1928	*Gay-Neck* by D. Mukerji, Dutton
1929	*The Trumpeter of Krakow* by E. Kelly, Macmillan
1930	*Hitty, Her First Hundred Years* by R. Field, Macmillan
1931	*The Cat Who Went to Heaven* by Coatsworth, Macmillan
1932	*Waterless Mountain* by L. Armer, Longmans
1933	*Young Fu of the Upper Yangtze* by E. Lewis, Winston
1934	*Invincible Louisa* by C. Meigs, Little Brown
1935	*Dobry* by M. Shannon, Viking
1936	*Caddie Woodlawn* by C. Brink, Macmillan
1937	*Roller Skates* by R. Sawyer, Viking
1938	*The White Stag* by K. Seredy, Viking
1939	*Thimble Summer* by E. Enright, Rinehart
1940	*Daniel Boone* by J. Daugherty, Viking

1941	*Call It Courage* by A. Sperry, Macmillan
1942	*The Matchlock Gun* by W. Edmonds, Dodd
1943	*Adam of the Road* by E. Gray, Viking
1944	*Johnny Tremain* by E. Forbes, Houghton Mifflin
1945	*Rabbit Hill* by R. Lawson, Viking
1946	*Strawberry Girl* by L. Lenski, Lippincott
1947	*Miss Hickory* by C. Bailey, Viking
1948	*The Twenty-One Balloons* by W. du Bois, Viking
1949	*King of the Wind* by M. de Angeli, Doubleday
1950	*The Door in the Wall* by M. de Angeli, Doubleday
1951	*Amos Fortune, Free Man* by E. Yates, Aladdin
1952	*Ginger Pye* by E. Estes, Harcourt Brace
1953	*Secret of the Andes* by A. Clark, Viking
1954	*And Now Miguel* by J. Krumgold, T. Crowell
1955	*The Wheel on the School* by M. De Jong, Harper
1956	*Carry On, Mr. Bowditch* by J. Latham, Houghton Mifflin
1957	*Miracles on Maple Hill* by V. Sorensen, Harcourt Brace
1958	*Rifles for Watie* by H. Keith, T. Crowell

(See the website that accompanies this textbook for weblinks to a complete list of winners and honor books.)

INSIDE CULTURALLY ENRICHED CLASSROOMS

Creating a Multicultural Classroom

As stated previously, at this point in every chapter I will describe methods of building a multicultural language arts program.

Teachers who have been most successful in expanding the communication spectrum for students from diverse cultures weave four themes throughout their curriculum (Hornberger, 1990). They consistently motivate students by selecting content about experiences that are common in all cultural groups. In this way the sharing of an individual student's cultural experiences is in a context that is meaningful and exciting for the entire class. Also, peers listen more intently to culturally and personally relevant questions such as "What is different in your family's dinner and routine than that of the three bears and why?" than to a fact-oriented question such as "What was the name of the person who entered the three bears' home?"

Literature Card 2

CALDECOTT AWARD–WINNING BOOKS

1938	*Animals of the Bible* by D. Lathrop Lippincott	1960	*Nine Days to Christmas* by M. Ets, Viking
1939	*Mei Li* by T. Handforth, Doubleday	1961	*Baboushka and the Three Kings* by N. Sidjakov, Panassus
1940	*Abraham Lincoln* by E. d'Aulaires, Doubleday	1962	*Once a House* by M. Brown, Scribner's
1941	*They Were Strong and Good* by R. Lawson, Viking	1963	*The Snowy Day* by E. Keats, Viking
1942	*Make Way for Ducklings* by R. McCloskey, Viking	1964	*Where the Wild Things Are* by M. Sendak, Harper Collins
1943	*The Little House* by V. Burton, Houghton Mifflin	1965	*May I Bring a Friend?* by B. Montresor, Atheneum
1944	*Many Moons* by L. Slobodkin, Harcourt Brace	1966	*Always Room for One More* by N. Hogrogian, Holt
1945	*Prayer for a Child* by E. Jones, Macmillan	1967	*Sam, Bangs and Moonshine* by E. Ness, Holt
1946	*The Rooster Crows* by M. Petershams, Macmillan	1968	*Drummer Hoff* by E. Emberley, Prentice Hall
1947	*The Little Island* by L. Weisgard, Doubleday	1969	*The Fool of the World and the Flying Ship* by U. Shulevitz, Farrar, Straus, Giroux
1948	*White Snow, Bright Snow* by R. Duvoisin Lothrop	1970	*Sylvester and the Magic Pebble* by W. Steig, Windmill
1949	*The Big Snow* by B. & E. Haders, Macmillan	1971	*A Story—A Story* by G. Haley, Atheneum
1950	*Song of the Swallows* by L. Politi, Scribner's	1972	*One Fine Day* by N. Hogrogian, Macmillan
1951	*The Egg Tree* by K. Milhous, Scribner's	1973	*The Funny Little Woman* by A. Lent, Dutton
1952	*Finders Keepers* by N. Mordvinoff, Harcourt Brace	1974	*Duffy and the Devil* by H. Zemach, Farrar, Straus, Giroux
1953	*The Biggest Bear* by L. Ward, Houghton Mifflin	1975	*Arrow to the Sun* by G. McDermott, Viking
1954	*Madeline's Rescue* by L. Bemelmans, Viking	1976	*Why Mosquitoes Buzz in People's Ears* by V. Aardema, Dial
1955	*Cinderella* by M. Brown, Scribner's		
1956	*Frog Went a-Courtin'* by Rojankovsky, Harcourt Brace		
1957	*A Tree Is Nice* by M. Simont, Harper Collins		
1958	*Time of Wonder* by R. McCloskey, Viking		
1959	*Chanticleer and the Fox* by B. Cooney, T. Crowell		

(See the website that accompanies this textbook for weblinks to a complete list of all winners.)

Goldilocks and the Three Bears

Successful teachers also add structure, clarity, redundancy, enthusiasm, and appropriate pace to this culturally based content to maximize student engagement. Structure and clarity are employed in shaping the purpose and focus of language arts lessons; they are not used to suppress students' thinking, voices, and choices. Redundance is applied as needed, typically in summarizing and reinforcing new lesson content. Enthusiasm is expressed toward the content of language arts. Finally, appropriate pace and maximized student engagement are employed to maintain a continuously positive learning atmosphere (Block, 2000; Campbell & Ramey, 1995). During question-and-answer sessions such teachers also follow student responses by incorporating previous student answers into subsequent questions in a process linguists call **uptake** (taking a student's comment to move a class discussion forward). For example, Ms. Johnson asked the question above that compared the three bears' dinner to students' evening routines. Juan answered, "We eat tortillas and only some of us sit at the table because there are eight in my family and our table's too small." Ms. Johnson used uptake and said, "Juan has shown us how what we eat and how many eat together changes from family to family" (Cazden, 1988; Collins, 1982, 1989b). This continuous interweaving of writing, reading, and talking helps culturally diverse students relate topics of instruction to the next classroom comment and builds on their previous learning.

Second, most effective teachers ask culturally diverse students to employ the language arts to address broad social concerns. For example, such teachers ask students to read books with main characters from their cultural group and to focus book sharings on large, thematic, humanistic issues, such as identifying how people relate successfully to others. When these books are discussed in groups in which different cultural identities are represented, students learn various ways to interact productively with others.

Third, teachers who enhance cultural understanding ask students to demonstrate their language achievements orally, visually, and dramatically, as well as in writing. To illustrate, Ms. Johnson often asks Juan to talk in Spanish during show and tell so classmates see a competence in Juan's language abilities that they do not possess themselves. As a result, his preschool friends frequently ask Juan to teach them Spanish words, and as he does, his self-image expands.

Finally, teachers that are most successful with culturally diverse populations create classroom dialogues about how to engage prior knowledge, use text structure, and monitor comprehension, while being acutely sensitive to individual students' unique dialects and the beautiful language variety that they bring to the classroom (Hornberger, 1990; Heath, 1994; Cazden, 1994). For example, consider dialogues about how to engage schema and prior knowledge of cranes (discussed earlier in this chapter). If a culturally diverse student looks puzzled, the teacher would ask others to describe not only their thinking but also how the word is used in their culture and would find a way for the puzzled child to see a crane of the kind the students described. Table 1.2 summarizes principles for establishing a multicultural classroom and implementing a multicultural week.

RECOGNIZING AND REPORTING PROGRESS

Using Parent Observations

When parent–infant interactions go well, babies form strong emotional ties with their caregivers. The attached baby interacts extensively with the primary caregivers, who become the primary adult attachment object. Once attachment occurs, a baby does what it can to maintain proximity to primary caregivers, including crawling toward them, crying when they are out of sight, and clinging on to them. John Bowlby (1969) provided a comprehensive theory about both the course of attachment and the biological and social mechanisms that account for this attachment. The developmental course of infant–caregiver attachment has been studied extensively in the quarter-century since Bowlby's book first appeared, with Bowlby's perspective now enjoying a great deal of research support (e.g., see Sroufe, 1996, for a review of this literature).

Perhaps the most important finding in the attachment literature is that the more responsive the adult, and the more the adult is there to help when the baby needs

TABLE 1.2 MULTICULTURAL AWARENESS WEEK SCHEDULE (MAW)

MONDAY

Exploring the culture through pictures

- Present students with a variety of picture books that include visual representations of a culture and the time period being studied.
- Allow them to choose one picture that they find interesting, and have them write a descriptive essay about the picture.
- Have them employ any other writing techniques studied during the previous week in their descriptive essay.

TUESDAY

Silent reading of a biographical essay

- Make a few different biographical essays available for them to read and give them the freedom to choose the one that interests them most.
- After they finish reading, ask them to name five things that they find significant about that person and why they think that person is an important historical figure.

WEDNESDAY

Exploring the culture through music

- Present music that represents both the culture and the time period that is being studied.
- Listen to the music and have the students write an essay on how the music made them feel. They will be expected to write about their emotions and their initial reactions to the music.

THURSDAY

Movie day

- Choose a film that emphasizes the theme of the MAW.
- Have the students answer objective questions during the movie.
- Discuss the questions after the movie and the scenes that made the greatest impact on them.
- Have them write a reaction essay, expressing their opinions about the movie— why they did or didn't like it.

FRIDAY

Guest speaker

- Students choose to invite a guest speaker in on Friday who will talk about what was studied during that particular MAW.
- Ask the guest to share his or her personal experiences with the rest of the class.
- Ask the guest to read a story aloud to the class that reflects and integrates the topic of the MAW.
- Students will apply what they have learned this week in writing to be shared with parents or peers.

help, the more secure the emerging infant becomes. When researchers have measured both parental sensitivity early in the first year of a baby's life and security of attachment later in the first year, they have found a clear association between them (Sroufe, 1996, Chapter 10). This is important with respect to other aspects of language development. For instance, the more secure the attachment, the more effective the parent is in helping their child to explore the world.

Attachment security is also related to the quality of mother–child emergent literacy experiences during the preschool years. Dutch researchers Adriana Bus and Marinus van Ijzendoorn (1988) observed 1(½)-year-olds, 3(½)-year-olds, and 5(½)-year-olds, and their mothers as they watched "Sesame Street," read a picture book together, and went through an alphabet book—all prototypical emergent literacy contexts. Securely attached children were more attentive and less easily distracted during emergent literacy interactions. Particularly critical, secure dads were more oriented to reading and reading-related skills during their interactions (e.g., pretending to read). Also, mothers of more securely attached children expected more of their children, and the children met the expectations with pleasure and ease.

Parents can be taught to observe their children and be sensitive to them (e.g., Belsky, Rosenberger, & Crnic, 1995; van den Boom, 1994, 1995; van Ijzendoorn, Juffer, & Duyvesteyn, 1995). You can use the forms in Figure 1.1 and Figure 1.3 to help parents develop a family literacy environment that strengthens preschoolers' language development. You can also help parents understand what they can do to foster their preschoolers' emergent literacy. Such exercises are not schoollike, but playful and verbal. Parents can play with language in ways that are interesting to young children. Figures 1.3 and 1.4 can be given to parents and contain activities that fulfill these purposes.

•‣•

SECTION 3   TEACHERS AS CONTINUAL LEARNERS

Improving Our Professional Competencies

At this point in each chapter you can learn about activities that increase your teaching competencies. These competencies are related to the objectives presented in each chapter. These learning opportunities will always include a specific teaching ability, entitled "Professional Development Activity," that has been demonstrated to increase students' language learning and productive use of the language arts. You will also have the chance to use journal writing in a variety of ways and create samples of journal activities as models for your students in the section entitled "For Your Journal." The third subheading describes ways in which you can connect parents, classrooms, and communities.

PROFESSIONAL DEVELOPMENT ACTIVITY

Scaffolding

Scaffolding is *an instructional strategy that supports students as they attempt to use a competency for the first time* (Bruner, 1986). It is frequently singled out as one of the

Observing your own talk   NOT AT ALL | SOMETIMES | OFTEN

1. I asked questions to encourage my child to talk.
2. I used names and labels as I played so my child could imitate me.
3. I used specific words for color, size, and shape.
4. I described what my child and I were doing as we played.
5. I reminded my child of other related experiences when we played.

Observing your child's talk   NOT AT ALL | SOMETIMES | OFTEN

My child uses language . . .

1. to request help.
2. to engage me in play ("You be the . . . ").
3. to request information ("What . . . ?").
4. to plan the next activity or tell me how to play.
5. to label or name something.
6. to explain an activity or how a toy works.

Parents and Children Interacting

During play time, I remembered to . . .

- show kindness and interest in my child's ideas.
- join in play themes without dominating.
- allow my child to direct the action.
- follow my child's lead by respecting his or her ideas and ability to make decisions.
- look for ways to respond to and build on my child's ideas.

For each question, circle the O (often), S (some), or N (never). Then use the blank space to tell something about how you felt about that aspect of your playing together.

1. Do I observe how my child interacts as we play? For example, did I notice whether she was quiet? Excited? Does she want help? Or does she prefer to figure out things alone?   O   S   N

   I can improve by _____.

2. Do I approach my child slowly, with respect?   O   S   N

   I can improve by _____.

3. Do I allow my child to take the lead? Do I follow that lead?   O   S   N

   I can improve by _____.

4. Do I encourage my child's play by staying involved with the play theme and helping him or her to create new words and thoughts about it?   O   S   N

   I can improve by _____.

5. Do I use gestures, expressions, and a tone of voice to show I support my child and am there?   O   S   N

   I can improve by _____.

FIGURE 1.3 OBSERVING PARENTS AND CHILDREN: CHECKLIST TO GIVE TO PARENTS TO DEVELOP THEIR YOUNG CHILDREN'S LANGUAGE ARTS ABILITIES

Adapted from *Families at School: A Handbook for Parents* (pp. 10–21), by Adele Thomas, Lynn Fazio, and Betty L. Stiefelmeyer, 1999, Newark, DE: International Reading Association. Reprinted with permission of Adele Thomas and the International Reading Association. Copyright © 1999 by the International Reading Association. All rights reserved.

Children learn language by . . .

imitating sounds
singing songs
making rhymes
asking and answering questions
listening
explaining
doing finger plays
pretending
explaining their ideas
describing things
comparing things
telling stories
sharing books
labeling
following directions
describing patterns
playing make-believe

Children develop emergent writing and fine motor skills by . . .

gluing
lacing
drawing
tracing
cutting
stacking
tearing
sewing

Children learn social skills by . . .

sharing
taking turns
pretending together
talking together
cooperating
helping one another
expressing their feelings

Children learn to view analytically and learn about math, space, and time by . . .

sorting things
talking about the time of day
putting things in order
counting
grouping things
drawing and labeling shapes
talking about more and less
matching things
making patterns
creating charts and graphs
talking about above and below, under and over, on top of, underneath, and beside
recognizing numbers
doing puzzles

Children develop psycholinguistic abilities and gross motor skills by . . .

jumping
running
twisting
climbing
walking
throwing and catching
skipping
balancing
bending
bouncing a ball

Children develop thinking skills by . . .

completing patterns
pretending
using their senses
playing memory games
doing puzzles
sorting things
noting similarities and differences
dramatizing
answering "what if" questions

FIGURE 1.4 PARENTS' GUIDE TO YOUNG CHILDREN'S LANGUAGE ARTS DEVELOPMENT

most important instructional techniques teachers can employ (Graves, Graves, & Braaten, 1996). Scaffolding enables learners to handle complex tasks because you, as teacher, assume parts of the task yourself (Means & Knapp, 1991). You gradually reduce your support as a student becomes more competent, confident, and self-directing in that specific language ability. This technique performs the same role as does temporary scaffolding in building skyscrapers. You place temporary scaffolds around students' learning to structure the students' construction of ideas. As the task progresses and the students' thinking becomes more substantial, you gradually reduce the scaffold (your support).

Although Langer (1991) identified many scaffold actions and statements that you can use, these can be combined into five types: (1) modeling a complete language ability first, before the child begins; (2) inviting students to try a new language ability while you do the entire action with them, such as Ms. Johnson demonstrated when she held Juan's hand so he could write his name for his mother's letter; (3) cluing the first step in a new language process as a child is attempting it for the first time, and the child watches—for example, saying, "Try using Step 1 that I just completed"; (4) calling specific languaging abilities by name to clue students' self-initiated use, such as saying "Which decoding strategy would be most valuable to decode that word?"; and (5) providing two models and methods of engaging a specific languaging ability and asking students to exercise their preference (Block & Mangieri, 1995a, 1995b, 1996; Collins, 1992; Reed & Roller, 1991).

For example, Juan asked Ms. Johnson: "Would you help me? I can't think of a title for my story." Ms. Johnson used the fourth scaffold by asking a question such as: "What have you tried?" Then, Juan answered: "I want a short title, but I don't want it to begin with the word *My* like all my other titles." Ms. Johnson then used his reply to scaffold again. This answer documented what Ms. Johnson suspected. Juan already uses summarizing strategies well, and this is not the reason for his difficulty in generating a title. What he needs is a strategy to increase his creative thinking. So, Ms. Johnson chooses the fifth scaffold and says: "When you want to create something new, like a title, you can do two things. You can exchange some words with other words. For example, if you don't want your title to be *My Trip,* you could use words similar to *my,* such as *Juan's, Our, Mine, Me,* or *The.* The second strategy is to change the order. For example, instead of making your title *My Trip,* you can rearrange by putting the last part (the trip) first, and the first part (you) last, such as *The Trip I Took, A Trip That Took Juan by Surprise,* or *The Most Important Trip.*" Once the scaffold was complete, Ms. Johnson asked Juan which strategy he wanted to use for this title. Because she'd demonstrated both, he could more reliably select the one that would be the most successful for him.

FOR YOUR JOURNAL

Daybooks

Journals are notebooks, folders, diaries, or handmade booklets in which you and your students keep personal reflections about your and your students' lives, language, and language arts use. For Your Journal activities enable you to practice many ways to use journals with your students. There are 14 types of journals; each devel-

Scaffolding is usually used to teach students in a one-on-one situation, but this technique can be used to teach a classroom of students. A volunteer is scaffolding the concepts up *and* down *by asking students to move their hands up and down to learn the meanings of these terms when they hear, read, or write them.*

ops different aspects of the language arts. All promote fluency in writing and reading, encourage risk taking in thinking, provide opportunities for reflection, develop use of writing conventions, and validate personal experiences and feelings (Routman, 1994). You can experience the benefits of journal writing activities by performing this and subsequent For Your Journal activities at the end of each chapter. The purpose of this activity is to encourage you to create a professional and personal journal to increase your teaching effectiveness. This journal can become a diary of your teaching history and a tool by which you reflect on your teaching philosophy and resolve professional difficulties. It will also provide examples of journal entries to share with your students.

The first type of journal is a **daybook.** You and your students can make one by marking one section of a journal as a "daybook." At the same time each day for 5 minutes, you and they write in this daybook about the good and bad situations that occurred during the day. Daybooks are designed to contain brief, dated entries, with one week to a page so patterns between days can be detected. To experience how valuable this journal can be, write today's date, and the day of the week on the first page of your daybook journal section. Keep a journal about your teaching (or other aspect of your life if not teaching presently) for 2 weeks. In your entries, focus on what you do, when you do it, and how you do it—for example, "How did I teach to the whole child this week?" At the end of the observation period, critically analyze your journal entries to determine how your instructional behaviors distribute across the week.

To use daybook journals with students, have them stop for 5 minutes at the end of each day and record what they learned, what questions they want to ask at home or at school tomorrow, and what they learned about themselves and others.

CONNECTING CLASSROOMS, PARENTS, AND COMMUNITIES

Capitalizing on the Power of Play

At this point in every chapter you will receive information and resources to share with parents and community members to increase the connection between these important environments in students' lives. The first action you can take is to assist parents to play with language with their children.

The importance of playful activity for preschoolers through middle school students cannot be overemphasized. It is as Friedrich Schiller said, "Man only plays when he is in the fullest sense of the word a human being; and he is only fully a human being when he plays." Through play, students assume many new roles and responsibilities.

Play takes many forms. At one end of the continuum children participate in games and sports that follow rules and rituals. At the opposite end of the play spectrum, children engage in dramas by assuming the roles of others. In play everything is possible. Children can shift from a game with rules to a world of fantasy, often stopping midway to give directions and explain actions, or answer questions. The dynamic effect play has on learning and thinking has fascinated philosophers, educators, psychologists, and anthropologists through the ages (Courtney, 1999; Newman, 2000; Christie & Stone, 1999). They propose that play is pivotal in developing spontaneity and exercises the opposite of habit (Blatner & Blatner, 1988). Spencer (1914) presented the notion that play is the result of surplus energy. On the other hand, Aristotle believed that play can be a catharsis or safety valve for pent-up emotions. Huizenga (1955) further posits that in creating a poetic phrase, motif, or in expressing a mood, play is always a part. Some believe that through play students discipline the imagination and enter the adult world of the arts and sciences (Hartley & Goldenson, 1975).

Among the most famous theorists examining play's role in learning was Freud. Freud's explanation of play was that it is a projection of wishes and enables children to reenact conflicts so that they can master them. (An extension of this philosophy can be seen in contemporary physicians' reports of the value of humor as a healing tool.) Play also alleviates stress. Thus, designing playful creations is gaining importance in today's schools. This natural impulse to play, if encouraged, can become a lifelong way of learning. Although some believe that play is frivolous and unrelated to serious learning, Morrow and Rand (1991) cite several studies in which "symbolic play" demands higher levels of cognitive involvement than "serious" cognitive tasks. Dramatic play has also been shown to improve story comprehension and other literacy skills.

For all of these reasons, teachers are learning new ways to keep "the play impulse" alive in their students and to encourage parents to do so as well. Blatner and Blatner's (1988) research found that children's play continues into adulthood and has emotional, social, educational, and cultural benefits in the following ways. Play enhanced their flexibility of mind, initiative, improvisation, humility, sense of humor, effective communication, inclusiveness, ability to interact and be at ease with others, questioning, looking for alternatives, solving problems, and learning new techniques. For example, many students like to play, listen, and mimic. During such episodes of play they "try out" behaviors, language patterns, and emerging hypotheses about the environment, words, and ideas. They develop their own curriculum and find answers they need.

Finger Plays for Nursery and Kindergarten

You can assist parents to support their children's language play by valuing children's language inventions as they spontaneously occur. You can also encourage the efforts of parents and students to play with language by inventing fun words yourself. You may need to set aside a few moments each week to play with words (e.g., riddles, limericks, and tongue twisters). Finger plays are also among the favorite means of easing students into exploring learning through play in the classroom. Some of the best sources of finger plays include *Finger Rhymes, Hand Rhymes, Play Rhymes,* and *Finger Plays for Nursery and Kindergarten.* Examples appear in Table 1.3.

At the upper elementary and middle school level, play often occurs through role plays and is equally important at these ages for all the reasons stated previously. As students do in the primary years, older students use plays, dramas, and role plays to internalize society's messages and determine what role they want to have in their world. Because peers and respected adults are adolescents' main language models, role plays by peers and adults often enable these students to listen better and learn more than they do from direct instruction. Role play and drama also appear to provide a subtle escape from self that adolescents need to internalize values and think deeply. Plays and dramas also become important "celebrative events" that bond them to each other and school.

SUMMARY

Language is a system of patterns and rules, called phonological, morphological, syntactical, and pragmatic, that govern how people communicate their thoughts. Through instruction students can learn to operate these principles as they create and transmit ideas to read, write, speak, listen, spell, act, and use technology more successfully. Such language arts programs also (a) help students satisfy their needs to have a valuable place in the classroom community; (b) provide lessons that are

TABLE 1.3 FINGER PLAYS

Finger plays capitalize on the power of play to increase young children's creative and analytical thinking abilities. When introducing finger plays, remember to follow these basic guidelines:

1. Use motivating facial and verbal expressions.

2. Say the rhyme and show the accompanying actions that you create as symbols of the meaning of the word with hand movements, facial expressions, and body language.

3. Repeat the rhyme, if necessary.

4. Say to the children: "Please help me say it while I do the motions."

5. Repeat the rhyme again with the children and invite them to join you in duplicating the finger actions. At times do not say the italicized words below so students have to analyze and reflect unaided as to the sequence of words that should come next.

6. Recommended finger plays are:

   a. Little Jack *Horner*
      Sat in the *corner* . . .

   b. Hickory, Dickory, *dock!*
      The mouse ran up the *clock.* . . .

   c. Little Miss *Muffet*
      Sat on a *tuffet.* . . .

   d. I know a little *girl*
      Who had a little *curl.* . . .

   e. Little Boy Blue come blow your *horn;*
      The sheep's in the meadow, the cow's in the *corn.* . . .

   f. Ding, dong *bell,*
      The pussy's in the *well!* . . .

   g. Mary, *Mary*
      Quite *contrary.* . . .

   h. One, *two,*
      Buckle my *shoe.* . . .

   i. Humpty-Dumpty sat on a *wall;*
      Humpty-Dumpty had a great *fall.* . . .

   j. A dillar, a *dollar,*
      A ten-o'clock *scholar.* . . .

Then, you can move to activities like the samples below in which children supply their own rhyming words in a familiar context. These finger plays develop young students' creative and analytic thinking abilities.

I am thinking of a word.
It rhymes with *floor.*
It is kept closed in the winter.
What is it? (door)

I'm thinking of a word.
It rhymes with *thing.*
It is worn on the finger.
What is it? (ring)

I'm thinking of a word.
It rhymes with *dandy.*
It is good to eat.
What is it? (candy)

I'm thinking of a word.
It rhymes with *sweater.*
It is something we write.
What is it? (letter)

Next, to further advance their language and thinking abilities ask children to supply a rhyming word that completes a sentence. For example:

An animal that rhymes with *hat* is ____. (cat)

A little *mouse* ran into the _____. (house)

My new *bed* was painted ____. (red)

Finally, have the children generate the word that rhymes. Ask them to:

Name a vegetable that rhymes with *born.*

Name a word that rhymes with *night.*

Adapted from *The sourcebook: Activity for infants and young children* (2nd ed., pp. 216–227), by G. W. Makion, 1990, Columbia, OH: Merrill.

integrative and literature-based, and support research about language learning; (c) provide authentic learning experiences in which students complete processes and products that will be used in the real world; (d) enable students to use language and think simultaneously about their own ideas and questions; and (e) feature teachers who possess characteristics that correlate with high student achievement.

There are eight components of language arts instruction: speaking, listening, reading, writing, thinking, observing, technological competence, and analytical viewing. Research demonstrates that these should be taught interactively with a multicultural emphasis (and assessed by performance measures). Language arts teachers are most effective if they care about both their students' lives and the language arts and have personal goals and a strong and broad teaching repertoire. In Chapter 2 you will learn how these principles can be actualized in your classroom.

HOW TO DO IT: USING WHAT YOU'VE LEARNED

At this point in each chapter, you will have several opportunities to implement and think about what you have learned.

ASSESSING YOUR LEARNING

1. List the characteristics of the best language arts teachers presented in this chapter. On a scale of 1 to 10 rank your present capabilities in each of these criteria. Be prepared to share your reasons for each ranking in a class discussion.

2. *Volcano: The Eruption and Healing of Mount St. Helens* by Patricia Lauder received the Newbery Honor Book Award for Outstanding Children's Literature in 1985. This book's beautiful photographs and captivating writing can be used to increase students' viewing, listening, reading, and writing competencies in many different ways. The book provides a glossary of key terms on page 60. Read the book and describe the important language arts objectives you would develop by using this selection of children's literature as core instructional material in your literature-based language arts classroom.

3. Literature Cards 1 and 2 describe award-winning books that can be used in many ways to achieve the principles of effective instruction cited in this chapter. Select one or more of the titles from these cards and develop a lesson in which you use these books to implement one or more of the principles of effective language arts instruction.

4. Devise a system whereby you can regularly receive suggestions for improvement from students, peers, parents, and administrators. For example, one teacher wrote a letter to each of the above constituencies over the winter vacation. The letter asked for suggestions for her improvement in five areas.

5. Ask a group of elementary students to discuss and then write about the characteristics of a good language arts teacher. In this discussion and subsequent writing, ask students to defend their statements and give examples from effective teachers they have had. Ask how they feel and how much they learn when they set their own goals for learning the language arts, and when they are allowed to pick their own books. If you do not have access to a group of elementary students, ask peers to describe characteristics of good language arts teachers as evidenced by their own teachers. Compare their lists to yours and prepare a written summary of what you learned from this activity.

KEY TERMS EXERCISE

Many people enjoy evaluating their ability to learn new terms. After reading this chapter, you can improve your retention by thinking about the definitions of each term listed below. Place a checkmark in the blank that precedes each term whose meaning you know. If you are not certain of the meaning of any term, review the discussion of that term. If you learned the meanings of 25 or more of these terms after your initial reading, it is a good indication that your comprehension is strong. Congratulations.

_____ authentic language arts task (p. 22)

_____ bound morphemes (p. 15)

_____ constructivist theory (p. 5)

_____ culture (p. 27)

_____ daybook (p. 38)

_____ dialects (p. 16)

_____ disequilibrium (p. 8)

_____ equilibrium (p. 8)

_____ free morphemes (p. 15)

_____ grammar (p. 5)

_____ graphemes (p. 13)

_____ higher-level thinking (p. 4)

_____ International Phonetic Alphabet (IPA) (p. 4)

_____ journals (p. 36)

_____ language (p. 3)

_____ language arts (p. 3)

_____ language arts instruction (p. 3)

_____ learn (p. 8)

_____ listening (pp. 3–4)

_____ morpheme (p. 15)

_____ morphological clues (p. 15)

_____ morphology (p. 5)

_____ observing (p. 4)

_____ oral language (p. 3)

_____ phonemes (p. 4)

_____ phonemic awareness (p. 4)

_____ phonics (p. 4)

_____ phonological clues (p. 13)

_____ phonological language system (p. 13)

_____ phonology (p. 4)

_____ pragmatics (p. 16)

_____ psycholinguistic theory (p. 9)

_____ reading (p. 4)

_____ scaffolding (p. 33)

_____ schema (p. 6)

_____ semantic or morphological system (p. 15)

_____ semantics (p. 5)

_____ sociolinguistic theory (p. 11)

_____ Standard English (p. 16)

_____ syntactical cluing (p. 16)

_____ syntactical system (p. 16)

_____ syntax (p. 5)

_____ technological literacy (p. 4)

_____ uptake (p. 30)

_____ viewing (p. 4)

_____ writing (p. 4)

FOR FUTURE REFERENCE

Cairn, T. H., & Munsie, L. (1995). Parent participation in literacy learning, *The Reading Teacher, 48*(5), 392–341.

Cullinan, B. (Ed). (1992). *Invitation to read: More children's literature in the reading program.* Newark, DE: IRA.

Danielson, K. E., & LaBonty, J. (1994). *Integrating reading and writing through children's literature.* Boston: Allyn and Bacon.

Davidson, J. (1996). *Emergent literacy and dramatic play in early education.* Albany, NY: Delmar. (Describes the integration of the principles of this chapter at the preschool, kindergarten, and first-grade levels through numerous in-depth classroom examples.)

The education and care of young children: Report of the ASCD Early Childhood Consortium. Alexandria, VA: Association for Supervision and Curriculum Development.

Gay, G. (1995). *At the essence of learning: Multicultural education.* West Lafayette, IN: Kappa Delta Pi.

Lukens, R. J. (1995). *A critical handbook of children's literature.* (5th ed.). New York: Harper.

Monson, D. L. (1995). *Adventuring with books: A booklist for pre-K–grade 6.* Urbana, IL: NCTE.

Multicultural reference materials: Office of the Commissioner, Room 115 Education Building, New York State Education Dept., Albany, NY 12234; California Dept. of Education, Bureau of Publications Sales, P.O. Box 271, Sacramento, CA 95802–0271

National Council of Teachers of English. (1996). *1996 Caldecott calendar.* Urbana, IL: NCTE.

Taylor, R. L. (1995). Functional uses of reading and shared literacy activities in Icelandic homes: A monograph in family literacy. *Reading Research Quarterly, 30*(2), 194–221.

NEW WEBSITES

www.teleport.com/~dleahy/Truth/lesson.htm

Internet ready lesson plans and ideas categorized by content area. Excellent database resource.

http://encarta.msn.com/schoolhouse/lessons/

Well-organized index of lessons is categorized and searchable by content area. Complete lessons with related web links. Submit your own lesson plan for other teachers to share.

www.solutions.ibm.com/k12/teacher/activity.html

Monthly thematic units with lesson plans and web resources archived since 1995.

www.kings.k12.ca.us/math/lessons.html

Internet-infused lessons on math topics. Most lessons reflect NCTM standards regarding real-life content. The home page also has links to lessons for science, history, and language arts.

TOPICS FOR TEACHERS

1. New teacher page: www.geocities.com/Athens/Delphi/7862/management.htm

This site provides a plethora of information for the first-year teacher; well-organized ideas for starting the school year; and links for professional development including journals, organizations, and many classroom management resources.

2. Classroom discipline techniques: http://users.aol.com/churchward/his/techniques.html

Learn about 11 techniques for keeping control of your classroom plus find additional links to Four Steps to Successful Classroom Discipline with examples and a detailed explanation of the honor-level system model.

3. Checklist for teachers: www.ed.uius.edu/facstaff/m-weeks/majprof.html

Choose from an excellent collection of teacher resources including teaching styles, discipline models, and web resources and lesson plans for each of the content areas.

Multiage partnerships between kindergartners and preschoolers allow the younger children to overcome fears they may have about starting school by collaborating with their older counterparts.

CHAPTER 2

TEACHING THE LANGUAGE ARTS

Meisong, Juan, Allison, and Michael are now 4 years old and are entering their preschool, on the first day of school, full of wonder and excitement. The room was colorful and the walls were overflowing with posters, words, charts, and book jackets. Tables were covered with cloths, equipment, and writing materials. Their teacher, Ms. Diederick, told the children that the signs above these tables were Listening Circle, Play Center, Block Club House, Thinking Table, Computer Corner, and Discussion Den. The class library, a kitchen, some computers, and an easel were at the front. A large rug was laid out in the Discussion Den. Ms. Diederick said: "Please join me on the rug as I read *Charlie Brown Goes to School.*" Afterward, students talked about being anxious about coming to preschool today, shared the items that they had brought from home to show, made designs for their lockers, and (with Ms. Diederick's help) wrote their names to put on their desks. At 10:00 A.M. the kindergartners came to partner with Meisong and her classmates. They taught them how to work at each center. In 10-minute intervals, pairs changed centers, and everyone had the grandest time. At the end of the day, Meisong asked her partner and new kindergarten friend to come home with her. Ms. Diederick watched Meisong and Deanna laugh and skip along home. Her idea to use multiage partnerships had worked. The kindergartners had achieved her objective of removing the preschoolers' fears of going to school, and the preschoolers had given the kindergartners an opportunity to demonstrate how much they had learned the year before.

In this chapter you will learn how to (1) implement the principles in Chapter 1; (2) schedule short as well as extended blocks of time for language arts instruction; (3) maintain a positive classroom climate; (4) support students' risk taking; (5) involve students in planning what to learn; (6) monitor student-led, small-group discussions; (7) advance students' communication abilities daily; and (8) formalize your language arts teaching philosophy.

You will read examples from exemplary preschool language arts programs as you learn how to develop effective programs for all grade levels, from kindergarten through eighth grade. After reading this chapter, you should be able to master these

IRA, NAEYC, NCTE, TEKS, and other statewide and province-based standards for language arts professionals:

1. Creating student-centered classrooms
2. Grouping students to maximize low and high achievers' language learning
3. Integrating wordless books, big books, pattern books, and alphabet books in the language arts program
4. Developing a philosophy of teaching language arts
5. Developing lessons to exercise students' language abilities and to emphasize their prior experiences
6. Planning lessons for paraprofessionals and teaching assistants who work with the children in your room

SECTION 1   THEORETICAL FOUNDATIONS

Research on How to Organize Language Arts

Your year-long language arts program will need a master plan, daily schedules, appropriate instructional groups, and effective activities (e.g., Clay, 1998; Block, 1999; Allington, Pressley, Block, McWharton, & Morrow, 1999; Smith, 1990; and Rumelhart, 1993). These researchers found that even poorer readers read significantly more books than higher-achieving peers who were in classrooms that did not use the organizational systems and activities in this chapter (IRA/NAEYC, 1999; Neuman, 1999; Block, 1999).

Children who read voluntarily, and have an internally guided interest in books, achieve higher scores on standardized tests (Atwell, 1994; Sweet, Guthrie, & Ng, 1998). Similarly, voluntary reading correlates with higher levels of reading achievement, increased comprehension, vocabulary development, and reading fluency because students in literature-rich classrooms read significantly more words than students in traditional classrooms (Anderson, Hiebert, Scott, & Wilkinson, 1985; Ruddell, 1998). In addition, students in a literature-rich classroom took 9 minutes longer to select a book to read than students who learned to read without a literature-based approach: "Without exception, children in the literature-based classroom sampled text from one or more books before making their selections, either by reading parts of books to themselves or to another child. They also employed strategies like using the card catalog to find books on a desired topic or by a specific author" (Askov & Peck, 1982, p. 174). Achieving this level of student independence in language arts development is difficult without using the organizational structures described in the next few pages.

Such student ownership is also important in writing, critical viewing, drama, and reflection. In student-centered classes, children frequently meet to discuss the work they are doing. When these peer conferences are customary, students' abilities to speak, think, and write messages for specific audiences and purposes improve (Calkins, 1994; Collins, 1992b; Dodge, 1994). Such meetings, as well as small-group discussions and whole-class conversations, also expand language users' awareness of the necessity to match speakers' or writers' intentions to readers' and listeners' expectations, interests, and needs (Calkins, 1994; Graves, 1998; Fountas, & Pinnell, 1996; Clay, 1999). For example, students in one literature-rich second-grade classroom wrote an average of 18 books of 20 pages or more. In traditional classrooms, students wrote few books, and when they did, the manuscripts tended to be composed of one-page compositions from each member of the class (Hagerty & Hiebert, 1989).

Similarly, Stuart and Graves (1987) found that children produce better products when given the control to choose topics about which they want to write. **Journal writing,** where students write about topics of importance to them on a regular basis, also increases very young children's (including preschoolers') abilities to take risks, to write more specifically, and to communicate original thoughts (Bloodgood, 1999; Neuman & Roskos, 1997; Stanton, Shuy, Kreeft, & Reed, 1988). Moreover, young writers who write in journals regularly used more effective and complex syntax than peers who did not write in journals (Graves, 1998; Nystrand, 1989) and benefitted from peer as well as teacher critiques of their writings (Block, 1996; Collins, 1991b; Block, 1999; Calkins, 1994; Nystrand, 1989). These benefits occur in part because, when students respond to each writing, it is most often solely as interested readers. On the other hand, when teachers respond, it is usually as evaluators, measurers, correctors, or editors. Students in student-centered communication classes also appear to shift their perceptions of reading and writing from a skill to a meaning-emphasis process. Such a change does not occur in traditional classes, but rather in classes that apply the grouping systems that follow.

In summary, a literature-based, student-centered language arts program contains many benefits and special features, such as discussion periods, pupil compositions, self-selected readings, and the celebration and encouragement of students' creative and critical thinking. The purpose of our discussion up to this point has been to increase your understanding of the theory that supports a student-centered approach. The next discussion will help you plan 36 weeks of instruction so you can effectively transfer this theory to practice.

DEVELOPING A MASTER PLAN

Your **master programmatic plan** begins when you reflect on what you want your students to have accomplished by the end of the year. It will be helpful if you obtain a copy of your state's and school district's language arts objectives to become familiar with competencies that are your responsibility at your specific grade level. These objectives are likely to be similar to the following, which were prepared as national standards by a National Council of Teachers of English (NCTE) and International Reading Association (IRA) joint task force (1999):

- Students become considerate, effective speakers who express innovative ideas and insightful commentary that adds to others' thinking.

- Students choose to read widely for pleasure, and use printed materials to improve their lives.

- Students influence others through skillful and effective writing.
- Students listen actively and increase their listening vocabularies to more fully appreciate thoughts that others share in discussions.
- Students are comfortable and effective in thinking creatively and analytically.
- Students use viewing, observations, and interpretations of nonverbal language effectively to add meaning to their lives.
- Students become technologically literate and develop the desire to stay abreast of innovations in computing, electronic networking, and other technological communication aids.

Once you have identified year-long goals, you can develop semester-long and weekly goals. While your daily schedule will fluctuate occasionally, posting your schedule in the room, just as Ms. Diederick did for her preschoolers, is important for students (shown in Figure 2.1). An established procedure provides the security and structure students need to put forth maximum effort, take risks, and engage in intensely personal and meaningful work to attain their language goals. Such schedules minimize unnecessary interruptions. Regardless of the daily schedule you choose, a large part of the success of your language arts program rests on your ability to manage movement. Procedures include making sure students know how and when to move and store materials; having clearly marked, color-coded areas where students turn in their work so time is not wasted collecting papers; and ending the day by arranging furniture and writing opening activities for the next day. These procedures include students knowing how to move from station to station in the language arts room, throw away trash, sharpen pencils, leave the room, and raise or not raise hands during discussions. You can build this knowledge by demonstrating the procedures yourself, asking students to perform them, and then posing possible disruptive scenarios to the routine, such as "What will you do if I'm having a conference with a student and you need something?" "What must you do before going to a new activity?" "How many children should be at the class library at one time and why?" Students profit from practicing these procedures for several days at the beginning of the year and by having a signal to end activities and put materials away.

Ms. Diederick illustrated this by developing such class procedures on the first day of school with Meisong and all her classmates. She asked questions that have proved successful for many teachers: "What do you want our classroom to be like?" "What kinds of people do we want to be?" and "What do you need in our room to help you learn as much as you desire?" Meisong answered these questions first, by saying, "We should be nice to everyone." Then Juan chimed in, "I want to take care of all our pretty things." Michael added, "I want to be in charge of cleanup, and everyone can help me when they finish everything they do." Allison ended the discussion by saying, "I want all of us to do our best all the time."

When students play such prominent roles in deciding how their classroom will be run, the class will come together as a learning community more rapidly, and students can learn to balance the principles of fairness and sharing with their spontaneity and need for immediate feedback in language experiences. At times, however, even with these procedures in place, students who have not yet learned how to satisfy their belonging needs, ease frustrations, or alleviate personal affronts through positive means,

Time	Activity	
8:30	Settle In	
8:35	Morning Meeting, Journaling	
9:00	Reading and Writing Workshops	
10:00	Outdoors	
10:15	Snack	
10:30	Shared Reading	
11:00	Morning Work Time	
12:00	Lunch and Recess	
1:00	Story and Quiet Reading	
1:30	Math or Science Activity	
2:00	Choice Time	
2:30	Jobs	
2:40	Meeting [Changed to Journaling Time for today] 	

"When's lunch?" and "How long till recess?" are questions young students often ask. With a written schedule posted visibly somewhere in the room, children can find out for themselves. Also, because many young children cannot yet read, pictures (such as those shown above) posted beside the words are helpful. To allow flexibility in the schedule, velcro can be attached to the back of each activity so that they can be switched around or applied by the children themselves (as shown in the bottom square).

FIGURE 2.1 SAMPLE DAILY SCHEDULE TO POST IN YOUR CLASS

Created by Blythe Bader and Jennifer Walker, 2000, elementary education majors at Texas Christian University, Fort Worth, TX. Used by permission.

will need your help. You can help them (and simultaneously develop their language arts) in the following ways:

- If a student seeks attention continuously and disruptively, you can notice and compliment positive behaviors the first thing each morning.
- If a student becomes overly angry, you can develop a behavior contract with the student and place him or her in a positive leadership position.
- If a student projects helplessness, you can challenge her or him to complete a few steps in the task and set individual student goals that make positive contributions to the classroom community.
- If a student is revengeful and hurts your or peers' feelings, you can assign a project that the student shares with others to build his or her confidence in being valuable to others and the class. Many times, students who disturb others need people who are willing to care about them before they become willing to care about themselves or their communication abilities.

DEVISING DAILY SCHEDULES

Effective language arts instruction can be scheduled in four ways: learning centers; minilessons and workshops (so different amounts of time can be allocated to particular language arts objectives); thematic units (to integrate the language arts for in-depth learning); and multiage classes in which students of two or more age levels join the same community to learn together. You do not have to use only one of these organizational plans but can combine these scheduling options in a wide variety of ways. The benefits and limitations of each will be described next.

DAILY SCHEDULE 1: LEARNING CENTERS

Learning centers are usually designated sections in the language arts classroom where materials are continually available for students to work with alone or in small groups to master specific language arts objectives. Learning centers are particularly valuable for preschool through second grade students as they support their desire to achieve independence and develop group communication skills. They enable young children to engage with content intensely for short periods of time. For older students, learning centers satisfy the need to display unique talents, creativity, leadership, and cooperation skills. At both of these age levels, learning centers promote a sense of belonging, acceptance, and peer support. Learning centers also build intrinsic motivation because students select meaningful tasks and have a colorful working environment for "hands-on" activities. In addition, students tend to become deeply engaged in activities in a cooperative atmosphere in which they draw on one another's strengths to solve problems.

Although learning centers come in many forms, they need three essential elements to become highly successful:

1. The learning goal must be important to the group (e.g., the topics are ones that students enjoy and judge as important, such as imperishable beauty, leadership, truth, justice, philosophical issues, ethics, and sociopolitical concerns).

2. There must be individual as well as group accountability. All group members must see themselves as positively interdependent with others.

3. The materials and processes to be used at the center must be modeled in advance; three different types of sample end products should be on display; and opportunities to use auditory, tactile, visual, and kinesthetic learning styles should exist.

In preschool through grade 2, centers can also focus on social skills (e.g., performing actions in homemaking and eating at restaurants), building buildings in the block center, and creating objects in art and bookmaking centers. In the upper elementary school years, centers can also focus on in-depth studies concerning specific topics such as poetry and scientific subjects as well as stages of the writing process, such as editing. Daily schedules that include centers should ensure that students do not avoid the more difficult ones. The following procedures reduce the likelihood that this will happen.

You and your students can choose a theme for each center that is important to students and relates to their lives outside of school. A center pegboard is helpful, as it develops a record-keeping system that enables you to monitor at a glance what every student is working on and has completed. With this system in place, students are free to select activities that are of greatest value to them, and to indicate why they preferred these choices and elected to work alone, in pairs, or in groups. An example of the Center Choice Board that Ms. Diederick used is shown in Figure 2.2.

Language arts teachers often use a center rotation system in which students rotate from center to center every 20 to 30 minutes. In this way, every day three groups can meet with you during each one-hour center rotation period. Some teachers ring a bell once to end one center and a second time one minute later to alert students that work should already have begun at the next center. Many types of centers can be created, including those shown in Figure 2.3.

Writing Corner or Center: Students have a corner with many different important things to write about and with. For example, Ms. Diederick's children created attendance charts, labeled belongings, and "wrote" their own books using pictures and scribbles for words they could not yet write. The key to success in a writing center is that students are provided the materials and instruction to work independently of the teacher. They can read their works in pairs, write in journals, pair to study spelling words, or write in preparation for a discussion or presentation that will occur later in the day or week.

Listening Center: Students can use music as a background for writing poems and prose; use records and tapes to transcribe words for the class; tape-record stories or sets of directions; and listen to book tapes with which students read along as a narrator reads the story. Activities in the listening center can also include role playing about information students hear—even dressing up as favorite literary characters.

Reading Centers and Classroom Library Centers: Books from the Literature Cards in this textbook can be displayed on chalk ledges, for students to use in recommending their favorite books to peers. Pillows, bathtubs, lofts, rugs, and stuffed animals often appear in these centers. Steps that can be followed to establish highly effective centers are described in Figure 2.3. Students can also design the library classification and checkout systems they want to use.

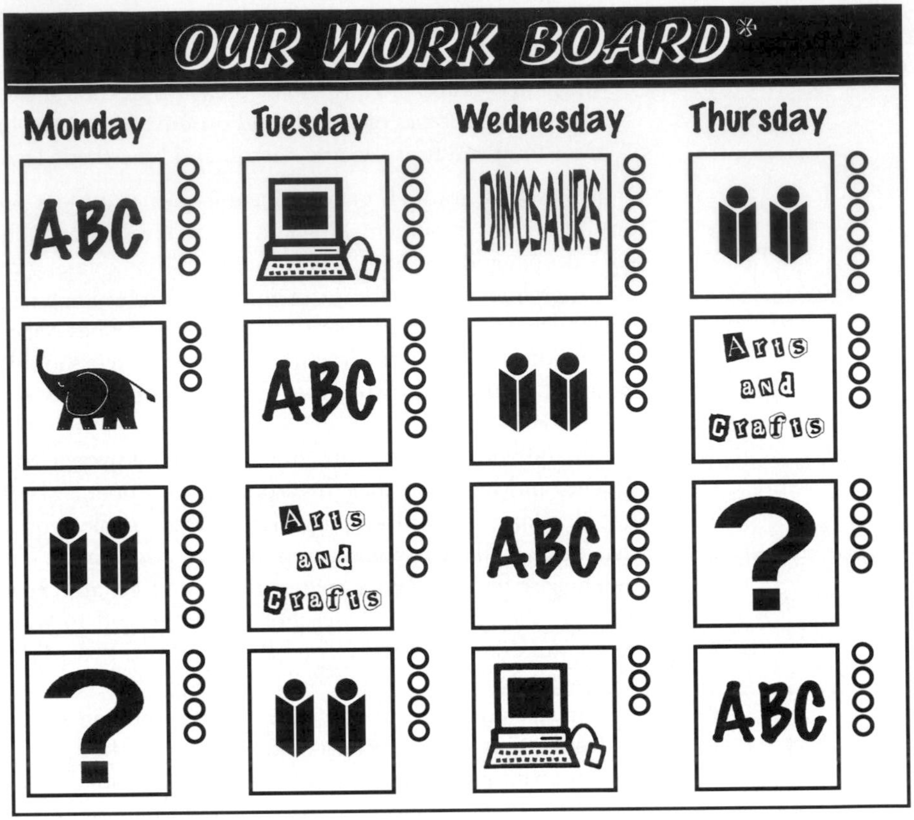
OUR WORK BOARD*
Monday
Tuesday
Wednesday
Thursday
ABC
DINOSAURS
Arts and Crafts

USING THE WORK BOARD ...

The Work Board can be used in a variety of ways. For structured times, the board can allow students to move from one activity to another in given time frames (30 minute sets). If center time is offered for one hour in the morning and one hour in the afternoon, each student will spend time in each of the four squares each day. During center time on Fridays, students can select from any square. This will also allow the teacher an opportunity to meet with students.

***The circles beside each picture denote how many children can go to that center on that day. Children choose where they want to work during center time by writing their names in the circles of their choice, or the teacher writes the children's names in the circles that designate in which center he or she wants them to work.**

FIGURE 2.2 LEARNING CENTER CHOICE BOARD

Created by Claire C. Graham, 2000, master of elementary education degree candidate at Texas Christian University, Fort Worth, TX. Used by permission.

Art Center Tips

1. Cover carpeted floors with a shower curtain (duct-taped firmly to floor) to prevent staining.
2. Have a hanging drying rack with spring clothespins nearby.
3. Keep only a day's supply of paint in the center, in paper cups, milk containers, etc., with one paintbrush per color.
4. Stuff newspaper in cracks in easel to pick up spills and between paint containers to keep them from tipping over.
5. Keep a supply of scrap paper in a crate nearby—include newspaper, butcher paper, brown paper bags, wallpaper, laminating film, and aluminum foil.
6. Use parents' old button-down shirts, worn backwards, as smocks.
7. Provide a scissors box—a large box with lots of paper and scissors. Kids can cut as much as they want; include paper with patterns and shapes on it.

Block Center Tips

1. Locate in a low-traffic area so buildings don't get knocked over.
2. If you don't have carpeting, get an area rug with a low nap for this center—it will be more comfortable and it will absorb the sound of falling blocks.
3. Get a bin for each shape of block, and attach a picture of each shape on its bin.
4. Make a line on the floor with tape the length of your storage shelf two feet away. This space is a "no building" area, so that children will have space to take blocks off the shelves without knocking over buildings.
5. Provide measuring tools (rulers, yarn, cut-outs of hands and feet) to measure size of buildings.
6. Set up a good rule—only build as high as your shoulders!

Dramatic Play Center Tips

1. Start with a basic home living theme with two areas, kitchen and office. Provide a play sink, stove, refrigerator, cabinet for dishes, table and chairs, high chair, ironing board, cleaning supplies, pots and pans, telephone, dishes, utensils, empty food containers, doll bed, and dress-up clothes.
2. Later, adjust this area to your theme. For example, if you are studying fire prevention, turn this center into a fire station. Make a fire engine out of a large box, and add clothes such as boots, helmets, and raincoats.
3. Have a specific place for everything!

(continued)

FIGURE 2.3 TIPS FOR SETTING UP LEARNING CENTERS IN A PRIMARY CLASSROOM

Created by Aimee O'Rourke, 2000, kindergarten teacher at St. George Catholic School, Fort Worth, TX. Used by permission.

Science Center Tips

1. Ideally, locate this near a window, a water source, and an electrical source.
2. Have a classroom pet! Guinea pigs are most highly recommended, but rabbits, gerbils, hamsters, rats, mice, birds, fish, snakes, lizards, and large insects are also recommended.
3. Include indoor plants, magnets, magnifying glasses, balance scales, kaleidoscopes, thermometers, rocks, shells, and insect homes (like ant farms).
4. Let the children take care of the living things!
5. Provide a new, self-directed experiment each week.

Library Center Tips

1. Locate this center in a quiet corner. Reading lofts are an excellent "hideaway" for reading and can be easily constructed, but if this is not an option, try filling a plastic kiddie pool with pillows and blankets or making a "reading house" from a large cardboard box—adjust to fit theme.
2. Children's books on tape can be found at public libraries—provide these along with simple tape players and headphones for a listening area.
3. Consider also having a puppet theater (made from a large box) and puppets which fit your theme where students can dramatize stories they have read, a flannel board with theme-related figures, a magnetic board with magnetic letters, or a chalkboard and chalk.

Manipulative/Math Center Tips

1. Keep a supply of carpet squares here and tell students that they must confine their work to a carpet square.
2. Provide puzzles, beads for stringing, geoboards, matching and sorting games, and math manipulatives.
3. Make sure to have a self-contained bin for everything.

Music Center Tips

1. A piano here is ideal—put different colored dots on one octave of the keyboard and write out songs using the dots in the correct order for the keys to be pressed. If you don't have a piano, autoharps are great and often come with prewritten song sheets to be placed under the strings.
2. Provide tape players along with fun songs for dancing, movement props, such as scarves and ribbons, as well as class-made instruments, like shakers and drums, and toy xylophones and rhythm sticks.

FIGURE 2.3 (CONTINUED)

Creative Arts Areas: In this center, students are allowed to use puppets, costumes, props, art media, and musical instruments to pretend, play, and relive stories. A portion of this area can be designed for paper, papier-mâché, and clay sculpturing of words, objects, and scenery to increase decoding and comprehension abilities. Recorders, autoharps, xylophones, bells, and tambourines are small instruments that students enjoy having available as well.

Sharing Area, Discussion Dens, and Student Display Areas: These centers are designed as group meeting areas for conversations and discussion. This area often also contains a table and bulletin board for displays of student products, a chalkboard, an overhead projector, and other materials such as charts and markers.

Content Topic Centers: When students become particularly involved in a content area, concept or career centers provide an opportunity for in-depth participation in a subject so that all learning modalities, all language arts, and multiple intelligences can be used to solve problems and satisfy students' questions. Ms. Diederick sets up a new career or concept center every 3 weeks. For example, Meisong and her other classmates didn't understand why some plants needed water to grow and others, which they saw at Walmart, "that grew on ceramic dogs, cats, and frogs" didn't. They created an experiment to discover why in a scientist learning center. So far Ms. Diederick has set up centers about automobile mechanics, beauticians, forest rangers, plumbers, veterinarians, post offices, offices, grocery stores, restaurants, airports, building centers, travel agencies, and banks. For each center, Ms. Diederick visited several establishments and brought real-world objects that were used in that business. She always included writing materials that denoted activities relative to each profession and reading materials that illustrated and described the activities of each professional group. These materials increased the quality of students' role playing and students' vocabulary growth.

DAILY SCHEDULE 2: READING AND WRITING WORKSHOPS

Before reading and writing workshops begin, the entire class meets together for approximately 5 to 10 minutes. The goal of this time is to inspire students to attempt tougher feats during their small group meeting times. In the process, students receive information about why the upcoming workshop was scheduled, such as what new growths in their abilities demonstrated that they were ready for each new higher challenge. This brief time also provides an overview of the day's activities, and enables you to introduce new books and materials that students can use in their reading and writing workshops.

Many of these "opening-of-the-day" class meetings also include a **morning message.** This is a time to greet the day, for teacher and students to share messages about themselves, about what happened the night before, and about what important events are taking place in their lives, and to introduce the work to be done during the day. A benefit of a morning message is that most students profit from having time to converse and chat together as they begin the day. This informal time also enables them to tell about new events in their lives and to get to know each other better (Calkins, 1994). As this message is constructed on the chalkboard, it also assists students to learn new vocabulary words and context clues.

Immediately following the class meeting and morning message, a minilesson is presented. **Minilessons** involve about 5 to 10 minutes in which you or students offer suggestions for ways students can improve in a specific area of language arts. Throughout the lesson, students discuss and share examples of their successful (and not so successful) uses of a language arts principle. There are four ways that minilessons can be conducted (Avery, 1993):

1. **Direct presentations** are minilessons in which you teach a concept and present examples of the language process in action, such as, "This is where your writing folders will go, and this is when you will use your folder. Watch how I write a memo and where I place it on the computer when I am finished."

2. Minilessons can also be **demonstrations by a student.** In these instances, students show samples of their work and highlight new language procedures and products by revealing how they use a language arts competency, such as how to write quotation marks.

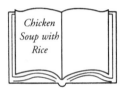

Chicken Soup with Rice

3. In **role play** minilessons, you and students can add humor and drama to make points. For example, to teach her preschoolers the difference between periods, exclamation points, and question marks, Ms. Diederick invented a game in which students made a different clicking sound at each point where one of these symbols appeared in the pattern book *Chicken Soup with Rice* by Maurice Sendak. She read to them aloud from the big book version so all could see the punctuation marks, and the children gave the appropriate sounds with glee! Alternatively, if you want to demonstrate an effective start to a cooperative group activity, you can ask several students to demonstrate it in a role play. Then, you can ask them to exaggerate behaviors that the class does not want to exhibit, such as procrastination and causing distractions for others.

4. Minilessons can be discussions in which all students **relate previous experiences** using some aspect of the language arts. By sharing what former students did when facing a language challenge before the class, students can modify their ideas to reach successful resolutions more quickly. These minilesson discussions enable students to become more objective about their shortcomings and generate higher expectations for themselves.

Minilessons are usually followed by "state of the class" inventories, which should take no longer than 5 minutes. During this period you can write each student's name on a chart, notebook, or blackboard and have them tell or write what they will be doing next, such as shared readings, writing alone, taking a personalized spelling test, rehearsing a dramatic presentation, or leaving the class to conduct interviews.

State of the class meetings are followed by reading and writing **workshops** in which students have from 30 to 50 minutes to do the activity they chose and to practice the suggestions offered in the minilesson. As shown in Figure 2.4, during this time students can work independently or in small groups in a wide variety of ways while you confer with individuals about their progress and questions. Students can move at their own pace. When finished with reading a book or a first draft of writing, students are ready for conferences with you, peers, or adult volunteers in the class. They can indicate this need by merely coming to the person in charge of

---

Sample Schedule 1: Centers

[The room is organized in centers.]

9:00–9:15 *Opening:* Morning Message when the class generates two or three paragraphs about ideas they had since the day before; goals for the day or week are posted; and important events in students' lives are noted. Students write in their journals, meet in pairs to share books to read, or share individual projects/proposals with classmates.

9:15–9:45 *Centers:* Students select (or are assigned to) one of these centers each day, and normally no one spends more than one day a week at each center. The types you can elect to use are Writing Center, Publishing Center, Silent Reading Loft, Library Center, Teacher Center, Reading Center, Shared Reading Center, Listening Center, Research Center, Working in Pairs Center, or Working Alone Center.

9:45–10:00 *Sharing:* Teacher or classmate reads to the class. This can also be the time for author's chair (students read to the class), a sharing time, and a time to set goals for tomorrow's work.

Sample Schedule 2: Minilessons and Workshops

8:50–9:00 Opening (same as in Schedule 1)

9:00–9:10 Students share and participate in a minilesson. At the end of this lesson, students refer to the class chart to see the group in which they have been placed based on their needs and the information in the minilesson.

9:10–9:40 Students complete their responsibilities in small groups. Group compositions change as new goals are set, e.g., during this time students may be assigned to edit a peer's paper, evaluate and work in their portfolios, participate in a teacher–student conference, or work in reading or writing groups.

9:40–9:50 *Sharing:* Teacher and students evaluate progress on learning the objectives of the minilesson and select groups from the chart for the next day's work. An example of a reading workshop follows.

Reading Workshop (50–70 min)		
Opening of Class and Morning Message (5 min) *Sharing Time (5–10 min)* *Minilesson (5–10 min)*		
Self-Selected Silent Reading and Written Response (SSR) (35–45 min):		

SSR (10 minutes)
1. Self-selected book
2. Reading their goal pages for literature-response group
3. Responding to literature
4. Record keeping
  a. Book time and title logs
  b. Signing up for individual reading conference
  c. Meet in pairs or with teacher
	Literature response (15–20 minutes)
	1. Group meeting for response
	2. New meeting
	3. Determine new response mode
		Individual reading conferences (10–15 minutes)
		1. Two a day
		2. Running records are made and analyzed
		  a. Taped
		  b. Retellings

Sharing time (children) (5–10 min) + setting goals for tomorrow		

FIGURE 2.4 SAMPLE SCHEDULES

The graphic in Sample Schedule 2 is from "Organizing for Effective Instruction: The Reading Workshop," by D. R. Reutzel and R. B. Cooter, Jr., 1991, *The Reading Teacher, 44*(8), pp. 548–554. Reprinted with permission of D. Ray Reutzel and the International Reading Association. Copyright © 1991 by the International Reading Association. All rights reserved.

conferences that day. At the beginning of each workshop, you may meet for a few minutes with a group of students who want to watch you demonstrate the minilesson objective again.

After workshops, sharing time begins. Students can share their insights, about the objective taught in the minilesson or present finished writings, reports, research, or dramas. As shown in Sample Schedule 2 in Figure 2.4, this sharing period is about as long as the minilesson and only one-third to one-quarter as long as the workshop. This sharing time is also when individual needs and praises concerning new language growths can be given. The following procedures promote smooth operation of minilessons and workshops:

- No one interrupts the teacher when conferences are being conducted.
- Student-group leaders resolve group needs or put unresolved issues in writing so time can be reallocated during another class period to address them.
- Students are responsible for assessing their day's work at the end of each workshop.

Additional information about conducting reading and writing workshops is described in detail in Chapter 6.

The strengths of minilessons and workshops are that students receive direct instruction in language arts competencies they need at the time of need, and all students receive some portion of your individual time. They also designate a portion of the language arts program (and provide a framework) for students to talk to you and their peers about their strengths and weaknesses. In addition, they emphasize the importance of student voice and choice in instruction.

Moreover, in a workshop, activity density and length can vary. Writers, readers, speakers, and listeners can work on projects they choose and at their own pace. For example, in a typical writing workshop a few students can compose independently, some can work together planning and researching a new topic, others can write first drafts, others edit and review, and a small group at a computer table can complete their final drafts of writings and presentations. You can hear the buzz of writers reading and talking about their compositions while you are providing feedback to individual students who request your help. The class is bustling with students using pencils, markers, paper, stamps, scissors, scotch tape, staplers, dictionaries, thesauruses, hole-punchers, yarn, peel-off vinyl letters, stencils, cloth tape for book spines, sample books that your former students wrote; and cumulative folders. The weaknesses of minilessons and workshops are that the language arts can become compartmentalized, less integrated, and involve tasks that do not have real-world outcomes. Special care must be taken to ensure that all projects serve authentic functions in students' lives.

DAILY SCHEDULE 3: THEMATIC UNITS

Thematic units are series of literary experiences organized around a central focus, overarching questions, content areas, genres, authors, or language arts topics (Wiggins & McTighe, 1998). In addition to the integrative benefits, thematic units enable students to become immersed in a topic so they learn it more completely. In the process they engage their choices, feelings, questions, and individualized explorations. As Brewer stated: "The linking of one subject to another with the flame of quiet enthusiasm could be the greatest gift any teacher can give" (1995, p. 281).

Thematic units are also called focus units, thematic studies, literature studies, and author studies. All units provide an organizational framework for read-aloud activities and study experiences through which students explore a group of related books in terms of their thematic content, literary devices, craft, and commonalities. Thematic units usually open with a whole class experience such as sharing in a teacher-read book, discussion, or community event. This experience prepares students to engage in independent and collaborative creative and critical thinking about language arts activities based on a theme.

Thematic units should extend for at least a week and rarely beyond 6 weeks (or one full grading period). For large themes, the time line might resemble the following:

WEEK 1: Class chooses and discusses a theme, creates list of issues to explore, and engages in self-selected readings to gain background about the theme.

WEEK 2: Initial integrated language arts activities are planned; students meet in groups to make preliminary outlines of due dates for projects and students volunteer to become responsible for specific tasks. Students also hold meetings (weekly throughout the unit) to share information about what they learned.

WEEK 3: Projects begin and students visit outside resources to answer questions raised during the previous week.

WEEK 4: All projects are completed, and many students elect to work outside of class time to complete their projects.

WEEK 5: This becomes a week of celebrative experiences. Each group has a day or part of a day to teach classmates as much of their group's work as possible. These experiences enable students to make public their learning and be introduced to books they did not read, which often results in better choices and increased learning during recreational reading periods in subsequent weeks.

It is important to remember that merely completing several activities associated with a theme does not constitute a thematic unit. Themes need powerful, real-world ideas and questions to bind students' projects together. These unifying ideas arise from students' needs and curiosities. For example, it would have been easy for Ms. Diederick to build a thematic unit by merely reading to the class several books written by the same author or selecting a content topic such as weather or "neighborhood helpers." Instead she capitalized on an intense and acrimonious discussion the class had about who their favorite author was. To resolve their differences, they decided to spend one week finding out who the favorite author was. The class became eager to learn, and a thematic study was inaugurated. Students wrote a survey, read it to all classes, tallied results, announced the winner (Eric Carle), and invited him to speak at their preschool. They wrote questions for his visit, discussed what he did as a writer that they liked, and told him. By the end of this unit, students had integrated and practiced all the language arts and were critiquing other authors' writings with more sophistication. They chose books based on more information about their preferences. This was a true thematic unit founded on students' questions, built on authentic activities, and culminating in experiences that students will perform as adults (e.g., working in groups to solve problems, selecting books, collecting data, preparing for guests, and interviewing speakers).

Benefits of thematic studies are that (1) you are free to help students look at problems, situations, or topics from a variety of viewpoints; (2) there is less emphasis on competition; (3) you can model more integrated language arts strategies; (4) assessment is holistic, authentic, and meaningful so that it provides an accurate picture of students' progress and development in independent language use; and (5) students understand the "why" of activities and events instead of just the "what" (Wiggins & McTighe, 1998; Berliner, 1994). A sample daily schedule for thematic units appears in Figure 2.4.

DAILY SCHEDULE 4: MULTIAGED CLASSES

Multiaged classes had their roots in the American one-room schoolhouse where students stayed with the same teacher throughout their entire educational careers. Today, in multiaged classes, students from two or three age levels become a community of learners for a day or longer. Sometimes a teacher remains with a class for 3 years, so students have only two teachers from kindergarten through fifth grade. This system follows a family grouping model and provides more opportunities to know students and to enhance their strengths. Because of more time spent together, older students have more opportunities to teach and demonstrate their newly evolved strengths to younger classmates. On the opposite side, younger students can learn from a greater number of more mature and more capable peers.

Students also have longer periods of high-quality **academic learning time** (the amount of time a student spends attending to relevant tasks while performing with a high rate of success) (Putnam, 1997; Bruner, 1986) and are likely to experience **eustress** (a state of being where they are so immersed in an activity of interest that they lose a sense of time). A caution to heed when using multiaged groups is to ensure that depth of study does not minimize breadth of coverage. You may need to refer to your yearly goals more frequently in this scheduling system to ensure that time is available to study each objective. Another deficit of this organizational option is that you have to be very objective and adept at identifying strengths in many types of students. A teacher may be unable to nurture a particular student's strengths, and that pupil may have that same teacher for up to 2 more years.

A major benefit of multiaged classes is that students learn a lot incidentally and through the expanded explanations of the many older and more accomplished language users in their classroom each day. Because of this, the curriculum can go deeper into topics of individual student's interest and need. Because student-led groups are more common, more one-on-one conferences can be held between peers and between you and students.

As an example of this positive benefit, Chase (1995) reported that in one multiaged class activity, students wanted to raise money for the school so they planted, harvested, and sold pumpkins. They used numerous language arts skills. Profits went to their school, with a percentage being saved to purchase equipment and seeds for next year's crop. By the second year students were so experienced with farming that they doubled their acreage and profits!

Last, I recommend that once your schedule is in place, you spend approximately 3 days demonstrating and having students practice behaviors and procedures to effectively manage each section of the schedule. On the first day of these practice sessions, you can ask students to work in the centers, in their workshops, on thematic unit activities, or in multiaged groups for only about 10 minutes. Then ask them to discuss the things they judged to have gone well, and patterns in their movements, procedures, and behavior that they want to improve. During the second and third days of these practice sessions, you can increase the length of time students engage in language arts activities until you have observed and discussed the success of one session in which the full time allocated for each division of your schedule has been completed as successfully as you and your students desire. At this time, you can ask students to elect officers to assume leadership roles in the classroom community. Each officer can decide on improvements he or she would like to make in the classroom and meet with you the week before they assume office to ensure that the classroom community continues to grow in a positive way. Each officer can maintain his or her office for a period of 2 to 3 weeks, provided there are enough offices for all students to have at least six different offices in one year. A list of officers that you might consider follows:

- *President:* answers questions when you are unavailable
- *Attendance:* takes the roll to the office and takes lunch orders to cafeteria
- *Horticulturist:* waters plants as needed
- *Line leader:* first in line
- *Mail carrier:* places notes in mailboxes; runs errands
- *Librarian:* keeps book collection orderly and checks out classroom library books
- *Chalkboard monitor:* erases and washes
- *Floor manager:* picks up litter; in charge of organizing furniture groupings for instruction
- *Science/math assistant:* distributes and puts away math and science materials
- *Hospitality chairperson:* guides classroom visitors
- *Ecologist:* saves electricity whenever possible and recycles paper
- *Computer monitor:* turns off computer monitor and organizes disks
- *Listening center manager:* turns off the tape recorder and puts away tapes; makes new audiobook tapes
- *Playground equipment specialist:* cares for equipment
- *Resource manager:* distributes and collects papers
- *Vacation director:* fills in for an absentee person in group meetings and prepares notes of work to be made-up for students who are absent each day

In closing, once you have selected and implemented a daily schedule, you can more appropriately select the group size and activities you and your students will use each day.

GROUPING FOR INSTRUCTION

When it comes to grouping, there is no "best" group size (Larrivee, Semmel, & Gerber, 1997). There is one *incorrect* grouping arrangement, however. Students should never always stay in the same sized group because no grouping system is powerful enough to address all their language needs.

A growing body of research also suggests that constant grouping into ability levels does not significantly increase students' achievement, and is likely to have detrimental effects on the self-concept and achievement of weaker students (Allington, 1999; Berghoff & Egawa, 1991). One reason is that less proficient students are those in most need of learning new ways to organize information, make valuable contributions to conversations, and write and read more challenging materials. Peer modelers for these students are absent when homogeneous groups are used. O'Keefe (1994) also found that because human beings are sensitive creatures, their learning is influenced by how close their teachers are to their desks. For instance, students in the front and center rows consistently participate to a significantly greater degree than those on the sides, and teachers tend to call on high-achieving students 3.5 times more frequently than lower-achieving peers (Dyson, 1999). The types of groupings that improve students' learning of language arts follow.

PAIRED GROUPINGS

Paired instruction builds listening, speaking, and thinking abilities because "he who teaches others teaches himself." While paired instruction has been used since the time of the Spartans, only recently has research documented its benefits. For instance, Putnam (1997) discovered that peer teaching is among the most effective forms of instruction. Students remember 95 percent of the language arts skills when they teach others, but only 10 percent of the information that they read without discussing. We also know that paired learning enables students to grow academically and socially. It can occur in two ways. In **dyadic pairs** two students are graded on one collaborative piece; in **peer tutoring** older or more capable language users work with younger or less advanced peers, and students receive separate grades for their work. Paired groupings can be self-chosen (or teacher-assigned) between stronger and weaker, same sex, mixed sex, or older and younger students.

The reason teaching others increases thinking and skills in language arts is that, as "teachers," students must increase their critical listening to generate alternative explanations and to rephrase and reteach the same idea to their partners. Other benefits are that (1) both rapid and slow learners have an attentive audience; (2) students share and develop language arts skills by managing greater responsibilities, which enhances their self-images; (3) many students develop higher-level thinking strategies such as using similies and metaphors to describe concepts they are teaching; and (4) most students experience greater enjoyment than they would working alone. Paired instruction also provides more intense, personal work than other grouping systems because there are fewer negotiations of an "agenda" and more opportunities for students to have one-to-one sharing and to think creatively.

Such partnerships may also be the most cost-effective way to raise language arts achievement because it yields greater achievement per dollar than any other educational investment (Fuchs, Fuchs, Karns, Hamlett, Daiths, & Katzaroff, 1996). In addition, in a recent study, when students helped each other, both attendance and achievement increased (Texas Education Agency, 1994). The following excerpt from a paired learning session in Ms. Diederick's class demonstrates the learning benefits that can accrue through dyadic pairs:

When a preschooler and kindergartner work together, they can organize knowledge in new ways. Peers can make suggestions that are not interpreted as negative evaluations, as can be the case when critiques come from their teachers.

Deanna: "Bad." I don't think it should be there. Maybe you could find a better word to describe them.

Meisong: Or maybe leave "bad" out?

Deanna: That might sound better. Why don't you put "toys" instead of "stuff"? It sounds kinda a little babyish or something.

Meisong: OK. Let's see. "Toys." I have the best toys. How do you spell "toys"?

Deanna: T-O-Y-S. You could give a name to your favorite toy, like a designer label. It could be anybody. You know, it's sorta . . . How about using a name or something to describe it?

Meisong: OK.

The following guidelines will increase the results of paired learning. First, assign two students who normally do not work together, blending weaker with stronger students. Also, before paired activities begin, decide whether students will be graded individually or as a dyad and discuss your decision with the students. Monitor pairs daily to ensure that work is progressing effectively. For example, Ms. Diederick uses paired learning for 10 minutes every day, selecting different students to work with each other on Mondays through Thursdays. Then, students select their own partners and materials on Fridays. In her class, kindergartners "read" to their preschool partner for 5 minutes, discuss the pictures and words, and then change roles. Ms. Diederick found that these paired students increased kindergartners' reading speed in 5 weeks' time, and preschool students reported that getting to read with a partner was their favorite part of their class.

SMALL GROUPS

Small groups are best when students need to explore a wide variety of perspectives or require longer than 10 to 15 minutes to share. Types of small groups are (1) **interest groups,** where students develop a communication tool or thinking ability about which they are curious; (2) **project groups,** where each student is an expert or in charge of different aspects of a project; (3) **homogeneous groups,** where pupils of comparable ability work to advance that competency; (4) **heterogeneous groups,** where students of different ability levels work together; and (5) **task- or process-specific groups,** where students meet to concentrate on a single task or one step in a process, such as writing.

Before students break into small groups, you should ensure that they clearly understand the objective, the tasks, and the activities in which they are to engage. Then students appoint a group leader (or the teacher does), and special responsibilities are assigned to other members, such as recorder (documents the work of the group and takes notes), summarizer (summarizes what has been decided in the group and writes a paragraph of the ideas to share with the class), courier (performs errands and brings materials to and from the group), interrogator (challenges group to defend their answers and uses questions that are specified in Chapter 3 of this textbook), and secretary (keeps the group on task, watches the time, assists those who were absent the day before to catch up on their work, and assumes responsibility as group leader when the group leader is absent). With these actions in place, small groups will run smoothly, and during small-group meetings you can either meet with individual students or stay with one group during the entire small-group working session.

Although group work has many benefits, it lacks the efficiency of independent work. It can be slow and cumbersome. On average, groups spend only 58 seconds discussing a single topic, and they jump from topic to topic without any logical connections (O'Keefe, 1994). However, when tasks require depth and diversity, the analytic abilities that group work stimulates enable small groups to surpass other grouping systems in their effectiveness in promoting learning.

COOPERATIVE LEARNING GROUPS

Cooperative learning groups differ from small groups in five ways:

1. Positive interdependence of group members
2. Individual accountability for one's own learning
3. Cooperative skills used to produce a product
4. Face-to-face interactions
5. Group reflection and goal setting (Antil, Jenkins, Vadasy, & Wayne, 1998).

Research has offered guidance about which types of behaviors promote the most language arts learning during cooperative group work. For example, studies demonstrate that students who construct explanations to clarify processes that help classmates arrive at their own solutions learn more than students who simply tell classmates the answers (Fuchs, Fuchs, Hamlett et al., 1997; Nattiv, 1994). Also, other researchers have demonstrated that cooperative groups enable students to engage in and resolve cognitive conflicts with peers, and they, in turn, learn more (e.g., Bearison, 1982; Nastasi, Clements, & Battista, 1990). In resolving these disagreements, children explain and justify their positions, question beliefs, seek new information, or adopt alternative frameworks and conceptualizations (Bell, Grossen, & Perret-Clermon, 1985; Tudge, 1985).

To be most effective, every student in the group should be held accountable for a portion of the learning responsibilities and every student's effort should be necessary to attain the highest possible group grade. Since the mid-1980s, cooperative learning has received a great deal of attention as a grouping system (Johnson & Johnson, 1995). When cooperative grouping began, students were homogeneously grouped. Research now suggests, however, that for lower-ability students, heterogeneous rather than homogeneous cooperative groups are more effective (Johnson & Johnson, 1995; Putnam, 1997). On the other hand, for gifted students heterogeneous cooperative groups may be less advantageous. Frequently they are thrust into leadership positions that they may not be prepared to assume and become domineering or nonparticipatory (Larrivee, Semmel, & Gerber, 1997; Stevens & Slavin, 1995; Webb, Nemer, Chizhik, & Sugrue, 1998). At the end of the chapter, you will find a list of several books that I recommend for further information concerning cooperative groups.

To avoid the problems of domineering and nonparticipatory students, you can assign every member in a cooperative group a number and each cooperative group a number, and then pose a question. Then all cooperative group team members can put their heads together, examine the possibilities, and construct an answer. Next, you pick a number by drawing a card from a stack. The first number drawn designates the person from each group who will answer the question you posed; the second number that you draw will indicate which group will respond first (Garmston & Wellman, 1994). It is also helpful to establish a time limit in which products and processes are to be completed and to not waver from it. Assigning specific tasks so every student has a responsibility and requiring a concrete product at the end of each cooperative group meeting reduces the inefficiencies in this grouping system, and increases its benefits as well.

LARGE GROUPS

Large groups can create positive and warm community climates, help students make decisions, develop class plans, resolve issues, see "expert" demonstrations, and become real audiences for student presentations. Large groups also meet many belonging needs, build bonds, and effectively create knowledge that is common to the whole.

Making effective large-group decisions requires time but the experience will provide valuable models for students to use in their adult lives. While it is easy to make decisions by majority rule, doing so has serious disadvantages. Minority voters often lose their commitment to carry out the tasks. Even majority voters have different motives, so it is likely that dissention will occur when the project begins. Majority rule can also create polarization, dissatisfaction, and resentment. Compromise can have equally severe problems. For one, the decision is likely to be based on no one's best idea, so no one gets what she or he wants, or feels highly committed to the task (O'Keefe, 1994). The best decision-making process is to reach a consensus so a win–win situation results. To do so, you and your class can (a) discuss the benefits and deficits of several options, (b) model how to ask questions to gain more famil-iarity about task requirements, and (c) take opposing ideas through stages of devel-opment so that the reasons behind people's dissension are clear. It takes time to reach consensus, but you will know it has occurred when students become enthusiastic, voice new possibilities, and ask to begin work on the consensus reached.

INDEPENDENT WORK

Independent work allows high-level, sustained reading, writing, thinking, and re-flection because students do not have to reduce their language learning speed to meet the needs of others. Independent work also provides maximum time for stu-dents to develop personal ownership of projects, and establishes many occasions for you to individualize instruction. **Individualization** is the process of providing spe-cial scaffolds, models, and assignments to meet the needs of one or a few students rather than the whole group.

A second purpose of independent work sessions is to enhance your ability to assist students in one-to-one settings, and help them work on their own more in-dependently and effectively. Recently, students reported that they want a quiet en-vironment when they work alone (Block & Mangieri, in press). For this reason it is helpful for the class to establish procedures that they want the learning community to follow during independent work. Such rules can be that all must work quietly,

Individualization is more than assigning different tasks to different students to meet individual needs. It is caring for and supporting each individual, and realizing when students need your assistance.

sit in one location the entire time, ask only one person for help in a whisper, go outside the classroom to talk to the teacher, and refer to a chart that lists quiet tasks to complete if they finish early. Ms. Diederick's students completed a list of tasks that they wanted to give as a gift to their kindergarten partners to display in the kindergarten room. The list, "Things to do during independent quiet working time when you finish your work early," read as follows:

1. Read around the room with a pointer.
2. Read from your book box.
3. Read a book to a partner.
4. Read a book quietly.
5. Listen to a book at the listening center.
6. Read books that your class has written.
7. Write in your journal.
8. Read from your writing folder.
9. Read or write at the overhead projector or chalkboard.

SECTION 2   PUTTING THEORY INTO PRACTICE

Activities for the First Week of School

To come to know your students well, you can complete the following activities in the first week of school. To build a warm and caring classroom of learners, you can move your desk to a corner of the room, away from the door, to create an inviting, open passage into the room and indicate to students that you are not the sole owner of the class. Put materials on shelves easy for students to reach, and have a chart ready on which you and students can post classroom rules. Secure 100 or more reading materials, including wordless picture books, magazines, newspapers, novels, and poetry, which are appropriate for your students' age (see recommended titles in the Literature Cards in this book). Borrow books from public libraries, and join a children's book club.

Harste (1989) found that most successful programs made a conscious effort to keep parents involved and informed. Allington and Cunningham (1996) identified "ten best jobs" and "five worst jobs for parent volunteers." In their research they found that the most effective activities for parents to engage in are finding children's stories in books, running the school bookstore, reshelving library books, collecting and distributing book club orders, using a word processor, reading students' writings with them, assisting students to publish a newspaper, reading to students, rehearsing reader's theater or other dramatic performances, monitoring students in the classroom so the teacher can work individually with students, and setting up and cleaning up projects. The least effective jobs were tutoring less able students or students with disabilities, drilling and practicing with students who have low language arts ability, providing seatwork assistance to low-achieving students, guiding oral reading groups, guiding small group lessons, or teaching whole class lessons.

You and your students can prepare methods to inform parents about your language arts program, and plan ways they can become involved. The letter on pages 82–83 of this chapter can be the first letter you send. It is also important to identify a special location on your desk where students can leave notes to you that no one else will read. In addition, you can send a note to each student during the week before school begins describing how happy you are to have them in your class. You can ask them to answer in writing a question about themselves and bring it with them on the first day of school. Tell them about something they will do on the first day of school to ease their anxiety about the new school year.

Finally, develop a record-keeping system and decorate the room. Create something special that helps students feel that they are exceptional (such as a large-pocket apple tree for library book checkout cards). In October have students design and build something distinctive they want to add to their room, such as a mock TV–puppet stage; a flannel board; or a platform for role playing, plays, and impromptu speeches. This enables them to contribute something concrete to make their room extraordinary.

On the first day of school you can institute a positive climate through the following activities. Read a book from Literature Card 3: "Books to Read the First Day of School." The characters in these books experience the same anxieties and problems that students have when they come to a new classroom at the start of the year. Also, reading and discussing these books assists in building a supportive, caring sense of community. You can also show students that they are important by learning their

Literature Card 3

BOOKS TO READ THE FIRST DAY OF SCHOOL

Preschool–Third Grade

Me at Preschool by J. Godfrey, 1985 Little Lions

The Kindergarten Book by S. Calmenson, 1983 Grosset & Dunlap

Berenstain Bears Go to School by S. Berenstain and J. Berenstain, 1985 American School

Getting Ready for School Book by E. Kingsley, 1989 Western

Pete's First Day at School by J. Clenen, 1993 Random House

School by C. Bellows, 1990 Macmillan

Starting School by M. Stanek, 1981 A. Whitman

Curious George Goes to School by M. Rey, 1991 Houghton, Mifflin

First Day of School by H. Oxenbury, 1993 Penguin Group

Time for School, Nathan! by L. Delacre, 1989 Scholastic

When You Go to Kindergarten by J. Howe, 1994 Morrow

Starting First Grade by M. Cohen, 1988 Spoken Arts

Starting School by L. Knopper, 1987 Franklin Watts

Morris Goes to School by B. Wiseman, 1991 Harper Collins

Back to School with Betsy by C. Haywood, 1986 Harcourt

Pete's First Day at School by J. Clenen, 1993 Random House

First Day of School by K. Jackson, 1985 Troll Assoc.

School Isn't Fair by P. Boehr, 1992 Aladdin Books

Fourth Grade and up

Charlie Brown Goes to School by C. Schultz, 1991 Holt

Louis James Hates School by B. Morrison, 1980 Learning Corp.

The New Teacher by M. Cohen, 1989 Collier Macmillan

Miss Nelson Is Missing and other books by L. Allard, 1989 Sundance Publishing & Distribution

I Like Books by J. Lee, 1992, 1993, 1994 Scholastic

names through peer interviews, and writing their names many times during the first day's activities.

Curriculum during the first weeks of school should also be filled with memorable experiences, such as hiking in the woods, cooking, and composing class-made stories (Allen, Michalove, Shockley, & West, 1991). For example, select a book like *A Taste of Blackberries* or *Charlotte's Web* and read the full book in 3 days, allowing students to talk together for long periods of time. Or, plan a field trip where every person in the class has a job to do to prepare the class for the wonderful experience. This builds a familylike environment. Building this group unity is as important as the time spent establishing classroom routines if students are to have the security they need to develop their language arts abilities. Books on Literature Cards 4 and 5 have been chosen by many teachers to read during the first weeks of school because they help students adjust to school.

INTEGRATING THE LANGUAGE ARTS

Predictable Books, Big Books, and Wordless Books

When you can begin the year by reading predictable, big, or wordless books, students with lesser literacy skills are not made self-conscious. **Big books,** which are 2 feet tall as shown in the photo on page 74, are large enough for younger students to see the words as their teachers read them aloud. These books can also improve students' decoding abilities, comprehension, and self-concepts as readers (Holdoway, 1997; Travers, 1994). Because any type of picture book can be made into a big book, many teachers ask children, adult volunteers, and older schoolmates to make big books for preschoolers, kindergartners, and first-graders. These books can be exact replicas of books from Literature Cards in this textbook, or can be original books composed by students.

Wordless picture books have no words but tell stories through pictures. Wordless books encourage children to make up their own stories. They enable students to use the framework provided to learn how the elements of a story connect and build on each other (Clay, 1999). Students of all ages enjoy telling the story they create from a wordless picture book into a tape recorder, transcribing it, and reading it to the class as a friend shows the pictures. **Predictable books** repeat a phrase over and over so students learn about the rhythm in written language and how to decode more rapidly because the words reappear in a familiar context. Predictable books also develop students' oral and written language competencies. Some repeat a phrase or sentence so frequently that students begin to read the refrain spontaneously as you read it, and they subsequently include those words in their written compositions.

Books can be predictable in many ways. For example, Maurice Sendak's book *Chicken Soup with Rice* (1962) uses different words in a predictable rhyming pattern. Second, some predictable books base plots around a real-world sequence that is familiar to young children, such as repeating the days of the week, the seasons, or counting from one to ten in the predictable order. Returning to *Chicken Soup with Rice,* Maurice Sendak realized the value of using such a *familiar plot* to connect students' past schema to new words as he moves his book forward with the months of the year. Predictable books can also repeat the identical words or sentences in each

Chicken Soup with Rice

Literature Card 4

BOOKS TO READ TO PRESCHOOLERS THROUGH THIRD-GRADERS THE FIRST WEEK OF SCHOOL

First Grade Takes a Test by M. Cohen, 1983 Dell
See You in Second Grade by M. Cohen, 1991 Spoken Arts
Sometimes I Hate School by C. James, 1991 Raintree
A Hippo Ate the Teacher by M. Thaler, 1981 Avon
When Will I Read? by M. Cohen, 1983 Dell
Will I Have a Friend? by M. Cohen, 1967 Macmillan
    McGraw Hill
Moog-Moog, Space Barber by M. Teague, 1990 Scholastic
The Best Teacher in the World by Chardiet and
    Maccarone, 1990 Scholastic
Leo the Late Bloomer by R. Krause, 1994 Windmill
Scrawny, the Classroom Duck by S. Clyner, 1992
    Bradbury
Frosted Glass by D. Cazet, 1987 Bradbury
The Flunking of Joshua T. Bates by S. Shreve, 1993
    Knopf
Ramona Quimby, Age Eight by B. Cleary, 1981
    Scholastic
Homesick: My Own Story by J. Fritz, 1991 American
Ramona the Pest by B. Cleary, 1982 Dell
The Latchkey Kids by C. Anshaw, 1986 Syndistar
School by E. McCally, 1995 Macmillan
Josie Smith at School by M. Nabb, 1991 Maxwell
    Macmillan
Why Mary Jo Shared by J. Mayudry, 1967 Scott,
    Foresman
Sometimes I Don't Like School by P. Hogan, 1992
    Raintree
This Is the Way We Go to School by E. Baer, 1993
    Scholastic
Miss Nelson Is Missing and other books by L. Allard,
    1989 Sundance
School Isn't Fair by P. Baehr, 1992 Aladdin
School Bus by D. Crews, 1984 Greenwillow
Charlie the Caterpillar by D. DeLuise, 1993 Aladdin
The New Teacher by M. Cohen, 1989 Aladdin
Patrick and Ted by G. Hayes, 1984 Four Winds
Runaway Bunny by M. W. Brown, 1972 Harper & Row
Teacher from the Black Lagoon, by M. Thaler, 1989
    Scholastic

Principal from the Black Lagoon by M. Thaler, 1993
    Scholastic
Timothy Goes to School by R. Wells, 1981 Dial
Noisy Nora by R. Wells, 1973 Dial
It Happens to Everyone by B. Myers, 1990 Lothrop
My Mom Made Me Go to School by J. Delton, 1993
    Bantam
Rooster's Off to See the World by E. Carle, 1991 Picture
    Book Studio

Good Books for a Thematic Unit on Developing
Friendships in Grades K–3

No Friends by J. Stevenson, 1986 Greenwillow Books
Chicken Sunday by P. Polacco, 1992 Philomel
Julius, the Baby of the World by K. Henkes, 1990
    Greenwillow
The Lettuce Leaf Birthday Letter by L. Taylor, 1995 Dial
Lizzie Logan Wears Purple Sunglasses by E. Spinelli, 1995
    Simon & Schuster
I Hate Company by B. James, 1994 Dutton
Without Words by B. Sonneborn, 1995 Sierra Club
Murphy and Kate by E. Howard, 1995 Simon &
    Schuster
Corduroy by D. Freeman, 1993 Puffin
Bootsie Barker Bites by B. Bottner, 1992 Putnam
George and Martha by J. Marshall, 1993 Houghton
    Mifflin
Angus and the Cat by M. Flack, 1989 Doubleday
Benjamin and Tulip by R. Wells, 1973 Dial Press
The Wednesday Surprise by E. Bunting, 1989 Clarion
Chester's Way by K. Henke, 1989 Puffin Books
George and Martha by J. Marshall, 1972 Houghton
    Mifflin
Best Friends for Frances by R. Hoban, 1969 Harper & Row
Your Best Friend, Kate by P. Brisson, 1992 Macmillan
    Child Group
Rainbow of Friends by P. K. Hallinan, 1994 Hambleton-
    Hill

*Brown Bear,
Brown Bear,
What Do
You See?*

episode, as illustrated in the book *Brown Bear, Brown Bear, What Do You See?* by Bill
Martin. Through this repetition, students almost immediately add individual words
to their reading, writing, speaking, and listening vocabularies.

Children today are influenced by mass media. The fleeting nature of so much instantaneously flashed information leaves little opportunity for students to learn how
to observe and view with exploration and reflection. Therein lies one of the most

Literature Card 5

BOOKS TO READ FOR FOURTH GRADE TO MIDDLE SCHOOL THE FIRST WEEK OF SCHOOL

Good Books about Beginning School in Grades 4–6

One of the Third Grade Thonkers by P. Naylor, 1991 Dell

Rent a Third Grader by B. Hiller, 1988 Scholastic

Teach Us, Amelia Bedelia by P. Parish, 1995 Scholastic

Fourth Grade Rats and other books by J. Spinelli, 1991 Scholastic

Regina's Mistake by M. Moss, 1990 Houghton Mifflin

In the Year of the Boar and Jackie Robinson by B. Lord, 1992 Teacher Created Materials

Nothing's Fair in Fifth Grade and other books by B. DeClements, 1987 Cornerstone Books

The Truth about Sixth Grade and other books by C. O'Shaughnessy, 1991 Scholastic

Harriet the Spy by L. Fitzhugh, 1990 Harper & Row

Kid in the Red Jacket by B. Park, 1991 Piper/Macmillan

Cosmic Cousins by N. Hayashi, 1991 Red Fox

Hoy Fue Mi Primer Dia De Escuela (I Started School Today) by K. Frandsen, 1984 Children's Press

Little Brown Bear Wants to Go to School by C. Lebrun, 1995 Children's Press

Barney Is Big by N. Weiss, 1988 Greenwillow

Every Kids Guide to Making Friends by J. Berry, 1989 Childrens

The Fair Weather Friend Activity Guide: A Story about Making Friends by J. Berry, 1991 Kids Media Group

Morton and Sidney by C. Demarest, 1993 Aladdin

If You're Not Here, Please Raise Your Hand by K. Dakos, 1995 Aladdin

Cousins by V. Hamilton, 1990 Philomel

Front Porch Stories at the One-Room School by E. Tatem 1992 Bantam Skylark

The Very Lonely Firefly by E. Carle, 1995 Philomel

Good Books for a Thematic Unit on Developing Friendships in Grades 4–6

Frog and Toad Are Friends by A. Lobel, 1970 Harper & Row

Best Friends by M. Cohen, 1989 Aladdin

Will I Have a Friend? by M. Cohen, 1989 Aladdin

The Moon Bridge by M. Savin, 1992, Scholastic

The Night the White Deer Died by G. Paulsen, 1978 Delacorte

The Friendship by M. Taylor, 1989 Bantam

Ludie's Song by D. Herlihy, 1990 Puffin

Different Dragons by J. Little, 1986, Viking

Jeremy Thatcher, Dragon Hatcher by E. Carle, 1991, Harcourt Brace Jovanovich

Words of Stone by K. Henkes, 1992 Greenwillow

Crazy Lady! by J. Leslie Conly, 1993 HarperCollins

The Faithful Friend by R. D. San Souci, 1995 Simon & Schuster

Phoenix Rising by K. Hesse, 1994 Henry Holt

Maniac Magee, by J. Spinelli, 1990, Scholastic

Henry and Mudge and the Happy Cat: The Eighth Book of Their Adventures by C. Rylant, 1990 Bradbury Press

I Like You, If You Like Me: Poems of Friendship ed. by M. C. Livingston

The Bracelet by by Y. Uchida, 1993 Putnam

Further Resources for Teaching about Friendship

From the Heart: Books and Activities about Friends by J. Irving & R. Currie, 1993 Teacher Idea Press

---

important values of wordless books and picture books for all ages. These books challenge students to think, discuss, play out in their minds, and look again (Barton, 1986). They also enable students to study art forms when you and they discuss different illustrators' techniques, the use of background and detail to relay meaning, and the uses of different types of media.

INSIDE CULTURALLY AND LINGUISTICALLY ENRICHED CLASSROOMS

Differing Cultural Values, Limited English Proficiencies, and Native American Languages

Students from minority cultural and linguistic backgrounds often hold differing values concerning the importance of the language arts. Researchers have demonstrated,

Displaying a different big book each week provides additional words and letters that kindergartners can point to as they read to their preschool friends.

however, that when teachers hold high academic expectations for these students, their behaviors improve as they try new forms of interacting with others to reach the high academic standards their teachers expect (Crawford, 1997; Moll, 1999). You can communicate your high expectations by seating linguistically diverse students near the front of the class; not allowing other students to interrupt your instruction when you are working with these students in small groups; not accepting off-task behavior; preparing instruction that includes their names as positive examples for others; conveying work standards explicitly; and making them accountable for their work (Crawford, 1997; Krashen, 1995; Haber, 1995).

At present, only a fraction of Limited English Proficiency (LEP) students are taught in special bilingual or English as a Second Language (ESL) classrooms (Canney, Kennedy, Schroeder, & Miles, 1999). By the year 2000, language minority students (ages preschool to 14) should comprise almost 42 percent of the total public school system (National Center for Educational Statistics, 1993). Such linguistic diversity is hardly unprecedented in our history, however, as at the time of the nation's first census in 1790, more than 300 languages were represented (Crawford, 1997).

Today, more world languages are spoken in the United States than ever before or in any other country in the world. There are approximately 137 to 175 Native American languages alone represented by students in the United States. These students, like the other LEP and English Language Learners (ELL) as they are sometimes called, may not speak English on a daily basis in their homes. For this reason, Congress decreed that Limited English Proficient children (LEP or ELL) face a number of challenges in receiving an education that will enable such children and youths to participate fully in U.S. society, including (a) a segregated language arts program; (b) disproportionate and improper placement in special education and other special programs resulting from inappropriate evaluation procedures; (c) the limited English proficiency of their parents, which hinders the parents' ability to fully participate in the education of their children; and (d) a shortage of teachers and other staff who are professionally trained and qualified to serve such children and youth (Oeri, 1994).

Moreover, only one-quarter to one-third of the parents of LEP students in preschool to grade 3 rate themselves as fully proficient in English, whereas 40 percent of them never speak English or speak it only rarely in their homes (Moss & Puma, 1995). Parents whose English is limited are often discouraged from full participation in their children's education not only due to their language barrier but because of their unfamiliarity with the instructional culture of U.S. schools. It is important for you to take actions to encourage their full participation. Specifically, you can translate parent meetings and materials into their language before sending them home. You can offer adult English classes after school. And you can send home taped books read in English that parents can listen to while their preschool through grade 2 children also listen and point to the words in the book as their parents follow along with them.

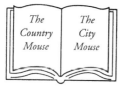

It is also important that in the classroom you do not misinterpret a lack of response from LEP, ELL, or Native American students as evidence of deficiency. Often, this absence of oral language is a culturally driven response to authority or an inability to verbalize an English response. It is helpful if you encourage LEP, ELL, and Native American students to share their history, culture, and language with the class. One method used by several teachers and researchers is sharing an American folktale, such as "The Country Mouse and the City Mouse," with your class. Immediately following that presentation, invite linguistically diverse pupils to share similar folktales from their countries. Doing so will assist them to find commonality among cultures, common forms of language, and similarities in vocabulary between two languages (Canney, Kennedy, Schroeder, & Miles, 1999; Morrison, 1990; Payne, 1999).

A third action you can take is to use the Total Physical Response (TPR) to explain assignments and to evaluate the language development of LEP students (Asher, 1982; Curtain & Pesola, 1994). TPR is when LEP students can observe you verbalizing actions as you do them. For example, Ms. Diederick would pick up her pencil and put it in her left pocket. As she did so, she would tell her daycare students:

"Ms. Diederick is picking up her pencil and putting it in her left pocket." LEP students would then repeat the statement and the action using their own names. For example, Juan said: "Juan is picking up his pencil and putting it in his left pocket."

In closing, Congress has recently ruled that Native Americans and the Native American languages have special status under federal law, which expands the purposes of language arts instruction. These policies can help serve the educational needs of these special language minority students in the United States, and are being developed from 2001–2003.

These special policies are being written because Native American languages have been declining for the past century owing to numerous factors, notably encroachments by the dominant culture and policies of linguistic genocide practiced by federal Indian schools until the 1960s (McCarty, in press). The threat of language extinction appears to be increasing—even on isolated reservations where tribal tongues survive among elders but more and more children grow up speaking only English (Crawford, 1996a). For example, according to the Alaska Native Language Center, only 20 Native American languages, 11 percent of those still spoken, continue to be learned by the youngest generations (Krauss, 1996). The remainder are moribund; that is, unless current trends can be reversed, they will soon have no living speakers.

Congress sought to counter this threat with the Native American Language Acts of 1990 and 1992. The first of these laws states a new federal policy "to preserve, protect, and promote the rights and freedom of Native Americans to use, practice, and develop Native American languages" as a matter of "self-determination" (P.L. 101-477). The second authorizes a grant program to assist Native Americans and other native organizations in preserving and revitalizing endangered languages (P.L. 102-524). As new policies are created, one valuable website that can assist your instruction is www.csun.edu/~hcedu013/eslplans.html. See Conversation Starters for the ESL/EFL classroom and Ernie's ESL/EFL activity page. For lesson ideas, check out these three websites: http://connect.bbn.com/Schools/TopTen/ESLLessonIdeas.html; www.multnomah.lib.or.us/ritnet/ear/lesl.html; and www.csun.edu/~hcedu012/eslindex.html.

RECOGNIZING AND REPORTING PROGRESS

Beginning-of-Year Assessments

Diagnosing students' preinstructional language strengths and needs during the first week of school is valuable. To do so, many teachers administer a reading attitude assessment, shown in Figure 2.5, as well as reading and writing inventories. You can also collect a writing (drawing) sample where students describe things about their listening, speaking, writing, and reading needs and strengths, and about themselves as people. To assess ability in reading from daycare environments through first grade, observe children's degree of involvement in book-sharing activities with big books and whether their eyes move left to right across the print or whether they look at your face as you read books.

You can call older students to your desk one at a time to read into a tape recorder. Students are to read from a page of children's literature at their grade level that you

Student-Friendly Reading Attitude Assessment

Name _____   Date _____

1. What do you do when you're bored? Number these activities 1 to 5 with 1 being the most likely.

 play on computer	 read a book	 play games	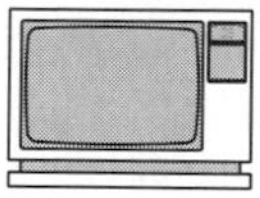 watch T.V.	 play outside

2. Circle what you like to read.

stories about far-away places	 stories about animals	 stories about sports	 scary stories	"I don't like to read"

3. If you had $10.00 to spend, what would you buy? If you had any money left what would you buy next?

food	 a book	 a new CD	 a game	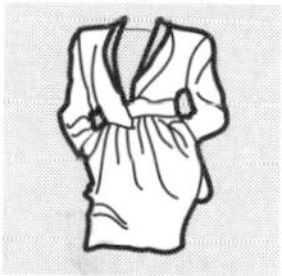 clothing

4. Do you think you are a good reader?

   a. Yes   b. No

5. Do you have a public library card?

   a. Yes   b. No

6. How often do you visit the public library?

   a. less than once a month   b. more than once a month   c. I never visit the library

7. How much time do you spend reading at home?

   a. less than 20 minutes a day   b. more than 20 minutes a day   c. I don't read at home

8. Do you often receive books for your birthday, Christmas, or other special occasions?

   a. Yes   b. No   c. Sometimes

9. What could I do, as your teacher, to help you be a better reader? Use the back to draw a picture or write a short paragraph.

FIGURE 2.5 READING ATTITUDE ASSESSMENT

Created by Robyn Dellamura, 2000, master of secondary education degree candidate at Texas Christian University, Fort Worth, TX. Used by permission.

have photocopied in advance. Before each student begins reading, write on the photocopied page the student's name and the counter number on the tape recorder at which the reading is to begin. During the reading, mark the errors each student makes (as they read the page from the book itself) on the copy that you have of that page as follows:

1. Circle the words that the student omitted.
2. Write correct words above the words read incorrectly.
3. Insert words that the child read that are not printed in the book.
4. Place an *R* above words that the child repeated.
5. Place a *P* above words you pronounce when the student does not attempt to decode it after a 6-second pause.
6. Place a double slash (//) after words when the student pauses for less than 6 seconds before continuing to read on.
7. Write *SC* above words for which the student self-corrects the pronunciation.

After you turn off the tape recorder, ask the student to retell what he or she learned from the reading. Make notes of the student's comprehension strengths, and any evidence of reading, listening, and speaking abilities and difficulties, as shown in the sample in Figure 2.6. Prompt students and ask questions for additional evidence of reading comprehension.

When each student returns to his or her seat, analyze why the student made the decoding and comprehension errors and indicate the types of instruction you want to provide. Make notes of these analyses on the sheet where you wrote down beginning counter times. Fast-forward the tape to leave a blank space that is the same length of time as the time that the student spent reading. You can use this space at the end of the year for a re-recording of the student's reading. Now you can begin a comprehensive assessment of grade-level reading ability and enjoyment for that child. When all the students have finished, you can group together students with similar needs for one day a week to address their specific decoding, comprehension, and oral reading needs.

At the end of the year, students can choose any selection they wish to read into the tape recorder, but they should not have read the piece previously. Call students to read in the same order as you did at the opening of the school year. Each student reads in the blank space that follows her or his first reading. After each student reads into the recorder, rewind the tape so each hears the beginning-of-year reading and then the end-of-year reading. Students enjoy this, and the tapes document their reading growth. An alternate plan is to use a separate audiotape for each student. This way students have their own tapes to put in their portfolios, and they can state their goals for the year on the tapes as well. After their end-of-year reading, students can replay their goals to hear whether they reached those they set for themselves. Then students can pass their tapes to subsequent teachers.

Many schools are using running records (Clay, 1999) rather than the above test. A full description as well as forms to use when conducting running records can be copied from the website that accompanies this textbook.

Jack looked at the little dog.
"Oh, yes," he said.
"We take care of all pets."

All day Ned and Jack took dogs.
They took big dogs.
And they took many little dogs.

Ned looked at the dogs.
Then he looked at Jack.
"We have many dogs," said Ned.
"How many do we have?"

"Let's see," said Jack.
"One, two, three . . .
One, two, three . . .
Oh, Ned. I don't know.
Let's say we have fifteen dogs."

"Look, Jack," said Ned.
"Here is a man with a big cat.
We don't want to take care of a cat,
do we?"
"Oh, yes," said Jack.
"We take care of all pets."

_____ main idea

_____ detail

_____ detail

_____ sequence

✗ inference

**COMPREHENSION
QUESTIONS**

1. What were Jack and Ned doing
   all day? (They were taking care
   of big and little dogs.)

2. How many dogs did they think
   they had? (fifteen)

3. Did the boys know exactly how
   many dogs they had? (no)
   Why do you say that? (They
   gave up counting and Jack said
   he didn't know.)

4. What was the last pet that was
   brought to Jack and Ned? (a big
   cat)

5. Why might Ned not want to
   take care of a cat? (Dogs don't
   like cats and they had many
   dogs; Ned thinks they have
   enough pets to care for.)

FIGURE 2.6 EXAMPLE OF INFORMAL READING INVENTORY: STUDENTS' ERRORS WHILE
READING ORALLY ARE SHOWN ON THE LEFT; ERRORS MADE WHILE ANSWERING QUESTIONS
AFTER READING ARE SHOWN ON THE RIGHT

SECTION 3   TEACHERS AS CONTINUAL LEARNERS

Beginning the Year

Knowing your teaching philosophy, keeping a personal journal, and developing effective communications with parents can become three of your most important teaching aids, especially at the beginning of the school year.

PROFESSIONAL DEVELOPMENT ACTIVITY

Your Teaching Philosophy

Sir Frederick Banting said, "You must begin with an ideal and end with an ideal!" To become the language arts teacher you want to be, you should formalize your philosophy of instruction. It determines how you will (a) answer parents' questions about your instruction, (b) decide how much time you will spend with single students each day, and (c) select material for your lessons. You can begin by writing answers to the following questions, which leads to the composition of a philosophy statement. By recording your most immediate thoughts below, you can begin to formalize your true teaching philosophy.

1. Visualize your ideal language arts program and mentally picture a typical day in action. As your students are engaged in successful language learning experiences, how many materials they are using, how many adults are in the room, what talents you are engaging. Now, complete the following statements:

In my ideal classroom, my students are _____ .

Other adults are _____ .

The three most important talents that I see myself using are: _____
_____ .

2. Describe how you will feel and what you will see in your students' eyes on the last day of school, if you have had a successful year.

_____ .

3. Picture your students leaving on this last day. Describe the most important language arts goal that they would have reached, in your professional judgement if your language arts program has been successful.

_____ .

4. Because great accomplishments start as smaller dreams, the fourth step in defining your philosophy is to identify your beliefs, goals, and visions of successful teaching. To do so, answer these three questions. What three values about language arts instruction will you never abandon?

_____ .

What could students do in your language arts class that would make you most proud?

_____ .

If _____ isn't occurring in your class, it will bother you. What will you do to ensure that this element will always be present in your class or in your teaching style?

_____ .

5. What types of support do you need to be the best teacher possible?

_____ .

What actions can you take to ensure that these supports are available?

_____ .

6. Think of someone who has a very different instructional philosophy from yours. What strength in that person's teaching style could you incorporate into yours to increase your program's effectiveness?

_____ .

7. After reflecting on your answers, compose a statement to describe your teaching philosophy. Do so by writing three sentences. The first describes your goal as a language arts teacher. The middle statement delineates the first methods that you'll use to implement this goal. The last describes how you will know you have implemented your philosophy effectively—how you will know you have been a successful teacher of the language arts.

Your teaching philosophy is: _____

_____

_____

_____

_____

_____ .

FOR YOUR JOURNAL

*Personal Journals and Introducing Journals to Preschoolers
and at the Beginning of the Year for Older Students*

Personal journals are places where students are allowed to write about any topic they choose. Students can even seal personal journal entries with a stapler or scotch tape if they do not want anyone else to read them. This type of journal is valuable for students of all ages, but more difficult to schedule for older students. For this reason, many upper elementary teachers assign personal journal writing as homework, and build other types of journal writing (e.g., interactive journals, learning logs, and reading response logs, which will be described in subsequent chapters) into the daily classroom schedule.

Scheduling personal journal writing as the first activity of the day enables younger students to build a sense of community. Scheduling it at the end of the day, in daybook fashion, increases students' review of (and reflection about themselves relative to) that day's events. Some teachers prefer to make journal writing a center into which all students rotate each day. Others schedule it immediately following the reading period so all students can respond in unison to their reading or engage in writing as soon as minilessons are concluded. Regardless of the time you select, students appreciate a consistently scheduled time for journal writing (Routman, 1994).

Many preschool (and kindergarten through grade 2) teachers invite parent volunteers and older schoolmates into the journal writing period to help young children write their thoughts in journals. Others teach that there are many forms of writing, and that young students can use any type: drawing pictures, scribbling, random letter writing combined with scribbling and pictures, invented spelling where beginning consonants represent words, and conventional writing. These teachers model how each of these would look on a page. After this modeling, most preschoolers come to believe that they can "write" and eagerly create compositions.

It is important to allow younger (and older) students to share their journal entries if they desire. Whereas some students need this experience to validate that their writings are valued by an appreciative audience, others are too shy to talk before a group unless they can read from their journals, and still others enjoy "showing off" in acceptable ways that increase learning. Because many view personal journals as treasured private places that no one else should enter, the sharing of personal journal entries should be optional.

CONNECTING CLASSROOMS, PARENTS, AND COMMUNITIES

Parent Letters

The following letter can be mailed to parents or guardians at the beginning of the year to originate a two-way communication system that should and often does continue throughout the school year.

(Date)

Dear Parents:

The next nine months will be a time of growth and exploration for your child. I look forward to sharing these exciting times and helping your child through challenging ones. I will use my professional background to teach and guide your child to the best of my ability.

As a parent, you are your child's first and most important teacher. I encourage you to become actively involved in your child's education. I am seeking ways in which you can share time with your children at home and in our classroom. Please take a moment to help me by filling out the enclosed sheet.

I would also like to meet you during this first month of school. If you can come to my room (#_____), please indicate the time you prefer.

Parent–Teacher Conference Times from September 1–30

Monday:	3:30, 4:00, 4:30	Date _____
Tuesday:	7:45, 3:00, 3:30	Date _____
Wednesday:	3:30, 4:00, 4:30	Date _____
Thursday:	7:45, 3:00, 3:30	Date _____
Friday:	3:00, 3:30, 4:00	Date _____

I cannot come during the hours listed. Please call me at _____

If you prefer a home visit, please call me to establish an appointment time.

Our class would enjoy and benefit from learning about one or more areas of your expertise. The attached form suggests several ways you can participate in activities to share. Please feel free to add ideas of your own.

Name _____

Address _____

Phone _____

1. I am willing to help in the following ways:

   _____ room mother/father/grandparent   _____ physical education
   _____ assistant room mother/father   teacher
   _____ phone committee   _____ field trips coordinator
   _____ sewing   _____ contacting people or
   _____ cooking for holiday parties   obtaining community
   _____ carpentry   resources for lessons
   _____ drama coach   _____ music teacher
   _____ dancing teacher   _____ Other: _____
   _____ arts and crafts leader   _____

   I suggest I assist the class by _____

2. I would enjoy working with you and the class at school in the following ways:
   _____ working with individual students in these subjects: _____
   _____

   _____ making games   _____ typing
   _____ library assistant   _____ working with small groups
   _____ reading stories   _____ preparing learning centers
   _____ ordering new books

3. I have the following special interest, talent, hobby, occupation, or materials I would be willing to share with the class by being a guest speaker on the topic of

   _____

   _____

4. The best time for me to help in the class is on
   _____ Monday   _____ Tuesday   _____ Wednesday
   _____ Thursday   _____ Friday   at _____ o'clock.

5. Is there any special information concerning you or your child that you would like to tell me that could advance your child's learning?

   _____

   _____

   Again I am looking forward to having your child as a student, and I am looking forward to meeting and working with you on behalf of your child.

Sincerely,

[*Note:* Before parents volunteer they need to confer with you. During this conference you can teach them the strategies they will use with students and establish a subsequent time to meet (in 3 weeks) and assess how valuable their volunteer work has been. By limiting volunteer periods to 3 weeks' duration, you can more easily reassign to other areas of responsibility parents who are not as effective or satisfied with their classroom role as they or you desire. Alternatively, you can increase the responsibilities for those who are highly successful within their roles.]

SUMMARY

Chapter 2 described four daily scheduling options—learning centers, units, mini-lessons and workshops, and multiaged classes—and the benefits and challenges of each option. Although all students are born with an innate ability for language, and all possess the need to communicate, students need to learn in many types of groups to attain their communication potential. Each grouping provides different advantages. Grouping systems include large and small groups, cooperative teams, paired instruction, and independent work. When special activities are included in the opening weeks of school, students develop a stronger sense of community and have expanded opportunities to talk, listen, read, and write in authentic ways. It is equally important to use achievement, attitude, and informal reading inventories or running records in these opening weeks to recognize students' preinstructional language strengths and needs. Predictable books, wordless books, and picture books are profitable genres to use at the beginning of school for students of all ages, but they have added value for preschoolers. The chapter closed with an opportunity for you to formalize your philosophy as a language arts teacher, practice personal journal writing for your students, and write an opening-of-school letter to parents. In the next chapter, you will learn how to increase students' speaking abilities.

HOW TO DO IT: USING WHAT YOU'VE LEARNED

The following provide several opportunities to think about and practice what you have learned.

ASSESSING YOUR LEARNING

1. "When young children can't yet read, it is important that you do not require them to write." Defend your position in favor of, or in opposition to, this statement.

2. If you are not teaching, observe a language arts lesson in an elementary school or reflect on your favorite language arts class when you were a child. List the principles of language learning from Chapters 1 and 2 that were in operation. Compare these principles to those cited in Chapters 1 and 2. Which grouping systems were being implemented effectively?

If you are teaching, in the coming week practice increasing your students' ability to take risks. Say to your students, "I'm glad you took a chance," "I like to hear that you have several alternatives in mind that you want to try," and "I like your question." Model how to say, "I don't know but I'm going to find out." You might also thank your students for the effective lessons that you have had together as soon after they occur as possible.

3. If you are presently teaching, share *Alexander and the Terrible, Horrible, No Good, Very Bad Day*. Follow this reading by using centers, a minilesson, or a thematic unit that you write to extend a language arts competency that you judge your students need. If you are not yet teaching, identify one of the most important books you've ever read, and reflect on why it was important to you. Visualize yourself sharing this book and its importance with future students. Describe how you will share it.

4. Design a system by which you will read the children's literature on the Literature Cards in this book. Enter the plan in your personal journal. You can begin this program by reading the Newbery and Caldecott Award books on Literature Cards 1 and 2 (pp. 29 and 30), and the wordless, predictable, and alphabet books in Literature Cards 3 and 4 (pp. 70 and 72). You can even make a mark in your textbook in some way to remind you what you have read and what you appreciated about each book.

KEY TERMS EXERCISE

Below is a list of the concepts introduced in this chapter. If you have learned the meaning of a term, place a checkmark in the blank that precedes that term. If you are not sure of a term's definition, increase your retention by reviewing the definition of the term. If you have learned 15 of these terms on your first reading of this chapter, you have constructed many meanings that are important for your career. Congratulations.

_____ academic learning time   (p. 62)

_____ big books   (p. 71)

_____ demonstrations by a student (p. 58)

_____ direct presentations   (p. 58)

_____ dyadic pairs   (p. 64)

_____ eustress   (p. 62)

_____ heterogeneous groups   (p. 66)

_____ homogeneous groups   (p. 66)

_____ individualization   (p. 68)

_____ interest groups   (p. 65)

_____ journal writing   (p. 49)

_____ learning centers   (p. 52)

_____ master programmatic plan (p. 49)

_____ minilessons   (p. 58)

_____ morning message   (p. 57)

_____ multiaged classes   (p. 62)

_____ peer tutoring   (p. 64)

_____ personal journals   (p. 81)

_____ predictable books   (p. 71)

_____ project groups   (p. 66)

_____ relate previous experiences (p. 58)

_____ role play   (p. 58)

_____ task- or process-specific groups (p. 66)

_____ thematic units   (p. 60)

_____ wordless picture books   (p. 71)

_____ workshops   (p. 58)

FOR FUTURE REFERENCE

Aronson, E. (1987). *Jigsaw classroom.* New York: Sage.

Gregory, C. (1995). *Quick-and-easy learning centers: Writing.* New York: Scholastic Professional Books.

Johnson, D., & Johnson, R. (1995). *Learning together and alone: Cooperative, competitive, and individualistic learning* (4th ed.). Boston: Allyn and Bacon.

————. (1995). *Circles of learning.* Alexandria, VA: Association for Supervision and Curriculum Development.

Juel, C. (1991). Cross-age tutoring between student athletes and at-risk children. *The Reading Teacher, 45,* 178–186.

Leto, D. J. (1995). Creating community with an after-school tutoring program. *Language Arts, 72*(2), 128–135.

Lynch, P. (1986). *Using big books and predictable books.* Richmond Hill, Ontario: Scholastic-TAB.

Macon, J., Bewell, D., & Vogt, M. E. (1990) *Responses to literature, grades K–8.* Newark, DE: International Reading Association.

Marantz, S. S. (1992). *Picture books for looking and learning: Awakening visual perceptions through the art of children's books.* Phoenix, AZ: Oryx Press.

Meichenbaum, D., Rothlein, R., & Fredericks, A. (1995). *The complete guide to thematic units: Creating the integrated curriculum.* Boston: Allyn and Bacon.

Opitz, M. F. (1994). *Learning centers: Getting them started, keeping them going.* New York: Scholastic.

Routman, R. (1994). *Invitations* (2nd ed.). Portsmouth, NH: Heinemann.

Schwarcz, J. H., & Schwarcz, C. (1991). *The picture book comes of age: Looking at childhood through the art of illustration.* Chicago: American Library Association.

Shannon, R. (1992). Reading instruction and social class. In P. Shannon (Ed.), *Becoming political: Readings and writings in the politics of literacy education* (pp. 1–32). Portsmouth, NH: Heinemann.

Slavin, R. (1989). *Using student team learning.* Baltimore: Johns Hopkins University.

Spann, M. B. (1995). *Quick-and-easy learning centers: Word play.* New York: Scholastic.

Wong, H. K., & Wong, R. T. (1994). *The first days of school.* Sunnyvale, CA: Wong.

ADDITIONAL RESOURCES FOR TEACHERS AND PARENTS

Books

Bodine, R., & Crawford, D. (1998). *The handbook of conflict resolution education: A guide to building quality programs in schools.* San Francisco: Jossey-Bass.

Cangelosi, J. S. (1993). *Classroom management strategies: Gaining and maintaining student cooperation.* New York: Longman.

Collins, C. (1987). *Acting-out children: New methods that eliminate their most negative classroom behaviors and teach them to make positive classroom contributions.* Ft. Worth, TX: Educational Research Dissemination.

Goldstein, S. (1995). *Understanding and managing children's classroom behavior.* New York: John Wiley and Sons.

Gootman, M. E. (1997). *The caring teacher's guide to discipline: Helping young students learn self-control, responsibility and respect.* Thousand Oaks: Corwin.

Harmin, M. (1995). *Inspiring discipline: A practical guide for today's classroom.* National Education Association.

Kauffman, J., Mostert, M., Trent, S., & Hallahan, D. (1998). *Managing classroom behavior: A reflective case-based approach.* Boston: Allyn and Bacon.

Websites

Behavior Management for the Classroom (voucher system):   www.happy-kids.com/school.htm

An Educational Internet Village—Teacher's Village provides resources for new teachers: www.teacherpathfinder.org/

THEMATIC UNIT: USING PREDICTABLE PICTURE BOOKS

Ms. Tiffany Diederick, from Overland Park, Kansas, has realized many benefits from using predictable books with her preschool children. This unit is one that she and her students created after they discovered that Eric Carle was their favorite author. As you read the unit, identify the daily schedules and grouping systems and specific ways that literature is integrated for these children.

Unit Goal.   The primary goal of this unit is to improve students' speaking, listening, reading, and writing abilities by studying the vivid works of Eric Carle.

Planning with Students.   Following a whole-class reading, the students will select one of Carle's works to explore individually.

Generalizations.   The students develop initial speaking, listening, reading, and writing behaviors. Specific language arts strategies to be learned are

Speaking skills—strategies for presentation to a group

Listening skills—strategies to identify specific detail

Reading skills—story mapping as a means of developing emergent reading concepts such as reading from left to right

Writing skills—prewriting skill development (i.e., movement from scribble to letter use)

Daily Schedule

Day 1: Teacher reads *Brown Bear, Brown Bear* to whole class; class makes a story map of Brown Bear and all he sees; teacher explains individual writing task for students to answer the question, "What do you see?"

Day 2: Teacher reads *Brown Bear, Brown Bear* to whole class; students compare their ideas of what they would see; teacher introduces *The Very Hungry Caterpillar, The Very Busy Spider,* and *The Very Grouchy Ladybug* for children to choose their story of emphasis.

Day 3: Small groups of children break into book groups and look through their stories with adult teaching aides; when it is time for them to meet with the teacher, they will read the story together using a big book.

Day 4: Read an Eric Carle book again. Play the Caterpillar game where each student is a character and the teacher is the narrator.

Day 5: Put together the "I see . . . " big book; determine which children will be what character for the Caterpillar play; have the students color their puppets to be laminated; the small groups discuss what makes Eric Carle's books special to touch and see.

Day 6: Present "I see . . ." book to the preschoolers. In the kindergarten room have groups of preschoolers and kindergartners pair so that they can read their group books together. Back in the preschool classroom, make the Caterpillar puppets to take home at the end of the day.

Day 7: Read all three Eric Carle books to the class again. Practice the puppet play with each student learning when to stand and say lines. Have students from different groups pair up to share their books.

Day 8: Practice the puppet play with each student saying lines. Have students from different groups pair up to share their books. The children should have seen and heard all of the books by now.

Day 9: Students perform the puppet play at a local retirement center or in the kindergarten classroom. While there, each group explains their book.

Day 10: Have the class draw a picture of their new friends at the retirement center or kindergarten and mail them a book of the pictures and their group-composed thank you note for allowing them to come and share their play.

Recognizing and Reporting Progress.   Make anecdotal records and save student samples of their books, puppets, and writings.

Kindergarten students must learn how to use their own speech as a vehicle for social exchange and interaction.

CHAPTER 3

ORAL COMMUNICATION

One day soon after Allison had told her rendition of the wordless picture book *Tuesday,* she asked Ms. Wooten if Meisong, Juan, and Michael could stay in from recess for a few minutes so she could read something to them before they left. Ms. Wooten agreed, realizing that it had been nearly a month since school began and Allison was still not volunteering to answer questions orally in class. What a breakthrough today might be! After everyone left for recess, the "Mighty Four," as they called themselves, gathered in the library corner. Allison opened the wordless picture book *The Cat In the Square* and began telling the most elaborate and ornate story that Ms. Wooten had ever heard about that book. Allison was using a melodic and expressive voice as well. After Allison finished, she told her friends that she liked the book because it reminded her of her small cat, Timothy. Meisong, Juan, and Michael began to tell Allison all about their pets and stuffed animals. Much too soon, the entire recess period had elapsed for these four students.

Ms. Wooten is aware, through her experience and through research, that approximately 30 percent of the students that will enter her kindergarten classroom have poor oral language abilities. These students must learn how to use their own speech as a vehicle for social exchange and interaction.

When students talk through experiences, they can more rapidly place them into perspective, cease worrying, and learn from them (Block, 1999; Clay, 1999; Norwicki & Duke, 1994). Thus, encouraging fruitful conversations in your classroom can transform how children interact and change your role as an educator.

Through the activities in this chapter you can help your students learn how to communicate their deeply felt emotions and ideas, and to acknowledge and appreciate the oral expressions of their classmates. They can also learn how to eliminate their speaking deficiencies. As Michael Halliday (1982, p. 11) stated: "A child doesn't need to know any linguistics in order to use language; but [you] need to know some linguistics to understand how the process takes place . . . [and] what is going wrong when it doesn't." By the end of this chapter you will have information concerning the following IRA, NCTE, NAEYC, and TEKS, and other statewide and province-based standards for professional development:

1. Why do students need oral language instruction?
2. What are the stages of oral language development?
3. What is dialect and how do you teach students with dialectical problems?
4. How do you ask, and help students to ask, effective questions?
5. What speaking difficulties can you help students to overcome?
6. How can you connect students' prior knowledge with new information through Think Alouds?
7. How can prekindergarten to second-grade students become more technologically literate with input devices (e.g., mouse, keyboard, remote control) and output devices (e.g., monitor, printer) so they can operate computers, VCRs, audiotapes, telephones, and other machines?
8. How can you use a variety of media and technological resources for directing independent oral language activities?

SECTION 1   THEORETICAL FOUNDATIONS

Students' Oral Language Needs

Leonard Bloomfield wrote that language learning is "doubtless the greatest intellectual feat any one of us is ever required to perform" (1933, p. 29). Students need your help to fully develop their speaking abilities for several reasons. First, many students will enter your K–8 classroom having had life-shattering experiences beyond their years. Most will likely have won more computer-based games, experienced more cities vicariously through more varied television programming, listened to more music, and solved more difficulties in their daily lives than you had at their age. Many will have lost much more than you through poverty and crises. In the process, they may also have survived so much that they develop the defense of silence, having lost the belief that what they have to say is important. Thus, many refrain from speaking. Without your instruction, these students may remain too afraid throughout their lives to risk speaking up to share their ideas (McClure, 1995).

When students' expressions are valued and understood by you, they can lose their fear of sharing orally. For example, before Allison entered kindergarten, she had not yet talked *at all* in her preschool class. Because Ms. Wooten's room contained effective and caring discussions and productive speaking development activities (as you will learn by reading this chapter), Allison's security increased and she began to share by inserting her reality into the classroom through speaking. For these reasons, 2 days after the "Mighty Four" read *Tuesday,* Allison spoke up during the class opening meeting. This was a very important event for her, her teacher, and her classmates. On that day, Allison's lips quivered as she related that her mother was hit by a car that sped through the school zone that morning. She told how her mother had turned to wave goodbye to Allison, and the car's driver didn't see her. "My mom's in the hospital right now," she said, and dropped her head. Her classmates expressed such sincere concern and appreciation that Allison's belief in her oral abilities increased. Through Ms. Wooten's expertise, a community of students had been built who supported and listened to each other during this and numerous other trials throughout the year.

Such classroom conversations are important because they enable students to relate prior experiences in which there is no right answer. Barnes (1975) was the first to call such speaking *exploratory talk*. **Exploratory talk** is characterized by questioning, hypothesizing, and improvising. When allowed to do so in classrooms, students can have a ready-made audience for testing and refining their positions and reasoning. When these exploratory talks involve other students of different persuasions, new knowledge is gained and students learn to converse with people of like and unlike minds (Cazden, 1994; Newell & Durst, 1993).

Students also need to be taught to speak effectively because oral communication is the medium by which people receive most of their information. Educators are becoming increasingly aware that more and more of your students' future professional and personal successes will depend on their effective use of speech. As Pericles stated: "The thinking human being not able to express himself stands at the same level as those who cannot think." Unfortunately, in many schools oral language instruction is overshadowed by reading and writing priorities. When pupils talk at school, they tend to do so only to give truncated answers or discuss topics for an average of no more than 58 seconds (Norwicki & Duke, 1994). In such classrooms, students often talk more at home than at school. In the most effective classrooms, however, teachers like you and Ms. Wooten develop oral language by connecting the familiar to the new and by augmenting students' exploratory talk and questions with a wide variety of audiovisually stimulating activities.

In such classrooms, students' oral language abilities improve because their teachers: (1) do not want everyone in a discussion to reach the same conclusion; (2) require students to find new information about the world; and (3) encourage students to question and state their judgments. For example, Ms. Wooten frequently says: "Who has a good question to ask about what Michael said?" and invites students to look at both sides of an issue by saying, "What if . . . ?" She frequently turns questions addressed to her back to the students. For example, if a student asks, "Why did Chris Van Allsburg name his book *The Polar Express* instead of *The Christmas Bell,* or something else?" her response would likely be, "Class, why do you think Mr. Van Allsburg thought *The Polar Express* was a better title?"

A third reason to develop students' speaking abilities is that those who have well-developed oral abilities are likely to have significantly higher reading and writing achievement (Ruddell & Ruddell, 1995; Cazden, 1998; Chall, 1999). This correlation is strong because words students speak become the first that they recognize and use in reading or writing. Moreover, by building students' oral vocabularies you can simultaneously increase the number of words they can decode when they read and write. Similarly, students who speak effectively will more quickly recognize the graphemes that represent the phonemes they say (Adams, 1999; Juel, 1991). Such students are also more likely to interact with friends who in turn point to printed words during conversations. Orally proficient students will also be less self-conscious about asking friends the meaning of unfamiliar words. These conversations create the schema necessary to store new word meanings. Moreover, the definitions students receive through them will probably be in terms that they can understand. And, in the course of that same conversation, students will likely say the new word they just learned. This immediate transfer further ensures that these terms will become a part of students' permanent speaking, listening, reading, and writing vocabulary. Reciprocally, being able to talk about what they have read or written strengthens their comprehension.

Students most easily learn to pronounce words that (1) have an appealing sound or are perceived to be "adult" words, (2) describe an incident that involves strong emotion, (3) have an immediate usefulness, or (4) are used by peers. Research has also revealed that the rehearsal of new words in a safe classroom environment increases the speed with which new words can become automatic in students' oral vocabulary (Block, 1998; Haggard, 1993; Templeton, 1999).

The fourth reason to develop students' speaking abilities is that oral language is the first language art that children use to express their original ideas. Unfortunately, for most students the words spoken at school are different from those spoken at home. Through your guidance, students can learn to adjust their speech appropriately for various audiences and purposes, and become successful speakers in school and throughout life. In the security of cozy, nonjudgmental small groups, which you can create through the activities in this chapter, your students are most likely to use the exploratory, thinking-aloud language that is so productive for learning. They can learn to speak to express honest feeling, and to consider other people's viewpoints. This will help expand their individual perspectives (Thomson, 1987; Dyson, 1999). Further, a strong oral language program increases the pleasure of learning because conversing with others adds pleasure to the school day.

The Little Engine That Could

Last, oral language skills build thinking, listening, reading, writing, and observing abilities in several ways. When communicating orally students have to explain more than when they listen, read, write, or observe. These explanations advance students' analytical skills. Speech also helps students stand outside their own knowledge and observe how their ideas influence others. Group talk assists students to hypothesize, test, and question their beliefs before they accept them as truths (Block, 1999; Dyson, 1999; O'Keefe, 1995). Further, if classroom discussions are curtailed, students miss opportunities to develop examples, make analogies, and relate experiences. These competencies have demonstrated an increase in students' abilities to infer, find themes, and locate main ideas during reading (Block, 2000; Pressley, 2000; Wepner, 1992). For example, as Juan and Allison demonstrate in their talk about *The Little Engine That Could,* they can help each other make important analogies and draw insightful conclusions. Had Ms. Wooten curtailed the following conversation, this episode, which helped build higher-level thinking may not have occurred:

Allison: My brother has that book. He read it to me when I couldn't tie my shoes . . . I don't know why.

Juan: Maybe he was trying to tell you that if the train could go . . . well, maybe, you can tie your shoes.

Allison: Yeah, like my bike . . .

Juan: What?

Allison: I saw my brother fall off his bike and it scared me, so I didn't want to learn to ride my bike. Daddy told me I could do it, but I thought I would fall.

Juan: Did your Dad make you ride it?

Allison: No, he just kept talking and told me I could do it if I wanted to.

Juan: Did you learn to ride?

Allison: Yes! I wanted to, so I could.

Juan: I don't know why that helped. Did the train do it because he didn't want the kids unhappy?

Ms. Wooten: The train didn't want the kids unhappy, but that wasn't the only reason he decided to go up the mountain. The train made it up the mountain because he wasn't afraid to try. He believed in himself. He kept saying, "I can do it," and . . .

Allison: So, telling himself he could do it helped him like it did me when I decided I could ride my bike.

Juan: Trying new things is good. We shouldn't always be afraid. If we keep saying we can do it, then we can make someone happy too.

STAGES OF ORAL LANGUAGE DEVELOPMENT

Students pass through stages in speaking abilities. When this developmental path is known, you can help individuals rewalk it and discover important landmarks they may have missed. Four distinct theories, as described next, explain how speaking abilities mature.

DEVELOPMENTAL THEORIES

Behaviorists contend that children learn to speak by **shaping,** which is the positive reinforcement of desired behaviors and the negative reinforcement of undesired ones (Bloomfield, 1933; Owens, 1984; Skinner, 1957; Wardhaugh, 1971). These researchers explain language learning as a process of imitating words and phrases that are rewarded by adults. These reinforcements help students discern and duplicate acceptable English-speaking patterns.

According to this theory, language learning occurs through children's need to respond to and create in their environment. This interaction happens in a part of the mind called the *language-acquisition device,* which is the section of the brain that receives information from the environment, analyzes it, and generates language rules (Chomsky, 1975; Watson, 1979). According to Chomsky and other behaviorists, the **language-acquisition device** organizes graphemes, phonemes, syntax, grammar, and semantic features into separate categories. Thus, these theorists propose that students learn to speak naturally when they are exposed to speech. Although many researchers support this theory, opponents propose that imitation or selective reinforcement cannot explain how students form sentences they have never heard before (Ferreiro & Teberosky, 1982; Pflaum, 1986). Because students can do this, however, these researchers suggest that learning to speak is more complicated than the behaviorists anticipated. Opponents of the behaviorist theory also argue that a language-acquisition device fails to explain why some of the more complex language forms must be taught before students understand or use them appropriately.

These opponents believe that the **cognitive field theory** better explains language development. They believe that students acquire language by creating hypotheses and structuring their own thinking. They posit that students create their own meanings, which explains why (1) each produces a different mental image when hearing a word (e.g., *dog*); (2) mental images mature over the years; and (3) single words can have multiple connotations. Cognitive theorists also state that rather than having innate "language-acquisition devices," students make rules about language subconsciously. Therefore, language learning is accelerated through an instructional program that makes students' subconscious rules more concrete and raises them to a conscious level so they can be used intentionally (Boomer, 1984; Page & Pinnell, 1979; Piaget, 1969; Canady, Kennedy, Morris, & Schmidt, 1997).

A third theory is **psycholinguistics.** Psychologists argue that language use, learning, and thinking are driven by students' innate capacity to seek and reflect on meanings gained through seeing, feeling, and doing. Psycholinguistic theorists recommend that oral language ability is best built through personal letter writing, conducting plays, participating in debates, and engaging in conversations. All these activities build an appreciation for the worth of clear thinking. These theorists posit that articulating and examining beliefs, sharing and exploring ideas, and talking through plans or problems are essential for learning to speak (Goodman, 1987; Smith, 1990).

Last, the **mastery** or **subskill theory** proposes that language and thinking mature through the sequential mastery of basic skills (Bloom, 1956). Subskill theorists believe that different working systems (skills, subskills, abilities, preferences, inclinations, dispositions, and prior knowledge) interact when students encounter material of variant difficulties. This theory also maintains that as much as 30 percent of language learning can be governed by students' attitudes, beliefs, and values.

STAGES OF LEARNING TO SPEAK

Regardless of which theory or theories most accurately explain oral language development, knowing them helps us to understand what students likely do as they learn to communicate. Although researchers work to obtain a definitive explanation of language acquisition, they have accumulated substantial evidence that most students pass through the following stages as they learn to speak.

Birth to age 2. Most children say their first, recognizable English words at about one year of age. (Children differ, however. Albert Einstein did not say his first word until age 4!) The first words children say are called **holophrastic speech.** One word is meant to convey as much meaning as complete thoughts and sentences do for adults. Most children begin to put two words together by age 2 (e.g., "Mommy come" . . . "All gone" . . . "Daddy toast"). However, when these two-word statements are used, they mean different things at different times. For example, when a baby says, "me milk" at breakfast, it probably means, "I want some milk." When said at lunch, it may mean, "I don't want any more milk." At the evening meal (on that same day) it may mean, "I can't reach my milk."

Ages 2–5. Speaking abilities expand rapidly during these ages. At this stage students acquire the ability to associate words with mental images and past experiences, an ability Piaget (1969) labeled **symbolic function** or **telegraphic speech.** Such speech derived its name from the telegraph, which uses content words to convey meaning. With telegraphic speech, children use single words to signify events, experiences, and things that are not present in the child's immediate environment (e.g., "Daddy gone bye-bye"). Soon, the need arises to use *function words,* such as *is, to, the, that,* and *of.* Only when children acquire function words do they move beyond a dependence on nouns and verbs to communicate. Most children learn to use endings on verbs and nouns (*-ed, -s, -tion*) before age 5. By age 3, children's speaking vocabularies reach 1,000 words and, in their next 3 years of life, their vocabularies increase fivefold. Thus, by the time Ms. Wooten's students reach her in kindergarten, most will have a speaking vocabulary of 6,000 words (Loban, 1976).

At some point between 2 and 5 years of age, children also begin to organize language into typical English sentences. Chomsky (1975) suggests that this reorganization results from the neurological development that causes maturation in the language-acquisition device. He hypothesizes that this device metamorphosizes in a manner similar to the transformation of larvae into butterflies.

Ages 6–7. When children are placed in the social setting of school, they begin to use language to **ritualize, instrumentalize, regulate, personalize, heuristicalize, imagine,** and **inform** (as explained on pages 99–101). Instructions you provide in kindergarten through second grade extend students' abilities to use their speech in each of these ways so they convey more accurate meanings. For example, when Juan said to Ms. Wooten, "Cinderella is happy," she modeled informative speaking by responding, "Yes, Cinderella solved problems, didn't she?"

Many students in kindergarten through second grade, however, still mispronounce words that contain *v, th, ch,* and *sh.* Many also substitute *w* for *r* and *l* in some words (Read, 1975). Although wide ranges of development can be expected during these years, the major oral language accomplishments expected from good language arts programs appear in Table 3.1.

Ages 8–13. From second through eighth grade, the quality of oral language relies greatly on the types of instruction students receive. Up to this point in the chapter, reasons why students need instruction to mature their speaking abilities, as well as theories that explain how oral language develops, have been discussed. Students also need instruction before they can use language for all the functions it can perform, such as making more effective requests, gaining control, relating, expressing feelings, giving information, imagining, and investigating. In the next section you will learn more about these functions as well as the daily dozen discussion strategies that you can use to improve students' oral communication, redirect their inaccurate answers, or eliminate their speaking deficiencies.

TABLE 3.1 LANGUAGE DEVELOPMENT GUIDE FROM BIRTH TO 6 YEARS OLD

5 TO 6 YEARS OLD

*10,000–15,000 word vocabulary**

- Enjoys stories. Follows sequence of several directions.

- Practices most grammatical rules in using language, uses complex sentences more frequently, carries on conversations. Participates in shared reading. Uses creative language. (A child describing a locomotive: *It just takes a big breath of air and holds it inside and that's what makes it go fast. It's like when you put air in a balloon and, poof, it blows itself away.*) Begins using humorous language intentionally.

- Draws pictures. Recognizes printed letters, words. Writes letters, words using invented spellings.

4 TO 5 YEARS OLD

*3,000–5,000 word vocabulary**

- Enjoys being read to. Follows sequence of two directions.

- Uses most basic rules of language. Pronounces most words correctly. Talks about pictures in books; tells stories about recent events. Begins to use more abstract language, transforms sentences into questions. (*I want Sally to come. Is Sally coming?*) Describes experiences as if language and activity are one. (*I'm making colors all over, I'm painting, pit, pat, pit, pat.*)

- Continues to scribble and draw. Recognizes printed letters and words. Writes letters to represent words.

3 TO 4 YEARS OLD

*1,000–2,000 word vocabulary**

- Enjoys being read to. Understands number concepts (e.g., one, two, three).

- Uses more complex sentences with adjectives, adverbs, verb past tenses. Generalizes knowledge about language, as in using invented word endings to convey past tense or degree. (*I eated breakfast today. I wented to the zoo. That dog was the nicest and bestest.*)

- Begins scribbling, drawing to communicate thoughts.

2 TO 3 YEARS OLD

*800–1,000 word vocabulary**

- Enjoys being read to. Points to objects in pictures. Follows prepositional directions. (*Put your toys in the box.*)

- Begins to listen to language, use language more dramatically. Uses simple and compound sentences, subjects, verbs, plurals, pronouns, prepositions, and concepts such as big and little. Puts words together to convey message. (*Milk all gone. He hugs, he kisses, he nice, nice teddy.**)

1 TO 2 YEARS OLD

*300–500 word vocabulary**

- Points to or looks at familiar objects or people when asked. (e.g., *"Where's the ball?"*) Follows simple spoken directions.

- Uses two or three word phrases. Communicates to meet need or share information by using telegraphic speech—nonessential words are omitted. (*Me milk. Doggie play. DaDa bye-bye. Not go. See truck.*)

- At 18 months, possesses about a 20-word vocabulary.

BIRTH TO 1 YEAR OLD

- Turns eyes and head to sound sources. Responds to own name, voices of others, environmental sounds.

- Plays with sounds, cooing and babbling. At about 6 months, begins to select and imitate sounds and single words that express thoughts and elicit responses. (*MaMa. Milk. No. Bye-bye.*)

---

*My research indicates that these examples are typical toward the end of the specified age range.

Created by Paula Pentecost, 2000, kindergarten teacher at St. Matthew Christian School, Fort Worth, TX, adapted from research by Walter Loban, *Language Development: Kindergarten through Grade Twelve;* Susan Mandel Glazer, *Oral Language and Literacy Development; Early Child Language Development,* webpages.marshall.edu/~sowards9/a.html, 1999. Used by permission.

FUNCTIONS OF LANGUAGE

Linguists are researchers who study language. They study the components of effective speech. Many kindergarten through second-grade students need your instruction before they can develop facility with each of these components and learn to express their thoughts more explicitly and effectively. The seven ways they can be taught to use language are described below (Halliday, 1976).

Effective speakers use language to make requests. When students use oral language to make requests, they are using language to meet needs. This is called the **instrumental function** of language. When students can't effectively speak instrumentally, their needs often go unsatisfied. Fortunately, by school age, most children can use instrumental language easily and nonabrasively—for example, they can say: "I would like . . ." "I want . . ." and "I need. . . ." If students are unable to make such requests, you can model how to do so by asking students what they want, like, and need, and by placing them in groups to learn from peers who assert themselves appropriately. For example, Juan heard Ms. Wooten say every day, "I want us to read [name of a book]." When students enact commercials and television situations and write letters or notes in your language arts program, they can also exercise and improve their instrumental language.

The Velveteen Rabbit

Second, effective speakers use oral language to control others. They speak to receive as well as to issue commands. When students speak for this purpose, they are exercising the **regulatory function** of language. One strategy that improves students' use of regulatory language is to stop the reading periodically and describe how a book character skillfully used regulatory language. To illustrate, when Ms. Wooten read *The Velveteen Rabbit,* she stopped at the incident when the boy was given a toy that was not his rabbit. She pointed out that the boy was using language to control his environment when he said, "Please give me my Bunny. He isn't a toy, He's REAL!" Students can also gain practice by performing role plays and playing word games, in which they give others directions such as, "Do this next." "This one goes here." "Move here."

In addition, you can assist students who are using language to make requests effectively as they interact with classmates during the day. For example, Michael wanted to borrow Juan's crayons at the art center. Ms. Wooten overheard Michael ask in a manner that made Juan not want to comply. So Ms. Wooten turned to Michael and said, "If I'm going to ask Juan if I can borrow his crayons, I'm going to decide how to do it before I try to ask him. I could say, 'Give me those crayons right now!' or I could say, 'May I borrow your crayons for just a minute? I'll bring them right back, and I'll be real careful when I use them.' Which one do you think he'll say yes to?" By modeling regulatory language in this way, Ms. Wooten assisted Michael in developing the sentence structures necessary to more effectively control his environment in the future.

When oral language is used to build strong personal relationships, it is serving an **interactional function.** For many students, speaking in school is the first time they will have had the opportunity to use language to function as a tool to increase their interactivity. These students may need instruction in how to (1) establish rapport, (2) include others in conversations, and (3) persuade. You can strengthen their interactional language skills by encouraging such talk with show and tell activities, storytelling, telephone conversations, and writing thank-you notes, as described later in this chapter.

When students speak to express feelings, attitudes, and worries, they are using the **personal function** of language. As students progress through the grades, most become more adept in expressing these thoughts and feelings. In the process, they come to realize their uniqueness from and unity with others. You can employ several strategies to develop personal language use, such as telling students your feelings, attitudes, and concerns. You can honor their concerns by asking follow-up questions such as, "If I understood you correctly, you feel . . ." Students also improve personal language when they keep personal journals, respond to literature, and tape-record their thoughts.

Informational function of oral language is the ability to give and receive new knowledge. Students display their abilities to use language informationally when they relay facts, report information, and ask questions. You can strengthen their ability to use informational language by asking students to give oral reports; read and interpret graphs, time lines, and maps; and share newspaper and magazine stories. Your goal might be to help students move beyond telling what they know, have heard, or read to explaining what they understand.

The **imaginative function** of oral language is the ability to stimulate the imagination and strengthen students' inventive qualities. Developing the students' imaginative use of language is becoming increasingly important because of our world's more rapid expansion in complexity and competitiveness. It is increasingly clear that students must learn to use language and all the language arts innovatively to succeed professionally and be able to advance to high levels in their chosen careers. Moreover, they must learn to adjust to rapid changes in patterns of communication, thinking, and lifestyles, which increasingly become rapidly outdated. You can develop this ability by asking students to imagine scenes from books you read before you show the pictures; by using phrases like, "Let's pretend that we're on an island"; and by including script writing as well as improvisation in your curriculum.

The **heuristic function** of oral language is the search for reasons behind actions and events. Today, students can more easily access large volumes of current and past knowledge. You can support their talk about relationships among these knowledge bases by teaching them how to ask "why," "what is . . . ," and "I wonder why. . . ." Students can learn to use heuristic language to satisfy their innate curiosities by conducting interviews, playing question-and-answer games, and keeping dialogue journals. Dialogue journals are journals in which you respond to students' individual questions, as will be described in more depth later in the chapter. In Table 3.2, you will find a list of books for ages 2, 3, 4, and 5 at each level of functioning. Each book contains characters that model the specific type of language function assigned to that book. By using these books—reading them orally, having parents read them to their children, and having children read them by themselves—children can learn by imitating the characters in these books how to use each of these language functions appropriately.

In summary, oral language can perform many functions. Your language arts program should improve students' abilities to (1) make requests to satisfy their needs (instrumental), (2) control their environment (regulatory), (3) perform rituals and engage in discourses with social grace (interactional), (4) express their individuality through their feelings and opinions (personal), (5) convey information to others (informational), (6) imagine and "field-test" new ideas (imaginative), and (7) ask "why" things are or are not as they appear or should be (heuristic). When students speak

TABLE 3.2 BOOKS THAT MODEL THE ORAL LANGUAGE FUNCTIONS

FUNCTIONS	AGE 2	AGE 3	AGE 4	AGE 5
INSTRUMENTAL Using language to meet needs	*Pass the Fritters Critters* by Cheryl Chapman	*I Really Want a Dog* by Susan Breslow	*Mother Mother I Feel Sick Send for the Doctor Quick Quick Quick* by Remy Charlip	*Pizza for Breakfast* by Maryann Kovalski
REGULATORY Speaking to give commands	*When You Were a Baby* by Ann Jonas	*Let Me Do It* by Janice Gibala-Broxholm	*Dunkel Takes a Walk* by Charles Martin	*Can I Keep Him?* by Steven Kellog
INTERACTIONAL Using language to build personal relationships	*My Hands Can* by Jean Holzenthaler	*I'm Busy, Too* by Norma Simon	*Ugly Bird* by Russell Hoban	*Big Sarah's Little Boots* by Paulette Bourgeois
PERSONAL Speaking to express ideas/thoughts	*What Do Toddlers Do?* by Debby Slier	*Sam* by Ann Scott	*Who's Afraid of the Dark?* by Crosby Bonsall	*I Wish I Had My Father* by Norma Simon
INFORMATIONAL Speaking to relay new information	*Baby's First Christmas* by Tomie dePaola	*All by Myself* by Anna Hines	*Trains* by Anne Rockwell	*Country Fair* by Gail Gibbons
IMAGINATIVE Speaking to build/strengthen imagination	*Where's Spot?* by Eric Hill	*Martin's Hat* by Joan Blos	*Angelina Ballerina* by Katherine Holabird	*The Monster and the Tailor* by Paul Galdone
HEURISTIC Speaking to find reasons for actions/events	*Spots, Feathers, & Curly Tails* by Nancy Tafuri	*Brown Bear, Brown Bear, What Do You See?* by Bill Martin	*How Come Elephants?* by Marc Simont	*Where Does My Spaghetti Go When I Eat? Questions Kids Ask about the Human Body* by Neil Morris

Created by Leslie Williamson, 2000, education major at Texas Christian University, Fort Worth, TX. Used by permission.

for these purposes, their messages can be misinterpreted, however, because of dialectical differences. Helping students eliminate these obstacles is another important component of your language arts program (Cox, Fang, & Otto, 1997).

DIALECTICAL DIFFERENCES

Dialect is the set of speech characteristics peculiar to a region, community, social group, or occupation, including jargon, slang, and coined words. The position of the National Council of Teachers of English (1994, 1999) and the International Reading Association (IRA, 1999) concerning dialect follows:

> We affirm students' right to their own patterns and varieties of language—the dialects of their nurture or whatever dialects in which they find their own identity and style. Language scholars long ago denied that the myth of a standard American dialect has any validity. The claim that any one dialect is unacceptable amounts to an attempt of one social group to exert its dominance over another. Such a claim leads to false advice for speakers and writers, and immoral advice for humans. A nation proud of its diverse heritage and its cultural and racial variety will preserve its heritage of dialects. We affirm strongly that teachers must have the experiences and training that will enable them to respect diversity and uphold the right of students to their own language.

In your program, you not only accept students' present speaking patterns, and strengthen their power of communication by making them aware of how variations in oral language can influence their listeners, but you teach them how to use traditional grammatical forms as well. What sociolinguists found in their research is that dialects are not ill-formed or half-formed variations of Standard English. Instead, each dialect constitutes a well-developed linguistic system in its own right, complete with rules for variations from Standard English and a path of language development for its speakers. For example, an African American child who says *pos* when he sees *post* is simply applying a rule of Black English, which requires a consonant cluster in ending position to be reduced to the sound of the first consonant (Pearson & Stephens, 1995). In other words, speakers of dialects express linguistic *differences,* not linguistic *deficits.* The goal of schooling is not, and should not be, to eradicate a dialect in the process of making each individual a speaker of Standard English. Instead, sociolinguists tell us that we should teach students to adapt their oral language to specific audiences.

By kindergarten, most students will have created their own linguistic speaking system, even if it contains nonstandard grammar. Furthermore, research has shown that students' mistakes in oral language can be used to understand the rule systems that these children have invented for themselves (Pearson & Stephens, 1995; Clay, 1995). It will take time and patience before some students can adapt linguistic patterns in their dialect to meet different audiences needs. You can accelerate this progress through activities like unison-choral readings, chants, and songs that contain Standard English sentence patterns. Such activities provide a reduced-risk setting in which students can practice Standard English. Such activities also minimize the embarrassment that some students could experience as they struggle to adapt their dialect to Standard English.

Because new words are continuously invented and standards for acceptable grammar are constantly changing, it is also important that students' personal speaking system and innovative uses of English are valued in the classroom. Such acknowledgments emphasize the fact that the goal of speaking is to communicate. Similarly, your language arts program should honor students' dialectical differences as demonstrations of language's beauty and multifaceted nature. Through your feedback, your students can come to realize that their thoughts are important, even though their language deviates from the norm in many ways. Students must choose what they want to adapt, if changes in speaking styles are to become permanent.

There are 25 dialects in the American version of English (listed by region in Figure 3.1). Although extensive, American dialects are neither as numerous nor as dis-

1. Northeastern New England Dialect
2. Southeastern New England Dialect
3. Southwestern New England Dialect
4. Upstate New York and Western Vermont Dialect
5. The Hudson Valley Dialect
6. Metropolitan New York Dialect
7. Delaware Valley Dialect
8. The Susquehanna Valley Dialect
9. The Upper Potomac and Shenandoah valleys Dialect
10. The Upper Ohio Valley Dialect
11. Northern West Virginia Dialect
12. Southern West Virginia Dialect
13. Western North and South Carolina Dialect
14. Delamarvia Dialect
15. The Virginia Piedmont Dialect
16. Northeastern North Carolina Dialect
17. The Cape Fear and Peedee valleys Dialect
18. South Carolina Dialect
19. South Atlantic Dialect
20. Gulf States Dialect
21. Southwest Dialect
22. Appalachians Dialect
23. Inland North Dialect
24. Great Lakes Dialect
25. Midwestern Dialect

FIGURE 3.I DIALECTICAL REGIONS IN THE UNITED STATES

Sources: From *A Word Geography of the Eastern United States,* by H. Kurath, 1949, Ann Arbor, MI: University of Michigan and *An Index by Region, Usage, and Etymology to the Dictionary of American Regional English,* Vols. 1 and 2, by American Dialect Society, 1993, Tuscaloosa: University of Alabama.

TABLE 3.3 CHARACTERISTICS OF AFRICAN AMERICAN AND VIETNAMESE DIALECT

AFRICAN AMERICAN DIALECTICAL FEATURES

PHONOLOGICAL SYSTEM DIFFERENCES

1. Consonant cluster simplification	des' (desk)
2. Deletion /l/	hep (help)
3. Voiced *th*	den (then)
4. Voiceless *th*	tin (thin)
5. Vowel neutralization before nasal consonants	pin (pen)

MORPHOLOGICAL AND SYNTACTICAL SYSTEM DIFFERENCES

1. Plural deletion	10 cent (10 cents)
2. Deletion of 3rd person singular	The girl walk fast. (The girl walks fast.)
3. Past tense deletion	The man call yesterday. (The man called yesterday.)
4. Existential *it* (there)	It was three apples in the basket. (Three apples are in the basket.)
5. Invariant *be*	He be hollin at us. (He is hollering at us.)
6. *Be* deleted	My momma name Annie. (My momma is named Annie.)

SEMANTICAL SYSTEM DIFFERENCES

1. Black English Vernacular (BEV) or African American Dialect is enriched by the rich lexical and discourse styles found in African American communities.

2. BEV is a semantically rich, rule-governed system. The claim that it is an illegitimate or linguistically inferior language system has been disproved in studies (Labov, 1975; Burling, 1973; Steffensen, 1978) and has been disproved in federal court (Labov, 1982; Smitherman, 1985).

3. Many surface features of Black English Vernacular are shared by some Standard English speakers from lower socioeconomic groups, but the distribution or frequency of specific features varies (Labov, 1975). Varieties in BEV (as in other types of dialect) develop along social, cultural, and economic boundaries.

tinctive as dialects in many other countries. For example, there are more dialects in Great Britain (about the size of Oregon) than in all of the United States (Farris, 1993).

As a general rule, when students' dialects interfere with their ability to communicate or comprehend, it is important to identify and suggest ways they can adapt the nonstandard features in certain types of settings. This is important because in their lives outside the classroom, students' incorrect word choices and nontraditional sentence structures can be interpreted as a lack of education. Moreover, without your instruction, some students' messages can be demeaned by listeners. Their listeners might think: "If this person uses inappropriate grammar, I'm not going to support his or her ideas. He or she obviously lacks education, and consequently the strength to bring these ideas to a successful conclusion, and I don't want to be judged dumb because I supported this person."

TABLE 3.3 (CONTINUED)

VIETNAMESE LANGUAGE DIFFERENCES

Based on the difference of the two sound systems, the following phonological system distinctions may cause difficulty for Vietnamese students learning English.

1. These sounds exist in English but not Vietnamese:

   /ĭ/ as in s<u>i</u>t   /o͞o/ as in b<u>oo</u>k   /ă/ as in c<u>a</u>t   /th/ as in <u>th</u>en

   /th/ as in <u>th</u>ank   /ch/ as in <u>ch</u>urch   /j/ as in bri<u>dg</u>e   /r/ as in <u>r</u>ed

2. There is difficulty in hearing the contrast between sounds as /ē/ in s<u>ea</u>t and /ĭ/ in s<u>i</u>t; /o͞o/ in f<u>oo</u>l and /ŭ/ in f<u>u</u>ll; /ĕ/ in b<u>e</u>d and /ă/ in b<u>a</u>d; /sh/ in <u>sh</u>oes and /ch/ in <u>ch</u>oose. Vietnamese hear these sounds as similar, thus cannot easily produce them accurately. There is only one sound for each pair in their language.

3. Sounds such as the voiceless stops /p/t/k/ that occur in English and Vietnamese, but have different articulations, also constitute problems. Most students assume they have the same sounds in both languages when they do not.

4. Final position of nasals /m/n/ and also the /l/ sound are pronounced differently in Vietnamese. Also different are the voiced and voiceless consonants in Vietnamese (e.g., /k/ in *dock* or /g/ in *dog* are the same because Vietnamese pronounce both of them as voiceless).

5. Clusters of consonants are particularly difficult, especially when they occur in the final position. When the final clusters contain voiced consonants, the difficulty becomes insurmountable for many students. They drop the excess consonant, pronouncing only one sound (e.g., a word like *minds* will be pronounced as if it had *one* consonant, *min*).

Adapted from *Collected Reading Techniques for Classroom Teachers* (p. 353), by J. Gipe, 1999, Upper Saddle River, NJ: Prentice-Hall, Inc. Copyright © 1999 by Prentice-Hall, Inc. Reprinted by permission.

Oral grammar and language differences can also transfer to students' writings as shown in Table 3.3 and Figure 3.2. Table 3.3 demonstrates features of Black and Vietnamese dialect. These dialectical features serve significant functions for many African American students because they are part of the markers of their African American identity (Tiedt & Tiedt, 1995). By studying Table 3.3, you can explain the exact differences between the two languages and Standard English to students so they can more effectively adjust their speech and compositions for different audiences. For example, in Figure 3.2A Michael's writing of "dewas" was representative of "there was." "Por" was written as it was because in the Black dialect the double /oo/ sound is pronounced as a long /o/. In Meisong's writing (displayed in Figure 3.2B) you can detect features of Vietnamese language that impinge on her speaking and composing of Standard English. For instance, Meisong wrote, "I wish that I have a turtle." Because her native language does not have changes in verb tenses to denote present, past, and future, the verb *have* makes sense to Meisong. She wrote, "Becues he hid in the dack very good" for "because he could hide in the dark well" and "ate all he food" for "ate all his food"; this made perfect sense to

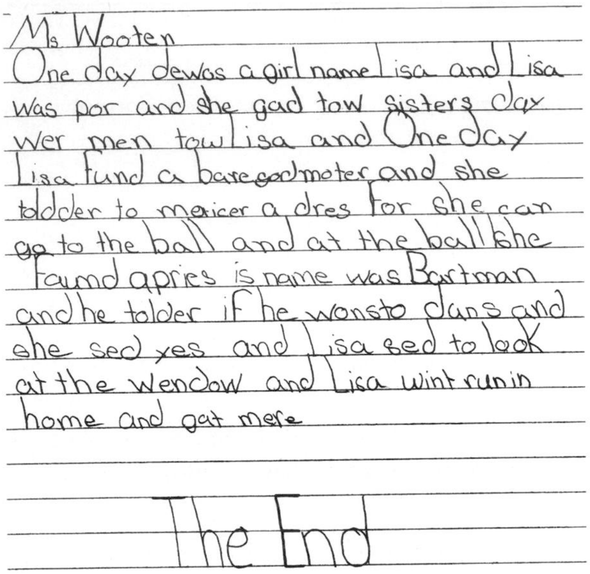

Ms Wooten
One day dewas a girl name Lisa and Lisa
was por and she gad tow sisters day
wer men tow Lisa and One day
Lisa fund a bare godmoter and she
tolder to maicer a dres for she can
go to the ball and at the ball she
faund a pries is name was Bortman
and he tolder if he wonsto dans and
she sed yes and Lisa sed to look
at the wendow and Lisa wint runin
home and gat mere

The End

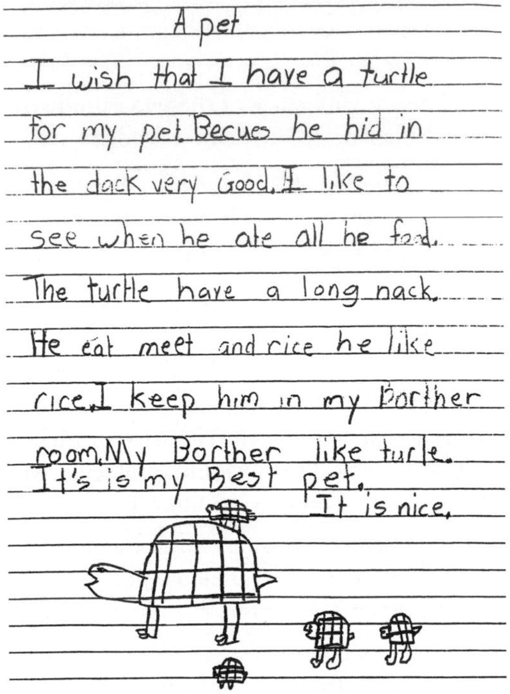

A pet
I wish that I have a turtle
for my pet. Becues he hid in
the dack very Good. I like to
see when he ate all he fad.
The turtle have a long nack.
He eat meet and rice he like
rice. I keep him in my Borther
room. My Borther like turle.
It's is my Best pet.
It is nice.

FIGURE 3.2A AFRICAN AMERICAN DIALECT INTERFERENCES
IN MICHAEL'S WRITING

FIGURE 3.2B BILINGUAL INTERFERENCES
AS DEMONSTRATED IN MEISONG'S WRITING

Meisong because qualifiers and personal pronoun derivatives do not exist in the Vietnamese language. When Ms. Wooten explained these differences, Michael and Meisong understood how to adapt their writing to look more like the Standard English of their classmates.

Part of communicative competence involves knowing when to adapt language to the appropriate settings, topics, and participants in a discourse. Therefore, many speakers shift between standard and vernacular features as appropriate to the formality of the social situation: Standard English for formal situations (e.g., commerce, education, law) and vernacular for informal settings. Moreover, speakers of any dialect vary their language according to the social setting.

ELIMINATING DISTRACTING VOCAL QUALITIES

Most students need your help to develop a melodic voice with appropriate pitch, tone, speed, and effective pauses. You can help students create a welcoming volume that makes hearing their messages easy and enjoyable. They can also learn to eliminate "crutch words" (e.g., *OK, ah,* and *you know*). These words are often used as "fillers of silence" by students who feel uncomfortable with the time it takes to translate their inner thoughts into words. They can be eliminated by teaching students to construct words to replace a crutch word. For example, if students use *OK,* you can teach them to substitute the following sentence as soon as they say the *O* in *OK:* "Oh, the next thing I want to say is . . . " Eventually, the crutch word as well as the substitute sentence will disappear from these students' speech.

Similarly, you can improve oral vocabulary by asking students to study a topic that has not been assigned to anyone else in the class. The student's vocabulary will expand as he or she explains this new knowledge to classmates. Students can also read their writings or children's literature aloud in small groups. In the discussions that follow, most will use the words they read to answer questions. In this way, they self-initiate the transfer of new words to their personal speaking vocabularies.

A third procedure to improve vocal qualities is to engage students in "conversation clubs." Students list topics they want to discuss and then they select the small group topic for which they have the strongest opinion or facts to report. During club meetings, you can complete a checklist of oral language for every student, and also determine which students do not (a) extend the discussion, (b) hold listeners' attention well, (c) check for the accuracy of their points without being told to do so, (d) ask questions to clarify, (e) state novel but provable points, (f) provide solutions, and (g) have inviting vocal habits. By marking these competencies on the Individual Students' Oral Language Needs Monitor (Table 3.4), you can assess individual

TABLE 3.4 INDIVIDUAL STUDENTS' ORAL LANGUAGE NEEDS MONITOR

Student's Name_____ Date_____

A check in each blank denotes that competence has been attained in that specific dimension of effective oral language skill.

___ 1. No diction problems: substitutions (*w* for *v*), omissions (*member* for *remember*), insertions, or distortions.

___ 2. Pitch holds listener's attention.

___ 3. Tone is inviting and pleasant.

___ 4. Speed is appropriate.

___ 5. Volume is appropriate.

___ 6. No crutch words are used.

___ 7. Content is interestingly presented.

___ 8. Vocabulary is good.

___ 9. Uses instrumental language: "I want."

___ 10. Uses regulatory language: "Do this."

___ 11. Uses interactional language: "We . . ."

___ 12. Uses informational language: "This is."

___ 13. Uses imaginative language: "I wonder."

___ 14. Uses heuristic language: "What is?"

___ 15. Is overcoming shyness.

___ 16. Participates in and enjoys celebrative experiences.

___ 17. Extends small-group discussions without coaxing.

___ 18. Checks for accuracy of spoken statements.

___ 19. Asks questions for clarification.

___ 20. States novel but probable points.

___ 21. Gives solutions or compromises for conflicting data.

___ 22. Dialect does not interfere with meaning.

___ 23. Stuttering, malocclusions, cleft palate are absent.

strengths and create instruction for those who do not exhibit one or more of these language use skills. Once you've taken these steps, both shy and second-language learners become more able to share their thoughts in groups.

In summation, it is important to develop students' speaking abilities and confidence because they should graduate from school having overcome timidity of thought and fear of speaking before others. Activities presented in the next section of this chapter will help you attain these goals. Each lesson incorporates principles from Chapters 1 and 2, culminates in real-world products, and addresses individual student needs.

SECTION 2   PUTTING THEORY INTO PRACTICE

Improving Students' Speaking Abilities

Your responsibilities to advance students' oral expression are exercised in many ways each day. In addition to the activities that follow, you can alter aspects of language that interfere with individual potential to have their speech understood and appreciated by others. Such alterations can most often occur in private one-to-one conferences.

ACTIVITIES THAT IMPROVE STUDENTS' SPEAKING ABILITIES

Among the activities that improve students' abilities to speak effectively are celebrative experiences, asking respondent-centered questions, conducting effective classroom conversations, making audio- and videotape recordings, organizing debates, engaging students in show and tell, presenting the Numbered Heads activity, and having panel discussions.

CELEBRATIVE EXPERIENCES

Celebrative experiences are events in which students exert extraordinary effort and invest strong emotions to make (or put on) a production or to reach a personally important goal. These goals are usually shared with an audience (e.g., giving a play or a speech to the community). Celebrative experiences are powerful because they require students to use all functions of oral language. They imagine, inform, command, share, identify, relate, and satisfy needs as they perfect their performances. When students have enough oral language skill to create vivid, celebrative experiences for others, their desire to further perfect their oral expressions intensifies. In addition, through celebrative experiences, many students create positive and successful experiences with oral language that transfer into pleasurable lifetime memories. Students also learn (a) to self-evaluate, and have a voice in the world; (b) to internalize language; and (c) to use language in school as it is used in the real world.

For all of these reasons, celebrative experiences should become a frequently occurring component in your language arts program. Although they can occur serendipitously, it is helpful to allot time during each grading period for at least one. During the first grading period, you can design the activity, but in subsequent periods you will likely find that students suggest ideas and want to assist you in planning these experiences.

ASKING EFFECTIVE QUESTIONS

Hilda Taba (1975, p. 3) stated that constructing effective questions is "by far the most influential teaching act." Effective language arts teachers question often and teach students to do so as well. Good questions, prepared in advance, elicit numerous thinking and language abilities. You can refer to Figure 3.3 throughout your teaching career to assist you in the preparation of such questions.

Effective questions are respondent centered rather than text centered. **Respondent-centered questions** are those that do not have one correct answer but enable students to defend the validity of their own personal response. **Text-centered questions** ask for only one answer, and that answer is usually given in a book or by a speaker. Text-centered questions merely elicit recall of previously stated information. Respondent-centered questions broaden the range of possible responses and teach students that most questions and problems in life do not have a simple, single answer. Likewise, such questions elicit longer responses and deeper thinking. Two ways you can create respondent-centered questions are (1) to ask questions for which you don't know the answers and (2) to place the word *you* with the verb in your question. To illustrate, contrast the following respondent-centered questions to the less powerful, text-centered ones.

1. Respondent centered: "Do you agree or disagree with the author of this poem, and why?" or "What do you think the author meant by . . . ?"
2. Text centered: "Who is the author of this poem?" "Who is the main character?"

By asking respondent-centered questions, you can also enable students to (1) engage in discussions more like those they have outside of school (i.e., in life we most often ask questions to find answers we do not know); (2) find out what others think by hearing what they say; (3) explore topics and argue points of view; (4) function as experts; (5) interact among themselves; and (6) receive immediate information about their comprehension and learning (Dyson, 1999; Block, 2000).

A high-quality classroom discussion consists of a good mixture of teacher- *and* student-initiated questions. When students ask the teacher questions about the topic or the reading, they are showing that they are interested and comfortable, as well as confident enough to risk asking a question in class. The more comfortable students feel, the more questions they ask. Moreover, high-quality discussions curtail the traditional scenario of (a) teacher question, (b) student response, and (c) teacher evaluation followed by the next teacher question. They also "encourage students to take into account more than just content, more than just their own experiences, more than just the wisdom of the world and the experience of others. Questions facilitate an intellectual process" (Christenbury & Kelly, 1983, p. 1). You can increase questioning abilities through the "Ask Me 'Til It's Perfect" activity.

In the "Ask Me 'Til It's Perfect" activity, students are divided into small groups and draw a simple picture (such as a house, tree, and sun for kindergartners). One

Directions: Model how to give good answers to each question. Then ask these questions of students who need to increase their abilities to (a) express their feelings and opinions, (b) elaborate, (c) think about their own thinking processes, (d) interpret, and (e) draw more valid conclusions.

AFFECTIVE
- How did this text make you feel?
- What did you like best about the text?
- What will you remember most about the text?
- Which character would you most like to be? Why?
- Did this text change your opinions about _____?

ELABORATIVE
- Does this text remind you of anything else? What characteristics do they share?
- What did you mean by _____? Can you give us an example?
- Can you describe _____?
- How could you advertise this book?
- Can you guess what question I would ask about this?
- What would you like to ask the author of this story?
- Why do you think the author chose this title? Can you think of another descriptive title?
- Why is this an important story to share?

METACOGNITIVE
- What were your thoughts when you decided what to do? How did you decide?
- Why did you choose this text to read?
- Can you describe your thinking? I need to hear the details.
- Did you have to remember what you already knew? What was helpful to remember?
- Did your thinking change as you read the text? How?
- What are you assuming about this text?
- Are you getting it?

INTERPRETIVE
- What do you need to do next?
- Can you think of another way we could accomplish this?
- What can you do when you become confused?
- What do you do when you come to difficult words?
- What do you do when you do not understand the content or the context?
- How did you arrive at this answer? What helped you the most?
- How can we discover if this is true?
- What difference does that make?

CONCLUSIVE
- Why is this text better than that one?
- That's right—How did you know?
- Is there a better way to present the ideas in this text?
- What are your reasons for saying that?
- What does the author mean by _____?
- Why does this go here and not there?
- What is the evidence for believing that?
- How do you know this is true?

FIGURE 3.3 QUESTIONS THAT INSPIRE CONVERSATION

Created by Elizabeth J. Keenan, 2000, master of elementary education degree candidate at Texas Christian University, Fort Worth, TX. Used by permission.

student from each group studies the details in the picture. Those students then return to the students in their group and describe the picture. Those who have not seen the picture can ask as many questions as necessary to clarify the mental picture they are forming. Then, when they are satisfied that they have the picture in mind, they can draw the picture based on that mental image. The winning group is the one whose picture is closest to the original drawing.

Technically, conversations depart from the normal structure of classroom discourse (teacher question followed by student response followed by teacher evaluation). Such conversations typically include only a few questions that clarify ideas and information ("What do you mean?"). They include more questions that probe for new information and deeper insights.

CLASSROOM CONVERSATIONS

Classroom conversations differ from class discussions in that conversations involve substantial contributions and reflections by both teacher and student (Newell & Durst, 1993). Such "caring talk" can occur between strangers, but a good conversation can only come to life between people who take delight in each other's presence. Thus, students must enter into conversations specifically for the delight in it (Peterson, 1992, p. 50).

Students benefit from being taught conversational discourse skills such as how to keep a conversation moving smoothly, how to express dissenting opinions productively, and how to free oneself to be oneself. Many teachers develop these abilities by convening learning centers called conversation clubs, after the model introduced by Stanley (1990) and expanded by Peterson (1992) and Echevarria (1995). During the first conversation club, students can share qualities of good small-group conversations and list procedures and statements members can make to create such conditions in future conversation clubs and group-work settings. A list constructed by kindergartners in Ms. Wooten's room and a list created by fourth-graders are shown below as examples of the types of oral language goals sought during conversation club meetings.

Our kindergarten conversations are good because

1. We look at who is talking.
2. We do not interrupt.
3. Two people do not talk at the same time.
4. We thank each other.

Our fourth-grade conversations are awesome because

1. We extend each other's comments by telling a reason why we agree with each other or why we see it slightly differently.
2. We keep our conversations open-minded by asking, "What didn't we consider?" and "What question should we have asked that we didn't?"

3. We trust each other and share ideas that are hard to express.

4. We ask questions and refer to previous comments not only to be courteous and show our interest, but also to listen better and truly understand someone else before we speak out.

5. We end our conversations on a positive note.

Six instructional actions can develop students' conversation skills.

1. At the beginning of the year, you can read *How to Carry on a Discussion* (Stanley, 1983), *Noisy Nora* (1997), *Me Duele la Lengra* (1997), and *Martha Speaks* (1992) to the class. From these books, students can learn to emulate how Peter Fieldmouse develops good discussion skills in group work, and how Martha Dog, Mariano, and Nora learn not to dominate conversations.

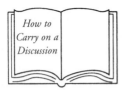

2. You can tell students that you do not want immediate answers but prefer that they take a moment to think before they speak. Also, you can request more than one student's opinion or point of view ("Give me another interpretation." "What do you think another reason could be?" "I'd like to hear two points of view about . . ." "I appreciate the time you took to reflect on your answer").

3. When students ask you to repeat a question, restate it as closely as possible to the original wording because students report that a loose paraphrase confuses them (Collins, 1988).

4. Refrain from restating student answers; students may interpret your doing so as meaning that their answers are not adequate without adding your authority to them.

5. In selecting items for a conversation, relate topics to the world of your students. (For example, in discussing *The Little Engine That Could*, Ms. Wooten related the moral of the story to students' lives: "You must think you can"; see the results of the conversation Juan and Allison had, on pages 94–95.) Further, by asking questions in relevant ways, you not only establish topics of interest but also encourage students to treat them on their own terms.

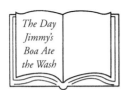

6. Use **deliberate silence.** Sollon (1983) found that when students finish a response or falter, their thinking is assisted by their teacher being deliberately quiet. Ms. Wooten demonstrated this strategy in a conversation that occurred while she was reading a book from Literature Card 6. Ms. Wooten selected *The Day Jimmy's Boa Ate the Wash* to build her kindergartner's listening abilities. Juan raised his hand and the following conversation began:

Juan: I think Jimmy got tricked. Does anyone agree?

[Ms. Wooten was deliberately silent.]

Michael: If he were here I'd say, "Boa, you shouldn't have tricked him."

[Ms. Wooten was deliberately silent.]

Allison: Maybe you should ask if he did it.

AUDIO- AND VIDEOTAPE RECORDINGS, PANEL DISCUSSIONS, AND DEBATES

To build oral language abilities, you can also tape-record a practice session of a speech that students are to give in a public forum (such as a presentation to a boy

CHILDREN'S LITERATURE TO INCREASE ORAL AND LISTENING ABILITIES: GRADES K TO 4

Best Books for Kindergartners Selected
by Kindergarten Teachers

Corduroy by Don Freeman
The Carrot Seed by R. Krauss
Cherry Tree by R. Bond, 1991 Boyds Mill
The Way to Start a Day by B. Baylor, 1986 Aladdin
I Know an Old Lady Who Swallowed a Fly by N. Bernard
    Wescott
Chicka, Chicka Boom Boom by B. Martin
Q Is for Duck by K. Greenaway
Over in the Meadow by F. Rojankovsky
Love You Forever by R. Munsch
Zoo by Gail Gibbons
Little Blue and Little Yellow by Leo Lionni
Barn Dance by B. Martin
The Day Jimmy's Boa Ate the Wash by Trinka Noble
Sylvester and the Magic Pebble by W. Steig, 1987 Simon
    & Schuster
The Z Was Zapped by Chris Van Allsburg
Whose Mouse Are You? by R. Kraus
If You Give a Mouse a Cookie by L. Numeroff
Little Bear by E. Minarik
When Will I Read? by M. Cohen
The Popcorn Book by Tomie dePaola
Ten Black Dots by Donald Crews
Feet by P. Parnall, 1988 Macmillan

Best Books for First-Graders Selected
by First-Grade Teachers

Ira Sleeps Over by B. Waber, 1972 Houghton Mifflin
Alexander and the Terrible, Horrible, No Good, Very Bad
    Day by J. Viorst, 1972 Atheneum
Osa's Pride by A. Grifalconi, 1990 Little, Brown
Fantastic Mr. Fox by Roald Dahl, 1988 Puffin
The Jolly Postman by J. & A. Ahlberg, 1986 Little
A House Is a House for Me by M. Hoberman, 1993
    Puffin
King Bigood's in the Bathtub by A. Wood, 1985
    HarBrace
Chocolate Fever by R. Kimmel Smith, 1994 Dell
Chickens Aren't the Only Ones by Ruth Heller, 1981
    Putnam
Where the Wild Things Are by Maurice Sendak, 1988
    HarpC Child Books
Amazing Grace by M. Hoffman, 1991 Dial
Miss Nelson Is Missing by H. Allard, 1993 Houghton
    Mifflin
The True Story of the Three Little Pigs by J. Scieszka,
    1989 Viking
Heckedy Pig by A. Wood, 1992 HarBrace
One Fish, Two Fish, Red Fish, Blue Fish by Dr. Seuss,
    1987 Random

The Art Lesson by Tomie dePaola, 1994 Putnam
First Grade King by K. L. Williams

Best Books for Second-Graders Selected
by Second-Grade Teachers

James and the Giant Peach by Roald Dahl, 1988 Puffin
How Much Is a Million? by D. Schwartz, 1993 Morrow
Owl Moon by J. Yolen, 1987 Putnam
Tikki Tikki Tembo by A. Mosel, 1989 Henry Holt
Skinnybones by B. Park, 1989 Knopf
Amelia Bedelia by P. Parrish, 1992 HarpC Child Books
Doctor de Soto by W. Steig, 1982 Farrar, Straus & Giroux
Charlotte's Web by E. B. White, 1990 Buccaneer
Madeline by L. Bemelmans, 1993 Puffin
The Courage of Sarah Noble by A. Dalgliesh
In a Messy, Messy Room J. Gorog, 1990 Putnam
Flossie and the Fox by P. McKissack, 1986 Dial
Fat Chance, Claude by J. Nixon
Ramona the Pest by B. Cleary
My Father's Dragon by R. Gannet
Molly's Pilgrim by B. Cohen
A Job for Jenny Archer by E. Conford
Beans on the Roof by B. Byars
Herbie Jones by S. Kline
The Show and Tell War by J. L. Smith

Best Books for Third- and Fourth-Graders Selected
by Third- and Fourth-Grade Teachers

Mufaro's Beautiful Daughters: An African Tale by
    J. Steptoe, 1987 Lothrop
Knots on a Counting Rope by B. Martin & J.
    Archumbault, 1993 Henry Holt
Koko's Kitten by F. Patterson, 1985, Scholastic
Ramona Quimby, Age 8 by B. Cleary, 1981 Morrow
Julian's Glorious Summer by A. Cameron, 1987 Random
    Books
Freckle Juice by J. Blume, 1984 Macmillan
James and the Giant Peach by R. Dahl
Sarah, Plain and Tall by P. MacLachlan
Did You Carry the Flag Today, Charley? by R. Caudill
The Mouse and the Motorcycle by B. Cleary
Pippi Longstocking by A. Lindgren, 1988 Puffin
The Chocolate Touch by P. Catling
Stuart Little by E. B. White
The Seven Treasure Hunts by B. Byars
The Tale of the Bluebonnet: An Old Tale of Texas and *The*
    Legend of the Indian Paintbrush by T. dePaola,
    1988 Putnam
Rumplestiltskin by P. O. Zelinsky, 1986 Dutton
Rip Van Winkle by M. Gipson, 1975 Doubleday
The Tale of Rabbit and Coyote by T. Johnston, 1994
    Putnam

scout or girl scout meeting). Then, as they critique the tape themselves, you and the students can refer to Table 3.4 to note areas for improvement. Class discussions and formal presentations can also be videotaped. A first tape recording can enable students to judge which discussion skill they want to improve; a second can be done during a "dress rehearsal" to refine their performance prior to "opening night" or as a posttest assessment on the night of the performance.

Panel discussions are formal discussions that present information. In panel discussions, participants are assigned different topics to research. They discuss their topics before an audience whose members are less knowledgeable about the topic, and they ask questions. Often, local-access cable television networks welcome student panel discussions on talk shows. Through such broadcasts, students learn to use facts (from their research) to support their opinions and develop interactional, heuristic, informative language functions (items 11–14 and 16–23 in Table 3.4), and group thinking and problem-solving abilities.

Debates are formal presentations that showcase opposing viewpoints. In a debate, two or more pupils present one position on an issue and two or more present an opposing position. Each speaker states a proposition and then takes notes for a rebuttal. Team members are allowed to confer with partners during the debate, and other class members judge the merits of each side using the Debate Score Sheet in Figure 3.4. A typical time frame for such a 4-member debate follows:

First speaker, "pro" position of the issue	3–5 minutes
First speaker, "con" position of the issue	3–5 minutes
Second speaker, "pro" position of the issue	3–5 minutes
Second speaker, "con" position of the issue	3–5 minutes
First speaker's rebuttal (con position)	1–2 minutes
First speaker's rebuttal (pro position)	1–2 minutes
Second speaker's rebuttal (con position)	1–2 minutes
Second speaker's rebuttal (pro position)	1–2 minutes

SHOW AND TELL

Show and tell is an activity in which students describe important thoughts and events in their lives. It develops personal, informative, and interactive language functions. Before show and tell, students can make rules. They might require that (1) speakers bring something they judge to be of interest to a lot of people (students are less self-conscious when they have an object to show and tell); (2) speakers prepare three points to make and two questions to ask listeners at the end of the sharing; (3) listeners ask questions; and (4) listeners either state something they enjoyed or appreciated about each presenters' talk, preparation, or thoughts or ask a question. By applying these rules over the course of several show and tell presentations, many speakers and listeners will develop the ability to give more specific compliments and suggestions for improvements, and extend conversations.

Even with such preplanning, two difficulties can arise during show and tell lessons:

DEBATE SCORE SHEET

Directions: Single points can be awarded for

1. Making opening statements that are short, clearly explained, and adequately supported. (one point)

2. Using appropriate facts. (one point)

3. Wording opinions correctly. (one point)

4. Making rebuttals that point out poor explanations or faulty supports, or asking questions about something left unsaid. (one point)

5. Listening carefully—which is taught prior to holding the first debate. (one point)

TEAM A MEMBERS

	OPENING	REBUTTAL	CLOSING	TOTAL POINTS
1.				
2.				
3.				
4.				
5.				

TEAM B MEMBERS

	OPENING	REBUTTAL	CLOSING	TOTAL POINTS
1.				
2.				
3.				
4.				
5.				

After hearing the debate I voted for Team _____ because _____

_____ .

_____

Debate Judge (student's name)

FIGURE 3.4 DEBATE SCORE SHEET

1. Students may direct their talk to you rather than to their classmates. You can eliminate this problem by taking a seat at the same level as the students and near the back of the group. Then, after telling students the order for presenters, you can give two directives before show and tell begins: Each student is responsible for introducing the next presenter and for assisting that next speaker with props and providing verbal prompts when necessary if that person loses his or her train of thought. With these directives in place, show and tell can become a more authentic activity, one in which a speaker is in charge of an audience that bestows its respect and attention during the event.

2. Students may have trouble deciding what to discuss. You can assist them by sending home a list of topics that will be studied in other content areas. Parents can help plan show and tell topics related to the new topics. Students can also create their own flannel board stories to show and tell, show and tell with partners, take roles in a commercial, or demonstrate displays or models that they create. They can fill bags ("Me Bags") with objects from home that they want to share.

Show and tell increases students' abilities to perform items 6–12 and 22–23 on the Individual Student's Oral Language Needs Monitor (Table 3.4), as well as Divisions 1, 2, and 6 of thinking abilities (presented in Chapter 12).

If a few of your students are afraid to speak in front of the class, read to the class Joan Detz's book, *You Mean I Have to Stand Up and Say Something?* (1985). Her humorous treatment of this apprehension decreases student fears.

INTEGRATING THE LANGUAGE ARTS

As students learn the functions of language, you can read from and have books from Literature Cards 6 and 7 in the classroom for students' self-selected reading. These books improve students' use of each language function because the characters in them employ these functions masterfully. By reading the books on Literature Cards 6 and 7, students can learn to appreciate their own and peers' dialects and enhance their own unique, oral expressions. Literature Cards 6 and 7 contain some poetry and choral readings designed for these purposes.

A method of integrating language arts, literature, and oral language development is to use wordless picture books (listed on Literature Card 12) as described on p. 215.

NUMBERED HEADS

Numbered Heads is an activity for small groups of students. Each student takes a number (e.g., 1 through 4). All students work together to find answers to questions that you pose orally or that students have posed orally prior to beginning this lesson. Then you call one of the numbers (e.g., 2), and all the students who were designated as 2s in their groups are required to give their group's answer to the question. This system makes everyone responsible for learning and gives all students the opportunity to speak before the class.

Some teachers carry the Numbered Heads activity one step further by having students take two numbers. The first number that they draw (e.g., 2, as described above) designates the student's individual number. The second number drawn (e.g., 3) designates the student's group number. If the teacher calls number 2 and number 3, this designates the student with individual number 2 and group number 3.

Scaffolding impromptu oral presentations, by providing props and friends for support, assists oral language development.

The student with this set of numbers is the first to give the answer for their group. This activity is continued until all students have been chosen to speak.

Turn to Your Friend and Share is a slight variation of Numbered Heads that can be used spontaneously in almost any situation to build students' oral language abilities. In this activity, when you ask a question, students turn to a partner and share their ideas about the question. The partners decide on an answer they will share if their group is called on. After a few moments have elapsed, you call on three different pairs to share their ideas. You can then ask a second question and continue this activity.

One of the first indications that your oral language program is successful will be that students bring more and more of their lives into the classroom. Students will burst into class with stories to tell that are alive with new thoughts and language uses they have learned on previous days. As Ms. Wooten discovered, by October of every school year, she had to keep a pencil and pad in her morning robe because she had become overwhelmed with stories she wanted to tell her class. She had to jot them down. As she moved from room to room, busily getting ready for school, she put her thoughts on post-it notes. When she told her students about her habit, they began to do the same, bringing little pictures to class to remind them of stories and ideas they wanted to share.

Literature Card 7

CHILDREN'S LITERATURE TO DEVELOP STUDENTS' READING, SPEAKING, WRITING, AND LISTENING VOCABULARIES: GRADES 5 TO 8

Favorite Books for Fifth- and Sixth-Graders

Where the Red Fern Grows by W. Rawls, 1961 Doubleday

On My Honor by M. D. Bauer, 1986 Houghton Mifflin

The Sign of the Beaver by E. Speare, 1983 Houghton Mifflin

Roll of Thunder, Hear My Cry by M. Taylor, 1976 Bantam

A Blue-Eyed Daisy by C. Rylant, 1985 Dell Yearling

Homesick: My Own Story by J. Fritz, 1982 Dell Yearling

Anne of Green Gables by L. M. Montgomery, 1914 Grosset & Dunlap

The Cay by T. Taylor, 1987 Doubleday

Tuck Everlasting by N. Babbitt, 1975 Farrar, Straus, & Giroux

Indian in the Cupboard by L. R. Banks, 1981 Doubleday Books

The Secret Garden by F. H. Burnette, 1993 Macmillan

The Lion, the Witch and the Wardrobe by C. S. Lewis, 1950 Macmillan

The Whipping Boy by S. Fleischman, 1986 Greenwillow

Slave Dancer by P. Fox, 1991 Dell

The Great Gilly Hopkins by K. Patterson, 1978 Harper Trophy

My Side of the Mountain by J. C. George, 1975 Puffin

Monkey Island P. Fox, 1991 Orchard Books

Animal Farm by G. Orwell, 1993 Knopf

Anna, Grandpa, and the Big Storm by C. Stevens, 1982 Puffin

Call of the Wild by J. London, 1995 University of Oklahoma Press

The Deadly Mandrake by L. Callen, 1978 Little, Brown

Mrs. Frisby and the Rats of NIMH by R. C. O'Brien, 1971 Atheneum

The True Confessions of Charlotte Doyle by Avi, 1990 Orchard Books

There's a Boy in the Girl's Bathroom by L. Sachar, 1988 Knopf

Shiloh by P. Naylor, 1991 Atheneum

Weasel by C. C. DeFelice, 1990 Macmillan

Parallel Time: Growing Up in Black and White by B. Staples, 1994 Pantheon Books

Beauty: A Retelling of the Story of Beauty and the Beast by R. McKinley, 1978 Harper & Row

Favorite Books for Seventh- and Eighth-Graders

The Witch of Blackbird Pond by E. Speare, 1958 Houghton Mifflin

Cheaper by the Dozen by F. Gilbreth, 1948 T. Y. Crowell

Beowulf, 1940 Oxford University Press

A Day No Pigs Would Die by R. Peck, 1974 Knopf

The Pearl by J. Steinbeck, 1974 Viking Press

The Scarlet Letter by N. Hawthorne, 1900 Pocket Books

To Kill a Mockingbird by H. Lee, 1960 Lippincott

Adventures of Huckleberry Finn by M. Twain, 1985 University of California Press

Lord of the Flies by W. Golding, 1962 Coward-McCann

Death of a Salesman by A. Miller, 1949 Viking Press

Adventures of Tom Sawyer by M. Twain, 1962 Harcourt, Brace & World

Catcher in the Rye by J. D. Salinger, 1951 Little, Brown

Great Expectations by C. Dickens, 1962 Collier Books

Johnny Tremain by E. Forbes, 1967 F. Watts

Red Badge of Courage by S. Crane, 1972 Pocket Books

A Separate Peace by J. Knowles, 1959 Macmillan

The Summer of My German Soldier by B. Greene, 1973 Dial

A Wrinkle in Time by M. L'Engle, 1962 Ariel Books

Treasure Island by R. L. Stevenson, 1992 Viking

Hatchet by G. Paulsen, 1983 Dial

The Wind in the Willows by K. Grahame, 1980 Holt, Rinehart & Winston

Amzat and His Brothers: Three Italian Tales by P. Fox, 1993 Orchard Books

Sing Down the Moon by S. O'Dell, 1973 Dell

Of Mice and Men by J. Steinbeck, 1965 Modern Library

1984 by G. Orwell, 1949 Harcourt, Brace & World

A Light in the Forest by C. Richter, 1953 Knopf

The Hobbit by J. R. R. Tolkien, 1977 H. N. Abrams

The Great Gatsby by F. S. Fitzgerald, 1993 Macmillan/Hudson River

The Black Pearl by S. O'Dell, 1967 Houghton Mifflin

The Chocolate War by R. Cormier, 1974 Pantheon Books

Across Five Aprils by I. Hunt, 1965 Tempo Books

In closing this section of the chapter, students pass through stages in oral language development, and variations in the process can be addressed by private conferences with individual students and outside support from specialists. Specific

Writing the words that students say in their native language and asking them to teach these words to the class demonstrate that their dialect and home language are valued.

lessons that build oral language competencies include audio- and videotape recordings, show and tell, classroom conversation, debates, Numbered Heads activity, and using literature and wordless picture books. By cultivating students' abilities to ask questions, you can also advance their speaking and thinking abilities.

INSIDE CULTURALLY AND LINGUISTICALLY ENRICHED CLASSROOMS

Ten Lessons That Enrich Bilingual Students' Learning

The National Center for Research on Cultural Diversity and Second Language Learning at the University of California at Santa Cruz has determined that three approaches to bilingual education can increase these students' oral language development. The first is the **immersion approach.** This approach is an instructional practice that enhances LEP, ELL, and bilingual students' abilities to learn English as rapidly as possible without any special intervention. The philosophy is that such programs bolster students' self-esteem enough that they learn English through daily exposure to it and through doing the activities that will be specified in this section of the chapter.

The second approach is called the **ESL approach.** In this approach, instructional practices are specifically designed in both Spanish and English. The philosophy of this approach is that by helping students to achieve competency in their native language system, you can decrease the difficulty of learning a second language. Teachers who speak Spanish deliver instruction to LEP, ELL, and bilingual students in structured lessons before they are taught how to read and write and speak English.

The third approach is called the **bilingual approach.** This approach uses instructional practices in which LEP, ELL, and bilingual students learn how to read and write in their native language and learn oral English concurrently. In bilingual approaches, students are taught to read and write in English while they learn to speak in both Spanish and English. The philosophy of this approach is that most young children cannot read or write either language, so teaching them to read or write Spanish will only delay their ability to read and write English more rapidly.

Recent studies have demonstrated that, regardless of the approach used, we must move beyond arguing over which way to teach English to how to best meet the individual needs of bilingual students (Fitzgerald, 1995; McLaughlin, 1995). Regardless of the philosophy of instruction and approach followed in your school, bilingual students can improve their oral speaking abilities. That is the purpose of the 10 lessons that are described below.

The National Center for Research on Cultural Diversity and Second Language Learning has identified several principles to guide the implementation of these lessons.

Principle 1.   Bilingualism is an asset and should be fostered in students.

Principle 2.   There is an ebb and flow to children's bilingualism. It is rare for both languages to be equally effective in all children.

Principle 3.   There are different cultural patterns in language use among bilingual students.

Principle 4.   For some bilingual students, code switching, which is the interchanging of two different languages in a single sentence, is a normal language phenomenon.

Principle 5.   Bilingual children come to learn a second language in many different ways based on the number of prior experiences they have had with that language, the number of opportunities their teachers make available to them to speak both languages in the classroom, and how individually motivated they are to learn both English and Spanish.

Principle 6.   Language must be used to communicate meaning; responses to students' oral expressions, whether in Spanish or English, must acknowledge the meaning they have conveyed.

Principle 7.   Language flourishes best in a language-rich environment that is based on the principles outlined in Chapters 1, 2, and 3 of this textbook.

Principle 8.   Children should be encouraged to experiment with language. This principle can be applied with the language play activities that are described in Chapter 1.

Principle 9. Paying particular care to the wording of questions, the pace of a lesson, and the strategy used to activate prior knowledge will significantly increase students' achievement in learning Spanish and English.

Principle 10. All classroom activities should engage bilingual students' "funds of knowledge" (Moll, 1999).

Funds of knowledge have been defined by Moll as resources and experiences available to bilingual students outside of school. Research has shown that when you tap into English language learners' funds of knowledge, both their oral language and their academic achievement will accelerate. Students whose teachers translate each learning experience into knowledge with real-world examples enable bilingual students to visualize incidents in their life outside of school and to express them during oral language lessons.

The first lesson to build bilingual students' oral language abilities uses tongue twisters. Bilingual students and second-language learners can learn to discriminate English letter sounds more rapidly if they repeat tongue twisters and invent their own to challenge classmates. (One of the best sources for tongue twisters that students enjoy is *Fast, Freddie Frog* by Ennis Rees [1993], published by Wordsong Boyds Mills Press in Honesdale, PA.) Also, if students are encouraged to use their native language as well as English while listening throughout the day, their comprehension improves. For example, Ms. Wooten regularly asks her students, "How would you say that in Spanish?" If the student does not know, he or she goes to a bilingual student in the class. Being bilingual is valued as something very special in Ms. Wooten's class.

If some students speak nonstandard English, they profit from extensive instruction in exercises that help students hear the differences between initial, medial, and final parts of English words and sentences. Such exercises begin by asking students to say which sentence begins or ends with a word you specify. When your students are comfortable performing this listening task, you can couple the activity with meaning clues by creating riddles, such as: "I'm thinking of something we all wear. The name of these articles begins like *shine*. Everyone has these objects on today. What word am I thinking of?" [shoes]

Word games and jokes also increase vocabulary, verbal fluency, and listening abilities of bilingual students. Some word games, such as the following (used with permission from *The Reading Teacher's Book of Lists*, 3rd ed., 1993, Prentice Hall, p. 285), also help increase phoneme awareness.

Hink Pinks	*Answers*
What is an uncovered seat?	bare chair
What is a library burglar?	book crook
What is a strong beautiful plant?	power flower

Jokes

Why is 10 afraid of 7? Because 7, 8, 9.

What kind of bird goes "Bang Bang"? A fire quacker.

What goes "Tick-tick, woof-woof"? A watch dog.

Where do cows go on vacation? Moo York.

What do you get if you cross a cat and a lemon? A sour puss.

What do you get if you cross a centipede and a parrot? A walkie-talkie.

Another facet of bilingual students' oral language development is their access to multicultural literature. A list for your use appears in Literature Card 8. As Barry (1998) states, "an important role of multicultural literature is the connection it allows students to make between home and school" (p. 36). A broad spectrum of literature also sparks ESL and bilingual learners' interest in speaking, without which they might otherwise be bored by characters with whom they have seemingly little in common.

To this end, a blank alphabet book may be the ideal English language introductory tool for a kindergartner who is a non–English speaker (Dobervich & Thacker, 1999). Presenting students with their own blank books on the first day of class signifies active participation and learning. Emblazoned on each page is a letter of the English alphabet, along with a blank space to write new and important-to-them vocabulary words. Similarly, a campus tour book is another valuable way to welcome bilingual students into a new classroom environment. Accompanied by a buddy or teacher, ELL, LEP, or bilingual students can tour the school building and take pictures of students at each location. Once the photos are compiled, the words that name each location are added below the pictures. The pictures provide a visual cue to the English word that designates that location. Then, the students will have also created their own picture books that they can tell or read to the class.

A fourth activity involves books on tape. Such books promote both listening and reading vocabulary as well as comprehension of English words. Through listening to the rhyme and rhythm of English words and sentences, bilingual students' confidence improves as they become familiar with spoken English, particularly word sounds. They also become more adept at recognizing and using colloquial words, and other types of figurative language that is unique to English (Moll, 1999; Mulhern, 1997).

Partnered reading (Cassady, 1998) is a fifth activity that builds bilingual students' oral language. In diverse classroom settings, LEP students need to be supported by more proficient speakers. If they are left alone, they can reach deadends and not know how to continue. Thus, partners reading with them can provide clues or word meanings. (Ms. Wooten has found that she uses partnered reading a lot because her native kindergarten English speakers are sometimes more adept at creating relative meaning for LEP students than she is!)

Student hypothesizing is a sixth strategy. When bilingual students stumble on an unknown word, they often inquire: "What word is that?" Instead of telling them or defining the unknown word, the student hypothesizing method proceeds by you asking: "What do you think would make sense there?" This method forces children to draw on context, pictures, and patterns to discern the correct word or to say a Spanish word that would make sense (Francisco & Krashen, 1998).

Julie High, author of *Second Language Learning through Cooperative Learning* (1996), suggests a seventh activity called Who Am I? In this activity, bilingual students use basic identifying adjectives to discover a "mystery animal" (High, 1996).

Literature Card 8

DUAL LANGUAGE BOOKS IN SPANISH AND ENGLISH

Good Books with a Lot of Pictures

Las Navidades: Popular Christmas Songs from Latin America by L. Delacre, 1990 Scholastic

The Book of Pigericks by A. Lobel, 1986 Altea

Moon Rope/Un Lazo a la Luna by L. Ehlert, 1992 Harcourt Brace Jovanovich

Tortillitas Para Mama and Other Nursery Rhymes/Spanish and English by Griego et al., 1981

Family Stories/Cuadros de Familia by C. L. Garza, 1990 Children's Book Press

Tierra Amarilla: Stories of New Mexico by S. Ulibarri, 1971 University of New Mexico Press

Carlos Planta un Girasol by K. Petty, 1997 Scholastic

Martha Planta un Rabaro by K. Petty, 1997 Barcelona, Spain: Destino

Solomon, the Rusty Nail by W. Steig, 1985 Farrar, Straus & Giroux

Good Books to Tell You a Lot in Spanish and English

⌐ *Clifford the Big Red Dog* by N. Birdwell, 1988 Scholastic
└ *Clifford el Gran Perro Colorado* by N. Birdwell, 1989 Scholastic

⌐ *The Very Hungry Caterpillar* by E. Carle, 1979 Collins Publishers
└ *La Oruga Muy Hambrienta* by E. Carle, 1989 Philomel

⌐ *Is Your Mama a Llama?* by D. Guarino, 1989 Scholastic
└ *¿Tu Mama es Una Llama?* by D. Guarino 1993 Scholastic

⌐ *Alexander and the Terrible, Horrible, No Good, Very Bad Day* by J. Viorst, 1972 Atheneum
└ *Alexander y el Dia Terrible, Horrible, Espantoso, Horroroso* by J. Viorst, 1989 Macmillan

⌐ *The Grouchy Ladybug* by E. Carle
└ *La Marquita Malhumorada* by E. Carle, 1992

⌐ *Bread and Jam for Frances* by R. Hoban
└ *Pan y Mermelada Para Francisca* by R. Hoban, 1995

Taking a Walk/Caminando by R. Emberly, 1990 Little, Brown

⌐ *Brave Irene* by W. Steig, 1991 Farrar, Straus & Giroux
└ *Irene la Valiente* by W. Steig, 1991 Farrar, Straus & Giroux

Me duele la lengua by A. Decis, 1997 Barcelona, Spain (Edebé)

Carlota y los dinosaurios by J. Mayhem, 1998 Barcelona, Spain: Serres

Good Books If You Are Just Beginning to Learn about Spanish or English

My First 100 Words in English and Spanish by K. Faulkner, 1992 Simon & Schuster

My First Phrases in Spanish and English by K. Faulkner, 1993 Simon & Schuster

On the Pampas by M. Brusea, 1991 Henry Holt

Noisy Nora by R. Wells, 1994 Santillana

Mrs. Frisby and the Rats of NIMH by J. Conly, 1986 Harper & Row

My First Book of Words and Mi Primer Libro de Palabras by L. Shiffman, 1992 Scholastic

⌐ *The Giving Tree* by S. Silverstein
└ *El Arbol Generoso* by S. Silverstein, 1991

Chicken Sunday by P. Polacco, 1992 Scholastic

Iguana Dreams: New Latino Fiction by D. Poey & Suarez, 1992 HarperCollins

Mariposa by L. Fernandez, 1983 Editorial Trillas

Books That Have Several Chapters in Spanish and English

⌐ *Blubber* by J. Blume, 1982 Bradbury Press
└ *La Ballena* by J. Blume, 1983 Bradbury Press

⌐ *Ramona the Pest* by B. Cleary, 1968 William Morrow
└ *Ramona la Chinche* by B. Cleary, 1984 William Morrow

⌐ *Number the Stars* by L. Lowry, 1989 Houghton Mifflin
└ *¿Quien Cuenta las Estrellas?* by L. Lowry, 1990 Espasa-Calpe

⌐ *Roxaboxen* by A. McLerran, 1991 Lothrop, Lee & Shephard
└ *Roxaboxen* (Spanish version) by A. McLerran, 1992 Scholastic

⌐ *The Cricket in Times Square* by G. Seldon Thompson
└ *Un Grillo en Times Square* by G. Seldon Thompson, 1992

Diario Ana Frank by A. Frank, 1971 Plaza y Editores, S. A.

⌐ *Tuck Everlasting* by N. Babbitt, 1975 Farrar, Straus & Giroux
└ *Tuck Para Siempre* by N. Babbitt, 1992 Trumpet Book Club

⌐ *Nine Days to Christmas: A Story of Mexico* by M. H. & A. Labastida, 1959 Viking
└ *Nueve Dias para Navidad* by M. H. & A. Labastida, 1991 Puffin Books/Viking Penguin

Each student has a picture of a different animal taped to his or her back. Through questions and answers, students try to determine the animal's identity. As a catalyst in classes with very low English proficiency students, you could list on the board sample questions that students might use to discover their animal's identity.

Another variation is called the Mystery Classmate. Students cooperatively write descriptions of classmates, then read them aloud for the class to guess the identity of this student. High (1996) asserts that this activity will actively engage students because their high personal involvement increases their interest in speaking English effectively.

In the opening scenario of this chapter, Ms. Wooten demonstrated how to use wordless books as a powerful aid to assist bilingual children with language production. This works because, as bilingual students explore the pictures, they simultaneously use language to create a story about the pictures. Cassady (1998) found that the following activity with wordless books "enhances creativity, vocabulary, and language development for readers of all ages, at all stages of cognitive development, and in all content areas" (p. 379). To begin, you can "read" a wordless book aloud. As you describe the pages, share aloud the story in your head. In this way, you will model vocabulary orally, turning the thoughts we usually keep tucked inside our heads into concrete and audible English. You will also demonstrate to bilingual students that the "right" English word does not always exist.

Next, you can read two pages of a story and urge more fluent bilingual students to "read" these same two pages in Spanish. LEP students continue to read in English to their partners. As students' oral language skills advance, they can share their stories aloud with the entire class. A low-risk opportunity is afforded through this activity, and creativity is developed. Such buddy conversations are brief but focused periods of time when two students simply talk and share ideas about a story between themselves. This provides bilingual students with a smaller, more private forum to practice transforming their ideas into coherent English sentences. The native English speaking buddy can be taught to model short sentences, clear speech, and comprehensible vocabulary.

An eighth activity is to use visuals to reinforce concepts and vocabulary. A clear area of consensus among researchers is that vocabulary learning should play a major role in successful programs for English language learners (see McLaughlin, 1995, for a synthesis of this research). Moreover, the standard method of presenting up to 20 new vocabulary words at one time to bilingual students is not effective in helping English language learners develop vocabulary; using lists of 7 or fewer words is more effective. With shorter lists, students can work on derivatives and try to match concepts over relatively longer periods of time (Echevarria, 1998; Moel, 1999).

The ninth activity is to use visuals to reinforce concepts and vocabulary. It is particularly valuable to use visuals during instruction that range from complex semantic maps (Reyes & Bos, 1998; see p. 196 in this text for an example) to those based on text structures, such as compare–contrast "think sheets" (see several samples in Chapter 12). Visuals are especially successful in supporting English language development because they help students visualize the abstractions of language (Rousseau et al., 1993; Saunder et al., 1998).

A tenth activity to develop speaking abilities is "code switching" from English to their native language in directions and discussions. For example, you can provide an

TABLE 3.5 BOOKS THAT TEACH ENGLISH IDIOMS AND PHRASES TO BILINGUAL STUDENTS

CONVERSATIONAL POEMS FOR CHORAL READING

Fleischman, Paul. *I Am Phoenix.* Illus. by Ken Nutt. Harper, 1985.

———. *Joyful Noise.* Illus. by Eric Beddows. Harper, 1988.

Hoberman, Mary Ann. "An Only Child" in *Fathers, Mothers, Sisters, Brothers.* Illus. by Marylin Hafner. Little, 1991.

Hopkins, Lee Bennett. *Side by Side: Poems to Read Together.* Illus. by Hilary Knight. Simon, 1988.

Joseph, Lynn. "Pulling Seine" in *Coconut Kind of Day.* Illus. by Sandra Speidel. Lothrop, 1990.

Merriam, Eve. *You Be Good and I'll Be Night.* Illus. by Karen L. Schmidt. Morrow, 1988.

———. "Windshield Wiper" in Kennedy, X. J. *Knock at a Star.* Little, 1982.

"O Won't You Sit Down," African-American spiritual, in Bryan, Ashley. *All Night, All Day.* Atheneum, 1991.

There's a Hole in the Bucket. Illus. by Nadine Bernard Westcott. Harper, 1990.

Weil, Zaro. *Mud, Moon, and Me.* Illus. by Jo Burroughs. Houghton, 1992.

Wolman, Bernice, sel. *Taking Turns: Poetry to Share.* Illus. by Catherine Stock. Atheneum, 1992.

IDIOMS

Ciardi, John. "This Man Talked about You" in *I Met a Man.* Illus. by Robert Osborn. Houghton, 1973.

Kennedy, X. J. "Telephone Talk" in *The Kite That Braved Old Orchard Beach.* Illus. by Marion Young. M. K. McElderry/Macmillan, 1991.

Lee, Dennis. "The Secret Place" and "Secrets" in *The Ice Cream Store.* Illus. by David McPhail. Scholastic, 1991.

Livingston, Myra Cohn. "I Never Told" in *I Never Told and Other Poems.* M. K. McElderry/Macmillan, 1992.

———. "Secret Passageway" in *Worlds I Know and Other Poems.* Illus. by Tim Arnold. M. K. McElderry/Macmillan, 1985.

McCord, David. "Secret" in *All Small.* Illus. by Madelaine Gill Linden. Little, 1986.

Prelutsky, Jack. "I Had a Little Secret" in *Beneath a Blue Umbrella.* Illus. by Garth Williams. Greenwillow, 1990.

Seabrooke, Brenda. "Clues" and "Secrets" in *Judy Scuppernong.* Illus. by Ted Lewin. Cobblehill/Dutton, 1990.

Viorst, Judith. "Secrets" in *If I Were in Charge of the World and Other Worries.* Illus. by Lynn Cherry. Atheneum/Macmillan, 1981.

---

in-depth description of a topic in English, followed by a brief description in their native language. An excellent follow-up activity is to distribute English questions about a topic that you want second language students to ask each other. If their partners ask these appropriately, students can place a checkmark beside the question, and the pair can work together to write, in English, an answer to that question. If the pair finish early, they can write new questions to ask a second pair.

As a slight alternative, bilingual students can meet in pairs (with those who have well-developed speaking abilities) to read the books listed in Literature Card 8, which are printed in both Spanish and English, and in Table 3.5. As they read, they can also analyze the special English idioms and phrases that these books contain and discuss how to incorporate them into their daily conversations.

RECOGNIZING AND REPORTING PROGRESS

Anecdotal Records

In Chapters 1–3 you have read examples of how Ms. Johnson, Ms. Diederick, and Ms. Wooten observed their students' language abilities and used these observations to create personalized instruction for individual students. In this section you will learn why such assessments are important and how to record them in the form of **anecdotal records.**

Anecdotal records are handwritten notes about single-student, small-group, and whole-class actions that indicate progress in communication and/or thinking abilities. Although many teachers use mental anecdotal records to guide instruction, more and more are using a formal, anecdotal record-keeping system to document their students' language progress. The first step in devising such a system is to select a record-keeping format that is comfortable for you. For example, you can carry a clipboard with post-it notes for writing notes throughout the day; use separate sheets in a spiral notebook for posting notes on each student's page at the end of the day. You can write notes on individual student notecards or use individual file folders to sequence these anecdotal records. Some teachers set aside a specific time at the end of the week to make anecdotal notes; a few record different categories of anecdotal records on a different day. Regardless of the form you devise, the following guidelines will increase their effectiveness.

It is important to write the first thoughts you have as you document incidents. These more immediate reactions will likely be specific and less judgmental descriptions of the salient features of that event than would be possible if you reflect longer than a day before you write. To write the best anecdotal record, observe specific dimensions of students' craftsmanship: (1) note the products and activities that an individual (or class) is using; (2) write the exact comment that a student makes about their reading, writing, speaking, listening, and thinking processes; (3) note specific points that were learned in the process; and (4) list questions that you want to ask that student in the future. Your records should also be objective and nonemotional, capable of being shared with parents, principals, and other school administrators at all times. You can also consistently and faithfully uphold students' privacy by sharing individual records only with that student. For example, here is one of the notes Ms. Wooten made during the first month of school:

> 8/31—Allison is struggling with oral descriptions. She wants to tell fictitious stories, but doesn't know enough about the topics to do so. She does not use personal language. I will model how to tell personal narratives, which I think will help her learn to do so very soon. I will also ask her to tell me about her brother tomorrow.

When you set aside time in each grading period to analyze anecdotal records, it can take as few as 20 minutes per grading period to note one or two patterns of behavior and to establish new instructional goals to guide students' learning for the next term. Although you may want to change the anecdotal record-keeping system during the course of a year, it is best to keep each system in place for one full grading period so students can learn the procedures you use.

It is important to realize that when you experience difficulties with your recording system, you may be attempting to record too much or too frequently (Paradis, Chatton, Boswell, Smith, & Yovich, 1991). By changing your system, you can avoid frustrations, as one of Ms. Wooten's colleagues explained:

> I was really excited about keeping anecdotal records. I got all organized, made about 3 entries each week for every student, and then it was *only* Sept. 28 when I couldn't keep up, so I stopped altogether. I realized I was attempting to do so much record-keeping that I was too stressed and fatigued to teach as well as I desired. I changed to one record for each child every 2 weeks and what a difference it made.

In closing, to devise a record-keeping system that appeals to you, you might consider the following strategies used by Ms. Johnson, Ms. Diederick, and Ms. Wooten:

- Use blank mailing labels. Based on the work of Pils (1991), Ms. Johnson carries a stack of mailing labels in her pocket all day. When an important event occurs, she pauses and writes about it on a mailing label. At the end of each day, she takes a few minutes to remove the backing from each label and places it on an individual student's page, or the full class record page in her spiral notebook. In this way, she doesn't have to sit down at the end of each day to try to remember the details about these significant events.

- Ms. Diederick sets aside 45 minutes each week, while her preschoolers are napping, to make whole-class and individual-student anecdotal entries. These entries document the class's and each student's most important accomplishment of the week. Setting aside this special time ensures that she makes a specific assessment of every student weekly.

- Ms. Wooten schedules one hands-on performance experience each grading period for the explicit purpose of obtaining anecdotal records for every student whose predominate learning style is tactile or kinesthetic.

DEVELOPING TECHNOLOGICAL COMPETENCIES

Keeping Abreast of Innovations, E-Mail, Chatrooms, and Key Pals

As constructivist theory suggests, students comprehend more of what they create for themselves. The implications are that technology can support students' learning by facilitating their construction with a high level of interactivity and experimentation. The technological supports recommended in odd-numbered chapters throughout this textbook meet this criteria. Each produces dynamic and interactive representations that would not be possible without technology's support. In these chapters you will learn about technology specifically designed to develop each of the language arts. You will read about specific audiocassettes, videotapes, and records that support students' oral language development. By listening to many expert language users on these technologies, students begin to emulate varied sentence structures and phraseologies in their personal speaking registers. In every state in the United States and every Canadian province there are government-supported educational service centers. These centers can provide many of these records, videotapes, and audiocassettes for you at no charge. Personnel within individual school districts can tell you about this resource center.

In addition, subscribing to one of the following journals will keep you up to date on technological developments. If the subscription to the journal is free, it is marked with an *. For those that have a charge, you might want to ask your principal to order a subscription that can be placed in the teachers' lounge or faculty resource library.

*1. Ask ERIC Virtual Library (CNN Newsroom Classroom Guides and Discovery Education Online) gopher ericir.syr.edu, or telnet ericir.syr.edu; login as gopher. (Other computer access databases are The Computer Database, Microcomputer Index, Education Resources Information Centers, and Resources in Computer Education.)

2. Learning and Leading
with Technology
1787 Agate Street
Eugene, OR 97403-1923
1-800-336-5195

3. Classroom Computer News
Intentional Education, Inc.
341 Mt. Auburn Street
Watertown, MA 02171

4. Educational Computer Magazine
P.O. Box 535
Cupertino, CA 95015

5. Electronic Learning
Scholastic, Inc.
902 Sylvan Avenue
Englewood Cliffs, NJ 07632

6. School Courseware Journal
1341 Bulldog Lane, Suite C
Fresno, CA 93710

7. Courseware Report Card
150 W. Carob Street
Compton, CA 90220

8. Swift's Directory of Educational
Software for the IBM PC or
Apple Computer
Sterling Swift Publishing
Company
7901 South Interstate Highway 35
Austin, TX 78744

9. Hyperlink Magazine
P.O. Box 7723
Eugene, OR 97401

10. Only the Best
Customer Service
R. R. Bower Co.
P.O. Box 762
New York, NY 10011

*11. Educational Software Preview
Guide
Publication Sales
California State Department
of Education
P.O. Box 271
Sacramento, CA 95802
($2.00 charge for mailing)

*12. T. H. E. Journal
150 El Camino Real, Suite 112
Tustin, CA 92680-3670

13. Spoken Arts (for oral language
development resources)
Department B
310 North Avenue
New Rochelle, NY 10801

14. Listening Library, Inc. (for oral
language and listening development resources)
One Park Avenue
Old Greenwich, CT 06870

Moreover, as new learning technologies are transforming many U.S. schools, there are considerable disparities that exist in access. Specifically LEP, ELL, and bilingual students have the lowest access to new computer technology of any sub-component of the student population (Dunkel, 1999; McLaughlin, 1995). The Internet provides many opportunities for students to explore **e-mail exchanges** and **chatrooms.** E-mail accounts are becoming more and more affordable in schools, and chatrooms have been set up specifically for students to develop better understandings of different cultural experiences.

To begin either of these programs, you may want to contact classrooms in other countries that have already established such e-mail and chatroom exchanges. One location that you may find very helpful is Intercultural E-Mail Classroom Connection (www.stolaf.edu/network/iecc). It contains up-to-date mailing lists of teachers and other cultural contacts for which your students can exchange e-mails. At this site your students can become key pals. Key pals are pen pals in technology. Key pals interact with pen pals from around the world. Important new friendships may develop with students from different cultures and linguistic backgrounds. While bilingual, LEP, and ELL students practice their first language, English-speaking students can learn a second. The following sites are available so that your students can develop key pal contacts:

1. **Key Pals**   www.keypals.com/p/keypals.html
2. **Intercultural E-Mail Classroom Connections**   www.stolaf.edu/network/iecc
3. **E-Mail Classroom Exchange**   www.iglou.com/xchange/ece/

As the year progresses, you can study the same subject or discuss issues that have international implications so that your students come to understand and respect the perspectives that exist in our global society. In Chapter 5, you will read about learning strategies of particular value to ESL and bilingual students that can be created from the interactive CD-ROM storybooks and software. Such technology is entering more and more schools and public libraries as a resource that has been proven to maximize ESL and bilingual students' learning.

These CD-ROM programs are exceptional tools because they integrate live pictures and scenery with auditory support. Such technological applications are preferred over videos for second-language learners because students can interact simultaneously with the content area, visual stimuli, and audio reinforcement. Moreover, if students do not understand the narration or want to see a word again or an action conducted again, they merely have to click a button and the process, word, or term can be reviewed. Moreover, such interactive visual stimuli draws students to listen more carefully to the sounds of the words they're hearing at the same time that active illustrations help students obtain meaning. Technology not only allows students to work at their own pace, but is a powerful tool to combine active listening with other areas of their literacy development as they surmount any oral language barriers they might have.

SECTION 3   TEACHERS AS CONTINUAL LEARNERS

Teaching Oral Language

By performing think-alouds and using dialogue journals, your students will rapidly increase their oral language abilities. In addition, when you include parents in a unit to teach telephone skills, families who use English as a second language can improve their own speaking abilities while strengthening their children's English speaking abilities.

PROFESSIONAL DEVELOPMENT ACTIVITY

How to Do a "Think-Aloud"

Modeling is one of the most effective ways to demonstrate thinking and communication processes. **Modeling** is the process of demonstrating how to think about or perform a language arts objective by talking about it immediately before or after students perform it in class. In a model, you demonstrate each step in the process.

Think-alouds are a special type of modeling. A think-aloud is a very powerful teaching tool because it demystifies thinking, writing, reading, speaking, and listening by deliberately bringing to the surface the language arts processes going on in the mind. For example, Ms. Wooten gave her kindergartners these two think-alouds. The first is how to learn new words to add to their speaking vocabularies. Her think-aloud began:

> *Gracious.* Now what does that word mean? Whenever I don't know a meaning, I put all the information together that the author has already given me to see if I can figure it out. I know that it describes Grandma as a person. But what is its meaning? It must also have something to do with the way Grandma acts. I know this because of the next few sentences. These sentences describe how she treats friends who come to dinner. Because she is so kind to everyone, *gracious* must mean something like *kind.* In Spanish *gracious* means thank you, so the English word is similar.

Ms. Wooten's second think-aloud models how to make predictions while reading:

> Boys and girls, I want to share with you how I think when I read. Before I read a book, I do a number of things. First, I look at the title. The title usually tells me a lot about what the story or book will be about. Second, I look at the pictures to make a prediction about what the big idea is and what may happen. For instance, in this book, *The Girl Who Loved Wild Horses,* I think about this girl who is from a Native American culture. Then, I make a prediction about all I know about horses and Native American cultures, and I begin reading, checking what I read against the prediction I have in my head. After I find out whether my first prediction was right, I make another one about what will happen next. And I keep doing that until I finish reading. So, I always have a prediction in my head about what will happen next. Finally, after I finish reading, I think again about the main idea of the story and try to apply it to my life.

Fourth-grade students who were taught reading comprehension strategies with such think-alouds were more aware of their comprehension abilities than students who had instruction without think-alouds (Baumann, Seifert-Kessell, & Jones, 1992). Think-alouds will be most effective if they explicitly connect pieces of information, provide adequate explanations, and describe cause-and-effect relationships (Loxterman, Beck, & McKeoun, 1994). In summary, by performing think-alouds frequently in your class you can employ one of the best methods of showing an end product before the class tries to replicate the thinking and oral or written language arts process to be learned.

FOR YOUR JOURNAL

Dialogue Journals

A **dialogue journal** is a written conversation, or a talk on paper, between a student and a teacher (Atwell, 1984; Calkins, 1983; Graves, 1983). Stanton (1980) emphasizes that dialogue journals are intended to provide all students with an opportunity to share privately with the teacher their reactions, questions, and concerns about school experiences without any threat of reprisal or evaluation. Dialogue journals require thinking, but they do not demand a finished product. Dialogue journals also provide an opportunity for teachers and students to communicate meaningfully through writing, so that the writing a child does has a purpose and an audience. Dialogue journals build students' oral language skills as well as their reading and writing, but it also helps teachers know each student in a deeper and more personal way. Observational notes from one study confirmed that students (as young as age 5) did not hesitate to write to their teachers; stayed engaged in their writing until they finished their entries; and seemed to enjoy conversing with their teachers in print (Wrenn, 2000).

Most teachers require students to write a minimum of one dialogue journal entry per week, and they keep dialogue journals in a special center so that students can access their journal any time an important question or thought crosses their minds. Each weekly entry can be addressed to the teacher or to a peer. At the beginning of the year, it might be easier for your students if you model a think-aloud on how to write a dialogue journal entry. You might also make a list of possible questions and thoughts that students can write, such as the following:

- What you notice
- What you think and feel
- What you wonder about
- What you like and don't like
- How well you read and why
- What you wonder about yourself as a reader or writer
- What the book said and meant to you
- Unknown words you do not know

Dialogue journals can also have additional benefits for bilingual students. To illustrate, Juan's mother wrote a letter to Ms. Wooten, which became a dialogue journal that she and Mrs. Martinez, Juan's mother, continued for several weeks. In the initial journal entry, Mrs. Martinez wrote the following to Ms. Wooten:

Dear Ms. Wooten,

   Thank you so much for sending home the books *Family Stories/Cuadros de Familia* and *Rhymes/Spanish and English* for me to read aloud to Juan. I think he likes them because they describe hard times that a family had and because he loves animals so much. I like how realistic the author makes the characters. One word I couldn't understand in a sentence I was trying to read to Juan was: "His eyes began to *smart.*" What does this mean? I am about halfway through both books. We are both looking forward to reading and talking about the rest of them.

Mrs. Martinez

Dear Mrs. Martinez,

   I am so pleased that you and Juan are enjoying the books. I thought he would like them. "His eyes began to smart." *Smart* can have other meanings besides the most common English meaning that someone is very wise. It can also mean for something to sting. That is what it means in this sentence. Have your eyes ever smarted? That's what the word means. Could you tell me what kind of experiences Juan would like to read about next? If he liked these books, I would like to give you Cynthia Voight's book called *Homecoming.* I don't have it in our library yet, but I can ask Laurel, our librarian, to order it from our Educational Service Regional Center if you would like to read that book next week.

Ms. Wooten

CONNECTING CLASSROOMS, PARENTS, AND COMMUNITIES

Developing Telephoning Skills

Telephoning teaches students to use effective oral skills and has a built-in application to the real world. It also develops students' regulatory, instrumental, interactive, personal, and informational functions of language, as well as items 9–12 on the Individual Student's Oral Language Needs Monitor (see Table 3.4). It is especially valuable for students learning English as a second language. If possible, you can teach these skills by using real or simulated telephones, which many telephone companies will bring to the classroom. Prior to instruction, you can ask students to brainstorm skills that make telephone conversations clear. Strategies for teaching how to answer and make telephone calls (for kindergarten through second-grade children) are shown in Figure 3.5.

You can solicit parents' aid by providing them with a copy of the list of telephoning skills that your class develops. Then you can ask each student to call a different classmate's parent to provide information about a future class event (e.g., what to bring, when, where, and other information concerning a special classroom project). As parents listen to the student on the telephone, they can make comments on the checklist of skills about how well that student met each of the criteria the class developed. They can place these comments in an envelope to be returned to you. After reviewing all parents' comments, you can summarize the class successes and weaknesses and share them with students as a whole-class performance assessment.

There are two additional ways that teachers are using the telephone to enhance the language arts program. The first is that they are installing answering machines and a telephone line in their classrooms so parents can call to leave messages. Teachers also can put messages on their incoming lines so parents hear about upcoming events or special information in case teachers are unavailable to answer the phone because they are teaching. Dodge (1999) also created the concept of **phone friends.** Phone friends makes each student an assistant to other students who are absent or unsure of an assignment. A phone friends' list is compiled in class and posted at each student's home so that students have each other's phone numbers in case they have questions regarding a homework assignment or need help in a particular subject area. A sample form that can be used for this activity is available on the website that accompanies this textbook.

●∙•∙●∙•∙●∙•∙●∙•∙●∙•∙●∙•∙●∙•∙●∙•∙●∙•∙●∙•∙●∙•∙●∙•∙●∙•∙●∙•∙●∙•∙●∙•∙●∙•∙●∙•∙●∙•∙●

SUMMARY

In this chapter, you have read about the stages of oral language development, seven functions of oral language, reasons to develop students' speaking abilities, and methods of doing so. You have also read about the importance of integrating literature,

MODIFYING PHONE CALLING FOR YOUNG KIDS

by Color Coding Each Number

1 9 1 4 7 5 3 2 8 6 9

CREATING A PICTURE PHONEBOOK

so Young Children Can Call

Grammy and Pop-Pop and Other Important People

TAKING MESSAGES: YOUNG CHILDREN CIRCLE THE CORRECT CHOICES

While You Were Out . . .

TEACHING CHILDREN TO USE MESSAGE PADS

To _____

Date _____ Time _____ ☐ AM ☐ PM

WHILE YOU WERE OUT

M _____

of _____

Phone (_____) _____
　　　　Area Code　　　Number　　　Extension

TELEPHONED		PLEASE CALL	
CALLED TO SEE YOU		WILL CALL AGAIN	
WANTS TO SEE YOU		URGENT	
	RETURNED YOUR CALL		

Message _____
_____
_____
_____
_____
_____
_____

　　　　　　　　　　　　　　Operator

FIGURE 3.5 TEACHING HOW TO TAKE PHONE MESSAGES AND TELEPHONING SKILLS

Created by Jennifer Rioux, 2000, master of education degree candidate at Texas Christian University, Fort Worth, TX. Used by permission.

anecdotal records, audiovisual technological aids, code switching (and ten methods of instructing bilingual students), think-alouds, and dialogue journals into your language arts program. In the next chapter you will learn how to strengthen students' listening abilities and discover how closely speaking and listening development are related.

HOW TO DO IT: USING WHAT YOU'VE LEARNED

The following provides opportunities to reflect on and practice what you have learned.

1. How do students learn language by imitating others?; and, How do students learn language through a "language acquisition device"?

2. Why does an effective oral language program increase achievement in reading, writing, and other scholastic areas?

3. What are the seven functions of language and describe one method that you can use to develop students' abilities to use each?

4. There were 10 activities described to assist students to learn English whose first language is not English. State the grade you are teaching (or the grade level you most desire to teach if you do not have your own classroom presently. Rank order your choices of these 10 activities, stating the reasons why you rated them as you did. Your ranking will be based on the developmental level of students at the grade you specified.

5. Design a lesson that uses one of the books from a literature card in this chapter to improve a student's oral language abilities.

6. Select one question from each of the five categories in Figure 3.3. If you are teaching, write these questions, one per day, at some point in your lesson plans for next week. Focus on asking that question several times that day. At the end of the week, assess the effects of these questions on student's oral language development. If you are not teaching presently, identify a question from each category in Figure 3.3. Match these questions to five activities in this chapter. State why you judge that you will ask each question in the course of teaching each of the activities you selected and how doing so will enrich the learning experiences of your future students.

KEY TERMS EXERCISE

The following list contains new concepts that were introduced in this chapter. If you learned the meaning of a term, place a checkmark in the blank that precedes the term. If you are unsure of a term's definition, it will increase your retention if you pause for a moment and return to the page where that term's definition appears. If you have learned 35 of these terms on a first reading of this chapter, you have constructed an understanding of a majority of the most important terms you need to develop your students' oral language abilities. Congratulations!

_____ anecdotal records   (p. 125)

_____ behaviorists   (p. 95)

_____ bilingual approach   (p. 120)

_____ celebrative experiences   (p. 108)

_____ chat rooms   (p. 128)

_____ classroom conversations
(p. 111)

_____ cognitive field theory   (p. 96)

_____ debates   (p. 114)

_____ deliberate silence   (p. 112)

_____ dialect   (p. 101)

_____ dialogue journal   (p. 130)

_____ e-mail exchanges   (p. 128)

_____ ESL approach   (p. 120)

_____ exploratory talk   (p. 93)

_____ funds of knowledge   (p. 121)

_____ heuristicalize   (p. 97)

_____ heuristic function   (p. 100)

_____ holophrastic speech   (p. 96)

_____ imaginative function   (p. 100)

_____ imagine   (p. 97)

_____ immersion approach   (p. 119)

_____ inform   (p. 97)

_____ informational function   (p. 100)

_____ instrumental function   (p. 99)

_____ instrumentalize   (p. 97)

_____ interactional function   (p. 99)

_____ language acquisition device
(p. 95)

_____ linguists   (p. 99)

_____ mastery or subskill theory
(p. 96)

_____ modeling   (p. 129)

_____ numbered heads   (p. 116)

_____ panel discussions   (p. 114)

_____ partnered reading   (p. 122)

_____ personal function   (p. 100)

_____ personalize   (p. 97)

_____ phone friends   (p. 132)

_____ psycholinguistic   (p. 96)

_____ regulate   (p. 97)

_____ regulatory function   (p. 99)

_____ respondent-centered questions
(p. 109)

_____ ritualize   (p. 97)

_____ shaping   (p. 95)

_____ show and tell   (p. 114)

_____ students hypothesizing
(p. 122)

_____ symbolic function/telegraphic
speech   (p. 97)

_____ text-centered questions   (p. 109)

_____ think-alouds   (p. 130)

_____ turn to your friend and share
(p. 117)

FOR FUTURE REFERENCE

The following resources describe oral language development. Some also provide more examples of language arts programs in action in preschool, kindergarten, and first-grade classrooms.

Avery, C. (1993). *And with a light touch: Learning about reading, writing, and teaching with first graders.* Portsmouth, NH: Heinemann.

Benedict, S., & Carlisle, L. (1992). *Beyond words.* Portsmouth, NH: Heinemann.

Bishop, R. S. (1987). Extending multicultural understanding through children's books. In B. Cullinan (Ed.), *Children's literature in the reading program.* Newark, DE: IRA.

Blatt, G. T. (Ed.). (1993). *Once upon a folktale: Capturing the folklore process with children.* New York: Teachers College Press.

Bosma, B. (1992). *Fairy tales, fables, legends, and myths: Using folk literature in your classroom* (2nd ed.). New York: Teachers College Press.

Cullinan, B. E. (Ed.). (1993). *Children's voices: Talk in the classroom.* Newark, DE: IRA.

Jody, M., & Saccardi, M. (1996). *Computer conversations: Readers and books online.* Urbana, IL: NCTE.

Pierce, K. M., & Gilles, C. J. (Eds.). (1993). *Cycles of meaning: Exploring the potential of talk in learning communities.* Portsmouth, NH: Heinemann.

Routman, R. (1994). *Invitations. Changing as teacher and learners K–12.* Portsmouth, NH: Heinemann.

Routman, R., & Butler, A. (Eds.). (1995). *School talk.* Urbana, IL: NCTE.

Wolfram, W., & Christian, D. (1989). *Dialects and education: Issues and answers.* Englewood Cliffs, NJ: Prentice-Hall.

ADDITIONAL RESOURCES FOR KINDERGARTEN TEACHERS AND PARENTS

Books

Douglas, K. M. (1997). *Simple centers for kindergarten.* Grand Rapids, MI: Instructional Fair–TS Denison.

Fisher, B. (1996). *Inside the classroom: Teaching kindergarten and first grade.* Portsmouth, NH: Heinemann.

Fisher, B., & Holdaway, D. (1998). *Joyful learning in kindergarten.* Portsmouth, NH: Heinemann.

Fleming, M. (1997). *25 emergent reader mini-books: Easy-to-make reproducible books to promote literacy.* New York: Scholastic.

Kurth, M. J. (1998). *Kindergarten themes.* Cypress, NY: Creative Teaching Press.

Martinez, D. (1998). *Kindergarten homework.* Cypress, NY: Creative Teaching Press.

Merrick, S. M. (Ed.). (1996). *How to manage your multi-age classroom.* Huntington Beach, CA: Teacher Created Materials.

Websites: Online Resources (in English and Spanish) Recommended Books in Spanish for Young Readers

For additional high-quality books in Spanish for young children, please visit the Center for the Study of Books in Spanish for Children and Adolescents online at **www.csusm.edu/campus_centers/csb**. Under "Recommended Books" users can access our searchable database of commendable books in Spanish published around the world for children and adolescents.

More than 4,000 in-print books that deserve to be read by Spanish-speaking children and adolescents (or those who wish to learn Spanish) are in the database. Books have been selected because of the quality of art and writing, presentation of material, and appeal to the intended audience.

To provide equal access for the Spanish-speaking world, bibliographic information, grade/age level, subject headings, and a brief description for each book are available in both English and Spanish. Weekly updates of recent titles are provided.

U.S. Dealers of Books in Spanish for Children and Young Adults

AIMS International Books, Inc., 7709 Hamilton Avenue, Cincinnati, OH 45231-3103, 800-733-2067, 513-521-5590, fax: 513-521-5592

Bay Books, 1029 Orange Avenue, Coronado, CA 92118, 619-435-0070

Lectorum Publications, Inc., 111 Eighth Avenue, Suite 804, New York, NY 10011, 800-345-5946, 212-929-2833, fax: 212-727-3035, online: www.lectorum.com

Los Andes Publishing, Inc., P.O. Box 2344, La Puente, CA 91746, 800-LECTURA, online: www.losandes.com

Mariuccia Iaconi Book Imports, 970 Tennessee Streeet, San Francisco, CA 94107, 800-955-9577, 415-821-1216, fax: 415-821-1596, online: www.mibibook.com

Reading and Language Arts Resources for Professionals: Young Children's Oral Language Development www.tapr.org/~ird/Dimsdle/rdgprof.html

Resources for Parents

Green, L. (1996). *Improving your child's schoolwork: An A to Z reference guide.* Rocklin, CA: Prima Publishing. 287p.

This book is filled with ideas to assist parents in understanding their child's needs and improving their education. Includes strategies and resources.

Green, L. J. (1998). *Finding help when your child is struggling in school.* NY: Golden Books. 289p.

This book helps parents identify problems, use school resources, communicate with schools, and build children's self-confidence. This helps parents get involved in their child's education by helping them understand how to take advantage of school resources.

Hirsch, E., & Holdren, J. (Eds.). (1996). *What your kindergartner needs to know.* New York: Doubleday. 292p.

This book is a great resource for letting parents know what schools generally cover during kindergarten. It has a great reading and writing section with pieces of literature and writing activities.

Holdren, J., & Hirsch, E. (Eds.). (1996). *Books to build on: A grade-by-grade resource guide for parents and teachers.* New York: Dell Publishing. 361p.

This book is a collection of literature and book titles appropriate for each grade level. This book will assist parents in selecting quality literature for their children.

Jacobson, J. R. (1998). *How is my first grader doing in school?* New York: Simon and Schuster. 192p.

This book shows parents how to assess their child and gives parent-friendly activities to do with the child. Great reading and writing sections.

McGuinness, D. (1997). *Why our children can't read and what we can do about it.* New York: The Free Press. 384p.

This book talks about the flaws in current literacy practices and gives suggestions on how to fix them.

Reviews from parent council: To maintain a creative-learning environment for children. (1996). Vol. 4, number 1. Austin, TX: Richardson. 218p.

This book has reviews of children's books, audio selections, computer programs, learning aids, parenting materials, and videos. This will help parents locate and select quality resources for their children.

Routman, R. (2000). *Conversations: Strategies for teaching, learning and evaluating.* Portsmouth, NH: Heinemann. 469p.

This book demonstrates how to develop oral language abilities. It contains numerous classroom-tested practices and more than 30 forms to evaluate students' growth in expressing themselves.

A major responsibility in a student-centered language arts program is developing listening abilities, which should begin by first grade.

CHAPTER 4

LISTENING DEVELOPMENT:
A STUDENT-CENTERED APPROACH

A major responsibility in a student-centered language arts program is the development of listening abilities. Mr. Stone was well aware of this fact and chose to teach first grade because he knew he could structure his language arts program to meet the special language needs of children in this age group. He loved to see the eagerness with which first-graders connected to their peers. However, he was aware that they had not yet developed the skills to do so successfully. They tended to be bossy and demanding in play situations. They needed his guidance to learn how to make rules, participate in cooperative play, and share. As a matter of fact, it was not uncommon for his first-graders to change the rules (which some call cheating) or change the story (which some call lying). They also displayed a tendency to be very competitive and to insist on being first. He knew that, when the children tattled (which increased as their speaking vocabulary improved), it was usually to show him that they knew the rules and not to be cruel to others. Although their dependence on adults was decreasing, they still continually turned to Mr. Stone for direction, praise, and approval.

Mr. Stone enjoyed the tendency for 6-year-olds to be curious learners. At this age they are very interested in the process of learning to write, read, draw, and listen, but unlike older children, first-graders derive more pleasure from the process of creating than from the final product. For this reason, finding ways to help his first-graders enjoy revising their writing was difficult.

Last, Mr. Stone appreciated the fact that 6-year-olds wanted to be in perpetual motion. They would squirm as they sat, and found it difficult to listen. They used full-bodied gestures when they spoke. Quite often during the independent silent reading, they would read aloud without even realizing it. In the classroom, his first-graders needed to move from movement-based activities to quiet activities and back again. For these reasons, the activities in this chapter provide a means to actively engage students while developing their listening skills.

As this chapter proceeds, you will also become familiar with the structure of Mr. Stone's classroom and how it contributed to developing his students' listening abilities.

Imagine for a moment that you are inside Mr. Stone's, Meisong's, Juan's, Michael's, and Allison's first-grade classroom. When you enter, you are struck by the students' thinking and listening abilities. In-depth discussions are in progress. You experience the positive and supportive atmosphere in which listeners are able to ask their friends questions. When Mr. Stone sees you approach, he introduces you to the class, and, without being asked to do so, the students stop talking immediately to hear what Mr. Stone has to say. After your introduction, they arrange themselves on the rug for a class meeting, which begins their language arts lessons each day. Meisong and Allison reach for your hands and walk you to a spot that they have prepared.

After everyone is settled, Mr. Stone says: "Today, let's move from left to right. Everyone can share something good that happened to them yesterday, or you can pass if you wish." Michael shared: "My dad played catch with me last night for a really long time. Juan is coming to my house today after school." Juan added: "Yes, our editing committee is inventing a new game that we're going to tell you about tomorrow." "My puppy isn't sick anymore," Allison declared. "I brought some *real* bamboo for our project!" Meisong said eagerly. Everyone else listens carefully, nodding their heads in affirmation. A few more students talk. A few students pass. No one feels pressured to participate.

This class meeting was the beginning of the language arts lesson. Students talked about ideas, projects, and drawings that they completed at school or at home the day before. In this time, they followed the "listening time rules" (see p. 153) that they created. Mr. Stone and the students continued to express enthusiasm and encouragement to the speakers. Michael and Allison told the class that they worked eagerly at school and at home to finish their projects so they could tell their friends about them in tomorrow's language arts class meeting.

The purpose of this chapter is to help you learn how to develop your pupils' listening abilities and to learn more about first-grade language arts instruction so exchanges such as those above can regularly occur in your classroom. By the end of the chapter, you will have gained information to assist you in mastering the following IRA, NCTE, NAEYC national standards, as well as statewide and province-based objectives for professional development in the language arts:

1. What principles guide effective listening instruction?
2. How can you teach students to listen more effectively?
3. How can you build students' listening, speaking, writing, and thinking abilities through interviews, oral histories, and simulated newscasts?
4. How can you help students to recognize propaganda and listen more effectively in groups?
5. What activities strengthen the five levels of listening ability?
6. What are the qualities of exemplary first-grade language arts teachers?
7. How can you involve parents in their children's language arts development?
8. How can you adapt instruction to meet the needs of different learners to accomplish different purposes?

SECTION 1   THEORETICAL FOUNDATIONS
Students' Listening Needs

> *"Know how to listen and you will profit even from those who talk badly."* —Plutarch

"**Listening** is a highly complex and interactive process by which spoken language is converted to meaning in the mind" (Lundsteen, 1979, p. 1). The best listeners keep an open, curious mind. As a matter of fact, Husius argued that "listening without a specific purpose, that is listening *without wanting anything from it . . .* opens up fuller access to the totality of the other [person]" (p. 121). They constantly search for new ideas, and integrate what they hear with what they already know. They also evaluate many points of view. They are personally involved in what they hear and stay alert by outlining and creating mental examples on their own. Good listeners also ask questions that assist speakers to expand their own thinking about a topic.

WHY STUDENTS NEED LISTENING INSTRUCTION

Developing students' listening abilities is important for several reasons. First, becoming an expert listener may be among the most important competencies that students can develop because they will spend more than 50 percent of their lives listening (Cooper, 1991). As researchers have found, most students and adults listen five times more frequently than they write, three and one-third times more frequently than they read, and twice as much as they speak (Wolven & Coakley, 1985; Lundsteen, 1979; Werner, 1994). Ironically, by the time students graduate from high school, they will typically have received writing instruction each week for 12 years; about 1,274 hours of reading instruction; 141 to 283 hours of oral language instruction; but less than *6 hours of listening instruction.* This disproportionate allocation of instructional time is limiting many students' active, efferent, and aesthetic listening abilities (Burley-Allen, 1982; Wolf, Miera, & Carey, 1996).

Second, accurate and perceptive listening abilities can minimize misunderstandings and help students sustain satisfying and productive relationships. The success with which students interpret messages and appreciate aesthetic sounds can also increase their mental health, social pleasure, and professional success (Block & Mangieri, 1994; Elliott, 1995).

Third, as demonstrated by Mr. Stone's class meetings, effective listening abilities strengthen students' abilities to use other language arts. For example, effective listening sparked these students' desires to share orally, write, and read more. Good listening abilities also expand students' reading comprehension and writing competencies. If they have listened effectively to alternative ideas and others' personal stories, their schema expands and will be reflected in an increased competence in speaking, reading, and writing (Wells, 1993; Cazden, 1994; Udall & Nurst, 1991).

Another reason it is important to allocate more time to listening instruction is that without it many students become confused when they hear unique oral language patterns (Chomsky, 1969). Also, without effective listening strategies most people will remember only 25 percent of the information they hear.

PURPOSES FOR LISTENING

Listening is different than hearing. Hearing is the reception of sound. **Sound** has been defined as "an onrushing, cresting, and withdrawing wave of air molecules that begins with the movement of an object . . . and ripples out in all directions [in sound waves]" (Ackerman, 1990, p. 177). As stated previously, for listening to occur, listeners must set a purpose and interact mentally with the incoming sounds and information to assimilate all that they hear into a comprehensive whole from which they obtain meaning. To achieve this goal, there are five listening skills that must be developed: (1) to distinguish sounds; (2) to understand messages; (3) to receive information; (4) to interpret and evaluate what one hears; and (5) to enjoy, appreciate, and respond to meaning (Wolven & Coakley, 1979). Students pass through phases before they develop competence in each of these (Jacobs, 1986). To begin, infants' limited consciousness appears to distinguish sounds only when a personally relevant and immediate need arises. As they grow older, people begin to **half-listen,** choosing to hear only what is important to them.

For example, research has demonstrated that immediately after listening to a 10-minute presentation, the average adult will retain only about 50 percent of what was said. Within 48 hours, the same person's retention rate will decrease dramatically to the point of recalling only 25 percent of the orally presented information (Gibbs, Hewing, Helbert, & Ramsey, 1985).

As these data demonstrate, an alarming amount of information is lost between the reception and recall stages of the listening process. There are many reasons for this loss. Some of it occurs because listeners' attention is selective—part is conscious, and part is a result of automatic processing. Also, according to Friedman (1978), our nervous system typically attends to a single stimulus for only 5 to 8 seconds before requiring a change. Still more is lost through misinterpretation. In addition, during auditory processing, it is not uncommon to discard the sequence or degree of similarity or contrast among ideas (Friedman, 1978; Gans, 1994). Last, once we store information we have heard, the memory's fateful reproduction of what was actually received may not be retrieved (Kupfermann, 1991). Thus, to listen more effectively, your students must learn how to receive more; discriminate accurately; attend completely; listen efferently; listen actively; and listen appreciatively.

Although people often use the terms *hearing* and *listening* interchangeably, it is after messages enter the brain that instruction can significantly impact the quality of thinking students do with the words received. Medical specialists can use audiometers to discern hearing ability levels. Thus, determining whether a hearing loss is present is an important first step in your listening curriculum.

Research reports that up to 10 percent of today's students have a mild to severe hearing loss that interferes with listening. Many of these losses have not been diagnosed (Gans, 1994; West, 1995). Although students with severe hearing losses are being taught to listen in special programs, it will often be your responsibility to identify the 10 percent (or two or three) of the students in your class each year who have mild to serious, undiagnosed hearing losses. These students may reveal their hearing loss through behaviors such as speaking in very loud voices, offering points in classroom conversations that were just made by another classmate, being unable to make certain sounds, and turning the volume of record players and tape recorders up too loud. Hearing loss can also delay language development, personal vocabulary recognition, and reduce achievement in subjects in which listening is required.

Mild hearing losses can also result from allergies that impair the ear canal (West, 1995). Physicians are advocating that teachers become more involved in the diagnosis of probable hearing losses because parents may be too close to the problem to see it clearly. Many parents think that a child with hearing difficulties is just not paying close enough attention or is ignoring their oral directions. Thus, when a child in your room has multiple ear infections, head congestion, speaks in a loud voice, or if it is hard to gain his or her attention, your first "suspect" should be hearing loss. Such an assessment may eliminate the negative implication that a student is being defiant, and this, rather than an inability to hear, is the cause of his or her inattention.

LEVELS OF LISTENING ABILITY

Effective listening instruction increases students' abilities to learn from what they hear. Because distinct activities are needed to improve each of the six types of listening, descriptions of these activities follow.

LEVEL 1. RECEIVING
Ensuring Students Can Hear

If you suspect a student has hearing difficulties, you can stand a short distance behind the student and call his/her name. Then, you can ask a question. If the student is not deeply concentrating, and has no hearing difficulty, he or she will turn to face you. If the student does not turn around, you can contact the school nurse who can administer auditory tests such as these:

1. The Sequential Tests of Educational Progress
2. The Stanford Achievement Test Series
3. The California Achievement Tests/Listening Test
4. The Brown-Carlsen Listening Comprehension Test
5. The Detroit Tests of Learning Aptitude

Students who have receptive listening problems can also be discerned because their body image, expressive language, and developmental characteristics will differ from those of their peers, as listed in Table 4.1.

Researchers have determined that there are five reasons why children have difficulty receiving information. The first, **fading theory**, suggests that students lose information because it fades from memory unless it is used rapidly or frequently enough. Thus, when students are asked to recall or retell what they hear but can't, the difficulty may be that it faded from memory too rapidly to be recalled. Second, the **distortion theory** suggests that the longer information remains in long-term memory, the more it is mingled with and indistinguishable from other stored information (Gans, 1994). In this instance, a student might recall information not presented in the context just heard.

TABLE 4.1 POSSIBLE INDICATORS THAT A STUDENT HAS A HEARING LOSS

The following can be considered symptomatic of a listening problem:

- A need to have instructions repeated
- Distractibility, restlessness, daydreaming, poor attention and concentration in learning situations
- A tendency to misinterpret what is being said, which produces odd reactions and impedes communication with others
- Difficulty with following and/or participating in conversations in a noisy environment
- Poor balance or coordination
- Excessive body movement when speaking or listening (fidgety)
- Poor posture: overly tense and rigid (hypertonic) or insufficient tonicity (hypotonic)
- The tendency to withdraw or avoid communication in learning situations and/or social situations
- A lack of curiosity or interest in learning
- Lack of interest in oral communication and, in extreme instances, avoidance or active refusal to use language as the medium through which to communicate with others

Third, the **suppression theory** proposes that students consciously forget unpleasant information. A strong indication that this is the cause of a student's difficulty is the student's inability to recall *any* information that was just presented. The fourth theory is the **processing breakdown theory.** Students who suffer from this phenomenon may not be able to answer a question but feel as if the answer is on the "tip of their tongue." Processing breakdowns occur when a student has poor retrieval cues and weak coding systems in his or her long-term memory. If this is the cause of receptive difficulties, special programs to build long-term memory skills are needed. These programs can be implemented by auditory technicians and speech therapists. The final theory, the **never-learned theory,** means just that. For students who experience this difficulty, aural material was never learned to begin with and therefore cannot be recalled. Students with this difficulty often exhibit other slow-learning traits or learning disability symptoms. Activities to assist these children will be presented in the last section of this chapter.

Once you have determined whether a student has any of these receiving problems, you and the student can decide on a program to overcome their individual difficulties. This program can begin in small homogeneous groups. If each group includes an expert listening peer who performs think-alouds about his or her already perfected ability to receive information in a specific way, receiving abilities can improve rapidly.

Children with impairments to receiving aural input will be limited in the quality of their speech and vocabulary development. Because such students can have halted, sporadic, or distorted reception, they can lack auditory discrimination, which is necessary for phonological and syntactical success in reading, writing, and speaking. Without your instruction, such students could spend several years believing everyone hears as they do, and unnecessarily be detained from achieving higher levels of understanding and enjoyment of language.

LEVEL 2. AUDITORY DISCRIMINATION
Instruction to Distinguish Sounds

The second type of listening is to discriminate between sounds and words, and between individual sounds within words. Children must be able to hear **phonograms.** Phonograms are the single sounds within words. It is important to teach phonograms because children can recognize that individual sounds are coherent phonological units in and of themselves. After learning this skill, they can recognize **onset** (the beginning sound of words, usually the beginning consonant or consonant blend) and **rime** (the ending vowel and syllable of a word) relatively easily. Students can also splice these back together again, creating several different words that rhyme. Another advantage of teaching phonograms as the second level in your listening program is that it assists students in decoding instruction. Auditory discrimination of phonograms provides students with a means of decoding many of the basic beginning words they must read. The most common phonograms to teach are listed in Table 4.2.

As you will notice in Table 4.2, there are eight groupings of words that make up the 38 phonograms that determine the most frequently occurring sounds of basic English words. Two activities using Table 4.2 can assist your students in developing auditory discrimination. The first is to separately introduce the sounds in each of these eight divisions. You can have students create rhymes and use the rhythm of the language as the first method of teaching auditory discrimination. When you do so, you are incorporating rhyming and other creative thinking processes to improve students' listening abilities.

Rhyming is the rhythm and sound pattern of the English language that rhythmically groups together similar sounds so that they produce word associations. These associations assist students' memories and auditory discrimination, which in turn assists their learning in two ways. The rhyme itself creates automatic word associations through similarity of sounds. Beginning your lessons by introducing the words *jay, say, pay, day,* and *play,* which contain the most frequent sound of our language, the phonogram /ay/, is an exercise in using rhyming.

Second, rhymes and poems increase students' semantic rhythm. They create a context in which students can find clues to the meanings of new words, as Mastropieri and Scruggs (1991) discovered. Indeed, some memory experts suggest that the associations children make during these lessons are whimsical, fun, and playful, and children retain more of what they learn, as discussed in Chapter 1 (Gans, 1994). Because auditory discrimination lessons can be so enjoyable, they actually improve students' ability to retrieve information. To illustrate the power of rhyme, think how

TABLE 4.2 MOST COMMON PHONOGRAMS IN RANK ORDER BASED ON FREQUENCY OF OCCURRENCE IN MONOSYLLABIC WORDS*

FREQUENCY	RIME	EXAMPLE WORDS TO TEACH IN AUDITORY DISCRIMINATION LESSON
First most frequent out of every 100 monosyllabic words contain:		
26	-ay	jay say pay day play
26	-ill	Hill Bill will fill spill
Second most frequent out of every 100 monosyllabic words contain:		
22	-ip	ship dip tip skip trip
Third most frequent out of every 100 monosyllabic words contain:		
19	-at	cat fat bat rat sat
19	-am	ham jam dam ram Sam
19	-ag	bag rag tag wag sag
19	-ack	back sack Jack black track
19	-ank	bank sank tank blank drank
19	-ick	sick Dick pick quick chick
Fourth most frequent out of every 100 monosyllabic words contain:		
18	-ell	bell sell fell tell yell
18	-ot	pot not hot dot got
18	-ing	ring sing king wing thing
18	-ap	cap map tap clap trap
18	-unk	sunk junk bunk flunk skunk
Fifth most frequent out of every 100 monosyllabic words contain:		
17	-ail	pail jail nail sail tail
17	-ain	rain pain main chain plain
17	-eed	feed seed weed need freed
17	-y	may by dry try fly
17	-out	pout trout scout shout spout
17	-ug	rug bug hug dug tug

many times in your life you have recited the following verse to help you remember the days in the months:

Thirty days has September,
April, June, and November
All the rest have thirty-one,
Except for February, which has twenty-eight
Until leap year makes it twenty-nine.

TABLE 4.2 (CONTINUED)

FREQUENCY	RIME	EXAMPLE WORDS TO TEACH IN AUDITORY DISCRIMINATION LESSON
Sixth most frequent out of every 100 monosyllabic words contain:		
16	-op	mop cop pop top hop
16	-in	pin tin win chin thin
16	-an	pan man ran tan Dan
16	-est	best nest pest rest test
16	-ink	pink sink rink link drink
16	-ow	low slow grow show snow
16	-ew	new few chew grew blew
16	-ore	more sore tore store score
Seventh most frequent out of every 100 monosyllabic words contain:		
15	-ed	bed red fed led Ted
15	-ab	cab dab jab lab crab
15	-ob	cob job rob Bob knob
15	-ock	sock rock lock dock block
15	-ake	cake lake make take brake
15	-ine	line nine pine fine shine
Eighth most frequent out of every 100 monosyllabic words contain:		
14	-ight	knight light right night fight
14	-im	swim him Kim rim brim
14	-uck	duck luck suck truck buck
14	-um	gum bum hum drum plum

*For a complete list of all example words, see Fry (1998).

Adapted from "The Most Common Phonograms," by Edward B. Fry, 1999, *The Reading Teacher, 51*(7), pp. 621–622.

More activities that you can use to teach rhyme are discussed next and in Chapter 5. If you refer to Table 4.2, you can see that, within eight lessons, you can introduce to your children the most common phonograms and advance rapidly their auditory discrimination. You can conduct an activity to increase auditory discrimination abilities and develop students' auditory discrimination of sounds, nuances of words, and nonverbal communication. For this activity, pair the students with partners. Give each student a sheet of paper and pencil. Each pair of partners can sit side by side as they listen to you read a story. Prior to reading the story, you can identify words that contain (1) consonants that frequently begin English words, such as *b, d, f, g, h, l, m, n, p, r, s, t, v;* (2) short vowel sounds; or (3) consonants that frequently appear at the end of words, such as *d, g, l, m, n, r, s, t.*

As you read, you can stop at the end of a sentence that contains one of the words you've identified. Ask students to write the word they heard that had the sound of a consonant (at the beginning or end) or the long or short vowel that you specify. Then, ask students to write the word they think they heard and a second word they know that contains the same sound. Using the phonograms in Table 4.1, you can teach this lesson with a sentence containing the phonogram /ay/. For example, say the sentence, *The cow ate hay.* Then follow with the instruction: "Boys and girls, write the word that has the /ay/ sound." Next, tell students to write another word they know that ends with the /ay/ sound. Students should write a word like *say* or *ray.* After you've finished reading and asked for several words, tell students the correct words, and have students check a partner's paper (misspellings do not constitute errors). There are two purposes for asking students to write a second word that contains the same sound. First, generating words to match a spoken sound strengthens auditory discrimination; and second, hearing (in their internal speech) other words with the same sound immediately following a stimulus sound highlights the unique sound of each onset and rime in both words. At the end of this activity, through a review of students' papers, you can discern which sounds each student does and does not discriminate.

Clinical studies have identified that the underlying problem in many students' auditory discrimination and reading disorders is an incompletely developed **auditory conceptual function.** The auditory ability to register and compare the sequence of sounds within spoken words is also called **phoneme segmentation** or **phonological awareness.** The primary cause of auditory conceptual function is neurophysical—and it occurs throughout the population, regardless of race; sex; cultural factors, such as education and socioeconomic status; or even intelligence.

Secondary symptoms of this auditory discrimination difficulty are adding, omitting, substituting, and reversing sounds and letters in reading, spelling, and speech. It is often (incorrectly) thought that students make these errors because they are not paying attention. However, mispronouncing words or seeing letters inverted or scrambled may be caused by students misjudging the sequence of phonemes (the sounds) within spoken words, or not grasping how our alphabet represents words. These errors may result in spelling "gril" for *girl* and "cret" for *correct,* or read "steam" for *stream,* "litter" for *letter,* "saw" for *was,* or "dad" for *bad.* Students with this difficulty cannot determine whether what they say matches what they see.

The evidence is increasingly clear that auditory conceptual function, or phonological awareness, is directly related to literacy skills (see Chapter 5). It is important that its presence is diagnosed. A published test, the Lindamood Auditory Conceptualization (LAC) Test, is available for evaluating phoneme segmentation ability. A lack of auditory conceptual function in this area prevents a person from being able to use phonics. A severe lack usually can be seen in reading and spelling errors that are grossly unphonetic or in students with an inability to read and spell. Even a minor lack in development can adversely effect a person's ability to recognize and self-correct reading and spelling errors.

One reason that this factor has escaped detection until recently is that a person can say a word without being conscious of its component sounds. It had been thought that if you could say a word, you could also discriminate its sequence of sounds. This is not true for a significant percentage of the population. Whereas only

4 percent of the population is color-blind and cannot discriminate colors, 30 percent have auditory conceptual difficulty from a moderate to severe degree (Block, 1997; Stanovich, 1998).

The problem can be resolved with specific treatment. The solution is conscious input to the brain from another sense modality: *feeling*. Feeling the action of tongue, lips, and mouth as they produce speech sounds adds another dimension to the sounds that each letter, onset, and rime makes. The sequence of sounds and letters involved in reading and spelling can be reinforced with this additional feedback to the brain. Through the integration of auditory, visual, and motor information, students can overcome auditory conceptual weaknesses and become self-correcting readers, speakers, listeners, and spellers.

One widely used program is the Lindamood-Bell Auditory Discrimination Program. In this program, students are taught to *feel* various mouth positions for English sounds, as shown in Figure 4.1. Because these positions and feelings are given catchy labels—"lip poppers," "tip tappers," "nose sounds," "skinny sounds," "scrapers," "lip coolers"—students find them easy to learn. As students duplicate your mouth position, they learn to feel and make the sounds of individual words and

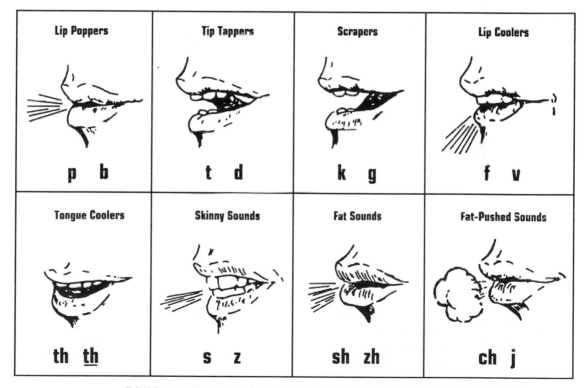

FIGURE 4.1 MOUTH POSITIONS TO TEACH STUDENTS THE AUDITORY CONCEPTUAL FUNCTION (PHONEMIC AWARENESS)

Source: From *Letter Sound Labels* (p. 32), by C. H. Lindamood and P. C. Lindamood, 1979, New York: Harcourt Brace Jovanovich.

letters that they are not able to pronounce or recognize auditorily (and retain visually) without this special instruction. The program also uses colored blocks or felt to represent sounds; students are asked to arrange the blocks in the order the sounds occur in the words, adding a tactile dimension to the learning process. The program assists readers with learning differences because it ties letter-to-sound matches to consistent, concrete, sensory, and visual stimuli. Two similar programs are the Williams ABD Program, which uses textured letters, and the Elkonin Method, which uses picture associations to reduce the complexity of auditory discrimination.

Once auditory conception is in place, you can use another effective method to diagnose auditory discrimination. Cut out small pictures and glue them three to a row. Number each row and place a pictorial line marker for younger students as illustrated in Figure 4.2. The line marker in the first line is an apple. Ask children to put their finger on the apple to ensure that those who cannot read numbers are on the correct line to do their work. Then ask students to circle the picture that depicts a word you say in each row. If you create items to assess students' reception of words such as *behind, under, above, in, over,* and *out,* you can also discern two listening components. When students do not circle the correct picture, either they have not received the instruction, or they do not know the meaning of the word. If you suspect the first cause, refer the student for further auditory discrimination testing. If the second cause is likely, you can provide instruction by modeling the meaning of each preposition. For example, you can ask students to place objects in

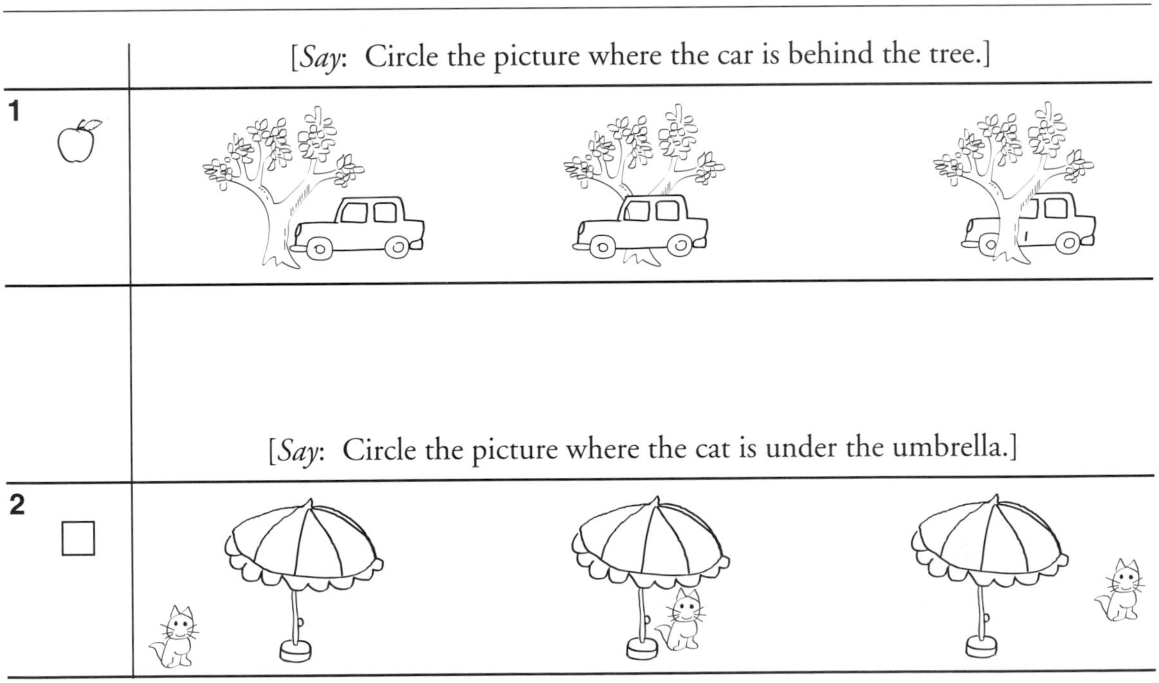

FIGURE 4.2 SAMPLE ITEMS FROM AN INFORMAL TEST TO DIAGNOSE AUDITORY DISCRIMINATION

specific locations that are *under* or *behind* another object, such as putting a ball *on* a table.

Students' discrimination abilities develop in a progression from gross distinctions to skill in detection of minute changes in tone, pitch, intonation, and volume. After you have analyzed students' levels of discrimination, you can group them for instruction in small needs-based groups. Such instruction can include asking them to listen for 10 words that begin with a particularly difficult sound and to watch your mouth as you say this sound. Then, you can ask them to orally read a book that has several words containing a sound they need to discriminate into a tape recorder (e.g., students who need to discriminate the *b* sound could read *Brown Bear, Brown Bear* [Martin, 1973]). By playing back this tape, students who need this instruction can hear the differences between the *b* sound and other sounds. To verify that they hear this difference have them close their eyes so they cannot see others in the group and raise a hand when they hear the *b* sound on the tape. If students cannot yet read, you can do as Mr. Stone does and read the story into the tape for them. Then students listen and raise their hands for you as described above.

Mr. Stone's first-graders also enjoy imitating sounds, rhythms, and onomatopoeia (words that sound like their meanings). You'll find such sounds, rhythms, and words in books and records like *Cat Goes Fiddle-I-fee* (Wood, 1994); *Wheel Away* (Dodds, 1991); *Thump, Thump, and Rat-a-tat-tat* (Boer, 1989). Students can improve their auditory discrimination by reading aloud and listening to predictable books and poetry. Favorites for these students include *Poems for Two Voices* (Fleishman, 1988); and all those that are listed in Literature Card 6, Chapter 3. Young students also profit from writing about sounds in "sound stories" ("Z-Z-Z-Z roars the street car" for *z*, and "brrroom goes the truck" for *b* and *r*). Mr. Stone reads such books aloud and his students write the beginning sounds of the words.

LEVEL 3. ATTENDING TO A MESSAGE
Teaching Students to Pay Attention

Many students need to be taught how to pay attention. One of the first stages of auditory attention is **selective attention**. Selective attention involves the ability of the sensory register to filter sounds into the mental control processing for meaning schematic folder. Gans (1994) identified a number of variables that influence the degree to which children select one piece of information over another for processing. Among those variables are the intensity of the stimuli when they are presented; the number of times that they have heard a particular stimuli; the degree to which the stimuli are concrete rather than abstract; the amount of contrast or novelty involved in its presentation; and the speed with which the stimuli are presented. Because there is a constant bombardment of environmental noise in students' lives, the elements of greatest intensity, extensity, concreteness, contrast, and speed will receive priority attention. It is for these reasons that MTV and video games capture students' interest so completely.

To teach selective attention, you can select an audiocassette of someone reading a selection of children's literature. Before you begin the lesson you model how to set a purpose for listening by performing a think-aloud. You can perform this think-aloud for 3 consecutive days using different books that they will hear on tapes. The purposes for listening that you model include (1) answering a question on a topic about which you are curious, (2) gaining information to improve life, (3) evaluating the value of a selection, or (4) predicting the ending of, or author's purpose in writing, a selection. Then, you can have students choose the purpose they want to fulfill before you start the tape on the fourth day. On the fifth day, you can ask students to write or tell their own purposes for listening to a tape or book that you read. They can also describe why and how they set their purposes.

Students who are at least as old as the first-graders in Mr. Stone's class can also advance their attending skills by learning the 10 steps to becoming a good listener in Table 4.3. To teach these steps, find a picture in your textbook and describe it to the class. Your students will draw what is described. Compare their drawings to the picture you described.

When this activity is complete, you can ask students to engage in a second activity. Divide the class into five groups. Students in one group choose to use step 1

TABLE 4.3 STEPS TO BECOME A GOOD LISTENER: A GENERIC LISTENING GUIDE THAT CAN BE USED IN MANY SUBJECT AREAS AND CONVERSATION CLUBS

1. Anticipate a sequence of ideas and the elements of a work.

2. Show sensitivity to what others have to say.

3. Relate the ideas of others to your own ideas.

4. Understand that books and other media are concerned with people, places, things, and ideas.

5. As soon as you begin to listen, try to hear the sentence that tells what the subject is; ask yourself what the total focus of the person's talk is. Pick the most important details the person relates.

6. Pay close attention to all words that tell directions such as *north, south, east, west,* or *up, down, here, there, over, under, above.* As soon as you hear such a word, picture in your mind the effect that word has on the topic.

7. Listen for the words that signal order, such as *first, second, last, after, before,* and *also.* Try to put yourself in the place of the person speaking, and in your mind, perform the order of the activities he or she is describing.

8. As you listen, picture what is described. This mental picture will help you distinguish the most important details and how they relate to each other. As you hear each detail, tie it to the detail immediately preceding it. The person talking had a very important reason for putting these details together, and you need to think about what that reason is.

9. Pay special attention to words such as *and, or, but, yet,* and *because.* These words tell you how two ideas are related to each other.

10. Ask questions of the person talking to clarify the points being made.

from Table 4.3 as they anticipate a sequence of ideas in a book that you read aloud and then relate details to this main idea. Another group chooses to use step 2: showing sensitivity to what others have to say, and so on. Each group can practice a different listening strategy. For instance, a third group tries to relate other students' ideas to their own. A fourth group focuses on the people, places, things, and ideas in the book. They also try to explain why these details were included in the story. A fifth group listens to the main ideas in the book. When all group assignments have been made, you read the book. When the book is finished, each group presents their attending strategy to the class. Then each group writes about how their listening abilities improved because they learned all 10 strategies. Next, rotate groups until every student has practiced all 10 steps in Table 4.3.

A third lesson to increase students' ability to pay attention is called bracketing. **Bracketing** means to "file" some thoughts away and then return to think about them at a more appropriate time. Bracketing enables people to concentrate more completely on the task at hand. To teach it, you can perform a think-aloud of bracketing methods that you use, such as stopping to make a note when your mind begins to wander to a different topic, designating a specific time after school hours to think about a personal problem, and intentionally refocusing your mind on a topic when it begins to wander. Once you've modeled how these methods free your mind to concentrate on the speaker's message, you can ask students to select one of the strategies in Table 4.3. Then, you can request that they listen for 20 minutes and discuss the effects of bracketing on their ability to pay attention. You can also teach that if they find themselves thinking of what they want to say when they should be listening, they can "bracket" these thoughts by noting them on a sheet of paper, and then they can return to their listening with more focus and concentration.

In closing, if some students have a very difficult time attending, you can ask these students to discuss how they want to improve their listening. For instance, Meisong, Allison, and others in Mr. Stone's class, held such a discussion and posted in their room the following list of behaviors that they wanted to follow during class meetings, and at other listening times:

Listening Time

1. Look at the speaker
2. No put-downs
3. Ask questions
4. Concentrate

Mr. Stone also taught his class the following chant, which you can also ask your students to memorize and say frequently when they want to increase their ability to attend to a speaker's message:

My eyes are on the speaker that I see,

My mind is not on me;

My hands are folded as quiet as can be,

Because I'm listening perfectly!

Two games that children of all ages enjoy also can build their ability to pay attention. Students must be instructed to use the specific strategies listed in Table 4.3 before games begin. The first is call chain stories. A **chain story** is when someone in the class begins a story by introducing a character in a sentence. The second person in the circle describes the setting in which that character lives. The third person in the circle describes the time period in which the character is living. The next student in the circle adds a description of events. The story continues until the third person from the end of the circle holds up a red card and stops the series of events with a resolution or with an ending. Once that student holds up the red card, the last two students get to tell what happened as a result of the ending. After the first story is complete, students tend to add more details to their subsequent involvement in this activity.

A second activity, called the **Gossip Game,** is one that children enjoy equally well. Before starting, caution students that they will be assessed on how well they implement one or more of the steps in Table 4.3. At the end of the game, ask children to discuss how well they implemented the step and divide the class into groups of five. Gossip begins with student or teacher whispering a paragraph to the person next to them. That student in turn whispers the paragraph into the next person's ear. This continues until all five people in each group have heard the paragraph. The last person having heard the paragraph tells the first person what he or she heard. The group then discusses what could have been done to duplicate what they heard more perfectly.

After all groups have had a few moments for discussion, call the class back together again and have them report on what they will do to improve their listening abilities the second time the game is played. For the second game, and all subsequent games, the student must read a printed paragraph to the first person hearing the paragraph. This way, the student who tells the paragraph at the end can be monitored by the first student, who rereads the printed paragraph that began the game. The group that is the first to duplicate the exact paragraph wins.

LEVEL 4. BUILDING EFFERENT LISTENING ABILITIES
Teaching Students to Comprehend

Efferent listening comprehension is defined as behaviors used to understand speakers' meaning, categorize information, monitor one's own comprehension during listening, ask questions for clarification, follow sequential ideas, and take notes. The term *efferent* means to receive, attend, and comprehend with a predominant purpose of gaining new information, obtaining new facts and perspectives, and learning about content areas or subjects in books. This type of comprehension is contrasted with aesthetic comprehension in which you listen to learn more about yourself and others, to appreciate and enrich your life, or to empathize and affectively respond to others or situations (Rosenblatt, 1978).

To gain information most effectively, you can teach listening comprehension by helping students to (1) recognize and use the order of information being presented, (2) ask questions of themselves and the speaker, and (3) take notes. You can teach order by showing students how to place information in categories or columns that they write as they listen, by outlining, noting main points or phrases, or creating a semantic map.

By presenting book talks and preparing listening guides, students are encouraged to ask questions and develop their speaking and listening abilities.

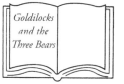

For example, before Mr. Stone read *Goldilocks and the Three Bears* aloud, he demonstrated how he organized information as he listened. He read the first two pages. Then, Mr. Stone said that in his mind he thought about each of the opening sentences he heard. He told how he knew that the author was introducing the most important characters in the story and that in both pages the story moved forward describing how Goldilocks saw what each member of the bear family did. He said that his mind recognized that the order this author used was to describe what each of the bears did and how Goldilocks discovered these things. Because he detected this, his comprehension improved. On each page as Mr. Stone read, he was looking for the discoveries that Goldilocks would make about Papa Bear, Mama Bear, and Baby Bear, in that order.

Last, to show students how they can order thoughts by making columns on a page, Mr. Stone wrote *Papa Bear, Mama Bear,* and *Baby Bear* at the top of an overhead acetate. As he and the class listened to the rest of the story, they wrote what they heard, in the order in which the events occurred. After everyone shared what they heard and wrote, Michael said: "This note-taking system can help me in social studies too."

To conclude this lesson, Mr. Stone also shows how students can improve their comprehension by asking themselves questions as they listen, such as "I'll listen to see if I get any clues." "Why don't I understand this?" "What can I do to understand it better?" "Should I take notes?"

Another method of building listening comprehension is to use listening guides (Castello, 1976). A **listening guide** is a partially completed outline created by a speaker to show listeners the relative importance of the speaker's points. Before the speech begins, you or the speaker can create and distribute a listening guide. Some guides require that students complete missing parts to an outline of the speech. Students also can create their own listening guides to accompany talks they give to a small group of classmates. Classmates can complete the guide while the speech is being delivered, and, when it is finished, the speaker can show the completed listening guide he or she made prior to the speech. When students compare their guides to the ones the speaker completed, it often leads to discussions of what they can do to improve their listening abilities.

The conversation club is another activity that builds efferent listening comprehension. As described in Chapter 3, you can place students in such groups based on topics they choose to discuss. As students converse freely for a few minutes about their topics, each writes about what a person in the group was doing to be an effective listener. At the end of the conversation club, students can also write objectives they want to achieve to strengthen their own efferent listening abilities in future meetings. These objectives can be saved and referred to before the next meeting. See Table 4.3 for an example of a listening guide made by a colleague of Mr. Stone's. This guide can be adapted for younger listeners.

Students can also build their efferent listening abilities by engaging in activities in which they have to follow complex directions. For example, one of Mr. Stone's favorite activities to develop students' listening comprehension is having them create origami projects. **Origami,** the traditional Asian paper-folding craft, involves making simple objects such as boats, birds, or flowers by folding brightly colored tissue paper. To begin this activity, Mr. Stone explains that learning to follow directions is a skill that can be developed through practice. Repetition helps the mind learn how to hear details precisely and consecutively. Mr. Stone then reads the directions for making an origami dove from the book *Origami Made Easy.* As he reads each direction, students fold their papers according to what they hear. After each direction, students show their partners the way they folded their papers. If there are differences between their work, they decide who folded the paper correctly and why; for example, they may determine that one word in the directions was not accurately heard. After the seven directions for the dove are completed, students divide into groups of four. One student in each group reads the directions for another origami object to other group members, who follow the directions step by step. After each project is complete, students show their origami objects to other groups and discuss what they learned about following directions, as well as hints they can suggest to improve future episodes of efferent listening.

Lastly, you can use videotapes or records that accompany children's literature to develop students' listening comprehension. To do so, you can play a videotape or record of a story that children have or have not heard before. Then you stop the recording before a significant event and ask students to tell you, based on all the details they have gathered from their listening, what the upcoming event is. Sources for records and videos for this activity follow:

- *All Ears* (a record series to develop listening comprehension), published by Penguin, 375 Hudson Street, New York, NY 10014-3657
- Records by Weston Woods, Weston, CT 06883
- Multimedia materials by Random House, 400 Hahn Road, Westminster, MD 21157
- Pied Piper, P.O. Box 320, Verdugo City, CA 91466
- The Listening Library, Inc., 1 Park Avenue, Old Greenwich, CT 06870-9978
- *Read with Me Books and Cassettes* (books and audiotapes for students), Mulberry Books, William Morrow, 105 Madison Ave., New York, NY 10016, (212) 889-3050
- Additional references in *Films and Filmstrips for Language Arts: An Annotated Bibliography*, 1111 W. Kenyon Road, Urbana, IL, 61801-9905, (217) 328-3870.

LEVEL 5. BECOMING AN ACTIVE LISTENER
Teaching Students to Invest Themselves in Listening

An **active listener** is someone who brings enthusiasm and energy to the listening process and invests part of him- or herself in sharing information, ideas, feelings, or dilemmas. Your students will learn to do so best when they participate in meaningful discovery discussions in which you actively listen to them. In such situations, they observe how you do not let distractions interfere with the oral exchange in which you are engaged. They will also observe how you question while listening to understand and build on each person's comments.

The degree to which students become active listeners is also based on students' personal interest, level of commitment, and the context in which they are listening. Students can increase their interest and commitment by talking about times when they had fun listening, such as when they were on the playground, hearing a good story being read, or listening to a presentation about a subject in which they were very interested. When students discuss these events, they learn how they invested themselves as they listened, by having new ideas, by having a desire to add to what they hear, and by realizing other people have the same thoughts that they have.

A second method of teaching active listening abilities is to invite a guest speaker to class. Before the presentation, you can teach students how to (1) listen for the speaker's goal, (2) identify three ideas that are important to that goal, (3) summarize, and (4) develop questions to ask the speaker, as described in the next section of this chapter.

Students' active listening abilities also improve when you ask interesting and challenging questions. To demonstrate, place yourself in the following scenario and attend to the type of thinking that each question elicits in your mind. The students in Teacher A's class were listening as she read the book *Cinderella*. Teacher A then asked the students: "What did the fairy godmother use to make the carriage?" "What did Cinderella lose at the ball?" and "What time was Cinderella supposed to leave the party?" As each of these questions were answered, fewer and fewer of her students became actively involved in listening. Alternatively, when Mr. Stone finished reading the same fairy tale he asked the following questions that increased students' active listening: "Why do you think Cinderella did not run away from her wicked stepmother?" "What is the difference between love at first sight and real love, and which type do you think the prince had and why?" The students began actively listening and investing themselves in the discussion. Mr. Stone also opened the discussion so students could ask their own questions. When he did so, Michael asked: "If everything else the fairy godmother gave to Cinderella turned back into its original form, why didn't the glass slipper change back as well?" All his students began enthusiastically to answer Michael's question! Students in Mr. Stone's class were more actively listening than the students in Teacher A's class because they wanted to know the answers to the questions asked. They wanted to invest themselves in listening because they were asked challenging, high-level, critical-thinking questions (as listed in Figure 3.3).

A third method of developing active listening is to use radio broadcasts. Radio broadcasts enable students to hear stories as they were told on the radio years ago. To begin this lesson, you can order a set of tapes of old broadcasts from Cassette Library, P.O. Box 5331, Baltimore, MD 21209; or from the *Tune-In Series,* Sunburst Communication, Pleasantville, NY 10570. These broadcasts include Sherlock Holmes's adventures; Superman episodes; The Shadow; Hopalong Cassidy, Gene Autry, and Lone Ranger western episodes; George Burns and Gracie Allen specials; and Jack Benny shows. You can divide students into small groups to listen to one broadcast and then enact and embellish it for classmates who did not hear it.

LEVEL 6. LISTENING APPRECIATIVELY AND REFLECTIVELY

Students who listen to appreciate the beauty and value of a language experience are listening appreciatively and reflectively. They listen, read, or think to savor the pleasure of a personal meaning (Rosenblatt, 1938, 1978, 1985). During aesthetic listening students form mental images, make comparisons to their lives, and become engrossed in the personal benefits they are receiving. As they hear what is said, sung, recited, dramatized, enacted, or discussed, they also take meaningful mental side trips. Their minds don't wander from the subject, but often reflect on a salient insight or resolution to a personal dilemma that emerged through the active listening in which they were engaged. An important distinguishing feature of reflective listening is that during these side trips, students do not lose the speaker's train of thought. They contemplate a personal response to the material they hear while simultaneously listening to the speaker's new information. The generic listening guide in Table 4.3 can assist students to do so with greater ease.

In closing this discussion, we have come full circle and return to reemphasize a principle stated in Chapter 1: That is, it is important to remember that you are the most important element in building students' listening ability. Often, best listening requires patience. If you include every student in your listening audience and demonstrate that their listening is important to you, most students will begin to share their ideas, feel more supported in their work, and value their classmates listening to them. As Duckworth stated, "It is a matter of being present as a whole person with your own thoughts and feelings. It is a matter of working very hard to find out what those thoughts and feelings are, as a starting point for developing a view of the world in which people are as much concerned about other people's security as they are about their own" (1987, p. 120). The following lessons improve all the levels of listening ability described above, and enable students to learn more from what others say for the rest of their lives.

SECTION 2   PUTTING THEORY INTO PRACTICE

Improving Students' Listening

Students do not significantly increase their listening abilities merely listening to others during the day. They do so by including the following activities in their language arts program. Without these lessons, most students develop only one listening strategy. They try to remember everything they hear, and often become confused as soon as they misunderstand a word or mishear a speaker's intent. To avoid these difficulties, the following lessons teach students to predict, question, detect propaganda, use purpose-posing journals, and engage in family story projects.

DIRECTED LISTENING THINKING ACTIVITY

The **directed listening thinking activity** (DLTA) is a lesson that teaches students to use the details they hear to predict what will occur next (Stauffer, 1980; Lundsteen, 1989). This lesson begins by asking students to survey and set a purpose for listening. Students then listen as you relate part of a story or pieces of information from a content area. You can stop at a point, in the series of information, at which students will have received enough information to make an accurate prediction and defend it. Then discuss why they heard or did not hear previous points in the message accurately, what distracted them, and which level of listening ability they will strengthen in the next DLTA activity.

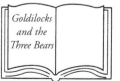

Goldilocks and the Three Bears

This activity has a counterpart called the directed reading thinking activity, or DRTA (Stauffer, 1969). This activity includes all the steps above but students read silently instead of listening. For example, Mr. Stone used *Goldilocks and the Three Bears* as a DRTA. After teaching students to use columns to categorize their thinking as they listened and read, he asked them to make predictions about what was going to happen next in *Goldilocks*. Then, he asked students to read silently to page 17, close their books, and write the ending they envisioned. Once predictions were made, students described the strategies they used to do so. Such fairy tales and first-person narratives are powerful genres to use as reading and listening materials for DLTA and DRTA lessons. Fairy tales are effective because their plots are predictable and the endings are characteristically happy. First-person narratives are also effective because students must attend to every detail to identify who the narrator is.

A first-person narrative can be used effectively at every grade level for DLTA lessons and in fourth through eighth grades in DRTA lessons (see Figure 4.3). In Figure 4.3 there are six points, marked by broken lines, at which students can stop to make predictions. To begin this lesson you cut this figure on the broken lines and give students one clue at a time to read. After students describe who they think the narrator is and why, you can provide the next clue. [The answers to Figure 4.3 appear in the Answer Key at the end of the book.] A list of six other books that can be divided easily for DLTA or DRTA lessons appears at the end of this chapter.

THE LANGUAGE EXPERIENCE APPROACH

The **language experience approach** (LEA) is one of the most effective methods of increasing listening abilities. It uses speaking, listening, reading, and writing abilities simultaneously to reinforce each other (Lee & Van Allen, 1963). The philosophy of this approach is that children who cannot read or write well can say what they think. After you write what they say, they can read what you wrote. Nessel and Jones (1991), who have written a book about using LEA to build listening abilities, recommend the following steps for such lessons:

Mondays: Discuss a stimulus event and write students' thoughts on a chart. Students illustrate or read more about the event, and the dictated story on the story chart is read repeatedly to strengthen their reading and listening vocabularies.

Tuesdays: Students reread the story they created Monday. Depending on the grade level, they either underline known words, circle new words, or use a thesaurus to add new words to sentences.

Wednesdays: You implement a lesson that students need based on the story, such as how to identify main ideas when speakers talk or how to decode words.

Thursdays: Older students design their own independent activity to build individual strengths by using the story as a common theme, and younger students practice the Wednesday lesson independently.

Fridays: Students engage in an alternative activity, such as preparing word cards for the new words learned from the story, creating challenges for classmates, or reviewing what they learned from the week's work.

As demonstrated in one of Mr. Stone's lessons, you can challenge students' thinking, listening abilities, and creativity during such LEA lessons, by asking respondent-centered questions:

Mr. Stone: [Saying playfully] Once, a long time ago, when your grandparents' parents were children, fish had feet. How many feet did they have?

Allison: Four!

Juan: Five!

Meisong: Six!

Michael: Eight!

Mr. Stone: Seven!

[Note to teacher: Cut on dotted lines after photocopying for students.]

CLUE #1

Lunch made me sleepy, so I curled up to take a nap. With sleep came a wonderful dream. I was stretched out on a lovely green lawn with the sun warming my body. Birds were singing gaily overhead, and little yellow daffodils peeked out through the grass. I reached out to touch one—and suddenly there was no sun.

A heavy shadow had shut out the light. Something grabbed me and I cried out, fighting to get free. It was no use; I was traveling through space. This was no dream. It was real. I had been captured, and there was nothing I could do about it.

- -

CLUE #2

Soon I felt something solid at my feet. I could move, but it was hard to stand. My legs felt limber. Where was I?

Cautiously, I stepped forward, OUCH! I bumped into a wall and again in the other direction, but every time there was a wall. Four walls and no door. I'm in a cell!

All of a sudden there was a blast of cold air from above. I looked up but could see nothing. Where was the air coming from? Suddenly I knew: there was no roof on my cell! I had discovered a way out.

- -

CLUE #3

Stepping carefully toward a wall, I attempted to reach the opening. I wasn't tall enough, so I sat down again to think. The cell was still rocking. Maybe I could throw myself against one of the walls and tip the cell over. Again and again I rushed the wall, but I finally gave up, defeated.

Sitting down, I tried to gather the energy for one more try. If that didn't work—Wait, the movement stopped!

A minute later I heard an earthshaking bang as I felt a different motion. My cell was moving up and down, not back and forth. I couldn't keep my balance. I said to myself I'd conquer whatever it was. I'd be ready. In an instant there was a horrible crunch, and the wall nearest me was ripped away. Beyond the opening I could see a dazzling light.

- -

CLUE #4

"Now's your chance," I told myself, cautiously crawling to the opening. At first, I saw nothing but a shiny wood floor. Then I saw *them*!

Feet! Giant feet! They seemed to surround me, so I quickly retreated. I could be ground to smithereens out there! Of course, that's what they were planning—that's why they made it easy for me to escape! Well, I'd fool them; I wouldn't move.

No, I couldn't stay. I had to try to get out.

- -

CLUE #5

Once again I crept to the opening, but the feet were still there. Then I noticed something else. Near two of the feet, four round posts rose from the floor. The posts were topped by a thick, low roof. I could easily squeeze under it, but those giant feet couldn't.

I took a deep breath and moved quickly. Racing out of my cell, I skidded under the thick roof. I made it! My legs felt like rubber again, but I was safe for a moment.

- -

CLUE #6

What would happen next? I wondered. I didn't have long to wait, however, for I heard voices high above the roof.

"Oh, Donald, she's afraid of us!"

"Well, naturally," came the reply. "That must have been a frightening trip for such a little _____."

FIGURE 4.3 DLTA OR DRTA STORY: READ ONE CLUE AT A TIME AND THEN PREDICT WHO THE NARRATOR IS

Michael: Nope. How would they walk?

Mr. Stone: [As he writes on the chart] Once, a long time ago, when your grandparents' parents were children, fish had feet. Some fish had four feet, some fish had five feet, some fish had six feet, no fish had seven feet, but some had eight. What did these fish wear?

Juan: Shoes . . .

Mr. Stone: What kind?

Juan: Blue ones because fish like the ocean.

Michael: Orange.

Mr. Stone: They like colors. I never saw blue, yellow, and orange shoes for fish. What were they made of?

Michael: Scales. And when they walked, they sounded *tick-tick.*

Mr. Stone: [Pointing to the language experience chart as all read it aloud] Once, a long time ago, when your grandparents' parents were children, fish had feet. Some fish had four feet, some fish had five feet, some fish had six feet, no fish had seven feet, but some fish had eight feet. The fish wore blue and orange shoes made of scales.

Mr. Stone: But! [dramatic pause and Mr. Stone gasps] But!

Michael: One didn't. [Michael quickly jumps in to add his creative ideas.]

Mr. Stone: One didn't what?

Michael: One fish didn't wear those shoes. Those scales on his feet. [long silence as Michael thought]

Mr. Stone: Why?

Michael: Because he had different kinds of feet. Round ones.

Mr. Stone: Hmmm. Fish with round feet. Hmmmm.

Juan: Oh! Hey, listen to me! They were round like a horse foot.

Michael: No, they were round like something else; it's my answer.

Juan: No, they were, uh, uh. He wore horse's shoes and when he walked he sounded like a brontosaurus walking. When he walked, he sounded like thunder!

Michael: Yes! [Juan and Michael high-fived their hands as the class cheered for the great ending to their language experience story.]

INTERVIEWING

Because interview talk shows have become such a popular television programming format, most students enter school already familiar with interviews and how adults conduct them. Good interviews blend a twelve-step, planned process and spontaneous questions posed after having completed extensive research on a topic. In addition, if students read *Mama and Her Boys* (1987) by Lee Hopkins before they begin this lesson, they can learn other listening strategies from the main character, a young boy who interviews the school's custodian for the school newspaper. From this encounter a special relationship develops. Similarly, students can learn from *The Kidnaping of Aunt Elizabeth* (Parte, 1995) how to interview relatives as they share stories about their youth.

TABLE 4.4 TEACHING STUDENTS HOW TO CONDUCT SUCCESSFUL INTERVIEWS

Name _____ Date _____

STEPS FOR CONDUCTING EFFECTIVE INTERVIEWS

1. State the purpose of the interview first. Tell the interviewee the purpose.

   The purpose is: _____

2. Begin with a question that seeks background information about the topic. This question builds trust between two people and increases the chances that they will better understand each other.

3. Next, ask for a description of an experience that led to the present problem. This description will be better if you use follow-up questions that begin with the words:

   How _____

   When _____

   Where _____

   What _____

   Who _____

   Why _____

4. Then, ask the person to give an example. This example will ensure that you understand the intent of the speaker.

5. Paraphrase what the person says if you aren't sure you understand what was said.

6. Ask for an interviewee's definition of simple words that could mean different things, such as *difficult, happy,* and *good.*

7. Listen carefully so you can follow up with a question that begins with one of the words in #3 above.

8. Spend at least 30 minutes reading information about the topic before you go to your interview.

9. Take notes in the spaces directly below each question so the interviewee will not have to wait too long while you write.

10. You may want to use a tape recorder, but first ask the interviewee if it is acceptable.

11. Write a thank-you note as a follow-up to the interview.

12. After each interview, critique yourself and find ways you can improve.

To begin, teach the steps to effective interviewing found in Table 4.4. As shown there, students are to ask whether they can tape-record the interviewee, are to have read about the topic, and are to have constructed at least six questions (as shown in item 3 of Table 4.4). As students read items 4–12, you can explain what they mean—such as paraphrasing and taking notes on a "questioning page." When students have no more questions, you can perform a mock interview of a colleague or principal, another adult, or a student to model the steps in the process.

Once this demonstration is complete, you can also ask students to analyze interviews by television newscasters or sports broadcasters based on the twelve steps in Table 4.4. Following this viewing, students profit from discussing the effective listening strategies that both the interviewer and interviewee used. When students are ready, they can conduct interviews about topics of interest to them. For example, first-graders in Mr. Stone's class interviewed family members to determine if they could remember what it was like when they were their age. These interviews also led into the Family Study Projects, which your students will likely enjoy, presented at the end of this chapter.

Throughout this process, students learned how not to ask too general a question during an interview or in life. For example, instead of asking, "What do you think about me?" they learned to ask force-choice questions, such as "Which of the following characteristics of our family are most important to you and why?" They also learned to ask comparative questions, such as, "In what way was _____ better than now?" and "How is this different from _____?"

A second type of interview your students will likely enjoy is oral histories. **Oral histories** are interviews with individuals who have survived an incident or participated in a historical event. Students can begin an oral history by researching a subject such as the Holocaust, the civil rights movement, the Vietnam War, or the history of their hometown. They interview people living in the area who had personal experiences with the topic, using approximately 20 questions about each person's experiences, perspectives, and interpretations of the event. When students add these firsthand data to their research to prepare for the interview, many come to view history as a living subject that involves not only famous but average people from all walks of life.

Before students begin oral history projects, they can read *Canon in the Courtyard Square: A Guide to Uncovering the Past* or *My Backyard History Book* by David L. Weitzman (1985, 1975). These books demonstrate how they can use their oral history interviews to gain data that will improve their community. In planning an oral history, students can work in groups and assume different responsibilities:

• One can create the questions for the interviews.

• One can make copies of the surveys.

• One can conduct the interview.

• One can compile the data from the completed surveys and write the first draft of the oral history.

• One can write a proposal to present the results and a plan for improving some aspect of their city to appropriate community officials.

Other ways to use interviews in the classroom to build students' listening abilities follow:

1. Create an interview center by having pictures of people in different occupations. The students choose a profession they are interested in and write questions for a mailed interview.

2. At the beginning of the school year, students can interview each other to become better acquainted with their classmates.

3. Students can write a talk show that has to do with what they are studying. For example, if they are doing a unit on bears, they can create a talk show in which they interview a zookeeper. This can be a culminating activity in which students present all the research they have completed during their interviews with different people related to their topic.

LISTENING TO DETECT PROPAGANDA

One of the most important active listening skills is the ability to detect propaganda. The following lesson helps students do so.

In the *Platonic Dialogue,* Plato wrote, "Seeking truth through discussion is better than through persuasion." **Propaganda** is a method of trying to persuade people to change their ideas or behavior by deliberately slanting ideas and information to further a person's own cause or to damage an opposing cause. This propagandized persuasion usually occurs subtly, through the propagandist's choice of words, which can have either good or bad connotations. For example, *conversationalist* and *chatterbox* have the same dictionary meaning, but the first is more positively interpreted than the second. Television advertisements and public speakers use at least 10 different propaganda statements that students can learn to recognize. You can share these, as described in Figure 4.4 either on an overhead transparency or as a handout. Once students have discussed these devices, you can explain how knowing about them can help overcome propaganda's harmful effects. Students can choose one or more of the following activities to reinforce their learning.

1. Examine articles from the editorial pages and/or advertisements from various newspapers and discuss each in terms of biases, radical ideas, and attempts at sensationalism. The same procedures can be used with magazine articles, pamphlets, and books.

2. Explore several books or articles by the same author to trace the origins of, or changes in, that author's interests, viewpoints, opinions, or causes.

3. Read two biographies about the same person. Check facts and sources and compare the objectivity of each, one to the other.

4. Watch television commercials to detect which types of propaganda devices are used.

INTEGRATING THE LANGUAGE ARTS

Your students can reinforce what they learned about listening by reading a book of their choice from Literature Cards 9 and 10. These books are designed for use in kindergarten through grade 8. These books contain main characters who use various strategies to improve their listening. Once students have finished reading their books, they can discuss different strategies their characters modeled. These books also contain poetry that students enjoy reading aloud.

DEVICE	EXAMPLE/ DESCRIPTION	DID AUTHOR USE?		EVIDENCE
1. Bandwagon 	claiming everyone is doing it: e.g., "Is your house the only one on the block not protected by Alpha Alarm?"	Yes ☐	No ☐	_____ _____
2. Repetition 	repeating favorable words: e.g., *bargain, best, first, sale*	Yes ☐	No ☐	_____ _____
3. Transfer 	transferring of feelings about one thing to another: e.g., "If you like your mother, you'll like our pie."	Yes ☐	No ☐	_____ _____
4. Testimonial 	famous person promoting something: e.g., "I'm a famous baseball star. I am strong because I eat Sugar Flakes cereal every morning."	Yes ☐	No ☐	_____ _____ _____
5. "Better Hurry" or "It's Free" 	convincing you that there is a good reason to take action immediately or that you can get something for nothing: e.g., "Better hurry, only a limited supply is available."	Yes ☐	No ☐	_____ _____
6. Glittering Generality 	using glowing words or phrases: e.g., "All patriotic citizens will agree . . ."	Yes ☐	No ☐	_____ _____
7. Name Calling 	referring to competitors as undesirables: e.g., "The greedy crooks at the other store just want your money. We want to help you."	Yes ☐	No ☐	_____ _____

FIGURE 4.4 TEACHING STUDENTS TO RECOGNIZE PROPAGANDA DEVICES

The books on Literature Card 10, in particular, develop students' abilities to discriminate letter sounds and sounds in the environment. If you read these books aloud, students can repeat individual words and write them down. This integration

Literature Card 9

CHILDREN'S LITERATURE THAT DEMONSTRATES THE NEED FOR AND METHODS OF LISTENING EFFECTIVELY

Listen Rabbit by A. Fisher, 1964 Crowell, New York

Sounds of a Summer Night by M. Garelick, 1963 Young Scott Books, New York

Henry and the Monstrous Din by R. Hoban, 1967 World's World, New York

Morning, Noon, and Nighttime Too by L. Hopkins, 1980 Harper & Row, New York

The Silent Concert by M. Leister, 1970 Merrill, New York

If You Listen by C. Zolotow, 1990 Harper Audio, New York

A Friend Can Help by T. Berger, 1979 Macdonald, New York

What Is That Sound? by Mary O'Neill, Macmillan, New York

The Silly Listening Book by J. Slepian & A. Seidler, 1967 Follett, New York

The City Noisy Book, The Country Noisy Book, and other noisy books by M. Brown, 1994 Trophy, New York

Kartusch by S. Cosgrove, 1984 Fernandez, New York

Gossip by J. Pienkowski, 1990 Random House, New York

Horton Hears a Who by Dr. Seuss, 1982 Random House, New York

The Other Way to Listen by B. Baylor & P. Parnall, 1978 Scribner, New York

High Sounds, Low Sounds by F. Branley, 1975 Crowell, New York

Is Anyone Listening? by W. Carley, 1974 Garrard, New York

Listen! And Help Tell the Story by B. Carlson, 1965 Abingdon Press, New York

That Man Is Talking to His Toes by J. Hann, 1976 Four Winds, New York

Small Boy Is Listening by H. Zemach, 1959 Houghton Mifflin, Boston

The Listening Walk by P. Shower, 1994 Scott Foresman, New York

The Listening Book by D. Safier, 1952 Caxton Printers, New York

Kermit's Mixed-Up Message by J. Barkan, 1987 Scholastic, New York

Sounds of Home (Series) by B. Martin, Jr., 1966 Holt, New York

of the language arts will strengthen their auditory and reading abilities as well as their speaking, listening, and writing vocabularies.

FAIRY TALES AS A VALUABLE RESOURCE IN LISTENING DEVELOPMENT

Fairy tales are fast paced, have dramatic and exciting plots, contain easily identifiable good and bad characters, and are one of the favorite types of literature of first-graders. In a review of research, Norton (1993) found that whereas fairy tales appeal to students of many ages:

1. Children's interest in fairy tales emerges at the preschool age and peaks between the ages of 6 and 8;

2. After age 8, interest in fairy tales gradually declines as curiosity about realistic fiction escalates; and

3. Young children particularly enjoy listening to, reading, and giving their opinions about fairy tales because they believe in magic, that animals have consciousness much like humans, that wrongdoing should be punished, and that good behavior should be rewarded.

Literature Card 10

POETRY BOOKS TO INCREASE LISTENING ABILITY

Good Books for Kindergartners and First-Graders

Hard to Be Six by A. Adoff, 1991 Lothrop

OUTside INside Poems by A. Adoff, 1981 Lothrop

Make a Circle, Keep Us In by A. Adoff, 1975 Delacorte

Think of Shadows by L. Moore, 1988 Macmillan

I Feel the Same Way by L. Moore, 1967 Atheneum

ABCDEFGHIJKLMNOPQRSTUVWXYZ by K. Kuskin, 1963 Harper & Row

Soap Soup by K. Kuskin, 1992 HarperCollins

Listen to a Shape by M. Brown, 1979 FranklinWatts

Let Them Be Themselves by L. B. Hopkins, 1992 HarperCollins

Through Our Eyes by L. B. Hopkins, 1992 Little, Brown

Under the Sun and the Moon and Other Poems by M. W. Brown, 1993 Hyperion Books

Listen, Children, Listen: An Anthology of Poems for the Very Young by M. C. Livingston, 1972 Harcourt

Something New Begins by L. Moore, 1982 Atheneum

Fresh Paint by E. Merriam, 1986 Macmillan

Good Books for Second- and Third-Graders

Today We Are Brother and Sister by A. Adoff, 1981 Lothrop

Little Raccoon and Poems from the Woods by L. Moore, 1975 McGraw Hill

I Thought I Heard the City by L. Moore, 1969 Atheneum

All My Shoes Come in Two's by M. A. Hoberman, 1957 Little, Brown

Click, Rumble, Roar: Poems about Machines by L. B. Hopkins, 1987 HarperCollins

I'm Mad at You by W. Cole, 1978 HarperCollins

Rainbow Writing by E. Merriam, 1976 Atheneum

Out in the Dark and Daylight by A. Fisher, 1980 HarperCollins

The Child as a Poet: Myth or Reality? by M. C. Livingston, 1984 Horn Book

Flamboyan by A. Adoff, 1988 Harcourt Brace Jovanovich

All the Small Poems by V. Worth, 1987 Farrar, Strauss & Giroux

The Kite That Braved Old Orchard Beach: Year Round Poems for Young People by X. J. Kennedy, 1991 McElderry/Macmillan

Good Books for Fourth- and Fifth-Graders

Tornado! by A. Adoff, 1977 Delacorte

Always Wondering: Some Favorite Poems of Aileen Fisher, 1991 HarperCollins

The Philharmonic Gets Dressed by K. Kuskin, 1982 Harper & Row

Fathers, Mothers, Sisters, Brothers: A Collection of Family Poems by M. A. Hoberman, 1991 Little, Brown

Creatures by L. B. Hopkins, 1985 Harcourt Brace Jovanovich

Don't You Turn Back: Poems by Langston Hughes by L. B. Hopkins, 1969 Alfred A. Knopf

Who Shrank My Grandmother's House: Poems of Discovery by B. J. Esbensen, 1992 HarpC Child Books

Why Am I Grown So Cold?: Poems of the Unknowable by M. C. Livingston, 1982 Atheneum

Climb into the Bell Tower: Essays on Poetry by M. C. Livingston, 1990 HarperCollins

I Am the Running Girl by A. Adoff, 1979 Harper & Row

Sam's Place: Poems from the Country by L. Moore, 1973 Atheneum

Working in the Dark: Reflections of a Poet of the Barrio by J. S. Baca, 1992 Red Crane Books

Independent Voices by E. Merriam, 1968 Atheneum

Oh Such Foolishness by W. Cole, 1991 HarperCollins

Good Books for Sixth-, Seventh-, and Eighth-Graders

If You're Not Here, Please Raise Your Hand: Poems about School by K. Dakos, 1990 Macmillan

Old Possum's Book of Practical Cats by T. S. Eliot, 1967 Harcourt Brace Jovanovich

Joyful Noise: Poems for Two Voices by P. Fleischman, 1988 Harper & Row

Birches by R. Frost, 1988 Henry Holt

Looking for Your Name: A Collection of Contemporary Poems by P. B. Janeczko, 1993 Orchard

The Trees Stand Shining: Poetry of the North American Indians by H. Jones, 1993 Dial

Sports Pages by A. Adoff, 1986 J. B. Lippincott

My Friend's Got This Problem, Mr. Candler: High School Poems by M. Glenn, 1991 Clarion Books

Back to Class: Poems by MellGlenn, 1988 Clarion Books

Black Mesa Poems by J. S. Baca, 1989 New Directions

If I Could Only Tell You: Poems for Young Lovers and Daydreamers by E. Merriam, 1983 Alfred A. Knopf

Poems: The Dreamkeeper and Other Poems by L. Hughes, 1994 Knopf

Poem-Making: Ways to Begin Writing Poetry by M. C. Livingston, 1991 HarperCollins

All the Colors of the Race by A. Adoff, 1982 Lothrop

The thematic unit at the end of this chapter models how fairy tales can be used to increase listening abilities and other language arts skills. Moreover, Table 4.5 lists various versions of many popular fairy tales so students can (1) listen to various versions of the same fairy tale and discuss their differences; (2) reenact various plots to emphasize cultural influences reflected in each; (3) hold reading workshops to respond to a version of their choice; and (4) explore what features distinguish fairy tales from other genres.

INSIDE ACADEMICALLY DIVERSE CLASSROOMS

Oral and Written Language Learning Disabilities

New materials are being developed to address these special students' needs. Among them are the (a) Read and Stamp program in Tampa, Florida (Halem, 2000); (b) Lepria's Touch and Learn program in Lincoln, Massachusetts (Hook & Marsh, 1992); (c) Caption Vision from the Consumer Electronics Group of Electronic Industries Association (Koskinen, 1993); (d) Text Sets; (e) Running Start from the Reading Is Fundamental (RIF) program in Washington, D.C.; and (f) many early language development tutorial programs for less able readers, such as Reading Recovery and the America Reads program, which are described in more depth in discussions of remedial readers' special needs in Chapter 6.

The Read and Stamp program enables children to select the stamp that corresponds to the noun in a story, so that when they read a sentence they can stamp a blank with a picture of the word that should appear there. For example, if their story is about a black dog running to a house, they would select a stamp and stamp a picture of a dog in the first blank, and stamp a picture of a house in the last blank. These materials enable students, with a good oral language background, to translate oral words into printed symbols.

The Touch and Learn program assists students who have oral language learning difficulties to develop vocabulary and word attack skills. It is designed to diagnose specific phonetic and phonic decoding problem areas and to provide additional training so that students can begin to reinforce their automatic oral and written word recognition skills. Touch and Learn is a software program that spans a wide range of learning differences for beginning students. Students can advance at their own pace. They touch the computer screen to answer oral and written questions.

The Caption Vision program was created so that students can see words printed on the television screen as they hear them. This is an effective tool for building reading, language, and comprehension skills, expanding vocabulary, and improving students' spelling and punctuation (Beentjes & Van Der Voort, 1988; Goldman & Goldman, 1988; Koskinen, 1993).

The Text Set program is an approach to instruction in which books of various readability level (that relate to a common topic) are studied. Text sets enable students at various levels of reading proficiency to read independently about a subject. Teachers also read books orally to children with reading difficulties to build their listening vocabulary so that this background knowledge assists in the decoding and comprehension of the next book. Some sets contain the same main characters in

CINDERELLA

Ashpet: An Appalachian Tale by J. Compton, 1994, Holiday
Cinderella by A. Ehrlich, 1985, Dial
Cinderella by C. Perrault, 1970, Viking
Cinderella by J. Grimm, 1976, Little Brown
Cinderella by M. Brown, 1980, Aladdin
Cinderella by P. Galdone, 1978, McGraw Hill
The Egyptian Cinderella by S. Climo, 1989, Crowell
Korean Cinderella by E. Adams, 1990, Dial
The Korean Cinderella by S. Climo, 1993, HarperCollins
Moss Gown by W. Hooks, 1987, Clarion
Mufaro's Beautiful Daughters: An African Tale by J. Steptoe, 1987, Lothrop
Prince Cinders by B. Cole, 1987, Putnam
Princess Furball by C. Huck, 1989, Greenwillow
Sydneyrella and the Glass Slipper by B. Myers, 1987, Macmillan
Tatterhood and Other Tales by B. J. Phelps, 1978, Feminist
That Awful Cinderella by A. Granowsky, 1995, Steck Vaughn
The Paper Bag by R. Munsch, 1983, Annick
The Rough-Face Girl by R. Martin, 1992, Putnam
The Turkey Girl: A Zuni Cinderella Story by P. Pollock, 1996, Little, Brown
Yeh-Shen by A. Louise, 1990, Putnam

JACK AND THE BEANSTALK

Jack and the Bean Tree by G. Haley, 1990, Viking
Jack and the Beanstalk by B. S. de Regniers, 1985, Atheneum
Jack and the Beanstalk by D. Johnson, 1976, Little, Brown
Jack and the Beanstalk by J. Jacobs, 1992, Aladdin
Jack and the Beanstalk by L. Cauley, 1983, Putnam
Jack and the Beanstalk by S. Kellogg, 1989, Dial
Jack and the Beanstalk by W. de la Mare, 1984, Holt
Jack and the Beanstalk Incident by T. Palusen, 1990, Ariel Books
Jack and the Beanstalk: Giants Have Feelings, Too by A. Granowsky, 1996, Steck Vaughn
Jack and the Giant: A Story Full of Beans by J. Harris, 1997, Rising Moon
Jack and the Wonder Beans by J. Still, 1997, Putnam

THE OLD LADY WHO SWALLOWED A FLY

I Know an Old Lady by A. Mills and R. Bonne, 1961, Rand McNally
I Know an Old Lady Who Swallowed a Fly by Westcott, 1980, Little, Brown
There Was an Old Woman by A. Jackson, 1997, Dutton
There Was an Old Woman by S. Kellogg, 1980, Four Winds

THE GINGERBREAD BOY

The Bun: A Tale from Russia by M. Brown, 1972, Harcourt Brace Jovanovich
The Gingerbread Boy by H. Ziefert, 1995, Viking.
The Gingerbread Boy by P. Galdone, 1975, Seabury
The Gingerbread Man by J. Aylesworth, 1998, Scholastic

The Gingerbread Rabbit by R. Jarrell, 1964, Collier
Journey Cake, Ho! by R. Sawyer, 1953, Viking
The Pancake Boy: An Old Norwegian Folk Tale by L. B. Cauley, 1988, Putnam
The Runaway Pancake by P. C. Asbjorsen and J. Moe, 1980, Larousse
You Can't Catch Me! by J. Oppenheim, 1986, Houghton Mifflin

THE THREE LITTLE PIGS

The Fourth Little Pig by T. Celsi, 1992, Steck Vaughn
The Three Little Javelinas by S. Lowell, 1992, Northland
The Three Little Pigs by G. Bishop, 1989, Scholastic
The Three Little Pigs by J. Marshall, 1989, Dial
The Three Little Pigs by M. Zemach, 1988, Farrar, Straus, & Giroux
The Three Little Pigs by P. Galdone, 1970, Seabury
The Three Little Wolves and the Big Bad Pig by E. Trivizas, 1993, McElderry
The True Story of the Three Little Pigs! by J. Scieszka, 1989, Viking

GOLDILOCKS AND THE THREE BEARS

Bears Should Share!: Goldilocks and the Three Bears by A. Granowsky, 1995, Steck Vaughn
Deep in the Forest by B. Turkle, 1976, Dutton
Goldilocks and the Three Bears by L. B. Cauley, 1981, Putnam
Goldilocks and the Three Hares by H. Petach, 1995, Putnam
Somebody and the Three Blairs by M. Tolhurst, 1990, Orchard
The Three Bears by P. Galdone, 1972, Clarion

LITTLE RED RIDING HOOD

Little Red Cap by J. Grimm, 1983, Little, Brown
Little Red Cap by L. Zwerger, 1983, Morrow
Little Red Riding Hood by J. S. Goodall, 1988, McElderry
Little Red Riding Hood by P. Galdone, 1974, McGraw-Hill
Little Red Riding Hood by T. S. Hyman, 1983, Holiday House
Little Red Riding Hood: The Wolf's Tale by D. Rowland, 1991, Citadel
Lon Po Po: A Red-Riding Hood Story from China by E. Young, 1989, Philomel
Red Riding Hood by B. S. de Regniers, 1972, Atheneum
Red Riding Hood by J. Marshall, 1987, Dial
Ruby by M. Emberley, 1990, Little, Brown

THE PRINCESS AND THE FROG

A Frog Prince by Z. Berenzy, 1989, Henry Holt
The Frog Prince by E. H. Tarcov, 1974, Scholastic
The Frog Prince by E. Isele, 1984, Crowell
The Frog Prince Continued by J. Scieszka, 1991, Viking
Pondlarker by F. Gwynne, 1990, Simon & Schuster
The Princess and the Frog by R. Isadora, 1989, Crowell

every book, and some sets describe subtopics within a content area or unit. Examples of these text set books are shown in Table 4.6.

The Running Start program is a 10-week intervention designed for first-grade children. Children with oral or written language learning difficulties are challenged to read 21 books (or to have the same number of books read to them orally) during a 10-week period. At the outset of this program, a private foundation called Reading Is Fundamental (RIF) donated as many as 80 books to the library of each teacher in the Running Start program. Over a 10-week period, parents and older children visit the classroom on a regular basis to assist teaching reading and writing to children who have oral language learning difficulties. Before the 10 weeks is over, many children are able not only to read these books to themselves, but to listen with greater intensity as other children read books to them. Information about this

TABLE 4.6 SERIES BOOKS AND TEXT SETS FOR PRESCHOOL TO MIDDLE SCHOOL READERS

SERIES BOOKS

Series books are easy readers because the reader builds up a store of information about the characters and the author's style that makes the decoding and comprehension of subsequent books in the series more predictable.

N. Bridwell's *Clifford, the Big Red Dog* series, Scholastic
M. Rey's *Curious George,* Scholastic
Mercer Mayer's *Little Critters,* Scholastic
Pat Reilly Giff's *The Polk Street School Kids,* Dell
Judy Delton's *Pee Wee Scouts,* Dell
Else Minarik's *Little Bear* books, Harper & Row
Cynthia Rylant's *Henry and Mudge* books, Macmillan
James Marshall's *George and Martha* books, Sandpiper

TEXT SETS

The Broadway Ballplayers Series by Maureen Holohan (1998). The Broadway Ballplayers, Inc. (P.O. Box 597, Wilmette, IL 60091, 1-888-LET ME PLAY [1-888-538-6375]. #1 Friday Nights by Molly (1997); #2 Left Out by Rosie (1998); #3 Everybody's Favorite by Penny (1998); #4 Don't Stop by Angel (1998); #5 Sidelines Blues by Will.

Francine Pascal's Sweet Valley Jr. High Series (1999). Bantam Books (1540 Broadway, New York, NY 10036). *Get Real.* Jamie Suzanne.

The Wolfbay Wings Series. Bruce Books. Laura Geringer/HarperCollins. (10 East 53rd, New York, NY 10022, USA). #1 Woodsie (1997); #2 Zip (1997); #3 Cody (1997); #6 Shark (1998); #7 Billy (1998). ISBN 0-06-027899-4. 94pp.

Thumbprint Mystery Series (1998). Contemporary Books (4255 West Touhy Avenue, Lincolnwood, IL 60646-1975, USA). 30 softcover books.

Voyager: Reading and Writing for Today's Adults (1999). New Readers Press (U.S. Publishing Division of Laubach Literacy, Department S99, P.O. Box 888, Syracuse, NY 13210-0888, 1-800-448-8878). Nine levels of readers, workbooks, and teaching guides. Prices vary.

Basic Life Skills at Work: The Factory Mystery (1997). Micro-Intel Inc. (1200, Papineau, Suite 301, Montreal, PQ H2K 4R5, Canada).

program can be obtained from RIF, Smithsonian Institution, Room 500, 600 Maryland Avenue SW, Washington, DC 20024.

Several definitions of specific literacy difficulties have been proposed, but the definition created by the National Advisory Committee on Handicapped Children in 1999 is the most widely accepted. This definition reads:

> Children with special (specific) learning disabilities exhibit a disorder in one or more of the basic psychological processes involved in understanding or in using spoken or written language. These may be manifested in disorders of listening, thinking, talking, reading, writing, spelling, or arithmetic. (p. 3)

There are immediate signs that a learning disability may exist. One is, in misspelling a word, students do not misspell it the same way twice. Another is when students cannot repeat sentences in order even though they can repeat single words in proper order. Some students need special programs such as those above before their oral and written language abilities can improve. When these programs are implemented as early as first grade, their effects can be most dramatic.

Literacy differences can begin in the motor, sensory, or cranial regions of the peripheral nervous system. It is important to remember that just because an individual's language learning can best develop through alternative oral learning programs does not mean that it cannot culminate in abilities just as powerful as those of students whose competencies develop through traditional instructional approaches. The easiest and most effective modification in the classroom for students with special academic language learning needs is to allow extra learning time. One way to do so is with computers. Pairing two students at a computer enables a student with learning differences to brainstorm orally with a partner before beginning to write or read. Another benefit of the computer is the tactile experience. When students type ideas, the motor and the sensory avenues in their cognitive processing unite more rapidly. In this way, their words more easily attach to their mental processes. Moreover, when their brainstorming segment is printed out, students with learning differences have something tangible they can use to group common ideas together.

Similarly, older students with language learning difficulties may take hours to respond to one essay question. If necessary, this extra time should be allowed. Some benefit from writing ideas on individual note cards. By laying the note cards in front of them, they can find the most logical organization of their thoughts. Unless they can manipulate information with their hands, their writing will only reflect a small portion of their knowledge. Students with listening difficulties benefit from reading materials and taking tests apart from the rest of their class. In this way, they can read the material out loud or to themselves without feeling self-conscious. In this setting, they can also read questions to a tutor who can verify that they read each word in the question correctly (Lee & Jackson, 1992).

RECOGNIZING AND REPORTING PROGRESS

Rating Scales to Assess Oral Language Arts Processes

Rating scales are assessment instruments that rank language arts objectives on a continuum. These assessments are particularly valuable for rapidly moving, oral language arts processes. Two examples follow, and several others (ready-to-be-used assessment rating scales of other oral and written language processes) can be printed for your use from the website that was created to accompany this textbook. Figure 4.5 is an example of one rating scale on which students' speaking abilities are ranked from 1 to 5. Figure 4.6 assesses three language arts processes and demonstrates how students can self-evaluate their own speaking and listening abilities.

The benefits of rating scales are that students' language abilities can be measured against their own best past performances. They also enable students' strengths in speaking, listening, and other language arts processes to be championed even when areas for improvement exist.

SECTION 3   TEACHERS AS CONTINUAL LEARNERS

Listening to Students, Their Stories, and Their Voices

> *To understand children we must hear their words, follow their explanations, understand their frustrations, and listen to their logic.*   —Ferreiro and Teberosky (1982)

To become a more effective listening teacher, you can do the following activities that not only can enhance your listening abilities, but simultaneously can enable students to strengthen theirs. Truly listening to students is a skill *and* an art. You can increase your skills by practicing to listen to students' stories as if every word a student says to you is the most important word that they have ever said. Having this mental framework can focus your attention more completely on the total messages that students are communicating, in their entirety, including the desire that generated subtleties and implied meanings which can hide behind students' words. When you receive the full intent of students' words, you have listened to **students' voices.** Student voices can be defined as the values, prior experiences, and purposes that surround the oral message that a child is delivering and the child's unique interpretations and style of orally expressing who he or she is. When you understand the story and the child's voice simultaneously, you have elevated your listening skills to an art form. In the following professional development activity, you can increase your skills in telling stories and in helping students to tell better stories and enhance their abilities to express their voices.

PROFESSIONAL DEVELOPMENT ACTIVITY

Storytelling

Stories rarely lay out all the facts, events, and ideas in a step-by-step fashion as occurs in textbooks. Instead, stories are constructed with suspense, plot buildups, surprising twists and turns, and multiperspective accounts that become memorable to the listener or reader (Wiggins & McTighe, 1998). Because a narrative "whatever their medium . . . words, films, oral recitations . . . holds the interest of an audience by raising questions in their minds and delaying the answers" (Lodge, 1992, p. 14),

STUDENT SELF-ASSESSMENT FOR GROUP WORK DURING CONSENSUS BUILDING

Name _____   **Date** _____

Put an "x" on the line at the point that best describes your involvement today in your group.
5 means "the whole time" and 1 means "not at all."

1. I offered my opinion to the group.   5   4   3   2   1

2. I responded to others' statements or opinions.   5   4   3   2   1

3. I feel that I need to work on _____ .

4. A group skill I think I am good at is _____ .

5. Overall, the grade I think I deserve today is _____ .

ASSESSMENT OF EFFECTIVE CONVERSATIONAL SKILLS

RULES FOR GOOD DISCUSSIONS:	MICHAEL	ALLISON	MEISONG	IVAN	GROUP AS A WHOLE
1. Listened to others well	✓	✓			✓
2. Thought before they talked	✓	✓			✓
3. Talked effectively and in a normal voice	✓		✓	✓	
4. Stuck to the subject	✓	✓	✓	✓	✓
5. Did not put down someone's idea	✓	✓	✓	✓	✓
6. Took turns well	✓	✓	✓	✓	✓
7. Encouraged everyone to participate	✓	✓	✓		
8. Asked questions	✓	✓	✓	✓	✓
9. Did not interrupt a person speaking	✓	✓			

(Conversations become higher level.)

The progress I think the group made in having a good conversation is that _____

_____ .

For the most part all group members were able to hold conversations about their picture without any help. Occasionally I asked an open-ended question that led to more discussion. General rules for moving thoughts to higher levels in group conversations have not been learned. I will plan a lesson to address this need.

FIGURE 4.5 EXAMPLES OF HOW RATING SCALES CAN BE USED TO ASSESS SPEAKING, LISTENING, AND COOPERATIVE GROUP SKILLS

NAME ___Michael___   SCHOOL ___Lad___

PRIMARY GRADES STUDENT SELF-EVALUATION

I WAS A GOOD SPEAKER   **RATING SCALE**

1. I spoke so everyone could hear me.   1   2   3   4   (5)
2. I looked at people when I spoke to them.   1   2   3   (4) 5
3. I contributed my fair share to the discussion.   1   2   3   4   5
    more than I should have   Why?   I saad de mst
    [I said the most]

    less than I should have   Why?

4. I feel people in the group paid attention to what I said. 1   2   3   4   (5) YES
5. I was afraid to talk during the discussion.   NO   (1) 2   3   4   5

I WAS A GOOD LISTENER

6. I listened to each student.   1   2   3   4   (5)
7. I looked at each speaker.   1   2   3   (4) 5
8. I did not interrupt other speakers.   1   (2) 3   4   5
9. I thought about what others said.   1   2   3   4   (5)

I SHARED MY IDEAS WELL

10. I had read the book.   1   2   3   4   (5)
11. I explained my ideas clearly.   1   2   3   4   (5)
12. I backed up my ideas with reasons.   1   2   3   4   (5)
13. I helped keep the discussion on the topic.   1   2   3   4   (5)
14. I was prepared for the discussion.   1   2   3   4   (5)
15. I think that everyone could understand my ideas.   1   2   3   4   (5)
16. I took notes and listened actively.   1   2   (3) 4   5
17. I built on other students' ideas ("piggy-backed").   1   2   (3) 4   5
18. I examined ideas before accepting or rejecting them.   1   2   (3) 4   5
19. When I disagreed, I backed up my reasons with   1   2   3   4   (5)
    information from the book.

FIGURE 4.6 EXAMPLES OF A STUDENT SELF-ASSESSMENT RATING SCALE OF SPEAKING AND LISTENING

it engages students' learning more actively than other types of instruction. Through their illogical and sequential format, they are easier to recall than textbook accounts:

> We do not easily remember what other people have said if they do not tell it in the form of a story. We hear, in the stories of others, what we personally can relate to by virtue of having in some way heard or experienced that story before ourselves. (Schank, 1990, p. 83)

Storytelling is relating a tale to listeners through voice and gesture. It differs from reading aloud or reciting poetry because storytellers use the responses of the audience to tailor a story to match their audience's interests. Storytelling, as an ancient language arts form, has survived precisely because of its personalized and interactive nature (National Council of Teachers of English, 1995).

Storytelling binds generations together to help us solve problems, make sense of the world, and communicate community values. It is therapeutic for both speakers and their listeners. When students hear your stories, stories about other people's lives, and literary stories, they (1) receive a framework for their language development, (2) hear multiple perspectives, (3) subtleties of meanings, and (4) learn how to emphasize certain points. Moreover, when you tell stories about your past, you model how to use sensory details to retrieve and relate vivid memories. Listening to stories also sharpens children's perception of the importance of details in all language arts, especially when you instruct them to "observe natural storytelling taking place around them each day, and to note how people use gestures, facial expressions, body language, and variety in tone of voice to get stories across" (NCTE, 1995, p. 2).

One of the most beneficial methods of developing students' listening abilities is to welcome and celebrate the stories that they tell about their lives. "From the stories we hear as children we inherit the ways we talk about how we feel, the values we hold to be important, and what we regard as truth" (Meek, 1992, p. 105). To illustrate, I would like to turn to the importance that such stories had in the lives of two famous children's authors: Roald Dahl and Patricia Polacco. Roald Dahl hated school until a woman began coming to visit his English boarding school. This woman came once a week and told stories to children. It is this volunteer storyteller that Roald Dahl credits for leading him to his writing ability and his desire to create many well-loved children's books such as *Charlie and the Chocolate Factory.* Similarly, Patricia Polacco was 5 years old when her grandmother died. She always remembered the stories that her grandmother told her. Today, Patricia is a well-known author of numerous children's books like *The Keeping Quilt.* Most of these stories are family stories that her grandmother shared with her.

When you listen to students' stories you can help them shape and reshape their lives and imagine what could have or should have happened. As an example, Dyson and Genishi (1994) shared the experience of a first-grader, who told a story about a starfish in his bathtub. In sharing this story, Anthony cast himself as a student experienced with starfish and as a family member. By telling this story and having a teacher who appreciated it, he was also able to enter into an ongoing classroom dialogue in which he could be accepted and appreciated by his peers:

Anthony: One time, um, I saw a little baby starfish in the tub.

Teacher: Oh my goodness! Did someone put it in there to play with you?

Anthony: No. It just came out of the drainer. [The other children laughed, but Anthony was quite serious.]

Teacher: One thing we just learned about starfish is that they live in what kind of water, salt water or fresh water?

Children: Salt water!

Anthony: It was in the fresh water.

Teacher: I don't think I ever heard of a freshwater starfish.

Shawnda: A starfish came up the drain! [with great amusement]

Anthony: I picked it up and showed it to my mommy and then it started moving.

Shawnda: A STARFISH CAN'T COME UP NO DRAIN!

Teacher: It's an amazing story, Anthony. [said with appreciation; and Anthony, who has been quite distressed by the laughing, smiles contentedly]

Shawnda: I TELL YOU . . .

Teacher: Shawnda, I know. I know that, and you know that, but Anthony needs his story.

Anthony smiled at Shawnda, quite agreeing with his teacher (adapted from Dyson & Genishi, 1994, p. 1).

As a teaching tool, stories are one of the best vehicles for passing on factual information because, as already described, data lingers longer in children's minds when presented in narrative. Familiarity with storytelling can become a valuable prerequisite for understanding text (O'Keefe, 1994). The more practice students have in telling and hearing stories, the easier their task becomes when they read stories, especially ones that contain flashbacks, interior monologues, and embedded information (Gersten & Dimino, 1990; Roney, 1996). They learn to question characters' personalities and motives, obstacles, expected outcomes, and themes best by listening and telling stories (O'Keefe, 1994).

Finally, storytelling can become a survival technique for students who do not feel as competent as their peers in reading or writing. Their comfort in the oral mode can become the path they use to reach the written modality. Moreover, community bonds are formed when stories are told: "Shelly tells the story of how her grandmother cooks chitlins for Thanksgiving dinner, Billy tells about doing detective work to retrieve his stolen bike, and the teacher tells about the horror she felt when she fell on the subway" (Pierce & Gilles, 1993, p. 47). Everybody belongs when the classroom is a place where everyone listens to everyone else's stories. In your storytelling lesson you can:

1. Ask a librarian to model storytelling.

2. Have students select a story they want to tell from a worldless picture book or from Literature Cards 6 and 7 in Chapter 3.

3. Ask students to read the story three or four times until they know the feel and flow of the story.

4. Have students memorize their opening lines, which can be an imaginative, fanciful, or fictitious reason for telling the story.

5. Provide time for students to practice telling the story to a small group, or before a mirror, and use the checklist in Table 3.4 to evaluate this practice session.

6. Allow students to choose the day they want to tell their stories, allowing one story per day until all have told their first story.

FOR YOUR JOURNAL

Purpose-Posing Journals

Purpose-posing journals are journals in which students write their purposes for listening or reading before they listen and read. You can also use purpose-posing journals as a first step in a DRTA or DLTA activity. When purpose-posing journals are used often, the mental process of predicting and establishing one's own purposes for listening or reading become more automatic and habitual. To introduce this type of journal, you can write three key questions on the board about a reading or listening experience that you are about to assign. Then, you can ask students to write as complete an answer to each question as they can in their journal, prior to reading or hearing about that experience. Next, you ask them to (a) leave space after each answer to record facts that they gain from reading or listening, and (b) summarize what they learn. After the reading or listening is completed, you can also have students write how posing purposes for a topic before they listened or read aided their learning.

To experience the power of using journals in this way yourself, write in your journal answers to the following questions about topics that will be discussed in Chapter 5 of this textbook. Write as much as you know about each topic before you read Chapter 5. Leave space following each answer. After you've read Chapter 5, you can return to this journal entry and summarize other points you learned. When finished, you can write how this experience aided your thinking and learning.

1. What was your most memorable experience about learning to read? What principles of instruction do you suppose were in operation to make this experience so important to you? (Write your answer and then leave space.)

2. What do you expect to learn in Chapter 5, "When Sound Meets Print: Teaching Phonics and Vocabulary"?

3. List the strategies that you use to **decode** (pronouncing and assigning meaning to unknown words). How can you or do you teach these strategies to students?

   Bonus Question: What are the characteristics that differentiate exemplary from less-than-exemplary first-grade teachers? (Write your answer and then turn to the book at the end of this chapter for a report of research findings designed to answer this question.)

CONNECTING CLASSROOMS, PARENTS, AND COMMUNITIES

Family Story Projects

Parents can help students listen more actively and share their stories at school, especially when you involve them in family story projects (Leseman & deJong, 1998). **Family story projects** are activities in which parents, relatives, siblings, or significant others in students' lives share significant family memories in stories. You can initiate family story projects by asking family members to tell a story during the evening and having students write the stories they hear. Or, parents can write stories and ask you to read them to the class. Either way, these storytelling experiences enable parents to model the importance of storytelling and listening in their own lives to share a personally significant event in their lives with their children. This activity also enables you to root instruction in the real world of students' homes.

An effective way to begin family story projects is to send a letter home to parents explaining to them why you would like for them to share stories with their children. You can use information from pages 82 through 84 to assist you in writing that letter. Then, you can conclude by either making a form or making a list of suggested story topics that parents might use. For example, they could tell stories about how they set their personal goals. A story might begin:

"Some changes I would like to make are . . ."

"I'm tired of _____."

"I think I'm going to _____, and this is why _____."

"I wonder how I would go about doing _____."

Another topic could be personal strengths.

"Some time ago, this happened to me, which enabled me to _____."

They could also talk about stories they value concerning their children, stories they value about their own childhood, stories about their hopes and dreams, or very special moments that they want their children to remember.

Some parents find it easier to write stories. For these parents, Thomas, Fazio, and Stiefelmeyer (1999) recommend that you provide for parents "sample memory book openers." Some sample memory book opener examples that they recommend are

Dear _____,
You loved _____. I wanted to share with you how this happened when you were younger.

Dear _____,
One of my favorite times in life was when I did _____.

Dear _____,
You have your own way of doing things. One thing about you that I most appreciate is _____.

Dear _____,
Another family member that we both admire, _____, taught me how to _____.

Once the project is initiated, many students also ask their parents to come to school and share their stories. In Mr. Stone's first grade, for instance, Meisong's mother came to demonstrate how rice is planted, harvested, and cooked in Vietnam; Michael's father brought an African drum to school, allowed all students to beat a rhythm and taught about Kwanzaa; and Juan's aunt came to tell about Juan's great-great-grandfather's involvement in Mexico's fight for independence and Cinco de Mayo.

Mr. Stone's students became so interested in family stories that he followed these experiences by filling the classroom library with books that describe family memories and traditions from differing cultural groups:

Ackerman, Karen. *Song and Dance Man.* New York: Viking, 1994.

Bechard, Margaret. *Star Hatchling.* New York: Viking, 1995.

Day, Nancy Rains. *The Lion's Whiskers: An Ethiopian Folktale.* New York: Scholastic, 1995.

Duke, Kate. *Aunt Isabel Tells a Good One.* New York: Simon & Schuster, 1995.

Flourneoy, Valerie. *The Patchwork Quilt.* New York: Atheneum, 1995.

Geras, Adele. *My Grandmother's Stories: A Collection of Jewish Folk Tales.* New York: Dial, 1994.

Hoffman, Mary. *Amazing Grace.* New York: Dial, 1991.

Hoffman, Mary. *Boundless Grace.* New York: Dial, 1995.

Howard, Elizabeth Fitzgerald. *Aunt Flossie's Hats (and Crab Cakes Later).* New York: Simon & Schuster, 1995.

Johnson, Angela. *Tell Me a Story, Mama.* New York: Greenwillow, 1995.

Kurtz, Jane. *Pulling the Lion's Tail.* New York: Simon & Schuster, 1995.

Leedy, Loreen. *Who's Who in My Family?* New York: Holiday House, 1995.

McDonald, Megan. *The Potato Man.* New York: Macmillan, 1995.

Nodelman, Perry. *The Same Place but Different.* New York: Simon & Schuster, 1995.

Orr, Katherine Shelley. *My Grandpa and the Sea.* New York: Scholastic, 1994.

Polacco, Patricia. *Thunder Came.* New York: Dial, 1994.

SUMMARY

Increasing students' listening abilities is one of the most important objectives in your language arts program. When you know and can recognize on which levels of listening they do well and for which they need more instruction, you can individualize and personalize your program. Levels of listening ability are receiving, discriminating, attending, listening actively, and listening appreciatively. This chapter describes activities to diagnose and increase students' abilities on each of these levels. It also presented several methods of teaching listening interactively because doing so enhances students' speaking, reading, viewing, thinking, and writing abilities. Examples of such integrative instruction are the directed listening or reading thinking approach (DLTA or DRTA), the language experience approach (LEA), interviewing, listening guides, and storytelling. Fairy tales can assist students to develop listening abilities more rapidly. A unit that used fairy tales to enhance listening abilities appears at the end of the chapter.

One of the most effective assessments of listening, speaking, and reading processes is the rating scale. Such instruments enable you to record specific aspects of students' growth in the somewhat internally guided processes of listening and speaking. For students who have special listening needs, you can implement special programs, such as Read and Stamp, Touch and Learn, Caption-TV, and Running Start.

Chapter 4 closes with a discussion of how purpose-posing journals and family story projects can increase students' listening abilities and build stronger connections between the classroom, community, and parents. In the next chapter you will learn how to develop students' decoding abilities and vocabularies.

HOW TO DO IT: USING WHAT YOU'VE LEARNED

The following provide opportunities to reflect on and practice what you have learned.

ASSESSING YOUR LEARNING

1. If you are teaching, design a listening activity using fairy tales. Assess your lesson by using a rating scale to identify the communication abilities students developed.

2. Select one of the activities in this chapter. Before you teach it to a group of elementary students, administer an informal pretest concerning the type of listening the activity is designed to develop. Then teach the activity and, if possible, wait one day before posttesting to determine students' growth. After the posttest, ask students how much they learned about the lesson's objective. Once these tests are complete, you can analyze the value that your instruction held for these students.

3. What proportion of your language arts program do you want to delegate to developing your students' listening abilities, and why? Defend your position.

4. Place yourself in Mr. Stone's situation. During the third month of school he received a new student who was a recent immigrant to the United States. Implement what you have learned in this chapter to respond to Santiago, Mr. Stone's new student:

Mr. Stone's students wrote questions in the problem-posing journals before they began their experiment to determine the fastest-growing vegetable seeds. As they began to plant the 10 different vegetables that they had selected, Santiago came to Mr. Stone and asked, "Where is my *semilla*?" Mr. Stone replied, "Are you asking for your seed?" "Yes," said Santiago, "I'm going to *plantala*."

In order to assist Santiago in learning English, Mr. Stone said, "Here is your seed. You also need dirt and a cup," and he held up the hand that held the dirt and the one that held the cup as he said these words. To this instruction, Santiago responded, "Where's mi *diario*?" Mr. Stone did not know the word *diario*. What would you have done next if you were Mr. Stone? To check your answer against what actually occurred, you can turn to the Answer Key at the back of the book.

5. Throughout this chapter, we have discussed the importance of sharing good literature with children. We also described the value of introducing variant versions of fairy tales to children. Select two books from Table 4.5 that are of interest to you. Read them back-to-back to children and have them describe what it is that they've learned about the commonalities and differences that exist between the cultures represented in each of the books, as well as what they have learned about how stories have been used throughout the generations to communicate the values that a culture esteems.

KEY TERMS EXERCISE

In this chapter several new terms were introduced. If you know the meaning of the following terms, place a checkmark beside that term. If you do not, return to the page on which that term was introduced and reread its definition. In doing so, you will retain these concepts more readily. If you know as many as 25 vocabulary words before you return to reread those that are unknown, you will have learned most of the information about listening development during your first reading of this chapter. Congratulations.

_____ active listener   (p. 157)

_____ auditory conceptual function (p. 148)

_____ bracketing   (p. 153)

_____ chain stories   (p. 154)

_____ decode   (p. 178)

_____ directed listening thinking activity   (p. 159)

_____ distortion theory   (p. 143)

_____ efferent listening comprehension   (p. 154)

_____ fading theory   (p. 143)

_____ fairy tales   (p. 167)

_____ family story projects   (p. 178)

_____ gossip game   (p. 154)

_____ half-listen   (p. 142)

_____ language experience approach (p. 160)

_____ listening   (p. 141)

_____ listening guide   (p. 156)

_____ never-learned theory   (p. 144)

_____ onset   (p. 145)

_____ oral histories   (p. 164)

_____ origami   (p. 156)

_____ phoneme segmentation (p. 148)

_____ phonograms   (p. 145)

_____ phonological awareness (p. 148)

_____ processing breakdown theory (p. 144)

_____ propaganda   (p. 165)

_____ purpose-posing journals (p. 178)

_____ rhyming   (p. 145)

_____ rime   (p. 145)

_____ selective attention   (p. 151)

_____ sound   (p. 142)

_____ storytelling   (p. 176)

_____ students' voices   (p. 173)

_____ suppression theory   (p. 144)

FOR FUTURE REFERENCE

Books about Listening Abilities or First-Grade Students

Barton, B. (1986). *Tell me another: Storytelling and reading aloud at home, at school, and in the community.* Portsmouth, NH: Heinemann. Provides valuable information about improving storytelling abilities as well as providing many suggestions for captivating books at every age level that students and teacher can tell effectively as their first storytelling experience.

Biagi, S. (1986). *Interviews that work.* Belmont, CA: Wadsworth. Provides samples of many types of interviews that students can simulate as if they were news broadcasters, sports commentators, anchor persons, and feature reporters.

International Listening Association, Center for Information and Communication Sciences, Ball State University, Muncie, IN 47306-0535. This is a network of professionals interested in, and knowledgeable about, the area of listening, listening instruction, and recent research concerning the development of more advanced listening abilities.

Newkirk, T., & McClure, P. (1992). *Listening in: Children talk about books (and other things).* Portsmouth, NH: Heinemann. Provides transcripts of children's dialogue, introduces many possibilities for extending children's talking and listening to literature, and how to extend the oral and listening abilities of children from diverse cultures. Focuses on the development of these oral language abilities in a second-grade class.

Nichols J. B., & Hazzard, S. P. (1993). *Education as adventure: Lessons from the second grade.* New York: Teachers College Press. Provides additional information about life in a second-grade classroom.

Trousdale, A. M., Woestehaff, S. A., & Schwartz, M. (Eds.). (1994). *Give a listen: Stories of storytelling in school.* Urbana, IL: NCTE. Describes storytelling and its benefits and relates how teachers can rediscover the power of oral storytelling for themselves and their classrooms.

RESOURCES FOR PARENTS

Cheney, M. (1997). *How to develop your child's gifts and talents in vocabulary.* Los Angeles: Lowell House. 176p.

This book includes how children acquire language and learn new words from context; games to play; and words to know.

Fuller, C. (1997). *Teaching your child to write: How parents can encourage writing skills for success in school, work, and life.* New York: Berkley Publishing Group. 211p.

This is a very practical guide for parents to learn ways to encourage their children to develop writing skills. The activities suggested include writing for fun (e-mails, friends, newspapers, plays, etc.). Kids who learn to become better writers are better able to express themselves creatively.

Gardner, J., & Myers, L. (1997). *10 simple and effective methods to develop your child's love for reading.* Hulbrook, MA: Adams Media Corporation.

This is a book that gives parents specific strategies and activities to do with their children at home to show them how much fun reading can be. It teaches children to ask questions, notice patterns, predict endings, make connections, think logically, and learn new words. All those strategies help children to develop oral language and to write their own stories.

Itzkoff, S. W. (1996). *Children learning to read: A guide for parents and teachers.* USA: Praeger. 216p.

This book presents parents and teachers with the learning stages through which children must pass in order to become fluent, independently literate readers and writers. It explains the developmental dangers unique to each child that parents and teachers may have to confront and help the child work through. This book illustrates the learning process, and points to successful and failed strategies used by teachers today in our classrooms.

Jacobson, J. R. (1998). *How is my first grader doing in school? What to expect and how to help.* New York: Simon & Schuster. 192p.

This book contains fun, easy-to-do activities designed to teach children important skills. There are several reading exercises that include identifying letters, letter sounds, sight words, phonics, predicting, identifying new words, and reading comprehension. This book also lists exceptional read-aloud selections for parents and children including picture books, riddles, poetry, and easy-to-read books. It also includes oral language activities.

Leonhardt, M. (1996). *Keeping kids reading: How to raise avid readers in the video age.* New York: Crown. 264p.

This book discusses specific read-aloud activities to use with young children, such as plays, poetry, having the child read his or her favorite book from the author's chair, and book parties for young children and their friends. Also addresses how to incorporate technology into building students' enjoyment of reading.

Leonhardt, M. (1997). *99 ways to get kids to love reading and 100 books they will love.* New York: Three Rivers Press. 121p.

This book includes tips for different levels and ages of readers; offers help in choosing books; and discusses the importance of creating routines.

ADDITIONAL RESOURCES FOR TEACHERS

Bode, B. A. *Dialogue journal writing as an approach to beginning literacy instruction.* ERIC No. ED300816.

Hannon, J. *How will changing our kindergarten journal format to include student/teacher dialogue affect student population.* ERIC No. ED408047.

Lopez, E. B. *Dialogue journal: Writing in kindergarten and the first grade classsroom.* ERIC No. ED324115.

Nos, N. (1997). *Enhancing 1st grade literacy instruction: Practical, innovative teaching strategies.* Bellevue, WA: Bureau of Education and Research.

Woolfolk, A. (1995). *Educational psychology.* Needham Heights, MA: Simon and Schuster.

Websites

1. To prepare creative lessons: www.pbs.org/learn

2. For students to use:
   www.thekids.com/kids/stories/fables/
   www.hminet.com/store/catalog/cgrws
   www.hminet.com/monsters

Younger Readers

Allard, H. (1985). *Miss Nelson has a field day.* Boston: Houghton Mifflin.

Amstutz, A. (1994). *Mystery tour.* New York: Mulberry.

LeMieux, A. (1995). *Super snoop Sam Snout and the case of the missing marble.* New York: Avon.

Older Readers

Adler, D. A. (1985). *The fourth floor twins and the fish snitch mystery.* New York: Viking.

George, J. (1996). *The case of the missing cutthroat: An ecological mystery.* New York: HarperCollins.

Seabrooke, B. (1995). *The haunting of Holroyd Hill.* New York: Dutton.

THEMATIC UNIT: EMPHASIZING NATIVE AMERICAN FOLKLORE FOR KINDERGARTEN THROUGH SECOND GRADE[1]

This unit (as well as Literature Card 11) contains a list of fairy tales that first-graders can read during the unit. Why are fairy tales a particularly valuable genre for first-grade students? What would you have done, in addition to the activities Mr. Stone's students completed, to improve students' listening abilities?

Preschool to first-grade children especially need daily exposure to traditional tales, beautiful folk literature, and a variety of children's classics. By reading these books orally to children, you will model fluency, express the value of reading for pleasure, and provide young children with many examples of story structure, book language, and new vocabulary. Simultaneously, children can participate in non-threatening shared rereadings of the book, such as chanting sections, singing along with you, tracking print together as you point to words, or engaging in activities that are designed to highlight words, patterns, and print conventions from traditional fairy tales and folk literature. In the process, many young children internalize the concepts of letter–sound correspondence, directionality, phrasing, and punctuation, all so valuable as they turn their attention to print, which is discussed in Chapter 5.

Generalizations

Because folk tales are deeply rooted in oral tradition, this unit is designed to help students develop strong speaking and listening abilities. It will

- Help students understand the link between the oral tradition of folklore and the benefits of improved speech, storytelling, and listening abilities
- Make students more comfortable speaking in front of groups
- Help students articulate thoughts and ideas more clearly
- Develop the skill of persuasive speech
- Develop confidence, poise, and a sense of "stage presence"
- Help students recognize common characteristics found in folk tales
- Improve speaking and listening abilities by reciting or dramatizing various folk tales
- Help students understand how folk tales apply to daily-life situations
- Strengthen interpersonal skills by working in small peer groups

Process in Action

1. You can introduce the unit by defining folklore and stating the various characteristics found in folk tales. It is very important to stress that folk tales are an oral

Note: Although the content in this unit focuses on folklore from the Native American culture, students should be given the option to study additional folklore from their own and other cultures as well.

[1]Ms. Lydia Wooten is an exceptional kindergarten and first-grade teacher and wrote this unit. Ms. Wooten resides in Frederick, Maryland.

Literature Card 11

FOLK LITERATURE

Folktales and Fairy Tales with a Lot of Pictures

Thirty-Three Multicultural Tales to Tell by DeSpain, 1998 August House

Ol' Jake's Lucky Day by A. Ivanov, 1984 Lee & Shepard Books

Cornelius by L. Lionni, 1983 Pantheon

The Cobbler's Song by M. Sewell, 1982 Unicorn

Monkey and the White Bone Demon by Z. Xiu Shi, 1984 Viking

The Goose and the Golden Coins by L. Cauley, 1981 Harcourt

Molly Whuppie by W. De La More, 1983 Farrar, Straus & Giroux

The Magic Stove by M. Ginsbury, 1983 Coward-McCann

Moonsong Lullaby by J. Highwater, 1981 Lothrop, Lee & Shepard

Legend of the Milky Way by J. Lee, 1982 Holt, Rinehart & Winston

Why Mosquitoes Buzz in People's Ears by V. Aardema, 1976 Dial

Strega Nona by T. de Paola, 1975 Prentice-Hall

The Wolf's Chicken Stew by K. Kasza, 1987 Putnam

Good Books to Tell You a Lot about Folktales and Legends

Moon Game by F. Asch, 1989 Aladdin

Her Seven Brothers by P. Goble, 1993 Aladdin

Star Boy by P. Goble, 1991 Aladdin

Wiley and the Hairy Man by M. Bang, 1987 Aladdin

Penrod Again by M. Christian, 1990 Aladdin

The Gold Coin by A. Ada, 1994 Aladdin

Turtle Knows Your Name by A. Bryan, 1993 Aladdin

The Silver Cow: A Welsh Tale by S. Cooper, 1991 Aladdin

What Happens Next? by J. Donmaska, 1983 Greenwillow

Giant Treasury of Brer Rabbit by A. Hessey, 1990 Derrydale Books

John Henry by J. Lester, 1994 Dial

Good Books If You Are Just Beginning to Learn about Legends and Folktales

Mathew's Dragon by S. Cooper, 1994 Aladdin

The Completed Hickory Dickory Dock by J. Aylesworth, 1994 Aladdin

Buzz Buzz Buzz by B. Barton, 1995 Aladdin

Wild Wild Sunflower Child Anna by N. Carlstrom, 1991 Aladdin

Such a Noise! by A. Brodmann, 1989 Kane/Miller Book Publishing

The McBroom Series by S. Fleischman, 1992 Greenwillow

Folktale Plays around the World by P. Nolen, 1982 Plays, Inc.

The Ghost-Eye Tree by B. Martin Jr., & J. Archambault, 1985 Holt, Rinehart & Winston

Books That Have Several Chapters about Folktales and Legends

If You Had a Horse by M. Hodges, 1984 Scribner's

The Trouble with Adventures by C. Harris, 1982 Atheneum

Monkey & the White Bone Demon by Z. Xier Shi, 1984 Viking

Magical Tales from Many Lands by M. Mays

Cut from the Same Cloth: American Women of Myth, Legend and Tall Tales by R. San Souci, 1993 Philomel

Pondlarker by F. Gwynne, 1992 Aladdin

Pecos Bill by A. Dewey, 1994 Mulberry

Febold Feboldson by A. Dewey, 1984 Greenwillow

tradition, thus easily and clearly making the connection to teaching speaking and listening competencies in the course of this unit.

2. You can read aloud the book *The Girl Who Loved Wild Horses* by Paul Goble.

3. You can ask students to volunteer any characteristics of folklore they recognize in the book. You can write the responses on the chalkboard, dry-erase board, or flip-chart.

Students can write their own folk or fairy tales as an exercise in appreciating the traditional qualities of the genre and in developing their storytelling abilities.

4. You can teach various strategies of speaking aloud and listening effectively. For this lesson it would be helpful for you to model or demonstrate how to do so.

5. Students can be given options for class presentations.

The end result will be a presentation in which the students demonstrate and assess their speaking skills. Students can select from the following options:

- Organize the class into judge, jury, prosecution, and defense. Hold a mock trial: *The People versus Goldilocks.* Is she guilty of breaking and entering? Should she be punished? If so, what should the punishment be?

- Pair students. One student reads an American version of Cinderella to his partner. The other must pay close attention. The reader can stop to ask questions or ask for predictions.

- Read *Mufaro's Beautiful Daughters* (Steptoe) to the class. Have the class discuss similarities and differences between the African and American versions of

Cinderella. Make a Venn diagram of these on the board. There are two centers in the room. One has many countries' versions of Cinderella to read at the students' own pace. The other has historical and geographical information on Africa. The class splits into two groups and visits the centers alternately.

- Model a think-aloud for learning new words from context clues through use of the surrounding text and pictures. Students silently read *Puss in Boots* (Perrault) and use the techniques they have learned. Monitor the room, answering questions for the students.

- Have students write their own fairy tales.

- Have students read their finished stories to a kindergarten class. Students discuss in class what they have learned in this unit.

Integration of the Language Arts

Students have the opportunity to study and learn in a variety of ways to accommodate their various learning styles so that every student has the chance to succeed. An interesting art activity integrates Native American symbols and different art media. After a class discussion about how Native Americans communicated ideas, experiences, and feelings through pictures, students can transfer various Native American symbols onto crushed brown-paper bags, which have a look of leather (see Figure 4.7).

Resources

Native American Folk Tales

Baylor, Byrd. (1995). *And it is still that way: Legends told by Arizona Indian children.* New York: Scholastic.

Begay, S. (1992). *Ma'ii and cousin Horned Toad.* New York: Scholastic.

 sun rising   leave tepee   hunt   feast   sun rising   leave tepee

FIGURE 4.7 NATIVE AMERICAN SYMBOLS

Belting, N. (1992). *Moon was tired of walking on air.* New York: Houghton Mifflin.

Bernhard, E. (1993). *Spotted Eagle and Black Crow.* New York: Holiday House.

Brachac, J. (1993). *The first strawberries.* New York: Dial Books for Young Readers.

Second-graders, eager to master new skills, are challenged by the difficulty of integrating the processes involved in phonics decoding and vocabulary instruction.

CHAPTER 5

WHEN SOUND MEETS PRINT: TEACHING PHONICS AND VOCABULARY

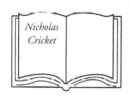

Nicholas Cricket

Ms. Hulsey is reading Nicholas Cricket and Allison and her second-grade friends are engrossed in the story's beautiful melody created by many words that they have never heard before. This is the first day of a decoding strategies unit that Ms. Hulsey developed after having conversations with students who wanted to learn to decode and remember "really big words." For example, yesterday Ms. Hulsey held a discovery discussion with Allison:

Ms. Hulsey: I would like for you to read a few words for me.

Allison: O.K. [She stumbles through a list of words.] I didn't get a lot of them right, did I?

Ms. Hulsey: Why do you think you are having problems reading?

Allison: I can't read good.

Ms. Hulsey: Tell me about the times when it is easy for you to read and you enjoy it.

Allison: When all the words are little. Like when I read the Curious George books.

Ms. Hulsey: I understand. What do you do when you run into big words?

Allison: I look at all the letters. Then I look at them again. I try to see if I know how they would sound like, but it's hard. I can't.

Just as Mr. Stone chose to teach first grade, Ms. Hulsey chose to teach second grade because she truly enjoys assisting students like Allison to overcome difficulties as they learn to read. She is well aware that second-graders are eager to master new skills. At this age children draw the same picture or write the same story about the very same thing over and over again, striving to achieve perfection. Many second-graders love to make lists. The genre of mysteries begins to intrigue this age group;

yet, at the same time, they enjoy having a schedule and a routine that they depend on and expect their routines to be followed exactly.

Like first-graders, most second-graders find transitions a bit uncomfortable. Ms. Hulsey realizes that children at age 7 are usually able to listen in a group discussion and appreciate the contributions of others. Allison can learn by imitating her friends, which is another characteristic of second-graders, yet, like most second-graders, she continues to have difficulty grasping and integrating the steps of the processes involved in phonics, decoding, and vocabulary instruction. Thus, Ms. Hulsey has several challenges before her, and she will use the activities in this chapter to address Allison's special decoding needs.

Why do some students instantly recognize 95 percent of the words they hear and read while others cannot? During the last 15 years there has been more research designed to answer this question than ever before (Adams, 1990; Clay, 1999; Stanovich, 1998; Stanovich & Cunningham, 1993). Through this research we have come to define **decoding** and **vocabulary development** as language processes in which students construct meaning from spoken and written messages through symbol awareness, word analysis, strategic thinking, association, and reflection. The purpose of this chapter is to describe how to increase students' abilities to recognize words when they listen and read, and to use a more precise and vivid vocabulary when they speak and write.

Oral vocabulary differs from reading and written vocabulary by its psychological and physical distance from the audience, by the amount of time people have to produce the language, and by its degree of permanence (Chafe & Danielewicz, 1986; Olson, 1977; Rubin, 1988; Tannen, 1985). This chapter describes methods that enhance phonics sight word and vocabulary instruction through balanced program that blends enriching literature and direct instruction. By the end of this chapter, you will be able to master the objectives from IRA, NCTE, NAEYC, TEKS, and other statewide and province-based professional competencies for language arts teachers:

1. What strategies enable students to become independent decoders and use more expansive vocabularies?

2. What can you do when readers can't decode?

3. How can you meet students' special vocabulary needs?

4. How can you teach the phonemic, morphemic, semantic, syntactic, and pragmatic systems of language?

5. What is emergent literacy and how can it be enhanced in children?

6. How can you become well versed with individualized and group instructional interventions targeted for students with greatest literacy needs?

7. What are some of the instructional technologies that support literacy learning, such as multimedia resources, interactive books, and multimedia encyclopedias?

•‍•

SECTION 1   THEORETICAL FOUNDATIONS

Developing Vocabularies as a Parallel Support for Phonics Instruction

Parallel distributed processing is the term psychologists use to explain how the brain associates words with their meanings (Seidenberg & McClelland, 1989; Stanovich & Cunningham, 1992: Cunningham & Stanovich, 1997). According to this theory, the brain uses many sources of information simultaneously as it searches for a word's meaning. It detects patterns in sounds it hears and symbols it sees. Information also comes from a word's spelling (orthography); sound (phonology); meaning-bearing units in the context of sentences (syntax and semantics); broader clues such as gestures, body language, plot sequence, knowledge of the speaker's or author's prior word choices; and the student's background knowledge. You can support the brain's abilities to perform these parallel distributed processes in many ways. Each is described below and illustrated in Figure 5.1.

Students can expand their vocabulary and decoding abilities with the instruction and experiences with literature described in this chapter (Purcell-Gates, McIntyre, & Freppon, 1995). The parallel support of direct instruction and emersion in vocabulary-rich literature fosters a richer, broader knowledge of written and spoken language than would be possible with one or the other in isolation.

Such an integrated approach also affords more chances for students to read, speak, listen, and write. This is important because one of the major differences between proficient and less proficient readers is that the former typically read more than the latter, and they recognize the meanings of most words instantly and automatically (Samuels, 1998; Juell, 1996; Clay, 1999; Cunningham, 1999). It seems that the occasional unfamiliar word grabs the attention of better readers immediately. They stop and invest energy in figuring it out. On the other hand, for less proficient readers, so many words are unknown that such pauses and reflection seem futile.

A second action is to read aloud. Research demonstrates that reading aloud to young children significantly increases their (1) expressive language skills, vocabulary, syntax, length of utterance, and written output; (2) comprehension; and (3) book skills, including print knowledge, decoding, story structure, and literary language (Dickinson & Smith, 1994; Muler & Snowling, 1999; Morrow, 1999). Furthermore, studies confirm that students who come to school from richly literate homes have a more expansive speaking, listening, reading, and writing vocabulary than students who have had limited exposure to a variety of spoken and written language (Ruddell & Ruddell, 1995). Evidence suggests that their vocabularies are broader and deeper because they have had daily encounters with words, have been read to, have tried to read books with significant others in their environment, have watched others write important messages for which they have paused to contemplate the exact word choice they desired, have written themselves, and have talked with someone about words they do and do not know. From all these experiences, such students come to value what words can do and to understand that specific words must be consciously selected to communicate accurate messages.

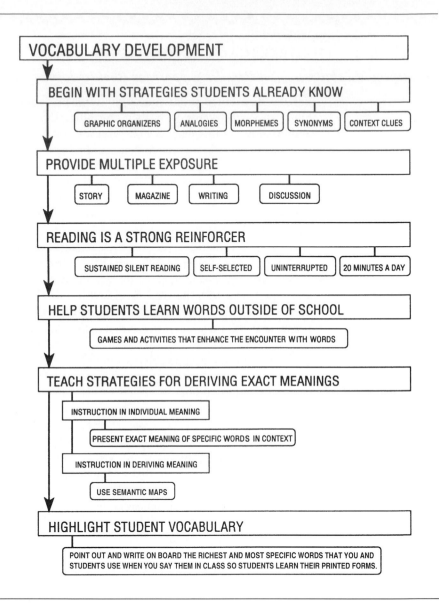

FIGURE 5.1 INSTRUCTION THAT BUILDS STUDENTS' ORAL AND WRITTEN VOCABULARIES

Moreover, the level of a student's reading ability is influenced by the level of that student's oral language development (Dyson, 1999; Purcell-Gates, 1998). Similarly, a student's dialect also determines the ease with which a student can handle formal features of printed English. Equally important, by second grade, children's ability to expand continuousal their oral vocabulary significantly affects their advancement to higher levels of reading success throughout their lives (Carver, 1998; Chall, Jacobs, & Baldwin, 1990; Carver, 1998). For these reasons, researchers strongly recommend that teachers of every grade read books regularly to increase students' oral and written vocabularies.

In summary, the kind of instruction students need to learn phonics and to increase their vocabularies is not to memorize new words in isolation or use unintegrated worksheets. Instruction must complement the parallel distributed processes that the brain uses to learn words. This requires stimulating and meaningful activities; more frequent use of quality literature as an instructional tool; varied and heterogeneously constructed reading groups; introduction to multiple decoding strategies; and activities that integrate a student's individual reading, speaking, listing, writing, observing, and thinking strengths. This instruction has increased importance because half the words used by present high school graduates are those they learned in the first and second grades (Collins & Mangieri, 1992; Nagy & Herman, 1984).

BUILDING VOCABULARIES

Each lesson incorporates six principles of language arts instruction.

1. The vocabulary section improves comprehension when both the definition of the word and the context in which it is used is understood by students.

2. Only key words from target passages should be taught. They should be words that are essential for comprehension and are repeated in various reading materials that students experience throughout their lives (Beck, Perfetti, & McKeown, 1982; Carver, 1998).

3. Words must be taught thoroughly and used by students in many different ways (Templeton, 1998).

4. Words should be taught in semantically and topically related groups (Heimlich & Pittleman, 1986).

5. The number of words taught should be limited to seven (Block & Mangeri, 1996).

TEACHING VOCABULARY WHILE READING ORALLY TO THE CLASS

The first method is applied to times when you read aloud to the class. On some days when you read, develop student's vocabulary rather than reading only for pleasure, as described later in this chapter. On days when vocabulary development is your goal, you can ask students to identify vocabulary that is new to them. Also, when you write vocabulary words on the chalkboard prior to reading, students can hear and see new words as you read. Alternatively, you can write the words as you read in the order that they appear in the story. When, you finish reading, students can say and write the words in contexts that they create.

Similarly, when introducing a unit or a book, you can ask students to anticipate words they may encounter. For example, if they are to read a story about Thanksgiving, have them suggest words that are likely to be in the story (e.g., *turkey, cranberries,* and *dinner*). Then you can teach them that when a new word appears, they can anticipate how it might relate to the theme of the reading (or speech being

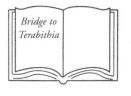

heard). For example, new words that might appear in a Thanksgiving story are likely to be *turkey* rather than *tunnel* and *dinner* rather than *dimmer.*

Because word boundaries are almost impossible to identify in oral language, writing new words you say for students immediately after saying them, can increase students' vocabulary. For example, after Ms. Hulsey read the last chapter of *Bridge to Terabithia,* Allison asked: "Did the author choose the name *Terabithia* for a particular reason?" In her answer Ms. Hulsey told Allison how expressive her choice of *particular* was and she wrote that word on the board. Then, she gave its meaning, and used it in her response to Allison's question. Last, she asked other classmates to give their answer to Allison's question, selecting classmates who needed to build their speaking vocabularies. These students responded with phrases similar to, "The particular reason I think she chose the name *Terabithia* is. . . ." Through this instruction, Ms. Hulsey enabled students to use a new word soon after it was heard. This increases the likelihood that the word will become a part of students' self-initiated vocabulary.

SEMANTIC MAPPING OR WEBBING

Webbing, or semantic mapping, is a visual organization in which thoughts and ideas are diagramed to demonstrate their relationship to each other. Researchers have established that graphically connecting ideas together increases vocabulary development, reading comprehension, and writing abilities (Johnson & Pearson, 1984; Templeton, 1998). Such semantic maps, concept maps, and webs assist students to understand levels and categories of meaning and to organize their thoughts. Further, when these key words and phrases are categorized and illustrated during the introductory portions of a lesson, students receive a meaning-based focus on concepts as they are unveiled.

To teach semantic mapping, you can write the main concept to be read or written in the center of the chalkboard or overhead in a circle. Extending from this center you can make spokes that demonstrate the categories of concepts to be included in this reading or writing experience. Words within each of these categories denote the different meanings and ideas that are related to each concept, as illustrated in the semantic web Allison created to write a story about shopping, shown in Figure 5.2. Then you can explain how semantic maps create a diagram of the schema that an author followed when he or she wrote so that the relationship between new vocabulary words and concepts in these writings can be learned more easily.

You can also use semantic webs in content areas or to introduce a book, or unit or to solicit students' background knowledge relative to a topic. You write the title of the book, unit, or concept in the center of the web. If you use the web as a pre-reading or prewriting activity, you can ask students to identify and discuss definitions, descriptions, synonyms, and phrases that they think are related to each word on the map. Then, as they read the book and explore the unit, students can verify and extend their definitions. As a follow-up experience, students can increase the number of words included in each category. When students construct webs, as Allison did, they can use these maps as outlines to help organize and clarify their ideas before giving an oral presentation or writing a composition.

FIGURE 5.2 EXAMPLE OF A SEMANTIC MAP

When you use semantic webs to introduce thematic units, children can generate the information that they already know and what they want to learn. For example, some students may suggest that a study about a country include its cultural traditions while others may be concerned the current issues, people, politics, or economy. From the resulting web of these concepts relative to this country, children can learn new words (and generate new ideas) in a context that deeply interests them.

DECODING AND ENCODING

When students encounter an unknown word, they must decode it. When they say or write a word that they are thinking, they **encode** it. In other words, decoding changes printed letters or spoken sounds into meaning, encoding translates thoughts into spoken or written words. This chapter describes strategies that assist students to decode printed and oral words. To teach these strategies, you can use need-based groups in which only students who need to learn a specific strategy are present. Thus, because you are personalizing decoding instruction, the membership in decoding instructional groups will likely change with each strategy taught.

Decoding does not merely mean to use phonics, sight words, structural analysis, and context clues. To decode, students must learn that certain strategies work more effectively with certain types of words. For example, the word *eight* is better learned by employing sight word than phonic analysis strategies. It is also important that readers internalize both the rationale for using a decoding strategy and ways in which that process can work in concert with others to gain meaning. After each activity in this chapter is taught, you can demonstrate and ask students to practice integrating more than one decoding strategy to derive meaning.

Moreover, as readers gain more confidence in their decoding abilities they will not only sustain their positive attitudes but increase their speed of word recognition. Such fluency is related to high levels of comprehension for students as early as first grade (Lesgold & Resnick, 1982; Bosch, Bon & Schreider, 1995). Most readers need to be taught the following types of decoding clues: (1) basic sight words (the 300–400 most frequently occurring words in our language); (2) content-specific sight words; (3) signal sight words (words that authors use as highways to carry meanings); (4) syntactical and semantic context clues (what words are likely to appear in certain spots in a sentence); (5) structural analyses (prefixes, suffixes, and affixes, that add meaning to base words); (6) phonics and letter-to-sound correspondences; (7) dictionary usage skills; and (8) combining these clues.

TEACHING SIGHT WORD STRATEGIES

Without a well-developed sight vocabulary student's read very slowly. Frequent stops lock their short-term memory into processing single words. When this occurs, they are limited in their ability to gain meanings from sentences or to use the rhythm of printed words, matching speech to print, to make sense. There are three types of sight words that you can teach: content-specific, high-frequency, and signal sight words.

Content-Specific Sight Words.   These words appear only when particular subjects are read. You can teach students that when they are reading and come to a long word that they have never before seen, the word is usually a content-specific sight word. If they pause to think about the subject about which they are reading, that word most often describes something about the subject (e.g., it could be an object that is used relative to that subject, or a descriptive detail, or an event that occurs relative to the subject). With this instruction, students can come to learn the meaning of many content-specific sight words independently.

You can also teach content-specific sight words through imagery. Students can remember content-specific sight words more easily when their meaning is portrayed in clever drawings attached to the words. Therefore, you can create an image of a word, and after showing the meaning-associated image, you can discuss how the meaning relates to the passage being read. Thus, when a reader can't remember a word, you can associate a picture with the meaning of the word. For example, Ms. Hulsey used this activity in a needs-based group to teach Allison and four other students how to image the meaning of *yarn:*

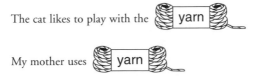

The cat likes to play with the yarn

My mother uses yarn

Then, Allison and her friends wrote several sentences to practice writing the new word that they had learned.

Teaching High-Frequency Words.   High-frequency words are defined as the words that appear most frequently in printed English, as shown in Table 5.1. Recognizing a word by sight means that the reader has identified a word instantly by the unique **configuration** of the total word's shape (e.g., elephant), by the unique combination of its letters, or by its position in a certain location in the sentence (e.g., "*Once* upon a time . . ."). Unfortunately, many of the basic sight words (*the, to, that*) do not contain a picturable meaning or unique configuration. Therefore, you can best teach the works in Table 5.1 by (a) emphasizing the location in sentences where they likely appear (e.g., *the* comes before nouns while *they* replaces nouns), (b) assisting students to memorize their configurations, or (c) learning through repeated reading experiences so that these words reach a level of instant recognition. Such instruction is important because when students know 5,000 of the most frequently occurring words in our language by sight, virtually all reading material they select in the future will have 93 percent recognizable words. For this reason alone, the time your readers spend in the following basic sight word lessons will be very profitable. For a complete list of the words most frequently occurring in English, see *3,000 Instant Words* by Elizabeth Sakiey and Edward Fry (1984).

Basic sight word instruction is most effective when you teach the most frequently appearing words first. These words have been identified by Fry, Fountoukidis, and Polk (1985) and appear in Table 5.1. When students can read the first 25 by sight, they will be able to read about one-third of all the words they will ever encounter in print; when they can read the first 100 words, they will recognize about half of all the words they will ever read.

Basic sight words can also be learned through configuration. **Configuration** is defined as the visual image formed by the letters in a word—for example, the configuration of *the* is the and the configuration of *that* is that. To turn configuration into an instructional tool, select words from Table 5.1 that are distinct in their configurations and lengths, such as *a, that, one, it, therefore.* Then ask students to draw their personalized, unique configuration around each one, which will help them remember that word's meaning and sounds. For example, *a* means "only one"; Allison drew the following configuration to learn the word a .

Next, you can ask students to write words with their unique configurations on one side of a notecard, with one word per card. Immediately after drawing each configuration, ask students to turn the card over and print the same word without its configuration. When all words have been completed, have readers study their configured words by saying each word aloud or silently until they can recognize them instantly. Then have students read the words on the back side of the card (without the configuration) to a partner. If they cannot read a word, instruct them to refer to the side with the configuration. Last, ask them to read a page from their present selection of children's literature in which these words appear to their partners. For any word the student misses, you can have partners show the configured version without giving any other prompt. If the configuration does not lead to their peer's immediate recall of that word, have them point out the position the word holds in a sentence in the book. If neither of these prompts is effective, ask students to explain what they were thinking when they drew the configuration and teach partners to work to make the configuration more distinct. For example, Allison stated: "*That* is a word that tells me something is about to be said about the words that came before it; *of*

TABLE 5.1 THE MOST FREQUENTLY OCCURRING WORDS IN ENGLISH

WORDS 1–20	WORDS 21–40	WORDS 41–60	WORDS 61–80	WORDS 81–100
the	at	there	some	my
of	be	use	her	than
and	this	an	would	first
a	have	each	make	water
to	from	which	like	been
in	or	she	him	call
is	one	do	into	who
you	had	how	time	oil
that	by	their	has	now
it	word	if	look	find
he	but	will	two	long
was	not	up	more	down
for	what	other	write	day
on	all	about	go	did
are	were	out	see	get
as	we	many	number	come
with	when	then	no	made
his	your	them	way	may
they	can	these	could	part
I	said	so	people	over

Common suffixes: *-s, -ing, -ed*

usually means only a little bit, such as only one detail will be given. I can remember *of* is little and don't have to concentrate so long when I see *of* ! I like *of*s best!"

Teaching Signal Sight Words.   This third type of sight word is defined as words that designate (1) cause-effect relationships; (2) order (3) summation, (4) more of the same, (5) something different or changes in thought. Table 5.2 displays signal sight words that readers profit from learning. The following steps are an effective method of teaching them:

1. Make an overhead of a page from a selection of children's literature that you just read or will read to the class.

TABLE 5.2 SIGNAL SIGHT WORDS

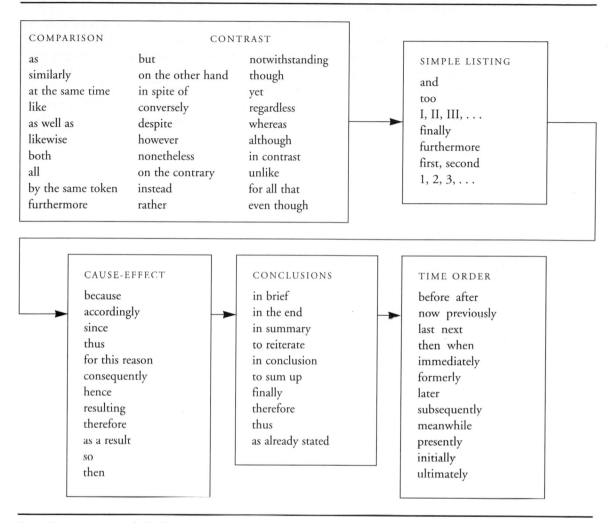

COMPARISON	CONTRAST	
as	but	notwithstanding
similarly	on the other hand	though
at the same time	in spite of	yet
like	conversely	regardless
as well as	despite	whereas
likewise	however	although
both	nonetheless	in contrast
all	on the contrary	unlike
by the same token	instead	for all that
furthermore	rather	even though

SIMPLE LISTING

and
too
I, II, III, . . .
finally
furthermore
first, second
1, 2, 3, . . .

CAUSE-EFFECT	CONCLUSIONS	TIME ORDER
because	in brief	before after
accordingly	in the end	now previously
since	in summary	last next
thus	to reiterate	then when
for this reason	in conclusion	immediately
consequently	to sum up	formerly
hence	finally	later
resulting	therefore	subsequently
therefore	thus	meanwhile
as a result	as already stated	presently
so		initially
then		ultimately

Source: From *Reason to Read: Thinking Strategies for Life through Literature,* Vol. 1 (p. 138), by C. Block and J. Mangieri, 1995, Palo Alto, CA: Addison-Wesley. Used by permission.

2. Highlight a few words that appear in the different categories in Table 5.2, for example, a "continuation" and a "sequence" sight word.

3. Ask students to explain the difference between two words and what each signals about upcoming words in text.

4. Ask students to read silently. When they come to a signal sight word, ask them to raise their hands, tell you what it means, and how they are using its meaning to understand upcoming words.

Presenting the same word repeatedly in different sentences also assists students' mastery of sight words. You can create such repeated exposures by using the **language**

experience approach (LEA), which requires students to say or write a sight word several times, as Ms. Hulsey did.

Ms. Hulsey designed a lesson in which her students observed a bees' nest; she read to them about bees, and invited to class someone who worked on a bee farm. Then Ms. Hulsey held a small-group lesson with students who needed sight word instruction, asking them to tell all they learned about bees. Most students began their sentences with the word *they.* She wrote these sentences, one after the other on a chart until the list of students' thoughts was complete. Next, students read the LEA aloud resulting in a choral reading where the sight word *they* was seen repeatedly in a context that had meaning to the students.

Bees

They were busy.

They were noisy.

They were different sizes.

They don't want to hurt people.

They are magical.

They make honey.

The next day these students experienced a similar activity featuring the word *the;* the following week the lesson emphasizes the word *that.* With each consecutive lesson, students reviewed the previous weeks' charts. As a result, the students learned these words rapidly.

A third method that builds students' strategic decoding of sight words is to identify a sight word that appears several times on a page in a book that a student has chosen to read. Before the student reads that page, call attention to the sight word and what meaning it adds to each sentence. After the student finishes reading, ask for the pronunciation and meaning of that sight word.

•

PHONICS

My teacher always tells me to sound it out, but I don't know what that means. I just move my finger and my lips cuz she does. Please don't tell her. I should have learned [to sound it out] in kindergarten [but I didn't]. I don't think any of the kids in Care Bears can sound the words out either. (Michael, 1994, p. 55)

Phonics is the science of matching speech sounds to printed letters. In 1986, Congress decreed that the Department of Education was to study the effects of phonics instruction on reading achievement. After 4 years of work, the study, *Beginning to Read: Thinking and Learning about Print* (Adams, 1990), was published and recommended:

Programs for all children, good and poor readers alike, should strive to maintain an appropriate balance between phonics activities, and the reading and appreciation of informative and engaging texts. As important as it is to sound words out, it is important only as an intermediate step. Sounding words out should not be the end goal, but a way of teaching what [students] need to know to comprehend text. The only reason for reading words is to understand text. Many teachers downplay the teaching of phonics, or relegate it to seat work, in an attempt to introduce students to texts as early as possible. But treating phonics as a poor relation is a poor strategy, particularly for children who have little experience with reading before they start school. Only through explicit phonics instruction will such children learn to sound out words on their own, and be able to read independently without difficulty—a key factor in determining whether they can understand what they read. (Adams, 1990, p. 248)

There are a variety of instructional phonics methods. One of the first was based on the linguistic method (Bloomfield & Barnhardt, 1961). Leonard Bloomfield reasoned that children had trouble pronouncing single sounds because sounds were taught one at a time. Instead, he proposed that children learn to sound out patterns in words, (e.g., as *cat, rat,* and *fat*). Since 1961 this method has been called the analytical approach and has developed into approaches such as **word making,** in which children put together words that have the same vowel and ending consonant or same vowel and beginning consonant or consonant cluster. For example, teachers have taught children to "make words" by:

1. Lining up according to the first letter of their last name
2. Identifying letter clusters such as *Stan* and *Stacy,* by lining up in alphabetical order
3. Learning color words
4. Learning animal words
5. Learning number words
6. Learning theme words
7. Learning rhyming words (such as *tree* and *see*)
8. Learning words from a particular word family that has an ending rhyme (such as /op/,/at/, /in/)
9. Learning words with one syllable
10. Learning words that start with a consonant and vowel (such as *cat, cattle, car,* which all start with *ca*)
11. Learning words that have the same vowel sounds (such as *pig, sit, tin*)
12. Learning words with silent letters (such as *bomb,* with a *b* at the end; *phone,* with a *p* at the beginning; *ghost,* with a silent *h*)
13. Learning contractions
14. Learning compound words
15. Learning words with prefixes and suffixes
16. Learning homophones
17. Learning words with the same root (such as *medical* and *medicine*).

During the last 30 years, the linguistic approach, and word making have been followed by **word sorts.** Word sorting is when children place words in categories, either by sound, look, or meaning. In using this method, children compare and contrast individual words on word cards and line them up in a row or put them on a word sorter slotted chart. In latest research studies, such word activities have been identified to assist children in improving their phonics abilities (Freppon & Dahl, 1998; Stahl & Duffy-Hester, 1998).

There is wide (but not unanimous) agreement among researchers that early literacy acquisition depends, at least in part, on awareness of the phonology of the language, especially in languages that use alphabetic routing systems, word making activities, linguistics approach, and analytical phonics (Adams, 1990; Share & Stanovich, 1995). **Phonological awareness** is defined by Stanovich as "the ability to phonologically segment, analyze, and synthesize the speech stream" (1998, p. 552). In addition to developing phonological awareness, children must also learn the **alphabetic principle.** The alphabetic principle is the phenomenon in English that each speech sound or phoneme is represented by a distinct graphic or graphemic symbol that readers can read.

The results of a recent survey by Ehri and Oakhill (1999) suggest that the majority of phonics lessons in preschools appear to use the **balanced approach.** In kindergarten, however, only a third of the classrooms observed continue to teach phonics using literature. The number drops so that by first and second grade only a fifth of all classroom teachers have learned to implement a balanced approach to phonics instruction. A balanced approach means that children are exposed to more than just environmental print or book discoveries on their own. Exposure to environmental print alone is demonstrating to be insufficient as an instructional aid; environmental print is unable to teach elementary school-aged children all the phonics generalizations necessary to become independent automatic readers.

In addition to exposure to quality literature, children learn to read best when participating in word games and when they develop word identification skills such as rhyming knowledge, lowercase letter knowledge, sound correspondence, alliteration detection, nursery rhyme knowledge, and phonics generalizations that are described next in this chapter. Such instruction has proven to have long-term effects, as Hanson and Farrell (1998) demonstrated. Children who are taught with a balanced approach in kindergarten continue to develop their literacy skills and surpass the scholastic and reading achievement of peers not taught with such a balanced approach to instruction when these children reach their high school years.

How to Teach Phonemic Awareness and Phonics.   What is necessary before you can teach phonics? It has been demonstrated that teachers themselves must have a depth of explicit knowledge necessary to navigate students through the complexity of English orthology and phonology (Ira, 1997, 1998; Venezky, 1998). If you are interested in determining your ability to understand phonics, there are two steps you might take before you read on. The first is to read the information in Table 5.3. In this table, you will find information about understanding words that students must use either consciously or subconsciously to be able to decode.

What is the best way to teach children phonemic awareness and decoding skills? This question has been debated throughout the twentieth century. In response to this question, the International Reading Association has consistently maintained that

no single approach to reading and writing instruction can be considered best for every child. In response to many requests for *positional phonics,* the role of phonics in reading instruction

TABLE 5.3 PHONICS GENERALIZATIONS AND UNDERSTANDINGS ABOUT WORDS THAT STUDENTS NEED TO LEARN

1. High-Frequency Words
2. Letter–Sound Relationships and Patterns
   a. Consonants
      - Consonant Clusters (e.g., *s* clusters: *st, sp, sn, sm, sl, sc, sk, sw, spl, str, spr, scr, squ*)
      - Consonant Digraphs
      - Alternative Sounds *r*
   b. Vowels
      - Long and Short
      - Vowel Combinations
      - Two Sounds of *oo*
      - Vowels with *r*
      - Silent *e*
      - Phonograms
      - Open and Closed Syllables
3. Word Structure, Word Meaning, and Other Categories
   a. Contractions
   b. Compound Words
   c. Affixes
      - Inflectional Endings
      - Prefixes
      - Suffixes
   d. Synonyms
   e. Antonyms
   f. Homonyms
   g. Plurals
   h. Possessives
   i. Clipped Words
   j. Abbreviations
   k. Syllabication
   l. Greek and Latin Word Roots
4. Phonic Definition
   a. Like single consonants, a *consonant cluster* can be the onset of a word, like *spr* in *spring.*
   b. Referred to as *consonant digraphs,* sometimes two consonant letters represent one sound that is different from either of the sounds alone (e.g., *ch*eese, *wh*ere, *sh*oe, *th*is).
   c. There are two common sounds for *th* (*thought* and *this*).
   d. The sound of *f* can also be represented by two other consonant clusters, *ph* (*phone, photograph*) and *gh* (*cough, laugh*).
   e. Sometimes consonants are doubled, as in *little, runner, summer, puffin, dress, bell.*
   f. Sometimes clusters of consonants may be referred to as *final digraphs* (a letter cluster at the end of a word) such as *ck, nk,* and *ng.*
   g. The sound of *k* can be represented by a *c* or a *k,* as in *car* or *key.*
   h. *C* and *g* make two sounds, as in *car, face,* or *giraffe, get.*
   i. Sometimes consonants are silent, as in *knowledge* or *wrap.*
   j. *Qu* sounds like *kw,* as in *quiet.*
5. Syllable Rules
   a. Words have parts that you can hear.
   b. Some words have just one part and others have more than one part.
   c. You can clap and count the parts of words.
   d. Every syllable has a vowel sound.
   e. Usually, endings and prefixes are syllables in themselves.
   f. When you have a prefix, the spelling of the root word does not change (*reread*).
   g. When a word has two consonants in the middle, divide the syllables between the consonants (*bet-ter*).
   h. Syllables ending with a vowel have long vowel sounds (*ho-tel*).
   i. Syllables ending with a consonant have short vowel sounds (*mat-tress*).
   j. When a word ends with *le,* the consonant preceding it joins the cluster to make a syllable (*trou-ble*).
   k. Letter clusters such as *th, ch, wh, sh, ck, nk,* and *ng* usually stay together in a syllable.
   l. Affixes and endings are syllables that have meaning.

and position statement of the International Reading Association was adopted by the Board of Directors in January 1997 and stated: the teaching of phonics is an important aspect of beginning reading instruction and must be taught in the primary grades. Phonics instruction is necessary to promote independence in reading and must be embedded in the context of the total reading language arts program. (IRA, 1997, p. 1)

It will be important for you to develop the ability to teach phonics in the context of using authentic experiences, with authentic being defined as increasing students' power to use the elements of English orthography, as defined in Table 5.3, in activities that they will be doing throughout their lives beyond school. That is, authentic instruction will involve reading books, stopping to analyze words that are unknown, writing about the reflections they have as they read, and asking for better definitions by seeking reference materials to identify the meaning and pronunciation of individual words.

Recent research suggests that such instruction does not occur through particular packaged programs. Instead, it occurs through teachers being able to respond to the messages and clues that students give them, and to provide explicit explanations that are effective and adapted to individual students' needs (Duffy & Hoffman, 1999).

Phonics programs that can supplement your instruction include Sequoyah Literacy Systems (100 Galleria Parkway, Suite 1340, Atlanta, Georgia 30309), the Advantage Program of Accelerated Reading (P.O. Box 8036, Wisconsin Rapids, Wisconsin 54495–8036), Preparing Young Children for Reading Success (Debeck Education, P.O. 33738 Station D, Vancouver, B.C., Canada), the Benchmark Word Identification Program (2107 N. Providence Rd., Media, Pennsylvania 19063), and the Saxon Approach (Oklahoma City, Oklahoma), among others (Baumann, Hoffman, Moon, Duffy-Hester, 1998).

Theodore Clymer (1963) was among the first to analyze the usefulness of single rules to teach children about phonics and our language. Since that time, several studies have described the 45 different rules that are usually taught to children about the English language, shown on the website that accompanies this textbook (Clymer, 1963, reprinted 1996). The phonics generalizations in and of themselves are not as important to teach as the information in Table 5.3. Children must learn not only the rules of our language that apply to single letter sounds, but also how sounds are blended together: how *r* controls vowels, the Anglo-Saxon letter–sound correspondence, syllable patterns, morphing patterns; Greek and romance language letter–sound correspondence, syllable patterns, morphing patterns; and each of the other divisions of high-frequency words, word structures, word meaning, and other categories, as described in Table 5.3. When you begin to develop your phonics program, it is important for you to develop each element in Table 5.3. Table 5.4 describes the level at which each component in Table 5.3 needs to be introduced to children. By the end of second grade, most children should have mastered all the basic knowledge concerning phonics.

Phonics instruction has been criticized by some because, in the past, it was instructed incorrectly or overemphasized. As you may recall, when you were in elementary school, your teacher probably taught phonic principles as rules to be memorized, perhaps as many as one hundred. You may have also completed worksheets by matching sounds of letters and words you heard to pictures. Then, you

TABLE 5.4 PHONICS: MASTERY EVALUATION FOR TEACHERS

PHONEMIC AWARENESS
1. How many phonemes are in the word *umbrella*?   a. 1   b. 2   c. 5   d. 6   e. 7
2. How many graphemes are in the word *umbrella*?   a. 3   b. 4   c. 5   d. 7   e. 8

Vowels: Long and Short

Vowel sounds may be expressed in two ways: long and short. Mastery of each of these sounds will be evaluated in this section.

LONG VOWEL SOUNDS
Read each of the following sentences. Choose the word with the same vowel sound as the underlined word in each sentence.

_____ 3. The <u>raging</u> flood is destroying the beautiful homes.

   a. blue   b. clap   c. plate   d. mark

_____ 4. The old bus <u>broke</u> down on the way to the game.

   a. sport   b. cot   c. desk   d. pole

_____ 5. The <u>bright</u>, hot sun is shining on the window.

   a. quiet   b. perfect   c. thought   d. craft

_____ 6. The computer malfunctioned because it needs to be <u>cleaned</u>.

   a. crowd   b. poor   c. enough   d. class

_____ 7. The <u>cute</u> puppies were sleeping next to their mother.

   a. butter   b. mule   c. clasp   d. trick

SHORT VOWEL SOUNDS
For each word listed below, underline the letter(s) that make the short vowel sound.

   8. stamp   10. truck   12. humble   14. butter   16. crept
   9. popped   11. dimple   13. intern   15. cotton   17. gamble

Vowel Generalizations: Sandwich Words (CVVC) vs. Layer Cake Words (CVCE)

The placement of vowels in a word determines the sounds that they represent. Mastery of recognizing these placements will be evaluated in this section.

SANDWICH WORDS
For each word below, indicate with a checkmark the correct explanation of the vowel sound in that word.

18. **sail**   _____ long *a* sound   _____ silent *a*   _____ short *i* sound
               _____ short *a* sound   _____ long *i* sound

19. **float** _____ long *o* sound   _____ silent *o*   _____ short *a* sound
               _____ short *o* sound   _____ long *a* sound

20. **please** _____ long *e* sound   _____ silent *e*   _____ short *a* sound
               _____ short *e* sound   _____ long *a* sound

(continued)

TABLE 5.4 (CONTINUED)

LAYER CAKE WORDS

For each group of words below, circle the words that represent the sound indicated at the top of each group.

21. *a-e*	22. *i-e*	23. *o-e*	24. *u-e*
pane	slide	sloan	slug
tall	cliff	group	huge
sale	price	broke	blunt
crate	grim	pole	trust

Digraphs: Consonant and Vowel

Particular combinations of consonants and vowels create digraphs. Mastery of these digraphs and their sounds is evaluated in this section.

25. In the group of words below, circle the words that contain consonant digraphs. Underline the words with vowel digraphs. In the space to the right, write the digraph.

beam ___ seam ___ charge ___ rough ___ brain ___ plead ___

stain ___ phase ___ creed ___ throw ___ which ___ enough ___

Consonant Blends

Combinations of consonants create consonant blends. Mastery of recognizing these blends is evaluated in this section.

26. Underline the consonant blend in each word below.

blanket	plow	strange	program	clock	standard
sprain	trauma	draw	smash	flock	drake

Diphthongs

Combinations of vowels create diphthongs. Mastery of recognizing diphthongs is evaluated in this section.

27. Circle each word below that contains a diphthong. In the space to the right, write each diphthong for the word.

couch ___ four ___ gray ___ spoil ___ train ___ crew ___

convoy ___ own ___ plan ___ coat ___ fowl ___

Created by Brandy Horton, 2000, master of elementary education degree candidate at Texas Christian University, Fort Worth, TX. Used by permission.

learned exceptions to phonic "rules." Because so many phonic "rules" were taught, when you came to an unknown word, often you either did not remember the rule it followed, or the word you needed to decode was an exception to that rule. Today, you will teach your students only 14 phonic generalizations because these are the most prevalent in our language. That is, the 14 phonic generalizations shown in Table 5.3 enable students to decode English words with that pattern 8 out of 10 times because the letter-to-sound correspondence specified by these generalizations will be followed in 80 percent of the phonetically regular English words in which they appear. You will teach these phonic generalizations in needs-based small groups just as you taught sight word strategies.

Phonic Generalizations.   Phonics should be the first strategy students use to decode words when a word is phonetically regular (e.g., phonics should be used to decode *hat* because it contains the English word pattern like *cat, rat, bat,* and *sat*). After you teach and give examples of a phonic generalization, demonstrate how you can use that generalization in conjunction with context clues and structural analysis to decode many new words. Then read a sentence from a book and perform a think-aloud to decode one word in that sentence that adheres to the phonics generalization you are introducing. (Big books work very well for this section of the lesson because you can point to each word phonetically regular as you describe how you decoded it.) Next, ask one student to read aloud until he or she comes to the next word on that page that adheres to the same phonic generalization. This student explains the thinking he or she would use to decode that word if it was unfamiliar. Reading continues in this way until all students have had a chance to verbalize applications of the phonics generalization you introduced in this lesson.

A valuable step in teaching phonic generalizations is to model how to select from all the generalizations that are taught. To do so, you can make an overhead transparency of a page from a book, stop at a difficult word, and do a think-aloud of how you decoded it. You can also model how you think about meanings of words surrounding the one you know. Next, model how you select and apply one of the sound-to-letter generalizations to decode that difficult word. Reiterate this modeling until students volunteer to do a think-aloud for you when you stop at a difficult, phonically regular word. Without this oral modeling, students may never learn how to select a generalization on their own, how to apply it to a word, and how to use the sounds of letters to trigger meaning from their listening vocabularies.

The last step in this instructional series is for students to learn to use the 14 generalizations rapidly and independently. As Adams (1990) states, skilled reading is the result of a reader's speed and competence in perceiving the individual letters in words as well as the spelling patterns that make up words. To this end, researchers advocate sufficient practice in

- learning letter names and phonemes, as well as developing phonemic awareness;
- learning recurring spelling patterns; and,
- learning the most common sequence of letters within words.

For younger students, teachers like Ms. Hulsey tape big letters to the classroom floor. During free time and before dismissal each day, she asks her second-graders, one at a time, to stand on a particular letter that she names. The most dependable phonic generalizations appear in Table 5.4, which you can use as a self-assessment of your knowledge. After you have answered each question, you can turn to the answer key at the back of the book to identify how many generalizations you know.

Realizing you must know phonic generalizations to teach them, you can learn any phonics rules that you did not master in Table 5.4 by referring to one of the following books:

Teaching Phonics for Today: A Primer for Educators by Dorothy Strickland, 1998, International Reading Association, Newark, Delaware

The Phonics Awareness Handbook for Kindergarten and Primary Teachers by Lita Ericson and Moira Fraser Juliebo, 1998, International Reading Association, Newark, Delaware

Teacher's Guide for Evaluating Commercial Phonics Packages by Jean Osborne, Steven Stall, and Mercy Stein, 1997, International Reading Association, Newark, Delaware

When decoding and vocabulary recognition occurs by making comparisons to other spoken or written words it is called *decoding by analogy* (combining word parts and phonic generalizations). This ability to quickly and accurately pronounce phonically regular words that are not sight words consistently distinguishes good readers. By combining such word family instruction with reading and writing in which students are encouraged to use rhyming words to figure out how to pronounce or spell unknown words, less proficient readers can learn how to look for patterns in words. For example, you can teach a key word, such as *cat* for the /at/ phonogram and then say: "If this word is *cat,* then this word is (*hat*); if this word is *cat,* then this word is (*bat*)."

Then you can write five words that each represent a different phonogram, such as *day, flew, flag,* and *red,* and an irregular sight word, such as *the.* You can model the decoding by analogy strategy by reading a page from a book that contains a difficult word. As you perform a think-aloud to demonstrate the strategy, you can ask, "Is there any part of this word that you know, such as a meaning, sound, or spelling pattern?" An example follows with the difficult word, *incumbent,* in italics (Gaskins, Gaskins, & Gaskins, 1991, p. 216):

"The Senator was an *incumbent,* and so won the election easily." I can't think of a word that would make sense in this blank, so I think I'll try to decode it by analogy. I need to look for spelling patterns. I know a spelling pattern is the vowel and what comes after it. So, the first spelling pattern in this word is *I-n. I-n* is a word I already know, *in,* so I'll move on to the next spelling pattern. In this case that will be *u-m.* We have talked about the key word *drum,* so I will use that to help me with the second chunk. The third spelling pattern is *e-n-t.* I know the word *tent.* I already know the first chunk is *in.* And, if I know *d-r-u-m* is *drum,* then *c-u-m* is *cum.* And, if I know *t-e-n-t* is *tent,* then *b-e-n-t* is *bent.* The word is *incumbent.* Let's see if that makes sense in the sentence. "The senator was an incumbent and so won the election easily." Yes, that makes sense. I have heard that word on the news. I'm not exactly sure what it means though. I'll look it up. It says that an incumbent is a person who holds an elective office or position.

Students then complete a structured language experience approach and use the five words you introduced in a story that they compose on chart paper. Next, students perform a chant and a check spelling exercise using the five words introduced to reinforce their awareness of the spelling pattern in the five key words. They write these words from memory or copy them from the chart. Then they write a word that has the same word part but one that they have not yet been taught. For example, after *cat* is written and taught, students must write *hat* without having been taught that word that day.

Blending Made Easy.   Blending is difficult for many readers. Gliding individual sounds together in a word is an abstract concept. It is also difficult to learn merely by watching someone else's mouth as they blend or by seeing the steady movement of a hand beneath a word as it motions the speed of blending together its parts. However, Rosenshine and Stevens (1984) found that time spent in blending activities (for students functioning at first- and second-grade reading levels) results in higher achievement and increased vocabularies.

Unfortunately, past instructional approaches to blending were not as effective as desired. Because they asked students to say every sound separately, students' blending often resulted in unrecognizable words. For example, say each of the following sounds separately: /p/, /e/, /a/, and /t/. Now, say the sounds rapidly together. Did you say "peeaht" instead of "peat" as in *peat moss*? Another difficulty in past blending lessons is that whenever students had to separate a stop consonant phoneme (/b/, /ch/, /d/, /g/, /k/, /g/, /j/, /k/) from other letters, they had to say the /uh/ sound before they could blend it to the next letter in the word. For example, say these letters slowly and separately: /d/, /e/, /a/, /r/. Now, say the sounds again separately but a little bit faster: *duhear.* Therefore, regardless of how hard teachers pushed readers to say separate sounds faster and faster, correct blending did not result; many never approximated the spoken word that was represented.

Miller (1993) developed a more effective way to teach blending. Ask readers to say the correct medial vowel sound first, based on their use of the phonic generalizations in Table 5.3 to decode English words that contain the *cvc, cvcc,* and *cve* patterns. Then, have them attach the consonant sound that follows that vowel to that vowel sound and blend these two phonemes together. For example, for the word *d,* the student would say the sound /a/ and then /at/ as a single, blended sound. Last, the student would be asked to add the last sound: /rat/. Miller (1993) suggests extending this activity by demonstrating that changing one phoneme changes the word (e.g., *rat* becomes /rate/).

Another blending activity is to have students change words that begin with a single consonant to ones that begin with blends or digraphs or vice versa. You can write words that begin with consonant blends but ask students to say the base word first and then blend in the additional consonant sounds:

stop	top	_top (stop)
black	lack	_lack (black)

Moreover, when readers learn that there are only 120 major word patterns and 3,000 basic sight words that account for the largest majority of words that they will ever read in life, the goal of achieving rapid decoding becomes a reality for them. To illustrate this fact, readminister these blending activities one week later and demonstrate to students how much their blending abilities have improved by noting the increased number of phonetically regular words that they can read following instruction.

In closing, some readers enjoy taking pre- and posttests to see visible results of how much they have learned. (Table 5.4 presents in a nonthreatening format samples of every phonic generalization). In addition, it does not take long to analyze test results. A score of 80-percent accuracy indicates students' self-initiated use of phonetic analysis.

STRUCTURAL ANALYSIS

Structural analysis is analyzing morphemes, prefixes, suffixes, and word parts within multisyllable words to decode and determine meaning. Students in second grade and above must learn how to use as the first decoding strategy for decoding long words. For example, if students do not know the word *repeatedly,* they should think, "This is a long word so I should use structural analysis. I know the prefix *re* means 'to do again,' *peat* is the root word, *ed* means 'in the past,' and *ly* means the action is continuing, so the word *repeatedly* means something is being done over and over." You can also teach morphemes as students need them, in small-group settings.

Students in kindergarten through second grade should learn the meanings of the endings *-s, -ed,* and *-ing,* and to decode. Older students can learn to use Greek, Latin, and other foreign root words, prefixes, and suffixes to decode new words.

For example, in a unit that Ms. Hulsey taught to second-graders, she wrote on the board: "A prefix is a group of letters that go in front of a word. A prefix changes the meaning of a word. When you peel it off, a word must be left." Then she wrote *undeliverable* and *under.* Then she taught the three major kinds of spelling changes that occur in suffixation: (1) consonant doubling (thinning, swimming, begged); (2) *y* to *i* (worried, flies, busily); and (3) deleted silent *e* (shaking, unbelievable). There are 100 English suffixes; most determine a word's part of speech, tense, or provide other clues to meaning. Internet sites are also valuable to learn the root words of a variety of languages. Following are three that were recommended by Leu and Kincer (1995):

The Human Languages Pages: www.june29.com/HLP/

This website contains 2,000 links to language sources and words and phrases from different languages.

Say Hello to the World Project: www.ipl.org/youth/hello

This website provides audioclips demonstrating how to say *hello* in various languages and includes basic vocabulary they would need if they ever traveled to that country.

Youth Division of the Internet Public Library: www.ipl.org/youth

This website contains information for teachers and students about more than 100 additional activities that teach structural analysis.

SECTION 2   PUTTING THEORY INTO PRACTICE
Teaching Content Vocabulary Sight Words, Phonemic Awareness, and Phonics

The purpose of this section is to report on new methods that have been created within the last 5 years to build students' vocabulary. It is important to build on the knowledge that each individual student has accumulated about the English language before they entered your classroom. You can do this by asking students questions, such as "How did you decode that word?"; and "How did you know its meaning?" Children can verbalize which phonics principles, vocabulary concepts, structural analysis clues, or sight word knowledge they used at that moment. After considering how a student answers and how that student demonstrates his or her skills in each reading opportunity, you can decide which of the following activities (or which activities from Chapters 6 or 7) would best move the child forward. Your decision should be based on the principle that each activity is designed to develop. For instance, four activities in this chapter are designed to develop vocabulary words that might be encountered outside of the semantic web or semantic unit being studied in school. Three methods describe how to teach sight words that a child may come across but that may not be related to a field of study or a thematic unit. Similarly, in this chapter specific types of books are discussed that you can read aloud or use for shared readings, assisted readings, or repeated reading activities to help develop phonics concepts, such as long $\bar{e}$. Most of the words in these books contain that particular phonemic element.

TEACHING CHILDREN TO INCREASE THEIR VOCABULARY

Shared reading is a method in which the children share in the reading. They can read along chorally after you finish; they can read the specific word that has the phonetic sound in it, such as a /p/ sound; or they can pick a book you displayed and read it with a partner.

In **assisted reading,** children join into pairs, or you and a student read together, or a student and an older tutor in your classroom sits with the student. In assisted reading, you read one page and the child reads the next page. Before the child begins reading, you stop and ask the child to tell you what he or she thinks will occur on the next page. Or you can ask a question. Your partner reads the next page and has a chance either to ask a question or make a prediction about the next page. Then you read a page, make a prediction, or ask a question. Then your partner takes a turn, and so forth.

Repeated reading is an activity that also can be used to develop any of the lessons in Chapters 5, 6, and 7. Repeated reading is when you or a more able reader reads a page followed by a rereading of that same page by a less able reader. This activity is based on the principle that repeated exposure to words, and hearing words correctly introduced the first time, can increase the chance that less able readers will learn to recognize the meaning, the vocabulary, the sight, and the phonemic principles related to that individual word on a first reading.

The following activities are suggested specifically to develop vocabulary, sight word knowledge, phonemic awareness, phonics, and structural analysis.

Categorical Comparisons of Properties and Illustrations.   One of the most effective ways of teaching vocabulary is to teach it thoroughly (Rasinski, 1998). In this activity, children place a word in the center of a diagram, as shown in Figure 5.3. For example, Ms. Hulsey's children wanted to learn what the word *feline* meant. She wrote the word *feline*. She asked the students what category it is in. She explained

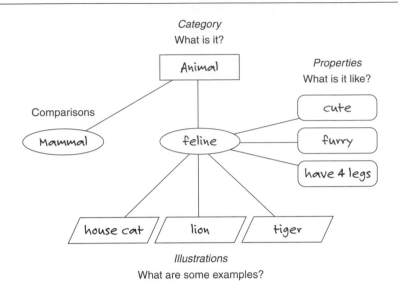

FIGURE 5.3 THE CATEGORY-COMPANION-PROPERTIES-ILLUSTRATION METHOD TO TEACH THE WORD *FELINE*

that a feline can be compared to other types of animals, such as mammals. The children associated felines with properties such as cute, furry, and four legs. They included examples: house cat, lion, tiger. These second-graders had eight words they used to assist their retention of the word *feline.*

Picture books, as shown in Literature Card 12, can be used in many, many ways to develop vocabulary. It is important to show children how words that describe the same concept often sound alike, look alike, or have the same group word as a meaning. The picture books listed in Literature Card 12 are designed for young children all the way up to eighth-grade children.

Verbal–Visual Word Association Strategy.   This strategy was developed by Hopkins and Bean (1999). It is most useful in developing content-area vocabulary. The activity begins by asking children to move beyond rote memorization of words and their definitions (Eeds & Cockrum, 1985). In this strategy, students are taught how roots and prefixes can also assist them in understanding the meaning of a word. You would first model the strategy and then students would be asked to implement the Verbal–Visual Word Association Strategy for at least one of the new words they come across each time they read.

To implement this strategy, you divide a rectangle into four parts, as shown in Figure 5.4. You show how the prefix has a meaning that contributes to the definition of the word. In the upper lefthand area, the student writes the portion of the word that adds to the meaning of the unknown word. In the upper righthand area, the stu-

Literature Card 12

PICTURE BOOKS TO DEVELOP VOCABULARY

Picture Books for Prekindergarten through Kindergarten

The Philharmonic Gets Dressed by K. Kuskin, 1982 Harper & Row

Fathers, Mothers, Sisters, Brothers: A Collection of Family Poems by M. A. Hoberman, 1991 Little, Brown

Creatures by L. B. Hopkins, 1985 Harcourt Brace Jovanovich

Don't You Turn Back: Poems by Langston Hughes by L. B. Hopkins, 1969 Alfred A. Knopf

Who Shrank My Grandmother's House: Poems of Discovery by B. J. Esbensen, 1992 HarpC Child Books

Why Am I Grown So Cold?: Poems of the Unknowable by M. C. Livingston, 1982 Atheneum

Climb into the Bell Tower: Essays on Poetry by M. C. Livingston, 1990 HarperCollins

I Am the Running Girl by A. Adoff, 1979 Harper & Row

Sam's Place: Poems from the Country by L. Moore, 1973 Atheneum

Working in the Dark: Reflections of a Poet of the Barrio by J. S. Baca, 1992 Red Crane Books

Independent Voices by E. Merriam, 1968 Atheneum

Oh Such Foolishness by W. Cole, 1991 HarperCollins

Good Books for Sixth-, Seventh-, and Eighth-Graders

If You're Not Here, Please Raise Your Hand: Poems about School by K. Dakos, 1990 Macmillan

Old Possum's Book of Practical Cats by T. S. Eliot, 1967 Harcourt Brace Jovanovich

Joyful Noise: Poems for Two Voices by P. Fleischman, 1988 Harper & Row

Birches by R. Frost, 1988 Henry Holt

Looking for Your Name: A Collection of Contemporary Poems by P. B. Janeczko, 1993 Orchard

The Trees Stand Shining: Poetry of the North American Indians by H. Jones, 1993 Dial

Sports Pages by A. Adoff, 1986 J. B. Lippincott

My Friend's Got This Problem, Mr. Candler: High School Poems by M. Glenn, 1991 Clarion Books

Back to Class: Poems by MellGlenn, 1988 Clarion Books

Black Mesa Poems by J. S. Baca, 1989 New Directions

If I Could Only Tell You: Poems for Young Lovers and Day-dreamers by E. Merriam, 1983 Alfred A. Knopf

Poems: The Dreamkeeper and Other Poems by L. Hughes, 1994 Knopf

Poem-Making: Ways to Begin Writing Poetry by M. C. Livingston, 1991 HarperCollins

All the Colors of the Race by A. Adoff, 1982 Lothrop

Good Vocabulary Books with a Lot of Pictures for First- and Second-Graders

The Silver Cow: A Welsh Tale by S. Cooper, 1983 McElderry Books

The Magic Stove by M. Ginsbury, 1983 Coward-McCann

Mother Crocodile: An Uncle Amadou Tale from Senegal by R. Guy, 1981 Delocorte Press

All Clean! by H. Ziefert & H. Drescher, 1986 Harper & Row

Use Your Head, Dear by Aliki, 1983 Greenwillow

Daydreamers by E. Greenfield, 1981 Dial Books

Our Granny by M. Wild, 1994 Ticknor & Fields

Jeff's Hospital Book by H. L. Sobol, 1975 Holt

I'm Not Oscar's Friend Anymore by M. Sharmat, 1975 Dutton

My Dentist and other books by H. Rockwell, 1975 Greenwillow

One Step, Two . . . and other books by C. Zolotow, 1981 Lothrop, Lee & Shepard

Out! Out! Out! and other books by M. Alexander, 1968 Dial

Where the Wild Things Are by M. Sendak, 1963 Harper & Row

Is Your Mama a Llama? by D. Guarino, 1989 Scholastic

Big Wheels by A. Rockwell, 1986 Dutton

All Gone! by H. Ziefert & H. Drescher, 1986 Harper & Row

Good Vocabulary Books to Tell You a Lot about the Subject for Third- to Fifth-Graders

Mooncake by F. Asch, 1988 Aladdin

Thirteen by R. Charlip and J. Joyner, 1994 Aladdin

A Little Pigeon Toad by F. Gwynne, 1990 Aladdin

Ruth Low Thrills a Nation by D. Brown, 1993 Ticknor & Fields

No Peas for Nellie by C. Demarest, 1991 Aladdin

Who Sank the Boat? by P. Allen, 1983 Coward-McCann

The Wish Card Ran Out! by J. Stevenson, 1981 Greenwillow

The Wrong Side of the Bed by E. Ardizzone, 1970 Doubleday

Elephant by I. Redmond, 1993 Knopf

Busybody Nora by J. Hurwitz, 1990 Morrow Jr.

Rosie's Walk by P. Hutchins, 1972 Weston Woods

A House Is a House for Me by M. A. Hoberman, 1978 Viking

Whose Baby? by M. Yabuuchi, 1985 Philomel

Cock-a-Doodle-Doo! by H. Ziefert & H. Drescher, 1986 Harper & Row

Tri = three	Tripod
The camera stood atop the tripod so that the photographer could take a picture without holding the camera	

FIGURE 5.4 THE VERBAL–VISUAL WORD ASSOCIATION METHOD TO LEARN THE WORD *TRIPOD*

dent writes the unknown word. In the lower lefthand area, the student writes the definition that was found in the dictionary or a sentence from a book in which the word appeared. In the lower righthand area, the student draws a picture to help him or her personally remember the word.

As shown in Figure 5.4, one day Allison came across the word *tripod*. She used the Verbal–Visual Word Association Strategy to teach herself the meaning of that word. She already knew that the word *tri* meant three, so she put *tri* and *three* in the upper lefthand area. Then she wrote the word *tripod* in the upper righthand area. She then wrote a sentence using the word. Because she knew that the word *tri* meant three, she read the sentence over again to determine the meaning of *tripod*. The sentence in the book that she was reading said: "The camera stood atop the tripod so that the photographer could take a picture without holding the camera." She wrote that sentence in the lower lefthand area. Then she drew a picture of what she thought a tripod would look like. When she finished, she realized that she had seen tripods before and that she knew what they were. To verify, she took her drawing to Ms. Hulsey who congratulated Allison on becoming a more automatic reader.

TEACHING STUDENTS TO INCREASE THEIR SIGHT VOCABULARY

One activity that students particularly enjoy is sight word tic-tac-toe. In this method, children simply draw a tic-tac-toe board and write a sight word that they learned in one of the squares. If another child can say the word, that child puts his or her mark over the word. If a student does not know the word, the student that wrote the word has the opportunity to say the word, tell the other child what it possibly means, and use it in a sentence. If that child does all three, his or her *X* or *O* is placed over that word. The second player then writes a word. If the first player can tell the meaning of that word and pronounce the word, then that player gets to put his or her *X* or *O* on the word. This strategy continues until the entire sight word game is complete.

Folder games are also very popular with students because they can be made by older tutor students, children's aids, or parent volunteers; they are easily available for student use.

A third activity has been used in many different forms throughout this century. It was first introduced in the United States in 1967 by Sylvia Ashton Warren in the classic book *The Teacher.* This activity is called a **word bank.** In personal file boxes, file folders, or large plastic storage bags, children place words they want to learn. Many people recommend that children attach words to pictures or draw a picture on the back of a word and place the word in the picture so that the **gestalt** (defined as the whole visual image) of the picture can assist the child in learning it (Johnstone, 1998).

Then students write the sentence in a book in which a word appeared; plus they draw a picture after interacting with a class peer who assists in learning the word. If the peer doesn't know the word, he or she can ask the teacher or a teacher's aid. When children hunt for words that they do not know, they learn to attend carefully to print it in their word banks as they copy each letter onto a card.

TEACHING STUDENTS PHONEMIC AWARENESS

It is important to assess how much phonemic awareness young children have. Children can have difficulty with phonemic awareness up until grade 2, as Ms. Hulsey discovered with Allison. The first step in determining a child's level is to test for phonemic awareness. One test is available later in this chapter. There are two additional tests available on the companion website to this book so that all aspects of phonemic awareness can be assessed. Once you have identified whether a child needs practice in one of the aspects of phonemic awareness, there are several teacher resource manuals and resource kits that can be used in the classroom. One that has been highly recommended by Ms. Hulsey and other primary teachers is the Scholastic Phonemic Awareness Kit (1998). This kit uses two puppets to teach children to blend and to segment sounds.

TEACHING STUDENTS PHONICS

One of the most valuable lessons for children is to learn each of the phonics generalizations that are presented in Tables 5.3 and 5.4. Introduce one phonemic element at a time using students' questions about words. When you have introduced a book and read it aloud, stop and ask the children what they think is the most important thing they want to learn from that book. If they ask you about a specific word, you can use the learning experiences from this book for teaching the phonetic elements that appeared. If, on the other hand, children are more curious about the meaning of the book, use that particular book sharing session to focus on comprehension instruction. In a student-centered language arts program, you can follow the lead of the children, as Ms. Hulsey did in the following example.

Mrs. Hulsey was conducting a science unit on insects. As she was reading a book about spiders, the word *heritage* appeared in a sentence: "It was the heritage of spiders to rule the landscape." Allison raised her hand and asked how she could learn the word *heritage.* Allison's verbal–visual association of the word *tripod,* as shown in

Figure 5.4, was still fresh in her mind. She pointed out that the word *age* was in *heritage*. Ms. Hulsey said, "Yes, Allison, you are using the verbal–visual association strategy perfectly. *Age* does relate to *heritage*. If you see the word *herit* at the beginning of a word, you can remember that it means something was passed down." She asked the students to tell the class about things inherited from grandparents. The class began to share. Ms. Hulsey turned back to Allison and said, "Now, let's put *herit* and *age* together with their meanings. What do you think is the meaning of *heritage*?" Allison said, "It's when people pass things down through the ages—*heritage.*" Ms. Hulsey said, "Yes, you are developing your vocabulary well." In this example, the phonic principle cannot be properly applied to *heritage*. If Ms. Hulsey had presented the word phonetically, the children would have sounded out the word as *her-i-tage*. Because this strategy would not have illuminated the meaning of *heritage* it is not the correct strategy to use for this word. Thus, part of teaching phonics is to teach children to use it proactively.

Proactive phonics is a method of teaching children how to decide the best strategy to use to decode a new word. It is designed to support structural analysis and context clues. Children are taught to study the sound of the word, the way the word looks, and the parts of the word and its meaning—all at the same time. Teaching phonics proactively means that children are instructed to determine whether the sounds of the word, the way the word looks, or the parts of the word and its meaning give the best clues to decoding the word. The second component of proactive phonics is to ask students, "What have you tried?"; "What do you want me to help you do to decode this phonetically regular word?" If a word is phonetically irregular, strategies other than phonics should be used to decode the word, as shown previously with the phonetically irregular word *heritage*.

Another strategy, the **talk-to-yourself chart,** was developed by the Benchmark School (1996). It enables children to learn that certain sounds in our language are represented in print by more than one letter. For example, in the word *rock*, the k sound at the end of the word is spelled with *ck*. As shown in Table 5.5, there are six

TABLE 5.5 "TALK-TO-YOURSELF" CHART

Ms. Hulsey used the "Talk-To-Yourself" Chart for her students to learn the phonetic generalization that /k/ can be represented as *ck*.

1. The word is *rock.*
2. Stretch the word.

    I hear *3* sounds.
3. I see *4* letters because /k/ is spelled *ck*. (Students reconcile the number of letters they see with the number of sounds they hear.)
4. The spelling pattern is /ck/.
5. This is what I know about the vowel: /ock/.
6. Another word on the word wall with the same vowel sound is *sock.*

sentences that children are to complete with a phonetically regular word they do not know. They do these with a partner. First they write the word they do not know. In this example, they would have written, "The word is *rock.*" When they stretch the word, they hear three sounds, but they see four letters because the k sound is spelled *ck.* Students then reconcile the number of letters they see with the number of sounds they hear, so they deduce that the spelling pattern for /k/ is *ck.* Second, they know that the vowel sound would be /ah/, a short sound because of the *CVC* phonic generalization. Another word on the word wall with the same sound is *sock.* By going through each of these steps, children are improving not only their phonics recognition skills, but also their spelling ability.

TEACHING STRUCTURAL ANALYSIS

Teaching students Greek, romantic language, and Anglo-Saxon root words is a very important component of structural analysis instruction. In the Anglo-Saxon language, words created to represent new concepts usually are formed by combining two already existing words. Many root words can be found compound words, such as *sunshine* and *cowboy.* The romance languages, however, use many prefixes and suffixes to form new words; *predicate, admit, submarine,* and *telephone* are examples of this. The word *international,* was formed by adding a prefix that meant going beyond *nation.* If a word has several prefixes and suffixes, it usually has been derived from a romance language. The Greek language, however, keeps the meaning of a base concept but may alter the spelling. For example, the words *physics* and *psychology* both have to do with science. The suffix *ology* means "the study of." In words such as *television, telephone, chrometer, thermometor, automobile, automatic,* you find other spelling alterations.

When children are aware that the English language is formed from three types of basic language roots, it is easier for them to understand that they can break words in many different ways. That is, children can learn that certain compound words retain their spelling and their sound when put together because they come from an Anglo-Saxon origin. This knowledge helps them learn to pronounce words they do not know. They can learn to break down compound words because they can see that the root words are words in and of themselves.

In addition, children can also learn that a word derived from a romance language maintains the root word in the middle. They can look for prefixes and suffixes while understanding that the root word is the main meaning of that word. Similarly, if they know that certain Greek words have a root that occurs at the beginning or end of the word and that that root may affect the spelling and sound of the word, they can better decode that word. Once they learn that *auto* means "self-running," they can use that information and that listening vocabulary to figure out the pronunciations and meanings of words like *automobile* and *automatic.*

With this type of instruction, children seem to thrive at the detective work they can do in a fun-filled atmosphere, under your guidance or alone, to help them develop their structural analysis skills, which are a major part of building students' spelling skills. Chapter 9, which focuses more on assisting children with spelling, introduces other methods used for structural analysis, such as architect design.

INSIDE CULTURALLY AND ACADEMICALLY DIVERSE CLASSROOMS

Identifying Decoding Difficulties

Many states require language arts teachers to diagnose dyslexia and other decoding difficulties. **Dyslexia** is "a disorder manifested by difficulty in learning to read despite conventional instruction, adequate intelligence, and sociocultural opportunity. It results from fundamental cognitive disabilities which are frequently of constitutional origin" (World Federation of Neurology, 1970, p. 11). This fall nearly 3 million new students will begin kindergarten, and by the end of their school career 250,000 of them (1 in 12) will be diagnosed with some form of dyslexia. This literacy difficulty is one of the most misunderstood and misdiagnosed.

The causes of dyslexia are often erroneously attributed to "everything from emotional problems to brain damage to inner-ear dysfunction" (Levinson, 1985, p. 34). In addition, dyslexia is commonly perceived as a disease in which students merely have trouble putting written letters and words in proper order. Unfortunately, reality goes far beyond this simplistic perception, as the following self-reports illustrate:

> *When I look at a word, my eye goes from the end of the word to the front, and then my mind will translate it from the front to the end. When I look at a word, I look at it from back to front, and then I mentally tell myself to flop it back the other way.*
>
> —Heather, college student

> *If someone put the words "pound," "proud," and "pruned" on a line and asked me to pick out "proud" I have serious doubts as to whether I could accurately perform the task because the words look the same to me.*
>
> —Anonymous adult who has dyslexia

> *For me, printed symbols were not stationary, but three-dimensional and freely floating on the page. Letters appeared as three-dimensional entities and would revolve independently. Therefore, I could not discern a "b" or "d" from a "p." I could not fathom how to tell the difference between these three letters. In addition, the order of the letters was not stationary. To this day, I type "eht" and not recognize that it should be "the."*
>
> —Thomas Fleming, Director of Department of
> Commerce Law Library (Cody, 1985, p. 24)

Although dyslexia manifests itself differently in individual students, readers with dyslexia frequently exhibit delayed spoken language, errors in letter naming, difficulty in learning and remembering printed words, reversal of letters in words, repeated spelling errors, cramped and illegible handwriting, difficulty in finding the right word when speaking or writing, slow writing speed, reduced oral language comprehension, and directional spatial confusion. A checklist to assist in diagnosing dyslexia appears in Table 5.6. Also these readers experience the added burden of being incorrectly judged lazy by uninformed peers and adults.

Readers also have other decoding difficulties. For example, in addition to phonological processing differences, some students have auditory perception problems that make it difficult to follow oral directions; visual perception problems that impair their memory for written words; poor fine motor skills that inhibit their handwriting; or speech articulation difficulties that interfere with their being understood (Hyde, 1992). On the other hand, many have remarkable abilities in areas other than language, such as exceptional visual-spatial or artistic abilities.

TABLE 5.6 CHECKLIST OF POSSIBLE DYSLEXIA CHARACTERISTICS

If a student demonstrates 10 or more of the following characteristics, he or she should be referred for further assessment.

1. Is your child late or irregular in speech development?

2. Does your child have trouble keeping attention focused on one thing?

3. Does your child have trouble controlling a crayon or scissors?

4. Does your child have difficulty jumping rope, skipping, swimming, or doing other things that require repeated rhythm movements?

5. Is your child clumsy?

6. Do your child's language difficulties persist into adolescence?

7. Does learning to speak a foreign language seem to be an impossibility for your child?

8. Does your child reverse words, reading *was* instead of *saw,* or make internal word mistakes, such as reading *want* for *went* or *house* for *horse?*

9. Is your child's handwriting difficult to decipher? Do letters look different each time your child writes them?

10. Is your child a poor speller?

11. Does your child have trouble finishing tests in the allotted time period?

12. Does your child have difficulties singing in tune?

13. Does your child seem slow in sports?

14. Is reading aloud painful for your child?

15. Does your child reverse numbers?

16. Does your child have to hold a book out farther than a normal 14 inches in order to read?

17. Are word problems (the ones that begin "If Johnny has 6 apples . . .") difficult for your child?

18. Are reading skills far behind peers for no explanation?

19. Does your child confuse left and right?

20. Have other family members been poor readers?

21. Is your child immature when compared to peers?

22. In infancy, were there reversals in speech?

23. Was your child confused by concepts such as *up* and *down,* or *yesterday* and *tomorrow?*

24. Does your child have serious difficulty in learning and remembering printed words or symbols?

25. Does your child have difficulty following simple instructions?

Source: Adapted from "Diagnosing and Treating Dyslexia," by D. Kaercher, May 1995, *Health,* pp. 10–11; and *Symptoms Indicating Dyslexia,* by C. Drak (a national expert on the subject and a dyslexic himself), 1994, Chicago, IL: The Orton Society.

RECOGNIZING AND REPORTING PROGRESS

Assessments That Can Be Used for Testing Vocabulary, Decoding, and Structural Analysis Skills

In addition to the following test, there are several tests available on the website that accompanies this textbook. These tests are both formal and informal. Among them are a checklist for emergent readers, a checklist for novice readers, concepts of print tests, and teacher self-evaluations for children. The Yopp-Singer Test of Phonemic Segmentation can be used to assess whether children can hear separate phonemes. A second type of test uses verbal prompts during one-on-one sessions with children. These prompts enable young readers to become aware of their behaviors and learn to solve problems in decoding by themselves. The following questions have been recommended by Ruzzo (1999):

> *Prompt Attention to Meaning:* "Does that make sense?"
>
> *Promote Attention to Language Structure:* "Does that sound right?"
>
> *Promote Attention to Visual Information:* "Does that look right?"
>
> *Prompt to Integrate Meaning and Visual Clues:* "Does it look right and sound right?"
>
> *Prompt Reading Awareness:* "How do you know?" "Were you right?" "How do you know?" "You said _____. Does that make sense?" "Go back and think about what would make sense." "Do you know something about that word that can help you?"

A third assessment strategy is to teach students to look beyond themselves for help. Taylor (1996) recommended that, in kindergarten through first and second grade, we help children develop phonemic awareness by asking them to write words and draw boxes around them. For example, they write the word *wild.* They draw a box around *w,* around *i,* and around *ld*—the three sounds they hear. Similarly, when they write the word *boat,* they draw a box around *b,* around *oa,* and around *t.* By doing this two letters can be shown to come at the beginning of a word, at the end of a word, or in the middle of a word. Children soon learn that several letters can go together to make one sound. Once you teach this method, you can use it as an assessment strategy to assist children to learn this concept.

Another phonics test, the name test, was developed by Cunningham (1992). It was validated by Duffelmeyer, Kruz, Merkley, and Fyfe (1994) and Duffelmeyer and Black (1996). There are other aspects of phonemic awareness that need to be assessed if children have difficulty hearing the differences between sounds (e.g., print concepts, morpheme deletion, syllable deletion, phoneme identification, syllable identification, and phoneme deletion). A test for each of these is available on the website that accompanies this book.

Many states are also requiring that teachers diagnose dyslexia. For example, Texas law related to dyslexia (Texas Code Senate Bill 21.924) states that, in accordance with the program, each school district shall provide for the treatment of any student determined to have dyslexia-related disorders. Specific reading disorders must be diagnosed by the regular classroom teacher as soon as any decoding problems are noted. To assist in this purpose, Table 5.6 is a checklist for possible high-risk dyslexia candidates. By determining whether a child possesses a majority of these characteristics, you have an objective indicator to refer that child for further testing. Even if the child does not have dyslexia, if a majority of the cases in Table 5.6 are present, this may be an indication that the child would benefit from additional instruction to meet their vocabulary and decoding learning style differences.

DEVELOPING TECHNOLOGICAL COMPETENCIES

Electronic Books and Multimedia

Electronic books (also called interactive texts) are books on CD-ROM (compact disk—read-only memory) that contain auditory soundtracks and visual movements. These computer disks enable students to watch animation, be surprised by questions characters ask of them as they read on the computer screen, and engage in hundreds of click-and-explore surprises in which words are defined and sidetrips to develop vocabulary are possible. Most electronic books have interactive features by which students can stop the computer's reading and enacting of a story as often as they desire. For example, in the series *Magic Tales: Stories That Magically Come to Life* (Davidson Publishers) students hear nine original songs that encourage them to play with language and read along. In this series, students can read the Russian folk tale *Magi and the Magic Geese;* the African folk tale *Imo and the King,* and the Japanese folk tale *The Little Samarai.* Ms. Hulsey's class compared the cultures depicted in these after all the students had read them.

Electronic books are particularly valuable for vocabulary development because children can access voice-synthesized pronunciations and definitions (and even Spanish translations) by pointing the cursor at unrecognized words and pressing a key. Such series include Discis Books, Living Books (Broderbund), and Stories and More (IBM). In these books the child or computer reads the book and the student presses a key for the computer to turn the page. Vocabulary Development: Words, Words, Words by Troll Associates (100 Corporate Dr., Mahwah, NJ 07430), Vocabulary Works by Modern Curriculum Press (13900 Prospect Rd., Cleveland, OH 44136), and Vocabu-lit by The Perfection Form Co. (1000 N. Second Avenue, Logan, IA 51546), develop students' vocabulary with audiocassettes, filmstrips, and computer assistance. Target words are presented on the screen and in filmstrip scenes and their meanings are compared. Additional recommended software to build students' vocabulary appears in Table 5.7.

Multimedia refers to computer software that combines sound, movement, words, and visual images to convey information. The technologies of multimedia and communications are receiving considerable attention and an increasing variety of product offerings are coming to the market at affordable prices. Many teachers report that the activity with the greatest potential for improving the teaching and learning process is student-constructed multimedia. The book *Multimedia in the Classroom* by Agnew, Kellerman, and Meyer (1996) provides the necessary background on current and future hardware and software, discussion of pedagogy, and lesson suggestions.

Another development is the introduction of interactive multimedia materials, which combine the capabilities of computers with such multimedia devices as laser

TABLE 5.7 COMPUTER SOFTWARE THAT BUILDS DECODING ABILITIES

1. Eta Language Arts Program: Basic Vocabulary Kit (Educational Teaching Aids)
2. Reading Reinforcement Skill Text Series (Charles E. Merrill)
3. Filmstrips: Read On! Series II (ACI Films)
4. Common Words (Charles E. Merrill)
5. Vocabulary Laboratories (Holt, Rinehart & Winston)
6. LEIR—Language Experiences in Reading, Levels I, II, and III (Encyclopedia Britannica Educational Corporation)
7. Supermarket Recall Program (William Orr)
8. Sight Words for Survival (Lakeshore Curriculum Materials)
9. Reading Joy Gameboard Kits (Reading Joy)
10. Sight Word Labs: Set 1 and Set 2 (Developmental Learning Materials)
11. Breakthrough to Literacy (Longman)
12. Cove School Reading Program (Developmental Learning Materials)
13. Curious Creatures (Curriculum Associates)
14. SuperSonic Phonics (Curriculum Associates)
15. Working Phonics (Curriculum Associates)
16. CornerStone Language Arts (Courseware)

videodiscs. In a Martin Luther King, Jr., interactive multimedia package (ABC Interactive Video, 212-456-4060), for example, students use a workstation equipped with a videodisc player and monitor connected by cable to a computer. The computer provides a large amount of print information, such as the verbatim speeches of King, summaries of news events from his life, a time line of important events, a glossary, and digitized photographs. Students also use the computer to control the videodisc player, clicking on icons to combine videos of television news clips and King's speeches for their own presentations.

Mapping.   Students can use a computer-based atlas and encyclopedia as tools to learn more about geography and to create informative maps for their own autobiographies. Software suggestions are The New Grolier Multimedia Encyclopedia (Grolier), World Geography (MECC), and Picture Atlas of the World and ZipZapMap (National Geographic Society).

Graphing.   Students can compare a pen pals' life to theirs, so endless opportunities for graphing arise. Students can also create graphs showing military experience, education, family size, leisure activities, favorite school subjects, and so on. Software suggestions are The Graph Club (Tom Snyder) and The Cruncher (Davidson).

Researching.   As topics like the Great Depression, World War II, the space race, and famous people come up in discussions, students often want to know more. They can elaborate on these moments and people in history through software such as History in Motion (Scholastic), GTV: A Geographic Perspective on American History (National Geographic Society), The New Grolier Multimedia Encyclopedia (Grolier), Microsoft Bookshelf (Microsoft), and How the Leopard Got His Spots (Microsoft) or HyperStudio (Rodger Wagner) or Multimedia Workshop (Davidson) to combine graphs, maps, charts, and other visual information with text.

The following multimedia programs can also be ordered to increase students' language arts encoding/decoding abilities and content-area vocabulary:

AT&T Learning Network. Mac. Bridgewater: AT&T Easy Link Services.

Discis Books. Mac. Buffalo: Discis Knowledge Research.

Everybody's Reading! Video recording. New York: Scholastic.

Living Books. Mac. Novato, CA: Broderbund.

Mac Usa. Mac. Novato, CA: Broderbund.

Magic Slate. Apple. Pleasantville: Sunburst Communications.

Oregon Trail. MECC, 6160 Summit Drive North, Minneapolis, MN 55430-4003, 800-685-6322.

Scholastic Network. New York: Scholastic.

Success with Reading. Apple. Jefferson City, MO: Scholastic.

The Writing Center. Mac. Fremont, W.VA: Learning Company.

Additional multimedia have demonstrated that they increase students' reading and writing abilities as they increase their vocabularies (Levin, 1997; Moreno & Meyer, 1999). Examples of these multimedia kits include:

Time Detectives for Hire (Rand McNally, Skokie, IL) is a set of historical mysteries in which students travel back in time with four young detectives to solve American historical mysteries. In the process they learn many valuable historical terms through pictures and graphics.

Bird and Cat: DK Eyewitness Books (DK Multimedia, New York) is the first of two releases in which students enter a natural history museum in which each floor is devoted to a different animal. Students can learn about 100 species of cats as well as numerous content-specific words related to their habits and habitats.

The World's Best Poetry on CD (Roth Publishing, Inc., Great Neck, NY) contains over 22,000 full-text poems from 2,500 poets and full-length essays that trace the evolution of poetry in various ethnic groups as well as pictures of selected poets.

Adventures with Edison, Blue Tortoise, and Red Rhino (Corel Corp, Ottawa, Ontario, Canada) are three CDs that reinforce science, reading, math, and creative thinking skills. In Adventures with Edison students experiment and explore scientific principles, lead a search through museums, and produce their own music videos. Based on the children's book *Blue Tortoise,* this CD recounts the story of the tortoise's race to the picnic with the narrator reading aloud in either English or Spanish, as is the case in Red Rhino.

Story Starters: Science (Pelican Publishers, New York) is a content-specific, graphics-adorned, "talking" word-processing package. Story openers, clip art, and background information concerning many topics in life science (plants, animals, ecology), physical science (matter and energy), earth science (earth, space, and weather), and the human body are available on this CD-ROM.

The Super Storytree computer program (Brackett, New York) helps students write a class "Choose-a-Path Adventure Story" with alternate series of events and various endings. Once the story is perfected, it is programmed into a computer in the school library so schoolmates can read their adventure. Through this activity students assess their abilities to work in mathematically oriented industries, computer-driven jobs, and occupations that combine creative and highly technical skills.

SECTION 3   TEACHERS AS CONTINUAL LEARNERS

Using Children's Literature Daily

In this section of the chapter, you will learn how you can use children's literature to increase students' vocabulary and decoding abilities. You will read about the steps that make reading aloud enjoyable and meaningful for students, how journals can be converted into publishable books and how language deviations interfere with decoding.

PROFESSIONAL DEVELOPMENT ACTIVITY

Reading Aloud Effectively

Reading aloud has been cited as the most important activity for building the knowledge students require for vocabulary decoding, comprehension, and later reading success (Anderson, Hiebert, Scott, & Wilkerson, 1985). Reading aloud has many benefits, which include inspiring students to write, demonstrating the rhythm and flow of the English language, promoting students' motivation, improving vocabulary, broadening genre appreciation, building comprehension, encouraging visual imagery, and developing concepts of print.

Reading aloud to students is one of the best methods of advancing communication and thinking abilities, as well as developing students' vocabularies and an appreciation for literature. It also develops a sense of story—a schema for how stories work. Moreover, reading aloud to preschool and kindergarten children helps them learn the difference between written and spoken language. For example, when students are read to, they see the connection between what they hear and the symbols that make meaning in print (Sticht & James, 1984). Another reason for the power of this instructional activity is that for one section of each day, you become "face-less." As you read, students can befriend an author they have come to love. These authorial friends have a closeness to your students that you and others do not; authorial friends have not corrected students' errors or asked them to take risks. These friends always see students at their very best. Authors can unconditionally transport their student friends to places they've never been, especially when the following books are shared: *Indian in the Cupboard; The Book of Three; The Black Cauldron; Corduroy; Goodnight Moon; The Terrible, Horrible, Very Bad Day; Make Way for Ducklings; Sylvester and the Magic Pebble;* and *The Very Hungry Caterpillar* (for younger students). Authors also keep their interest from day to day with "cliff-hanging" chapter endings (e.g., *Summer of Fear* and *The View from the Cherry Tree*).

Moreover, when you read to students, slower readers are on equal footing with better, fluent readers. In sharing the beauty and power of the written word, each student experiences the effects that precise, well-chosen words can have on thinking. Through this realization, students often become convinced that the hard work required to create such language is worth it. The steps in an effective reading-aloud experience follow.

Step 1. *Select and practice.* Become a good oral reader. Practice reading the book, preferably out loud, before you share it with students. Vary the genre you read to build your students' literary tastes. Vary your voice for each character, and use your voice to create sound effects and build suspense.

Step 2. *Decide on an objective you want to achieve.* The objective can be to (1) call attention to an aspect of the author's style that students can use to improve their writing (2) enjoy and share students' responses to the book at the end of the read aloud; (3) strengthen a listening comprehension skill, such as asking students to describe what was happening in their thinking as they listened; (4) increase students' speaking ability by having them note a particularly vivid phrase they want to use in their conversations; or (5) build reading vocabulary, by placing new words on the board at the reading's end.

Step 3. *Create a captivating introduction for your reading.* This introduction can be an interesting fact about the author of the story (for a list of books that describe author's lives, see Chapter 11), an insight that you gained through reading the book, or a description of the first time you read the book when you were a child and what it meant to you.

Step 4. *Decide how students will give a response to the reading.* Before you read, decide how you will elicit students' responses when the oral reading is finished:

a. Sample questions to ask and comments to make at the end to solicit students' responses follow:

- Was there anything in the story that troubled you?
- What images, feelings, or memories did the reading stimulate?
- What was there about the reading that influenced you most? Why?
- Were you disappointed or surprised by what was read?
- What questions or comments come to mind?

- Don't worry about how important a thought or issue may be to others; if it's on your mind, it's important and I want to hear it.

b. Instead of asking students to retell the story to assess their listening and reading comprehension, select a crucial detail and ask students what role that detail played in establishing meaning.

c. To strengthen students cause-and-effect thinking, ask them to explain why characters behaved as they did. Older students can also discuss whether character actions were prudent or imprudent, appropriate or inappropriate, rational or irrational.

d. To build students' interpretive thinking, ask them to state the theme or moral of the book. Also have them identify generalizations that were not adequately supported.

e. Have younger students re-create the story on flannel boards, as a group or in pairs.

Step 5. *If you are going to read a multichaptered book, read from this book daily until it is finished, so students are not left hanging.* Each day ask students to share ideas and feelings about events and ask, "What is likely to occur in tomorrow's reading?"

Step 6. *When you read, sit down.* Pull students close. Make sure that everyone is comfortable. Put a sign outside the room asking people to come back to the room at a specified time (when the oral reading time is over). This reduces interruptions between students and their authorial friends.

As a closing note and to reemphasize the importance of reading orally, Beverly Cleary and Russell Baker stated that the turning point in their lives (the point when each decided to become a writer) occurred when a teacher of theirs read something they had written, aloud to the class. Both writers say that through this activity, they realized for the first time that others could and did enjoy their writing.

You can take steps to enhance the reading experience before you read, while you read, and after you read. Specifically, before you read, you can put a piece of construction paper over the cover of a book to build children's total imagery, or show the cover of the book and ask them to predict what the book will be about. You can introduce the author and connect students' experiences to the book, discuss the genre, introduce the main characters, and then help students set their own purposes before the reading begins.

During reading, you can allow students to comment. If students prefer not to comment, you can have them raise their hands and ask someone in class to list the names of the students in the order that they raise their hands. When the reading is finished, the students then have the opportunity to contribute in the order that they raised their hands to say something about the book. You can also cover words in the book. You can cover all but the first letter or all but the first letter and vowel (use post-it notes). So children use their phonetic skills, their vocabulary knowledge, and their structural analysis skills to decode the words in the book.

After reading, it has proved to be most fruitful to allow students to make the first comment. By doing so, you can be sure that students have a chance to tell you what they thought was most important about this shared oral reading. Table 5.8 lists books that children most often request to have read aloud. The list was compiled

TABLE 5.8 BOOKS STUDENTS ASK TO HAVE READ ALOUD

The following books are favorites of teachers and students. After each title are the grade levels of students who most appreciate having the book read aloud.

When Bluebell Sang by Lisa Campbell, 1992, New York: Aladdin (preschool)

Ask Mr. Bear by Marjorie Flack, 1991, New York: Aladdin (K–1)

When the Dark Comes Dancing: A Bedtime Poetry Book, compiled by Nancy Lerrick, New York: Philomel (preschool–3)

Yang the Youngest and His Terrible Ear by Tensey Namioka, 1992, New York: Little, Brown (2–4)

"More, More, More" Said the Baby: Three Love Stories by Vera B. Williams, 1991, Fairfield, NJ: Greenwillow (4–6)

Golden Bear by Ruth Young, 1992, Bergenfield, NJ: Viking Penguin (2–6)

Cherry Tree by Ruskin Bond, 1991, New York: Boyds Mills (1–4)

The Wall by Eve Bunting, 1990, Burlington, MA: Clarion (4–8)

Osa's Pride by Ann Grefalconi, 1990, New York: Little, Brown (5–8)

Not Even Mrs. Mazursky by Jane Sutton, 1984, Minneapolis, MN: Dutton (2–6)

Front Porch Stories at the One-Room School by Eleanora E. Tate, 1992, New York: Bantam (3–8)

Winnie-the-Pooh by A. A. Milne, 1984, New York: Simon & Schuster (K–8)

The Trumpet of the Swan by E. B. White, 1986, New York: Scholastic (3–8)

Charlotte's Web by E. B. White, 1984, New York: Scholastic (2–8)

Molly's Pilgrim by Barbara Cohen, 1985, New York: Dial (3–6)

Ramona the Pest by Beverly Cleary, 1989, New York: Simon & Schuster (3–6)

The Great Christmas Kidnapping Caper by Jean Van Leeuwen, 1991, New York: Bantam (1–4)

A Certain Small Sheperd by Rebecca Caudill, 1991, New York: Simon & Schuster (2–6)

Jump: The Adventures of Brer Rabbit by Van Dyke Parks and Malcolm Jones, 1990, New York: Scholastic (1–3)

The Hundred Penny Box by Sharon Ball Mathis, 1989, New York: Scholastic (3–8)

James and the Giant Peach by Roald Dahl, 1988, New York: Scholastic (3–8)

The Best Christmas Pageant Ever by Barbara Robinson, 1990, New York: Dial (3–8)

---

from contributions made by each of the teachers represented in this textbook and by researchers.

In closing, it is important to stop at suspenseful spots each day. When reading a picture book, be sure the children can see the pictures clearly. If you have a child who needs to keep his or her hands occupied during reading, ask that child to hold the book for you. This diminishes classroom management problems.

FOR YOUR JOURNAL

Bookmaking

Following 10 steps during journal writing can assist students to write their own book.

1. Students should choose the type of book they want to make from those presented in Figure 5.5. The first book your students write should be 8 or 16 pages long so that the text can be combined into the books described in Figure 5.5.

2. Students do not have to write the title first, but instead write an outline of the beginning, setting, conflict or problem, and end of their stories. Then students decide whether their stories will be humorous or serious.

There are many ways to publish a book, here are a few suggestions ranging from the very simple to more complicated methods.

SCROLL

Book is written on a long sheet of paper, one page at a time is revealed. Dowels can be fastened at each end.

ACCORDIAN

A long sheet of paper is folded fanlike to make pages or individual sheets of paper are joined with tape. When pages are folded together, shapes can be cut paperdoll style so the pages are not severed. Stiff covers can be added.

RING BOUND/YARN BOUND

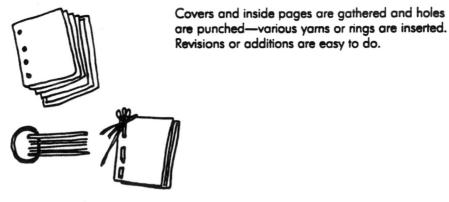

Covers and inside pages are gathered and holes are punched—various yarns or rings are inserted. Revisions or additions are easy to do.

FIGURE 5.5 TYPES OF BOOKS STUDENTS CAN MAKE

LIBRARY BOUND

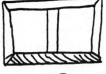

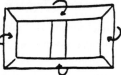

The inside pages are stitched and then the end papers are glued into stiff covers. (A, B, C, D, E)

FANCY OR PLAIN ENDPAPER

FOLDED AND SEWN BOOKLET

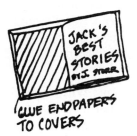

JACK'S BEST STORIES BY J. STARR

GLUE ENDPAPERS TO COVERS

COMB BOUND

Covers and individual pages are gathered and brought to a comb binder which a library or copy center might have.

CENTER SEWN BOOKLET ON INSIDE COVERS.

FIGURE 5.5 (CONTINUED)

3. Students should illustrate their stories with clear, simple pictures when the book is in the revising stage.

4. Students rewrite sections to "grab readers' attention" by making characters more whole and complete, establishing the sense of time and place quickly in the first two pages, showing the thinking processes of the characters so the story becomes more action-filled, adding richness in details to create a better mood, making the dialogue believable, utilizing a stylistic feature from one of their favorite authors, and taking chances to write a great opening sentence.

5. Students discover their book's visual identity by laying every two pages side by side, and overlapping a single picture between two pages. Any student having trouble drawing pictures should be told to "draw faster" because the more creative side of the brain will likely take over when speed increases. Students should complete at least two drawings a period. Once drawings are complete, students can improve them by making the most important lines heavier and wider. You can also hold up classmates' best drawings as samples to stimulate students' ideas for the next day's work.

6. When books have been assembled, you need 10 minutes to describe how to design the book's front cover; the book title should be easy to read, and the cover design should suggest the book's contents without crowding the space. After you've given these guidelines and shown students a few samples, allow only 20 minutes for students to make their covers. With such a tight time limit they won't have time to tell themselves they can't do it. Tell students that they will have the opportunity to show their cover at the end of this 20 minute period.

7. Students complete the backs, flaps, and spines of their books by bringing a picture of themselves, and asking another student in the room to read their stories and write a review for their front flap. The front flap tells just enough of the story to intrigue a reader. The back flap includes a few sentences about the author. The spine has the author's last name at the top, the title of the story in the center, and the title of the "publishing company" (the class) at the bottom.

8. Host an "unveiling of the books" with refreshments. Invite parents, principal, librarian, and students from other classes. Each student holds up his or her book and gives a one-minute synopsis. While refreshments are eaten, books are displayed on the chalkboard ledge for all to see. Books are then placed on display in the school library or public library for a week before students are allowed to take them home as gifts or to keep for themselves. The day books go off display, students select the class in the school in which they would like to read their book and do so.

9. When the students have completed this first book and have learned all the steps, they can make other books from journal entries using the processes described in Figure 5.5.

10. Parents can also become coauthors with their children, and write about special events in their families. For example, young children and their parents can take Polaroid pictures of cooking together and attach these photographs to a recipe book that they write together.

CONNECTING CLASSROOMS, PARENTS, AND COMMUNITIES

SSE (Sustained Silent Evenings)

Throughout the first five chapters of this book, you have read about the many benefits of immersing children in literature. From preschool to grade 2, children benefit from being read to daily at school and at home. By grade 2, most students also benefit from sustained silent reading programs. In this vein, Sustained Silent Evenings (SSE) has been created to provide opportunities for children in grade 2 and above to watch their parents read silently as they spend the same time reading silently to themselves. A Sustained Silent Evening is when parents set aside a certain amount of time for reading and writing; for second grade, 20 minutes is recommended; for third grade, 30 minutes; and for fourth grade through sixth grade, 45 minutes. From seventh grade on, children in middle school and high school should spend time silently reading once a week or writing with their parents in the same room. They should share what they read or write about that is of value to each of them. Adolescents involved in these activities build a stronger foundation than those who do not have this experience (Block, 1990).

With this in mind, it is valuable for your children to send home a letter to parents specifying that research has indicated that the top three variables that discriminate against more and less effective schools in literacy relate to the amount of parent involvement, the amount of volunteer reading at home, and the amount of actual reading that children do silently in class (Postlethwaite & Ross, 1992). In this letter, you can outline the steps that they can take to set up SSE. They can share books with young children. They can read aloud a book with their child. They can use the questions from Figure 3.5 to have discussions about that book. Give the children take-home sheets with the books each child selected for parent reading. These take-home sheets are copies of the literature cards in this book. For example, Allison selected books that are used in the thematic unit at the end of Chapter 6. When a book from that unit was selected, Ms. Hulsey sent home Literature Card 15 to Allison's mother. After an SSE on Monday night, Tuesday night they went to the library and Allison was able to read five more books on subsequent evenings that week that were similar to the one read the previous night. A list of books that are recommended for family reading nights (SSEs) can be found on the website that accompanies this textbook.

A final step you can take for parents to develop SSE periods is called "Caught Reading." In this program teachers tell students that you will make random calls to their homes between seven and eight o'clock in the evening. Two students will be called each Monday night. If they are engaged in a Sustained Silent Evening that evening with their parents before eight o'clock, they win the "Caught Reading" contest, and at the end of 6 weeks all the children who were caught reading during that period receive a reward selected by the class related to literacy.

SUMMARY

The purpose of this chapter was to describe how instruction can increase students' decoding abilities. Several activities were described, (1) teaching students to anticipate word meanings as they read (2) making semantic maps; (3) teaching content-specific words; (4) learning basic sight words, phonics generalizations, structural analysis, semantic and syntactic context clues; and (5) using caption vision, SSE, and reading aloud to students.

I also suggested several types of literature that are particularly valuable to strengthen students' vocabularies: higher-interest books that have a low density of new vocabulary terms, language play books, predictable pattern books, serial books, books that repeat highly specific phonic elements, and holiday books. The Five-Finger Method and teaching the decoding differences between languages are particularly valuable instructional interventions for special needs students. The **Five Finger Method** teaches children to raise one finger for each word they do not know on a page. If all five fingers are raised before they reach the end of a page, they might enjoy a less difficult book for independent, silent reading. In Chapter 6, you will learn how to increase students' abilities to use multiple decoding strategies simultaneously.

HOW TO DO IT: USING WHAT YOU'VE LEARNED

The following provide opportunities to reflect on and practice what you have learned.

ASSESSING YOUR LEARNING

1. If you are presently teaching, you can increase students' vocabulary this week by writing on the board vivid and melodious phrases the class has heard so students can see the printed versions. Write at least one of these on the board by the end of the week.

If you are not teaching presently, listen to others and make a journal entry of three words or phrases used in an especially influential or lyrical manner. To increase your vocabulary, try to use these words or phrases yourself, either in speaking or writing. In so doing, you can strengthen your awareness of the beauty of words, which is one of your best means of building your future students' desire to expand their vocabularies.

2. If you are not teaching, observe a reading program in action in an elementary school. What decoding strategies are in use? If you are teaching, videotape yourself conducting a reading lesson. Review the principles for reading instruction in this chapter and decide which principle you want to improve in your class during the next 2 months.

3. If you are presently teaching, teach one or more of the lessons in this chapter and compare your results with one or more colleagues or classmates. If you are not teaching presently, read one of the books from Table 5.8. Using the procedures of the

Professional Development Activity in this chapter, design an oral reading activity in which that book can be used to increase students' vocabulary or decoding abilities.

4. List the decoding strategies that increase decoding abilities. In a second column, list instructional activities that strengthen readers' use of each strategy. When finished, make copies of this form to use as an assessment record of individual students' progress. You can write the date that each instructional activity was taught and the effects.

5. After having read the information in this chapter, pretend that you are at a party and someone asks you how students learn to decode words. In your explanation, respond to the debate that exists between proponents of phonics instruction and those who favor whole-word recognition. It is necessary to address this issue in your comments because the person at the party just heard a news story on TV that phonics instruction is on the rise again.

6. What can you do when children select books that are too easy or too difficult; leave their books at home; or do not complete the required readings before they come to school the next day?

KEY TERMS EXERCISE

In this chapter there were several new terms introduced. If you know the meaning of each of the following terms, place a checkmark beside that term. If you do not, return to the page on which that term was introduced at this time to reread its definition. In doing so, you will retain these concepts more readily. If you know as many as 18 vocabulary words before you review those that are unknown, you will have learned most of the information about teaching phonics and developing vocabularies during your first reading of this chapter. Congratulations.

_____ alphabetic principle   (p. 204)

_____ assisted reading   (p. 213)

_____ balanced approach   (p. 204)

_____ configuration   (p. 199)

_____ content-specific sight words
(p. 198)

_____ decoding   (p. 192)

_____ dyslexia   (p. 220)

_____ electronic books   (p. 223)

_____ encoding   (p. 197)

_____ gestalt   (p. 217)

_____ high-frequency words
(p. 199)

_____ language experience approach
(p. 202)

_____ multimedia   (p. 223)

_____ parallel distributed processing
(p. 193)

_____ phonics   (p. 202)

_____ phonological awareness   (p. 204)

_____ proactive phonics   (p. 218)

_____ repeated reading   (p. 213)

_____ shared reading   (p. 213)

_____ signal sight words   (p. 200)

_____ structural analysis   (p. 212)

_____ talk-to-yourself chart   (p. 218)

_____ vocabulary development
(p. 192)

_____ webbing   (p. 196)

_____ word bank   (p. 217)

_____ word making   (p. 203)

_____ word sorting   (p. 203)

FOR FUTURE REFERENCE

Vocabulary Decoding, or Second-Grade Students

Adams, M. J. (1990). *Beginning to read: Thinking and learning about print.* Cambridge, MA: MIT Press.

Anderson, R., et al. (1985). *Becoming a nation of readers: The report of the commission on reading.* Washington, DC.

Clay, Marie. (1991). *Becoming literate.* Portsmouth, NH: Heinemann Educational Books.

Cunningham, P. M. (1995). *Phonics they use: Words for reading and writing* (2nd ed.). New York: HarperCollins.

Ehri, L. C. (1991). Development of the ability to read words. In R. Barr, M. L. Kamil, P. B. Mosenthal, & P. D. Pearson (Eds.), *Handbook of reading research* (Vol. 2, pp. 383–417). White Plains, NY: Longman.

Fraser, J., & Skolnick, D. (1994). *On their way: Celebrating second graders as they read and write.* Portsmouth, NH: Heinemann. [Provides additional, day-to-day experiences of what it is like to be a second-grade teacher in a student-centered classroom.]

Heimlich, J., & Pittelman, S. (1986). *Semantic mapping: Classroom applications.* Newark, DE: International Reading Association.

Holdaway, D. (1990). *Independence in reading* (3rd ed.). Portsmouth, NH: Heinemann Educational Books.

Miller, H., O'Keefe, T., & Stephens, D. (1991). *Looking closely: Exploring the role of phonics in one whole language classroom.* Urbana, IL: NCTE.

WEBSITES

These websites may be used for the grade level that you are seeking.

www.dallas.isd.tenet.edu/depts/reading/index.html

A list of books for grade levels K–3 that can be sent home for parents to read aloud.

www.kids-space.org/story/story.html

Storybooks 1998: of kids, by kids, and for kids

www.schoolexpress.com

School Express: Reading Worksheets

www.disney.com/educationalproductions/index.html

Disney Educational Productions: Edu-Station

www.zaner-bloser.com

Zaner-Bloser

wwwkidswriting.miningco.com/mbody.htm

Mining Company: Creative Writing for Kids

www.billybear4kids.com/games/mapedit/spell1.htm

Billy Bear for Kids: Games

www.oplin.lib.oh.us/EDUCATE/SUBJECTS/writing.html

Language Arts Writing

www.riggsinst.org/contents.htm

riggsinst.org/index3.shtml

ftp.riggsinst.org/70orton.htm

The Riggs Institute

www.ala.org/alsc/notable98.html

> The American Library Association: 1998 Notable Books for Children

www.ala.org/parentspage/tfp2.html

> Kids Connect at the Library: Tips for Parents

The following list may be more specifically used for the third grade:

www.pbs.org/wgbh/arthur/teachers/index.html

> Teacher's Corner

www.teachnet.com/lesson/langen.html

> Language Arts: General Lesson Ideas

ADDITIONAL RESOURCES FOR TEACHERS

Bear, D. R., Templeton, S., Invernizzi, M., & Johnston, F. (1996). *Words their way: Word study for phonics, vocabulary, and spelling instruction.* Upper Saddle River, NJ: Prentice-Hall. 384p.

Bernstein, R. (1994). *Phonics activities for reading success.* West Nyack, NY: The Center for Applied Research in Education. 296p.

Ericson, L., & Juliebo, M. (1998). *The phonological awareness handbook for kindergarten and primary teachers.* Newark, DE: International Reading Association. 122p.

Fitzpatrick, J. (1998). *Reading strategies that work.* Cypress, CA: Creative Teaching Press.

Heilman, A. W. (1998). *Phonics in proper perspective.* Upper Saddle River, NJ: Prentice-Hall. 141p.

Kohl, H. (1998). *Reading: How to.* Portsmouth, NH: Boynton/Cook. 224p.

Olmstead, J. (1992). *Reading with young children: A parent's guide.* Portland, OR: Olmsted Press.

ADDITIONAL RESOURCES FOR PARENTS

Books

Cheney, M. (1997). *How to develop your child's gifts and talents in vocabulary.* Los Angeles, CA: RGA Publishing Group.

Green, L. J. (1996). *Improving your child's schoolwork: 1,001 ideas arranged from A to Z.* Rocklin, CA: Prima. 288p.

Kaye, P. (1997). *Games for learning.* New York: Noonday. 251p.

Kropp, P. (1996). *Raising a reader: Make your child a reader for life.* New York: Doubleday. 206p.

Lawrence, L. (1998). *Montessori—read and write: A parent's guide to literacy for children.* New York: Three Rivers Press. 160p.

McGuinness, C., & McGuinness, G. (1998). *Reading reflex: The foolproof phono-graphix method for teaching your child to read.* Simon and Schuster. 353p.

CD-ROM

Curious George Learns Phonics

> Ages 4–6. Young Readers Series, Houghton Mifflin Interactive ($38.99 Barnes & Noble)

Kid Phonics (Sets 1 and 2)

> Ages 6–9. Davidson ($36.99 Barnes & Noble)

Reader Rabbit (Sets 1, 2, 3)

> Grades 2 and 3. The Learning Company ($14.99 CompUSA and Barnes & Noble)

Phonics for Kids

> Ages 3–10, Cosmi, Inc., 1997, Swift Jewel ($8.00 CompUSA)

Amazing American History

> Grade level 3 and up, Cosmo, Inc., 1997 ($1.88 [on sale] CompUSA)

Animals on the Move

Ages 10 and up (can be modified for a third grade level), Expert Software, 1998 ($9.99 CompUSA)

Cassette Tapes

Rock 'n Learn Phonics

By Brad Caudle and Richard Caudle, 1997, Rock 'n Learn, Inc. Conroe, TX ($15.95 Barnes & Noble)

Flash Cards

Phonics—Flash Cards with the Muppets

1993, American Education Publishing ($3.49 Barnes & Noble)

Phonics Made Easy

School Zone Publishing Co., Grand Haven, MI ($2.59 Barnes & Noble)

Games

Learning Games (Torrance, CA: Frank Schaffer Publisher)

#1 Set—Initial Consonants

#2 Set—Consonant Blends and Diagraphs

#3 Set—Short and Long Vowels

Lingo Bingo

Learning Resources, Inc., Vernon Hills, IL ($15.95 Mardel)

Vowels Bingo

Trend Enterprises, Inc. ($8.95 Mardel)

Quizmo Phonetic

World-Class Learning Materials, Inc., Baltimore, MD ($11.99 Mardel)

Participating in collaborative workshops helps third-graders learn decoding clues that enable them to decipher the meanings of words.

CHAPTER 6

TEACHING CHILDREN TO USE
MULTIPLE DECODING STRATEGIES

Mr. Evans was beginning his second year of teaching third grade. He chose third grade because it was the year of great discovery and wonderment in children's development. At this point in understanding the English language, children were able to use many different decoding clues to understand the meaning of words.

How did Mr. Evans develop his language arts program? During his first year of teaching, he took graduate courses at the University of Notre Dame that introduced him to the following methods: semantic clues, tilling the text, using dictionaries correctly, reading and writing workshops, the four-block method, and PRA. With this body of knowledge in his teaching repertoire, Mr. Evans structured his classroom day as follows.

Every morning at 8:30, Melsong, Juan, Allison, Michael, and their classmates burst into the classroom and immerse themselves in reading and writing. Every morning, they spend 10 to 15 minutes in a whole-class sharing of literature (using one of the methods in this chapter). Then Mr. Evans meets with separate groups for about 45 minutes, while other students read with buddies, as described later in this chapter, or worked individually at their desks or at learning centers.

All Mr. Evans' children became comfortable with the established routines of learning to decode using strategies that are beyond individual word clues. Throughout this chapter, you will learn how to use such strategies yourself. After reading this chapter, you will have developed the competencies to master the following IRA, NCTE, NAEYC, and TEKS, and statewide and province-based standards for professional development for language arts teachers:

1. How can reading be taught as a process rather than a set of isolated skills?
2. What is the nature and multiple causes of reading and writing difficulty?
3. How can you diagnose individual reading difficulties?
4. What are the instructional implications of research from psychology and other fields of sociology that deal with students with reading and writing difficulties?

5. How can you effectively implement strategies that include parents as partners in the literacy development of their children?

6. How can you supplement children's phonetic awareness and phonics knowledge to better use this tool to identify new words in the English language?

7. How can you employ effective techniques and strategies for the successful and effective ongoing development of independent reading abilities?

SECTION 1   THEORETICAL FOUNDATIONS

Teaching Students to Decode Using Beyond Word Clues

Recent research revealed that, in the United States, primary kindergarten through fourth-grade teachers believe that the goal of reading instruction is to develop not only students' skills and strategies, but also their motivation to read and independent appreciation of literature. Such teachers embrace literature-enriched classrooms that combine reading children's literature and basal anthology selections. Such teachers spend at least 2½ hours per day using a variety of strategies, reported in Chapters 1 through 5 and in Chapter 6, to organize their day. These activities enable teachers not only to read to children, but to read with children, and enable children to read by themselves and with peers. Children also engage in self-selected independent reading, and such teachers create opportunities for discussion and expression daily. Last, the majority of primary-grade teachers in the United States today believe that engaging children in the oral and written responses to literature activities in this chapter, through scheduled journal writing and process writing periods, and directly teaching the phonics skills in Chapter 5 and in the beyond words skills in this chapter, are the best routes to develop independent journal readers.

Each of these teachers also develops their reading program by capitalizing on the strengths of each stage in young children's literacy development. For example, Mr. Evans began to plan his reading program, taking into consideration that, unlike many 7-year-olds, the 8-year-olds in his third-grade class generally do not enjoy working and playing alone. His third-graders are likely to enjoy forming book clubs, reading and writing workshops, and spending time planning who they want to include in the various activities that they can choose to do. Although each of the activities that Mr. Evans uses in third grade are used throughout all primary grades, special adaptations are made to meet the special needs for each grade level. Again, to illustrate, Mr. Evans capitalized on his third-graders' enthusiasm for team games, group projects, and small group discussions. He knows that his students look forward to assuming larger responsibilities and playing roles in classroom plays, and they value establishing traditions by the time they reach 8 years of age. They take pride in any special task they can accomplish as a group.

In addition, Mr. Evans' third-grade children appear to enjoy abstract thinking when it relates to real experiences. Because of this, he uses many of the students' ideas in developing his units. One example is the Sim City, which stands for a simulated city, that his third-graders created to show what they had learned as they read about various cities across the United States. Mr. Evans noted that Meisong, Juan, Michael, and Allison, from the first day of his class, began to select books that had more specific details in them than the picture books and vocabulary books that had been used in prior years. These four students began to create imaginative plays that served as important learning tools for them, and they became leaders of many of the projects that Mr. Evans continued throughout the year.

Throughout the discussions in this chapter, you can begin to blend whole language concepts with more direct instructional approaches to teach children decoding and comprehension. **Whole language** is an approach to literacy instruction built on the natural development of literacy competencies through exposure to whole selections of literature that are completed for the enjoyment and pleasure of reading. Whole language also includes the use of children's input in the design of the objectives to be covered. Whole language favors children's literacy development over the explicit teaching of basic reading skills. Students read and write daily in such approaches.

Recent research indicates that a whole language emphasis in preschool through first grade is sufficient to teach children basic concepts of print and to erase any initial disadvantage that children may have have prior to coming to school (Whitehurst et al., 1999). Other research suggests that, by third grade, directed instruction is a valuable component to add to the whole language experience so that children learn to blend together many skills as they confront more difficult words (Block, in press; Pressley & Block, in press).

Further, good and poor readers at the third-grade level do not differ significantly in abilities to substitute a word that is syntactically correct for a word that sounds incorrect when read orally. Regardless of the type of phonic instruction they have received, good and poor third-grade readers exhibit a high degree of proficiency with single consonant combinations, short vowels, long vowels with the final *e,* multisyllabic words, and other medial vowels. Posing a particular problem at the third-grade level are a majority of children who still cannot recognize independently, without further instruction, single consonants with two sounds, such as *c* and *k,* or combination vowels *oi, aw,* or *ai.* Most difficult are closed syllables such as *supper,* certain open syllable words such as *computer,* and words that contain more or less frequently occurring phonic elements (National Reading Panel Progress Report, 1999).

Also by third grade, good readers' errors are semantically correct 50 percent of the time, on average. That is, most third-graders make errors that have a semantic content sense. Before third grade, however, children's errors, on average, make sense within the sentence less than 34 percent of the time (National Reading Panel Progress Report, 1999). Last, research has recently demonstrated that when third-graders do not know a word, they go through six stages to try to decode the word independently. Typically, third-graders first try to say the beginning consonant and then the whole word. For example, if they do not know the word *bat,* they say *ba,* and then try to say *at.* The second strategy they use is to try to break the word into parts or chunks, even if the chunks do not correspond to syllables. For example, Meisong, in trying to recognize the word *trust,* divided it up into these sounds:

tra, us, t, so that it had three parts, which she blended together to arrive at the word *trust.* The third strategy is to divide the word into syllables or approximate syllables. They try a series of different pronunciations for the approximations until they can correctly pronounce the word that has been stored previously in their listening vocabulary.

By the fifth attempt to decode a word, children resort to strictly phonetic degenerations of the word. If, after sounding out the word letter by letter, they still cannot recognize it, they perform a unique combination of strategies that they can learn from this chapter and others in this book. Oddly enough, this same pattern is followed by good and poor readers. The only difference between them is the intensity and tenacity with which better readers persevere until they successfully decode an unfamiliar word. Also, better readers tend more frequently to use the graphic similarities between words, context clues, and the semantic clues introduced in this chapter (National Reading Panel Progress Report, 1999). For this reason, it is important to expose greater numbers of less able readers of all ages and stages of development to the strategies in this chapter.

In the next pages are eight strategies for assisting students to integrate multiple beyond single word clues in decoding. These eight strategies are not presented as recipes because, as was stated by O'Neal (1996, p. 52):

> Recipes, which began as such useful things, have become tyrants leaving even the most well-meaning cooks unsure of their own instincts. A slavish devotion to recipes robs people of the kind of experiential knowledge that seeps into the brain . . . most chefs are not fettered by formula; they've cooked enough to trust their tastes. Today, that is the most valuable lesson a chef can teach a cook.

In reading instruction, Mr. Evans is a chef. We can observe his classroom to understand how to blend eight different methods of teaching decoding so that all students' varied learning needs can be met.

In addition to modeling how to use context clues, decoding strategies can be taught with the **adding more phonics** method, **Which Word Do You Know?** method, and **contextual wedges.** The adding more phonics word approach teaches children that, once they have read to the end of a sentence, they can go back and reread that sentence and add additional phonics clues from the context in which the word appears to sound out the remaining letters of an unknown word. When students use the adding more phonics approach, they are not only using context clues and phonics, but also employing their predictive thinking abilities to decode unknown words. If their first attempts at decoding are inaccurate using this method, you can say, "That's a possibility. Go back and reread the sentence, putting that word and meaning in the proper place. Tell me whether the word you just said makes sense and why."

The Which Word Do You Know? approach can be used anytime students read a book or vocabulary words are introduced. This method begins either by listing words in sentences or pointing to unknown words in sentences and asking children to tell which words in the sentence they know and why. As individual children respond, they pronounce the word and describe its meaning, as well as explain what clues they used to discover the meaning.

SEMANTIC AND SYNTACTIC CONTEXT CLUES

Context clues are decoding strategies in which students use the position of a word in the sentence (syntactical context clues) and the meanings of other words in the sentence (semantic context clues) to determine the meaning and pronunciation of unknown words. For example, Mr. Evans modeled how to use context clues for the word *sputtered* in the following paragraph: "The car started the trip when it was low on gas. After one hour's drive the car sputtered to a stop." He showed his students how to look at syntactical context clues and determine that *sputtered* is a verb. Then, by using semantic context clues they can predict what the word means in reference to a car that is low on gas. Last, through rereading the sentence, they can say the sounds of the first letters in the word *sputtered* and think of words heard in the past as well as a meaning that would make sense in that sentence to decode that word.

It is important to teach readers that semantic context clues are valuable decoding tools, but when used as the sole decoding tool they can predict only about one-fourth of all content-specific words (Gough, Alford, & Holly-Wilcox, 1981). To help younger and less able readers learn how to use context clues, you can use a big book as Mr. Evans does. Cover with a self-stick note all but the first letter in a semantically rich word. You can cover five words in five distantly spaced sentences in the book so the chances that students can guess each word from the preceding semantic clues is high. For second-graders, you can cover six words; for third-graders, seven words; for fourth-graders, eight words; and for fifth-graders and above, cover nine words. Then, you can model how when students come to a word they don't know (the word that is covered with the Post-it note), they can say the sound of the first three letters, pause, and then continue reading, with the intent of using the first letter sounds and meanings in connection with the meanings of other words in the sentence to decode the unknown word. An example of such a modeling session that Mr. Evans used in his class is described below:

> [All the letters in the word *queen* are covered but *que.*]

> I have covered three words on this first page to illustrate what you can say to yourself and think when you come to words you don't know. You can put together the meaning of all the other words in the sentence to figure out these words, which is called using context clues. I'll show you how to do it. If I didn't know this word, I'd say to myself: "Once upon a time there was a handsome king and beautiful /que/ [pause] who lived in a large castle on the top of the highest hill in all the land." By reading to the end of the sentence, using what I know from previous stories, and the sounds of the first letter of my unknown word, I know that the word has to be *queen*. When we come to the next covered word, I want you to use context clues with me to decode the word. Then explain to me what you thought as you did so.

Contextual Wedges.   Another method of introducing the context clues decoding strategy was created by De Santi (1992). This method is called *contextual wedges*. To make a contextual wedge lesson, select a vocabulary word you want students to learn. Then create a contextual wedge for the word. A wedge is a three- to four-sentence paragraph in which the first sentence gives a general clue about the word's meaning. The second gives a slightly more specific clue, so students who use the context clues in both sentences come closer to recognizing the new word. By the time you write the third and fourth sentences, students who use all the context clues recognize that only one word can fit all syntactical and semantic clues in the passage. Once you've created the wedge, you can tell readers that sometimes an unknown word can be decoded by using the words around it—their meanings (semantics), the grammatical functions (syntax) they serve, and the context in several sentences. Then, have students read the sentences. Students should use the words they read, and the order in which they appeared, to decide the word that should fill the blank. You should accept three or four words that "make sense" in that blank and write these in that sentence. Ask students to describe the thinking processes they used to think of each word. Repeat this process with each sentence, until by the end of the passage, only one word makes sense by combining all clues. An example of the contextual wedge strategy used by Mr. Evans appears below. (You may want to test your context clues knowledge by marking the point at which you recognized the word being described.)

We use _____ to build many things.

It is best when _____ are straight and tall.

Many people travel far to see groups of _____ .

Throughout the year _____ are always changing color.

When a lumberjack cuts down _____ , he always yells "Timber."

Another method of teaching context clues is called **cloze exercises,** which are passages in which some words are replaced by blanks and students write the words they think should appear in the blanks. They also write their rationale for each word they choose. Each of the sentences in the contextual wedge above is a cloze sentence. Each contains a blank in which readers are to use semantic and syntactic clues to deduce the word that was omitted.

NAMING WORDS, DOING WORDS, PAINTING WORDS, AND READING STORIES TO TEACH SYNTACTIC CONTEXT CLUES

Most students benefit from being explicitly taught how to use context clues. To do so, you can create a lesson in which students dictate stories as a class. After a story or a series of sentences has been dictated in the morning message through a language experience approach or just to get ready for this lesson, you can teach how nouns and phrases can be found in specific spots in sentences. Then you can note that nouns and phrases are often known as **naming words.** When you have written *naming words* in a column to the right of the sentences the students have dictated, you can go back and ask the children to tell you each word in the sentences that names an object, person, place, or thing. As each word is identified, you circle it in a color such as yellow.

Then you can teach students that certain words—adjectives and adverbs—are called **painting words,** which enable us to draw pictures in our minds of what we are discussing. Again, we turn the students' attention to the sentences they dictated and ask them to point out the different words that help them to paint clearer pictures of objects in their minds. As they tell you a painting word, circle that word in blue.

Next, you can teach students that verbs are sometimes called **doing words** because they tell us what people are doing. Again, return to the paragraph and ask students to tell you which words are doing words and circle those in a third color like red. When students examine the sentences with painting, naming, and doing words circled, they can notice that some words between these circled words remain uncircled. These uncircled words are usually sight words, and, for the first time, sight words become easier for students to identify because of syntax clues. Specifically, as shown in Figure 6.1, sight words stand out when all other words are circled, and their repetitive nature becomes vivid to students.

When this repetition is revealed, less able readers can find that reading need not be the arduous task they once envisioned: they do not need to decode every new word that is unveiled to them in a sentence. With this knowledge in mind, students are ready to have read to them books from Literature Card 13. These books were specifically chosen because they repeat common phrases and use the same naming, doing, and painting words repeatedly. By having students pick out the naming, painting,

---

Example 1:   Between Naming, Doing, and Painting Words

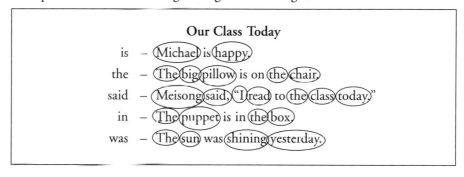

[Every child holds up the card of the word they choose after Mr. Evans asks them to decide which word should replace the picture that appears in the position of the missing word in that sentence (syntactical clues). He asks them the meanings of the words in that sentence.]

FIGURE 6.1 EXAMPLES OF THE BETWEEN NAMING, DOING, AND PAINTING WORDS ACTIVITY AND THE REBUS ACTIVITY TO TEACH SYNTACTICAL CONTEXT CLUES

Literature Card 13

BOOKS THAT INCREASE STUDENTS' ABILITIES TO USE SEMANTIC AND SYNTACTIC CONTEXT CLUES

A Woggle of Witches by A. Adams, 1971 New York: Scribner (139)

Animals Should Definitely Not Wear Clothing by J. Barrett, 1970 New York: Atheneum (65)

Arthur's Christmas Cookies by M. Brown, 1995 Boston: Little, Brown (150)

The Fireflies by E. Carle, 1995 New York: Harcourt (107)

May I Bring a Friend? by B. S. DeRegniers, 1964 New York: Atheneum (151)

Drummer Hoff by B. A. Emberley, 1995 New York: Simon & Schuster (30)

One Fine Day by N. Hogrogian, 1971 New York: Macmillan (150)

Good-Night, Owl by N. Hogrogian, 1995 New York: Simon & Schuster (51)

The Snowy Day by E. Keats, 1962 New York: Viking (157)

Peter's Chair by E. Keats, 1967 New York: Harper & Row (153)

Goggles by E. Keats, 1969 New York: Macmillan (149)

Leo, The Late Bloomer by S. Kellogg, 1973 New York: Dutton (78)

The Mystery of the Missing Red Mitten by S. Kellogg, 1974 New York: Dial (128)

The Comic Adventures of Old Mother Hubbard and Her Dog by A. Lobel, 1968 New York: Bradbury (91)

The Bear's Toothache by D. McPhail, 1972 Boston: Little, Brown (111)

Where the Wild Things Are by M. Sendak, 1963 New York: Harper & Row (139)

Noisy Nora by M. Sendak, 1973 New York: Dial (103)

*The numbers in parentheses following each entry indicate how many words are contained in the story.

and doing words, syntax clues become almost automatic for many children. In the process, sight words become manageable and new words become less difficult to decode.

For younger children, **rebus stories** serve the same function. A rebus story contains pictures or drawings inserted in place of the words that you want to teach children. For example, Mr. Evans was introducing rebus stories to his children by putting this sentence on the board: *The* (and then he drew a picture of a house) *is black.* He passed out, prior to this, three word cards. On one card was the word *house,* on a second card was the word *horse,* and on the third card was the word *hang.* When Mr. Evans read the sentence aloud, he put his hand under the house and didn't say anything. He asked the children to hold up the card that would fit in that sentence. Because each child held up one of the three cards he had given them, he easily determined which children recognized the word *house* and matched it with the picture that depicted its meaning.

USING DICTIONARIES AND THESAURUSES

Instruction in efficient dictionary and thesaurus use builds students' decoding abilities and vocabulary (Anderson & Pearson, 1984; Beck & Dole, 1992). Many students may have been dissuaded from using dictionaries as reading tools because they could have been

- required to look up words they didn't want to look up or told week after week to look up and write the definition of every word in their spelling list

- given a dictionary as soon as they began to write and may have received an inadvertent message that their teachers did not believe they could write well enough without using a dictionary, especially if they were told to use a dictionary more frequently than other classmates
- sent to a dictionary to look up a word without instruction about how to find meanings and understand diacritical markings
- required to use the dictionary when incarcerated for disciplinary problems (e.g., "Copy two pages from the dictionary instead of going to recess today.")

Through the following methods, however, students can come to enjoy and value dictionary use. This instruction should require approximately 2 weeks. During this time you can teach dictionary use skills as separate lessons and ask readers to practice alone or in pairs until each skill becomes automatic.

Dictionary Sword Drills.   Students can learn to use dictionaries through a game called Dictionary Sword Drills, in which you ask students to apply one of the objectives below to a specific word that you say. The first person or pair to find the word wins that round. For example, if students just learned to use the first letter of a word as a clue to the best place to open the dictionary (A–G words can more rapidly be located if the dictionary is opened near the beginning; H–R words if it is opened near the middle; and S–Z words if opened near the end). To illustrate, Mr. Evans said the word *zebra,* and the first student/pair to find that word and read its definition won that round of Dictionary Sword Drills.

The specific objectives in dictionary instruction are

- how definitions are ordered in dictionaries from the most general to the most specialized, instead of being ranked from the most to least commonly used;
- identifying which definition an author meant in materials students are reading;
- how to use the first letter of a word to open a dictionary at the most efficient place (as described above);
- knowing how alphabetical order of the first, second, third letters in a word determines the order in which that word appears in a dictionary;
- recognizing guide words and knowing their functions;
- understanding diacritical markings and primary, secondary, and tertiary accents;
- locating the parts of speech of a designated word;
- how to skim a dictionary page to locate a word quickly;
- understanding syllabication markings;
- how to know the preferred spelling of a word;
- using the information contained in the preface and appendices of dictionaries; and
- finding synonyms and antonyms in the definitions of words.

In addition, throughout the year, it is valuable for students to watch how often and for what reasons you turn to the dictionary. Research also suggests that students understand words better when dictionary definitions are translated into language they normally use (McKeown, 1993). Moreover, after you have taught the above skills, you can bring in a wide variety of types and sizes of dictionaries by checking them out from public and school libraries. Allow students to choose a specific type of dictionary for their own use. Some readers enjoy soft- rather than hardcover versions, thick rather than thin, or smaller rather than larger sizes. A list of popular ones to begin your classroom collection follows:

> **Picture Dictionaries:** *My First Dictionary* (contains approximately 600 words) by Oftedal and Jacob, published by Grossett and Dunlap; *Picture Book Dictionary* (contains approximately 1,000 words) by Hillerich, English, Bodzewski, and Kamatos, published by Rand McNally; and *My First Picture Dictionary,* published by Scholastic.

> **Beginning Dictionaries** (each dictionary in this section contains most words students read through third-grade readability levels): *The Ginn Beginning Dictionary* by William Morris, published by Silver Burdett Ginn; *My First Dictionary,* edited and published by Houghton Mifflin; *Scholastic First Dictionary,* edited and published by Scholastic; *Scott Foresman Beginning Dictionary* by Thorndike and Barnhart, published by Scott Foresman; *Webster's Beginning Dictionary* by G. and C. Merriam, distributed by Silver Burdett Ginn; and *American Heritage First Dictionary A to Z,* published by Houghton Mifflin.

> **Intermediate Dictionaries** (each dictionary in this section contains words up to sixth-grade readability): *Scott Foresman Intermediate Dictionary* by Thorndike and Barnhart, published by Scott Foresman; *Webster's Intermediate Dictionary* by G. and C. Merriam, distributed by Silver Burdett Ginn; and *The American Heritage School Dictionary,* edited and published by Houghton Mifflin.

> **Advanced Dictionaries** (each dictionary is designed for middle school and high school-aged students): *Webster's Third New International Dictionary* by G. and C. Merriam, distributed by Silver Burdett Ginn; *Webster's Ninth Collegiate Dictionary* by G. and C. Merriam, distributed by Silver Burdett Ginn; and *The American Heritage Dictionary of the English Language,* edited and published by Houghton Mifflin.

If you schedule dictionary lessons during November, your students can receive an added benefit. At the end, you can ask readers to write the title, author, publisher, place of publication, and publication date of their favorite dictionary on a piece of paper. Unbeknownst to students, you can then mail this information to their parents or guardians, explaining that this is the dictionary their child prefers and suggesting that they consider purchasing it as a Christmas, Hanukkah, or Kwanzaa gift. In this way students could have their favorite dictionary available for home use.

Last, do not require beginning readers to refer to a dictionary when they are first learning to write unless they choose to do so or you can help them locate the word they want to spell. The frustration of trying to find words they cannot spell can lower students' self-esteem. Most readers discover on their own the importance of referring to dictionaries to express their thoughts more exactly when writing. If you keep dictionaries at writing centers, in the reading–library corner, and on the desk from which you direct most writing lessons, readers come to expect that dictionaries can be a valuable partner in decoding and writing. When readers self-initiate this partnership through their desire to understand the precise meaning of words, they also increase their appreciation for the hard work that their favorite authors do to select "just the right" word when they write and how this work makes writing so much better!

How to Use Thesauruses.   By third grade, students should also be introduced to thesauruses. **Thesauruses** are books that contain synonyms and antonyms. When students use these books their vocabulary increases as does their specificity in word choice when writing. You can teach students to use thesauruses by having each select a word that he or she says or writes too frequently. Then, you and the student can look up the word in a thesaurus and read its synonyms. The students can select which new words they want to incorporate into their vocabulary. For example, Mr. Evans' class was using the word *said* too frequently. They made a SAID IS DEAD poster that listed 20 synonyms they could write to replace *said* in their compositions. Versions of thesauruses that elementary and middle school students enjoy include:

> *In Other Words: A Beginning Thesaurus* by Schiller and Jenkins, published by Scott Foresman and Company (third-grade reading level)
>
> *My First Thesaurus*, edited and published by McDougal, Little (third-grade reading level)
>
> *Young Writer's Thesaurus*, edited and published by McDougal, Little (fourth-grade reading level)
>
> *In Other Words: A Junior Thesaurus* by Schiller and Jenkins, published by Scott Foresman and Company (fourth-grade reading level)
>
> *Roget's International Thesaurus*, edited and published by Thomas Y. Crowell (sixth-grade reading level) (web.cs.city.ac.uk/text/roget/thesaurus.html)

When students compose on a computer, you can also teach them to use dictionaries, thesauruses, and other tools in word processing programs as described below.

ASK A FRIEND, TEACHER, OR COMPUTER

Students need to know that asking a friend, teacher, or computer what a word means is a valuable decoding strategy and that they are not "cheating" when they ask. Students should also learn that to become independent decoders they should use sight words, phonics, structural analysis, context clues, and decoding by analogy strategies first, but if these techniques do not unlock the word's meaning, they can ask you, a friend, or a computer what a word means. By doing so they can more quickly return to their reading, learn a new word, and have the shortest interruption of their train of thought as they read.

READING AND WRITING WORKSHOPS, GRAND CONVERSATIONS, AND BOOK CLUBS

In 1987, Nancy Atwell published *In the Middle: Writing, Reading, and Learning with Adolescents.* In this book, she described the "workshop" that she created for her reading and writing classes. Since that time, several variations of this concept have been created, such as book clubs (Raphael et al., 1992), literature circles (Short & Pierce, 1990), conversational discussion groups (O'Flahavan, 1989; O'Flahavan, Stein, Wieneck, & Marx, 1992), and grand conversations (Eeds & Wells, 1989).

Reading and writing workshops are instructional practices in elementary and middle school classrooms in which students engage in the same practices that readers and writers use outside of school. Students make choices about what they want to read; they use the different strategies to decode new words presented in Chapters 5 and 6; they talk to someone else about what they are reading or writing; and they identify their own ways of enjoying reading (Atwell, 1987). Research to determine the effectiveness of reading and writing workshops has been inconclusive. Some researchers have discovered that students from at-risk classrooms and culturally diverse, intercity student populations benefit from such instruction (Harris-Martine, 1999; Morriss, 1991). Others have studied seventh- and eighth-grade students and found a positive impact on student achievement and enjoyment of reading (Cline, 1993; Wells, 1993). On the other hand, Dionisio (1989) found that some students became so uncomfortable when talking about books that their involvement in achieving literacy growth decreased. Fawcett (1998) reported that evidence in favor of reading and writing workshops outweighs evidence opposing its effectiveness on student reading and writing achievement.

Writing workshops differ from reading workshops in that students begin their lessons with a minilesson and prewriting instruction. Such lessons include brainstorming, list making, story mapping, outlining, and generating possible topics and skills that can be used in a future writing. Immediately following this instruction, students draft their first writing. During this time, they are encouraged to express their thoughts during the drafting process and not to be encumbered by concerns about mechanics. At this stage the ideas are most important because these rough drafts are followed by periods in the writing workshop when students revise, edit, and publish. Researchers have discovered that writing workshops enable students to take their writing more seriously and to learn more about the writing processes involved in taking a work from a first draft to a published piece of writing they can enjoy (Stern, 1995).

How are reading and writing workshops organized? Workshops may vary depending on the teacher and the grade level but always involve a large block of time. The majority of reading and writing workshops are used for student selection of reading and writing experiences. The smaller portion of the instructional time is used for teachers to demonstrate minilessons, to record the status of individual student progress, and to assess group work as students engage in small group committees or workshop activities that are student-led. A component of reading workshops called *status of the class* is a method to record what each student is doing during workshop time (Atwell, 1998). During this time, the teacher calls each student's name and records the student's plan for the workshop that day or for the workshop on the next day. Students must also keep track of their own work using recording forms that are turned in weekly.

Many types of activities are engaged in during reading and writing workshops. First, 45 minutes are usually set aside three to five times a week for children to read and write about experiences that are significant to them. They can use predictable books, which are shown on Literature Card 14. They choose the type of workshop

Literature Card 14

PREDICTABLE AND PATTERN BOOKS THAT BUILD STUDENTS' DECODING ABILITIES

Predictable Books with a Lot of Pictures

Seven Little Rabbits by J. Becker, 1980 Scholastic

A First Book of Sounds by M. Bellah

The B Book by S. & J. Berenstain, 1971 Random House

Where Have You Been? by M. Brown, 1983 Dial

I Can't Said the Ant by P. Cameron, 1961 Coward-McCann

Klippity Klop by E. Emberley, 1974 Little, Brown

As I Was Crossing Boston Common by N. Farber & A. Label, 1975 Dutton

Drummer Hoff by B. Emberley, 1967 Prentice-Hall

A House Is a House for Me by M. Hoberman, 1978 Viking

The Very Hungry Caterpillow by E. Carle, 1989 Philomel

10 Bears in My Bed by S. Mack, 1974 Pantheon

Where Are You Going, Little Mouse? by R. Kraus, 1972 Weston

The Napping House by A. Wood, 1984, Harcourt Bracc Jovanovich

Polar Bear, Polar Bear, What Do You Hear? by B. Martin Jr., 1992 Holt, Rinehart & Winston

If You Give a Mouse a Cookie by L. J. Numeroff, 1985 HarperCollins

More Advanced Predictable Books

The Big Snow by Berta & Elmer Hader, 1993 Aladdin

Penrod's Pants by M. Christian, 1989 Aladdin

Just Like Daddy by F. Asch, 1989 Aladdin

Fortunately by R. Charlip, 1964 Four Winds Press

Don't Forget the Bacon! by P. Hutchins, 1992 Live Oak Media

You'll Soon Grow into Them, Titch by P. Hutchins, 1983 Greenwillow

I Know an Old Lady by R. Bonne & A. Mills, 1994 Scholastic

When I First Came to This Land by O. Brand, 1965 Putnam

I Once Knew a Man by F. Brandenbert, 1970 Macmillan

When Everyone Was Fast Asleep by T. dePaola, 1976 Holiday House

Busy Monday Morning by J. Domanska, 1985 Greenwillow

The House That Jack Built by R. Peppe, 1970 Delacorte

The Doorbell Rang by P. Hutchins, 1986 Morrow

When You Were a Baby by A. Jonas, 1991 Greenwillow

The Shopping Basket by J. Burningham, 1980 T. Crowell

Poor Esme by V. Chess, 1982 Holiday House

Predictable Books If You Are Just Beginning to Learn How to Read

Look What I Can Do by J. Aruego, 1988 Aladdin

Discovering Trees by D. Florian, 1990 Aladdin

The Milk Makers by G. Gibbons, 1987 Aladdin

Up Goes the Skyscraper! by G. Gibbons, 1990 Aladdin

Lisa Cannot Sleep by K. Beckman, 1992 Random House

The Three Billy Goats Gruff by M. Brown, 1987 Dial

The Friendly Book by M. Brown, 1987 Dial

A Dark, Dark Tale by R. Brown, 1981 Dial

Mr. Grumpy's Outing by J. Burningham, 1973 Weston Woods

Do You Want to Be My Friend? by E. Carle, 1976 HarperCollins

The Very Busy Spider by E. Carle, 1984 Philomel

The Little Fish That Got Away by B. Cook, 1985 Lothrop

Jimmy Lee Did It by P. Cummings, 1985 Lothrop

This Is the Bear by S. Hayes, 1993 Candlewick Press

The Grouchy Ladybug by E. Carle, 1989 Philomel

Jesse Bear, What Will You Wear? by N. Carlstrom, 1986 MacMillan

Whose Mouse Are You? by R. Kraus, 1972 Weston Woods

I Unpacked My Grandmother's Trunk by S. Hoquet, 1983 Dutton

Predictable Books That Have Several Chapters to Be Used as Students' First Chapter Books

Hardy Boy Mysteries by C. Dixon, 1950–1979

Nancy Drew Mysteries by C. Keene, 1950–1981

Encyclopedia Brown Saves the Day by D. J. Sobol, 1970 Camden

Encyclopedia Brown and the Case of the Mysterious Handprints by D. J. Sobol, 1986 Bantam

You Be the Jury by M. Miller, 1987 Scholastic

You Be the Jury II by M. Miller, 1989 Scholastic

You Be the Jury III by M. Miller, 1991 Scholastic

You Be the Jury IV by M. Miller, 1993 Scholastic

Ramona the Pest by B. Cleary, 1968 Morrow

Merry-Go-Round: A Book about Names by R. Heller, 1992 Scholastic

Fighting Words by E. Merriam, 1992 Morrow

Series TV: How a Television Show Is Made by M. Drucker & E. James, 1983 Clarion Books

One Sun: A Book of Terse Verse and Play Day by B. McMillan, 1990 Holiday House

Dr. Seuss's ABC by Dr. Seuss, 1963 Random House

The Listening Walk by P. Showers, 1991 Harper Trophy

Old Mother Hubbard by A. & M. Provenson, 1977 Random House

Sounds of a Powwow by B. Martin, 1974 Holt, Rinehart & Winston

Buzz Said the Bee by W. Lewison, 1992 Scholastic

(continued)

Literature Card 14

CONTINUED

I Love You, Good Night by J. Buller & S. Schade, 1988 Simon & Schuster

Stop That Noise! by P. Geraghty, 1992 Crown

Roar and More by K. Kuskin, 1990 Harper Trophy

It Figures by M. Terban, 1993 Clarion

Antics! An Alphabetical Anthology by C. Hepworth, 1992 Putnam

Books That Have Several Chapters about the Rhythm and Word Patterns in the English Language

The Dove Dove: Funny Homograph Riddles by M. Terban, 1988 Clarion

Eight Ate: A Feast of Homonym Riddles by M. Terban, 1982 Clarion

Sing a Song of Popcorn by B. de Regniers, E. Moore, M. White, & J. Carr, 1988 Scholastic

Shoes by E. Winthrop, 1986 Harper Trophy

A Giraffe and a Half by S. Silverstein, 1964 HarperCollins

Poems of a Nonny Mouse by J. Prelutsky, 1989 Alfred A. Knopf

If I Had a Paka by C. Pomerantz, 1993 Mulberry

Faint Frogs Feeling Feverish and Other Terrifically Tantalizing Tongue Twisters by L. Obligado, 1983 Viking

Oodles of Noodles by L. & J. Hymes, 1964 Young Scott Books

Tog the Dog by C. & J. Hawkins, 1986 G. P. Putnam's Sons

Zoomerang-a-Boomerang: Poems to Make Your Belly Laugh by C. Parry, 1991 Puffin Books

Moses Supposes His Toeses Are Roses by N. Patz, 1983 Harcourt Brace Jovanovich

Fox in Socks by Dr. Seuss, 1965 Random House

The Baby Uggs Are Hatching by J. Prelutsky, 1982 Mulberry

Time to Rhyme: A Rhyming Dictionary by M. Terban, 1994 Boyd Mills Press

they want to be involved in and the type of book they want to use. Workshop types for reading are small groups of shared reading experiences, minilessons or demonstrations, guided reading, independent reading, or inquiry or reading-to-learn workshops.

Reading aloud is when you read aloud to students as described in Chapter 5. This is an important component of reading workshops and usually lasts from 10 to 20 minutes each day that the reading workshop approach is used. **Shared reading** is any reading in which all participants have access and have read the same text, whether it's on chart paper, in a big book, in their own personal copies of books or stories, or on an overhead projector. During the shared reading, the teacher demonstrates how to read fluently or how to solve a decoding problem using one of the strategies in Chapters 5 or 6. Immediately following this demonstration, students read aloud and share in the reading so that they can demonstrate that they have learned the particular objective that the teacher has taught.

Minilessons or demonstrations are planned lessons that usually take less than 10 minutes in which you focus on an element of decoding, comprehension, or writing that students have not yet mastered. During this discussion and demonstration, you can use one of the books on the literature cards in this chapter. Children can practice the strategy that you demonstrate on subsequent paragraphs in the book, either through a shared reading experience or by reading silently while you walk from desk to desk, asking each child to demonstrate how to use the decoding strategy when you point to a random word.

Guided reading is focused reading instruction with a book that is selected by a teacher in response to an assessment of a particular group of students' needs. Most often, guided reading is conducted in **homogeneous groups.** Homogeneous groups are created with students who have the same needs in reading. This instruction requires about 25 to 30 minutes of reading/writing workshop time. It involves ongoing explicit reading instruction that continues until learners can demonstrate an increased achievement level using the strategies taught.

Independent reading is a component of the reading and writing workshop that is usually scheduled for 10 minutes for first-graders, 15 minutes for second-graders, 15 to 20 minutes for third-graders, or 20 to 30 minutes for fourth- through eighth-graders. During independent reading time, students choose books they want to read. They can read together with a partner or in small groups led by students. Usually, during independent reading time, students write or share orally at the end of that period what they learned from the book that impressed them. Some teachers allow small groups of students to read the same book, with one student becoming "the teacher," leading the group through the reading.

Literature studies is often initiated when students want to read more than one book by an author. Another word for literature studies is author studies, which are demonstrated in more depth in Chapter 7. A literature study is when students focus their conversations on their interpretation of the text rather than on skills instruction. Less capable readers are encouraged to respond in smaller groups so that their ideas and voices can be heard. During literature studies, the teacher expresses opinions, as if an equal partner with children in sharing the joy of literature.

Last, the **inquiry** or **reading-to-learn** component of reading workshops is when students use reading to pursue answers to questions they have. This grouping system can comprise a whole class, an individual, or a small group activity. Students spend approximately 10 to 15 minutes reading to find an answer to a question that someone asked.

Writing workshops contain write-alouds, shared writing, interactive writing, minilessons, guided writing, independent writing, and opportunities for response. A **write-aloud** is when the teacher demonstrates purposeful writing that he or she is doing. In a write-aloud the teacher describes something he or she has written using a chart board or an overhead projector, and talks students through how decisions were made, what thoughts transpired, and what revisions were made. Typical topics during write-alouds are how to write to a specific audience, how to choose more specific words, how to format for certain types of genres, and how to increase spelling and punctuation abilities. The benefits of the write-aloud approach are that students can see their teacher learning and can view their own writing processes from another writer's perspective. In doing so, they come to judge themselves more as authors and assume greater responsibility for perfecting their writing as a professional might.

Shared writing or **interactive writing** is when students and teachers compose together. This activity usually takes about 20 minutes, unlike write-alouds that usually take only 10 to 15 minutes. During the block of time reserved for shared writing in a writing workshop approach, teachers and students can write a thank-you letter to someone who visited their class, generate a note that they want to send home to parents, or write a newspaper article for the school newspaper. Students participate orally and contribute information, spelling, and punctuation strategies, as well as new strategies they have been using for composing and writing.

Minilessons can occur at any time during the other components of a writing workshop. A minilesson can be for one student, a small group, or for the entire class to teach something that several students seem to be doing wrong. During this time you can demonstrate how to select topics; different components of how to draft, revise, edit, and proofread writings; and how to use better conventions and more specific words. You can also conduct valuable minilessons during writing workshops on how to use dictionaries, thesauruses, and computers more effectively as writing tools.

Guided writing takes place as you move among students with a clipboard, responding and attending to their individual ideas and needs. Immediately after you have assisted a student with a writing obstacle or with writer's block, you can jot down on a post-it note attached to your clipboard the specific strategy taught or the specific question asked. Later you can paste it into the individual file folder or individual pages in your anecdotal record notebook. In future discussions you can review with the students all they have learned during their guided writing activities. Some teachers like to put students in small groups during this time so that they don't have to repeat the same comment over and over again.

Independent writing is when students take charge of their own writing. They usually select their own topic, draft, revise and edit, and make their own decisions about when they want to share their writings. During these individual writing periods, they are free to go to peers to elicit responses, to confer, and to share what they have written. These periods usually last about 10 minutes for first-graders, 10 to 15 minutes for second-graders, 15 to 20 minutes for third-graders, and 20 to 30 minutes above the third-grade level.

Opportunities for response is a period of time, usually about 20 minutes per writing workshop, in which teachers and students share what they have learned or have written as they completed their composition. It is also during this period that published pieces are displayed in the classroom, in the hallway, or taken to the library for others to read. A closing component of opportunities for response is when students take the **author's chair.** Taking the author's chair is when students sit in the teacher's chair at the front of the class and either read their writing as if it were a completed work or to have students suggest ways it could be improved before the final revising and editing.

Grand conversations are a variation of the reading and writing workshops. It was named for its resemblance to good dinner conversations, and was created to replace the traditional school question-and-answer recitations in which teachers ask a question, students respond, and students either ask a second question or critique the statements made by students. Grand conversations usually last for about 20 to 30 minutes during a class period. They take place primarily after the teacher has read a book or a portion of a book, and students become the directors of the discussion (McGee, 1998). For a grand conversation students sit in a circle so that they can all see each other. The teacher serves as the facilitator, but the talk is primarily among the students. Traditionally, literature discussions have been gentle inquisitions in which students dialogue among themselves (Tompkins, 1998).

Prior to holding grand conversations, you can increase the quality of these conversations in three ways. First, you can encourage students to make connections between each other's comments and demonstrate how to do so by using the comments displayed in Table 6.1 following the PRA model, introduced subsequently in this chapter. Second, you can teach them to end each grand conversation with a synthesis statement or a summary so that they practice the skills of summarizing in addition to learning to share and listen to varied opinions and interpretations of fact. Last, you can ask questions. By that, you can ask students to ask themselves questions such as: What does this text mean to me? What does the text mean in relation to other text read? and What does this text mean for interpreting the world around me? Such instruction has been determined as valuable towards increasing students' abilities to appreciate and value reading. To illustrate, Mr. Evans conducted all components of the writing and reading workshop with his third-grade children. He did so by reading aloud the book *Frog in Winter* during a read-aloud. He then highlighted the between, naming, doing, and painting words using a paragraph on a chart that the children selected from *Frog in Winter*.

After teaching students to use syntactic clues more effectively, the students did a shared reading and read five pages from the book. Students were given individual copies, met in small groups in a reading workshop, and conducted grand conversations using that book. They brought their conversations back to the group in a summary statement from each group leader. At the end of that time, the teacher called together a group of students for guided reading who had not yet learned how to use the syntactical approach as well as Mr. Evans would have liked. During this guided reading activity, other students were engaged in independent reading alone, in pairs, or in small groups to read another edition of the *Frog and Toad* series. Immediately following that, students made their own books, in a writing workshop format, in which they wrote their own *Frog in Winter* version of the story.

To conclude, Allison, who had had some difficulty the past year learning to read, stated that Mr. Evans was advancing her even higher in her reading ability. Following this lesson, she said: "Reading and writing workshops is when you take a great

TABLE 6.1 QUESTIONS TO ASK DURING PRA AND GUIDED READING LESSONS TO INCREASE STUDENTS' INDEPENDENT DECODING AND COMPREHENSION ABILITIES

How did you decode that word?	What do you know that might help?
How did you do that?	What could you try?
Why did you say that word?	It starts like that. Now check the last part.
Where's the tricky part? (after an error)	You made a mistake. Can you find it?
What did you do to get that meaning?	Try that again.
Were you right? How do you know?	Try it another way.
What could you try and why?	
What would you like me to teach you that would help you?	

book like *Frog in Winter* and you get to read it and really love it. That's real reading! When I read in my reading and writing workshops, I get to choose a favorite book from the library and find a quiet spot, or sit with Meisong, Juan, or Michael and read everything I want. I really love the stories and I love decoding the words."

Book clubs, a third variation of reading and writing workshops, are small groups in which reading and discussion of various books occur, and students are given the opportunity to read the same text or a different text about the same topic. In book clubs, generally, four to no more than six students of mixed ability levels meet together because they want to discuss the similar topic about the same book they've read or about different books they all read. During book clubs, children are free to write any type of report or summary of the activities that occurred during that time.

GUIDED READING AND THE FOUR BLOCKS APPROACH

Guided reading is when teachers use questions and comments to help children become aware of strategies they can use to decode and comprehend text. The strategies include the knowledge they have within themselves, the clues that exist within the text, and instruction from the teacher that assists them to overcome similar challenges with literacy in the future. In a guided reading lesson, which usually lasts 20 minutes, each reader is taught to develop effective strategies for processing novel ideas that occur within individual text. The students within a guided reading group are usually needing instruction on the same skill. Guided reading occurs by the teacher asking questions that would prompt students to solve decoding problems themselves. The types of questions that are used are cited in Table 6.1. Once students read silently, aloud, or the teacher does a read-aloud for this small group of students, the teacher pauses at a difficult point in the text and ask students what they have done to decode or comprehend that portion of the text. Then, the students tell how they can do so in the future and instruction moves on as they study a different component of the text. The books used during this instruction are at students' instructional levels rather than independent levels.

FOUR BLOCKS APPROACH

One of the more recent approaches for scheduling guided reading has been called the **four blocks approach** (Cunningham & Hall, 1998; 1999). The four blocks approach is when the 2½ (or more) hour block allocated for reading and writing workshops and instruction is divided into four blocks of time of approximately equal lengths. During these blocks, students learn to decode by working with words; engage in guided reading or a PRA lesson; engage in a writing workshop; and then have self-selected reading activities in which they can participate in shared reading and independent reading or independent writing. Ms. Kurowski, the second-grade teacher across the hall from Mr. Evans, uses the four blocks instructional approach for guided reading instruction. The schedule she follows is in Figure 6.2.

Ms. Kurowski values the four block system because she has access to an instructional aid or a second adult in the classroom with her. Essentially, children rotate through four different types of activities so that you have an opportunity to assess

8:20–8:50

Working with Words

Focus will be on Word Wall and high-frequency words. Students will practice recognizing, spelling, and decoding these words. 10 minutes for teacher to introduce new words, 20 minutes for activities including sorting words, rhyming, and guessing covered words in sentences.

8:50–9:25

Guided Reading

During this time, students will read from basal readers and teacher-selected materials at or easier than grade level. 10 minutes will be allotted for teacher comprehension instruction, 15 minutes for group reading, and 10 minutes for whole group discussion or activities.

10:00–10:30

Writing

Teacher will begin with a 10-minute minilesson modeling writing styles and thought processes. 15 minutes will be spent with students working on their writing projects. Final 5 minutes will be used for sharing works ready for publishing.

12:40–1:10

Self-Selected Reading

Teacher will read aloud for first 10 minutes, 15 minutes will be spent with students reading books and available materials. Students will also conference with teacher. 5 minutes will be reserved for students to share what they have read.

I will have another teacher working with me, so I plan to work with one group on Working with Words while another does Guided Reading. This should limit classroom noise and distraction.

FIGURE 6.2 DAILY SCHEDULE FOR FOUR BLOCKS INSTRUCTION

Adapted by Carol Kurowski, 1999, second-grade teacher, Tulsa, OK. CLKurowski@aol.com.

students in four different types of reading and writing experiences. As shown in Figure 6.2, one group of students works with words while another group meets with you in guided reading. Students can read from either a basal reader or material that you select that is at or easier than their grade level. Ten minutes is allowed for comprehension instruction, 15 minutes for group reading, and 10 minutes for whole group discussion. Then the group that met with you goes on to self-selected reading in which you read aloud for 10 minutes, the students read their own materials for 15 minutes, and share what they learned for 5 minutes. Students then engage in writing so that they have 5 minutes to share at the end of a 25-minute writing lesson in which you have modeled for 10 minutes and students have written independently for 15 minutes. Some teachers have all four blocks going at one time when an instructional aid is available. Other teachers engage the whole class in activities that are designed around these four different components and objectives of instruction.

In addition to the websites described in Chapter 1 (which serve up ideas, analysis, or in-depth information on topics) is another group of sites known as web tools. These are designed to perform specific functions or to solve specific problems. For example, you can teach students to get a fast definition of a word by consulting www.dictionary.com. Reference works that are searchable on the site include *Webster's Revised Unabridged Dictionary, Jargon File, The Elements, Easton's 1897 Bible Dictionary, Hitchcock's Bible Names Dictionary,* and *The CIA World Factbook.* The site also links to other online dictionaries and language resources, including *Roget's Thesaurus* (www.thesaurus.com) and *Bartlett's Quotations* (www.columbia.edu/acis/bartleby/bartlett).

If students are still having trouble with the meaning of a word, they can try OneLook Dictionaries (www.onelook.com). OneLook is not an online dictionary; rather, it is a specialized search engine that queries more than 450 online dictionaries to supply a list of links to definitions. The U.S. Postal Service's ZIP Code Lookup and Address Information site (www.usps.gov/ncsc) can help students find a zip code or the postal service abbreviation for a state. There's a similar troubleshooting service for the telephone, where students can find area codes (www.555-1212-.com). Similarly, BigBook (www.bigbook.com), powered by GTE's SuperPages service, offers listings from more than 5,000 Yellow Pages directories.

Learn2.com (www.learn2.com) offers step-by-step instructions and tutorials on a wide array of activities, hobbies, and tasks. The skills taught range from how to change a flat to how to make stained glass.

In the next section of the chapter you can learn how to help students learn to use all these beyond individual word clues in an integrated fashion.

SECTION 2   PUTTING THEORY INTO PRACTICE

Using Vocabulary and Decoding Strategies Simultaneously

The purpose of teaching each of the above strategies is to ensure that readers understand and practice the beyond single word decoding tools available to them. The following lessons help them use multiple decoding strategies simultaneously and interactively.

ACTIVITIES THAT HELP STUDENTS DECODE INDEPENDENTLY

Whereas some students may need only one of these activities before automatic decoding comes more directly under their command, others may require several before they develop independent decoding skills. The following activities teach students to use more than one decoding tool to unlock the meaning of a word. These activities are called the PRA approach, text sets studies, What to Do When I Don't Know a Word, reader-selected miscues, and What's in My Head?

THE PRA APPROACH

The **PRA approach** is an instructional program in which students are asked questions to ascertain what they already know about decoding a word and to discover what they want to learn to decode more accurately. This approach is based on three components that enable children to become automatic and independent decoders and comprehenders. The first component, **proactive phonics,** is when students learn to initiate letter–sound correspondence without your prompting. Proactive phonics begins with teaching the phonetic generalizations in Chapter 5. Students are then asked to go back to the beginning of words whenever they come to a word they don't know and use the sound of the initial consonant and vowel, plus the semantic and syntax clues around that word to guide their decoding of the letter–sound correspondence in the middle or end of that word. After they attempt letter–sound approximation, they are to read to the end of the word and then go back and pull themselves through the entire sentence a second time. This is repeated until the sounds of the words match the meanings of the words that fit the syntactical components. This first component of phonics is guided by questions such as "Why did you say that word?" as well as those listed in Table 6.1.

Once the proactive phonics component of instruction in the PRA approach has been implemented, you can turn to the second division of instruction. This division, called **concrete referent vocabulary instruction,** is the *R* in PRA. *R* stands for referent, meaning that students are taught to tie the meaning of words in their lives to individual words, individual sentences, individual textbooks, and library books as they read, rather than prior to reading or after reading. Specifically, students are taught how to think about what a word could mean and how it might be used in that context in relation to all the other words in the sentences. Also, it is at this point in the PRA approach that students are taught that most long unknown words in tradebooks, textbooks, and library books relate to the subject matter being taught. Children are also taught how to draw pictures that are meaningful to them for difficult sounds, sight words, and other words that don't have a unique meaning as do picturable nouns. For example, Meisong, in trying to learn the difference between the word *a* and *the,* drew a great big 1 around the word *a.* This reminded her that *a* is the first letter of the alphabet and means only one thing. It is a picturable painting word that comes before nouns. Putting together all those contexts, she was able to recognize the word *a* and its meaning consistently.

The third component of the PRA approach is called **activating thought-filled comprehension.** This component (the *A* in PRA) teaches children to use the sea of meaning that authors create, as well as the rhyme and rhythm of the English language, to deduce the meaning of individual sentences and words. Children are encouraged with the questions in Table 6.1, through shared reading experiences, and with the teacher's minilessons of how to use the sea of meaning that exists as you read. A demonstration of how activating students' thoughts can lead to automatic decoding skills follows. After Mr. Evans finished a shared reading of a trade book entitled *How Flowers Grow,* he left the book on the easel. He then pointed to the word *flowers* in a sentence. He said that even if he didn't know this word, he knew that it would have to be related to something that grows because this book was about growing things. He also knew that the author was talking about pretty things. He had seen the things that the pictures on the page showed in his own yard; they were flowers. So he thought that word might be *flower.* By looking at the beginning of the word, he emphasized the *fl* sound and was able to sound out the word *flowers.* When the children stopped at other long words in the book, such as *garden* or *hoe-ing,* they began to explain how they would activate their thinking about how plants grow to lead them to comprehend the meaning of the word.

TEXT SETS STUDIES

Text sets studies provide children an extra support by focusing their attention on certain kinds of books. Specifically, a text set is when all the books that are available for student choice are either books that come from the same series of books that you have read previously or books on the same subjects. Students can use knowledge gained from a prior book to help them understand the concepts in the present book. Concept books recommended by Mr. Evans are shown in Literature Card 15.

WHAT TO DO WHEN I DON'T KNOW A WORD

To begin this lesson, distribute Figure 6.3 to students who have been introduced to the strategies it describes. You can also encourage students to refer to a class chart that you made by enlarging this figure and posting it in the room. Then, you can explain that students can use these strategies interactively to unlock the pronunciation and meaning of words. You can do so by (1) asking students to read the strategies with you, (2) sharing the information below, and (3) soliciting students' comments about this information and figure.

As a general rule, students must memorize basic sight words. Therefore, when readers see a word that is repeated frequently in texts, they should ask themselves: "What clues about that word can help me memorize its pronunciation and meaning?" Help readers understand that trying to recognize sight words instantly is among their most effective decoding strategies. Thus, whenever they see small words that occur regularly, they can also ask you or a classmate for clues as to how they can better recognize and remember that word in the future. At this point, it is helpful for some children to use one of the steps in the PRA approach. Help them draw a picture around the word that can give additional clues as to what that word means and how it can be used in the future. For example, they could draw a box around the word *the* and turn the *e* into a smiley face. They could draw a box around the word *that* and make *that* look like a hat. These clues can be used when you teach the very first step in Figure 6.3 of the What to Do When I Don't Know a Word strategy.

The second strategy is teaching students to analyze words with familiar spelling patterns phonetically. The phonetic generalizations that they have learned can be compared and contrasted in conjunction with word parts in new words that look like they contain regular English spelling patterns. Thus, when students see words that have vowel and consonant patterns similar to those of other words, they should

Literature Card 15

CONCEPT BOOKS FOR TEXT SETS STUDIES

Alphabet

John Burningham's ABC by J. Burningham, 1967 New York: Bobbs-Merrill

The Most Amazing Hide and Seek Alphabet Book by R. Crowther, 1978 New York: Viking

Picture Book ABC by H. J. Fletcher, 1978 New York: Platt & Munk

City Seen from A to Z by R. Isadora, 1983 New York: Greenwillow

The Teddy Bear ABC by L. Johnson, 1982 New York: Green Tiger

Good Night to Annie by E. Merriam, 1980 New York: Four Winds

Puppy's ABC by H. Piers, 1987 New York: University

Alphabet by F. Pragoff, 1987 New York: Doubleday

Counting

Ten, Nine, Eight by M. Bang, 1983 New York: Greenwillow

All the Little Bunnies: A Counting Book by E. Bridgeman, 1977 New York: Atheneum

1, 2, 3, to the Zoo: A Counting Book by E. Carle, 1968, 1987 New York: Philomel

The Very Hungry Caterpillar by E. Carle, 1969 New York: Collins

Can You Imagine . . . ? A Counting Book by B. Gardner, 1987 New York: Dodd, Mead

26 Letters and 99 Cents by T. Hoban, 1987 New York: Greenwillow

The Midnight Farm by R. Lindbergh, 1987 New York: Dial

How Many? by F. Pragoff, 1987 New York: Doubleday

Miscellaneous

Is It Red? Is It Yellow? Is It Blue? by T. Hoban, 1978 New York: Greenwillow

Dry or Wet by B. MacMillan, 1988 New York: Lothrop

Step by Step by B. MacMillan, 1988 New York: Lothrop

Here Are My Hands by B. Martin, Jr., & J. Archambault, 1985, 1987 New York: Holt

Twinkle, Twinkle Little Star by J. Messenger (Illus.), 1986 New York: Macmillan

The Two Bad Mice by B. Potter, 1904, 1986 New York: Warner

Growing by F. Pragoff, 1987 New York: Doubleday

What Color by F. Pragoff, 1987 New York: Doubleday

Things That Go by A. Rockwell, 1986 New York: Dutton

The Three Little Pigs by J. Wallner (Illus.), 1987 New York: Viking

Poetry—Rhymes

Shakin' Loose with Mother Goose by S. Allen & J. Meadows, 1987 New York: Kids Matter

The Adventures of Simple Simon by C. Conover, 1987 New York: Farrar, Straus & Giroux

Drummer Hoff by B. Emberley, 1967 New York: Treehouse

Mother Goose by G. Fujikawa, 1968, 1987 New York: Grosset & Dunlap

Clap Your Hands: Finger Rhymes by S. Hayes, 1988 New York: Lothrop

Out and About by S. Hughes, 1988 New York: Lothrop

A Hundred Scoops of Ice Cream by N. Josefowitz, 1988 New York: St. Martin's

James Marshall's Mother Goose by J. Marshall (Illus.), 1979 New York: Farrar, Straus & Giroux

Nursery Rhymes by M. Tarant (Illus.), 1978 New York: Crowell

Sleepy Book by C. Zolotow, 1958, 1988 New York: Harper & Row

Everything Glistens and Everything Sings by C. Zolotow, 1987 San Diego: Harcourt Brace Jovanovich

Source: From *Reader's & Writer's Connection* (2nd ed.), by M. Heller, 1995, New York: Longman.

---

ask themselves: "What other word do I know that has letters like this that I know how to pronounce? What generalization have I learned that could apply to this word? What would make sense in this context?"

Third, you can teach students that as a general rule, long words can be decoded most effectively through structural analysis. When readers see long words they should ask themselves: "Is there any section of this word that I recognize, such as a prefix, root word, suffix, or part of a compound word?" Then, when recognizing or

Check to see whether the word is on my sight word list.

Sound it out if the word follows a regular English pattern.

Use structural analysis if it is a long word.

Look at other words in the sentence. Does that help me?

Quietly ask a friend or teacher.

Look in the dictionary or go to the computer.

Use the word in a sentence.

FIGURE 6.3 WHAT TO DO WHEN I DON'T KNOW A WORD

pronouncing part of the word, that section's meaning can signal the full word's meaning, especially when other contextual clues are considered.

Fourth, you can teach students to use the meanings of other words in a sentence and the syntactical role that an unknown word serves in that sentence as clues to meaning. Last, you can model how readers can apply sight word vocabulary, phonic generalizations, or structural analysis, and reread a sentence in its entirety. By doing so, they can say the sound of the first letter, pause, and then read on until they gain enough context clues to discern the meaning of the unknown word. Reading to the end of the paragraph may also be helpful.

As a general rule, if the above strategies are unsuccessful, readers should ask a friend or teacher or refer to a dictionary or a computer. If the meaning is still vague, they can reread the entire sentence aloud to be sure that they understand the word's meaning in the context in which it appears.

The next step in this activity is to demonstrate how readers can ask themselves the following questions when they come to a word they do not know:

"What type of word is this?" (e.g., It is a long word.)

"Which strategy should I apply first to decode this word while I also think of all the clues I have?" (e.g., If it's a long word, I know I may be most successful if I use the structural analysis decoding strategy first. I recall that many long words I read are content-specific sight words.)

"What makes sense at this point in the sentence, using what I know about the author's writing style, and begins with the letter _____?"

Once students understand the way decoding strategies interact, they can practice using them interactively with a partner. Specifically, you can ask pairs to select a book to read. One student can read aloud as the second follows along silently. When students come to a word they don't know, they should allow their partners to ask the questions above and refer to Figure 6.3. As students read, you can move from pair to pair to assess their decoding abilities and answer queries. After 10 minutes of reading, you can ask partners to switch roles and continue the activity.

For example, in one session Juan correctly read the word *lioness* and Mr. Evans asked how he decoded it. He said he knew the word *lion* was in the word, but that the word meant more than a lion. He also knew (from the context) that the word meant a mother and he thought how *prince* means royal and *princess* means woman, so *lioness* meant lady lion!

In Mr. Evans' class, when this activity ended, Allison and Michael asked whether they could meet with a small group of younger schoolmates to teach them what they had learned. Mr. Evans was delighted by their growth in abilities and confidence. He agreed. On the next day, while Allison and Michael taught these strategies in another class, Mr. Evans and the rest of the class discussed what they had learned and how confident they were in their independent decoding abilities. They also identified strategies in which they would like to become more proficient, and the class scheduled the following additional activities to reinforce these strategies.

READER-SELECTED MISCUES

Reader-selected miscues is an exercise in which students identify words and sentences that they do not understand (Rhodes & Shanklin, 1994). After students have been introduced to the strategies in this chapter, you can ask them to select a book they want to read, at their instructional reading level (neither too easy nor too difficult). Then, you can distribute five acetates to each reader and an acetate pencil or felt-tip marker. After demonstrating how they are to lay an acetate over the first page of the book, students read and underline difficult words or sentences on the acetate. Next, after they have read and marked five pages, they bring their books and acetates to you. By categorizing the common difficulties between the words and sentences that individual students marked, you can help each recognize which decoding strategies could aid in the future with similar words that are unknown.

WHAT'S IN MY HEAD?

Ms. Marjorie Downing, an elementary teacher at Benchmark School in Media in Pennsylvania, and Pat Cunningham, reading professor at Wake Forest University, created this activity. Its purpose is to help students integrate decoding strategies through mental word imaging, a strategy that has proved to increase students' decoding abilities (Muter & Snowling, 1998). Students enjoy the challenge it poses and the game format. To begin, you can select 25 words for which you have not taught the pronunciation and meaning and write them in groups of five on a wall poster. They can be words that students want to learn, which appear in a selection they read, or which provide background for a new subject area unit.

Next you ask students to number to five on their papers and write the correct word as soon as they work it out. Then give five clues to the first word you want them to write. Begin with the most general clue and progress in specificity until the last clue, which, combined with the previous four, eliminates all but one word from the list or sentences on the wall. The first clue you can give is telling students how many syllables the word has; whether it contains a prefix or suffix; or another structural analysis decoding clue.

The second clue can be based on students' knowledge of phonetic generalizations. For instance, you can state that the word you are thinking about begins with the same sound as another word [you say]; ends with the same sound (as a different one you say); rhymes with another word; or contains the same phonetic generalization (as a different word that you say), such as, "The word I'm thinking about rhymes with *cake*." The third clue integrates students' knowledge of syntactical clues and endings of words. For instance, tell students the grammatical function that the word serves or the vowel spelling pattern it contains, such as, "The word is a noun." The fourth clue can identify some aspect of the semantic function of the word, but be sure the semantic information you supply relates to at least two words on the wall. For example, you can say that the word names one of the birds about which the class will read this week. The fifth clue will give the definition of the word so that no other word on the wall matches that definition. Table 6.2 illustrates such sets of five clue cards that you can use for three different "What's in My Head?" activities.

INTEGRATING THE LANGUAGE ARTS

Using Predictable and Pattern Books to Teach Decoding

Previously in this chapter, you read about how text sets and concept books can be used to increase students' decoding abilities. Another type of literature that has proven to be very successful in increasing students' independent decoding skills are **predictable** and **pattern books**. Predictable books are of many types. Basically, these books are written with patterns or series of words that are repeated so that

TABLE 6.2 "WHAT'S IN MY HEAD?" SAMPLE WORD LISTS AND WORD CLUES

A. WORD LISTS

List 1:	*List 2:*	*List 3:*
bed	kind	eyes
room	forest	wild
day	king	claws
teeth	boat	world
yellow	thing	walls

B. CLUE CARDS

List 1:	*List 2:*	*List 3:*
Clue #1—It is a short word.	Clue #1—It is a one-syllable word.	Clue #1—It is a plural word.
Clue #2—It begins with the same sound as *bike.*	Clue #2—It begins with the /k/ sound.	Clue #2—It begins with the same sound as *club.*
Clue #3—It rhymes with the word *head.*	Clue #3—It rhymes with the word *ring.*	Clue #3—It rhymes with the word *jaws.*
Clue #4—It can be found in a house.	Clue #4—It has four letters.	Clue #4—It is part of an animal.
Clue #5—It is something you usually sleep on.	Clue #5—It usually goes along with a queen and it wears a crown.	Clue #5—An animal can scratch with these.
[The "What's in My Head" word is *bed.*]	[The word is *king.*]	[The word is *claws.*]

students can learn new words through the rhythm and rhyme of the English language. Pattern books are also of several types. These books have a specific type of sentence pattern, which is repeated, such as a question or statement, so that students learn to say that sentence and, in turn, learn the individual words within that sentence.

Specific types of predictable books can have a predictable last word to the sentence, a predictable rhyming pattern, or the use of a predictable word part, such as the morpheme *all* in the rhyme *Humpty Dumpty sat on the wall, Humpty Dumpty had a great fall.* This type of patterning uses a word part for the pattern and the predictable part of the word. Pattern books can start out by repeating a word, such as the color yellow: Yellow is the color of the sun; yellow is the color of butter. Another type of pattern book could be based on certain world events, such as a book of months: In January we do this _____; in February we do this _____.

These books are often used in read-alouds by the teacher or in minilessons. Used this way, you teach students a specific strategy that appeared in Chapters 5 or 6. Following your instruction, you introduce the book and do a think-aloud to show children how you used the strategy within the pattern of the book to decode an unknown word in a specific sentence of the book. Next, you ask students to do a think-aloud as they read that same or similar pattern on the next page in that book. Knowing that this pattern will repeat itself over and over again in the book, several children in your class have an opportunity to perform a think-aloud and to show you that they have understood your instruction.

To illustrate, Mr. Evans selected the pattern book *What Good Luck, What Bad Luck* written in 1995 by Robert Charlip. As he read this book, he wrote on the board the steps he was thinking to decode the word *seared.* Mr. Evans read:

> What good luck, what bad luck, said the fisherman to his son.
> They sat by the riverbank all day long, but it was beginning to turn to night.
> What good luck, what bad luck, said the fisherman to his son.
> We sat here all day, nary a fish did we see,
> but now as the sun is turning to night, we leave with glee.
> We are happy for having been together all day, without a fish to carry our way.
> We still have our memory of joys we shared, and the fish can all rest without being seared.

Then, Mr. Evans stopped and said: "Class, I used the first part of the word, *s,* and then I used the rhyming pattern that had appeared, *ear,* realizing that the fish would not be eaten, and that the fishermen would not cook any, to come up with the meaning of the word *seared* in this instance. As you can see, I combined phonics, semantics, and syntactical clues, as well as the PRA approach, using the sea of meaning that the author was giving me. Allison," Mr. Evans continued, "I would like for you to repeat this strategy and tell us what you did as I turn the page and we continue to see what good luck and bad luck the fishermen had." At this point, Mr. Evans erased the board and Allison began to read aloud. Following the reading, she then told the class the specific applications of the decoding strategies of phonics, structural analysis, and context clues that she used to deduce the word *lured* on the next page of this predictable pattern book.

Literature Card 14 contains numerous pattern books that can be used with children who are in preschool all the way through grade 2, as well as books that interest children in grades 3 to 8. In the process, you can have children select particular books of interest and have them share these books with you through read-alouds and shared reading experiences. On subsequent days, children can break into groups and practice using decoding strategies with new predictable and pattern books that they select. During these activities, you can monitor students' progress while they have multiple opportunities to practice integrating their decoding skills.

INSIDE CULTURALLY AND ACADEMICALLY DIVERSE CLASSROOMS

Remedial Readers

Remedial readers are students who are at least two grade levels below their grade placement in their reading ability. Specifically, a remedial reader in third grade would be any student who is reading two grade levels below or is functioning only at the first-grade level. Recent research from the Center for the Improvement of Early Reading Achievement (see www.ciera.org for a complete listing of these research reports) indicates that, in the past 20 years, the number of children diagnosed as remedial readers has steadily increased. Children with specific reading disabilities are now the single largest category of students that receive special services in schools today (Sternberg & Spear-Swerling, 1998). When a student has received the instructional strategies in Chapters 5 and 6 and are still not making adequate progress in reading, additional approaches are necessary. Students can receive these approaches in your classroom. Doing so can enable them to maintain progress alongside their peers and help them save face in front of their friends. Without such specific interventions, however, many of these students may continue to fall further and further behind in their reading ability or be incorrectly diagnosed with a more severe difficulty than really exists. To avoid both of these negative consequences, the following strategies are recommended.

First, students who are falling behind in reading ability need more intense, dense, and cognitively rich instruction than ever before. Such children should receive (a) multiple provisions for acquiring accurate and quick word recognition; (b) repeated instruction, which instills the desire and means for continuously increasing their vocabulary; (c) text that increases comprehension strategies, fluency, ease, and pleasure in reading; and (d) instructions that enable you to model thinking processes as well as the value and power that students can receive from deeply processing text. Such interventions should address the complex challenge of providing more time and scaffolds to remedial readers. You can do so by allowing them to meet with you more regularly, and using the PRA approach so that they generate more insights about their own reading difficulties and discover new joys from literacy.

A second strategy is to break higher-level comprehension and decoding thinking processes into concrete steps that can be visualized and used separately for children to learn before they become more automatic. An example of how a decoding thinking process was broken into concrete steps is shown in Table 6.1: What Do I Do When I Don't Know a Word? When remedial readers are given your support, they can learn to dissect the skills of reading into smaller and more manageable steps. Without your support, such thinking may never occur (Block, 2000).

Third, it is important for you to diagnose what aspect of decoding comprehension fluency or vocabulary with which individual children are having difficulty. Checklists and rubrics shown in the next section of this chapter can assist in this process.

A fourth step is to use videotaping. At the beginning of the year, you can ask each student to bring in a videotape from home. It does not have to be new. About once a month you can record remedial readers reading a passage from a book or from any type of reading material, such as a newspaper or magazine that they choose. As soon as the tape ends, ask the student why he or she chose the book, what he or she liked best about the book, and then share what he or she thinks is the most important improvement made in reading since last month. Then rewind the tape, allow the children to view it with you, and send it home for parents to review. At the end of the videotaping, the student makes a contract or completes one of the rubrics or checklists in this chapter.

A fifth strategy, recommended by Roller (1998), can be used with remedial readers. In her research, Roller found that five actions can be taken by teachers to improve the progress of remedial readers. First, it is important that teachers allow remedial readers to talk about the steps they are following so the remedial reader can hear the thoughts they are having as they read. Second, it is important not to use too many easy books, as this decreases students' motivation and opportunities to increase their decoding abilities. Third, it is important to teach only a few basic concepts from each book, and to ensure that these concepts are the essential ones for understanding challenging and interesting information that is at each remedial reader's interest level. Fourth, you can have remedial readers to read to younger students because the modeling and discussion that occur as they share these books can help remedial readers in their decoding and comprehension skills. In the process, they also learn to set goals for reading and to reflect on what they've read. Before they visit with younger students, they can practice the reading with you. You can space the visits so that they have plenty of time to prepare to read well each selection that they take. Last, Roller recommends that you frequently ask about their thinking processes and strategies. For example, you can ask, "How did you know that the word was *after* instead of *and*? What should I teach you next that would help you to improve your reading?" Then, by rewarding the good behavior of reading and looking for the words as they read, they begin to value the use of strategies.

Such work has proved to be more effective for many remedial readers than immediately placing them in restricted special education classrooms. When remedial readers are placed in such classrooms, many negative affective ramifications can occur. For example, a growing body of research suggests that pulling students out for special remedial instruction too frequently can have detrimental effects on the self-concept and achievement of some readers (Berghoff & Egawa, 1991; Clay, 1999; Olsen, 1994). Remedial readers need to have more able readers as models, and to learn new ways to organize new information, make valuable contributions to conversations, and read and write more challenging words. When pulled out and placed in homogeneous groupings outside of their regular classrooms too frequently, expert peer modelers are not available to assist them in developing these abilities.

Two of the most telling true stories can convince us to work harder and to try new strategies with remedial readers. The following story was written by Alan, a second-grader, as reported in Booth (1989).

> I am in the slow readers group.
> My brother is on the football team.
> My sister is a waitress at the Blue Dragon Diner.
> I'm in the slow group in reading.
> That is all I am in and I hate it.
> I hate it!

The second story comes from a parent letter that was addressed to a teacher who had not used the strategies in Chapter 5 and 6 to assist her son to read. The parent begins the letter by saying:

Let me tell you about my 7-year-old son, Billy. Billy started preschool, had done average work, and went on to kindergarten. They waited until spring of the kindergarten year to tell me he was immature. But now he was already 6. They told me to hold him back. I then started to watch him more closely.

Halfway through the second year of kindergarten, he still couldn't recognize the letters and sounds of the alphabet. Then the school teacher tested him and said he had an attention disorder. They then assigned him to special education. He went through first grade at the age of 7, with a class of seven children in his room. All of the children were more disabled than Billy. He did not have any peers to relate to in school.

By the middle of his first-grade year, our doctor said that the school had made a mistake, that he was not attention disordered, and that he would not order that Billy be placed on Ritalin. Thus, at 7 years of age, I put him in one-year vision therapy. He had already had 3 years of extensive tutoring at home 3 days a week at night, and he had been engrossed for 2 years in a reading study group at the university. All of this was expensive and was wearing our family out because we were running him back and forth for all of his special reading helps.

Now all this would not have mattered to us at all if any improvement had been made. Now, at age 8, he is a normal all-boy child in every way, but even at halfway through second grade, Billy still isn't reading. The teachers are still trying the same old methods that have been used with him for 5 years. I wish they would try some new strategies.

Sincerely,

Concerned Parent

Last, many computer programs are in the process of being developed for remedial readers. Among the most recent are Read 180 (Scholastic, 1999) and **Touch and Learn** (Lexia Learning Systems). These programs focus students' attention on comprehension and word meaning. The computer provides motivation, video clips, automatic word recognition feedback, as well as auditory and visual stimuli. Features also include automatic branching, customizable instruction so that you can add your own instructional words, a printed bar chart to indicate student program, and teacher reports for individuals or whole classes.

In closing, it is important to remember that you can meet the needs of struggling readers. You can do so not by placing them in a remedial reading group, but by pacing their instruction more intensely, densely, and with more cognitively enriched strategies. They can learn to manipulate plastic letters to learn words. They can write, develop their own word banks, use pictures to illustrate the words they're learning, be sent home with book bags that contain instructions on using and reinforcing strategies with parents at home; and each of the strategies in this chapter can be repeated at different levels of difficulty.

RECOGNIZING AND REPORTING PROGRESS

Reading Checklists and Rubrics

Many teachers use reading checklists and rubrics to grade the language arts. Reading checklists enable teachers, students, and parents to see individual skills students have mastered. Rubrics separate steps in a language arts process and report the degree of proficiency that students have attained. For example, if a rubric were used to measure how well students are decoding, a rubric would state: "above grade level," "at grade level," or "below grade level" proficiencies. Samples of checklists and rubrics appear in Tables 6.3 and 6.4. Other examples can also be downloaded from the website that accompanies this textbook.

SECTION 3   TEACHERS AS CONTINUAL LEARNERS

Improving Abilities to Teach Decoding Skills

PROFESSIONAL DEVELOPMENT ACTIVITY

Managing Small Groups

What are the other students doing when you are working in small groups? This is a difficult question for many teachers. One of the most important principles that exemplary teachers follow is that, when they are with a small group, they try to devote their entire attention to the group's learning. By doing so, those children feel that their learning experiences are important.

Conversely, if you allow yourself to be repeatedly distracted by children outside of the small group, your students in the small group can begin to experience a decline in motivation to improve their reading abilities. This is called the **slight rejection phenomenon.** The rejection phenomenon is when children sense that you have turned your attention away from their needs or a request they are making to meet the needs of someone or something besides them. If you do not return immediately, apologize to the students, and share with them the importance of their own individual needs, oftentimes students begin to feel that other things are more important to you than their learning.

Thus, to avoid the slight rejection phenomenon, it is important that you learn to manage students in small groups and that you set aside some specific types of activities that other students can engage in without your direct supervision. In Figure 6.4, there are several examples of activities that students can do while you are engaged in small group activities. You decide whether you want the remainder of the students to operate as a whole class, in small groups, in pairs, or as individuals. Then you select an activity in Figure 6.4 in the box that corresponds to the size of group you prefer to use that day. After giving instructions, modeling, and showing examples to the class, you can turn your attention to the intense instruction that is necessary and the focused attention you must give to those who are in your small group so they can reach their maximum potential.

FOR YOUR JOURNAL

Reading Response Journals

Students record their ideas and feelings about what they have read in reading response journals. Such journals have been reported to be one of the best ways to

TABLE 6.3 EXAMPLES OF THE TYPE OF CHECKLISTS THAT YOU CAN CREATE TO ASSESS EACH STUDENT'S INDEPENDENT DECODING, COMPREHENSION, VOCABULARY, AND WRITING ABILITIES

Name: _____   Objectives taught during the
Date: _____   _____ grading period

STRATEGIES THAT HELP ME COMPREHEND AND COMPOSE

When I come to an unknown word, I

_____ skip it and go on to "till the text" on subsequent pages for clues and then come back to it

_____ substitute a word I do know that sounds like it and makes sense by referencing my prior knowledge

_____ use context to figure out what it means

_____ look it up or ask someone

_____ say (or write) a blank to hold the spot and go on reading or writing until the word becomes clear

When I am reading and I don't understand what's happening, I

_____ use picture clues to help me figure out what's going on

_____ summarize by stopping for a few moments to do so before I read on

_____ reread the confusing parts

_____ reestablish my purpose and reread with this purpose in mind

Before I start reading, I

_____ till the text

_____ predict what it will be about

_____ set a purpose

During reading, I

_____ confirm my predictions

_____ use metacognitive strategies

_____ scan for the most important words

After reading, I

_____ reread the book

_____ think about how my life is like the book

_____ think about what I learned from the book

_____ summarize the entire plot

TABLE 6.4 SAMPLE RUBRIC FOR READING AND WRITING ASSESSMENT

Name: _____   Date: _____

STRATEGIES TO USE DURING READING AND WRITING

Directions: Choose one of the words (*often, sometimes, never*) and write it in the blank to record how regularly you ask yourself the following questions as you read and write.

Prereading and Prewriting

_____   Is this similar to anything I have read before?

_____   Why am I reading this?

_____   Why would this information be important for me to know?

_____   Do I have any questions about the text before I read it? If so, what are they?

During Reading and Writing

_____   Am I understanding what I'm reading?

_____   What can I do if I don't understand this information?

_____   Why am I learning this?

_____   Are these characters or events similar to others I have read about?

_____   How does this information differ from other things that I know about?

_____   Why is this difficult or easy for me to understand?

_____   Is this interesting or enjoyable? Why or why not?

After Reading and Writing

_____   Can I write a brief summary of the story?

_____   What did I learn in this story, or did I say what I wanted to say in my writing?

_____   Where can I go to obtain some additional information on this topic if I need to add it?

_____   Did I confirm (or do I need to modify) my initial purpose for reading or writing this text?

_____   Is there anything else that interests me and that I'd like to find out or write about this topic?

_____   Do I have some unanswered questions from this text?

Adapted from *Evaluation of Student's Metacognitive Thinking during Reading and Writing,* by R. Meinbach, M. Rothlein, and G. Fredericks, April 1995. Paper presented at the annual research meeting of the American Educational Research Association, New Orleans, LA.

	Pre-K–2nd	3rd–8th
Before the Bell Rings 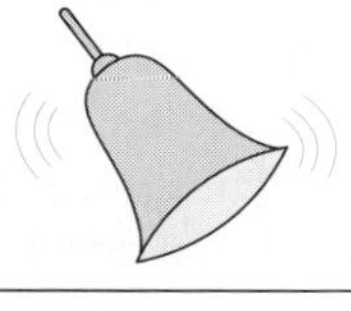	Journals Share with a partner what was enjoyed in a book read the night before Copy and respond to morning message	Dialogue journals Computers Respond to morning message Sharing with a peer what was enjoyed about library book read the night before
Reading Workshop 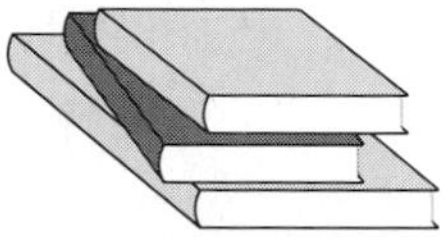	Independent reading and writing centers Partner reading Parent reads aloud to a group Multiage partner reading	Research projects Student-led instructional groups Partner reading Assisted reading Sustained silent reading
Large Group Instruction 	Theme-based art and centers Individual work Story response Reading readiness activities	Technology labs Story response A comprehensive, decoding, or thinking activity
Learning Centers 	Listening and writing center Language games Books on tape Dramatic play Partner reading	Peer tutoring Listening, reading, or writing Book-based project work
Writing Workshop 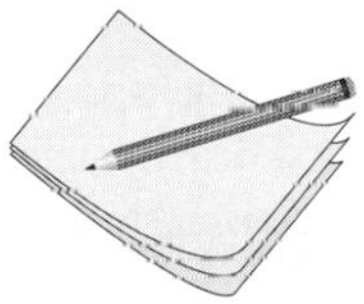	Book making Picture drawing to represent words Message making Letter writing	Sustained silent writing Letters to others Learning log Book making Writing to improve the school and/or community

FIGURE 6.4 WHAT CAN THE REST OF THE CLASS DO WHEN THE TEACHER IS WORKING WITH A SMALL GROUP?

Created by Sheron Marvin, 2000, master of education degree candidate and elementary teacher at Castleberry Independent School District, White Settlement, TX.

connect reading and writing (Leu & Kincer, 1995). They can be used in a variety of ways. First, you or the students read a section of a literary work. You stop and ask children to write their responses. Some responses can be shared orally and then recorded in a special section of the journal as starters for larger pieces of writing that individual children may want to pursue at a later date.

In a second type of reading response journal, students assume the role of a main character and make entries in their response journal as if they were the person in the story. In this entry, students make the response about what they would want to do before they actually read the next chapter. If the journals are used in this way, some starter sentences that you can put on the board before you introduce reading response journals follow. "The character I like best in this story is _____ because _____." "This character reminds me of myself or someone I know very well in that this person also _____." "If I were _____ at this point, I would _____." (Youngblood, 1985). Reading response journals have been used by many teachers within the past 10 years because children's choices are honored, and reading becomes authentic because the writing they do in response journals is shared with others (Rosenblatt, 1985; Spiegel, 1998).

CONNECTING CLASSROOMS, PARENTS, AND COMMUNITIES

Providing Tutorial Assistance

One-to-one tutoring is among the most effective forms of instruction (see Wasik & Slavin, 1993; and Wasik, 1998 for a review of this research). It increases the amount of time that students spend reading. In addition, many schools are turning to parents and training them to become tutors at school and at home for children with reading problems.

Tutoring sessions are best when they occur in 20-minute sessions or when individual children's needs demand greater amounts of time. Juel (1996) found that the more successful tutoring **dyads** (pairs of people working together for a common goal) had the following qualities. First, parents (or tutees) and their child devoted more time to reading books with familiar vocabulary words. They worked directly on teaching letter-to-sound instruction. Second, they used stories and word analysis activities found in Chapters 5 and 6 of this textbook. Third, they engaged children in figuring out grapheme/phoneme relationships for themselves rather than telling students the words they did not know. Fourth, these dyads allowed the tutee to do most of the reading, and the child was an active participant in asking questions about how to read better. Moreover, when parents were trained in a step-by-step fashion either orally or through written materials that were sent home, the effects of their tutorial greatly increased.

It is important that you closely supervise and record the progress being made during tutorial sessions that occur at home or at school. For instance, Wasik's research (1998) found only four common characteristics between the 17 tutorial programs used across the country. Educators were surprised. Specifically, the most successful programs (Howard Street Book Buddies, Reading One/One, Host, Reading Recovery, Success for All, Head Start, AmeriCorps, and Intergenerational Programs) all contained these components: (a) reading of new material by the student, (b) reading books in which either the words or the entire story were familiar to the student, (c) an activity that emphasized word analysis and letter–sound relationships, and (d) a writing activity that emphasizes a child's own thinking (and composing) about events in the stories read.

Moreover, Leeper and his colleagues (1990) identified characteristics that distinguish expert tutors from less effective tutors. In general, more effective tutors had been taught by teachers to make the interactions with their students intense, which can be accomplished by using the tables and figures in this textbook. Second, more effective tutors provided rapid feedback, which was highly personalized, and situationally contingent guidance to students. They frequently encouraged the child and asked for explanations, suggestions, reflections, and considerations, rather than providing directions, error corrections, or answers (Leeper, Aspinwall, Mumme, & Chabay, 1990).

•••

SUMMARY

The purpose of this chapter was to describe how instruction can increase students' abilities to move beyond interior word clues to increase decoding abilities. Several strategies assist children to develop these skills, such as syntax and semantic clues; using a dictionary and thesaurus; asking their friends, teachers, or seeking a computer's help; using reading and writing workshops; developing guided reading lessons in a four-block system or PRA lessons; and implementing book clubs and grand conversations. These activities have repeatedly demonstrated to strengthen students' abilities to recognize words when they read and to use more precise and vivid word choices when they speak and write.

In the second section of the chapter, four lessons were described that help students use both within word and beyond word decoding strategies simultaneously and interactively. These lessons involved the following activities: What's in My Head? What to Do When I Don't Know a Word, reader-selected miscues, the PRA approach, text sets and concept books, and patterned and predictable books. In addition, you received information about how to manage small groups, implement reading response journals, and set up tutorial programs at home and at school. You read about a unit that Mr. Evans completed at the third-grade level that employed text sets in a social studies class so students could create a simulated city. In the next chapter, we will turn our attention to increasing students' comprehension abilities.

HOW TO DO IT: USING WHAT YOU'VE LEARNED

ASSESSING YOUR LEARNING

1. Describe the order in which you will implement the activities in this chapter and provide your reasons for them.

2. Turn to Table 6.1 and rank order the three most important questions that you want to become an automatic part of your teaching repertoire. Once you have listed these three questions, describe why these are the most important and how they match your teaching style.

3. Discuss the benefits and deficits of using reading and writing workshops versus guided reading lessons, the four-block method, and PRA. Specifically, describe three benefits and three weaknesses of each in your discussion and modify the approaches to develop a system of reading instruction that you want to employ to maximize the benefits of all.

4. Write three new What's in My Head? activities with five sets of word clues that you can use with your students.

5. Create a checklist or rubric that can be used in your classroom to improve your ability to assess individual students' decoding abilities.

6. Implement two of the activities from this chapter and describe the effects of this instruction on a student.

7. Describe what you would do had you been Mr. Evans in the following true story that occurred in his class one day.

> Mr. Evans had prepared to make dinosaur nests with his third-graders. On that morning, he arrived an hour early and made sure that all the exciting "make believe" dinosaur eggs were ready, with an egg being placed at every group of tables. The bell rang and students were so excited they could hardly wait to begin. Then, Roberto, a Mexican American student who had only been in the class for a week and had never read a book aloud, handed Mr. Evans a book about dinosaurs that his father had bought him the night before. Roberto then asked: "Could you teach me to read this book so I could read it to the class after lunch?" To do so, Mr. Evans would have to put the dinosaur activity on hold.

What would you have done? Please write your answer to this scenario. Then turn to the answer key at the back of the book to read the action that Mr. Evans took. By checking your answer against Mr. Evans', you can discern if you implemented the principles of this chapter: to assist the class, to avoid the slight rejection phenomenon, and to capitalize on this zone of proximal development of wanting to learn to read.

KEY TERMS EXERCISE

The following are the new concepts that were introduced in this chapter. If you know the meaning of a term, place a checkmark in the blank. If you are unsure of a term's definition, you can increase your retention and return to the page where the definition appears. If you have learned 33 of these terms on a first reading of this chapter, you have constructed an understanding of a majority of the most important terms that you need to develop your students' independent decoding abilities. Congratulations!

_____ activating thought-filled comprehension   (p. 261)

_____ adding more phonics   (p. 244)

_____ author's chair   (p. 256)

_____ book clubs   (p. 258)

_____ cloze exercises   (p. 246)

_____ concrete–referent vocabulary development   (p. 261)

_____ context clues   (p. 245)

_____ contextual wedges   (p. 244)

_____ Dictionary Sword Drills   (p. 249)

_____ doing words   (p. 247)

_____ dyads   (p. 276)

_____ four blocks approach   (p. 258)

_____ grand conversations   (p. 256)

_____ guided reading   (p. 255)

_____ guided writing   (p. 256)

_____ homogeneous groups   (p. 255)

_____ independent reading   (p. 255)

_____ independent writing   (p. 256)

_____ interactive writing   (p. 255)

_____ inquiry   (p. 255)

_____ literature studies   (p. 255)

_____ minilessons   (p. 254)

_____ naming words   (p. 246)

_____ opportunities for response (p. 256)

_____ painting words   (p. 246)

_____ predictable and pattern books (p. 266)

_____ PRA approach   (p. 261)

_____ proactive phonics   (p. 261)

_____ reader-selected miscues (p. 265)

_____ reading aloud   (p. 254)

_____ reading-to-learn   (p. 255)

_____ rebus stories   (p. 248)

_____ remedial readers   (p. 268)

_____ shared reading   (p. 254)

_____ shared writing   (p. 255)

_____ slight rejection phenomenon (p. 272)

_____ text sets studies   (p. 262)

_____ touch and learn   (p. 271)

_____ Which word do you know? (p. 244)

_____ whole language   (p. 243)

_____ write-aloud   (p. 255)

FOR FUTURE REFERENCE

Resource Books for Teachers

Allington, R. L., & Cunningham, P. M. (1998). *Classrooms that work: They can all read & write.* Reading, MA: Addison-Wesley. 284p.

Au, K. H., Carroll, J. H., & Scheu, J. A. (1997). *Balanced literacy instruction: A teacher's resource book.* Norwood, MA: Christopher-Gordon. 367p.

Cooper, D. J. (1997). *Student-centered language arts instruction.* NY: Houghton Mifflin. 601p.

Fountas, I. C., & Pinnell, G. W. (1996). *Guided reading: Good first teaching for all children.* Portsmouth, NH: Heinemann. 405p.

Hindley, J. (1996). *In the company of children.* York, ME: Stenhouse.

Taylor, D. (1998). *Beginning to read and the spin doctors of science.* Urbana, IL: National Council of Teachers of English. 443p.

Books for Parents

Bernard, M. E. (1997). *You can do it! How to boost your child's achievement in school.* NY: Warner. 348p.

Calkins, L. (1997). *Raising lifelong learners.* Reading, MA: Addison-Wesley. 299p.

Cooper-Mullin, A., & Marmaduke-Caye, J. (1998). *Once upon a heroine.* Chicago: Contemporary Books. 349p.

Dietz, M. J. (1997). *School, family, and community.* Gaithersberg, MD: Aspen. 176p.

Dodson, S. (1997). *The mother–daughter book club: How to start a club of your own.* NY: HarperCollins. 274p.

Hausner, L., & Schlosberg, J. (1998). *Teaching your child concentration.* Washington, DC: Lifeline Press. 156p.

Hirsch, E. D. (1996). *Books to build on: A grade-by-grade resource guide for parents and teachers.* NY: Delta. 384p.

Lewis, V. V., & Mayes, W. M. (1998). *Valerie and Walter's best books for children.* NY: Avon. 640p.

McCaleb, S. P. (1997). *Building communities of learners.* Mahwah, NJ: Lawrence Erlbaum. 194p.

Odean, K. (1997). *Great books for girls.* NY: Ballantine. 416p.

Odean, K. (1997). *Great books for boys.* NY: Ballantine. 384p.

THEMATIC UNIT

THEMATIC UNIT: SIMULATED CITY*

Michael Evans, teacher at Saint Catherine School in Tulsa, Oklahoma, used this unit, called Simulated City, for his third-graders. It is an example of several methods by which students' vocabularies (listening, speaking, reading, and writing) can be developed in authentic activities that students enjoy. The duration of the unit is 3 weeks (15 days).

Day 1. Objectives—Introduction to the Sim City project. Have students learn about the process of elections and primaries. Learn the value of democracy. Discuss issues that one might consider when they are trying to decide for whom to vote.

Method—The students will read the story *Girls Can Do Anything* in their reading groups. They will discuss whether they think a girl could be president as the book states. I will use this book to springboard to a discussion of the role of the mayor (who happens to be female) and city council members. The students will discuss what they think are the qualities of good leaders and they will then be able to put forth their name for either the mayor or one of two city council positions.

Homework—students will write a campaign speech on why they are the best candidate for the position and create a campaign poster to hang in the room.

Day 2. Objectives—Discuss the terrain of different cities and how this effects them. Discuss the terrain of our simulated city. What is the terrain of Tulsa?

Method—The students will break into small groups and will each be given two real-life cities to examine. The group must report back to the class on how the city is a product of its environment. The students will learn that communities can be very different (e.g., fishing community or agricultural community).

Day 3. Objectives—Allow the students to participate in the democratic process. Let them experience the decisions made in a real campaign. Have them practice their public speaking skills. Create the atmosphere of the city in the classroom.

Method—Each student will be given 2 minutes to present to the rest of the class his or her campaign speech and poster. Following the speeches there will be a primary election in the morning. This will help narrow down the candidates. The remaining candidates will be allowed to give another speech in the afternoon and the final election will be held. The students will arrange their desks around the outside of the city. They will begin work on an art project to cover their desks with a mountain scene and establish the terrain of the city.

Day 4. Objectives—The rest of the class will be assigned their roles within the community (those not elected to positions) and will conduct research on them. Have them predict what issues will arise for each of their particular roles.

---

*Created By Michael Evans, 2000, elementary education teacher at Saint Catherine School, Tulsa, OK. Used by permission.

Students can use their language and spatial reasoning skills in a community effort to design, create, and perform services for a simulated city.

Method—The students will make certificates that will outline their roles in the community. This will be done with a great deal of fanfare so that the students are aware of just how important each role is to the community. Roles will include fire chief, police chief, banker, contractor, retailer, lawyer, doctor, grocer, mail carrier, priest, principal, and reporter. The students will write for their journal entry about what they think of their new jobs and anything else related to their respective positions in Sim City. During art class, students will create the terrain of Sim City.

Day 5.   Objectives—Utilize spatial reasoning skills in the creation of the city. Practice math measuring skills. Learn about the practice of plotting land. Discover the limitations that a budget can create.

Method—The students will gather as a community and discuss where each of the buildings in the community will be placed. They will have to vote on the location of each building and take into account factors like accessibility. They will be limited by a budget that will only allow the construction of eight roads. They will begin to construct these roads using their newly acquired math skills and measuring techniques. The roads will be named and the contractor will be responsible for the architecture and for creating the two city bridges.

Day 6. Objectives—Utilize math measuring skills to construct businesses. Learn what factors need to be considered for each particular business. Learn how to make blueprints and floor plans.

Method—The students are supplied with construction paper and various other materials. Following the completion of these buildings in the morning, the class will be visited by a local architect who will teach the class how to make blueprints and floor plans.

Homework—The students will make their own blueprints for the insides of their particular buildings.

Day 7. Objectives—Study the factors considered when selecting the site for a home. Continue to use math skills in the construction of their houses. Practice new writing skills. Review *how, who, what, why, where,* and *when* questions.

Method—Class discussion on the best locations for houses. What are the positive and negative aspects of building in various locations. For instance, it is nice to be close to the downtown area, but it is also a lot noisier. The students will then build their houses out of milk cartons and will choose a plot of land for their house in the city. The students will each write a fictional newspaper article for the *Sim City Times.* Each article will be tailored to individual interests and students can choose to work with a partner if they are willing to write a (longer) front-page story. Following the completion of the articles, the students will do a quick review of simple editing skills. They will cover capitalization and end punctuation. Following this review, they will self-edit their own work and then complete a final draft.

Day 8. Objectives—The students will learn to make choices based on a limited budget. The students will practice using negotiation skills.

Method—The students are broken up into four groups of five and they are each given a list of things that the city wants or needs. The price of each of these objects has been broken down into simple money problems. They are told that the city has an annual budget of $5.50 and, based on this, they must decide in their small groups what objects they would like the city to purchase. They will come together as a large group to discuss the conclusions of each group. They will be asked to name three benefits and three negative aspects concerning each of their choices.

Day 9. Objectives—Learn to write a persuasive essay. Learn a memory device that will help the students with their writing skills. (This lesson is adapted from the article, "Self-Regulated Strategy Development and the Writing Process: Effects on Essay Writing and Attributions," by Melissa Sexton, Karen R. Harris, and Steve Graham.) Practice oral reading skills.

Method—The students will use the budget worksheets that were provided the previous day. They will select their number one choice for what they would buy with the city budget. They will learn the different aspects of writing a good essay using the memory device acronym TREE: T = topic sentence; R = reasons (the topic sentence must be backed up with three good independent reasons); E = examine the reasons. Are the reasons listed really persuasive? Do they tell the reader why they should support the topic sentence? Make changes as necessary. Write a good concluding sentence to reaffirm the topic sentence; E = ending sentence. We will discuss each of these steps and then we will examine a sample TREE paragraph written on the chalk board. The students will be asked to locate and identify each of the parts of the TREE in the paragraph. The students will begin to work on their own TREE paragraphs to discuss how they want to spend the city budget. Following the completion of their work, they will present their papers to the class and they will vote on what additions they would like to make.

Day 10.   Objectives—Discuss changes that take place over time. Learn about the dangers of pollution.

Method—The students will learn about pollution that is produced by factories and how it effects the environment. Each student will receive a petri dish that they will coat with petroleum jelly. They will place the dishes outside and in 3 days they will be able to see the pollution that is produced in the Tulsa area. They will use this information to decide if they will place restrictions on the Sim City factory.

Day 11.   Objectives—Highlight the entertainment aspects of different cities. Show the students how different cultures influence the makeup of a community.

Method—The students will watch a Travelers video on Toronto. They will see all of the different ways in which different cultures can change a community. Following the video, the students will begin to work on creating a travel brochure for the Simulated City. They will include all of the best aspects of the city and try to come up with a creative slogan that will entice people to visit the city.

Day 12.   Objectives—The students will learn how to debate and formulate arguments. They will learn to list the positive and negative aspects of an issue.

Method—We will do a sample conflict which involves the whole class. We will discuss the positive and negative aspects of having classroom rules. On the board we will make two lists and compare them. Following this exercise we will divide into two groups and the students will be given a problem to debate. The city has experienced a flood and several of the homes and local businesses were damaged. They claim that the city is responsible for repairs because they failed to repair the damaged dam in the budget project. The city claims that the individuals are responsible because they selected the plots of land close to the river and they are aware of the dangers of flooding. They will discuss and then come together as a class to debate and vote on the issue.

Day 13.   Objective—Examine the results of the pollution experiment. Make a decision about the factory based on the results of the experiment.

Method—The students will see the pollution that is in the air. They will have to decide if they are going to close the factory to prevent pollution. They will have to decide if clean air is more important than all of the jobs that the factory provides. They will also be losing their number one export: Sim City Chocolate! They will divide into two groups for discussion before coming together as a class to debate and vote on the issue.

Fourth-graders prosper in a cooperative setting in which they can exchange their thoughts and feelings and, thus, expand their comprehension abilities.

CHAPTER 7

USING NONFICTIONAL AND FICTIONAL READINGS AND STUDENTS' WRITING TO INCREASE COMPREHENSION ABILITIES

Alison and Meisong were the first in their fourth-grade class to coauthor a series of books. Their books, entitled <u>Allison and Meisong at the Metropolitan</u> and <u>Allison and Meisong in Washington, D.C.</u>, began when Ms. Hopkins asked everyone to write about learning how to read. Allison, Meisong, Juan, and Michael wrote the following.

> When I first learned to read I wondered what the next word would be. I love books that make your mind jump with ideas for the ending.—Meisong

> I didn't really start to read until second grade. It was kind of late to start learning but I hadn't really been ready until then. I always wondered what people were writing. I was so happy when Ms. Halsey and Mr. Evans taught me how to read.—Allison

> I remember when I was in the first-grade library looking for as many horse books as I could find. I learned *so* much from those books. When I went to my first riding lesson, I already knew almost everything. From those materials, I'd memorized the stories and pictures. Now I own a horse and ride her in rodeos. I have won three blue ribbons. I don't know what I would do if I couldn't read.—Michael

> I guess you could say that if someone makes me read something boring, I will, but if I do it on my own I think it is a lot of fun.—Juan

Ms. Hopkins was aware of these and the rest of her fourth-graders' varied experiences with reading and writing. She also knew that, as children turn 10 years of age, they want to become more independent and are more strongly aligned with their peer group. She appreciates how well they respond to her efforts to help them improve their comprehension and writing abilities. Like many 9-year-olds, 10-year-olds embarrass easily and can be sensitive to teasing. They tend to form clubs and are becoming more loyal to their peers. Ms. Hopkins students often want and need an adult to listen when they talk over their ideas and feelings. Her language arts program provides a cooperative setting in which all of her children can share thoughts and feelings with their peers and her and can feel confident that they will not be put down.

The goals in comprehension instruction are not that different from those in an oral language program. They are to (1) develop students' abilities to analyze, interpret, and evaluate literary works; (2) become more comfortable with the power of words; (3) increase students' desire to communicate, learn, and experience pleasure through the literacy in their lives; (4) use their language arts periods to discover more about themselves; and (5) expand the positive purposes in their multicultural society, heritage, and future.

In real life, comprehension and composing are often self-initiated and demand planning and decision making. Similarly, desires to comprehend and compose are spurred when students face a challenge, or receive new information on which they want to act, and not merely when they are asked to receive facts passively. For these reasons, the best comprehension and composition instruction can begin with students' misunderstandings or desires to increase their own understanding about something that is of value to them. At these times, they can more automatically learn comprehension and composing strategies on which they can rely to create meaning. This chapter describes how to teach these strategies. Now, more than in any period in history, researchers are developing literacy strategies and unlocking the mysteries of how the mind comprehends and composes. By the end of this chapter, you'll have learned about these discoveries, and mastered knowledge concerning the following IRA, NAEYC, and NCTE standards:

1. How can you increase students' comprehension and composing abilities?

2. How can you increase students' motivation to read and write?

3. How can you employ the most recent computer-based and technologically related aids to enlarge students' comprehension?

4. How can you develop metacognition and oral reading abilities?

5. How can you conduct "author studies"?

6. How can you teach students metacognitive monitoring strategies?

7. How can you teach students to vary their reading rate and to write to a variety of audience?

8. How can students create multimedia products?

SECTION 1   THEORETICAL FOUNDATIONS

Comprehension and Composing Needs

Classroom practices in reading and writing have changed dramatically. In the past, many educators believed that students had to read before they could write, so composing instruction was postponed until children were well into the primary grades. Recent research has demonstrated that reading and writing abilities develop simultaneously. This knowledge concerning the integration of reading and writing has been called "the single most important change in the language arts instruction" in the last 20 years (Pearson, 1985; Godley & Mahiri, 1998).

Literacy is defined as the ability to read and write. Both reading and writing increase students' experience with written language. Both involve the intake of meaning: Reading instruction should result in the interpretation of (and aesthetic response to) information. Writing instruction should culminate in the ability to give meaning and ideas to many people. Teaching writing in conjunction with reading prompts learners to become more thoughtfully engaged. It also engenders a sense of authorship that leads students to "read more critically, more flexibly, and with a view to negotiating meaning for themselves" (Tierney & Shanahan, 1996, pp. 261–262).

Another similarity between reading and writing is that when students identify what works well for them in books, they often learn to include these features in their writing. For example, when Juan was in Ms. Hopkins's class, he reported the following qualities and characteristics in author's writings that made reading more enjoyable and more memorable for him: surprises; reversals in plots; action, suspense, or unusual happenings; changes in the usual order of things; events that aroused his curiosity; and well-developed characters with whom he could identify—feel happy or sad with.

Interestingly enough, teachers have not embraced nonfictional literature until recently. Up until about the 1990s, **nonfictional literature**, defined as literature that contains facts and events that actually occurred, was shunned in many classrooms for a number of reasons. First, with the advent of the whole language movement in the 1980s, early literacy instruction centered on reading many fictional stories. Second, elementary children have more difficulty comprehending nonfiction than they do fiction (Alverman & Boothby, 1982; Langer, 1998). Many quality nonfiction selections were not available prior to 1980. Thus, such books were less interesting than fictional books. Not surprisingly, as a result children also report that they prefer to read and write fiction over nonfiction by a 3-to-1 margin (Langer, 1986, 1998). This tide has turned as more nonfictional books are winning literary awards.

This chapter will describe how important it is for all language arts programs to contain ample doses of nonfiction reading and writing. Such experiences enable children to develop an appreciation and skills that are not possible if a program does not contain factual books. For instance, young children who are immersed in nonfiction books tend to choose informational books during story time (Putnam, 1991; Sulzby & Teale, 1987), and nonfiction becomes the preference for most male readers. Moreover, when children are taught how to read nonfiction books, new structures for writing and reading informational content become available to them. This breadth of structural knowledge can be used throughout their lives to add depth and breadth to their lives. For all of these reasons, fiction and nonfiction author studies have become an important component to students' comprehension development.

These author studies become memorable when children are encouraged "to live the literature of the author and to share the ways in which the author has moved, taught, and delighted them" (Skolnick & Frazier, 1998, p. 255). They become memorable when students add their own critical analysis and explore the biographical aspects of the authors and the events. When you and your students collaborate during the course of an author study, as described in the Professional Development Activity later in this chapter, students not only learn the value of fictional and nonfictional writings (and the textual clues that aid in decoding and comprehending each), but also gain a greater respect for their own abilities as authors and as critics who can identify the qualities of authorship that are most effective.

COMPREHENDING AND COMPOSING

The purpose of this chapter is to describe the recent history and effective methods of teaching comprehension. A basic tenet of this discussion is that understanding occurs on several levels simultaneously. To help students comprehend more completely, reading programs must differentiate the types of instruction that they provide. Just as students learn to employ a variety of strategies to decode new words, they must also learn to use a variety of comprehension strategies to ensure that meaning-making is under their direct control.

This new instructional approach presents comprehension as a crafting process—one in which understanding is constructed by students, authors, and teachers working together artistically to create knowledge. This process encourages readers to think independently about authors' intentions as they simultaneously learn content. In addition, this perspective views comprehension as more than a type of imprinting, whereby authors and educators impart ideas and universally accepted truths. Students are more than tabulae to be scripted or molds to be filled. They are sculptors themselves.

This approach is also influenced by sociopsycholinguistics. A reader's purpose, state of mind, experiences with the English language, and background knowledge are as important in making meaning as are the printed words and the social, historical, and political context in which every text is interpreted (Bakhtin, 1992; Bloome, 1986; Rosenblatt, 1978). Thus, if students are to craft a more enriched understanding, they must be taught how to experience a broad continuum of thoughts, bordered on one side by authors' intended meanings and on the other by their personal applications of those meanings to their lives. Through such lessons, books can more frequently become the windows through which students look at the world anew, see who they are, and increase their own personal insights (Galda, 1997; Gaskins, Gaskins, & Gaskins, 1991; Mangieri & Block, 1996; Pressley, Harris, & Guthrie, 1995).

Before students can reach these levels of crafting ability, schools must overcome the limitations of present forms of instruction. First, comprehension lessons should demonstrate how students can use authorial clues and comprehension strategies interactively. Methods of doing so are called *tilling the text* and are described in more depth later in this chapter. Second, teachers must model that it is useful to stop reading from time to time to craft meaning.

Further, comprehension lessons must not be too prescriptive, stifling, or depersonalized, on the one hand, nor too free-flowing and unmonitored on the other. When these conditions exist, students do not learn how to craft meaning unless a specific genre is very familiar to them (Block, 2000a, 2000b). Similarly, when free reading and unlimited choice of reading materials dominate direct instruction, many pupils do not develop adequate comprehension skills. Instead they continuously struggle to attain only a semblance of meaning. In these instances, the intense concentration necessary to make meaning gives way to the lazy, effortless task of reading merely to confirm their own ill-informed opinions and unsubstantiated beliefs. Alternatively, no matter how well students engage in comprehension strategies, if they do not have the opportunity to read what they want, they may never fall under the spell of wonder that such self-discovery of books casts. Braumann, Hotten, and White (1999) found that 20 percent of the total reading comprehension program should be spent in strategy instruction (described in more depth later in this chapter). A balance of self-discovery and strategy instruction is desirable.

A fifth limitation of some past comprehension lessons is that even though beginning and struggling readers spend time listening to high-quality literature, they often do not spend time learning how to read fiction or nonfiction or mastering enough comprehension strategies so that they can read silently and unaided. Likewise, without adequate instruction older readers are "making compromises with the demands of text (Mackey, 1997, p. 451)" In other words, rather than pausing to investigate a detail, many students merely "come up with a make-do interpretation that will enable them to keep reading" (Mackey, 1997, p. 454). They do not craft their own understanding, but instead engage in "good enough reading (Mackey, 1997, p. 460)." At this level of comprehension, students simply (1) accept that some ideas will remain vague to them, (2) skip too many words, (3) resist ferreting meaning from long sentences and paragraphs, (4) fail to capture enough of the authors' details to accurately interpret upcoming events, and (5) fill gaps in literal comprehension by inserting personal experiences rather than textual information. Moreover, when students realize that their limited understanding is not sufficient for complete comprehension, they merely read on word by word and hope that clarity will somehow magically emerge.

To overcome these limitations, three new types of comprehension lessons should be used. Type 1 lessons build eustress and positive values toward literacy. Type 2 lessons increase risk-taking through interactive, strategic thinking processes that produce a more complete comprehension during silent reading. Type 3 lessons strengthen students' desires to learn more about the reading process and about their own efficacy as valid crafters of comprehension. These lessons teach students how to integrate their literal, interpretive, applied, and metacognitive thoughts with past experiences, story grammar, and authors' writing styles. Students learn concurrently to realize the authors' purposes along with their own reading goals.

Each of these new comprehension lessons have a unique goal. When successful, Type 1 lessons culminate with students using reading to grow as human beings. Sustained silent reading periods and one-to-one conferences on a daily basis can accomplish this goal. Type 2 lessons increase students' repertoire of comprehension strategies. Lessons in this chapter are designed to reach this goal. Type 3 lessons enable students to learn more about themselves as readers and how they can continue to advance to higher levels of comprehension ability. One way to reach this goal is for students to meet in small groups with you to discuss strategies they are using to increase comprehension.

Comprehension is the process by which a reader or listener interacts with printed or oral material (Brown & Palincsar, 1990; Duffy & Roehler, 1989; F. Smith,

1988b). Through schema and previous personal and vicarious experiences, students reconstruct the sender's message. Comprehension is a complex process that requires students' engagement, use of schema, interpretation, and self-initiation of reading strategies. In this section you will learn how to teach comprehension at three levels: literal, interpretive, and applied.

Literal comprehension is "reading the lines" or understanding what the author said, such as recalling details and main points. To comprehend literally, students remember what was stated exactly as it was written. **Interpretive comprehension** is defined as "reading between the lines." Readers process ideas based not on what was stated but on what was implied by the author, including points the author intended the reader to deduce, interpret, rephrase, or infer from explicitly stated information. **Applied** or **critical comprehension** is defined as "reading beyond the lines," which occurs when readers evaluate, integrate, and use information and ideas read or heard to make decisions in their own lives (Raphael, 1989). To do so, students relate information inferred from text to their lives through creative and evaluative thinking.

Comprehension improves when your instruction builds bridges that connect authors' ideas and students' lives. You can fill gaps in students' background knowledge, expand concepts during reading and listening instruction, and alert students to the schemata they already possess before reading or listening (Prawat, 1991). In addition, substantial research suggests that students who have extensive prior experience with a genre and topic comprehend more than students who have less prior knowledge (Marzano et al., 1998; Yochum, 1990).

Strategies are self-initiated plans of action that readers and writers use to make meaning. They involve (1) intentional and deliberate thoughts, (2) flexible and adaptable skills, (3) reasoning, and (4) metacognition (Dole, Buffy, Roehler, & Pearson, 1991; Garner, 1987). **Metacognition** is a consciousness of one's own thinking processes before, during, and after reading, writing, speaking, listening, and viewing.

When readers encounter obstacles to comprehension, they need strategies to overcome their difficulties. Block (2000), Pressley et al. (1991) and Weinberg and Balaythy (1991) recommend students learn to predict, visualize, and summarize. Researchers have evidence that it takes many years for some comprehension and composing strategies to become automatic. (Gaskins, Gaskins, & Downer, 1995; Block & Cavanaugh, 1997; Pressley, 1994). Recent studies by Kletzien (1991) and Zabrucky and Ratner (1989) also demonstrate that while good and poor comprehenders use similar strategies, good comprehenders are more willing to persist in using them. Moreover, without your instruction, poorer readers tend to reuse only very few and often ineffective strategies.

Thus, self-initiated, value-filled comprehension occurs when students have learned the strategies (and possess a desire) to make emotional (aesthetic) and efferent responses to a selection before, during, and after reading (Rosenblatt, 1978). When readers and writers approach a reading or writing with an **efferent stance,** they tend to focus most of their attention on understanding what the author intended to be carried away from the reading or writing. They usually seek to learn information, as when they study a driver's manual, read a recipe, or write a news report. When readers and writers approach a reading or writing with an **aesthetic stance,** they focus more inwardly as the reading moves them to personal responses, ideas, and feelings that are stirred by the text or writing experience. In these situations, as the reading or writing activity proceeds, "the reader draws upon memories, senses, relationships with other things, savors the artistry of the author, and feels a range of sensations" (Zarrilla, 1991, p. 222). Students achieve both of these stances by asking questions, drawing inferences, and constructing hypotheses. They must also initiate effective strategies when their comprehension becomes unclear.

EMERGENT LITERACY

Reading and Writing Begin

Emergent literacy is a continuum of understandings that enable students to begin to read and write. Emergent literacy is one of the most interesting and controversial topics in education today (Morrow, 1999; Teale & Sulzby, 1986). Emerging literacy is a continuous process that begins during the first months of life can and can continue through third grade (Adams, 1990). In Chapter 3 you discovered the depth of research presently underway to better understand oral language acquisition processes. A comparable number of studies exists concerning emergent literacy and how young children come to understand written language.

From the 1930s through the 1970s educators believed that there was a "best time" to initiate reading and writing (and to some degree, speaking and listening) instruction. Educators believed that students had to reach a level of "readiness" be fore literacy concepts would imprint (Morphett & Washburne, 1931). This philosophical position, known as **reading readiness** dictated that children had to acquire a basic set of mental skills before instruction in reading and writing could begin. These competencies were believed not to be in place until students reached a mental age of 6½ for reading and 9 years for writing instruction. During the early 1980s new research revealed that students do not need such an accumulation of life experiences before literacy instruction can begin.

Research now indicates that children learn to read and write using traditional English words as early as 2 years of age; writing abilities often develop before reading; many students spell before they read; and, reading and writing can be learned in conjunction with speaking. Most children enter preschools and kindergartens knowing 14 of the 26 letters of the alphabet (Newman, 1999). Moreover, kindergarten children's literacy develops rapidly. For example, when a one-word label can no longer bear the weight of students' accumulated associations, they begin to write sentences and paragraphs.

YOUNG CHILDREN'S SPECIAL COMPREHENSION NEEDS

The first 6 years of a child's life are extremely important because this is when most language is acquired. Linguists and psychologists have also found that emergent literacy follows a similar path regardless of the language a child learns. For instance, signs of word recognition appear at about 6 to 8 months of age. At approximately 1 year, children write their first scribbled words. Children join words together by 18 months, and by age 4, most have internalized many of the basic rules that govern their language. Approximately 2 years later, students master language to such an extent that they can speak and "write" (scribble) sentences they never used before (Travers, 1982).

Because 4- and 5-year-olds talk to integrate subject matter, allowing for substantive conversations at school can accelerate their literacy growth. (Newmann, 1991; 1999).

Moreover, language development parallels motor and cognitive abilities and is connected to a child's biological makeup. For example, students' brains reach 90 percent of adult size by age 5. Research has also demonstrated that children who are advanced in oral language tend to have greater achievement in literacy as well. Further, this level is greater than those who have not used literary concepts before first grade. Studies also indicate that some children enter school with only 2 to 3 hours of print and text interaction with adults, while others have as many as 2 or 3 thousand hours of such exposures with adults (Teale, 1986). The former group of students rarely recovers from such limited literacy exposure (Adams, 1991).

YOUNG CHILDREN'S SPECIAL WRITING NEEDS

Most students demonstrate some of the following literacy understandings by preschool or kindergarten. They display an awareness that writing has meaning, and they use the same mark repeatedly (the **recurring principle**). When they realize that "real writing" is made up not of only one mark, but of a variety of marks, used repeatedly in many orders and directions, they demonstrate the **generative principle**.

As students become more aware of print conventions, they also realize that "adult writing" is ordered by the **linear principle,** and they only write horizontally. At this point, however, they are not usually clear about the left-to-right principle of English. Therefore, although they know that their writing should be written horizontally, they aren't sure where to begin. For this reason, some students write words backward or begin the first letter on the right and move backward across their page, moving right to left. Once students learn these principles, they turn their attention to individual letters and work to comprehend the **flexibility principle.** When students realize that adding marks to letters can transform them into different letters, they wield the principle of literary flexibility. Similarly, Marie Clay (1998) reports that it takes students considerable time to fully understand which features distinguish one letter from another. For instance, when children first begin to write they do not realize that *I* and *T* are different. As students begin to realize the flexibility of writing, they also initiate contrasts between letters, or use the **contrastive principle.** For example, they comment that *I* is like *T* but has two horizontal lines instead of only one.

The last developmental stage in emerging writing is when students intend their works to be read by others. They discover that others should be able to read what they have written. This stage has been identified as the **sign principle** (writings are like signatures of thoughts). An example of Juan's knowledge of the sign principle appears in Figure 7.1. In this picture, Juan demonstrates that he knows that the word *bird* can be used to communicate meaning, just as a picture of a bird can communicate meaning. Children learn these principles when you enable them to do the following tasks:

- Copy words from buildings and signs (environmental print) during field trips and use them in class.
- Retell, predict, and write stories, characterizations, new vocabulary words, and settings they discovered when read aloud to them.
- Find a word on the page that has been pointed out to them elsewhere.

FIGURE 7.1 EXAMPLE OF JUAN'S USE OF THE SIGN PRINCIPLE IN EMERGENT WRITING

Your class can take "reading walks" where you have labeled objects by "planting" signs for them to read in the schoolyard and neighborhood. This also can aid in their mastery of these important concepts. (Sulzby, Teale, & Kamberelis, 1989). **Dictation** is when you become your students' secretary and you write what they say. Dictation demonstrates the important links between thought, writing, and reading. It also allows you to offer alternative grammatical structures and elaborate on students' thoughts. Moreover, dictation helps students see that their language is valued and builds their courage to write something unaided and alone (Wuertenberg, 1986).

You can also write messages to your class every day that adhere to these principles: (1) use short words and sentences; (2) do not write paragraphs longer than three sentences; (3) use large letters and leave large spaces between words; (4) write interesting things, using students' names when possible, but write simply; (5) use only one thought per sentence; (6) post a "dictionary" or chart of definitions of longer words you use, and add to it throughout the year; and (7) as much as possible, try out your draft writings on a few students who arrive early, before duplicating it or having the entire class read it (Lowe, 1992).

Reading small, traditional-sized books (or big books) to young children also increases letter-naming knowledge (Mason, Kerr, Senha, & McCormick, 1990). Using big books with enlarged print enables children to approximate the intimacy of parent–child book sharing (Holdaway, 1979). Another valuable activity is to appoint a committee of three students each week to generate a letter that the class can mail to all parents about what they learned. Students then add one sentence of their own concerning something special that they learned. You serve only as editor, helping students correct the letters they make. As students take more and more responsibility for reporting what they learned, the quality of their letters increases.

By age 5, most children still print everything in all uppercase letters, and a few use both hands interchangeably for handwriting. Your responsibility, as a kindergarten teacher, is to develop hand dominance and fine motor skills, using the letters and words students write. If a student does not have hand dominance by the end of kindergarten, you may wish to consult with school specialists and parents to ensure that these slower-evolving abilities are not misinterpreted as learning disabilities. Moreover, most young children become easily frustrated because their motor skills cannot keep up with the speed in which they can create ideas that they want to write. In such cases, you can decrease this frustration by inviting older students into the room to write for them. By age 5½ most students have established their own penmanship style (Hilliker, 1986). In the next section, you will read about what can be done to assist students who have mastered and moved beyond these emergent literacy stages.

TILLING THE TEXT

Tilling the text refers to students' abilities to use all the clues in a text to fully engage in and comprehend each section that they read, just as soil is tilled and nourished before planting. Through such cultivation more nutritious fruits (meanings) can be produced. In essence, comprehension and composition advance when students learn how to (1) attend to an author's writing style as they read, by scanning the text for subheadings and print features (such as the length of paragraphs and amount of white space) to determine their own purpose for reading as well as the conceptual density of that material; (2) establish their own purposes for comprehension and composing; (3) use their own background knowledge to expand and not interfere with meaning-making; and (4) initiate metacognitive strategies to make meaning and overcome obstacles while comprehending and composing. Figure 7.2 demonstrates the strategies you can teach to increase student's abilities in tilling the text.

ATTENDING TO AUTHORIAL WRITING STYLES

Among the first steps in tilling the text is to recognize the logic that the author followed when dividing the topic into chapters and subtopics. In performing this analysis, readers and writers can be lead to realize that dense concepts and writing styles require more intense use of comprehension and metacognitive processes, and that each writing needs to be, and was, built by the author with a specific purpose in mind.

You can help readers understand the connections between events in a story (**story map** or **story frames**) and the types of paragraph structures that authors use. This understanding can increase students' abilities to predict while reading (Loxterman, Beck, & McKeoun, 1994). When connections between writing formats are made

Now I Get It!

Reading should be a fun and exciting experience for everyone. To help you to enjoy and get the most out of what you read, follow the steps on this sheet. And remember, you only get out as much as you put in, so give it your all!

Before you read:

1. Pick a place.

Where in the world do I want to go to read?
What type of environment do I need?

2. Scan the book.

What do I expect to learn about?
What do I want to learn?
What do I expect to feel?
What is my purpose for reading?

While you read:

1. Get involved.

Where do I want to go from here?
How does this book make me feel?
Have I ever experienced anything like what I am reading about?
Would I have done the same thing if I were the character/author?

(continued)

FIGURE 7.2 TILLING THE TEXT STRATEGIES

Created by Sarah Karr, 2000, second-grade teacher at Sacred Heart Elementary, St. Petersburg, FL. Used with permission.

2. Reread and question.

Am I understanding what I am reading?
What is not clear to me?
Why did that happen the way it did?
What do I need to go back over?
What things do I need to ask about?

After you read:

1. Reflect and evaluate.

What pieces are still missing in this puzzle?
Have I fulfilled my reading purpose?
What questions do I still not have answers to?
Did things happen the way I would have
expected them to?

2. Seek others and share.

Who can help me better understand what I have read?
Who might help to answer my questions?
Who would also enjoy hearing about what I have read?

3. Read more.

What will be the next books/topics I can check off my list?
What other books should I read next?
What will the purpose of my next reading be?

FIGURE 7.2 (CONTINUED)

clear, students also begin to think ahead more frequently and gain a greater sense of control over their own reading abilities.

In like fashion, students find it easier to make meaning in reading and writing when they recognize the function that single paragraphs perform in a text. The next section describes the functions of paragraphs and how to teach them. When you provide this information, many students often come to understand for the first time that sentences are put together in a predictable manner. As a result, reading can be viewed more like "a friend" because it begins to possess qualities of dependability and predictability.

PARAGRAPH FUNCTIONS

The most frequently occurring types of English paragraphs follow:

Introductory Paragraphs: Provide an overview for the entire text, and tell readers the purposes of the paragraphs that will follow.

Explanatory Paragraphs: Give reasons for an event, outcome, position, or author's ideas. Key words in this paragraph are *for example, specifically, for this reason.*

Descriptive Paragraphs: Delineate features and individual points after a main purpose or idea has been stated in a previous paragraph.

Cause and Effect Paragraphs: Present the results of one or more causative agents or actions that led to a specific event. Key words to indicate that a paragraph is describing a cause or an effect are *because, since, so that, so, if, as, for.*

Conditional Paragraphs: Specify what would happen if something else occurred or state the limits to the ideas presented in a previous paragraph. Key words in this paragraph are *if . . . then, unless, although, only if.*

Time or Spatial Sequential Paragraphs: Relate the order in which particular events or ideas occur or give the order that things described exist within a given space. Key words in this type of paragraph are *first, second, third, then, next, before, after, during, while, another, also, in addition, when, until, meanwhile, always, following, finally, initially.*

Question and Answer Paragraphs: Begin with a question and subsequent sentences answer the question.

Summarizing or Concluding Paragraphs: Report the most important points from previous paragraphs. Key words in this paragraph are *hence, therefore, as a result, thus, in summary, in conclusion, accordingly, consequently, finally, to sum up.*

To teach these, as you read a story to the class from an overhead transparency, you can pause to model how you identified the paragraph you just read. Then, you can make a game of identifying the functions of subsequent paragraphs—students read along with you and identify the function of each upcoming paragraph. You can conclude this work by asking students how knowing the purposes of paragraphs can assist them as they read new books silently, and if knowing the purposes that paragraphs serve can increase comprehension by increasing the predictability of the meaning in the next paragraph.

ESTABLISHING A PURPOSE

One of the most important actions you can take is *not* to tell students the purpose for reading a piece of material. When you establish readers' and writers' purposes too often, students may not learn to do so themselves. It often takes repeated trials before readers and writers trust that they *can* comprehend and compose effectively. To help them assume this ownership before they read or write, you can ask students to answer the questions below, and to scan the text to discern which parts capture their minds and attention. In the process, they can become more alert to those sections that may require their more intense concentration. Readers can do so when they have been shown, and then asked to describe, how they perform the following tilling-the-text thoughts before reading or writing:

- What motivates them to read or write; and when choice is not given, what do they do to establish a personal purpose for an assigned reading or writing?
- How can they activate their prior knowledge before, during, and after reading or writing?
- How can they add to their text-specific knowledge and vocabulary as they read?
- How can they focus and refocus their minds on meaning-making when their concentration is interrupted during reading and writing?

When such thoughts do not occur, students read only through "calling the words." **Word calling** is defined as reading all words accurately but not comprehending what they mean. Word calling usually emerges at some point after second grade because students have not been taught to answer the above tilling-the-text questions or to establish their own purposes for reading. Many word callers also become so obsessed with reading for accuracy that they literally forget to comprehend (Mackay, 1998; Dymock, 1993). Also by third grade, readers move into material for which they no longer can merely guess at the meanings of words and topics (by using their common sense and personal experiences) (Chall, 1983). Moreover, when they have not been taught to set purposes and analyze textual differences between fiction and nonfiction, many content-area reading materials become too conceptually dense for them to comprehend. Unless readers and writers learn the metacognitive strategies on pages 313–314, most will not stop as soon as they misunderstand or miscommunicate something (Baker & Brown, 1984; Block, 1999). Alternatively, as demonstrated by researchers such as Atwell (1998), Clay (1999), and Graves, Cooke, and Laberge (1989), students who establish purposes, preview their text, and revise their writings make better inferences about material read and written. These strategies help readers and writers relate new vocabulary to overarching concepts.

USING PRIOR KNOWLEDGE

There are many methods of increasing students' abilities to apply prior knowledge to reading and writing. The more automatically prior knowledge can be elicited while reading or writing, the more fully and effectively students will comprehend and write. Readers and writers who do not use prior knowledge as a tool often have (1) out-of-school culturally driven experiences that are disparate from in-school texts; (2) texts that are not clearly written to move distinctly from point to point; (3) vocabulary introduced prior to reading that does not relate to the central idea of the book, or that was taught in an isolated fashion; or (4) metacognition that is not engaged so inaccurate word choices are left uncorrected (Palinscar & Brown, 1984; Block & Mangieri, 1996; Dyson, 2000).

Equally important, readers and writers must recognize when their prior knowledge contains naive or incorrect information. In the process they must learn how to reconcile new and conflicting information. Without this instruction, students either ignore unknown vocabulary because they believe that they already have the needed meaning these words provide, or, when a conflict in information occurs, they stop thinking about what they are reading. To help students discern naive background knowledge, you can (1) demonstrate how they can probe their beliefs before reading; (2) model how you know when your background experiences are inadequate to accurately "read between the lines" in a book; (3) encourage students to place themselves in the story; and (4) identify the questions that they want to ask while they read.

Another method of integrating background knowledge is to ask what students are thinking as they read. Finding what background knowledge students are applying at a particular moment in a text helps students better understand whether that level of knowledge is adequate to reflect and remember what they read. Similarly, once they learn to make predictions as they read (see pages 521–522), they can analyze whether the first three predictions they made in the text are accurate. If they are, their background knowledge is interacting effectively with the author's intent, as well as their own purposes for reading.

In brief, readers and writers increase their comprehension when they learn to till their texts by recognizing the functions that individual paragraphs serve, establish their own purpose for reading, and analyze the support structures in fictional and nonfictional texts. When this knowledge is coupled with the following cognitive and metacognitive strategies, comprehension and composing abilities have a greater likelihood of becoming internally guided and valued by the majority of your students.

METACOMPREHENSION AND METACOMPOSING STRATEGIES

Metacomprehension and metacomposing tasks during reading and writing include (1) being aware of what one is thinking and why; (2) using self-initiated strategies to improve and sustain focus on reading and writing; and, (3) overcoming disruptions or obstacles in comprehension and composition (Baker & Brown, 1984; Paris, Lipson & Wynon, 1987). If students do not think metacognitively, studies have shown that they will have less knowledge about how to consciously organize their thoughts while reading or writing, and will not know what to do when they do not comprehend something or when they reach writing blocks (Wong & Palincsar, 1989; Johnston, 1985; Block, 1999). The purposes of metacomprehension and metacomposing are to develop knowledge and control of oneself and of literacy processes.

While expert readers use these strategies without being instructed to do so, they remain secrets to many readers and writers (Collins, 1991b; Johnston & Winograd, 1985). Unless taught, these students believe that putting the meanings of individual words together is the ultimate outcome of reading and writing. Moreover, without your instruction, many will have great difficulty applying efferent and aesthetic thoughts to literal comprehension (Borkowski, Carr, & Pressley, 1987; Wong, 1987; Scardamalia & Bereiter, 1984). Specifically, without the activities in this chapter, many students may never:

connect their past experiences to printed material while they read because they do not remember the ideas in the reading;

take risks or infer so reading becomes informative and enjoyable;

ask themselves questions before, during, and after reading;

scan or skim texts so they can connect ideas in their short- and long-term memories to the main conceptual premises in a text;

reread to eliminate confusion;

develop an inquiring mind so their mental images nurture a critical disposition and a quest for truth; and

engage and become personally committed to making their own meanings beyond the author's purpose so reading results in responses and actions that enhance their lives.

To use these strategies to improve their comprehension and composing, students must develop the attitude that they can learn from failure and establish a belief in their abilities to succeed in literacy. They must also allocate different levels of attention to separate components in reading or writing and develop persistence and the ability to commit to finishing a reading or writing task even when it becomes difficult. Equally important are the abilities to select a comprehension or composing strategy; to apply the strategy effectively to overcome confusion; to check their progress; and to determine the success of their strategic thinking during and after comprehending or composing.

SECTION 2   PUTTING THEORY INTO PRACTICE

Strategies to Improve Comprehension and Composing

The following instructional methods have proved to increase significantly readers' comprehension and composing abilities (Block, 2000, 1993; Block & Mangieri, 1996; Pressley & Harris, 1990; Wittrock & Alesandrini, 1990). Students learn these strategies faster if presented through direct instruction, using graphic and descriptive illustrations (thinking guides), as shown in the following pages (Block & Mangieri, 1995, 1996a, 1998b).

ACTIVITIES THAT INCREASE COMPREHENSION AND COMPOSING ABILITIES

In each of the following lessons, readers and writers are told why a strategy is useful and in what types of reading situations each will be most effective (Block & Mangieri, 1995; Schunk & Rice, 1989). There are six strategies to emphasize: asking questions before, during, and after reading and writing; explaining and interpreting; summarizing; inferring and predicting; imaging; and metacognitive thinking.

ASKING QUESTIONS

To introduce this lesson, you can share with students a common element that exists among people who have become highly successful in a variety of fields. These people ask questions of themselves and others when they become confused or want to understand something more completely. Students also can learn to ask good questions that will increase their understanding of themselves and the world around them. Tell students they will know that they have improved their abilities when they notice that they are asking more questions of themselves and others and others are understanding them better. Explain that these changes will likely occur within 2 weeks of practicing the strategy introduced in this lesson.

 To teach the strategy, ask students to read a book they select. After a few minutes have elapsed, ask them to tell you what they were thinking as they read. List their answers on a paper or chart. To start them thinking, write the following sentences on the board before you ask for their ideas. My mind is wandering. I don't understand this.

 After students have added what they were thinking to this list, you can write the following strategies on the board and tell them that these types of thinking can aid comprehension. These thoughts include (1) stopping during reading to think about new ways to use what you read; (2) rereading when something does not make sense; (3) predicting what will appear in the next sentence as you come to the end of one you are reading; (4) imaging; (5) summarizing each time a subheading approaches in a reading; (6) drawing conclusions about the author's purpose in providing each section of information and in choosing a specific type of paragraph; and (7) asking yourself or the teacher questions about the concepts read, such as:

- What does the author mean by "_____"?
- If I understand, the author meant _____. Is that right?
- Where will this point not apply? How does _____ relate to _____?
- What is the difference between _____ and _____?
- Would this be an example?
- Is it possible that _____? What else could we do?
- If _____ happened, what would be the result?

Students who posed such questions increased their comprehension more than students who simply discussed the material they read (Block, 1999; Graham & Block, 1994; King, 1994). These questions connect new ideas and integrate the author's main ideas into individuals' existing schema. This occurs because the act of generating questions is a knowledge-constructing activity. It requires reconceptualization, which in turn enhances learning and reinforces retention (King, 1994; Collins, 1992; Block & Mangieri, 1996; Block, 2000). Results from these studies also suggest that questioning connected new ideas to readers' own experience-based, background knowledge, so retention increased more than when students answered questions that only connected ideas in the reading or writing to each other.

K-W-L stands for What I Know, What I Want to Find Out, and What We Learned. It is an activity that can increase students' abilities to ask questions before and during reading. These questions are combined in a graphic (Ogle, 1989; Carr & Ogle, 1987). K-W-L teaches students that successful reading means asking questions and thinking about ideas while they read. To use this method, before students read (write, or listen), you can provide a blank chart as shown in Figure 7.3. Students complete the first two columns before they read and the last column during and after reading. The K-W-L chart in Figure 7.3 is an example that Ms. Hopkins created after Michael, Juan, Allison, and Meisong used the Kidsopedia Internet website to learn more about whales.

WHALES		
What We Know	*What We Want to Find Out*	*What We Learn—Still Need to Learn*
K (Know)	**W** (Want to know)	**L** (Learned)
They live in oceans. They are vicious. They eat each other. They are mammals.	Why do they attack people? How fast can they swim? What kind of fish do they eat? What is their description? How long do they live? How do they breathe?	D — They are the biggest member of the dolphin family. D — They weigh 10,000 pounds and get 30 feet long. F — They eat squids, seals, and other dolphins. A — They have good vision underwater. F — They are carnivorous (meat eaters). A — They are the second smartest animal on earth. D — They breath through blow holes. A — They do not attack unless they are hungry. D — Warm-blooded. A — They have echo-location (sonar). L — They are found in the oceans.

Final category description for column L, information learned about killer whales:
A = abilities, D = description, F = food, L = location

FIGURE 7.3 AN EXAMPLE OF THE K-W-L COMPREHENSION STRATEGY THAT MS. HOPKINS'S THIRD-GRADERS CREATED

Adapted from "K-W-L Plus: A Strategy for Comprehension and Summarization" by E. Carr and D. Ogle, 1987, *Journal of Reading, 30*(7), (pp. 626–631). Reprinted with permission of Eileen Carr and the International Reading Association. Copyright © 1987 by the International Reading Association. All rights reserved.

A third method is to teach students to make free associations and skim. In doing so, students can learn to retain thoughts that come to mind when they first look at a passage to be read. For example, you might ask, "What are you thinking about as you look at this picture and the first page of *The Old Man and the Sea* or *Make Way for Ducklings*?" To practice using this strategy, students say (aloud, to a partner, or to themselves) or write what comes to mind when they see or hear key concepts related to their reading. If this free association step is conducted in a group setting, student ideas are listed or mapped on the chalkboard. Key concepts can also be outlined in the order in which they occur in the reading–listening experience. Students benefit from this prereading discussion because classmates' ideas and words embellish their own schema before they read or hear new information. Afterwards students can state something new that they learned about skimming and free association, such as, "Today I noticed that when I set a real specific purpose for reading something, and if the text isn't talking about it right then, I can *read* the author's thoughts and also *think* about my purpose simultaneously. I remember what I read better this way." Table 7.1 is a form you can use for this activity.

Similarly, to teach the importance of sequential thinking during reading, listening, and speaking, you can introduce clue words that indicate order (e.g., *first, next, then*). Ms. Hopkins uses one method of doing so with her older students. She demonstrates and gives directions to only one-half of the class. The students who watched her demonstration then attempt to duplicate the recipe in writing. These pupils then give their recipe to a classmate who did not watch her demonstration.

TABLE 7.1 ACTIVE READING CHART TO INCREASE STUDENTS' ABILITIES TO ASK THEMSELVES QUESTIONS AND TO MONITOR THEIR COMPREHENSION WHILE THEY READ

What characters have we met so far?	What seems to be the main conflict/problem at this point?	What questions have I asked myself while I read?	What is my prediction about what will happen next?
Chapter 1:			
Chapter 2:			

(etc.)

Adapted from the original "Active Reading Chart" created by Carol Santa, 1996, in *Project CRISS* (p. 95), Dubuque, IA: Kendall/Hunt. Used by permission.

That classmate is to read the recipe and see if they know what Ms. Hopkins made. Afterwards the pair discusses their success and reads a story, stopping at each sequential clue in the book and describing what sequential reasoning it triggered. Younger students can complete a similar activity by putting sequential clue words on pictures that depict a story's order. As shown in Figure 7.4, Michael used this strategy when he was in Ms. Hulsey's first-grade class.

EXPLAINING AND INTERPRETING NONFICTION AND FICTION

When readers are asked to explain their reasoning, comprehension increases (Block & Mangieri, 1999; Block, 1999; Pressley et al., 1989; King, 1994). You can also assist students' detail recognition by telling them that the purpose of details is to identify who, what, where, how, and why, as they relate to the most important concepts, actions, and ideas in a story. You should not ask students to locate specific details that you give to them to find because this is not an authentic task. Instead, you can ask readers to point out details that they found important, interesting, effective, suspenseful, creative, or humorous, and to analyze why some details are more important than others. You can also assist them to analyze differences between detail types and discuss qualities that most effective details share. The Thinking Guide in Figure 7.5 can help you teach the thinking processes that students can use to improve their interpreting and explaining abilities.

FIGURE 7.4 MICHAEL'S FIRST-GRADE WRITING OF A RECIPE TO TEACH HIM SEQUENCE SKILLS FOR COMPREHENSION DEVELOPMENT

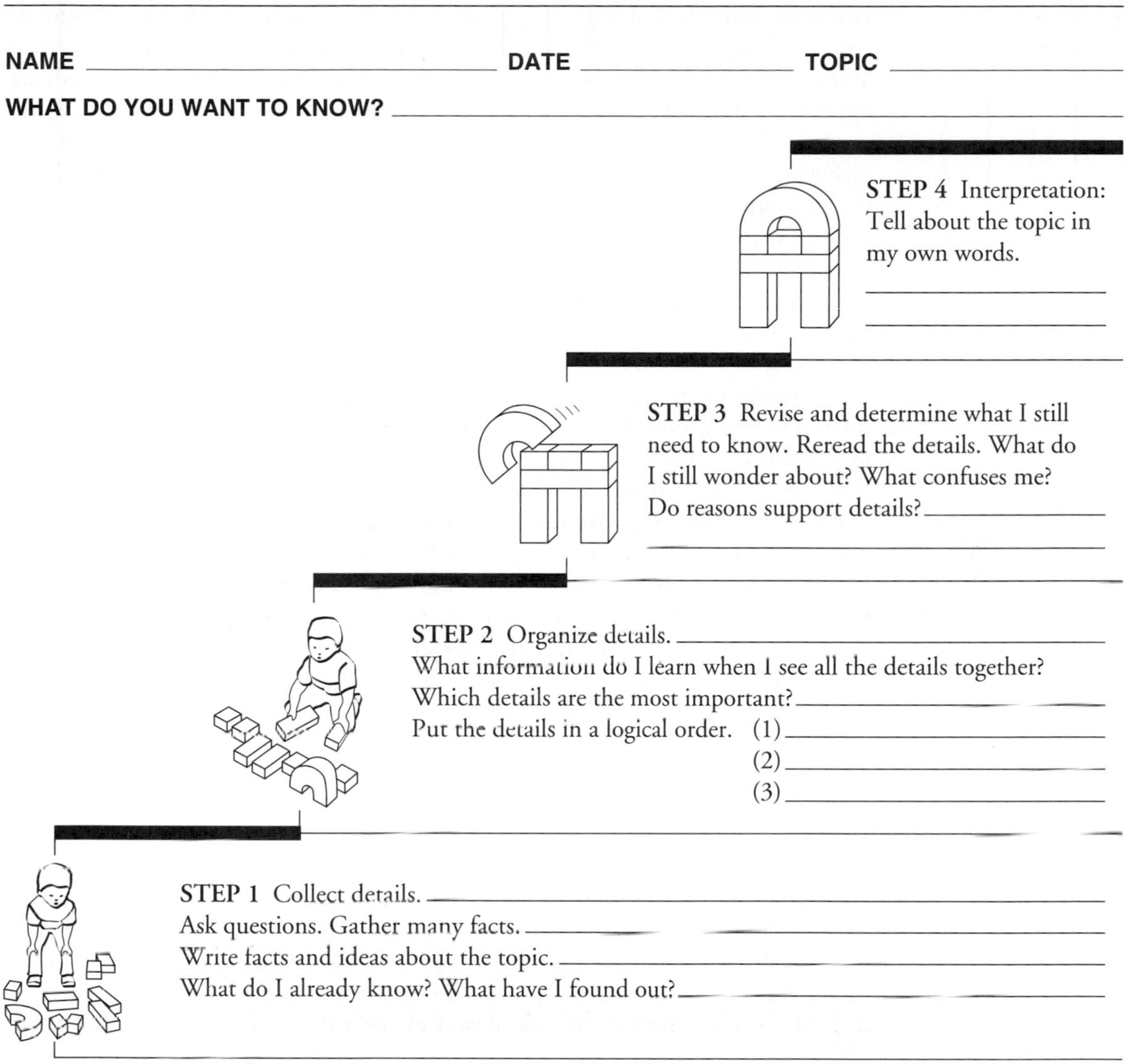

NAME _____ **DATE** _____ **TOPIC** _____

WHAT DO YOU WANT TO KNOW? _____

STEP 4 Interpretation: Tell about the topic in my own words.

_____

_____

STEP 3 Revise and determine what I still need to know. Reread the details. What do I still wonder about? What confuses me? Do reasons support details?_____

_____

STEP 2 Organize details. _____
What information do I learn when I see all the details together?
Which details are the most important?_____
Put the details in a logical order.   (1)_____

(2)_____

(3)_____

STEP 1 Collect details. _____
Ask questions. Gather many facts. _____
Write facts and ideas about the topic. _____
What do I already know? What have I found out?_____

FIGURE 7.5 THINKING GUIDE TO SHOW STUDENTS THE STEPS TO FOLLOW WHEN INTERPRETING OR EXPLAINING NEW INFORMATION

Adapted from *Reason to Read: Thinking Strategies for Life through Learning,* Vol. 2 (p. 134), by C. Block and J. Mangieri, 1996, Reading, MA: Addison-Wesley. Used by permission.

TEACHING MAIN IDEAS AND SUPPORTING DETAILS

Many students have difficulty locating a main idea in a paragraph. You can assist them with two types of lessons. First, you can explain to students that most authors place their main ideas as the first or last sentence in a paragraph. As you teach students this strategy, you can have them locate the main ideas with you as you show them on an overhead projector excerpts from books that they are reading or that you have read aloud to them. The next step in this lesson is students highlight, on copies of pages taken from books that the whole class is reading, the main ideas. They share with each other the pattern they discover the author of that particular book using. If you prefer not to copy pages from library books or basal readers, you can have children write the main idea on post-it notes besides the paragraph, or put a checkmark beside the main idea on a post-it note. As they share the books with their groups, the students can refer to the position in each paragraph where they found the main idea and how they identified it.

A second lesson for teaching mean ideas is to use a graphic. Children create a tabletop, write the main idea of a paragraph on the tabletop, and write the supporting details on the legs of the table. Alternatively, you can use a graphic similar to the one Michael completed in Ms. Hopkins's room. He was reading a nonfiction book about the history of Texas and came to information about El Paso, his home town. He wrote the main idea, "El Paso grew from a small town to a big city," vertically. Horizontally he listed all the details that helped him determine what the author was trying to communicate about the main idea.

In closing, your students might also enjoy giving headlines to nursery rhymes, with examples being found in English (1999), or writing headlines for newspapers. If you choose the latter activity, you can cut headlines from newspaper stories and, in a small group, give students several newspaper stories to read along with several headlines. They are to read the stories and then match the headline that represents the main idea that the reporter is trying to communicate in that story.

SUMMARIZING

When students create mental and written summaries of readings their retention increases by an average of 16 percent. Summaries also enhance their application of readings to life (Block & Mangieri, 1995; Stein & Kirby, 1992). Students can develop strategies of summarizing while they read and write when you teach how to delete redundant or trivial information and relate main ideas to three or fewer supporting pieces of information (as shown in Figure 7.6). Santa (1996) recommends that you do so by asking students to fold a sheet of paper into six parts. Have students reopen it and number each section to correspond to the first six paragraphs they read. As students read each paragraph, have them describe the thinking they used to delete redundancies and identify the central idea. Then ask students to write one summary sentence in rectangle 1 to record the first paragraph's main point. They do the same for the five remaining paragraphs and share their summarization strategies with classmates.

You can also model summary thinking visually by writing a summarizing paragraph as students watch by using the steps in the Thinking Guide shown in Figures 7.6 (e.g., see the summary paragraphs of *The Velveteen Rabbit* demonstrated in Figures 7.6 and 7.7).

The following books are excellent for teaching summarization because chapters have clear but implied summaries:

The Courage of Sarah Noble by Alice Dalgliesh, New York: Scribner, 1954.

A Weed Is a Flower: The Life of George Washington Carver by Aliki, Englewood Cliffs, NJ: Prentice Hall, 1965.

1. **DELETE DUPLICATION.**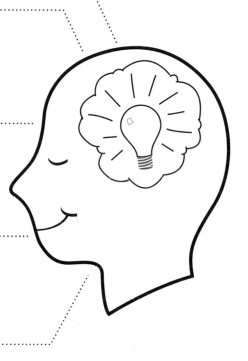
   - *Example:* There was a rabbit and in the beginning he was really splendid. He was fat and bunchy as a rabbit should be.

   - *Summary:* The splendid rabbit was fat and bunchy.

2. **COMBINE IDEAS WITH THE SAME SUBJECT.**
   - *Example:* He had a brown coat with white spots. He had thread whiskers and his ears were lined with pink satin. His spots made him stand out among plain red stockings.

   - *Summary:* His brown coat, white spots, and pink-lined ears made him stand out among the plain red stockings.

3. **RESTATE IN FEWER WORDS.**
   - *Example:* There were other things in the stocking: nuts and oranges, and a toy engine, and chocolate almonds, a mouse and candy canes; but the rabbit was the best of all.

   - *Summary:* The stocking was filled with Christmas treats, but the rabbit was the best gift.

4. **USE SUMMARY WORDS.**
   - *Example:* Summary words include *almost all, in conclusion, in brief, the main point, on the whole, ultimately, to sum up.*

   - *Summary:* In summary, the velveteen rabbit was the boy's favorite toy.

5. **REMOVE DETAILS THAT ARE NOT ABOUT THE MAIN SUBJECT.**
   - *Example:* On Christmas morning when he sat wedged in the top of the boy's stocking with a sprig of holly between his paws, the velveteen rabbit looked charming.

   - *Summary:* The velveteen rabbit looked charming.

FIGURE 7.6 THINKING GUIDE TO SHOW STUDENTS THE STEPS TO FOLLOW WHEN THEY ARE CREATING A SUMMARY

Adapted from *Reason to Read: Thinking Strategies for Life through Learning*, Vol. 2, (p. 138), by C. Block and J. Mangieri, 1996, Reading, MA: Addison-Wesley. Used by permission.

Jack Jouett's Ride by Gail Haley, New York: Viking, 1973.

The Drinking Gourd by F. N. Monjo, New York: Harper Junior Books, 1983.

The White Stallion by Elizabeth Shub, New York: Greenwillow, 1982; New York: Bantam, 1982.

Little House in the Big Woods by Laura I. Wilder, New York: Harper Junior Books, 1953, 1986.

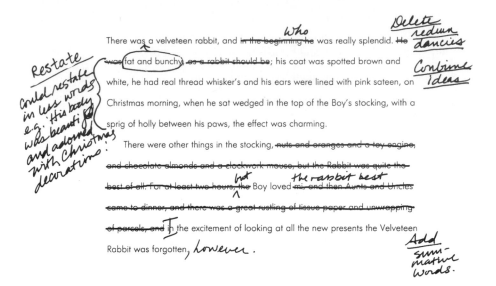

FIGURE 7.7 MS. HOPKINS DEMONSTRATED THE STEPS TO WRITE A SUMMARY OF <u>THE VELVETEEN RABBIT</u>

And Then What Happened, Paul Revere? by Jean Fritz, New York: Coward, 1973.

Columbus by Ingri D'Aulaire and Edgar P. D'Aulaire, New York: Doubleday, 1955.

Sarah, Plain and Tall by Patricia MacLachlan, New York: Harper Junior Books, 1987.

Johnny Appleseed by Carol Beach York, New York: Troll Associates, 1980.

INFERRING AND PREDICTING

Inferring is the process of judging, concluding, or reasoning from given information and is the first step in constructing meaning that is not literally stated. **Predicting** is a special type of inference in which the reader deduces the next event, action, or idea. Weaver and Kintsch (1991) analyzed text and found that as many as 12 to 15 inferences can be contained in every expressly mentioned statement in a passage. Therefore, the inferring strategy must become a cornerstone in students' strategic thinking before higher levels of comprehension are possible.

Inferring also enables readers to discern differences between unfolding events in a text and what they just stored in their short-term memories. You can teach young readers to infer by giving examples of inferences that they already make in their own lives. For example, you might say:

If your mother, father, grandmother, or grandfather told you to remember to take your umbrella to school, your brain would automatically think of rain, although no one said that word.

This is a thinking process and strategy you can use to make meaning, called *inferring;* you can do this when you read and listen. To infer, you take what the author said plus what you know and end up with what was meant. For example, listen to this sentence: "Nibbsie came running, with the stick in his mouth." You hear what I said, and your mind adds a few things based on what you know. By doing so, you create an entirely new thought that the author did not tell you. Nibbsie is a dog. You knew this because there were clues that he was a dog. As you read and listen in the future, look for clues and use more than one clue as you think. When you do so, you are inferring.

Another method is to give students a first-person story in which the narrator is identified only as "I," and students must infer to uncover who "I" is. Divide the story into paragraphs, and have readers use the first paragraph as their first inferring clue; then discuss their ideas and how they silently thought as they read to come up with these ideas. Continue in this manner, one paragraph at a time, until the correct narrator is identified and the inferences that led to this identity are explained by individual readers. Next, lay separate paragraphs on a table and have readers come to get and read them one at a time, at their own pace, until they are sure they have inferred the correct first-person narrator. When they make this inference, ask them to whisper it in your ear. Then, write the amount of time it took each student to make that inference, and allow them to change their minds if they choose to read on after their first inference. When all students have inferred at least once, identify the first few to accurately identify the narrator. Ask them to explain to the group the inference processes and strategy they used. Have students practice their inferring skills for a week as they silently read other texts.

Students should also explain the reasons behind their inferences and predictions. Such vocalizations transfer to faster mastery of metacognitive strategy use when reading silently (Block, 1995, 1999). Older students can also be taught to explain inferences by reflecting how they inferred specific traits of literary characters and friends. For example, Ms. Hopkins taught her fourth-graders to describe how authors want readers to infer characters' traits through the relationships they form with other characters. Books that Juan, Allison, Meisong, and Michael enjoyed reading to practice inferring are *The Great Gilly Hopkins; Sarah, Plain and Tall; The Eighteenth Emerging; Goodbye, Chicken Little; Julie of the Wolves; One-Eyed Cat; Sea Glass;* and *The Summer of the Swans.* Each of these books contained many inferences that students discussed. In addition, you can ask readers to make inferences from pictures that are age appropriate. With pictures, less able readers and writers demonstrated just as powerful inferences, predictions, and interpretations as more expert readers (Beal, 1990; Holmes, 1987). Another method is to remove the dialogue from the last two sections of a cartoon, and ask readers to write their inferences as the captions.

IMAGING

Imaging is defined as making a mental picture of scenes, actions, events, and characters in a text. The reason imagery instruction is so important to readers and writers is that it induces them to think actively while comprehending and composing. It also enables readers and writers to become immersed in the experience evoked by the language process (Fleckenstein, 1991). Moreover, because imagery evokes emotions, it is the best strategy to increase readers' positive, aesthetic response to reading. Images of feeling have also proved to be most powerful connector between the cognitive and emotional aspects of life and learning (Broudy, 1987).

Further, students who learn to create vivid mental images also tend to produce written texts that create high emotional engagement. Fleckenstein (1991) found that students who reported vivid mental images were using those images as conceptual or emotional pegs to investigate the motives behind the emotions they expressed. Thus, imagery contributes to the intensity of readers' and writers' engagement with text; connects the cognitive and affective dimensions of thought; provides a conceptual peg for retention; and provides an organizational system for literacy actions.

The first method to increase imagery is to tell readers that they can learn how to paint pictures in their minds as they read and write to increase how much they remember, and that these pictures are called *images*. Ask students to read picturable nouns and to describe the images these words evoked (McNeil, 1987). After students have described to a partner the images that underlined key words in a series of sentences, have them read an entire paragraph and describe how their images changed as they read each successive sentence.

Another method is to teach students to create similes that describe the main ideas they read. For example, Meisong wanted to describe how she had arranged all the snowballs she wrote about in her story. She wanted to communicate the splendor of this final product, which had taken her an hour to create. She wrote: "I formed 25 snowballs. I put them side by side in a perfect half-circle. It glistened in the sun. It was beautiful. Then," she said, "I wanted people to really see it in their minds as they read, so I added, 'It looked like a huge diamond necklace for a giant princess.' " By using the word *like* and knowing how to use similes to create effective mental images, Meisong left her writing experience with a strong feeling of accomplishment and pride.

The third method to develop imagery is to ask readers to tell you about an event about which they are going to write. In the process of describing it, they frequently create an image in their minds. For example, Michael told Ms. Hopkins about the following image before he wrote: "The second time Michael Jordan shot from the foul line he missed it. Patrick Ewing jumped up and wrestled it away from everyone else!" Following this explanation he wrote more details for this scene because he had created a vivid image of it in his mind before he began. Stories on tape (without pictures and books to be read along with them) have demonstrated to significantly increase imagery abilities (Block, 2000).

Last, Bellance and Fogarty (1990) have had success teaching imaging by asking students to personify human traits for inanimate objects or animals. This adaptation increases the speed and vividness with which students imagine new information while reading and writing. For example, the first student in a group can say, "An elephant is riding a bike." Then, a second student is asked to explain why the image is beneficial: "That's a good idea because the elephant can get around faster." Then this student names another trait that this elephant could possess: "He can also talk and says, 'What's for lunch?' " Then, a third student explains why the last trait was a good idea ("That's a good idea because the elephant can communicate with people and other elephants as he rides past them") and adds another idea to the visualization:

"He flies kites as he rides his bike." As each idea is expressed, another student explains it and adds to it. All comments are written on a chart. After seven entries, students reread the chart and describe the details of their mental images to each other.

METACOMPREHENDING AND METACOMPOSING

As mentioned in the opening section of this chapter, research indicates that many readers and writers lack metacognition, or self-direction strategies (Smey-Richman, 1988). This situation is especially alarming when related to the findings that (1) metacognition is crucial to the development of insightful comprehension and creative composition; (2) learning how to learn (a highly advanced metacognitive ability, has the most enduring effect on student achievement); and (3) the development of metacognition enhances readers' motivation as well as their positive attitudes toward reading (Dyson, 2000; Presseisen, 1987; Chipman & Segal, 1984; Cullinan, 1992). Because so many benefits result from increased metacognition, five activities to increase students' metacognitive abilities follow.

Metacognitive Lesson 1: Thinking about Their Thinking before, during, and after Language Arts Processes.   To begin this activity, demonstrate how metacognition should involve planning before students read, monitoring while they read, and reflecting after they read. You can show students, through your think-alouds (using overhead transparencies of text they can read along with you), how to (1) survey the material and answer questions that establish their purpose for reading and tie their prior knowledge to the text; (2) preview and skim to identify key words and subtopics; and (3) hypothesize and predict new information that may be included.

Goldilocks and the Three Bears

As you read, perform think-alouds to demonstrate how you (1) refine earlier predictions based on new information you read; (2) determine what is most important in a paragraph; (3) resolve confusion; (4) pause to reflect and elaborate as you apply the information to your life; (5) form images and similes to connect to personal events in your life; and (6) summarize. After the reading, demonstrate how you reflect, look back at details to check for misunderstandings, summarize in your mind or on paper, jot down a new idea the reading gave, create mental images as well as outlines as aids in retention. An effective next step is to ask students to write what they were thinking when they came to a paragraph that they particularly enjoyed. Periodically, kneel beside their desks, interrupt their reading, and ask them to tell you what they are thinking about as they are reading.

Metacognitive Lesson 2: Self-Monitoring and Explaining Metacognitions.   This activity begins by introducing the following symbols:

✓ = I know that I understand this paragraph.

? = I know that I don't understand this paragraph.

As students read, have them select one of these symbols to write beside paragraphs in the margin of pages photocopied from a book (or on an acetate that covers a page in a book) to indicate how well they comprehend each paragraph. After they mark about 10 paragraphs, ask them to meet with you for a discovery discussion to analyze what it was about the paragraphs that they misunderstood (see Figure 7.8).

STEP 1	STEP 2	STEP 3

Why am I confused?

- Is there a word I don't understand?
- Do I lack background in this area?
- Is a sentence too long?
- Was my concentration broken?
- Did I have to figure out unknown words?
- Did I understand the author's purpose?

Why don't I have enough information?

- I can get more by asking myself if I know:

  Who?

  What?

  Where?

  When?

  Why?

  How?

To trust my ability to put new information together to comprehend, I assess:

- Whether I know I have enough information about what I'm reading;
- Whether I put together all the words correctly to be sure I didn't confuse any ideas;
- If I have done both items above I can test my understanding by reading or thinking about the next part to see if that part logically connects to what I understand right now.

STEP 1   +   STEP 2   +   STEP 3   =   COMPREHENSION

FIGURE 7.8 THINKING GUIDE TO HELP STUDENTS EXPRESS THEIR METACOGNITIVE STRATEGIES TO IMPROVE COMPREHENSION

Adapted from *Reason to Read: Thinking Strategies for Life through Learning*, Vol. 1, (p. 159), by C. Block and J. Mangieri, 1995, Reading, MA: Addison-Wesley. Used by permission.

As you interact with students on a one-to-one basis (during this and subsequent activities, and as they write; read silently and orally; or speak, listen, or view), students can refer to Figure 7.8 to assist them to express their metacognition.

INTEGRATING THE LANGUAGE ARTS

Modeling a Literary Character's Comprehension and Composing Strategies

To this point in this chapter, literature and the language arts have been used interactively in many ways to enhance students' comprehension and composition abilities. Among the most powerful, however, is to call students' attention to their favorite character and that characters comprehension strategy use. There are four lessons that integrate language arts and literature to develop an understanding of the main character's comprehension strategy use. The first is particularly valuable for young children but can be used at all ages. This lesson involves children creating a language experience chart in which every child gets an opportunity to contribute what they learn from the characters of their favorite books and how those characters increased their comprehension with the particular questions they asked, summaries they stated, inferences they drew, or interpretations or explanations they gave of other characters in the book. After the language experience chart is created, every child receives a copy of the story. Double-space each copy and ask each child to follow along as he or she reads. While each child performs a choral reading of the story, he or she learns not only new comprehension strategies but also decoding skills.

A second lesson involves children writing a letter to a main character after the story is read. They write this letter from the perspective of another character in the book. For example, after Ms. Hopkins read *Charlotte's Web* to the class, Michael wrote the following letter to Charlotte as if he were Wilbur. That letter is shown in Figure 7.9.

For a third activity students write a report card for a main character. Children not only enjoy doing this, but it provides the opportunity for them to write comments about how they use their metacognitive thinking and all their comprehension strategies to evaluate the score that that particular character should receive. For example, as shown in Figure 7.10, Allison wrote a report card for the donkey in *Sylvester and the Magic Pebble* after she read it with Lucero, her fourth-grade classmate.

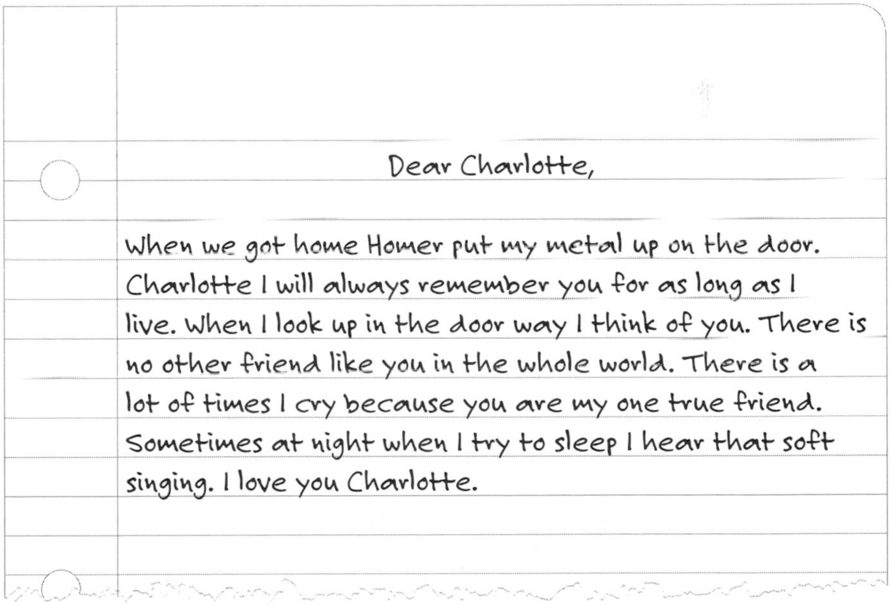

Dear Charlotte,

When we got home Homer put my metal up on the door. Charlotte I will always remember you for as long as I live. When I look up in the door way I think of you. There is no other friend like you in the whole world. There is a lot of times I cry because you are my one true friend. Sometimes at night when I try to sleep I hear that soft singing. I love you Charlotte.

FIGURE 7.9 MICHAEL'S LETTER TO CHARLOTTE, WRITTEN AS IF HE WERE WILBUR, AFTER READING CHARLOTTE'S WEB

	A	B	C	D
1	NAME		90–100	Excellent
2	Little Boy		89–80	Good
3	GRADE		79–70	Satisfactory
4	4th		69–60	Needs Improvement
5	TEACHER		59 & below	Failing
6	Lucero Cordero			
7		GRADE		COMMENTS
8	UNHAPPY	90		He wanted a donkey but they couldn't afford one. He asked his mom for a donkey but his mom said no. He dident pay attention to his mom of bring the donkey in the house. The little boy was disappointed because his mom wouldent let him keep the donkey. He told his mom what happend.
9	MANNERABLE	100		
10	WISE	60		
11	DISAPPOINTED	90		
12	HONEST	100		The kid was proud of the donkey because the donkey went up the stairs.
13	PRIDE	90		

FIGURE 7.10 DONKEY CHARACTER EMOTIONS REPORT CARD

Last, students enjoy sharing dramatizations and hobbies. Literature Cards 16 and 17 list books in which vivid characters describe how they use reading, writing, speaking, listening, and viewing to improve their thinking in intense problem-solving situations. Such work has proved to increase students' desire to apply the strategies in this chapter. As you will read at the end of this chapter, other types of literature to engage students' metacognitive thinking includes historical nonfiction and mysteries. Because the plot structure in these genres demands question-posing and self-monitoring of one's thinking, Ms. Hopkins's third-graders recommend this unit. They not only preferred nonfiction and mysteries in subsequent self-selected reading times, but also reported significant increases in their abilities to plan, sustain, and choose effective comprehension and composing strategies as a result.

INSIDE CULTURALLY ENRICHED CLASSROOMS

Using Choral Reading and Singing to Nurture Ethnic Textures in Reading and Writing

Fox (1988), Calkins (1991), Williams (1991), and Barclay (1992) attest to the power of singing and chanting to build vocabularies and thinking abilities, particularly for students from backgrounds where Standard English is not the predominant language or dialect. Students can sing along with records like the following where a printed

Literature Card 16

LITERATURE TO ENHANCE STUDENTS' COMPREHENSION

Favorite Books and Stories That Children
Like to Dramatize

Vingananee and the Tree Toad, a Liberian Tale by
    V. Aardema
Who Sank the Boat? by P. Allen
All Night, All Day by A. Bryan
Shiko and His Eight Wicked Brothers by A. Bryan
Mr. Gumpy's Motorcar by J. Burningham
Mr. Gumpy's Outing by J. Burningham
Hey! Get Off Our Train by J. Burningham
The Grouchy Ladybug by E. Carle
Rooster's Off to See the World by E. Carle
Bony-Legs by J. Cole
The Large and the Growly Bear by G. Crampton
The Legend of the Bluebonnet by Tomie de Paola
The Legend of the Indian Paintbrush by Tomie de Paola
Play with Me by M. Ets
Hattie and the Fox by M. Fox
The Chick and the Duckling by M. Ginsburg
The Gunniwolf by W. Harper
Ben's Trumpet by R. Isadora
The Snowy Day by E. J. Keats
Letter to Amy by E. J. Keats
Peter's Chair by E. J. Keats
Geraldine's Blanket by H. Keller
Anansi and the Moss-Covered Rock by E. Kimmel
The Carrot Seed by R. Krauss
The Story of Ferdinand by M. Leaf
Tacky the Penguin by H. Lester
How Many Spots Does a Leopard Have? by J. Lester
Frederick by L. Lionni
The Elves and the Shoemaker by F. Littledale
The Magic Fish by F. Littledale
Anasi the Spider, a Tale from the Ashanti by G. McDermott
Brown Bear, Brown Bear, What Do You See? by
    B. Martin Jr.
Listen to the Rain by B. Martin Jr. & J. Archambault
Stone Soup by A. McGovern
Too Much Noise by A. McGovern
Snow Lion by D. McPhail
The Funny Little Woman by A. Mosel

Mortimer by R. Munsch
The Napping House by A. Wood
Mouse Count by E. S. Walsh
The Mitten by A. Tresselt
Where the Wild Things Are by M. Sendak

An Author Study of Books by Mercer Mayer
That Children Like to Dramatize

Surf's Up, 1994 Golden
Top Dog, 1994 Golden
Just a Thunderstorm, 1993 Golden
Appleard and Liverwurst, 1990 Morrow
All by Myself, 1983 Golden
Just a Mess, 1987 Western
Just a Nap, 1989 Western
Just a Daydream, 1989 Western
Just Grandma and Me, 1983 Western
I Was So Mad, 1983 Golden
Just Grandpa and Me, 1985 Western
Just Me and My Little Sister, 1986 Western
Just Me and My Babysitter, 1986 Western
Just Me and My Puppy, 1985 Golden
Just Me and My Day, 1977 Golden
Just My Friend and Me, 1988 Golden
The New Baby, 1983 Golden
Merry Christmas Mom and Dad, 1982 Golden
Me Too!, 1983 Golden
Just Me and My Mom, 1990 Western
Just Going to the Dentist, 1990 Western
Just for You, 1975 Golden
When I Grow Up, 1991 Western
There's a Nightmare in My Closet, 1991 Greenwich
Just Me and My Little Brother, 1991 Western
Police Critter, 1986 Simon & Schuster
Just Go to Bed, 1992 Western
Little Critters This Is My School, 1990 Western
Rosie's Mouse, 1992 Western
What a Bad Dream, 1992 Golden
Purple Kiss, 1994 Golden
Just a Snowy Day, 1983 Western
A Monster Followed Me to School, 1991 Western

version of each song is included, or they can sing songs recorded by their favorite recording artists, for which they have written the words and their own sequels.

Rock-a-Doodle-Doo with Steve Allen and Jayne Meadows. Kids Matter, Ashland, Oregon 97520.

Literature Card 17

NONFICTION BOOKS ABOUT HOBBIES TO INCREASE COMPREHENSION STRATEGY USE

Primary Level

You're a Good Dog, Joe: Knowing and Training Your Puppy by K. Unkelbach, 1971 Prentice Hall

Coins You Can Collect by B. Hobson, 1967 Hawthorn

Exciting Things to Do with Color by J. Allen, 1972 Lippincott

The Little Pigs First Cookbook by Watson, 1987 Brown

How to Draw Cartoons by S. Hoff, 1975 Scholastic

How to Draw Silly Monsters and other how-to-draw books by F. Smith, 1985 Scholastic

Sports Cards by McLoone and Basta, 1979 Holt, Rinehart, & Winston

Splodges by M. Carrick, 1976 Viking

Create-a-Kite by Editors of Consumer's Guide, 1977 Simon & Schuster

Easy Origami by D. Nakano, 1985 Viking

Insect Pets: Catching and Caring for Them by C. Stevens, 1978 Greenwillow

Intermediate Level

Paint a Rainbow by J. Hawkinson, 1970 Whitman

Introducing Needlepoint by D. Lightbody, 1973 Lothrop

Cookie Craft by Williams and Williams, 1977 Holt, Rinehart, & Winston

Getting Started in Stamp Collecting by Hobson, 1982 Sterling

How to Paint with Water Colors by Zaidenberg, 1968 Vanguard

Creating with Burlap by Fressard, 1970 Sterling

Know Your Game: Baseball and other sports books by M. Bloom, 1991 Scholastic

The Drawing Book by J. Deacon, 1989 Scholastic

Collage by M. Marks, 1968 Dial

Drawing and Painting with the Computer by D. Bolognese and R. Thornton, 1983 Watts

Children's Plays for Creative Actors by C. Boiko, 1967 Plays

Easy Weaving by Lightbody, 1974 Lothrop

Jewelry from Junk by H. Sattler, 1973 Lothrop

Rock Collecting by Gans, 1984 T. Crowell

Model Cars and Trucks and How to Build Them and other books by H. Weiss, 1974 Crowell

Indoor Gardening by D. Fenton, 1974 Franklin Watts

Sing Along with Oscar Brand. Peter Pan Industries, 88 Saint Frances Street, Newark, NJ 07105.

Everything Grows! with Bruce McMillan (photo illustrator). Crown Publishers, 1989. This rendition of the popular Raffi song will probably be an instant hit with Raffi fans, and the repetitive and predictable text allows everyone to join quickly in the reading of this book.

Five Little Ducks with Jose Aruego and Ariane Dewey (illustrators). Crown Publishers, 1989. Aruego and Dewey's vivid colors and uncluttered illustrations bring this popular Raffi song to life.

There's a Hole in the Bucket with Nadine Bernard Wescott. Harper & Row Publishers, 1990. Wescott's illustrations bring the story to life and provide a humorous ending to a classic children's song.

Frog Went a-Courting with Wendy Watson. Lothrop, Lee, and Shepard, 1990. Watson uses this traditional song as a vehicle to transport readers to a miniature world she creates with her illustrations.

The Vivian Vinn method is another powerful way to build comprehension and composing strategies in culturally enriched classrooms. The Vivian Vinn method was invented by Mem Fox, the children's author. In this method, you say the first verse to a nursery rhyme such as "Little Bo Peep" and then you say: "I love it, I love it said Vivian Vinn; Tell me the rhyme. Let's say it again." Then, you point to a student who has his or her hand raised and that student says the first verse to a different nursery rhyme. Further, McIntyre (1991) discovered that making "Martian Songs" (repeating the sounds of vowels to rhythm) of the long and short vowel sounds for her first-grade students increased the number of vowel sound–letter correspondences they learned. Another is to ask students to create a rap song. The beauty of using singing as an instructional tool is that decoding, thinking, and oral literary–linguistic development become fun. Students often repeat the refrains on the playground and at home and gain esteem if they are the first "to know all the words" of the most popular songs on MTV and the radio.

In addition, when students interpret prose and poetry as a group (choral reading), they experiment with different vocal inflections and increase their interpretive thinking and reading skills. Choral reading begins by selecting a piece of prose or poetry that relates to a recent experience the class has had. This selection is divided into parts, and small groups of students read each part. Choral readings can also be completed by the class in unison, by pairs or groups of students reading a specific part, or in rounds (e.g., having each row read a line from "Three Blind Mice" at a different time). Before choral readings are begun, students set a personal objective (for their own speaking, reading, or thinking development). Then they evaluate their success at the lesson's end.

Many children also enjoy having a scale that they can use to judge the level of the book they are reading. This scale can be helpful in an initial screening of books that you might want to read to your class. Basically, a first-grade book usually contains one sentence per page with a picture. A second-grade book usually contains two or three sentences per page and a picture. At approximately the third-grade readability level, a book contains on average one full paragraph per page and a picture. At the fourth-grade level, a book contains two to three paragraphs with a small picture per page. By fifth grade, there are several pages without pictures and four or more paragraphs. By the sixth-grade reading level, a book contains six paragraphs per page and almost no pictures.

RECOGNIZING AND REPORTING PROGRESS

Students' Self-Assessment of Comprehension and Composing Strategies

There are a variety of ways in which you can enable students to self-assess their improvements in comprehension and composing processes. Examples of these types of assessments appear in Table 7.2, The Buddy Checklist, and in Chapter 14. The Buddy Checklist can be used when pairs read aloud to teach other. It enables you to build students' interactive use of decoding and comprehension strategies and to monitor several pairs of students as they work simultaneously.

DEVELOPING TECHNOLOGICAL COMPETENCIES

Working in Pairs with Computers and Hypertext

You can use the computer in many ways during comprehension and composing instruction, including telephone conferencing, networks, international computer databases, word processing, word processing with voice synthesizers, spelling checkers, computer thesauruses, editing programs, and branching software to provide

TABLE 7.2 BUDDY CHECKLIST FOR NONFICTION AND FICTION TO INCREASE STUDENTS' ABILITIES TO MONITOR THEIR COMPREHENSION WHILE THEY READ

Name _____

Buddy's Name _____

BUDDY READING

Directions: When your parter needs your help with a hard word, suggest one of these strategies. Check whether your suggestion worked. Go in order until you have suggested all seven strategies. Repeat.

	YES	NO
1. Think of what makes sense.		
2. Sound it out.		
3. Look for chunks in the word.		
4. Look at the picture.		
5. Look for endings you know.		
6. Look at another page where you saw the word.		
7. Go back and get a running start.		
Comments on my buddy's retelling of the part that was read:		
Comments on my buddy's use of the strategies:		

opportunities for students to create their own story endings. Through computers your students also have the opportunity to be taught by more high-quality examples than would be possible without it. That is because technology experts and educators outside your classroom take several months of concentrated work to develop each example in their software. You would not have the time to create and do the research connected with their creation.

Another important contribution technology makes to students' comprehension and composing abilities is that it makes information more vivid. Research has demonstrated that the more vivid the information one receives, the more permanent it becomes in long-term memory (French, 1990). Technology also enables students to view and discuss current events in the classroom. It adds variety and a change of pace, and it increases motivation for learning. **Hypertext** has the potential to change the purpose, process, and products of students' comprehension and compositions.

Hypertext refers to text that has computer links so that students can gain further information. It allows students to move through different information in a nonlinear sequence. For example, a hypermedia or hypertext program can present children's literature on a screen and allow students to click on words, phrases, or pictures to receive more information about the item they selected. This feature also provides readers with online support to enhance their background knowledge (because more information about a concept can be presented before a reader reads on). Such programs also enable students to draw graphics and program their own responses to information. For example, Michael's letter, which he wrote as Homer to Charlotte, was inserted in the *Charlotte's Web* file for his classroom. Any time a child clicked on the words "responses to *Charlotte's Web,*" they could read what Michael wrote. This program was used by Ms. Hopkins year after year. Inserting her children's best works inspired future students to rise above her past students' success.

A recent study demonstrated that grouping students in computer-based activities costs no more than traditional instruction (Fletcher, Hawley, & Piele, 1990). As a matter of fact, when two students work at one computer, the number of literal comprehension errors decreases. There is also better support for higher-level comprehension in pairs than when students work individually at the computer (Cole & Griffin, 1987). This appears to occur because two students are likely to have different skills. By working together and dividing the labor, their separate strengths interact to build greater understanding and accomplish more complex tasks. When group size is increased to three or more, however, the organization of the work breaks down and more off-task behavior occurs.

The quality of software varies. A list of computer software that has been demonstrated to increase students' comprehension and composing abilities, higher-level thinking, and problem-solving abilities appears in Table 7.3. An additional 30 titles appear in the website that accompanies this textbook.

●•●

SECTION 3 TEACHERS AS CONTINUAL LEARNERS

Increasing Comprehension and Composing Abilities

To review, this chapter has described the cognitive and metacognitive strategies that increase students' comprehending and composing processes. As students become internally guided language users, they profit from your modeling of how to engage in effective author studies, how to use interactive journals, and how to read more at home. The next section of this chapter describes how you can add these activities to your language arts programs.

TABLE 7.3 COMPUTER PROGRAMS THAT BUILD STUDENTS' READING AND COMPOSING ABILITIES, HIGHER-LEVEL THINKING, AND PROBLEM-SOLVING SKILLS

BEGINNING READERS/WRITERS	MORE-ADVANCED READERS/WRITERS
1. Reading Workshop (Mindscope) and Communication Computer Programs (Sunburst), A Newbery Adventure: Charlotte's Web (and others) (Sunburst) Enables students to involve characters in a wide variety of plots. 2. Kittens, Kids, and a Frog (Hartley Publishers), Storybooks and Storylords (Wisconsin Educational Network) Develops students' higher-level thinking and inferential comprehension by interfacing computer simulations and fantasy-based strategy lessons on videotape. 3. The Reading Comprehension Early Reader Series (Houghton Mifflin) Students answer higher-level comprehension questions about popular children's stories. 4. Scary Poems for Rotten Kids (Computer Tree) Simulates poetry readings with spooky music and program pauses and provides pronunciations as well as meanings of words a student references; also available in Spanish, French, and Cantonese.	1. Writing Adventure (DLM) Students make decisions that influence story outcome and can accept the challenge to construct a story, recount the adventure, and formulate a successful, appropriate conclusion. 2. Experience Recorder (Teacher Support Software) Prepares word banks for word recognition activities from stories written by classmates. 3. The Puzzler (Sunburst) Students make predictions about something in a story on the computer. Then more of the story is revealed and students confirm or reject their predictions. 4. Reading Realities Elementary Series (Teacher Support Software) Reading comprehension program where 1,400 students throughout the United States have written stories about issues they face, such as "So What If I'm Fat" and "My Parents Are Divorced" and students skim and type what they think the story will be about and how it will end before they read it.

PROFESSIONAL DEVELOPMENT ACTIVITY

Conducting Effective Author Studies

Author studies are studies that focus on an author that you and the children select that the children would enjoy reading. Once an author is selected, the children read books that the author has written. You also visit the website that accompanies the author's works and allow the children to obtain information about the author and the author's ideas about his or her books. On these websites you can often find references to magazines, CD-ROMS, and activities that you can incorporate into a unit study. The unit study can be an exploration into your understanding of an author's writing style and the major messages that the author intended to communicate. An author study usually begins with students listing on a chart the similarities

TABLE 7.4 WEBSITES THAT CHILDREN AND ADOLESCENTS CAN USE FOR AUTHOR STUDIES

Kay Vandergrift's Learning about the Author and Illustrator:
  <www.scils.rutgers.edu/special/kay/author.html>

The Scoop's Interviews of Authors and Illustrators:
  <www.friend.ly.net/scoop/biographies/>

Avon Books: <www.avonbooks.com>

Bantam Doubleday Dell Online: <www.bdd.com/index.html>

HarperCollins Authors: <www.harpercollins.com/authors/index.htm>

Houghton Mifflin: <http://hmco.com>

Little, Brown Books for Children—Featured Authors:
  <http://pathfinder.com/twep/lb_childrens/author/>

Penguin Putman, Inc., Online Catalog: <www.penguinputnam.com>

Random House Children's Publishing Catalog Search:
  <www.randomhouse.com/kids/catalog/>

Simon & Schuster; Simon Says Kids—Authors and Illustrators:
  <www.simonsays.com/kidzone/author_index.html>

Aliki: <www.acs.ucalgary.ca/~dkbrown/k6/aliki.html>

Jean Fritz, *Good Conversation: A Talk with Jean Fritz* (video), Weston, CT: Weston Woods
  <www.penguinputnam.com/catalog/yreader/authors/309_biography.html>

Kathryn Lasky: <www.xensei.com/users/newfilm/homelsk.htm>

Kathryn Lauber: <www.indiana.edu/~eric_rec/ieo/bibs/lauber.html>

---

between authors and then reading biographical information about an author. This information is available on the websites in Table 7.4, as well as the website that accompanies this textbook.

After students have read an author's biography or autobiography, they may enjoy viewing a videotape. References for purchasing videotapes also are available on the website that accompanies this textbook.

Once this information has been digested and children are more aware of their own particular values as authors, they often enjoy writing their own autobiography or biography. Author studies have proved to benefit the quality of children's discussions, as well as their degree of inferential thinking (Jewell & Pratt, 1999). Other researchers have documented that children form more sophisticated opinions and better relate to the interpretations that peers offer about authors and their works. They are better able to agree and disagree, offer supporting evidence, and have an increased motivation to comprehend and to write (Block, 2001; Langer, 1994).

On the website that accompanies this textbook are author studies about Mem Fox; James Marshall, who wrote the *George and Martha* series; and Eric Carl; as well as a list of 223 children's books that are written by authors who can be studied, an author study by Joanna Cole, and more than 625 nonfiction books that can be used in author studies. It is important to include nonfiction books because they help children understand the detail and care with which individual authors research their topics before they create fiction books. This knowledge spurs students to choose more specific words and details and to do more research before they write on their own. An example of an author study conducted by Ms. Hopkins's fourth-grade class is offered as a guideline to help you begin your own author study with your children. The following author study of Tomie DePaola was modified from a unit created by Mr. Ward Niccore, a fourth-grade teacher at White Rock School, Keller, Texas.

Planning with Students.   After learning of Tomie DePaola's work, Ms. Hopkins's students picked a specific book and wrote summaries. Students shared their summaries creatively by acting them out, using make-believe conversations with the main character, and adding a retelling of what might have happened if certain events had not occurred. In addition to learning how to summarize, they learned by engaging its instrumental, regulatory, interactional, personal, informational, imaginative, and heuristic functions. Ms. Hopkins's daily schedule follows.

Day 1.   She read *Strega Nona* to the whole class, and asked what Strega Nona and Big Anthony individually needed at the beginning of the story. (Strega Nona needed help and Big Anthony needed a job.) Using the instrumental function of language, Ms. Hopkins's class discussed students' needs and how they could use "I statements" to communicate them. A class discussion on "I statements" occurred. A video concerning DePaola's life also was shown (*A Visit with Tomie DePaola,* New York: Putnam).

Day 2.   Ms. Hopkins read *Strega Nona Meets Her Match* to the whole class. She asked students how nonfiction differs from fiction. She asked students to recall some of the commands Strega Nona gave in the story. Next, the students discussed how Strega Nona used her magic. Ms. Hopkins gave a minilesson on using commands "nicely" in the classroom.

Day 3.   The students read *Bill and Pete Go Down the Nile.* Before they finished, Ms. Hopkins shut the book at the climax and asked the class to predict how the story might end. The children formed into groups and wrote an ending, working together using the interactional function of language. Ms. Hopkins monitored and helped students use appropriate interactive speaking skills by joining each group and participating. The groups shared their predictions with the class.

Day 4.   Based on the students' choice, they joined a group that read either Tomie DePaola's *Mother Goose* or *Nana Upstairs, Nana Downstairs.* Using the personal function of language, the students wrote independently about how the book made them feel and about similar circumstances in their own lives. Students shared what they wrote in an open class discussion.

Day 5. Ms. Hopkins read Tomie DePaola's nonfiction book *Cloud Book* to the class. The class discussed the science of clouds and used the websites cited in Chapter 10 to learn more about clouds. Ms. Hopkins wanted students to use the informational function of oral language by sharing facts and asking questions. She assigned students to research a specific aspect of weather, such as clouds, rainbows, or hurricanes. After several days, the students opened weather shops. Half the class rotated through different weather shops, learning new facts about weather while the other half manned the shops. Students wrote one fact about each shop. Students began a chart to analyze the commonalities, themes, and differences of DePaola's books.

Day 6. Ms. Hopkins read *Big Anthony and the Magic Ring.* The class chose their favorite DePaola book and wrote summaries.

Day 7. Ms. Hopkins read *Clown of God* and asked students to complete the analysis chart of Tomie DePaola's books.

Days 8 and 9. The students shared their analyses of DePaola as an author and discussed what they learned to improve their own writing abilities.

FOR YOUR JOURNAL

Interactive Journals

Interactive journals are sections of journals where students ask you questions about their comprehension and composing processes and you answer in writing. In these sections students are free to express their thoughts, feelings, and opinions about the material read. Research has demonstrated that students who use such journals on a regular basis gain more control over their own learning, make more inferences, formulate significantly more questions about concepts, and better understand how well they are monitoring or editing their own thoughts (Costello, 1992; Handloff & Golden, 1995; Wollman-Bonilla, 1991).

In addition, interactive journals provide opportunities for you to reemphasize that what students think matters. They also enable you to teach children how to write the different audiences shown in Table 7.5. You can do so by posting sample questions and statements prior to a journal writing exercise. When you respond to a journal, as Ms. Hopkins demonstrates in Figure 7.11, you do so as if you were a friend teaching, not as a teacher trying to be friendly (e.g., response journals should not be marked in red with grammar corrections, for example). You can also bring interactive journals into a discussion by using one student's response as an introduction for a class activity.

TABLE 7.5 CATEGORIES OF RESPONSES TO LITERATURE TO TEACH STUDENTS DURING INTERACTIVE JOURNAL LESSONS

CATEGORY NAME	DEFINITION	EXAMPLES
Writing persuasively	Assessing or rating the author's or illustrator's style; classifying genre; pointing out use of language or literary devices; evaluating the literary work	"This book is scary and exciting." "The author is very creative." "The illustrations are beautiful and really go with the text."
Writing descriptively and "how-to"	Literal retelling of the story; listing of literal aspects of the work, such as names of characters	"This story is about a 10-year-old boy named Steve who has to move to a new neighborhood."
Writing personally, comparatively, and contrastively	Statements about how the student felt while reading and what book the student wishes to read next; statements expressing personal interest	"I'm glad the kids were able to get out of the house in time." "I like this book." "I wonder what will happen next."

Source: Adapted from E. Handloff and J. M. Golden, "Writing as a way of 'getting' to what you think and feel about a story," in *Response Journals* (p. 202), by L. Parsons, 1990, Portsmouth, NH: Heinemann.

Dear MsH

     I finished Sounder. It was a great book. The Charachters are realistic because of the language they use is from that time of slavery and thier discriptions are true to life. I also just read a book called "Alvin Jerald, TV Archerperson". It was a very easy book It was funny and I had no troble reading it. I just started Reading a book called "When the Phone Rang" So far it is a very sad book because 3 children have to learn to live without there dead parents I haven't had any problems with it and it looks like a good book

        Ben Grimes

9.26

Dear Ben,

     Its good to see that you know when a book is easy reading for you — and sometimes thats just what you need in life — a pleasant diversion.

     "When the Phone Rang" is a book a few students have read & enjoyed since the first week this month. I'm glad you made it your choice, too.

     Thank you for the contribution during the mini-lesson about character development. Your observations about the boy's emotional denial of his parent's death made an important point.

     Let me know how the conflict the children experience is resolved!   Ms H

WHALE OF A JOB.

FIGURE 7.11 EXAMPLES OF MS. HOPKINS'S STUDENT-TO-TEACHER INTERACTIVE JOURNAL ENTRIES

CONNECTING CLASSROOMS, PARENTS, AND COMMUNITIES

Helping Parents Build Home Environments That Increase Their Children's Comprehension and Composing Abilities

Many parents lack methods to assist their children to develop literacy, and they will request your help (Fitzgerald, 1993; Elkind, 1995; Morrow & Newman, 1995; Teale, 1986). Although some parents are already reading to their children on a regular basis, many initiatives can increase parent-and-child literacy interactions. **Parent involvement programs** are community- or school-based projects that help parents learn how to assist their children in literacy activities at home and as volunteers at school. **Intergenerational programs** include parents and children in literacy development as colearners. The **Home and Back with Books** program (Hong, 1995) encourages children to be responsible readers.

Home and Back with Books includes a contract, trade books that students select, color-coded reading-level tags, a guide that explains the role of these tags, and a reading log. All but the contract go home each night with students in a plastic bag and are returned to a special basket in the class each day. The contract explains the program to parents, sets the rules for daily reading and care of books, and requires child and parent signatures. Students select a book each day that they want to take home. Then students and teacher decide which of the book tags are to be included in the book bag. For example, when a child has selected a book at his instructional level, the teacher might say, "You know a lot about this subject and you like this author a lot. You know most of the words on this page, so maybe you can read those parts and your parent can read the rest. Let's give this book the 'Let's read together book' tag." For another book, you might say, "You really like this book and you read it so well. Why don't we choose the 'I can read myself book' tag for this one." Pretty soon students' metacognitive abilities increase and they know what they are capable of. They will say, "I think this is a blue-tag book." The contract explains to parents each level of reading that a tag denotes in more detail.

The following home activities also develop literacy and you can suggest them to your students' parents:

1. When reading a newspaper, magazine, or book, ask your child a question about what you have read. If your child is interested, point to the answer to the question as you read it to him or her.

2. When driving in the car, play tapes of children's books, which can be checked out from the public library.

3. Right before your child goes to bed, read to him or her.

4. Let your children see you writing notes and letters so that he or she associates writing with real-life functions. Read aloud some of their writing and see your children's reactions. Share letters from friends and relatives. Also be alert to occasions when your child can assist in writing (e.g., adding to grocery lists, making notes at the end of letters, and signing holiday cards).

5. Read and accept with enthusiasm your children's writings and attempts to read. The adoring audience your child most wants is you.

6. Find a special, quiet, well-lighted place for your children to read and write.

7. Be certain to hold meaningful conversations with your children daily. Three places where such conversations can happen are in the kitchen, as they help with chores; in the yard, as they throw a ball around; and at the dinner table.

•°•

SUMMARY

In the past, kindergarten teachers did not spend as much time developing reading and writing competencies, because it was believed that reading and writing were too difficult to learn until children reached a mental age of 6½ and 9 respectively. Today, teachers are using the activities in this chapter to advance students' literacy continuously from preschool on. By conducting effective reciprocal teaching episodes and by using interactive journals, Home and Back with Books programs, realistic fictional literature, comprehension strategy instruction, and assessment continuums, students can develop literacy competencies in a meaningful and productive manner. This chapter presented methods of tilling the text to help readers and writers establish a purpose, apply prior knowledge, analyze paragraph functions, apply comprehension strategies, and think metacognitively. In the next chapter you will learn additional ways in which you can help students improve their writing abilities.

HOW TO DO IT: USING WHAT YOU'VE LEARNED

The following provide opportunities to reflect on and practice what you have learned.

ASSESSING YOUR LEARNING

1. Why is it important to teach readers to till their texts, establish a purpose, apply their prior knowledge, analyze authorial styles, and think metacognitively to increase their comprehension and composing abilities?

2. How many comprehension strategies can you recall that advance readers' comprehension and composing abilities?

3. What types of technological supports help readers to comprehend and compose strategies?

4. When your students are ready to experience harder books, what have you learned in this chapter that can enable them to do so with less difficulty?

5. Teachers who read this chapter can increase their retention by drawing a graphic (or writing) to summarize what they learned. Realizing that using the summarizing strategy increases retention approximately 16 percent, you can benefit by writing or sketching what you learned. You may enjoy writing a summary graphic of what you have learned to reinforce the main concepts. Did you "till" this chapter, interpret, and think metacognitively as you read? Would doing so increase your comprehension?

6. Who is your favorite children's author? Sketch an outline of methods you can use in your classroom to draw your students closer to this author's qualities that are most endearing and valuable to you.

KEY TERMS EXERCISE

The following list contains new concepts that were introduced in this chapter. If you know the meaning of a term, place a checkmark on the blank beside that term. If you are unsure of a term's definition, increase your retention by returning to the page where the definition appears. If you have learned 25 of these terms on your first reading of this chapter, you have constructed an understanding of a majority of the most important terms that develop your students' comprehension and composing abilities. Congratulations!

_____ aesthetic stance   (p. 292)

_____ applied or critical comprehension   (p. 292)

_____ author studies   (p. 322)

_____ comprehension   (p. 291)

_____ contrastive principle   (p. 294)

_____ dictation   (p. 295)

_____ efferent stance   (p. 292)

_____ emergent literacy   (p. 293)

_____ flexibility principle   (p. 294)

_____ generative principle   (p. 294)

_____ home and back with books (p. 327)

_____ hypertext   (p. 321)

_____ imaging   (p. 311)

_____ inferring   (p. 310)

_____ interactive journals   (p. 325)

_____ intergeneralization programs (p. 327)

_____ interpretive comprehension (p. 292)

_____ K-W-L   (p. 304)

_____ linear principle   (p. 294)

_____ literacy   (p. 289)

_____ literal comprehension   (p. 292)

_____ metacognition   (p. 292)

_____ nonfictional literature (p. 289)

_____ parent involvement programs (p. 327)

_____ predicting   (p. 310)

_____ reading readiness   (p. 293)

_____ recurring principle   (p. 294)

_____ sign principle   (p. 294)

_____ story map or story frames (p. 296)

_____ strategies   (p. 292)

_____ tilling the text   (p. 296)

_____ word calling   (p. 300)

FOR FUTURE REFERENCE

Books about Comprehension, Composing, and Fourth-Grade Students

Atwell, N. (1998). *In the middle. New understandings about writing, reading, and learning.* Portsmouth, NH: Boynton/Cook.

Calkins, L. (1994). *The arts of teaching writing.* Portsmouth, NH: Heinemann.

Dyson, A. (1995). Individual differences in emerging writing. In M. Farr. (Ed.), *Children's early writing development.* Norwood, NJ: Ablex.

Holland, K. E., Jungerford, R. A., & Ernst, S. B. (Eds.). (1993). *Journeying: Children responding to literature.* Portsmouth, NH: Heinemann.

Maore, K. F., & Crowell, Caryl G. (1994). *Inventing a classroom: Life in a bilingual whole language learning community* (3rd ed.). York, ME: Stenhouse.

McClure, A., & Kristo, J. V. (Eds.). (1994). *Inviting children's responses to literature: Guides to 57 notable books.* Urbana, IL: NCTE.

Moffett, J., & Wagner, B. (1992). *Student-centered language arts K–12.* Portsmouth, NH: Boynton/Cook.

Moore, D., Moore, S., & Cunningham, P. (1998). *Developing readers and writers in the content areas K–12.* New York: Longman.

Nelms, B. F. (Ed.). (1989). *Literature in the classroom: Readers, texts, and contexts.* Urbana, IL: NCTE.

Parsons, Les. (1989). *Reading response journals.* Portsmouth, NH: Heinemann.

Peterson, R., & Eeds, M. (1990). *Response journals.* Portsmouth, NH: Heinemann.

Purves, A. C., Rogers, T., & Soter, A. O. (1990). *How porcupines make love!! Teaching a response-centered literature curriculum.* White Plains, NY: Longman.

Sulzby, E., & Teale, W. (1991). Emergent literacy. In R. Barr, M. Kamil, P. Mosenthal, and P. D. Pearson (Eds.), *Handbook of reading research* (Vol. 2, pp. 727–757). White Plains, NY: Longman.

Weaver, C. (Ed.). (1998). *Lessons to share.* Portsmouth, NH: Boynton/Cook.

Wollman-Bonilla, J. (1991). *Response journals: Inviting students to think and write about literature.* New York: Scholastic.

WEBSITES FOR NONFICTION

ALSC—Cool Sites for Kids:
www.ala.org/alsc/children_links.html

Comprehensive literature links for reading and writing with author resources and literature-based lessons. Sponsored by the American Library Association.

Doucette Index: www.educ.ucalgary.ca/litindex

An incredible search tool for indexing books and websites for literature-based lessons. Type in a title or author to get books and sites that contain lesson ideas and unit plans for the requested book and/or author.

Helping Your Child to Learn to Read:
www.ed.gov/pubs/parents/reading.html

U.S. Dept. of Education Site with activities and interactive links to assist parents in helping their child to read. Site is well organized and includes step-by-step guides and hints for both reading with and listening to your child.

Maureen's Read-Aloud Page:
www.bhs.edu/wmc/mis/readaloud.html

Read-aloud tips and recommendations for parents and teachers. "Stages for Read-Aloud" gives tips for age groups with relevant reading links to Web resources for each page.

The Read In: www.readin.org

A one-day read-in has been held since 1994. This site has all the registration, online events, and links to dozens of children's author websites.

Score Cyberguides:
www.sdcoe.k12.ca.us/score/cyberguide.html

Dozens of web-based instructional units centered on literary works. Each guide has teacher and student editions, objectives, detailed activities, websites, and assessment rubrics.

A fifth-grader's burgeoning awareness of her writing abilities can be communicated to her teacher through discovery discussions.

CHAPTER 8

THE WRITING PROCESS
AND WRITING WORKSHOPS

During a sunny, fall afternoon, Allison, Michael, Juan, and Meisong were engaged in a writing workshop. They were completing 10-minute writes about their books to share with the class. Other students were reading by themselves while others still were engaged in repeated readings with a friend. Mr. Conteras walked around the room with a clipboard in hand, taking notes as he held discovery discussions with "Monday" students. (Students were divided into five groups. This division told students which day of the week members of their group were responsible for planning and sharing their final drafts with the class.) During this time, he asked a student to read a page aloud and discuss what was read. He wrote in a conference log to note how their reading ability was improving. After 20 minutes, Allison rang a bell to signal that it was time for her and other "Thursday" students to lead the sharing period. One after the other, "Thursday" students (who had renamed themselves the Prime Time Playmakers) read stories they had drafted, revised, edited, illustrated, word processed, and bound into a book. Today was a special day because Allison had not shared for the previous four Thursdays. She needed the extra time to write something special about everyone in the class. Today she had invited a special guest who read her book and signed autographs for everyone in the room. Students whispered, "Who will the guest be? What did Allison write about me in her book?"

Meisong used this time to have a discovery discussion with Mr. Conteras. He sat beside her at the conference table, and she began: "Writing is great for me this year, and I wanted to thank you. Last year my mother told me to write about my life all the time. I had to write about me. I was bored. I think my life is disciplined and rigid. I didn't like writing last year."

"Why?" Mr. Conteras asked.

Sylvester and the Magic Pebble

"I like to use my imagination. I create new worlds. You let me do that. We can even write poems about what we learned in science, and everything. You taught us how to write believable people, realistic descriptions, and to express our true feelings. I've put all you've taught me into my mind. My imagination, put into my writing, brings new ideas deep within me. Without writing, I'd have parts of me undiscovered. Thank you, Mr. Conteras. Can you teach me to write in personification? I loved the fantasy book Sylvester and the Magic Pebble. The donkey really seemed like a real person, and I love the comedy routine Steve Martin does about 'Happy Feet'. I want to learn to write in personified language and use both these ideas together."

The purpose of this chapter is to help students write more effectively. During the last 2 decades research about the writing process has had a profound impact on instruction (Graves, 1983, 1994; Routman, 1994; Calkins, 1994). For some teachers, initiating "the writing process" consists of helping students follow predetermined, neatly fixed stages of prewriting (brainstorming, rehearsal, and generating topics); producing a first draft (free writing, drafting, or generating connected ideas); revising (rethinking the organization or improving ideas, often prompted through conference with others); editing (checking for spelling or punctuation); and publishing (producing a final copy in a published form). However, the writing process should not be taught as such a linear and rigid series of stages, but as a recursive and fluid experience that allows children to move in and out of these stages in interactive ways (Calkins, 1994; Graves, 1994; Routman, 1994).

Through the activities, workshops, minilessons, centers, journals, learning logs, and thematic units described in this chapter, you can learn how to guide students' discovery that writing can be a powerful communication tool, an instrument to unearth more about themselves, and a cultivator of innovative and profound thoughts. After reading this chapter, you will also have the information to master the following IRA, NAEYC, NCTE, TEKS and other statewide and province-based standards for professional literacy teachers:

1. What are principles that develop students' writing abilities?
2. What are the stages students pass through as writers?
3. What is the authoring cycle?
4. What types of lessons most effectively develop students' writing abilities?
5. How can you improve students' writing through writing workshops?
6. How can you help students develop ideas for writing and for communicating effectively?
7. How can portfolios be used to assess writing?

SECTION 1   THEORETICAL FOUNDATIONS

What Writing Does for Students

"In many current reading programs, writing is no longer seen as a separate subject. Writing, like reading, is viewed as a tool for thinking . . . as a vehicle for sorting out and clarifying thoughts" (Harste, 1989, p. 29). A good writing program enables students to evoke specific types of thinking, such as hypothesizing, questioning, citing evidence, making assumptions, validating hypotheses, evaluating, and using schema

(Block & Mangieri, 1995; Applebee, 1999). Writing has this power because the more frequently students reformulate content, the more they play with words, discover nuances of meaning, expand the clarity of their expressions, and organize their thoughts. When their compositions are appreciated by others, their feelings of significance as people can also increase. Thus, through a well-constructed writing program, students can learn to use a tool to sculpt their initial thoughts into wise ideas that others can treasure. In written form, students can discern whether their ideas can sustain thoughtful examination by others (Norton, 1995a; Graves, 1994). In addition, when they become comfortable and value writing, students can add many benefits to their lives. From writing grocery lists to noting ideas for a novel or concerto, most of us (like Hemingway and Mozart) quickly grab the closest piece of paper as a composition pad to capture and retain our impulses and insights. As research demonstrates, students who become accomplished writers also discover more connections, raise more questions, and recognize literary patterns and words more consistently than less-proficient writers (Block & Mangieri, 1995; Graves, 1999; Pressley, Wharton-McDonald, Allington, Block, Morrow, & Brooks, 2000).

BENEFITS OF WRITING

A good writing program provides many other benefits, such as strengthening students' self-images. The effects of such a program can be almost instant, as the following journal entry demonstrates:

> I was astounded when the teacher read *one of my paragraphs* in class. Until then I didn't know I could write, *or that I had anything to say.* [When she finished reading it and talked about my ideas,] I began to think I could do something right for a change. (Stuart & Graves, 1987, p. 8)

Writing increases self-image because most students are more courageous in their compositions than they are in their speech. Writing affords the time that many students need to cultivate their confidence and originality. In turn, as students grow in command of and enjoy writing, they can more ably express their deepest convictions, which expands their self-worth. Through creating their own aesthetically pleasing narratives, students can strengthen their appreciation for other people's writing. Similarly, when crafting a work to become more aesthetic, persuasive, or descriptive, they learn to communicate more specifically and effectively, and to stimulate others to action (Collins, 1992a; Temple et al., 1988). This demonstrated power bolsters their self-concept.

Writing also creates learning. Even at a young age, students want to find the best way to say things. From the first letter to their mother, dad, or grandmother that said "I love you" to the most skillfully crafted book a fifth-grader can prepare to read for parents at the elementary school graduation ceremony, students use their writing abilities to communicate ideas in a permanent fashion. The permanence of writing enables student writers to remember their messages longer; revisit ideas at a later date; stimulate memories; and make language connections to facts that are more fleeting in their oral language. On a linguistic and performance level, writing is the one language art that enables students to permanently apply what they have learned about language. By manipulating sentence structures and finding precise word choices through writing, students' speech becomes more exact, and listening and reading vocabularies expand. With these increases, learning becomes increasingly easier, and communications have more impact.

Have you ever noticed that some messages you want to write, and some you want to say? Sometimes you want to call someone to tell them something, and at other times you choose to write a letter. It seems that single facts, immediate decisions, quick stories, jokes, daily news, and bursts of emotion are more effectively and aesthetically communicated through speaking and listening. On the other hand, reflection over facts, long-range decisions, complex stories, historical accounts, and sophisticated concepts are most effective when penned. For example, Meisong demonstrated, in her discovery discussion with Mr. Conteras, that writing and reading her stories to classmates moved her beyond an egocentric perspective. Moreover, for students like Allison, Meisong, Juan, and Michael, who are experiencing the internal changes of preadolescence at the fifth-grade level, writing can satisfy their intensified needs to connect to peers, to avoid feelings of isolation, and to engage in more reflective peer discussions. Writing and reading their thoughts provide a depth of expression they crave and more meaningful collaborations than extemporaneous speaking can provide.

When peers ask questions about something they have written, students realize that they have helped their friends to solve problems, examine, reflect, and learn. By comparison, the connection between students' speaking, listening, and reading and the effects of these language arts on others' lives is not as immediately evident. Of the three, speaking comes closest, but when a student's speech is questioned, it is most frequently because there was a miscommunication, a missed meeting of the minds, or a need for clarification, not because the speaker used language so effectively that it created an important reflection or insight for classmates.

To mature a child's writing ability, we must move beyond teaching specific types of genre formats and merely increasing a student's technical knowledge. Instead, we must demonstrate how writing differs from speaking. For example, learning to write involves using a word order that is often different from how we talk. Recent research has demonstrated the following results:

- Students consistently use the writing process and writing workshops to plan, define their purpose, and adjust their writing style to audiences. On standardized achievement tests they outperform peers who have not been taught these approaches and strategies (Dahl & Farnan, 1998).

- Average writing ability was higher among students whose teachers consistently encouraged them to use several strategies associated with elements of the writing process (Csiw, 1998; Hallenbeck, 1995; Pressley, Wharton-McDonald, Allington, Block, & Morrow, 2000).

- Students who were consistently encouraged by their teachers to use various prewriting strategies tended to attain significantly higher scores than peers who were not taught the writing process (Godley & Mahiri, 1998; Pressley, Wharton-McDonald, Allington, Block, & Morrow, 2000).

In summary, a good writing program can assist students to think on a higher level, increase their feelings of self-worth, and learn with more confidence. Moreover, as Lucy Calkins stated: "As humans, we write to hold out lives in our hands and to make something of it. Writing allows us to turn chaos into something beautiful, to frame selected moments, to uncover and celebrate the organizing patterns of our existing" (1994, p. 253).

PRINCIPLES OF WRITING INSTRUCTION

A **writing program** should be student-centered and integrate the language arts. It should differ qualitatively from times in the past when "writing instruction" was merely assigning a topic, allowing one day or a week (or a semester in the case of term papers) for students to write on that topic, and then precisely marking every error (in red ink) so students could plainly see them. The programs of today follow different principles of learning as described next.

Writing Must Be Satisfying.   "The problem with writing is not poor spelling, punctuation, grammar, and handwriting. The problem with students' writing is no writing" (Stuart & Graves, 1987, p. 34). Students need to write daily for 15 to 30 minutes if they are to learn to communicate effectively. As writing satisfies more personal needs, it simultaneously becomes more satisfying and pleasurable for students. Also, by writing with your students while they write, you can model strategies that you use and show how important writing is to you. For example, by writing when they write, you can model how you (1) experience "writer's block" just as your students do and how you overcome it; (2) feel writers' "good days" and "bad days" (which heightens your sensitivity to students' similar experiences during discovery discussions); (3) use expert writing strategies so your instruction becomes more credible to your students; and (4) (and your students) can express truly important ideas to others if you just write long enough and think hard enough.

Student Writings Must Be Shared and Appreciated.   If students are to master writing, not only must they compose regularly, but their writing must be appreciated by readers. When students relay personally important information to significant audiences, they produce more varied prose and poetry, present information more cogently, and eliminate irrelevant details (Graves, 1994). Even when students write to peers at a distant school, the quality of their work is significantly better than when they write solely for their teachers (Cohen & Riel, 1989; Reinleing, 1998; Labbo, 2000). Because young writers flourish when parents, community members, and peers read their compositions, student writings can more easily be applauded when they are framed and hung in schools, corporate offices, central administration buildings, restaurants, public libraries, hospitals, storefront windows, and doctors' and dentists' reception rooms. Students can also make handmade books as gifts for classroom and school libraries or nursing homes and churches.

To illustrate, in Mr. Conteras's room, students decided to spend one week creating posters and books that described ways of solving problems. Because they were the oldest students in their school, they looked into problems that existed at their school as their content. Each group identified a problem to solve, wrote to have their proposal for a solution approved, and completed their finished products. Meisong and other "Monday" students created a schoolwide visitor's book that contained school rules, a map of classrooms, a page to record names of visitors, daily schedules of every class, room locations, and a one-page "advertisement" per class that highlighted the goals that each class had established. Michael and the other "Tuesday" students surveyed the school about rules they wanted during lunch. They condensed the data, had the school vote on lunchroom guidelines (as well as consequences for not meeting them), and posted the results in the lunchroom. Juan and the other "Wednesday" students researched how to make a tepee and called companies to donate the supplies. After they made it, they posted a laminated sign outside that stated which days of the month various grades had the exclusive right to occupy it during recess periods. Allison and the other "Thursday" students researched the history of their school and made a stand in the central hallway to display the beautiful scrapbook that culminated from their work. Lin and the other "Friday" students prepared a poster for their class that outlined an improved policy for making up work missed by absent students.

Students Need Your Support and Instruction.   Your interest, enthusiasm, and belief that students are real writers is what they need to *become* real writers. Their writing abilities heighten when you immerse them in factual, persuasive, descriptive, narrative, and poetic writings. Students who are slow starters, as well as those who are disinclined to write, need your assistance to learn strategies that can increase their motivation and conviction. Such guidance includes providing specific feedback to them and explaining which parts of their writing you most enjoyed and why.

WRITING DEVELOPMENT THROUGH THE GRADES

When you recognize the stages your students pass through as writers, you can more ably guide their learning. The discussion of emergent reading and writing abilities in Chapter 7 was designed to build your knowledge of the beginning stages; the discussion below concerns subsequent stages. Although these stages are labeled by grade levels, the labels can be interpreted liberally because students vary widely in their rate of development.

By preschool and kindergarten, writing is a normal form of expression for most students, even though such expressions may be unintelligible. Preschoolers write by scribbling, drawing, and lettering. For example, at age 1, children are communicating when they make one long mark on a piece of paper (or wall). By age 2, they often scribe a single letter, which to them is the representation of their entire name. By age 4, many children spend several minutes scribbling below a picture, and these scribbles "tell all about the picture." By age 5, many students can form real letters, use invented spellings, and write a few words to represent many sentences (Bridwell, 1980; Hawisher, 1987; Halliday, 1976; Maynor, 1982; Schidenz, 1998).

First-graders are "noisy" writers. They talk as they write, rehearsing what they want to say. Likewise, when compositions are complete, first-graders tend to read them aloud to "hear how it sounds." For most, writing is a pleasurable activity. They value the writing process more for the enjoyment of doing it than for the purpose of creating messages to be read. Because of this perspective, most first-graders compose for themselves rather than for an audience. They also prefer composing something new rather than revising yesterday's work. As a matter of fact, if required to rework a piece without originating any ideas themselves, many become inhibited and digress in writing abilities (Salinger, 1992).

Second-graders typically move from scribbling for personal pleasure to writing for an audience. They also become more interested in final products, spending considerable time revising and editing. Because they have had only a few years of writing experience, and because they are concerned with other people's opinions, they frequently destroy many drafts before they judge one to be "just right!" Second-graders also have been described as authors of opposites (Calkins, 1994; Skolnick & Frazier, 1998). At times they write with carefree confidence whereas at other times they laboriously and scrupulously chisel, but use only narrow, shallow words. For this reason, 7- and 8-year-olds tend to be less creative than first-graders (Calkins, 1994; Skolnick & Frazier, 1998). This decreased inventiveness is not a regression in composition ability. It is the initial compensation students make as they learn how to write for real audiences. Many second-graders have specific writing needs. They require instruction to expand topics and to use more vivid verbs. They also compose stories that imitate plots in their favorite books (e.g., they devise *John and the Three Dogs,* which replicates *Goldilocks and the Three Bears*) unless there is breadth and depth in their writing activities. Two examples of how to create breadth and depth was represented in the units in Chapters 4 and 6.

In third grade, the concern for written perfection becomes even greater. Eight-year-olds frequently become deeply concerned about spelling, punctuation, capitalization, handwriting, and grammar. Many copy new stylistic elements from authors that they enjoy and do so to excess (e.g., writing seven exclamation points at the end of sentences). Third-graders also tend to choose giant, all inclusive topics such as "My Life," "My Family," and "The World." They also tend to exaggerate, write seemingly endless dialogues, and report streams of irrelevant details.

Most third-graders need instruction in summarizing. Many do not know which details to omit during revision. Because of this and their concentration on global topics, they are likely to overlook important details, so their stories lose sequential meaning. For these reasons, third-graders grow rapidly as writers when taught how to narrow topics and revise and edit.

In fourth, fifth, and sixth grades, writing becomes increasingly more sophisticated. Students achieve a level of "cognitive flexibility that enables them to internalize revision strategies and other executive functions that assist in producing increasingly complex and formal written text" (Ruddell & Ruddell, 1995, p. 90). Pupils at these ages also develop their own stylistic features, and when taught revising strategies, apply them more automatically. Through your instruction, most learn how to eliminate unnecessary details, narrow writing to a single purpose, and select from many genre and sentence structures. They can learn to write persuasively, descriptively, and entertainingly, and even manage adultlike humor.

During fourth through sixth grades, you can introduce many revising strategies that move beyond the word level (i.e., the **sentence-combining techniques** and varying paragraph functions). Sentence-combining teaches students to write compound and complex sentences. Throughout these upper grades, students enjoy reading

Literature Card 18

BOOKS WHERE MAIN CHARACTERS USE WRITING TO IMPROVE THEIR THINKING

Good Books with a Lot of Pictures about Writing

Invincible Louisa by C. Meigs, 1961 Little, Brown

On the Way Home by L. I. Wilder, 1976 HarpC Child Books

Are You There God? It's Me Margaret by J. Blume, 1970 Chivers

Airmail to the Moon by T. Birdseye, 1988 Holiday House

The Jolly Postman or Other People's Letters by J. & A. Ahlberg, 1986 Little, Brown

Arthur's Pen Pal by L. Hoban, 1976 Harper & Row

Truman's Ant Farm by J. K. Rattigan, 1994 Houghton Mifflin

Dream Peddlers by G. Haley, 1993 Dutton Children's Books

Only Opal by B. Cooney, 1994 Philomel

Nobody Is Perfick by B. Waber, 1994 Houghton Mifflin

Captain Abdul's Pirate School by C. McNaughton, 1994 Candlewick Press

I Can Be an Author by R. Broekel, 1986 Children

Black and White by D. Macaulay, 1990 Houghton Mifflin

Good Books to Tell You a Lot about How to Use Writing to Improve Thinking

Nellie Bly: Reporter for the World by M. Kendall, 1992 Millbrook Press

Rag Doll Press by E. J. Taylor, 1985 Knopf

Three Days on a River in a Red Canoe by V. B. Williams, 1981 Greenwillow

Beethoven Lives Upstairs by B. Nichol, 1994 Orchard Books

Amber on the Mountain by T. Johnston, 1994 Dial Books

Learning to Swim in Swaziland: A Child's Eye View of a Southern African Country by N. K. Leigh, 1993 Scholastic

Just One Tear by K. L. Mahon, 1994 Lothrop

Red Means Good Fortune: A Story of San Francisco by B. D. Goldin, 1994 Viking

Pageant by K. Lasky, 1988 Dell

Your Own Best Secret Place by B. Baylor, 1991 Macmillan

The Island by G. Paulsen, 1988 Orchard

No Words to Say Goodbye by R. Kopelnitsky & K. Pryor, 1994 Hyperion

Libby on Wednesday by Z. K. Snyder, 1990 Delacorte Press

Dear Dragon by S. Joslin, 1962 Harcourt & Brace

Emily by B. Cooney, 1992 Dell

Good Books If You Are Just Beginning to Learn about How to Use Writing to Improve Your Thinking

Slim Down Camp by S. Manes, 1981 Houghton Mifflin

Loretta P. Sweeny, Where Are You? by P. Giff, 1990 Dell

Carry on Mr. Bowditch by J. Latham, 1955 Houghton Mifflin

Rapscallion Jones by J. Marshall, 1983 Viking

I, Trissy by N. Mazer, 1971 Delacorte Press

The Diary of a Church Mouse by G. Oakley, 1987 Atheneum

The Trumpet of the Swan by E. B. White, 1970

Zlata's Diary: A Child's Life in Sarajevo by Z. Filipovic, 1994 Viking

Sink or Swim by B. Miles, 1987 Avon

Dear Benjamin Banneker by A. D. Pinkney, 1994 Gulliver Books/Harcourt Brace

Arthur, for the Very First Time by P. MacLachlan, 1980 Harper & Row

Tar Beach by F. Ringold, 1991 Crown Books

The Ramona Quimby Diary by B. Cleary, 1984 Morrow

Books That Have Several Chapters That Show How Main Characters Use Writing to Improve Thinking

Courage at Indian Deep by J. Thomas, 1984 Clarion

Your Best Friend, Kate by P. Brisson, 1992 Aladdin

The Lost Garden by L. Yep, 1991 Julian Messner

The Last of Eden by S. S. Tolen, 1980 Warne

The Witch of Blackbird Pond by E. G. Speare, 1958 Houghton Mifflin

The Devil in Vienna by D. B. Orgel, 1978 Dial

Joshua's Westward Journal by J. Anderson, 1987 Morrow

My Journals and Sketchbooks by A. Politzer, 1974 Harcourt & Brace

Anne Frank: Diary of a Young Girl: The Definitive Edition by A. Frank, 1995 Doubleday

My Side of the Mountain by J. C. George, 1988 Dutton

Sarah, Plain and Tall by P. MacLachlan, 1986 Caedmon

Dear Mr. Henshaw by B. Cleary, 1984 Dell

Strider by B. Cleary, 1991 Morrow

To Be a Slave by Lester, 1986 Scholastic

Skylark by P. MacLachlan, 1994 HarperCollins

about peers and use classmates' experiences to advantage in stories they subsequently compose (Bridwell, 1980; Hawisher, 1987; Maynor, 1982). For this reason, books from Literature Card 18 are exceptionally valuable at this stage in students' writing development. Characters in these books use writing in a wide variety of ways to improve their thinking and to make contributions to the world. After reading one of these books aloud, you can ask students to explain the value writing held for the main character, who is about their age.

In summary, writing can become students' most disciplined and precise expression of thought. Through instruction, students learn to revise their compositions until they accurately depict their ideas. Young writers pass through stages as they grow. There are several principles that guide writing instruction; and students should become skillful in prewriting, drafting, revising, editing, and sharing their work. In the next section you can read how students can be taught these processes.

THE WRITING PROCESS

Today's writing programs simulate the processes expert writers use. As depicted in the following discussion and in Figure 8.1, these processes involve prewriting, drafting, revising, editing, incubation, recycling through these stages, and sharing finished compositions. Several actions and decisions are made by master writers during each of these stages. The amount of time spent in each stage, as well as the number of times individual students revisit each stage in the course of completing a single composition varies considerably.

PREWRITING

The **prewriting** stage is the first in the authoring cycle. During this stage students explore ideas, consider options, and corral their thoughts. When they are taught strategies to use during this prewriting step, students can learn how to take the time to write exactly what they want to say and consider ways of saying it. Murray (1989), Rose (1992), and Graves (1994) recommend that students pick their own subjects: "It is not the job of the teacher to legislate a student's truth. It is the responsibility of the student to explore his own world, with his own language and to discover his own meaning" (Murray, 1989, p. 13).

Through your guidance, students can learn prewriting strategies such as "drawing out" ideas, discussing vocabulary with a peer, outlining, taking notes about observations and from readings to use in subsequent compositions, brainstorming, freewriting, interviewing, and asking for critiques on initial thoughts. During this segment of the writing process, many students need to talk to peers and you. Conversing during the prewriting stage is critical and gives students the framework for events and ideas that they need to begin writing (Dyson, 2000; Graves, 1999):

> Taking time for oral sharing promotes language development, inspires confidence, and gives reluctant writers possible topics from which to choose. While some students are talking about what they might write about, others are developing and practicing good listening skills and getting ideas for their own writing. The oral language time also allows teachers the opportunity to probe and guide the student to an awareness of what he [or she] already knows but may not know he [or she] knows. It is a time for hearing the personal stories of our students. The time for talk also encourages very young children to move way from common, boring topics such as rainbows, hearts, and butterflies . . . it gives upper elementary students the opportunity to

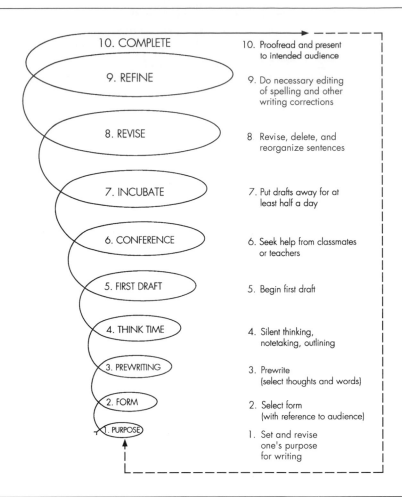

FIGURE 8.1 STAGES TO BE TAUGHT IN THE WRITING PROCESS

become astonishingly articulate about their fleeting, intangible ideas and when children can describe what they are doing as they write, it adds enormously to their dawning sense of deliberateness and their control over their writing. (Calkins, 1994, pp. 213 and 149)

Some students need your guidance to not spend too much time in the prewriting stage. You should discern whether their hesitancy to draft is due to a need for germinating ideas or writer's block. If they merely need more time to think, you can suggest that they turn to a partner, present their purpose, idea, and audience, and ask for that person's opinion about which aspect would be most exciting or interesting to begin the composition. On the other hand, if students are "afraid" to begin (writer's block), you can take actions to assist them, which are described in the next section.

DRAFTING

The **drafting stage** involves writing a first draft. During the drafting stage students put their thoughts on paper. Many follow the semantic web, outline, or mental notes that they developed during prewriting. In the process, they establish a voice such as talking informally to a friend, writing objectively for a research report, or writing to persuade others. Students erase, cross out, and draw arrows to clarify meaning, add new thoughts, and make new connections between their ideas. Some like to leave a blank line between each handwritten line (double-spacing their drafts) so that their subsequent revisions are less crowded.

It is during the drafting stage that you can conduct most of your formal, minilessons. Minilessons teach strategies such as (1) how to use stylistic features; (2) how to emulate vivid descriptions in children's literature; and (3) how to choose precise words. These minilessons can be scheduled when one or several students exhibit a need for specific writing skills.

As stated previously, during drafting, students sometimes develop **writer's block.** Writer's block comes from unorganized ideas. This problem can be overcome by advising students to write from what they know, what they care about, or what they want to think about. This suggestion is helpful because when students write about topics they know well, the organization of the composition evolves more easily, facts become more specific, and events are recalled more chronologically (Block, 2000, Linden & Whimbey, 1990). Students can overcome writer's block if you teach the following strategies.

1. *Do unfocused and focused freewriting* (Elbow, 1981). **Unfocused freewriting** is a process in which students write, rambling from topic to topic, for 5 to 10 minutes until they find an intriguing idea. **Focused writing** is similar, but it develops only a single topic by writing in a stream of consciousness about that idea. Donald Murray, a prominent researcher of the writing process, reports that freewriting is the strategy he uses to overcome writer's block: "These [freewriting] paragraphs provide no earth-shaking revelations, but they give me the opportunity to relive part of my life and to understand it better than I had before" (Murray, 1989, p. 14).

2. *Ask students questions as they write.* Ask the student, "Read to me what you have so far." Then ask, "What can you tell me about what you've written? Why do you think you're stuck now?" You can also teach students to ask a friend for help, as demonstrated below:

Meisong: Allison, I'm stuck. I don't know what else to say.

Allison: Read me what you have.

Meisong: [Reads all she has written so far]

Allison: Tell me what you want your readers to know next, and I'll take some notes while you talk. Don't worry if it sounds stupid. Just talk about what's really important to you.

3. *Prompt with a starter sentence.* Knowing several different ways to open a writing can often move students beyond their writer's block. You can post several sample starter sentences. Then you can read several opening sentences from books that their favorite authors have written. For example, Mr. Conteras modified this strategy slightly with Michael by saying: "Why don't you turn your paper over and write two types of sentences that you don't normally use. I'll be back in a minute, and we'll see which of the two we like best to use as a starter sentence for this writing." For younger students you can also suggest one-word exclamations to begin their writings such as "Oh!" "Wow!" and "Eek!" and suggest that they experiment with using compound subjects and predicates. For older students you can suggest an opening sentence that includes a gerund: "Howling loudly, the wind demanded my attention." You can also teach a minilesson early in the semester whereby students create a chart of starter sentences to "jump start" them over future writer's blocks. By posting these on a chart in a prominent place, students can refer to them as they write. As an example, the starter sentences that Mr. Conteras's fifth-graders wrote were:

> "I really don't know what I want to write next because . . ."

> "I remember a time in my life that is similar to [this part] so I'll add things I thought, wished, or that actually occurred, which can make this part of the story better."

> "I know a person like this, or if my main character were just like _____, this is what he or she would do next."

4. *Transcribe your students' thoughts. Tell the student: "Let me be your secretary; tell me what you want to write and I'll write it down."* Because students can more easily organize ideas orally, many writing blocks can be overcome if you write the first sentences that students compose as they speak their streams of consciousness. This "secretarial assistance" frees students to focus solely on connecting their thinking to their speaking, and eliminates the need to simultaneously restructure their thoughts into the grammatical principles and syntax of written language.

5. *Use factlines.* Another minilesson to increase the quality of first draft writing begins when the class experiences an event, audiovisual presentation, guest speaker, or field trip. After this you can ask students to turn a sheet of notebook paper lengthwise and use the left-hand margin line as a **factline.** On this line they make ^ carets and note the sequence of memories and insights that the experience created for them. Then, students can write their first draft below this factline and refer to it frequently as they write.

6. *Use 10-minute writes.* Developed by Ms. Marjorie Downer, a teacher at Benchmark School in Media, Pennsylvania, the **10-minute write** allows students approximately 10 minutes to write after a classroom reading. During this time, students (1) write comparisons of the story to their lives, (2) explain their interpretation of the moral or message, or (3) invent an imaginative sequel. You also can write for one of these purposes as students write. After 10 minutes have elapsed, you and students who volunteer can read what was written. You can express the most appreciation for students' writings if you read yours at about the midpoint of the sharing period. If you share first, you might intimidate some from sharing. If you share last, you might lead some to conclude you had "saved the best for last" and students will not have the last word.

7. *Conduct a poll.* To increase students' abilities to write persuasively you can conduct a poll. You can have students take a position about a current event or issue by posing questions: "How many think . . . ? or How many would . . . ?" Once students express their opinions orally, it becomes easier to draft their rationale and cite evidence of support. Similarly, to begin descriptive writings you can ask students to jot a scene, incident, or detail that first spurred their thinking about a topic. Explain to students that this initial thinking is often vivid and can occasion deeper meanings. It may not become the opening paragraph but may subsequently be moved to a later section in the composition. As Calkins explains, "the reason for putting concrete details on the page and lingering long enough to capture vivid, sensory particulars of it is that only then can students begin to know the fullness of an experience and to make their own new meaning from it" (1991, p. 279).

Last, at some times during drafting, students should be free to self-select spaces in the room where they want to write. Through this choice, most students feel more in charge, achieve a greater sense of solitude, and move more rapidly into a state of reflection to begin writing (Purcell-Gates, 1999; Graves, 1999).

REVISING

During the **revising stage** students rework drafts. Students begin to craft their art. Through revisings students "chisel and polish" to ensure that they have communicated precisely. They reorganize, insert, and delete words and phrases. Students can make better revisions when taught the following revising strategies:

REVISING QUESTIONS TO ASK MYSELF

1. Can I change a word to make my idea clearer?
2. Does each paragraph contain a main idea and vivid details?
3. Can I make an idea more powerful by rewriting or shortening any sentence?
4. Can I make stronger connections between ideas, sentences, and paragraphs?
5. Can I write an example so readers understand exactly what I mean?

Following this instruction, you can provide a revising learning center staffed by an older schoolmate, adult volunteer, or classmate who is esteemed as a revising expert. Moreover, because students learn from using peer revising reaction guides, such as the one displayed in Figure 8.2, a set of blank forms can be placed at this writing center. Then, students can ask a peer to complete one to help them revise. Figure 8.2 displays Meisong's story "Frisky Feet," which she wrote following her work in the discovery discussion with Mr. Conteras, and the comments Allison made about the personification story.

Subsequently, more advanced revising strategies can be practiced when students become members of an "editorial board." All students rotate into this board and meet once a week to select items for a newsletter to go home to parents. They make specific suggestions concerning classmates' "best works." As compositions pass through the board, specific notes can be made on each student's paper by using self-stick notes

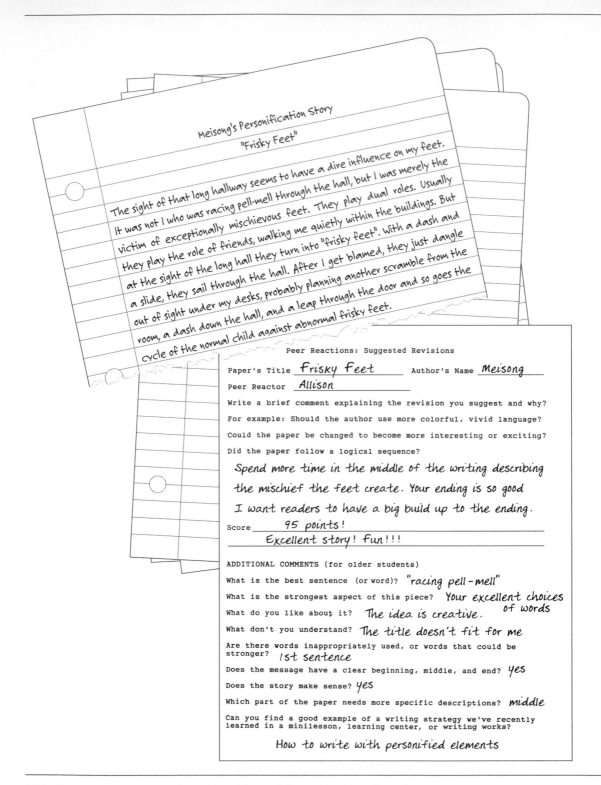

Meisong's Personification Story
"Frisky Feet"

The sight of that long hallway seems to have a dire influence on my feet.
It was not I who was racing pell-mell through the hall, but I was merely the
victim of exceptionally mischievous feet. They play dual roles. Usually
they play the role of friends, walking me quietly within the buildings. But
at the sight of the long hall they turn into "frisky feet". With a dash and
a slide, they sail through the hall. After I get blamed, they just dangle
out of sight under my desks, probably planning another scramble from the
room, a dash down the hall, and a leap through the door and so goes the
cycle of the normal child against abnormal frisky feet.

Peer Reactions: Suggested Revisions

Paper's Title *Frisky Feet*   Author's Name *Meisong*
Peer Reactor *Allison*

Write a brief comment explaining the revision you suggest and why?
For example: Should the author use more colorful, vivid language?
Could the paper be changed to become more interesting or exciting?
Did the paper follow a logical sequence?

   Spend more time in the middle of the writing describing
   the mischief the feet create. Your ending is so good
   I want readers to have a big build up to the ending.
Score_____ *95 points!*
           Excellent story! Fun!!!

ADDITIONAL COMMENTS (for older students)
What is the best sentence (or word)? *"racing pell-mell"*
What is the strongest aspect of this piece? *Your excellent choices*
                                                            of words
What do you like about it? *The idea is creative.*
What don't you understand? *The title doesn't fit for me*
Are there words inappropriately used, or words that could be
stronger? *1st sentence*
Does the message have a clear beginning, middle, and end? *yes*
Does the story make sense? *yes*
Which part of the paper needs more specific descriptions? *middle*
Can you find a good example of a writing strategy we've recently
learned in a minilesson, learning center, or writing works?
          How to write with personified elements

FIGURE 8.2 MEISONG'S STORY AND ALLISON'S PEER RESPONSE SHEET: AN EXAMPLE
OF HOW TO USE PEER EDITORS TO IMPROVE STUDENTS' REVISING ABILITIES

or a separate sheet of paper. Comments can include "This is where the piece works well"; "This is where I found the main ideas coming together well"; "We sort of see this part, but it's not very attention-getting"; "What kind of doll did she have?"; "Great simile! We like it!"; and "Fantastic ending sentence. It tied all your main points together." Additional discussions of the revising stage appear in Chapter 9.

EDITING

In the **editing stage,** students eliminate errors in spelling, punctuation, paragraph indentions, capitalization, and other writing conventions. Chapter 10 describes how to teach each of these communication competencies. The following activities can be used at the beginning of the year:

1. *Peer editing.* Students can select a revising partner and edit each other's drafts as Allison and Meisong did. Before they begin, you can model the information in Chapter 10 by reading one of your writings and showing on an overhead projector the editing changes that you made.

2. *Class "experts."* Students who have editing skills can become the "editing experts" for the class. These students can check classmates' drafts at learning centers, as described in Chapter 2.

3. *Minimal-mark editing.* You or student editors can place a dot or checkmark at the end of a line on a classmate's paper that contains an error. Then authors can find their own errors on marked lines and make corrections alone or in discovery discussions with you or peers.

4. *Sentence or paragraph of the week.* You can identify a noun–verb or capitalization–punctuation error many students make. Then you can demonstrate how to make the correct form. Subsequently, students can refer to their past writings and correct any occurrences of capitalization, punctuation, or tense errors. During the week, praise students who use this principle correctly in new writings. You can also display examples of students' well-crafted sentences or paragraphs on the board for classmates to read and possibly emulate so their writing style repertoires advance.

5. *Computer editors.* If students use word-processing programs, they can use spelling checkers and other error detection programs. You can help them to understand that these programs cannot replace their own thoughtful editing. For example, if you mean to type *road* but type *rode,* a spelling checker cannot detect an error because *rode* is in fact correctly spelled even though it is not the correct word.

SHARING–PUBLISHING

Writing is designed to be shared with others. Student compositions deserve to be recognized and celebrated. Thus, an important stage in the writing cycle is **sharing** students' written thoughts. You can arrange for a genuine audience by having students read their stories to peers in class or in other classes or put them in letters to pen pals, in a school newspaper, or in books they make to take home, to be used in doctors' or dentists' offices, or to be added to classroom or school libraries for peers to read. Students can also share their work with teachers in the school, parents, neighbors, principals, parents' friends, and relatives. They can also submit their works to publications that publish students' work, as listed on page 408.

Another method of sharing is to open the writing period each week by asking for the names of those who need someone to listen to their work or who want to sign up to share with a larger audience later in the week.

You can institute a program through the school librarian where students write their comments about a selection of children's literature on a book marker that remains in the book. When these markers are large enough for several students to write on the same one, students can use many schoolmates' comments to select a book.

One of the most popular methods for enjoying and sharing students' work is called **author's chair** (Graves & Hansen, 1983). An author's chair is a chair in the classroom that is used by students and teachers when they read their writings. An author's chair activity begins by an author sitting in the chair and telling the audience a purpose for listening to his or her writing (e.g., audience members can ask, "What do you want from us as an audience?" "How do you want to use us?"). The author might say: "I want you to tell me what I can do to make my characters more realistic"; "I want you to tell me how my writing has improved since the last time I read"; or "I just want to share what I have written with you to see what you think."

As the author reads, members of the audience may take notes about any suggestions they want to offer. They can also jot down what they liked about the writing. When authors finish, you can remind them that they are free to decide how (or whether) to use audience comments. The suggestions offered are viewpoints of others and may or may not be valid for their specific purposes. When suggestions are made, you can teach audience members to use sentences that begin with the word *I*. For example, audience members could say, "I think . . ."; "I wondered . . ."; "I liked . . ."; "I wasn't clear about . . ."; instead of "You need to do this"; "You weren't very clear about . . ."; and other comments with *you* as the subject. Doing so makes the authors less defensive.

In summary, writing instruction has become more authentic during the last 2 decades. Students engage in all phases of the writing cycle every year; they complete products read to real audiences; and they engage in speaking, listening, reading, and writing simultaneously to learn and think more effectively. They often collaborate when planning to write, revise, and share their work. Peer conferences, discovery discussions, minilessons, writing workshops, learning centers, and thematic units enlarge students' use of writing conventions, breadth of writing repertoires, and mastery of varied stylistic features. The writing workshop approach, as well as specific lessons that build students' writing abilities, are described below.

SECTION 2   PUTTING THEORY INTO PRACTICE

Increasing Students' Writing Abilities

The following activities increase students' writing abilities, integrate the language arts, and provide special strategies to increase the competencies of reluctant writers.

ACTIVITIES THAT BUILD WRITING ABILITIES

Writing workshops, factlines, 10-minute writes, progressive writing exercises, letter-writing units, and many computer programs are available to help students compose, select more precise words, construct clearer sentences, obtain data for writing, and create several genres for varied audiences. Also, as Meisong demonstrated, by fourth or fifth grades modern fantasy, mysteries, and science fiction expand students' writing style.

WRITING WORKSHOPS

Writing workshops are a method of dividing the language arts writing period into specific types of activities. Most often, a writing workshop is preceded by a mini-lesson you provide about something that several students can use to improve their writing. These minilessons traditionally take about 10 minutes. Immediately following, students engage in a writing worship. Most students are able to incorporate into their writing the strategy you have modeled. Others, however, take more time and may require your one-to-one assistance before their writing can reflect the instruction you just delivered.

Another feature of a writing workshop is an opportunity for you and the students to write quietly without any interruptions for 15 to 25 minutes, depending on the age of the student. Immediately following that writing, students are free to choose what they have signed up to do prior to the start of the writing workshop. They can move to the prewriting center and begin to make a list of ideas or browse through pictures to start thinking about what they want to write next. They can make a semantic web or talk to peers about how they want their story to begin. Others can go to the drafting or revising center where writing materials such as grammar books are kept to aid revising work. A peer editor who has been the revising expert can lead that group. Alternatively students can also choose to draft longer and stay at their desks. They can also write letters to pen pals, work at a computer, conference with the teacher, or join a circle that is being led by a peer, adult volunteer, or yourself. When students practice sharing their work, they are participating in the last stage of the writing workshop. The work can be shared with another class, and the stages of the work can be emphasized with different voices. At this particular stage in the classroom, which many teachers label the sharing section, students sometimes cut out felt characters to be used on felt boards, create word sentence strips or pictures to be used in pocket charts, or use overhead transparencies or puppets to aid them in the presentation of their stories.

Additional descriptions of a wide variety of writing workshops appear in several books (see Calkins & Harwayne, 1987; Calkins, 1994; Stuart & Graves, 1987; Graves, 1999; Routman, 2000). A sample schedule of such workshops follows:

9:00–9:10 Minilesson to strengthen some aspect of students' writing.

9:10–9:25 Sustained silent writing time (you and students write).

9:25–10:00 Writing stations (often called writing centers). Students go to the writing station that they select while you hold discovery discussions with a few students either spontaneously or in a systematic fashion as demonstrated by Mr.

Conteras in the opening scenario. Writing stations could be labeled "completing first drafts," "revising," "editing," and "preparing to publish and share." Because students write, edit, and illustrate at different speeds, students can rotate into these centers as their writing needs dictate.

10:00–10:30 Sharing time and planning for the next day's work.

Mr. Conteras uses four stations in his fifth-grade writing workshops. These can be used at other grade levels as well. The first is the Conference Station. It was created for students who seek assistance in drafting their writing. Mr. Conteras's class places material at this center to support brainstorming, semantic webbing, and talking about drafts in progress. He staffs this center with students who are very creative, enjoy planning, and like to help other students. The second is the Research Station. It is available to students who need help refining their work, finding information, choosing topics, or adding details to their writings. Resources at this center include dictionaries, grammar handbooks, encyclopedias, and a spelling rules chart. Students who staff this center are those who enjoy finding answers and answering detail-oriented and editorial questions. Third, the Illustration Station is for students who seek advice on illustrations or graphics to accompany their work, or want someone else to help them illustrate it. Materials at this center are markers, crayons, colored pencils, and art books. Students who staff this center are "artists-in-residence" (students who enjoy drawing). They are eager to give advice and to do sample pages to convey the images in their minds. Authors credit the artist if someone else illustrates their manuscripts. A Creative Sharing Station is also available for students. At this station students can improve their ideas before they write more or revise. Resources at this center include encyclopedias, atlases, and trade books. The staff are students who enjoy listening and collaborating to invent ideas. "Center Staff" people rotate each day so no student is away from his or her own writing for more than one day. Also, in Mr. Conteras's writing workshop plan, a student who chooses to work in the same center 2 days in a row can receive advise from two different "peer experts" in that center.

A sample of a six-day writing workshop schedule (that most students follow) appears in Figure 8.3. When writing is taught through such writing workshops, students can watch you model several strategies that support their composition abilities. For example, students can watch you brainstorm a list and a semantic web and freewrite on the same topic on the day that they meet with you at the prewriting learning center. These modelings can be followed by discussions about how students can use brainstorming when they are writing about a topic for the first time. They may profit most from semantic webs when they know a lot about a topic and want to organize it better; and they can benefit from freewriting when something is bothering them or they have a problem to solve. Students can spend several days performing each of these strategies with you until they judge that they can do so independently. When students feel confident in their prewriting skills, you can create a first draft learning center and students can learn the "tricks of the trade" for creating better first drafts with you at this center. This process can continue by subsequently establishing a revising learning center, editing learning center, and sharing–publishing center.

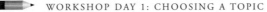

WORKSHOP DAY 1: CHOOSING A TOPIC

- Help students write about what they know.
- Focus on different activities to help students share out loud.
- Incorporate skills like brainstorming so students do not feel mentally confined.
- Let them write about anything that they find meaningful—they just need to write.

WORKSHOP DAY 2: DRAFTING

- Have students work in a worry-free environment to help the flow of ideas.
- Students should leave spaces between the lines so that desired corrections can be made by the writer later on.
- Make sure students know that great stories are not made overnight but that they also must begin somewhere as well.
- Use a temporary title to help students along in the process.

WORKSHOP DAY 3: RESPONDING & REVISING

- Students must understand that revision does not mean that the student's ideas are bad, but that writing is work in progress that must be refined to make it better.
- Conferences between partners, teacher and students, and groups help the response and revision process.
- Compare problem areas to other examples of written material so that students know what to model.

WORKSHOP DAY 4: IMPROVING WRITING

- Have students invent their own symbols to help personalize their style—all learning styles are not alike.
- Make certain students keep all prewriting materials along with drafts for their portfolios.
- Students should be focusing on more detail and style as they move through this particular workshop.
- Students should modify titles to reflect their work.

WORKSHOP DAY 5: POLISHING WRITING

- Have students evaluate whether their work is ready for editing or not.
- The piece of writing must be clear and concise.

WORKSHOP DAY 6: PROOFREADING

- All the details in terms of grammar and mechanics are cleaned up in this stage.
- Three phases of proofing should also be incorporated in terms of self-editing, peer-editing, and teacher-editing.
- A variety of forms should be used to have students reach their full writing potential.

FIGURE 8.3 CHARTING SIX WORKSHOP DAYS

Students also enjoy using learning centers in another way. These centers are patterned after the social event called a progressive dinner in which each stage of a meal is eaten at a different location. The purpose of progressive writing centers is to increase students' abilities to self-initiate strategies that improve their compositions at each stage of the writing process. They also establish a climate in which students can freely discuss many strategies, observe peers' effective writing styles, and compare different approaches to the same topic. Through this activity, students receive numerous models and become privy to the thinking processes of peers as they create, draft, revise, edit, and publish (Wepner, 1992). The steps of this activity are described below.

PROGRESSIVE WRITING CENTERS

To begin progressive writing centers, place groups of five students at tables. Ask students to select a topic that is important to the class and an audience to which they want their writing addressed. Then, ask students in every group to perform step 1 of the progressive writing activity prewriting.

Step 1. Prewriting.   Each group discusses the topic, jots down ideas related to it, and discusses prewriting strategies they might want to use. Then, every student completes a prewriting strategy (such as making a semantic map or list of ideas) on a sheet of paper. When finished, the entire group moves to the next table. (The prewriting step took 20 to 30 minutes in Mr. Conteras's fifth grade and 15 minutes in Ms. Hulsey's second grade.)

Ms. Hulsey's second-graders wrote about the following issues of importance to them:

1. Things that make us happy (books dedicated to, written for, and taken to our parents).
2. Being the oldest, middle child, youngest twin, or only child (with books or speeches being written to read to siblings, grandparents, or relatives).

Mr. Conteras's class wrote about the following issues that were important to them.

1. Building school spirit and eliminating fights at school. (Written plans to reach these goals are sent to the principal and vice principal.)
2. World peace. (After studying the 50th anniversary of the founding of the United Nations, and the hope that the new millenium brings, students wanted to create a cloth banner in which they could write their most important messages in India ink and add decorative emblems and illustrations of their concepts. This banner could be mailed to the United States ambassador to the United Nations.)

Step 2. Writing.   On the next day, at a new table, each group reads another group's prewritings aloud to each other. Next they discuss unique ideas from each prewriting that they want to include in their own first drafts. Then, each group member writes a first draft, taking as long as needed and even taking the draft home to complete before the next day's writing activity. In these first drafts, students are challenged to employ as many varied and vivid sentence patterns as possible.

Step 3. Revising.   On the next day, at a new table, members of each group read aloud the first drafts from another group's work. They discuss revisions that could be made to each. Then, each member of the group revises (adds/deletes/reorganizes) one of the first drafts at that table. (This step took approximately 30 minutes in both Ms. Hulsey's second-grade and Mr. Conteras' fifth-grade class.) Then students move to the next table.

Step 4. Editing.   At a new table, each group edits (mechanics/grammar/spelling) a revised story from another group's work. Before the compositions are edited, students read the revised stories to each other and discuss stylistic features in each that they judge to communicate well. (This stage was completed in approximately 30 minutes in Mr. Conteras's class.) Ms. Hulsey's second-graders modified this step by doing it together as a class. In their class, Ms. Hulsey described all the places where capitals should occur and then each student edited a writing for capitalization. Then she taught where periods, exclamation points, and question marks should appear and students checked for those. Subsequently, students edited for subject and noun agreement and used dictionaries to check for spelling errors.

Step 5. Creating final copy.   On the next day, at a new table, group members create a final copy of an edited piece written by the previous group. After having been shown and discussing several ways to make books and showcase work (see pages 230–231), students make a book and sketch illustrations as time permits. The next day each group returns to the table where they did their prewriting. They read the book that evolved from their prewritings. They also study how their original thoughts have been revised and crafted by peers. They identify one of the sentence structures represented in their final drafts that they want to incorporate into their own writing styles. Finally, students discuss and are taught strategies for writing effective titles for their stories (to build their summative thinking abilities).

Step 6. Sharing.   At the end of this lesson, some students read the final copy that was created from their prewriting. Some students in Mr. Conteras's and Mr. Stone's classes shared their stories with the class. After the sharing, students made a chart of new sentence structures they want to use in the future. They also selected the version they wanted to mail from the class to the ambassador and to their parents.

INTEGRATING THE LANGUAGE ARTS

Modeling How to Create Memorable Characters

Mr. Conteras integrated the language arts when he observed that his students were creating only one-dimensional characters. He read and asked students to read several books that model how to fashion more memorable characters, as listed in Literature Card 19. The class discussed how these authors made characters more memorable. Last, Mr. Conteras used the letter-writing unit that appears at the end of this chapter as one of the most powerful integrations of writing instruction with the language arts. Students write letters for purposes they select. In the process they draft, revise, edit, and craft their letters meticulously and witness the personal benefits

Literature Card 19

BOOKS THAT MODEL HOW MEMORABLE CHARACTERS ARE CREATED

To provide instruction in developing strong, believable characters, students read excerpts from three of the following books. Students compare these authors' strategies to create memorable characters in their own writings.

Did You Carry the Flag Today Charley? by R. Caudill, 1966 New York: Holt

Blue Skye by L. Littke, 1991 New York: Scholastic

Shoeshine Girl by C. Butler, 1975 New York: Cromwell

Queenie Peavy by R. Burch, 1966 New York: Viking

After the Goat Man by B. Byars, 1974 New York: Viking

Ramona the Brave and other books by B. Cleary, 1975 New York: Morrow

Inside Out and other books by A. M. Martin, 1986–1995 New York: Viking

The Sign of the Beaver by E. Speare, 1983 Boston: Houghton Mifflin

Terror on the Mountain by P. Viereck, 1990 Boston: Houghton Mifflin

Harriet the Spy by L. Fitzhugh, 1987 New York: Cornerstone

Something Special for Me by V. Williams, 1994 New York: Greenwillow

Johnny Tremain by E. Forbes, 1960 Boston: Houghton Mifflin

My Side of the Mountain by J. C. George, 1959 New York: Dutton

Caddie Woodlawn by C. Brink, 1937 New York: Macmillan

Class President by J. Hurwitz, 1990 New York: Morrow

Anastasia Krupnik by L. Lowry, 1979 Boston: Houghton Mifflin

Thank You, Jackie Robinson by B. Cohen, 1974 New York: Lothrop, Lee & Shepard

Best Friends for Frances by R. Hoban, 1994 New York: HarperCollins

Frog and Toad Are Friends by A. Lobel, 1984 New York: Puffin

Winnie the Pooh by A. Milne, 1926 New York: Dutton

The Tale of Peter Rabbit by B. Potter, 1963 New York: Golden Press

Like Jake and Me by M. Jukes, 1984 New York: Knopf

Call It Courage by A. Sperry, 1968 New York: Macmillan

Brave Irene by W. Steig, 1986 New York: Farrar, Straus, & Giroux

Roll of Thunder, Hear My Cry by M. Taylor, 1976 New York: Dial

Willie Bea and the Time the Martians Landed by V. Hamilton, 1983 New York: Greenwillow

Henry Huggins by B. Cleary, 1950 New York: Morrow

The Haunting by M. Mahy, 1983 New York: Atheneum

Summer of My German Soldier by B. Greene, 1973 New York: Dial

Katie for President and other books by A. Tolles, 1987–1995 New York: Dial

Mary Poppins by P. L. Travers, 1981 San Diego, CA: Harcourt Brace

Blowfish Live by the Sea by P. Fox, 1975 Englewood Cliffs, NJ: Prentice Hall

Bridge to Terabithia and other books by K. Paterson, 1984 New York: Ediciones

of engaging each stage of the writing process. Additional titles to use in your class to integrate the language arts to improve writing abilities are found on the website that accompanies this book.

INSIDE CULTURALLY ENRICHED CLASSROOMS

Building Additional Bridges to Improve the Writing Abilities of Second-Language Learners and Bilingual Students

Through writing, second-language learners have the opportunity to monitor their writing proficiency and, to some extent, their verbal ability as well. Following are five strategies that encourage their written expression. All these activities can be tackled independently or in a cooperative group setting.

Stop stories are an innovative way to create student interaction with literature through writing (High, 1998). In this activity, each student group receives an interesting picture. For 3 minutes, students write the beginning of a story in their own words about the picture. When the time limit approaches, the teacher calls, "Stop," and students pass their stories to their right. They read the story and have 3 minutes to add on to it. Finally, when all students in the group have contributed to each story, the original authors read their stories aloud. Through stop stories, ESL and bilingual students gain confidence in their abilities and learn to share their ideas with a small group, through a shared composition, before sharing a sole-authored work with the entire class.

Similarly, **two-sided stories** can be used effectively for very recent English speakers. This multidimensional approach begins with children creating stories in their own language (Miller, 1997). Students write several sentences in their native dialect, then illustrate their story on the left-hand side of the paper. Finally, the teacher or a native English–speaking buddy helps the student translate the story into English on the other side of the page. Two-sided stories are a wonderful literary experience because they emphasize the value of the child's native language while gently nudging him or her toward English competency. In the same way, the child feels that his or her ideas are important, no matter how difficult it is to write in English. An additional benefit is that every child is an author and has a story to share with the rest of the class, and native English speakers are able to celebrate the diversity and bilingual language abilities of their classmates.

A third strategy that promotes language transition through writing is the use of **literature logs.** Using literature logs, in which students write about and discuss experiences similar to those of the characters, helps students develop a personal connection to the story. (Goldenberg, Saunders, & Gallimore, 1998). This loosely structured writing practice also allows them to share their own thoughts instead of generating material that they think the teacher wants to read. Coupled with instructional conversation (teacher-facilitated small group discussion), learning logs have significantly increased writing ability for LEP students. When you use literature logs, some ESL students mix their languages as a first step to independent writing ability (see sample from Mr. Conteras's class in Figure 8.4).

Reflective writing is when students write for 10–20 minutes in their journals about something they have experienced or read. ESL students can write in any language that they desire. Reflective writing should be based on multicultural literature and experiences. Reflective writing provides an independent forum for students to express their thoughts and ideas (Noll, Lindahl, Valencia, & Salazar, 1998). This outlet encourages second-language learners to ask questions, express opinions, and make connections with various issues or media. A further extension of learning occurs when writing logs are chronicled in a notebook and students are asked to produce links from one week to another.

A fourth method, **modification of fairy tales,** is when students retell a traditional fairy tale in their own words. Cassady (1998) reports that, in addition to heightened writing ability, students demonstrate creative variety in their adapted fables. As part of multicultural activities, you can encourage students to select a folktale from their

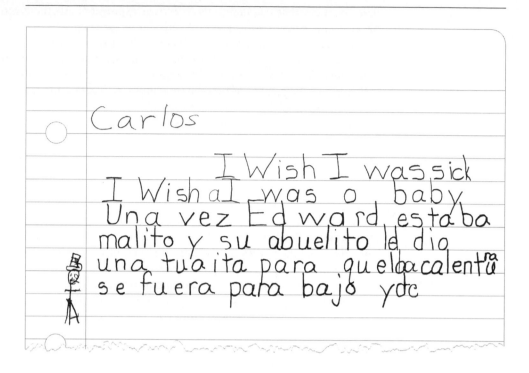

FIGURE 8.4 EXAMPLE OF THE BENEFITS OF LITERATURE LOGS FOR ESL STUDENTS

native countries (it may be an oral tradition) to arrange in their own words. Modified fairy tales should be shared in small groups until an individual volunteers to share their tale with the entire class.

RECOGNIZING AND REPORTING PROGRESS

Portfolios

Portfolios are one of the newer forms of writing assessments. Portfolios are collections of students' writing samples that have been analyzed and reflected on by the student and often by peers and teachers. These reflections are recorded as measures of progress as well as needs assessment for additional instruction. Portfolios take many forms. The most comprehensive are used as statewide assessments that every student at certain grade levels is required to complete. Several different types of writing are sampled in each portfolio. The categories and topics of writing include (a) how-to papers, (b) persuasive writing, (c) narratives, and (d) fictional and nonfictional genre.

Once every child has written a sample based on the specified criteria, the samples are graded according to rubrics that award points for separate dimensions of the writing process and mastery of writing conventions such as grammar, capitalization, punctuation, and spelling. This extensive use of portfolio as a measure of students' writing abilities can be found in Kentucky, Vermont, and in numerous school districts throughout the country, including Hawaii. Less extensive programs are located in individual buildings or individual school districts.

Students begin their portfolios in first grade and continue them throughout the elementary and sometimes middle and high school years. As a child is promoted from one grade to another, the portfolio is passed to the next teacher. Teacher comments, parent reflections, and student reflections, as well as book lists, spelling test scores, and other standardized test measures, are also included in many of the portfolios throughout the country. The least comprehensive portfolio is kept in a single teacher's classroom and is not passed from one teacher to another or from school to school. This type of portfolio is usually housed in a two-pocket folder that has three fasteners in the center to store papers.

This folder is used throughout the school year for students to store their writing. Writings in progress are usually stored in the pocket in the left-hand side of the folder. In the right-hand pocket are showcase portfolio pieces. **Showcase portfolio pieces** are writing samples that the student, teacher, or parent choose to represent the child's highest level of writing success. In this section of their showcase portfolio, students often have cover pages that describe which components of the piece made it a showcase piece.

For example, Michael chose the showcase pieces for his fifth-grade portfolio because they demonstrated how he improved the quality of dialogue so that you knew the characters better. Michael wrote something special about each piece he selected, but he also wrote an introduction about the importance of this collection of pieces. In that introduction, he stated that these pieces showed how he was beginning to develop his own voice as a writer; he knew that his talent as a writer sprang from detailed descriptions of characters he had developed throughout his life. Often, teachers ask students to grade their own portfolio work, by scoring either the entire collection or only their showcase. After they score their work, they defend it.

To complete the portfolio, the students self-assess their needs for improvement and set new goals. Oftentimes, one goal is set for first grade, two for second, three for third, four for fourth, and five for fifth. For example, returning to Michael's folder in December of his fifth-grade year, Michael wrote that he wanted to set five goals for the remainder of the school year: (1) improve his ability to describe characters by more effectively using dialogue between characters; (2) write better poetry; (3) write more complex sentences with descriptive phrases; (4) write shorter sentences that elicit more emotion; and (5) create better leads.

In addition to the two side pockets in a portfolio, many teachers fasten several introductory pages to the blank note paper that is stored in the center section of each folder. The initial pages are for students to record the titles and dates of their finished pieces. Often teachers ask students to rank, using a 5-star system, how well they think they did on each piece. A second page is for students to list topics they could write about that they have not yet written. This page is often added to during discovery discussions because, as you talk with students, you hear their ideas and can suggest that they write about them at a later date.

A third page is for students to record important growth they have discovered in their writing ability. On this page, many children put proofreading symbols, spelling words that they have learned, checklists that they want to use to improve their writing, as well as important insights that they have. For example, when Meisong finished her writing of *Frisky Feet,* she wrote down what she wanted to remember about how she had improved her writing ability: "I now realize that it is important for me to only include three adjectives or three items in a list, because if I include more than three, readers tend not to see how all of them fit together." Another page can contain frequently used words. Students can turn back to that page and quickly reference these words, which are usually the Dolch words that appear in Chapter 5. Students also like to keep their own dictionary of words to refer to for correct spellings. These are usually put in alphabetical order.

In classrooms in which portfolio assessments are used, students can work on their portfolios as part of a writing workshop or writing assignment. As they write they can date each draft, creating a continuous collection of writing samples in one location. Mr. Conteras values the portfolio system, and he uses the simplest system in which he keeps the portfolios throughout the year and sends them home with the students at the end of the year. Research supports that students who work with the system Mr. Conteras devised are very positive about maintaining their portfolios. Students appreciate the reflection time teachers make available to meet with them one-to-one at least once every 2 weeks to assess their portfolio (Dahl & Farnan, 1998). When portfolios are monitored with discovery discussions once every 2 weeks, most students do not find the portfolio process tedious or burdensome. They also report that they have less difficulty choosing their best works, feel that they have improved in their writing ability, and are able to set more realistic goals.

Mr. Conteras has devised the form in Table 8.1 to assist students to set new goals. In it, he combined the writing process with the portfolio process, and students identify in which areas of writing improvement they can work independently and in which they require the teacher's support or instruction. This form may be used in a wide variety of ways to improve students' writing processes or their portfolio self-assessments. Its use, as well as the process of portfolio assessment, writing workshops, and the writing process itself, have been demonstrated to significantly improve students' reading abilities (Kimenkov & LaPick, 1996).

SECTION 3   TEACHERS AS CONTINUAL LEARNERS

Writing Development

This section discusses how to conduct better conferences, called *discovery discussions,* with students. You will find reasons to use more peer conferences during the writing process so that students have an immediate reaction to their writing.

TABLE 8.1 MY PORTFOLIO REFLECTION SHEET: HOW MUCH I HAVE IMPROVED MY WRITING

Student _____ Date _____

Directions: Place an *I, S,* or *N* in the blank before each item.

I = does independently   S = does with support   N = needs additional instruction

PREWRITING SKILLS

_____ 1. Choose topic
_____ 2. Maintain focus on topic
_____ 3. Write diverse topics

FIRST DRAFT SKILLS

_____ 1. Brainstorm alone before writing
_____ 2. Use semantic maps or class charts or my portfolio to overcome writer's block
_____ 3. Keep a record of my thoughts and return to writing without much difficulty
_____ 4. Select relevant details to include

REVISING SKILLS

_____ 1. Willing to revise frequently
_____ 2. Selective about adding or deleting text
_____ 3. Use input of others
_____ 4. Self-reflective
_____ 5. Consider audience

EDITING SKILLS

_____ 1. Willing to edit
_____ 2. Able to work on mechanical aspects: (a) spelling, (b) handwriting, (c) punctuation, (d) capitalization

SHARING SKILLS

_____ 1. Able to publish
_____ 2. Persistent
_____ 3. Able to rework a piece after it is finished if a reader doesn't understand something
_____ 4. Share well orally

COMMENTS/INSTRUCTIONAL GOALS FOR NEXT TERM

_____ 1.
_____ 2.
_____ 3.
_____ 4.

PROFESSIONAL DEVELOPMENT ACTIVITY

How to Conduct Effective Conferences and Discovery Discussions

Conducting effective conferences is a very valuable professional ability. It takes time to develop because each conference has its own goals and constraints. There is no script to follow. Through one-to-one conferences, students' abilities can advance in areas that are most important at that time for that student, whether you had an idea of the area of need before the conference began or not. Conferences are beginning to be called **discovery discussions.** This term denotes a partnership with students in that both students and teachers can discuss new discoveries they have made or want to make. Discovery discussions are one-to-one conferences that are informal conversations between two people (you and a student) who value each other and each other's ideas *equally.* Discovery discussions provide one of the best opportunities for students to "tell their stories about who they are" in a specific writing. They also provide opportunities for you to (1) scaffold intensively in a student's zone of proximal development; (2) interact with each child personally to monitor his or her literary experiences, diagnose difficulties, offer guidance, and set practice where necessary; and (3) discuss the information each child provides in Table 8.1 (Block, 1999).

Discovery discussions can be scheduled in different ways. Students can sign up for a time to meet with you when they need your help with a specific problem or task. A daily chart can be available for students to request a conference and a regular 20-minute time period can be allocated for this purpose. Alternatively, you can schedule times to meet with all students during independent work and hold an individual discussion with every student each month. Discovery discussions can also be held impromptu to overcome specific writing problems (e.g., overcoming writer's block, tightening the main theme, creating vivid details, using sequence creatively, or incorporating varied sentence structures).

To begin a discovery discussion, you can ask students what they want to discuss. To become their trusted mentor, however, you cannot rush from one student to another, and you have to give students your undivided attention. Meeting individual needs varies. You may spend up to 90 minutes with one student and 30 seconds with another, yet give both what they need. The most important part of discovery discussions often occurs at the end of the conference, when students feel comfortable enough to risk asking a very important question or state a new insight. To evaluate each conference, you can mentally or literally note aspects that worked and didn't work well for you and that child. Moreover, by tape-recording some of your conferences, you can replay the tape, assess your growth as a mentor, and refresh your memory of specific reflections students made during a conference. Asking reflective questions is also very valuable. Examples of questions that teachers recommend follow:

- When you reread your writings where do you find "something that feels alive" (Calkins, 1994)?
- What part is most interesting to you?
- Where could this new idea go?
- What is this piece of writing really about (Graves, 1998)?
- What part do you want help with (Graves, 1998)?

FOR YOUR JOURNAL

Buddy Journals

Buddy journals are a section of students' journals that they trade with one another. One buddy writes an entry, and the other buddy writes a response. To begin buddy journals, you can allow interested students to choose someone with whom they want to communicate for a 2-week period. These students write in their journals twice a week and respond to their buddy's entries twice a week. On the last day of each week they discuss each other's comments. A sample buddy journal reflection sheet is provided in Table 8.2.

TABLE 8.2 BUDDY JOURNALS REFLECTION SHEET

Name _____

Buddy's Name _____

BUDDY JOURNALS

Directions: When you and your partner have completed six buddy journal entries, your partner will grade you on each of the items. If you agree with the grade, check *yes,* and write why. If you don't agree, check *no* and write why.

	YES	NO
1. Writing is clear and interesting. Grade _____ Writer's comment:		
2. Openings and closings are captivating. Grade _____ Writer's comment:		
3. Uses vivid words, good choices of nouns and verbs. Grade _____ Writer's comment:		
4. Does not repeat words or ideas unnecessarily. Grade _____ Writer's comment:		
5. Sentences are of different lengths and effective. Grade _____ Writer's comment:		
6. Spelling, punctuation, and capitalization are correct. Grade _____ Writer's comment:		

CONNECTING CLASSROOMS, PARENTS, AND COMMUNITIES

Letter-Writing Activities

A post office or letter-writing unit brings authenticity to the task of teaching letter writing. Letters students write after being taught letter-writing formats can be sent by (1) e-mail, (2) regular mail, or (3) simulated mail to classmates or schoolmates. Because letters are directed to a particular person, they allow students to envision a real audience. In this unit, students can prewrite by making a semantic map; brainstorming; making a list of questions they want to ask a friend or a company in the case of a business letter; and clustering freewritten notes that could have been jotted on different pieces of papers as a reminder of what they wanted to write. Next, students review the letter format in Figure 8.5 and write their first draft. When they become adults, they will most often revise and edit their own personal letters and ask others to critique their professional letters and memos. It is helpful to follow these same procedures during the revision and editing stages of letter writing in your class. When students get ready to share, they mail their final product (after you have proofread those that are mailed outside your classroom).

A post office center allows your students to express themselves through their writing. There are different kinds of letters: formal business letters, invitations, thankyou notes, personal letters (expressive writing). They can write letters to living heroes, favorite authors, sports teams, their parents, peers who are home sick, visitors to their classroom, pen pals, classmates, and you. By using a mailbox in the classroom, your students can send their peers postcards or drop you a line.

Pen pals are a great way to teach young writers how to send a letter. Pen pals can be obtained by having students write to an upperclassman, students from an-

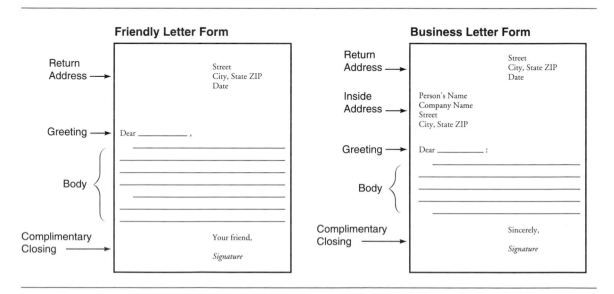

FIGURE 8.5 FORMS FOR FRIENDLY AND BUSINESS LETTERS

other school, college students in a teacher-education program, or the following organizations:

International Friendship League
22 Batterymarch
Boston, MA 02109

Student Letter Exchange
910 Fourth Street SE
Austin, MN 55912

League of Friendship
P.O. Box 509
Mt. Vernon, OH 43050

World Pen Pals
1690 Como Avenue
St. Paul, MN 55108

In addition, students can write letters to their parents informing them of important events, such as open houses, parents' picnics, or class plays. Younger students, especially those in preschool through first grade, can learn the value of writing clear letters by writing and drawing messages on postcards to other pen pals and parents. They can also write business postcards to obtain information as a class. Similarly, in 1990 the U.S. Postal Service began the four-star "Wee Deliver" program, which is a prepackaged letter-writing unit. To receive your free "Wee Deliver" starter kit and unit, send the name of your school along with the school's address, contact person, and telephone number to Literacy Initiatives, Corporate Relations, U.S. Postal Service, 475 L'Enfant Plaza, SW, Rm. 10541, Washington, DC 20260-3100.

Business Letters.   A format to teach business letters is shown in Figure 8.5. An effective strategy for teaching business letter writing is to allow students to write for information from companies that are involved in issues concerning thematic units they are studying, such as those that appear in this textbook. Students can also write business letters to companies that provide information about hobbies and other areas of personal interest. Many such addresses appear in a reference book that is updated every year entitled, *Free Stuff for Kids* (Lansky, Broberg, & Weiss, 1996). Students who become adamant about an issue profit from writing to their state or national leaders. The addresses of local and state officials appear in the telephone book, and the address for the President and United States senators and representatives appear below. By writing these letters, students learn that the proper salutation for judges and government officials is "The Honorable ____." Addresses for these officials at the national level are

President's Name
The White House
Washington, DC 20500

Senator's Name
Senate Office Building
Washington, DC 20510

Representative's Name
House of Representatives Office Building
Washington, DC 20515

Personified and Simulated Letters.   Students become more creative and tend to be less inhibited when they write letters as if they were animals from one of their favorite books (personified letters) or write as if they were literary or historical characters. If they choose to do the latter, students can write from the perspective of one main character to another. Such letters also develop students' abilities to write from a different point of view. For example, Mr. Conteras read the stories of *The Three Little Pigs* and *The True Story of the Three Little Pigs* after the progressive dinner activity described earlier had been completed. Students were free to respond to these books in any way they chose. Meisong wrote the following letter:

> This is why the wolf did it: He said that he was a long, lost cousin of the pigs. He was just wanting to meet them. That's why he blew their houses down. On the third house he just was trying to meet them but they, for some reason, put a pot of boiling water under the chimney. So they almost killed their family. Signed, Nelly, the Innocent Wolf

SUMMARY

In this chapter you learned that writing increases students' self-images, creates learning, expands students' creativity, and can increase students' higher-level thinking. In the most effective programs, students write to satisfy their needs, select their own topics, receive instruction to increase their writing power, and share their works with others. Students pass through stages as they develop. In preschool their writings are often unintelligible, and in first grade they typically talk to themselves as they write. By second grade they begin to understand that writing is to be read by an audience. By third grade, students can more easily learn strategies that make their writing more sophisticated, such as how to summarize and make characters more memorable. Today's writing programs also use prewriting, drafting, revising, editing, sharing, and publishing to increase students' ability to express themselves.

You discovered several methods that build students' writing abilities including writing workshops, progressive writing centers, writing different genres, building learning bridges for reluctant writers, word processors, conducting effective language arts conferences, employing buddy journals, and bookmaking. At the end of this chapter you will read about a thematic unit that Mr. Conteras used to develop students' letter-writing abilities. This unit can be used for students at every grade level. Chapter 9, will reveal additional information about individual components of the writing process, as Juan, Meisong, Michael, and Allison move into their sixth-grade class.

HOW TO DO IT: USING WHAT YOU'VE LEARNED

The following provide opportunities to reflect on and practice what you have learned.

ASSESSING YOUR LEARNING

1. If you have an available group of students, make a list of the ways they want to have their writing evaluated. Discuss with them how they can evaluate other students' writing, if they are teachers. Share your findings in class.

2. If you are teaching, work with two or more students or adult writers, ask them to describe what makes a good writer, and analyze characteristics of good writing they value. Have these older students or adult writers come to class to share a list of writing tips they follow. Before their visit, have your class brainstorm tips they use to write. Once speakers finish, ask students to determine whether their tips agree and why or why not.

3. How can you help a student who is just sitting there "looking into space" while others are freewriting? How can you help a student who experiences writer's block? Make a photocopy of either your or a student's entry. In class the next day, with that student's permission, edit the photocopied version on the overhead. Write the main point of the story (or your story) or the most important thing you want your readers to gain from these stories on a second sheet of paper. Have the class make the type of journal entry you illustrate. If you are not teaching, prepare a buddy journal entry and ask a friend to respond; ask the friend to write the most important thing he or she thought about your writing and to suggest how you can improve it. Make these revisions. Describe what you have learned about the peer editing process and how you can help students in your class use editing and buddy journals more productively.

4. If you are not teaching, select a book from Literature Cards 18 and 19 or *Sylvester and the Magic Pebble* and design a lesson. If you are teaching, practice telling your students: "Let me be your secretary; you tell me what you want to tell others and I'll write it down." Analyze the effects of this strategy in overcoming your students' writer's block. If you are not teaching, conduct a mock conference and tape-record it. You can confer with a classmate and analyze the tape to see whether you followed the principles in the Professional Development Activity in this chapter.

5. Meet with a colleague and study a selection of students' writings. Write what students would need based on these writing samples. To do so, first collect two or three samples of writing from one child. Second, assess the student's ability to use the writing processes demonstrated in the writing sample. Third, assign a grade to each of the writing samples using one method of grading (i.e., a checklist or rubric as described in Chapters 7 and 8). Then, share your results with your colleague. Together decide on a specific lesson that you would implement to improve that child's writing.

KEY TERMS EXERCISE

Below are the concepts introduced in this chapter. If you have learned the meaning of a term, place a checkmark in the blank that precedes it. If you are not sure of the definition of a term, increase your retention and reread its definition. If you have learned 18 of these terms on your first reading of this chapter, you have constructed an understanding of a majority of the most important terms that you need to develop your students' writing abilities. Congratulations.

_____ author's chair   (p. 348)

_____ buddy journals   (p. 361)

_____ discovery discussions   (p. 360)

_____ drafting stage   (p. 343)

_____ editing stage   (p. 347)

_____ factline   (p. 344)

_____ focused writing   (p. 343)

_____ literature logs   (p. 355)

_____ modification of fairy tales (p. 355)

_____ portfolios   (p. 356)

_____ prewriting stage   (p. 341)

_____ reflective writing   (p. 355)

_____ revising stage   (p. 345)

_____ sentence-combining techniques (p. 339)

_____ sharing   (p. 347)

_____ showcase portfolio pieces (p. 357)

_____ stop stories   (p. 355)

_____ two-sided stories   (p. 355)

_____ 10-minute write   (p. 344)

_____ unfocused freewriting (p. 343)

_____ writer's block   (p. 343)

_____ writing program   (p. 337)

_____ writing workshops   (p. 349)

FOR FUTURE REFERENCE

Books about the Writing Process and Fifth-Grade Students

Atwell, N. (Ed.). (1999). *Coming to know: Writing to learn in the intermediate grades.* Portsmouth, NH: Heinemann.

Bromley, K. (1994). *Journaling: Engagements in reading, writing, and thinking.* New York: Scholastic.

Cudd, E. T. (1989). Research and report writing in the elementary grades. *The Reading Teacher, 43,* 268–269.

Fiderer, A. (1994). *Teaching writing: A workshop approach.* New York: Scholastic.

Graves, D. H. (1994). *A fresh look at writing.* Portsmouth, NH: Heinemann.

Routman, R. (1994). *Invitations.* Portsmouth, NH: Heinemann.

Resources for Teachers

Bridges, L. (1997). *Writing as a way of knowing.* York, ME: Stenhouse.

> Provides thought-provoking essays and exercises to help develop writing skills and responses. It also examines journals, poetry, and dialogue writing.

Freeman, D. E., & Freeman, Y. S. (1996). *Teaching reading and writing in Spanish in the bilingual classroom.* Portsmouth, NH: Heinemann.

> ESL and bilingual teachers will find this book especially helpful. It thoroughly covers literature-based methods of teaching reading and writing to second-language learners. It also has a comprehensive list of children's literature in Spanish.

Gillis, C. (1997). *Writing outside the lines.* Portsmouth, NH: Boynton/Cook.

> The author gives suggestions for partnerships with community writers, poets, and authors. There is also an emphasis placed on writing for pleasure and children sharing their works with each other.

Hindley, J. (1997). *In the company of children.* York, ME: Stenhouse.

> This book guides teachers through the process of setting up writing workshops in all types of classrooms. It also discusses the teacher's role in writing and provides lots of ideas for minilessons in a variety of genres.

Moore, D. W., Moore, S. A., Cunningham, P. M., & Cunningham, J. W. (1998). *Developing readers and writers in the content areas k–12.* New York: Addison Wesley Longman.

> The authors share a wide variety of ways to integrate reading and writing into any content instruction. One in-depth section focuses on motivating students to read and examine the value of student inquiry.

Raphael, T. E., & Au, K. H. (Eds.). (1998). *Literature-based instruction: Reshaping the curriculum.* Norwood, MA: Christopher-Gordon.

> Children's responses to literature, multiracial identity, and literature selection in the classroom are all extensively discussed. Suggestions are provided that encourage the use of writing to explore culture and evoke personal response.

For Teachers of Writing

www-gse.berkeley.edu/Research/NWP/nwp.html

> Visit the National Writing Project home page, and from there visit sites of National Writing Projects (NWP) across the United States.

For Young Writers and Their Teachers

www.inkspot.com

> From this site, young writers can be part of a forum to exchange ideas with one another and with experienced writers. This page is linked to a site for writers of children's books and to a collection of works by young writers in the Young Writers' Showcase. Students can read works by other young writers and can also submit their writings to be published on the Web. There is an advice column called "Dear Kathy," where young writers can ask questions about writing that are answered by a professional writer. "Dear Kathy" is the author of Market Guide for Young Writers.

For Young Writers

www.kidpub.org/kidpub/intro.html

> KidPub is a delightful site where there are "more than 8,000 stories written by kids from all over the planet." It has become an exciting site where children can learn about HTML (hypertext mark-up language) formatting and publish their own stories on the Web.

Resources for Parents and the Community

Johnson, P. (1997). *Written and illustrated by children: Developing children's writing and illustration together.* Portsmouth, NH: Heinemann.

The author describes how primary students can be taught to create books that fuse their writing and drawing in profound ways.

Kaye, P. (1995). *Games for writing: Playful ways to help your child learn to write.* New York: Farrar, Straus, & Giroux.

Kaye, a renowned teacher and author of Games for Math and Games for Learning, now gives parents more than 50 ways to help their children become skilled, confident, and enthusiastic writers.

Linse, C. (1998). *The treasured mailbox: How to use authentic correspondence with children.* Portsmouth, NH: Heinemann.

Caroline Linse uses students' fascination for correspondence to help them develop writing skills. The result is classrooms of students enthralled with letter writing as a new and creative way of expressing themselves.

Miles, K. (1998, September). How to raise a child who loves to write. *Parenting Magazine, 63,* "Smart Starts" special learning section, 3–10.

Smith, J. (1998). *How children learn to write.* Boston: P. H. Brooke.

Smith examines the process children go through when learning the skill and art of writing. He also includes recommendations to enhance their writing over the course of their developmental stages.

Tucker, S. (1997). *Word wearings: Writing poetry with young children.* New York: Addison Wesley.

This book guides parents and children through the creative processes that encourage poetry writing. It can be adapted for children of all ages and encourages parents to take an active part in developing their child's writing abilities.

Wray, D. (1996). *Extending literacy: Children reading and writing nonfiction.* Boston: Routledge.

Wray encourages nonfiction reading and response through writing. Thorough instruction and a significant amount of exercises for parents are included.

THEMATIC UNIT: TEACHING MYSTERIES TO INCREASE COMPREHENSION AND COMPOSING ABILITIES[1]

Mysteries are among the best genres to develop students' comprehension, composition, and metacognitive abilities. Mysteries have crimes or problems to solve in which students must attend to clues in the text. Plots revolve around intrigue and complex characters. Although the solution must be logical, authors take great pride in subtly foreshadowing probable outcomes. As students read and write mysteries they must engage their metacognition and highest competencies in comprehension and composition. This unit on mysteries also provides many opportunities for students to imitate and manipulate language in their own writing so that their compositions become more intriguing, meaningful, and pleasurable.

Objectives

1. To discuss and learn what exclusive elements are found in a mystery.
2. To learn how to monitor consistently one's own reading activity and thinking processes (metacognition).
3. To improve writing abilities through learning to write subtle details, character qualities, and more complex plots.

Process in Action

Discuss aspects of mysteries. Introduce metacognition and lessons in this chapter.

Introduction Exercise.   The class breaks up into two groups and each is given a story to solve from George Shannon's *More Stories to Solve* (without solutions). Each group reads the story and discusses what the solution might be. Then the class does the following lesson that builds metacognition by letting students walk in someone else's shoes. Its purpose is to assist students in analyzing the metacognitive thoughts of characters in a story. The students use the main characters in the story and write the likely metacognitions of the opposing character. Students choose a partner and select a mystery of choice from the class library or school library (paired reading).

Mr. Conteras shows some examples of the Thinking Guide (in Figure 7.5) on the overhead projector. When the students are halfway through the book, they are to stop and complete the Character Frame about any two characters they choose in Figure 8.6. After it is finished, students answer the following questions: What has happened so far? Can I make any predictions using what I already know? Have I formed a picture in my head? What kinds of things do I still need to know before I can solve this mystery? Have I reread parts I didn't understand? Last, students write the ending of the mystery and share with classmates before all read the end of the book.

---

[1]This unit was written by Ms. Julie Hopkins, fifth-grade teacher in Fort Worth, Texas.

CHARACTER'S NAME, AGE, SIZE, APPEARANCE	LEVEL OF CHARACTER'S STABILITY OR VOLATILITY	INITIAL IMPRESSION AND WHY	WORDS CHOSEN TO SHOW PERSONALITY	ACTIONS THAT SUPPORT PERSONALITY TRAIT	CONVERSATION BY OR ABOUT THE CHARACTER THAT ILLUSTRATES TRAIT

What have you learned from this author that will improve your ability to create, in your own writing, characters that are more memorable?

FIGURE 8.6 CHARACTER FRAMES TO IMPROVE MY ABILITY TO UNDERSTAND LITERARY CHARACTERS AND TO INSPIRE MY ABILITY TO WRITE MORE MEMORABLE CHARACTERS (CAN BE SIMPLIFIED FOR GRADES K–3)

Removing Obstacles for Students

Have some mysteries available on videotape or the Internet for them to study prior to the lesson. For new mystery stories each month, see www.thecase.com/kids.

Sixth-graders begin to revise what they have written by concentrating on effective use of grammar, phrase, and word choices.

CHAPTER 9

REVISING TO CLARIFY MEANING

Today Meisong was anxious to read page 27 from <u>Volcano</u> by Patricia Lauer, and she was the first person to share. She read:

> In early summer of 1980 the north side of Mount St. Helens looked like the surface of the moon—gray and lifeless. The slopes were buried under mud, ground-up rock, pumice, and bits of trees. Ash covered everything with a thick crust. The eruption had set off thunderstorms that wet the falling ash. The ash became goo that hardened into a crust. The slopes looked like a place where nothing could be alive or ever live again. Yet life was there. (Laurer, 1993, p. 27)

Meisong said she realized that using phrases with the word <u>like</u> in them paint clear meanings because they compared new information to pictures seen before. "Above all, however," Meisong continued, "I like this book so much because, as I read it, I could feel how deeply the author feels about Mount St. Helens. I realized that when you really write, and rewrite to say <u>exactly</u> what you want, you can write about something in such a way that it makes other people care about it too. I want to write so well that something important to me can become important and beautiful to other people."

After she finished, Juan, who has become very poetic in the last two years, added: "I also realized something as you read. I realized that even expert writers can have their writing improved."

"Tell us more," Ms. Billick requested.

"Look at these sentences." Juan replied. "Instead of saying 'The eruption had set off thunderstorms that wet the falling ash,' I would have rewritten it to read, 'The eruption caused thunderstorms to weep. Their tears turned fallen ash to goo. When the sun reappeared, these massive tears transformed the earth into an impenetrable crust of steel.' "

Allison gasped: "Write that down before you forget it! It's beautiful!"

Scenes like this occur daily in Meisong's, Juan's, Allison's, and Michael's sixth-grade class because they have found that paraphrasing, rereading, and revising achieves deeper sincerity, clarity, honesty, and specificity in their writing. They are finding that mastering this depth is just as exciting as discovering a new idea in a book.

The purpose of this chapter is to develop students' abilities to paraphrase what they say and hear, to reread to increase depth of understanding, and to revise their writing. In the process they will learn how to use appropriate word orders, sentence structures, paragraph functions, and story grammar. By chapter's end you will also have received information concerning the IRA, NCTE, NAEYC, TEKS, and other statewide and province-based professional standards so that you can answer the following questions:

1. How can you include revising instruction in students' self-selected reading, writing, and speaking activities?

2. How can students learn to build more effective sentences?

3. How can students make more appropriate grammatical choices?

4. What are traditional, structural, and transformational/generative grammar?

5. How can you intensify students' use of idioms, metaphors, and figurative language to clarify and strengthen their spoken and written communication abilities?

6. What is the NCTE and IRA position concerning grammar instruction?

7. What methods increase ESL students' grammatical awareness?

8. How do you measure students' correct grammar usage?

SECTION 1   THEORETICAL FOUNDATIONS

Students Need to Revise

> *When Confucius was asked what he would do if he had the responsibility for administering a country, he said he would improve language. If language is not correct then what is said is not what is meant; if what is said is not what is meant, then what ought to be done remains undone; if this remains undone, morals and arts would deteriorate, justice would go astray; if justice goes astray, the people will stand about in helpless confusion.*
>
> —Confucius, 551–479 B.C.

Revising refers to the strategies students use to clarify their meanings. Revising focuses on improving word choices, sentence variety, paragraph organization, and clarity of ideas. Research documented that teaching strategies through traditional grammar worksheets does not improve most students' revision abilities (Elley et al., 1976; Petrosky, 1977; Hillocks, 1987). Conversely, when children listen to and read well-crafted writings, write often, and discuss their exact meanings and word choices; the study of grammar can become a pleasurable experience.

EFFECTIVE GRAMMAR INSTRUCTION

Grammar is the description of the structure of our language. It is comprised of principles that govern word choice, word order, usage, sentence structure, sentence type, dialect, paragraph form, paragraph function, and story structure. In 1987, "*the teaching of formal grammar* [emphasis added] was found to have a negligible or even harmful effect on the improvement of writing because it usually displaced some instruction and practice in actual composition" (National Council of Teachers of English, 1987). Other studies show that papers written by students who studied grammar through traditional worksheets for 2 years had more errors than students who merely wrote daily instead (e.g., Noyce & Christie, 1989; Elbow, 1981; Linden & Whimbey, 1990). With such data concerning the negative effects of teaching grammar, why should you teach it?

REASONS FOR TEACHING GRAMMAR

Researchers interpret the above data to mean that the *traditional methods* of teaching grammar did not call on students' self-initiated use of grammatical principles. Although grammatical principles are important to learn, the methods of teaching them need to be revised (Noden, 1999; Howie, 1979). Many of the past instructional methods violated the principles of language learning described in Chapter 1. These methods asked students to memorize rules through isolated exercises. This approach was comparable to asking students to become better runners by studying leg muscles on anatomical charts. We cannot teach our students to use powerful verbs by merely asking them to conjugate *see.* Instead, they must learn to use stronger verbs when they revise their own or a partner's paper. In the process most notice (or you can teach them) that to strengthen weaker sentences they must increase the precision of the verb. Through such lessons, many students self-initiate the selection of more effective words as they write.

Newer methods (presented in this chapter) can increase students' precision in spoken and written language (LeGuin, 1998; Willis, 1996; Noden, 1999). They do so by making students' subconscious grammatical knowledge explicit through the conversations and revising they use to internalize grammatical principles. These new methods also help students select between a variety of grammatical structures (Applebee et al., 1988; National Assessment of Educational Progress, 1987; Stuart & Graves, 1987). Without this instruction, students seldom reword or combine sentences, rearrange material, or improve meanings (Paul, 1990; Noden, 1999; Weaver, 1998).

What type of grammar should be taught? Although educators agree that students must possess a knowledge of grammatical principles, there are several theories about how the syntax of English should be taught.

TRADITIONAL GRAMMAR

Traditional grammar is a system of describing our language by sorting English words into categories, or parts of speech, as shown in Figure 9.1. Traditional grammarians propose that students learn to speak and write grammatically when they combine these parts of speech correctly. Traditional grammar was the first type of instruction offered in U.S. schools. It is based on the rules that govern Latin, and is modeled after instruction offered in Great Britain. Traditional grammatical theory treats English words as if their meanings are signaled through word endings.

Nouns

Traditionally, a noun is defined as the name of a person, place, or thing.

I. *Derivational Affixes*
   -age   coverage, village
   -ance   clearance, importance
   -ee   trustee, employee
   -er   employer, dancer
   -ment   pavement, government
   (also: -cy, -ity, -ness, -ster, -ism, -ist, -ship)

II. *Inflectional Affixes*
   To make plurals:
   -s   coats, pigs
   -es   dishes, ditches
   But note the irregular plural forms:
      children, women, oxen, men, deer, geese, feet
   Also, *mass nouns* are not commonly pluralized:
      communism, milk

Verbs

Traditionally, verbs are defined as words that name actions, or states of being.

I. *Derivational Affixes*
   -ize   socialize, criticize
   -ify   classify, mystify
   (also: -en, -ate, en-, and be-)

II. *Inflectional Affixes*
   -s, -ed, -ing, and *to* . . .

III. *Auxiliary Verbs*
   be/is/am/are/was/were
   have/has/had
   might/may
   shall/should
   will/would
   can/could
   must

Adjectives

Traditionally, adjectives are defined as words that modify nouns.

I. *Derivational Affixes*
   -y, -ive, -able, -ful, -less, -ar, -ary, -ic, -ish, -ous, -en*, -ed*, and *-ing**

II. *Inflectional Affixes*
   -er and *-est*

*Not to be confused with verb inflectional affixes.

Adverbs

Traditionally, adverbs are defined as words that modify verbs.

I. *Derivational Affixes*
   a-, -ly, -ward, -where, and *-wise*

FIGURE 9.1 COMPONENTS IN AN INSTRUCTIONAL PROGRAM OF TRADITIONAL GRAMMAR

Whereas Latin and Old English followed this treatment, modern English does not (aside from the meanings of plurality and verb tense). Moreover, with the increasing frequency of individual words that have multiple meanings (e.g., *run, tire, read,*

Prepositions

Traditionally, prepositions are rarely defined, except as they fall into *sentence test frames.*

The first frame identifies all but 9 of the 42 prepositions.

1. The ant crawled _____ the door.

   The following prepositions fit this slot:

about	behind	from	round
above	below	in	through
across	beneath	like	to
after	beside	near	toward
against	beyond	off	under
along	by	on	underneath
around	down	opposite	up
at	for	over	with
before			

The following prepositions do not fit this slot:

among	of
but (meaning *except*)	regarding
concerning	since
during	until or till
except	

Some prepositions in the second group fit this test frame:

2. The old man was silent _____ the war.

The others—*among, but, except,* and *of*—fit this test frame:

3. No one was talking _____ the girls.

FIGURE 9.1 (CONTINUED)

and *bat*), a principle of traditional grammar (that English words are only one part of speech) has been violated in modern English. Today, single English words can describe an action (verb = *run* home); things (noun = home*run, run* in a stocking, 5K *run*); a gerund (*run*ning the race, *run*ning the campaign) or an adjective (the *run*ning faucet).

A second weakness with traditional grammar principles is that traditional grammarians profess that modern English has more than eight categories of words. Because of these weaknesses you can supplement students' knowledge of the roles and functions of words by teaching common sentence patterns and pointing out how their favorite authors use a variety of sentence structures to convey meaning. Students enjoy identifying and comparing their favorite authors' most frequently used word order, sentence structure, and paragraph organization to other authors and to their own.

STRUCTURAL OR DESCRIPTIVE GRAMMAR

Structural or **descriptive grammar** is a theory of grammar that does not prescribe a "correct" form, but reports language as it is used today (Bloomfield, 1933; Fries, 1963). This principle helps students understand subtle differences of meanings between spoken and written language, as well as differences between regional dialects. In descriptive or structural grammar, words are divided into functions, with many words serving more than one function. For example, students are taught that while all sentences contain subjects, all subjects are not always nouns as traditional grammar might lead them to believe. When you teach structural grammar, you can introduce these word functions, within basic sentence patterns, as demonstrated below:

Noun markers	*The* birds fly.
Verb markers	The mailman *is* coming.
Negatives	He is *not* sad.
Intensifiers	He is *very* happy.
Conjunctions	The trees *and* flowers are signaling spring has arrived.
Phrase markers	The rain caused Rover to run *for* shelter.
Question markers	*What* is the proper way to teach grammar?
Clause markers	The party will be held *before* we leave school.

According to structural grammarians, modern English is comprised of word patterns, sentence orders, word classes, functions, and inflectional changes. An effective strategy to demonstrate descriptive grammar is to write out a story told orally and give it to students. Then distribute a second account of that same story as it would be recorded in a printed form. Ask students to compare the grammatical differences between oral and written language. As they describe these differences, they are to chart the principles that govern written English. You also can ask students to select their favorite sentences from one of the following books: *Where in the World Is Henry?; Goodnight Moon; A Dark, Dark Tale; The Cock, the Mouse, and the Little Red Hen; What Good Luck!; Millions of Cats; The Little Red Hen; The Three Billy Goats Gruff; The Chick and the Duckling; Where's Spot?; Good-night Owl!; Brown Bear, Brown Bear, What Do You See?; Roll Over!; Have You Seen My Duckling?; Alexander and the Terrible, Horrible, No Good, Very Bad Day; Do You Want to Be My Friend?; Elephant in a Well; Ask Mr. Bear; The Gingerbread Boy; Rosie's Walk; There Was an Old Woman; The House That Jack Built; The Great Big Enormous Turnip; I Know an Old Lady Who Swallowed a Fly; Mommy, Buy Me a China Doll;* and *The Judge.* Next, ask them to analyze why the sentences they selected are so memorable. Most often these analyses lead students to appreciate how rephrasing can change emphasis and clarify meaning.

TRANSFORMATIONAL-GENERATIVE APPROACH

This third theory of grammar explains how English speakers generate sentences they have never heard before. The theory of **transformational-generative grammar** explains what we do when we invent and change sentences and why the same thought takes on slightly different meanings in different sentences. Transformational-generative grammarians propose that the creation of sentences involves a deep structure and a surface structure of psycholinguistic knowledge. **Deep structure** refers to the meaning of the sentence and why that meaning can be conveyed in several forms. **Surface structure** is the specific syntax selected to communicate the deep structure. The surface structure is what is spoken, written, or sung.

To help students understand the difference between deep and surface structure, ask them to picture a white, furry rabbit. Then ask them to describe the rabbit in one sentence. Their sentences are written on the board and likely resemble the following: *The rabbit is furry and white. The furry rabbit is white. The white rabbit is furry. The rabbit I see is furry and white. The rabbit I see is white and furry. The rab-*

bit is white and furry. Once several samples have been written, explain how each sentence communicates the same meaning in different ways. You can also explain how transformational grammar enables us to understand how people can create a wide variety of active sentences, passive sentences, negative sentences, questions, and imperatives to depict the same underlying, deep meanings (see Figure 9.2).

Another set of grammar rules apply to oral English. Students need to learn how stress, juncture, gestures, body language, and pitch carry meaning, and how, in written language, capitalization, punctuation, and story grammar substitute for these oral rules to convey meaning. When students have been introduced to these three sets of English language principles, they need to learn to generate them independently. In the next section you can read how to nurture this independence for your students.

SENTENCE-COMBINING APPROACH

The goal of grammar instruction is for students to elect to use appropriate English syntax when speaking and writing. You can help students self-correct their grammar through the following instructional approaches. Because most 5-year-olds have

TRANSFORMATION *Simple Transformations*	DESCRIPTION	SAMPLE SENTENCE
1. Negative	*Not* or *n't* and auxiliary verb inserted	Lions roar. Lions don't roar.
2. Yes-No Question	Subject and auxiliary verb switched	Did the lion stalk the jungle?
3. *Wh-* Question	(*who, what, which, when, where, why*) or *how*	Why do lions roar?
4. Imperative	*You* becomes the subject	You see lions.
5. There	*There* and auxiliary verb inserted	There are cautious lions.
6. Passive	Verb changed to past participle form	Cubs are made hunters by lions.
Complex Transformations		
1. Joining	Two sentences joined using conjunctions	
2. Embedding	Sentences combined by embedding one into the other	Lions are animals. Lions are cautious. Lions are cautious animals.

FIGURE 9.2 COMPONENTS IN AN INSTRUCTIONAL PROGRAM OF STRUCTURAL (DESCRIPTIVE) GRAMMAR

While the teacher looks on, a sixth-grader helps first-graders learn about grammar after examining the sentences the younger children write. The sixth-grader uses the same sentences to show the first-graders how to vary their vocabulary by writing new beginning and ending phrases.

mastered the grammatical principles of spoken English and have thousands of words in their listening vocabulary, your job is to help them apply these principles to writing. The sentence-combining approach assists by increasing students' awareness of what language is, and cultivates their flexibility and revising abilities so that they originate more powerful sentences (O'Hare, 1973).

The sentence-combining approach begins with samples of students' own writings. You explain why grammar principles are so complex—for example, "Verbs are complicated to study, not because some ancient, devious grammar teacher conjured up conjugations to confuse students, but because as English was used over the centuries, people adopted things from other languages in an unplanned way." You can also ask students to talk about what they want to say *exactly.* "Talk almost always moves their writing forward. At every grade level, there is always more to include, more to tell. Often, talk will not only lead to longer and more fleshed-out texts, but it will also help the lilting sound of oral language to appear on the page. If we teach children the rhythm of writing, their texts will become longer and more precise" (Calkins, 1994, p. 116). Older students can create selective **cloze paragraphs** in their writings with correction fluid or self-stick notes, where the only words deleted are the verbs. A cloze paragraph is one in which words are deleted and blanks are inserted in their places. Students can guess what word can be written in the blank by knowing the rules of grammar and using them in conjunction with semantic context clues. Next, have students exchange these selective clozes with a partner. Once partners have filled the blanks in the sentences, you can ask students to compare their choices to classmates' originals and discuss how each student can improve his or her verb choices in future writing. Next, students can commit this goal to a written contract. Students' writing samples can be assessed in the future to note increased grammatical strength and whether their goals were met.

Similarly, younger students can be taught the positions, power, and functions of words through chants, choral readings, nursery rhymes, and language experience stories. For example, as you read books out loud, pause at a powerful sentence and ask why its order is so memorable. Young students can also learn by making compound subjects, predicates, and sentences. To illustrate, you can ask them to read two sentences where all words are the same but one. Then have them combine single words from both of these sentences to make one (e.g., *Rover eats kibble* + *Rover eats beef* = *Rover eats kibble and beef*). A major difficulty with students before reaching third grade is that they either "overcombine" or "undercombine" sentences as they write. Through discovery discussions you can correct the improper emphases individual students are placing on either overly short (or long) sentences in their writing.

Once students are skilled in word choice and sentence length, they can be taught to combine phrases more effectively (e.g., *Fluffy is my little kitten* + *Fluffy is my pet* = *Fluffy is my little pet kitten*). Books for younger students that contain such vivid phrase placements include *Where the Wild Things Are; The Snowy Day; Madeline; Blueberries for Sal; The Biggest Bear; Sam, Bangs, and Moonshine; The Happy Owls; A Bear Called Paddington; Mother Goose; Crow Boy; The Dead Tree; If I Found a Wistful Unicorn; Find the Cat;* and *At Mary Bloom's*.

After these lessons have been taught, you can also increase students' grammatical awareness by asking them to write a report of the steps they followed in a science experiment. When you receive this report, you write their opening two sentences on the board. You model how meaning is clarified and made interesting when redundant words and phrases are eliminated. To illustrate, Michael and Juan's first report for their sixth-grade teacher, Ms. Billick, read:

> We put dirt in cups. We put seeds in the dirt. We put the seeds one inch deep in the cups. We watered the seeds once a week. We watered the seeds on Mondays. We watered the seeds six times. The seeds made stems. The stems made leaves. Flowers came out this Wednesday!

After the above grammar lesson, their revised report read:

> After putting six inches of dirt in small paper cups, we planted pansy seeds one inch deep. We watered the seeds each Monday for six weeks. During the fifth week, stems sprouted and leaves developed. On Wednesday of the seventh week, flowers bloomed!

Last, students can practice combining sentences by using their own writings and revising them to adhere to the following phrase placement rules:

1. *Adverbs and adverbial phrases.* When they appear at the end of the sentence, they are subordinate to the main point. When placed at the beginning, they add detail or enhance the flow and beauty of the total message: for example, *The deer leaped gracefully and gently over the brook* versus *Gracefully and gently the deer leaped over the brook.*

2. *Adjective phrases* make images more vivid and convey relative importance, such as, *The fragile, budding gardenia bush grew* versus the emphasis in *The fragile gardenia bush was budding.*

3. *Prepositional phrases* added to the beginning, middle, and end of sentences embellish images and reveal substitute meanings (e.g., *For the longest time I have yearned to move west* versus *Moving west has been my deepest yearning*).

REFINING MEANING THROUGH PRECISE WORD CHOICES

When students are skilled in all three aspects of sentence combining (at the word, phrase, and sentence levels), they can learn how to use sentence patterns to enhance meaning. For younger children, this instruction can begin by embellishing basic sentence patterns in a language experience story. After writing several sentences, you can demonstrate how two sentences (with different subjects and verbs) can combine to make a more powerful statement. Explain to young students that doing so is important for their writing to become more interesting.

For older students refined meanings can be taught through a "cued format" (O'Hare, 1973). In cued refining activities, students learn to improve three weak sentences by communicating more effectively with one stronger sentence. For example:

1. The main sentence is presented: *They ate fruit.*

2. Word(s) to be inserted from a second sentence are underlined: *The fruit is <u>an orange</u>.*

3. Word(s) to be deleted are crossed out: *~~They ate~~ an apple.*

4. Connecting words, such as *and,* are written in parentheses after the sentence they connect.

5. Students combine these four parts into one sentence: *They ate an orange and an apple.*

6. They then discuss how the combination improved meaning.

Once students are skilled in combining cued sentences, they can learn to add prepositional phrases to sentences—for example, *JoAnn went* is the sentence, and *to the store, in the van,* and *to buy groceries* are the phrases. *JoAnn went to the store in the van to buy groceries* is the resultant combined form.

You can also project a **kernel sentence** (a sentence with only a noun and a verb) on the overhead projector. This kernel sentence concerns a topic or experience the class has just completed, such as, *We sang.* In this lesson several students are asked to come to the board and add to this sentence. Once statements are complete, each is analyzed. Beneath the statements students write where the sentences can be combined (students put grammatical rules and sentence expansion concepts they followed to create the statement in their own words). Students then meet in cooperative groups to create a chart of these self-generated grammatical rules, which is later posted above the editing committee table for future reference.

Another activity begins when you copy a page of children's literature that has a particularly powerful message. As you read the page orally, ask students to read silently. Students check sentences that they like and discuss why they prefer these sentences. Then they write (in their own words) the grammatical rules that govern each sentence they selected. They add these rules to the chart described above. Last, you can assess how students use these rules in their next composition.

The following activity can also be used at all age levels. It is called **writing imitations** (Linden & Whimbey, 1990). Students read one of the following literature sources and replicate a sentence from that book to integrate its appealing nature and communicative power in their writing and speaking (e.g., *The Polar Express* can illustrate effective compound sentences): *The Borrowers; The Twenty-One Balloons; The Cricket in Times Square; A Wary Snake in a Fig Tree; The Space Child's Mother Goose; Jump or Jiggle; A Chocolate Moose for Dinner; The King Who Rained; How a Horse Grew Hoarse on the Site Where He Sighted a Bare Bear; Ask Mr. Bear; One Was Johnny; Drummer Hoff; Mommy, Buy Me a China Doll; The Rainbow of American Folk Tales and Legends; Tall Tale America; Heroes in American Folklore;* and *Whoppers, Tall Tales and Other Lies.* Finally, you can give students an increasing number of ideas and transformations to make varied sentence types. You also can teach them the purposes of phrase markers such as *though, but, yet,* and *in this case.*

In closing, students can assess their own growth in grammatical awareness. They can write a pre- and then a postinstructional story. They can compare their prewriting to their postwriting and describe how their increased conscious knowledge of grammatical principles positively influenced their writing ability. The benefits of the sentence-combining approach can be immediate, even for first-graders, as shown in Figure 9.3, which was written by Michael after only one grammar lesson.

Translation: My favorite candy is skittles because it tastes good and they are my favorite color.

FIGURE 9.3 MICHAEL'S FIRST-GRADE, POSTINSTRUCTIONAL WRITING SAMPLE DEMONSTRATING THE SENTENCE-COMBINING APPROACH OF GRAMMAR INSTRUCTION

REVISING COMMITTEES APPROACH

The **revising committees approach** method of teaching grammar follows an **impromptu mode of instruction**, providing grammar instruction as needed. This approach teaches grammar individually and in minilessons while students are revising their writings. A form to accompany this approach can assist students in developing grammatical awareness (see Figure 9.4). Students check the description within each category of the writing evaluation form in Figure 9.4 that best depicts a peer's level of competence. You can also use this form as an assessment for your entire class

WRITING OVERVIEW		
MEANING	SPECIAL FLAIR	
	VERY CLEAR	
	GAPS IN MEANING	
	CONFUSING	
ORGANIZATION	EFFECTIVE	
	APPROPRIATE	
	IRRELEVANT	
	NO FOCUS	
CONVENTIONS	ADDITIONAL MEANING	
	CORRECT MECHANICS	
	SEVERAL ERRORS	
	ERRORS INTERFERE	
THOUGHT QUALITY	ACCURATE	
	LOGICAL	
	ILLOGICAL	
	INACCURATE	
WORD SELECTION	EVOCATIVE	
	COMPLETE	
	SOME PRECISION	
	LACKS PRECISION	
STORY STRUCTURE	CAPTIVATING	
	SMOOTH	
	SOME CONFUSION	
	LACKS STRUCTURE	

FIGURE 9.4 AN ENTIRE CLASS WRITING EVALUATION RUBRIC

by writing students' names across the top. (An enlarged ready-to-use version of this form appears on the website that accompanies this textbook.)

When students discover a new and effective sentence structure or word choice in a peer's paper, they can ask their peers what they were thinking when they implemented that choice. In this way, students can learn to incorporate this structure into their future compositions. This revising committee approach works well because students work together to apply grammatical principles.

Last of all, the revising committee approach uses students' self-initiated discussions about grammar. An example of one such discussion among Michael, Juan, and Allison in their sixth-grade class appears below. As they disagree about the use of the correct grammatical time frame in which they want their story to occur, they internalize verb tense knowledge.

Michael: [reading] "In Lancaster, Wisconsin, a small eight-year-old boy found a lost cat." *Found* is past tense. Is he finding him right now?

Allison: Are we telling the story over again or is it really happening right now?

Juan: Half the story is past tense and half the story is present tense.

Allison: I think it's present tense because, see, he says, "How long will I have to stay?"

Michael: How about "While they were gone, Tommy started walking around"?

Juan: What do you like, past or present?

Michael: [aloud to himself] She's going to say present.

Allison: Present tense. Just keep it present tense.

(Adapted from Nessel & Dixon, 1981, p. 235)

As a final note, you can teach students all three descriptions of grammar and use each of these instructional approaches. Rather than being mutually exclusive, when combined they complement each other. The six daily lessons that follow illustrate how such an integration can occur. These lesson plans also demonstrate ways to teach impromptu oral grammar lessons, increase students' sensitivity to point of view, and show how to use students' writing samples as the content for grammar lessons.

SECTION 2   PUTTING THEORY INTO PRACTICE

Teaching Students How to Revise

Language arts textbooks are the traditional material used to teach grammar. The way in which these books are used is crucial to their success, however. No longer should you ask students to memorize rules in artificial contexts and isolated, end-of-chapter drills. Instead, you and your students should refer to pages in the text that describe specific grammatical principles at points when students need them to improve their writing or speaking. Lessons should be on an individual or small-group basis and determined by the errors students make in their speaking and writing. In this modified textbook approach, textbooks are rarely referred to for large-group instruction. Rather, grammar textbooks serve as reference manuals, much like dictionaries and encyclopedias. When students lack a certain grammatical principle, you can develop minilessons, and students refer to examples in the text as a way to internalize the principle they need. Next, the principle is applied to students' writings rather than through the drill and practice exercises in grammar books. Last, you can ask students to use the principle in their writing that day and assess their skill.

ACTIVITIES THAT DEVELOP REVISING ABILITIES

Teaching oral and written grammar lessons, recognition of differing points of view, idioms, and oral rephrasing are among the best lessons to increase students' abilities to rephrase when speaking and writing, to paraphrase when speaking and listening, to reread when confused while reading, and to revise when writing.

ORAL–WRITTEN GRAMMATICAL AWARENESS

Developing students' ability to use correct oral and written sentence structures and word choices is important. Some researchers recommend that students as young as 5 years old learn to clarify their ideas. They support the position that such instruction should begin when a student asks a question about spoken or written English (Purcell-Gates, 1999; Graves, 1998). They suggest impromptu teaching begins by responding to students' questions with minilessons on grammar. For example, if a first-grader asks, "What is a noun?" you should provide the definition. Following this explanation, the student can read one of the books concerning grammatical awareness on Literature Card 20. After reading, you can conduct a discovery discussion to identify the child's favorite nouns in the story, emphasizing the importance he or she should place on selecting such specific, vivid nouns when speaking and writing.

As a second illustration, study the following example of an impromptu lesson. Loretta, a student in Ms. Billick's class said, "I ain't got no pencil." Ms. Billick could have replied, "You do not have a pencil," but this correction would not have been effective because it does not model the appropriate grammatical structure. (It uses second-person point of view rather than first-person.) Instead, Ms. Billick responded by using the correct grammatical principles for Loretta's sentence—that is, "I don't have a pencil, either. Let's find one." With this explicit, first-person example Loretta could hear how to use Standard English by making the following choices:

1. Omitting *ain't*.
2. Adding the verb *do* to the predicate to indicate present tense.
3. Changing the nonstandard negative contraction *ain't* to the standard negative contraction *don't*.
4. Changing the verb tense from present to present perfect.
5. Eliminating a double negative—that is, changing *no* pencil to *a* pencil.

Literature Card 20

LITERATURE THAT DEVELOPS GRAMMATICAL AWARENESS

Good Books with a Lot of Pictures about Grammar

Mine All Mine by R. Heller, 1997 Grosset & Dunlap

Alphabet by S. Boynton, 1983 Workman

Guinea Pig ABC by K. Duke, 1983 Dutton

A Children's Zoo by T. Hoban, 1985 Greenwillow

The Very Hungry Caterpillar by E. Carle, 1979 Collins

The Z Was Zapped by C. Van Allsburg, 1987 Houghton-Mifflin

It's Not Easy Being a Bunny by M. Sadler, 1983 Beginner Books

Amazing Animal Alphabet Adventures by R. & M. Chouinard, 1988 Doubleday

If You Give a Mouse a Cookie by L. Numeroff, 1985 Harper & Row

Hailstones and Halibut Bones by M. O'Neill, 1989 Doubleday

Where the Sidewalk Ends by S. Silverstein, 1984 Columbia

Smoky Night by E. Bunting, 1994 Harcourt

A Kettle of Hawks and Other Wildlife Groups by J. Arnosky, 1990 Lothrop

All About Where by T. Hoban, 1991 Greenwillow

Over in the Meadow by P. Galdone, 1988 Simon & Schuster

Good Books to Tell You a Lot about Grammar

The Girl Who Wouldn't Get Married by R. Grass, 1983 Four Winds Press

I Think I Thought and Other Tricky Verbs by M. Terban, 1984 Clarion

Nice or Nasty: A Book of Opposites by N. & M. Butterworth, 1987 Little, Brown

Over, Under, and Through and Other Spatial Concepts by T. Hoban, 1973 Macmillan

Slithery Snakes and Other Aids to Children's Writing by W. Petty & M. Bowen, 1967 Appleton-Century-Crofts

A Cache of Jewels and Other Collective Nouns by R. Heller, 1987 Grosset & Dunlap

Kites Sail High: A Book about Verbs by R. Heller, 1988 Grosset & Dunlap

Many Luscious Lollipops by R. Heller, 1989 Grosset & Dunlap

Merry-Go-Round: A Book about Nouns by R. Heller, 1990 Grosset & Dunlap

More Than One by T. Hoban, 1981 Greenwillow

A Snake Is Totally Tail by J. Barrett, 1983 Atheneum

Herds of Words by P. MacCarthy, 1991 Dial

Checking Your Grammar by M. Terban, 1994 Scholastic

Up, Up and Away: A Book about Adverbs by R. Heller, 1991 Grosset & Dunlap

Good Books If You Are Just Beginning to Learn about Grammar

A Funny Fish Story by J. Wylie, 1984 Children's Press

A Seed, a Flower, a Minute, an Hour by J. Blos, 1994 Aladdin

The Day Jimmy's Boa Ate the Wash by T. Noble, 1980 Dial

Brown Bear in a Brown Chair by I. Hale, 1983 Atheneum

Bicycle Bear by M. Muntean, 1983 Parents Magazine Press

Silly Goose by J. Kent, 1983 Prentice-Hall

Snake In, Snake Out by L. Bancheck, 1978 Crowell

Inside, Outside, Upside Down by S. & J. Berenstain, 1968 Random House

Animalia by G. Base, 1986 Henry Abrams

Chicken Soup with Rice by M. Sendak, 1976 Weston Woods

The Vanishing Pumpkin by T. Johnson, 1983 Putnam

Summer Is . . . by C. Zolotow, 1983 Crowell

Some Things Go Together by C. Zolotow, 1969 Crowell

A Children's Zoo by T. Hoban, 1981 Greenwillow

Grammar by B. Martin Jr., 1993 Simon & Schuster

Books That Have Several Chapters about Grammar

How to Improve Your Grammar and Usage by M. Rowk, 1994

Super, Super, Superwords by B. McMillan, 1989 Lothrop, Lee & Shepard

Esteban and the Ghost by S. Hancock, 1983 Dial

The Important Book by M. Wise, 1949 Harper

Word Works: Why the Alphabet Is a Kid's Best Friend by C. Kaye, 1985 Little, Brown

"The Grammatical Witch" in *Best Witches* by J. Yolen, 1989 Putnam

Alpha Beta Chowder by J. Steig, 1992 Harper

"An Unassuming Owl" (who and whom) in *The New Kid on the Block* by J. Prelutsky, 1984 Greenwillow

"Where Do Those Words Come From?" by C. Pomerantz in B. S. De Regniers *Sing a Song of Popcorn*, 1988 Scholastic

Jiggle Wiggle Prance by S. Noll, 1987

I Never Saw a Purple Cow and Other Nonsense Rhymes by E. C. Clark, 1991 Little

Grammar Smart Junior: Good Grammar Made Easy by Liz Buffa, 1995 Random House

How to Make Grammar Fun and Easy! by E. Ryan, 1992 Troll

In a Pickle and Other Funny Idioms by M. Terban, 1983 Clarion

Thus, a minilesson structured similarly to the following can help students overcome oral grammatical difficulties:

Loretta: I ain't got no pencil.

Ms. Billick: I don't have a pencil either.

Loretta: Where can I get a pencil?

Ms. Billick: When I don't have a pencil, I _____. What are you going to do in the future when you don't have a pencil?

Loretta: When I don't have a pencil, I'll_____.

Ms. Billick: Would you like me to tell you what you did to make your meaning clearer?

Loretta: Yes.

Ms. Billick then told Loretta the five changes listed on the previous page and explained that incorporating these principles into her speech would make her language easier for others to understand. She then said that less formal language may communicate well in casual settings, but standard English usually communicates better in formal settings. Next, she asked Loretta to select a book listed on Literature Card 21 to learn more. The next day Loretta told the class a new, oral grammatical principle she had discovered in that book.

Written grammatical errors can also be addressed by such individualized minilessons. For example, a successful minilesson to eliminate run-on sentences involves peer editors. Such editors can make a slash mark between the sixteenth and seventeenth words of any sentence in a classmate's writing. This slash indicates that the sentence exceeded preferred sentence lengths. Then, two students work together to revise the longest sentences. A second minilesson to reduce sentence length has students read their writings aloud, but to themselves. Any time they take a breath before the end of a sentence, the student can use this breath as a clue that the sentence may need to be reduced in length. Reading their writings aloud is also an effective strategy to assist students in locating inappropriate verb tenses and noun–verb agreements.

To sum up, the lessons up to this point in the chapter have demonstrated how using the modified textbook, revising committee approach, minilesson, sentence-combining approach, and peer editors can improve oral and written grammar. The following lessons can expand your instructional repertoire by depicting three ways to teach grammatical concepts in small, need-based student groups.

RECOGNIZING DIFFERING POINTS OF VIEW

As a language arts teacher, part of your responsibility is to prepare students to contribute to an international family of human beings. Students' lives are increasingly influenced by points of view that vary greatly by national and cultural heritage. The purpose of this lesson is to (1) increase students' sensitivity to points of view, (2) present methods of discerning how points of view impact ideas, and (3) teach strategies to resolve conflicts between differing points of view. To begin this lesson, you can teach students that events can be explained from four perspectives. For exam-

Literature Card 21

**BOOKS FOR STUDENTS WITH DIFFERENT DIALECTS OR WHO HAVE
DIFFICULTY WITH ENGLISH SPEAKING PATTERNS**

*The following books increase students' awareness of various dialects and demonstrate common sentence
pattern and word usage in the English language.*

I Hate English! by E. Levine, 1989 Scholastic
What Do I Say? by N. Simon, 1967 Whitman
Nathaniel Talking and other books by E. Greenfield, 1973 Black Butterfly Children
His Own Where and other books by J. Jordan, 1971 Crowell
Amelia Bedelia (Series) by P. Parish, 1963 Harper & Row
The King Who Rained and other books by Gwynne, 1970 Simon & Schuster
Sounder by W. Armstrong, 1987 ACB-Clio
Animals Should Definitely Not Act Like People and other books by J. Barrett, 1980 Atheneum
When the Sky Is Like Lace by Horowitz, 1975 Lippincott
Amifika by L. Clifton, 1975 Holt, Rinehart & Winston
Git Along, Old Scudder by S. Gammel, 1983 Lothrop
My Brother Fine with Me by L. Clifton, 1975 Holt
Lordy, Aunt Hattie and other books by J. Thomas, 1973 Harper
Secret Dreamer, Secret Dreams by F. Heide, 1978 Lippincott
Victor by C. K. Galbraith, 1971 Little, Brown
Dmitry, A Young Soviet Immigrant by J. Bernstein, 1992 Lippincott
The Boy Who Wouldn't Talk by R. Bouchard, 1989 Viking

My Special Best Words by J. Steptoe, 1974 Viking
The Friends by R. Guy, 1973 Holt, Rinehart & Winston
Wind in the Willows by G. Grahame, 1983 Adama Books
He Who Run-Far by H. Fredericksen, 1970 Young Scott
Morris Goes to School by B. Wiseman, 1970 Harper & Row
A Hero Ain't Nothing But a Sandwich by A. Childress. 1973 Coward, McCann, & Geoghegan
Harold and the Purple Crayon by M. Johnson, 1955 Harper & Row
The Phantom Tollbooth by R. Juster, 1961 Random House
Amos and Boris and other books by W. Steig, 1971 Little, Brown
Annie and the Old One and other books by S. Miles, 1971 Little, Brown
Cajun Night Before Christmas by H. Jacobs, 1994 Houghton Mifflin
The Magical Adventures of Pretty Pearl by V. Hamilton, 1983 Harper & Row
What Happened to Heather Hopkowitz by C. Herman, 1995 Aladdin
The Chinese Daughter by E. F. Lattimore, 1960 Morrow
The Night Journey by K. Lasky, 1981 F. Waurn

ple, Ms. Billick taught the following about point of view: (1) **first person,** uses the words *I* and *we*; (2) **second person** is one person telling another what to do and uses the word *you*; (3) **third person** reports events to people who are not present, using the words *they* and *he* or *she*; and (4) **omniscient point of view** sees all and knows all and uses the word *one*. She explained how one's perspective can alter an interpretation.

Father Water, Mother Woods

To demonstrate this, she read *Father Water, Mother Woods: Essays on Fishing and Hunting in the North Woods* (1994). This book incorporated several points of view. After reading the book, she divided students into response groups and asked them to retell the story from a different point of view. Each group shared the rendition that they decided to depict and described how their point of view established a new perspective on story events. Following these sharings with a second practice session of taking a new point of view, students selected a current event involving more than one country. After studying the cultural and societal values of the country their group selected and contacting officials from the ambassadors' or consulate offices, each group prepared position papers about the current event from their country's perspective, and compared them to classmates' reports.

As a third lesson, you can have students role-play situations in their lives in which they are in conflict with another person. In these role-plays, students assume the role (and point of view) of the person with whom they are in conflict. Classmates assume the role of the student and others involved in the difficulty. After the enactment, each student writes what was learned from assuming another person's perspective.

USING YOUR OWN, FAMOUS PEOPLE'S, OR STUDENTS' REVISIONS AS SAMPLES

You can make a transparency of Thomas Jefferson's first draft of the Constitution (see Figure 9.5) to open a discussion of the importance of grammatical principles (or you can use any writing sample that shows how revisions are made). Point to each change the author made and do a think-aloud for each addition, deletion, substitution, and reorganization. Then follow up by revising one of your compositions on the overhead as students listen and watch. Students can review before-and-after revisions of their classmates' writings in group settings as each author describes the reasons behind their changes. Doing so enables students to recognize new ways others combine sentences, and they learn new phrase placements that they are likely to emulate.

Once students are comfortable with basic grammatical principles, you are ready to use their grammatical awareness to expand their creative, expressive abilities. The

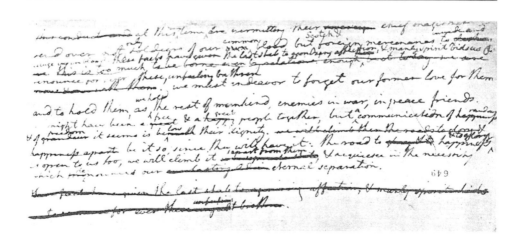

FIGURE 9.5 A PHOTOGRAPH OF THOMAS JEFFERSON'S FIRST DRAFT OF A SECTION OF THE DECLARATION OF INDEPENDENCE

following lesson demonstrates how to do so with idioms, figurative language, metaphors, similes, personifications, and proverbs.

TEACHING IDIOMS, FIGURATIVE LANGUAGE, METAPHORS, AND SIMILES

An **idiom** is a complex expression whose meaning cannot be derived from the meanings of its individual words (such as, "raining cats and dogs"). **Figurative language** refers to phrases that convey a feeling or thought that is characterized by painting an image (such as, "so nervous that my stomach has butterflies in it"). **Metaphors** are figures of speech that make a comparison between two things that have something in common, but the words *like* or *than* are not used to make the comparison (such as, "clouds are billowy pillows"). **Similes** are metaphors that make comparisons between two things with the words *like, as,* or *than* (such as, "soft as silk"). **Personification** is a figure of speech in which nonhuman things are given human qualities (such as Meisong's story about frisky feet in Chapter 8). **Proverbs** are sayings that describe a truth about life (such as, "You can't judge a book by its cover").

These advanced grammatical structures occur frequently in literature and in conversational speech. This lesson can help students to better understand other people's literal and inferred meanings and to write and speak more precisely and vividly. Each of these literary devices differs in the extent to which its literal meanings relate to its implied meanings. As you would expect, students have an easier time when introduced to a device whose literal meanings are more closely related to their personal experiences.

Once you have read a book that contains several of these devices, you can develop students' awareness of their power and build up their self-selected use of each type. You can begin by describing how such expressions are used (and the importance of learning what they mean) by showing the cartoon in Figure 9.6 on the overhead.

You can also place an idiom, proverb, or figurative language on the board every day for 2 months. Ask students to reflect on its meaning and discuss it, in a half-minute activity at the end of school as everyone prepares to leave for home. Then you can encourage students to use the device in a writing assignment, or you can use it in the next morning message. (See Table 9.1 for examples.)

Another effective lesson is to guide students to reconcile opposing positions in proverbs, idioms, and figurative language. As Manzo (1981) found, "Most often

FIGURE 9.6 EXAMPLE OF THE NEED TO LEARN FIGURATIVE LANGUAGE

Source: NANCY reprinted by permission of United Feature Syndicate, Inc.

TABLE 9.1 EXAMPLES OF PROVERBS, IDIOMS, AND FIGURATIVE LANGUAGE TO INCREASE GRAMMATICAL SKILL

PROVERBS

Stretch your feet only as far as your sheet will permit. (Spanish)

Look before you leap.

You can't judge a book by its cover.

The genius, wit and spirit of a nation are discovered in its proverbs. (English)

There is no proverb which is not true. (Spanish)

A stitch in time saves nine.

Every man has his price. (originally Lord Chesterfield)

What soon grows old? Gratitude. (Greek)

You do not teach the paths of the forest to an old gorilla. (African)

Lend to one who will not repay, and you will provoke his dislike. (Chinese)

Only in the grave is there rest. (Yiddish)

IDIOMS AND FIGURATIVE LANGUAGE

hold your horses	if the shoe fits, wear it	wet behind the ears
hit the ceiling	keep something under one's hat	under the weather
killing two birds with one stone	knock someone's socks off	between the devil and the deep blue sea
don't beat around the bush	let the cat out of the bag	give someone the cold shoulder
you don't have a leg to stand on	monkey business	keep your shirt on
he had me in stitches	out of the woods	bury your head in the sand
all ears	play it by ear	in one ear and out the other
at the end of one's rope	raise a stink	white elephant
bend over backward	shake a leg	straight from the horse's mouth
cat got your tongue?	smell a rat	chip off the old block
dressed to kill	spill the beans	get into someone's hair
elbow grease	spread oneself too thin	paint the town red
eyes bigger than your stomach	tongue-in-cheek	thinking cap
for the birds	wet blanket	feather in your cap
go to bat for someone	straw that broke the camel's back	

World Treasury of Proverbs

this . . . step has the most profound effect upon intellectual growth. Through it students come to realize that most things are set in a dynamic tension to one another. Life and learning are a process of reconciling seemingly opposing positions" (1981, p. 414). Proverbs can be found on the website that accompanies this book and in *World Treasury of Proverbs; Book of Proverbs, Maxims and Famous Phrases; In a Pickle;* and *Mad as a Wet Hen.*

If students wish to learn more about idioms, the following books can be helpful: *Hog on Ice and Other Curious Expressions* (Funk, 1948); *Tenderfeet and Ladyfingers;*

Eight Ate; A Feast of Homonym Riddles; In a Pickle and Other Funny Idioms (Terban, 1983); *Put Your Foot in Your Mouth and Other Silly Sayings* (Cox, 1980); *From the Horse's Mouth* (Nevin & Nevin, 1977); *Chin Music: Tall Talk and Other Talk* (Schwartz, 1979); and *A Surfeit of Similes* (Juster, 1989).

The following books contain different expressions commonly used in various regions of our country, or have literal illustrations of idiomatic expressions: *Amelia Bedelia* books by Peggy Parish, *The King Who Rained* by Fred Gwynne, and *The Burning Questions of Bingo Brown* by Betsy Byars. More books that contain vivid examples of figurative language are *The Sixteen Hand Horse* by Fred Gwynne, *The Dove, Guppies in Tuxedos,* and *Mad as a Wet Hen* by Marvin Terban, *Corduroy* by Don Freeman, *The Napping House* and *Quick as a Cricket* by Audrey Wood, and *Thirteen* by Remy Charlip and Jerry Joyner.

Native American books like *The Girl Who Loved Wild Horses* and *Dancing Teepees: Poems of American Indian Youth* by Virginia Driving Hawk Kneve (1989) also contain many metaphors and can be used as models of their use in clarifying meaning. *A Writer* by Goffstein (1984) is a 50-page book that carries one sustained metaphor throughout. This metaphor was of a writer's work being compared to a gardener's. Ms. Billick also showed a movie to demonstrate a different version of the metaphors expressed in *Dancing Teepees.* During these minilessons, students learned to

- Note and appreciate the gems in their writing
- Imagine many types of figurative language
- Make decisions about how to improve past and future writings and record these thoughts
- Study qualities of good writers
- Study specific types of figurative language
- Develop self-evaluation
- Record insights about the connections between reading, writing, speaking, revising, listening, viewing, and thinking
- Ask themselves: "Can I say this better by using an idiom, metaphor, or figurative language phrase?"

USING ORAL REPHRASING TO INCREASE WRITTEN REVISIONS

Ms. Billick has taught every grade level since she began her career. Through this time she ascertained that a few minilessons are valuable and enjoyable to students of all ages and refine their revision thinking in consecutively advanced ways. Using oral rephrasing as a prelude to revisions in writing is one of these. With this competence in hand, students draw secret pals from a jar of classmates' names. For one week, students note in their journals the observations they make of that person, being sure that the person does not know they are being watched. At the end of the day, students refer to these notes as they describe their observations to the class without mentioning the person's name or giving obvious clues. The class guesses which of them was being observed and tells the speaker which detail was most valuable to them. When all have spoken and learned how to phrase details, the class writes a description of an object in the class using as many details as possible. When finished, students mount their writings on a bulletin board. Then classmates revise their friends' sentences with colored markers. In Ms. Billick's class, for instance, Juan changed Meisong's opening sentence:

> Meisong originally wrote: "The object is round, and is eight inches in diameter."

> Juan suggested the revised sentence to incorporate more specific images: "The object is the same size as a basketball."

In summary, Graves (1994) stated, "Until I discover what I want to say with conviction, my nouns can be thin and colorless and the verbs lifeless and imprecise" (p. 171). The energy and force that revision provides can also enhance students' abilities to choose more precise, vivid, and imaginable words.

INTEGRATING THE LANGUAGE ARTS

SSR, SSW, SSE, and Author's Theatres to Build Grammatical Awareness

Ms. Billick uses SSR (sustained silent reading) or DEAR (drop everything and read) times and SSW (sustained silent writing) time in her class every day, and encourages SSE in which parents and students set aside time one night a week to read and write together. These sessions are times in the day when teachers, students, and in some schools all members of the school staff stop and read books silently (or write silently) about topics of their choice. These SSR, DEAR, SSW, and SSE times end with sharing sessions. At this time, Ms. Billick and other teachers use an optional practice called Author's Theatre in which students can choose classmates to act out the stories they write. This not only adds legitimacy to their role as authors and play writers, but also encourages children to bring their "play lives" into the official world of school (Dyson, 1995, p. 325). Through these media, they not only integrate language arts and literature but also use the "remarkable posers of 'meaning making'—the processes of invention and crafting." Students must use many advanced grammatical concepts to transform narratives into plays. Because this activity is enjoyable, it adds value to the learning process (Dyson, 1999).

INSIDE CULTURALLY ENRICHED CLASSROOMS

Attention to Cultural Sensitivity in Stories

Story grammar, grammar, and the need for revision vary according to some students' cultural values. For example, Meisong is from the Vietnamese culture and often omits inflectional endings such as *ed* and *s*. For this reason she profits from the paired and group revision activities in this chapter. Similarly, Ms. Billick became concerned that her Native American students were writing long stories that did not seem to "go anywhere" and did not contain the climax and ending components of story grammar. In discussions with Gail Martin, a teacher-researcher with Arapaho students in Wyoming, Ms. Billick discovered the reason these students' stories rambled along with no definite start or finish. Distinct differences exist between Arapaho stories and stories told and written at school. Arapaho stories are not written down. They are told in what we might call "serial form," continued night after night. A "good" story in that culture lasts at least 7 nights for a minimum of 3 hours a night. Also, these stories never really end because Arapahos believe there is no ending to life and no need for conclusions. After discovering this, Ms. Billick encouraged her Arapaho students to describe in the opening paragraph what was most important to them personally about a story and then begin their tale. She also taught them to summarize points made thus far in their tales, with a written concluding paragraph, so they could learn English story grammar without interfering with their cultural heritage.

Another method of strengthening and responding to students' cultural sensitivity is to assist students who are writing in a second language to increase their revision abilities by teaching them the English vocabulary that addresses their basic survival needs, which are the topics most often described in their work. For example, Ms. Billick asks students to write (on a chart that is displayed over the revising center table) their first language equivalent or to create a drawing for each English word. This chart remains in the room until all students are using these phrases appropriately in their revisions. The chart Ms. Billick's room created is shown in Figure 9.7 along with a list of additional survival words you may want to teach your students.

Sarah, Plain and Tall

Similarly, students who speak a different language must be taught the structure of the English sentence, the order of adjectives and adverbs, and subject and verb agreement. An effective method is to introduce these concepts orally and to use objects as you do so. For example, bilingual students hear and then say the words *under, up, on, beside, table, chair, book, in, over, behind* as they place a book in appropriate locations relative to a chair or table. Another method is to provide **story frames**. These frames provide the basic structure of English sentences so students with cultural interferences can focus mainly on the content they want to communicate. As shown in Figure 9.8, Meisong was able to communicate an in-depth character analysis of her favorite character in *Sarah, Plain and Tall*. This is a task she would not have been able to complete without Ms. Billick's assistance in making the story frame for her.

RECOGNIZING AND REPORTING PROGRESS

Writing Rubrics

Throughout this chapter rubrics have been recommended to evaluate students' rereading, rephrasing, and rewriting abilities. **Rubrics** are continuous descriptions that assess the quality and progress of student work in many categories. Teachers use rubrics to rank standards, to evaluate writing samples, and to report writing progress to students and parents. Rubrics can provide benchmarks for achievement in specific areas that students need to master before their writing competencies can improve. As shown in Figure 9.9, the Kentucky Department of Education has developed rubrics for every grade level. These rubrics are samples of how you can assess your students' writing abilities. Other examples of rubrics include the

run　　　　walk　　　　sit　　　　eat

happy　　　sad　　　angry　　　thinking　　　sleeping

dreaming　　　hungry　　　thirsty　　　sick

Essential Survival Words

1. Poison
2. Danger
3. Police
4. Emergency
5. Stop
6. Hot
7. Walk
8. Caution
9. Exit
10. Men
11. Women
12. Warning
13. Entrance
14. Help
15. Off
16. On
17. Explosives
18. Flammable
19. Doctor
20. Go
21. Telephone
22. Boys
23. Contaminated
24. Ladies
25. Girls
26. Open
27. Out
28. Combustible
29. Closed
30. Condemned
31. Up
32. Gentlemen
33. Pull
34. Down
35. Detour
36. Gasoline
37. Inflammable
38. In
39. Push
40. Information
41. Lifeguard
42. Private
43. Quiet
44. Look
45. Wanted

Essential Survival Phrases

1. Don't walk
2. Fire escape
3. Fire extinguisher
4. Do not enter
5. First aid
6. Deep water
7. External use only
8. High voltage
9. No trespassing
10. Railroad crossing
11. Restrooms
12. Do not touch
13. Do not use near open flame
14. Do not inhale fumes
15. One way
16. Do not cross
17. Do not use near heat
18. Keep out
19. Keep off
20. Wrong way
21. No fires
22. No swimming
23. Watch your step
24. Watch for children
25. No diving
26. Stop for pedestrians
27. Post office
28. Slippery when wet
29. Help wanted
30. Slow down
31. No admittance
32. Proceed at your own risk
33. Step down
34. No parking
35. Keep closed
36. No turns
37. Beware of dog
38. School zone
39. Dangerous curve
40. Hospital zone
41. Out of order

FIGURE 9.7 SURVIVAL WORDS TO TEACH BILINGUAL STUDENTS

Story Frame: Character Analysis

Directions: Please fill in the missing information. Use your own ideas from reading the book and seeing the film.

Sarah is an important character in the story *Sarah, Plain and Tall*. In the film version she is played by the actress Glenn Close. Sarah is important to the story because _She comes and gets them help in bad times_ .

The book tells us that Sarah is homesick for Maine. She _swims in the lake_ and _works in her garden_ to remind her of home. The film helps us to understand Sarah's feelings by _saying stuff like "I wish I had never come here"_ .

The film also showed _that she wanted to make a difference in their life_ .

In the story Sarah was a _strange woman,_ and _she was a nice woman_ .

In the film Glenn Close made her seem _very strong-hearted_ and _very independent and did what she wanted to do_ .

Both the story and film showed Sarah _was going to be very hard also she did what she wanted to do_

I think that Sarah was _very kind and loving,_ but I wish that _they didn't stop when they got married_ .

Meisong 6th grade

FIGURE 9.8 STORY FRAME TO TEACH CHARACTER ANALYSIS

Source: Adapted from "I Liked the Book Better: Comparing Film and Text to Build Critical Comprehension," by P. Duncan, 1993, *The Reading Teacher, 46*(8), p. 722. Reprinted by permission of the International Reading Association. Copyright © 1993 by the International Reading Association. All rights reserved.

following: focused wholistic scoring sheets for writing; checklists for evaluating practice essays and persuasive essays; analyses of the composing process; analyses of spelling skills; checklists for evaluating skills in using punctuation marks; writing assessments of content, style, and mechanics; reading continuum checklists; and writing evaluation checklists, among others.

GRADES 3–4

	IDEAS AND CONTENT WRITING	ORGANIZATION WRITING	STYLE WRITING
6	Stays fully focused on topic/task Includes thorough and complete ideas and information Shows active interest in topic	Has clear order	Risks using dynamic words Is fluent and easy to read
5	Stays mostly focused on topic/task Includes many important ideas and information Shows active interest in topic	Has clear order	Takes risks with words Is fluent and easy to read
4	Is partially focused on topic Includes some important ideas and information Shows some interest in topic	Has some order	Takes some risks with words Is readable
3	Strays from focus on topic Includes some ideas and information Shows some interest in topic	Has some order	Uses ordinary words Is mostly readable
2	Strays from focus on topic Includes very few ideas or little information Shows little interest in topic	Has little order	Uses ordinary words Is hard to read
1	Has no focus on topic Includes almost no ideas or information Shows little or no interest in topic	Has little order	Struggles with words Is hard to read

FIGURE 9.9 EXAMPLES OF ANALYTIC WRITING DEVELOPMENT RUBRICS

Source: From the Kentucky Department of Education, Lexington, KY.

DEVELOPING TECHNOLOGICAL COMPETENCIES

Child Safety, Classroom Home Pages, and Grammar Resources on the Computer and Internet

Child Safety.   Parents express concern that Internet searches could result in students accessing inappropriate information. You can restrict access to certain sites without limiting students' knowledge gains from the Internet with blocking software such as the following: Surfwatch—www.surfwatch.com/; Cyber Patrol—www.solidoak.com/cysitter.htm; or Net Nanny—www.netnanny.com. You can also use Internet sites that screen out inappropriate material (e.g., Yahooligans—

GRADES 5–8

	IDEAS AND CONTENT WRITER	ORGANIZATION WRITER	STYLE WRITER	VOICE WRITER
6	Stays focused on task/topic Includes thorough and complete ideas and information	Organizes ideas logically	Commands dynamic vocabulary Demonstrates writing technique Uses varied sentence patterns	Effectively adjusts language and tone to task and reader Shows active interest in topic
5	Stays mostly focused on task/topic Includes many important ideas and information	Organizes ideas logically	Uses dynamic vocabulary Demonstrates writing technique Uses some varied sentence patterns	Effectively adjusts language and tone to task and reader Shows active interest in topic
4	Stays partially focused on task/topic Includes some important ideas and information	Organizes ideas logically	Uses ordinary vocabulary Attempts varied sentence patterns	Attempts to adjust language and tone to task and reader Shows some interest in topic
3	Strays from focus on task/topic Includes some ideas and information	Attempts to organize ideas logically	Uses ordinary vocabulary Relies mostly on simple sentences	Attempts to adjust language and tone to task and reader Shows some interest in topic
2	Misunderstands task/topic Includes very few ideas or little information	Does not organize ideas logically	Uses limited vocabulary Relies mostly on simple sentences	May use language and tone inappropriate to task and reader Shows little interest in topic
1	Has no focus on task/topic Includes almost no ideas or information	Does not organize ideas logically	Struggles with limited vocabulary Has problems with sentence construction	May use language and tone inappropriate to task and reader Shows no interest in topic

FIGURE 9.9 (CONTINUED)

CHECKLIST FOR EVALUATING PRACTICE ESSAY ANSWERS
AND PERSUASIVE ESSAYS

	BELOW AVERAGE	AVERAGE	ABOVE AVERAGE
1. The writer answered the question directly.	1	2	3
2. There was an introductory sentence that restated the essay question or took a position on the question.	1	2	3
3. The essay was organized with major points or ideas that were made obvious to the reader.	1	2	3
4. The essay had relevant details or examples to prove and clarify each point.	1	2	3
5. The writer used transitions to cue the reader.	1	2	3
6. The writer had knowledge of the content and made sense.	1	2	3

GUIDELINES FOR PERSUASIVE ESSAYS

	BELOW AVERAGE	AVERAGE	ABOVE AVERAGE
1. Posed a problem and students took a stand and defended it.	1	2	3
2. Had appropriate length and clear statement of thesis.	1	2	3
3. Used sound inferences, good organization.	1	2	3
4. Stated relevant alternative positions.	1	2	3
5. Fairly portrayed position and gave reasons for it.	1	2	3
6. Grammar, punctuation, and style.	1	2	3
7. Stated conclusions and avoided exaggerations.	1	2	3

FIGURE 9.9 (CONTINUED)

AN ANALYSIS OF THE COMPOSING PROCESS (K–8)

PREWRITING

How does the student determine a purpose (topic and form) for writing?

_____ From a personal experience?

_____ From listening to and talking about a story, poem, or nonfiction?

_____ From reading a story, poem, or nonfiction?

_____ By taking the teacher's suggestions literally?

_____ By imitating a friend's ideas?

_____ By first drawing a picture or creating a piece of art?

WRITING

While writing, does the student need absolute quiet?

_____ Talks quietly with peers about the content of the work in progress?

_____ Appears to maintain a relatively relaxed posture in the use of pen or pencil and paper?

_____ Seeks help in a reasonable way with spelling, grammar, and punctuation?

_____ Comfortably uses invented spelling?

_____ Revises and edits while writing, as evidenced by scratched out words and phrases, arrows, erasures, and so on?

_____ Uses a word-processing program with ease?

_____ Considers the initial draft to be the final draft?

FIGURE 9.9 (CONTINUED)

www.yahooligans.com/) and Berit's Best Sites for Children (http://db.cochran.com/db_HTML:theopage.db) are two such sites.

Creating a Classroom Home Page. It is relatively easy to create a home page for your class. Doing so facilitates communication with children around the world. When students have the opportunity to pose their questions and post their writing, they become more involved because it is exciting for them to receive comments from around the world.

In only four steps, classroom home pages can be made. First, students decide what to place on the home page. Second, students design the graphics. Third, students enter data and format the information into HTML code. **HTML code** is the computer programming language most often used to design home pages. There are Internet locations that explain HTML codes and contain tutorials that explain the steps to set up a home page. The most frequently used Internet sites for this purpose are A Beginner's Guide to HTML—www.ncsa.uiuc.edu/General/Internet/WWW/; HTML Tools—www.utoronto.ca/webdocs/HTMLdocs/misc_tools.html; Setting Up a Web Site for Your School: An Online Presentation—www.fred.net/nhhs/ html2/present.htm.

The last step is to place your home page on a server so that it becomes part of the Internet. This can be accomplished in two ways. You can ask your school or school district to place your home page on the Web as most districts have a server already dedicated to Internet use (Leu & Kinzer, 1995). Alternatively, you can access the American School Directory (ASD) at www.asd.com. It has a mission to provide every school in the United States with its own home page server access.

Grammar Internet Sites and Major Search Engines.   The following list offers the most comprehensive child-friendly search engines for your students:

- **Searchopolis**   www.searchopolis.com

   An outstanding filtered search engine, easy to use and fast. Organized by subject categories, the site also offers access to reference materials such as a dictionary, a thesaurus, and an encyclopedia.

- **Ask Jeeves for Kids**   www.ajkids.com

   Children type in a question for Jeeves to answer, an easy-to-use format young-sters tend to like. A built-in spell-checker helps bypass snags—like looking for Pludo instead of Pluto.

- **Scholastic Web Guide**   www.scholastic.com/webguide

   An annotated index, growing larger by the month, of thousands of teacher-selected educational sites.

- **Homework Central**   www.homeworkcentral.com

   Organized according to subject area with more than 75,000 links, all carefully screened and evaluated. An excellent research aid for students of all grade levels.

- **KidsClick!**   http://sunsite.berkeley.edu/kidsclick!

   Developed by librarians, this site has limited content but no advertising and a unique feature: Results can be organized by grade level.

- **Yahooligans**   www.yahooligans.com

   A scaled-down version of the Yahoo site for adults, with restricted options and streamlined categories appropriate for kids.

- **Lycos SafetyNet**   www.lycos.com/safetynet

   A "Search Guard" feature is optional, but teachers can ensure its use by register-ing with a password.

- **GO Network**   www.go.com

   The "GOguardian" filter is optional and can be easily switched off by children. (*Scholastic Instructor, 59,* 71)

The following Internet sites enable your class to review quality literature written by children: The Book Nook—i-site.on.ca/booknook.html; World of Reading— www.worldreading.org/; Multicultural Book Review—www.isomedia.com/homes/

jmcle/homepage.html; and Aaron's Book Review—www.concentric.net/~Bbickel/books.html. The following websites enable students to revise their writing rapidly:

- Revise stories

  www.wisc.edu/writing/Handbook/CommonErrors.html

  Provides an editing checklist of 12 common errors and gives specific examples of correct and incorrect usage.

  www.wisc.edu/writing/Handbook/RespondingPeers.html

  Discusses how to talk to a classmate about his or her paper.

- Ask Miss Grammar   www.protrainco.com/info/noframes/grammar.html

  Students can e-mail questions about language to grammar experts and authors and access informational articles such as "Problematic Pronouns."

- CyberKids   www.cyberkids.com/

  A kids' magazine with many great reading opportunities. Each year the magazine invites submissions for writing, art, and musical compositions from students, ages 7–11, for a contest. After a preliminary screening, readers vote for the winners, which are then published. This is a great location for free reading time and for submitting really fine work for publication. Set a bookmark!

- www.urich.edu/~writing/rushed.html

  Investigates warning signs of a rushed paper.

- http://awesomelibrary.org

  Long list of links for language arts activities including revising.

- http://121.ed.psu.edu/default.html

  A list of activities for revising and a place for students to go online.

Grammar Programs.   Research demonstrates that when two students work at one computer, the number of low-level writing errors decrease and there is better support for higher-level activities than when students work individually at a computer (Cole & Griffin, 1987).

Technology can best support the rephrasing and revising processes through programs in which two students can write books, plays, and readers' theater scripts. *The Storybook Weaver* series is such a word processor with pictures. This software provides guidance for student revision in terms of topic and structure by offering a framework to support writing, as well as spell-checking and thesaurus features. On each page, below the text, the computer allows students to draw or paste predrawn figures. The following bookmaking and grammar-development programs function in similar ways to advance students' revising abilities:

Animal Farm: The Novel Approach. Interactive Learning (Students can use graphics and detail direction formats to learn how to write effective stories.)

DeOrilla a Orilla. Mindscape, From Shore to Shore (Students write in Spanish and communicate with other Spanish-speaking students around the world.)

Explore-a-Story. Teacher Support Software (Students follow animated stories until the story stops and students become the writers. Students can write, edit, illustrate, and print their own books.)

Ghostwriter. MECC, 6160 Summit Drive North, Minneapolis, MN 55430-4003, 800-685-6322

Grammar Gazette. MECC, 6160 Summit Drive North, Minneapolis, MN 55430-4003, 800-685-6322

Grammar Toy Shop. MECC, 6160 Summit Drive North, Minneapolis, MN 55430-4003, 800-685-6322

Great Pumpkin Letter Writing Campaign. Miliken (Fourth- and seventh-graders from different cultures and geographic regions write to each other.)

Group Grammar. Tom Snyder Productions, 80 Coolidge Hill Road, Watertown, MA 02172-2817, 800-342-0236

HBJ Writer. Harcourt Brace (Contains features like "Freewriting" [helps students discover ideas], "Nutshelling" [for focusing ideas], and "Planning" [to guide organization].)

Hillary and the Beast. Tom Snyder Productions, 80 Coolidge Hill Road, Watertown, MA 02172-2817, 800-342-0236

Hint and Hunt. Developmental Learning Materials, One DLM Park, Allen, TX, 800-527-4747

Immigrant. Harvard University, Graduate School of Education, Cambridge, MA (Helps students improve descriptive narratives.)

Jack and the Beanstalk. Tom Snyder Productions, 80 Coolidge Hill Road, Watertown, MA 02172-2817, 800-342-0236

KidPix. Broderbund, P.O. Box 6125, Novato, CA 94948-6125, 800-521-6263

Kid Works 2. Davidson & Associates, P.O. Box 2961, Torrence, CA 90509, 800-556-6141

Language Experience Recorder. Teacher Support Software

Language Master 4000. IBM (Thesaurus and spellchecker.)

Sentence Combining. Miliken Publishing Company, 1100 Research Boulevard, St. Louis, MO 63132 (Teaches how to write effective sentences.)

Show Time. MECC (Students write short plays following program directions.)

Storybook Weaver. MECC, 6160 Summit Drive North, Minneapolis, MN 55430-4003, 800-685-6322

Story Tree. Scholastic

Student Stories. MECC, 6160 Summit Drive North, Minneapolis, MN 55430-4003, 800-685-6322

Substance Abuse. Tom Snyder Productions, 80 Coolidge Hill Road, Watertown, MA 02172-2817, 800-342-0236

SuperPrint. Scholastic Software, P.O. Box 7501, Jefferson City, MO 65102, 800-541-5513

Syll-a-Search. Developmental Learning Materials, One DLM Park, Allen, TX, 800-527-4747

Teddy Bearrels of Fun. Developmental Learning Materials, One DLM Park, Allen, TX, 800-527-4747

Writer Rabbit. Apple

Writing a Character Sketch. MECC (Writing a narrative)

The Writing Notebook. Humanities Software, P.O. Box 590727, San Francisco, CA 94159 (Intermediate students' word processor.)

SECTION 3   TEACHERS AS CONTINUAL LEARNERS

Increasing Revising Abilities

Developing the ability to teach story grammar, to use homework journals, and to solicit parents' aid in publishing students' writings in children's magazines are three ways to significantly increase revising abilities.

PROFESSIONAL DEVELOPMENT ACTIVITY

How to Teach Story Grammar

Story grammar is a rule system that describes the regularities found in stories. It is the episodic ordering of story events. Such structure gives unity and coherence to stories.

In the process of learning story grammar, most students come to learn about characterization, which is important to stories. "When characters cope with problems and circumstances that seem universal, they teach us to see the rich potential for goodness, love, faith, hope, and honor (as well as fear and evil) that is in all of us" (Eeds & Peterson, 1994, p. 14). Similarly, teaching about settings is important because children can learn how to add to a story's illusion, which helps readers bring stories to life in their imaginations and adds to the meaning of the story (Eeds & Peterson, 1994). You can teach the basic episodic structure of story grammar by presenting Figure 9.10 to students. First explain setting, problem, goal, climax, and outcome by giving several examples from books you've read aloud to the class. Then show Figure 9.10, which illustrates the story grammar in E. B. White's *Charlotte's Web*.

Once this lesson is taught, students can read one of the following books, which have clear episodic structures. They can then fill in a blank story grammar chart, using Figure 9.10, in response groups with a book of their choice. Each group can read a different book. Groups can also develop a dramatization of the story. Once the story grammar is complete, each group can tell its story (or gives its dramatization) to classmates, who in turn complete Figure 9.10 for that group's story. The class then compares their work to the story grammar the group created before the storytelling or the enactment. Excellent books for this activity follow:

Grades K–3: *Going to Squintum* by C. Van Allsburg, *Jumanji* by C. Van Allsburg, *Little Tim and the Brave Sea Captain* by E. Ardizzone, *A Bargain for Frances* by R. Hoban, *Rumpelstiltskin* by R. Zelinsky, *The Ugly Duckling* by H. C. Andersen,

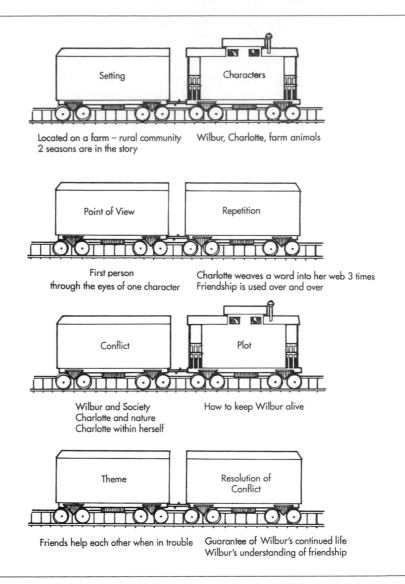

FIGURE 9.10 ELEMENTS OF STORY GRAMMAR THAT CAN BE TAUGHT

Ira Sleeps Over by B. Waber, *The Pied Piper of Hamlin* by M. Mayer, *Rapunzel* by B. Rogasky, and *The Treasure* by U. Schulevitz.

Grades 4–8: *Mrs. Frisby and the Rats of NIMH* by L. O'Brien, *Julie of the Wolves* by J. George, *Call It Courage* by A. Sperry, *Tales of a Fourth Grade Nothing* by J. Blume, *The Summer of the Swans* by B. Byars, *Island of the Blue Dolphins* by S. O'Dell, and *The Witch of Blackbird Pond* by E. G. Speare.

A second method is to introduce each section of story grammar separately. To do so, you can read or have students read a book that contains particularly vivid examples of separate story grammar entities. Some examples follow.

Portrayal of Personalities (Characterization)

James and the Giant Peach

Students should also be taught how appearance, actions, dialogue, and monologues of what the character thinks are authorial tools to develop memorable characters. Books that exemplify strong characterizations appear in Literature Card 19 (in Chapter 8). Especially vivid demonstrations of characterization are found in the following stories: *James and the Giant Peach* by R. Dahl demonstrates appearances; *The Pinball* by B. Byars demonstrates the power of character actions in conveying character; and *Roll of Thunder, Hear My Cry* by M. Taylor, *Ida Early Comes Over the Mountain* by B. Burch, *Anastasia Krupnik* by L. Lowry, and *Dear Mrs. Henshaw* by B. Cleary demonstrate how monologues by characters can reveal their moral fibers.

Conflicts in Stories (Problem/Goal)

There are four types of conflicts:

1. Conflicts between characters and nature (as seen in *Little Tim and the Brave Sea Captain* by E. Ardizzone, *Julie of the Wolves* by J. George, *Island of the Blue Dolphins* by S. O'Dell, and *Call It Courage* by A. Sperry)
2. Conflicts between the main character and society (as seen in *The Witch of Blackbird Pond* by E. Speare, *The Island of the Skog* by S. Kellogg, and *Zoar Blue* by R. Hickman)
3. Conflicts between characters (as seen in *A Bargain for Frances* by R. Hoban and *The Westing Game* by E. Raskin)
4. Conflicts main characters have within themselves (as seen in *The Cabin Faced West* by J. Fritz and *The Cay* by M. Taylor)

FOR YOUR JOURNAL

Homework Journals

Sometimes schools have a policy that students must be assigned homework. Such a policy is founded on research that students who complete homework have higher achievement (Valentine, Nye, & Lindsay, 1999). **Homework journals** are a viable means of providing meaningful work and avoiding busy work. You can ask students to write in their journals each night about one of the following: reading a self-selected book and recording their responses (using the response forms provided in this chapter and Chapter 14); discussing a topic with someone at home and recording the information shared; or, reflecting or writing about a goal they set for the week and recording their work to reach that goal. Students are to work on their journal writing for 20 minutes each day at home based on the option they choose. Students can also record the starting and stopping times of their work and have it initialed by an adult (so another person has some contact with the homework and can provide encouragement, critique, and feedback) and write a brief evaluation of the day's work. Before journals are sent home for the first time, it is helpful to write a letter to parents explaining the reasons for the work and the procedures. Every day you can read the signatures and comments from home.

An abiding problem in journal writing is to create the time to write responses to *every child's journal*. One solution is to buy a five-tier stand in which students place their folders. The first tier contains one-fifth of the students' journals to grade on Mondays, the second tier contains one-fifth of the students' journals to grade on Tuesdays, and so on. Students can turn in their journals each day so they can write every night. You can spotcheck some journals in the tiers that you do not normally grade on that day. Other strategies to reduce the amount of time spent grading journals are having students write specific information about journal entries to which they would like your response and grading only the entry that each student selects as the best each week.

To practice using homework journals this way and to provide samples for your students, you can set a communication goal for yourself each week. Every night you can work, read, or discuss a personal goal that you establish for 20 minutes. Then you can record your work in your journal. This can set an example for your class before they engage in homework journals for a 6-week grading period.

CONNECTING CLASSROOMS, PARENTS, AND COMMUNITIES

Magazines That Publish Students' Writings

Once students have learned to revise and make publishable final drafts, parents can help you locate publishing outlets for these works. The following magazines, online magazines, book companies, and competitions publish students' work. Parents can subscribe to these magazines so that students can see peers' writing as models. You can subscribe to the magazine of your students' choice from the following list to ensure that new magazines arrive in your classroom library regularly.

American Girl
830 Third Avenue
New York, NY 10022

Blue Jean
P.O. Box 90856
Rochester, NY 14609

*Books for Students
by Students*
Landmark Editions,
Inc.
1402 Kansas Avenue
Kansas City, MO
64127

Boy's Life
1325 Walnut Hill Lane
Irving, TX 75602

*Children's Digest &
Children's Playmate*
P.O. Box 567
Indianapolis, IN 46206

The Children's Magazine
8655 East Via De Ventura
Suite G-15
Scottsdale, AZ 85258

*Cobblestone,
The History Magazine
for Young People*
Cobblestone Publishers
20 Grove Street
Peterborough, NH
03548

Crayon Power
P.O. Box 1006
Bloomfield, NJ 07003

Creative Kids
P.O. Box 8813
Waco, TX 76714-8813

*Cricket: The Magazine
for Children*
P.O. Box 300
Peru, IL 61354

Ebony, Jr.
Johnson Publishing
Company
820 South Michigan
Avenue
Chicago, IL 60605

Falcon Magazine
P.O. Box 1718
Helena, MT 59624

*Highlights for
Children*
803 Church Street
Honesdale, PA 18431

Jack and Jill
P.O. Box 567
Indianapolis, IN 46206

Kid's Career Connection
726 E. Main St.
Lebanon, OH 45036

Kid's City (6–8 years)
Children's Television
Workshop
One Lincoln Plaza
New York, NY 10023

Kids Magazine
P.O. Box 341
Grand Central Station
New York, NY 10017

Merlyn's Pen
The National Magazine
of Student Writing
P.O. Box 1058
East Greenwich, RI
02818

*Mountain Standard
Time*
10144 89th Street
Edmonton, Alberta
CANADA T5H1P7

Read
245 Long Hill Road
Middleton, CT 06457

Scholastic Inc.
(Dynamath, Super
Science Red, Super
Science Blue,
Storyworks, Math
Power, Scope)
P.O. Box 3710
Jefferson City, MO
65102

Sesame Street Magazine
1 Lincoln Plaza,
3rd floor
New York, NY 10023

Spinoff (for gifted
children)
P.O. Box 115
Sewell, NJ 08080

*Stone Soup: The Maga-
zine by Children*
P.O. Box 83
Santa Cruz, CA 95063

3-2-1 Contact (8–14 years)
Children's Television
Workshop
One Lincoln Plaza
New York, NY 10023

Voices from the Middle
NCTE
1111 Kenyon Road
Urbana, IL 61801

Weekly Reader
(Current Science,
Current Health I)
3001 Cindel Drive
P.O. Box 8019
Delran, NJ 08075-9833

Wombat
365 Ashton Drive
Athens, GA 30606

Writes of Passage
817 Broadway
New York, NY 10003

Writing
245 Long Hill Road
Middleton, CT 06457

Young Author's Magazine
3015 Woodsdale Blvd.
Lincoln, NE 68502

Young Publish-a-Book
Contest
Raintree Publishers
P.O. Box 1367
Milwaukee, WI
53201-1367

Zillions
P.O. Box 53016
Boulder, CO 80322

Magazines—www.yahooligans.com/Entertainment/Magazines/

A central site for online kids' magazine. Many great resources.

Africa Online: Kids Only—www.africaonline.com/AfricaOnline/coverkids.html

A great magazine all about Africa.

Cyberkids—www.cyberkids.com/

Art, stories, and puzzles all contributed by kids.

HiPMag Online—www.hipmag.org/

An online magazine for children with hearing disabilities and impairments.

Internet Public Library—http://ipl.org

Sponsors an annual writing contest. See both Youth and Teen Division Writing Contest pages.

Keypals—www.keypals.com/p/wwwsites.html

Connect with another classroom at your grade level to engage in revision conferences over the Internet. Send drafts of student work over the Internet and seek suggestions from your partner class for improving student work.

Little Planet Times—www.littleplanettimes.com/

A great magazine for kids by kids.

Literature Card 22

ADDITIONAL MAGAZINES FOR CHILDREN BY TOPICS

These can be used in language art centers, creative dramatics, libraries, and thematic units in a variety of ways. Addresses and subscription information can be found in the current editions of *Magazines for Libraries* or *The Standard Periodical Directory* under the heading <u>Children and Youth-For</u>.

These books are available for use in the reference section of the public library. Recommended age range for magazines is in parenthesis following most of the titles. *These magazines are highly recommended.

General Interest

Turtle (2–5)	*Children's Magic Window* (6–13)
Sesame Street (2–6)*	*Child Life* (7–9)
Children's Playmate (5–7)	*Children's Digest* (8–10)
Wee Wisdom (6–12)	*Children's Own—The*
Highlights for Children (2–12)*	*Newspaper for Kids*
Muppet (7–13)	*Peanut Butter* (4–6)
Bear Essential News for Kids	*Humpty Dumpty* (4–6)
Micky Mouse (4–8)	*Kid City* (6–10)*
Snoopy (4–8)	*Creative Kids* (6–14)
Jack and Jill (6–8)	*Hot Dog* (7–9)
	New York News for Kids

Math/Science/Nature

Your Big Back Yard (3–5)*	*Zoobooks* (5–14)
Super Science I (6–9)	*National Geographic World* (8–14)*
Dolphin Log (7–15)	*Scienceland* (5–8)
3-2-1 Contact (8–14)*	*Naturescope* (6–14)*
Super Science II (9–12)	*Owl* (8–14)*
Chickadee (4–9)*	*Kind News*
Ranger Rick (6–12)*	*Dynamath* (9–14)*
Odyssey (8–14)*	

History/Social Studies

Cobblestone (8–14)*	*Streetwize Comics*
Think, Inc. (8–12)	*National Geographic World**
Buried Treasure	*Zillions* (8–14)*
Weekly Reader	*Calliope* (9–12)
Faces (8–14)*	*Scholastic News*
Skipping Stones	

Writing/Literature

Stone Soup (6–13)*	*Plays* (8–18)*
Sprint (8–12, low reading level)	*Short Story International: Seedling Series* (10–12)
Shoe Tree: The Literary Magazine by and for Children (8–14)*	*Creative Kids* (6–14)*
Cricket (6–12)*	

Sports/Hobbies/Crafts

Kidsports (8–14)	*Pack-o-Fun* (5–13)
Sports Illustrated for Kids (8–14)	*Children's Suprises* (5–12)

Available in Braille

Wee Wisdom (6–12)	*Children's Friend*

Of Interest to Girls

Barbie (4–12)	*Young Miss* (8–12)
Hopscotch (6–12)	*Teen* (13–18)
American Girl	

Of Interest to Boys

He Man and the Master of the Universe (4–12)	*G.I. Joe* (8–12)
Boy's Life (8–17)	

National Geographic Kids—www.nationalgeographic.com/kids/

One of the best magazines for children to explore the world around them.

Wordsmiths: Teen Voices @ Teen Link—www.nypl.org/branch/teen/vox.html

Sponsored by the New York Public Library, open to all teenagers ages 12 to 18. Submit up to three poems or two short stories (no more than five typed pages). Include name and age. Send e-mail submissions to teenlink@nypl.org. Include mail address and/or e-mail address for notification of when work is printed. Selected entries are posted on the web page for at least 2 weeks.

Writes of Passage—The Online Service for Teenagers—www.writes.org

An online source for students and teachers. This site expands on the *Writes of Passage* literary journal and gives young writers the chance to write and share stories, poems, and essays. Includes interviews with writers, writing tips, interactive writing activities, and the WP Teachers' Guide.

The Young Author's Magazine Internet Classroom—www.yam.regulus.com/

Offers a variety of educational opportunities. Includes a Poetry Submission Center and a Short Story/Essay Submission Center for works by students in grades K–12.

Young Writer's—www.realkids.com/club.shtml

Clubhouse provides useful information for young writers on the craft of writing. Includes a Teacher's Lounge resource for classroom teachers.

Zuzu—www.zuzu.org/

A hip magazine with poetry, artwork, recipes, and mystery pictures.

•°•

SUMMARY

"The craft of clear writing is not a mystery. . . . Simple writing is easy to describe, hard to perform, yet, it can be learned and practiced by persons who have something to say and the courage to communicate" (Murray, 1982, p. 103). Students must blossom as people before they can blossom as writers. The activities in this chapter were designed to engage students in deeper levels of interpretation and critique as they refine their revising abilities. Gradually, students can improve with the assistance of peers and with teachers who know how students master the layers of story meaning and elements of grammar that work to create and enrich students' communication. In Chapter 10 you will learn how to improve students' spelling and handwriting.

HOW TO DO IT: USING WHAT YOU'VE LEARNED

The following provide opportunities to reflect on and practice what you have learned.

ASSESSING YOUR LEARNING

1. Prepare a three-paragraph statement for parents that clarifies the differences between traditional, descriptive, and transformative-generative grammatical theories.

2. Choose one of the selections of children's literature on Literature Card 20. Develop a lesson to enhance your students' grammar awareness with that book using the revising committee approach.

3. Examine a language arts grammar textbook. Identify the theory of grammar on which it is based. Determine whether it uses any activities from this chapter to enhance students' knowledge. Make a list of pages to refer to for minilessons with your students.

4. If you are teaching, or if you are assigned to teach first grade in the future, what modifications can you make to writing, conferencing, and grammar programs to accomodate first-graders' need to vocalize as they write? If you are teaching in a third-grade classroom or above, ask your students to collect from their reading and writing, on a special page in their journal, favorite advanced grammatical structures. Spend some time at the end of a grading period sharing their opinions about why these grammatical structures are interesting.

5. Brooke is a student in Meisong, Juan, Michael, and Allison's class who has difficulty revising. She rarely changes a word she writes. After reading the following story that she wrote in 10 minutes, which activity would you first use with Brooke to develop her revising abilities? You can check your answer against the Answer Key at the back of the book and read the activity that Ms. Billick initiated on the day following her reading of Brooke's first draft.

> Brooke lives with her Mom and 11 year old sister, Cara. She also has three step-brothers, 10 year old twins, Mike and Scott, and 14 year old Chip who lives with her Dad. Brook has two cats, Taffy and Patches, and one dog, Doc. At home Brook likes to play with her friends. Her favorite color is green. Her favorite food is pizza. Her favorite sport is baseball. Brook's birthday is January 2nd.

6. After reading about the animals in the science fiction books in the thematic unit, Ms. Billick asked her students to describe what they would want if they could project into the future. Michael wrote simply, "My new bike." At this point, Ms. Billick could have taught a minilesson on sentence fragments, but instead she provided more appropriate feedback. Based on what you learned in the Professional Development Activity, what would you have done if you were working with Michael? After writing your answer, you can turn to the Answer Key at the back of the book to read what Ms. Billick did and compare her teaching strategy to yours.

7. Ms. Billick had the following experience with Juan. After engaging him in the sentence-combining approach and reading several books about hobbies from Literature Card 17 (in Chapter 7), she said: "Think about your hobby." After a minute, Juan wrote one sentence about collecting baseball cards. Ms. Billick then asked: "Who is your favorite player?" Juan responded: "Nolan Ryan." Using what you have learned in developing students' revising abilities, how would you have responded to Juan. If you would like to compare your answer to the one Ms. Billick actually gave, you can turn to the Answer Key at the end of the book.

KEY TERMS EXERCISE

Below are the concepts introduced in this chapter. If you have learned the meaning of a term, place a checkmark in the blank that precedes that term. If you are not sure of the definition of a term, increase your retention and reread its definition. If you have learned 20 of the terms in this chapter, you have constructed an understanding of a majority of the most important terms that you need to develop your student's revising abilities.

_____ cloze paragraphs (p. 380–381)	_____ homework journals (p. 407)
_____ deep structure (p. 378)	_____ HTML code (p. 401)
_____ figurative language (p. 391)	_____ idiom (p. 391)
_____ first person (p. 389)	_____ impromptu mode of instruction
_____ grammar (p. 374)	(p. 384)

_____ kernel sentence   (p. 382)

_____ metaphors   (p. 391)

_____ omniscient point of view
(p. 389)

_____ personification   (p. 391)

_____ proverbs   (p. 391)

_____ revising   (p. 374)

_____ revising committee approach
(p. 384)

_____ rubrics   (p. 395)

_____ second person   (p. 389)

_____ similes   (p. 391)

_____ story frames   (p. 395)

_____ story grammar   (p. 405)

_____ structural or descriptive
grammar   (p. 377)

_____ surface structure   (p. 378)

_____ third person   (p. 389)

_____ traditional grammar   (p. 375)

_____ transformational-generative
grammar   (p. 378)

_____ writing imitations   (p. 383)

FOR FUTURE REFERENCE

Books about Grammar, Revising, and Sixth-Grade Students

Atwell, N. (Ed.). (1990). *Coming to know: Writing to learn in the intermediate grades.* Portsmouth, NH: Heinemann.

Bryson, B. (1990). *The mother tongue: English and how it got that way.* New York: Morrow.

Dyson, A. H. (Ed.). (1989). *Collaboration through writing and reading: Exploring possibilities.* Urbana, IL: NCTE.

Guin, V. (1998). *Steering the craft.* Urbana, IL: NCTE.

Noden, H. (1999). *ImageGrammar.* Portsmouth, NH: Heinemann.

Paul, R., Binker, A. J. A., Jensen, K., & Kreklan, H. (1990). *Critical thinking handbook: 4th–6th grades.* Rohnert Park, CA: Foundation for Critical Thinking, Sonoma State University.

Tiedt, I. M. (1989). *Teaching writing: From topic to evaluation.* Needham Heights, MA: Allyn & Bacon.

Tierney, R. J., Carter, M. A., & Desai, L. E. (1991). *Portfolio assessment in the reading–writing classroom.* Norwood, ME: Christopher Gordon.

Weaver, C. (1998). *Lessons to share.* Urbana, IL: NCTE.

Willis, M. (1993). *Deep revision.* Urbana, IL: NCTE.

Spelling skills are strengthened when students read scripts to perform a play, use dictionaries, and invent word games.

CHAPTER 10

SPELLING AND HANDWRITING INSTRUCTION IN THE LANGUAGE ARTS PROGRAM

The Macmillan Book of *Greek Gods and Heroes*

Every Friday, Michael led the editing center. One day, three of his classmates came to discuss their spellings. He asked them to read their reports from <u>The Macmillan Book of Greek Gods and Heroes</u> and explain how they had invented the spellings for words they did not know. As each word was spelled, he wrote it on a chart, along with a synopsis of their explanations. After six words had been described, he passed out six note cards to each. They pulled out the rhyming dictionary and wrote words that had patterns similar to those on the chart that they wanted to learn how to spell. After all had identified words, they laid their cards on the table. Michael described a mnemonic aid they could use to spell each word in the future. Following this explanation, they played The Harry Potter's Wizard Sorts, a game Michael created based on the principle that sorting words into word families increases spelling accuracy.

The Harry Potter's Wizard Sort began by having every student turn their cards face down. Then the first student, Michael, turned up one card, and all the other students tried for 3 minutes to recall the words with similar patterns on the unturned cards. Then he turned these remaining cards over, and everyone checked the number of words that they remembered and wrote correctly. Students kept their own scores. After all had had a turn, total points for correctly spelled words were counted. For the rest of the week every word spelled correctly with these spelling patterns added one point to students' total scores. The students kept their scores secret. Michael and Mr. Sullivan, their seventh-grade teacher, decided how to reward those who had exceeded the goals they had established for themselves. Everyone agreed that spelling instruction had never been such fun and so effective!

Several research findings in this chapter will show that the success of this activity (and of others in this chapter) rests on (1) the fact that students are more successful when they correct their own spelling in their writings, (2) simultaneously learn words that share common semantic or visual features, (3) learn how to sort words based on word families, and (4) grade themselves after learning words that relate to a generalization. Moreover, spelling activities should provide real-world follow-up practice opportunities as soon after instruction as possible; allow students to set their own goals; and integrate their understanding of sound–symbol relationships by incorporating invented spelling during the drafting stages of writing. The lessons in this chapter will help you teach students how to use word patterns, letter-to-sound relationships, dictionaries, mnemonic aids, and imagery to spell correctly. You can also learn how to teach handwriting, punctuation, and other writing conventions. In addition, by the end of the chapter you will have the answers to the following questions, which represent standards for professional development from IRA, NCTE, NAEYC, TEKS, and other statewide or province-based professional standards:

1. Why is it so difficult to spell correctly?
2. How can you teach spelling, punctuation, and capitalization?
3. What strategies build students' use of correct manuscript and cursive penmanship?
4. How can you teach handwriting to left-handed students?
5. What is the position of IRA, NCTE, and NAEYC concerning invented spelling?
6. How can you diagnose the cause of spelling difficulties?
7. What are the stages of spelling development?
8. What are the roles of word walls and parents in students' spelling and handwriting development?

SECTION 1   THEORETICAL FOUNDATIONS

Why Teach Spelling and Penmanship?

The philosophy and strategies for spelling and writing convention instruction changed during the latter part of the 1980s. During this period, many teachers became disenchanted with testing a list of words that students could spell with 100-percent accuracy on Fridays but misspell in their own writings the next week. Researchers identified several reasons why drilling on spelling and writing conventions wasn't working in our schools.

It isn't easy to learn to spell. Spelling, capitalization, and punctuation probably demand the most difficult, constant attention of all the language arts. Even adults consciously have to attend to them each time they write. The difficulty arises from the fact that these tasks must be attended to in conjunction with other thinking tasks—for example, when students spell, they are also writing, creating, and paragraphing. Other language arts (reading, speaking, and listening) can occur without simultaneously executing these tasks and often without continually checking form.

Moreover, the ratio of time students spend speaking and listening is 3 times greater than the time spent writing. This difference reduces the opportunities students have to practice spelling, punctuating, and capitalizing. This decreased time, in turn, reduces students' exposure to the spelling patterns that frequently appear in English. As Vygotsky stated, "The child must learn that one can draw not only objects but also speech" (Vygotsky, 1978, p. 4). Perera also noted that "written language has to be more explicit than speech because it stands alone" (Perkinson, 1991).

Moreover, young children receive positive reinforcement when they stumble and stutter as they learn oral language, but receive criticism for invented spellings. When they share their first writings, parents often read the many correctly spelled words without lavish praise. Instead of supporting the beginning attempts to spell, many parents criticize incorrect spellings. Such negative reinforcements often inhibit students' desire and ability to spell correctly. Equally damaging are students whose teachers find and correct all spelling, punctuation, and capitalization errors for them. These students do not learn to self-initiate their own editing.

Words in the English language are difficult to spell. The English writing system is complex in several ways. First, the system has no one-to-one relationship between phonemes to graphemes; for example, the /g/ sound can be spelled *j* and *g*. Also, for those phonemes that have more than one spelling, it is not always possible to predict the correct spelling. Equally important, because our written language is an imperfect alphabetic system, few sounds have unique spelling representation. Specifically, 26 letters must represent 44 to 46 sounds and more than 26 dialectical variations. To represent these sounds, letters combine to make hundreds of spelling patterns. For instance, to spell even single, spoken sounds, the English language requires 5 hundred different letter combinations (Horn, 1947). For the 21 single consonant sounds in our language, there are 68 spellings. Worse yet, for the 5 single short vowel sounds there are 53 spellings!

When students learn to spell through an integrated language arts curriculum, however, this complexity is reduced because spellings can be based on the semantic relationships between theme-related words, such as drawing a flag and teaching all the words that have *flag* in them, such as *flagship, flagging,* and *flagpole.*

Another reason it is so difficult to learn to spell is because spellings and writing conventions have been altered by changes from Old to Middle to modern English. In the transition, sounds of numerous words and word orders in sentences changed, but their spellings remained constant. For example, when Old English changed to Middle English, the sound of *p, w,* and *k* at the beginning of the word was eliminated but the spelling remained (e.g., *know, wren, wrong, pneumonia*). Therefore, as today's students spell and compose, the reasoning that originally supported the correctly spelled words no longer applies. Students who do not know the spelling of such words are most often asked just to memorize them.

Presently, as many as 75 percent of the new words added to our language are borrowed from other languages and their spellings are foreign (Henderson, 1990). For example, when students learn to spell *lieutenant, ballet,* and *chic,* English spelling rules do not apply. Although these words are treated as English words, they are spelled by the rules that govern the French language. Students must know common morphemes (*-in, -en, -an,* etc.) that appear at the beginning or end of words. Positioning is also an important principle for spelling and writing conventions and a difficult one for some students to learn. Spelling a word correctly involves knowing the position in the word in which the letter is to appear (e.g., /f/ is spelled *f* at the beginning of words [*fir*], but *ff* or *lf* or *gh* at the end of words [*buff, half,* and *rough*]).

Becoming a good speller typically requires experiences above and beyond those provided by reading connected text. Even though learning to read does not automatically make children good spellers, learning to spell does benefit their reading. It does so, in part, by improving children's ability to focus on the individual sounds or phonemes within spoken words. Other research suggests that young children find it easier to use an alphabetic strategy in writing than in reading. Thus, children may be able to use spelling as an entry point into the writing system. Children's spellings also provide an excellent window to their knowledge of phonology and orthography. Clarke's (1988) research suggests that encouraging children to invent spellings while they are engaged in creative writing helps them to appreciate the alphabetic principle. Once children have grasped this principle, inventive spelling is no longer superior to traditional spelling.

The ability to read a word does not always guarantee that a child is able to spell that word. Beginners have been reported to read words **logographically**—by means of visual clues (Byrne, 1992; Frith, 1985; Gough, Juel, & Griffith, 1992). Ehri (1992) referred to this strategy as **prealphabetic reading.** Children who use this approach may identify *dog* by virtue of the "tail" at the end of the word rather than by linking the letters in the printed word to the sounds in the spoken word. A child who uses a logographic strategy to recognize printed words does not focus on all the letters and so may be unable to remember and reproduce the full spelling.

Even when children begin to link spellings to sounds, they do not do so completely. Instead, children may read by means of partial clues, connecting some of the letters in a spelling to pronunciation but ignoring other letters (Ehri, 1992; Perfetti, 1992). This approach sometimes allows children to read words correctly. For example, a young child may identify *bar* in reading by connecting the letter *b* to the phoneme /b/ and the letter *r* to the phoneme sequence /ar/. Because the child has not linked the letter *a* to its own separate phoneme in the spoken word, the child may not remember this letter when attempting to spell the word and may therefore produce the error *br* (Treiman, 1998).

Further research also shows that tasks that require a child to focus on the exact spelling of a word—whether copying the word, spelling it out loud, or forming the word using letter tiles—are superior to reading as a means of learning the spelling of that word (Bear & Templeton, 1998). They also need some type of direct instruction in spelling. Clarke's (1988) findings suggest that, as children become better spellers, fewer benefits are gained from invented spelling. As time goes on, children should be encouraged to spell words correctly, for example by looking for words in a dictionary or a personal word bank, rather than inventing their own spellings.

Children may need some type of direct instruction in spelling. One possibility is to embed spelling instruction in each child's independent writing experiences. Using this approach, the teacher selects certain invented spellings for consideration and helps the child to understand how the spellings can be improved. This approach may be called **guided invented spelling.** Because it is integrated into the context of writing, it is an example of what Tracey and Morrow (1998) called **authentic instruction.**

Currently, many teachers who encourage invented spelling do not offer children much guidance on how to improve their spellings. For example, the teachers in the invented spelling classrooms studied by Clarke (1988) seem not to have commented on the correctness of the children's spellings or helped children to improve their spellings. The children usually read their stories to the class and the teachers commented on the content of the stories, which marked the end of the writing process. In the classroom studied by Treiman (1993), the teacher wrote the conventional spellings of the words on the child's paper but did not discuss how the child's spellings differed from the conventional ones and did not improve the child's spelling.

Guided invented spelling may be very helpful if well and sensitively done. This instruction is tailored to individual children, giving them immediate feedback on the errors they have just made and teaching them what they need to know at that particular time. However, as yet no body of research systematically addresses the effectiveness of guided invented spelling (Mangieri & Block, 1999; Treiman, 1998).

In summary, both of the positions discussed in this section, invented spelling and direct instruction, have some merit. The research reviewed so far shows that spelling helps children master the alphabetic principle and also has a positive impact on reading. Proponents of the whole language approach are thus correct to suggest that writing should not be put off until the middle or late elementary grades but should begin much earlier. However, contrary to the belief of whole language advocates, research shows that children do not automatically become good spellers as a result of reading a lot. One cannot count on transferring knowledge from reading to knowledge of spelling. Children should certainly read good literature, but they should also spend time focusing on individual words. This can be accomplished with individual instruction—what I have called *guided invented spelling*—and with group activities, or, ideally, with both.

Although children need to spend some time studying isolated words and sounds, this study does not have to be meaningless or boring. Fortunately, a number of interesting and motivating activities can help children learn about words and their spellings. These are presented in Section 2 of this chapter. Memorization of word lists may be one part of such instruction, but it should by no means be the only part. Indeed, the systematic study of words—their spellings, meanings, and derivations—provides an important foundation for all reading and writing.

In addition, oral spelling should transfer to pencil and computer spelling. Second, prior research (Berninger, Abbott et al., in press) showed that children with both handwriting and spelling disabilities spell more poorly than children with only spelling problems, and children with spelling problems spell words of moderate or low predictability more poorly when using a pencil than a computer. Furthermore, Fashola, Drum, Mayer, and Kang (1996) demonstrated that bilingual and ESL students' decoding and spelling errors must be analyzed through reference to the orthographic rules that govern both their functional languages.

If students are to develop legible penmanship, they must also use proper hand position in their grip, place the features of letters appropriately, and position their pencil on the correct starting point of the line. Accomplishing all of these positions is not easy. Moreover, your instruction must not only train these positions, but also build students' small muscles and sustain their desire to improve their penmanship. During the 1980s the emphasis on penmanship instruction decreased. The reduced amount of time elementary teachers spent in developing manuscript and cursive writing skills raised the concern of junior and senior high school students' teachers and parents. By the 1990s increasingly larger proportions of our students' writing was becoming illegible.

In brief, there are several reasons why students need to be taught spelling, capitalization, punctuation, and penmanship. Methods of instruction during the 1970s and 1980s had several deficiencies and led to new approaches to spelling, handwriting, capitalization, and punctuation instruction (Ehri & Wilce, 1987; Fitzsimmons & Loomer, 1978; Hillerich, 1985; Hodges, 1981). You can use students' invented spelling and word patterns to develop students' knowledge of orthography. You can also use textbooks and word lists in new ways. And last, you can augment the editing step of your writing program to emphasize the correct use of principles that govern proper manuscript and cursive penmanship, described in the next section.

The difficulty in learning to spell was most clearly demonstrated when Hanna et al. (1966) programmed a computer with 300+ English spelling principles. Even though the computer used every English rule it "knew," it could correctly spell only 49 percent of 17,000 randomly selected English words. Considering this fact, it is a testimony to our educational system that most students can spell 80 percent of their words correctly! Although present instructional methods in spelling are making a difference, the information in this chapter can increase the impact your instruction can have on students' abilities.

STAGES IN SPELLING DEVELOPMENT

Preschool children's invented spellings are governed by a set of principles different from those that guide traditional spelling (Read, 1975; Treiman, 1998; Bear & Templeton, 1998). Their spelling develops in stages labeled precommunicative, semiphonetic, phonetic, transitional, and correct spelling (writing) stages (Gentry, 1982). However, recent research suggests that students progress at different rates in their construction of graphophonemic and orthographic knowledge, and an individual child may use a variety of spelling strategies on a given occasion. Therefore, examining what a given child knows may be more beneficial in facilitating future learning than trying to place that child in a specific developmental stage (Frerichs, 1996).

Precommunicative or Prephonetic Stage.   The prephonetic stage is when students scribble, writing is unreadable, and students do not understand that writing is to be composed of letters. Often their scribbling is vertical rather than horizontal. No letter-to-sound relationship is demonstrated.

Semiphonetic or Early Phonetic Stage.   The second stage of invented spelling evolves the moment children realize that letters and not lines or numbers are the things that "spell." They write one or more letters to represent a word. Interestingly, the letters that they write may not appear in any part of the correct spelling of that word. Children believe that a single letter can represent an entire word (or sentence) because it takes them so long to write one letter they feel as if they have written their entire thought (Flood & Lapp, 1991). See Allison's 4-year-old brother's spelling as an example. Randy attempted to write a *w* to stand for his entire name (see Figure 10.1).

Instruction for students in this stage of knowledge includes reading a book while you move your finger below the print; labeling objects in the classroom; pointing to the initial letter as you say printed words; bringing environmental print to the classroom; composing rebus stories; and chorally reading students' favorite chants.

Mwwww (ForRAndy)

FIGURE 10.1 SAMPLE OF ALLISON'S 4-YEAR-OLD BROTHER RANDY'S EARLY PHONETIC STAGE IN SPELLING DEVELOPMENT

Phonetic or Letter Name Stage.   The third stage begins when students use the basic English phonograms, such as /an/, /at/, /in/, /en/, /on/, /up/, and /us/. Although students in the phonetic stage use a letter or word for each thought they want to communicate, their spelling and writing conventions are incorrect. They write only the sounds they hear, such as *u* for *you*. Their writing is logical and systematic, however, such as *kr* for *car* and *n* for *in*, as illustrated in Figure 10.2. As a general rule, students' spelling will represent at least one-half of the sounds and the majority of the letters found in the traditional spelling of that word.

frt The GrL
cits a Pardv
si zrs

TerShe cuTs
Hr Har ②

Teh sheo
is Brd.

Translation:

1. "First the girl gets a pair of scissors."

2. "Then she cuts her hair."

3. "Then she was bald."

FIGURE 10.2 PHONETIC OR LETTER NAME STAGE IN SPELLING DEVELOPMENT

From "SSW: Sustained Spontaneous Writing," by K. Bromley, 1985, *Childhood Education, 62*(7), pp. 23–29. Copyright © 1985 by the Association for Childhood Education International. Reprinted by permission of Karen Bromley and the Association for Childhood Education International, 17904 Georgia Ave., Ste. 215, Olney, MD 20832.

Instruction for students at this stage includes memorizing basic sentence patterns and the capitalization and punctuation that accompanies them, such as their own name, high-frequency words, their friends' names, *Mother,* and *Father.* Temple, Nathan, Burris, and Temple (1988) have found phonetic spellers also benefit from segmentation activities in which an important word is rewritten several times on a strip of paper and students are to draw lines between each word; for example:

spell|spell|spell|spell|spell|spell|spell|spell|spell|spell|spell|spell|spell

Transitional Stage.   In this stage, pupils learn to pay attention to visual patterns and clues in words and sentences, to the letter-to-sound correspondences they represent, and to the basic rules of English orthography (Adams, 1990; Hillerich, 1985). When students use the right letters, but place them in an incorrect order, they have reached this advanced writing level (Wilde, 1989). Students also develop a spelling memory and use a visual coding mechanism, as shown in Figure 10.3. During the transitional stage, students benefit from instruction that emphasizes:

1. Short vowel patterns (*cvc*), long vowel patterns (*cvce* and *cvvc*), and consonant blend/digraph spellings, such as *br, pl, st, th, ch,* and *ph*

2. Spelling words with *m* or *n* before other consonants, which letter name spellers usually omit in words such as *lamp, find,* and *stand*

3. Spellings at the end of words; words ending in *-ve* (such as *move, have,* and *love*), and words that end with a double consonant (such as *ball, fall, miss,* and *pass*)

4. Spelling of past tenses of verbs (*-ed*)

5. Rules that govern capitalization and punctuation that appear in their own writings

Correct Spelling Stage.   It is at this stage that students understand the idiosyncrasies of English orthography. They often self-initiate proofreading to be sure they have spelled and written sentences correctly. They write prefixes, suffixes, silent consonants, irregular spellings, and complex sentences correctly. Most students reach this stage between ages 8 and 9. However, many do not use traditional spelling and writing rules for many years beyond third grade, especially if instruction in these rules is not provided.

HOW TO TEACH SPELLING, CAPITALIZATION, AND PUNCTUATION

Today, students' spellings are defined in two ways. **Traditional spelling** is the correct spelling of words. Students use traditional spelling when they spell words as they appear in the dictionary and adhere to the spelling rules that govern them. Students can also use **invented spelling** when they spell a word and the spelling they choose is not the correct spelling of that word. Other writing conventions you are required to teach are **penmanship** (the art or practice of writing with a pen, pencil, or other hand-held writing instrument), **capitalization** (the act or process of scripting or printing with capital letters at appropriate points), and **punctuation** (the act, practice, or system of inserting standardized marks in written matter to clarify the meaning and separate structural units in sentences).

I lic horses be kus
They aer butufol anamols
I lic blak horses whin they
Swet be kus they luk lic
Strip of blak liting
I lic Mar hoses bekus they
can hav babys and in som port
of my lif I whont to be abol to
ras hoses

FIGURE 10.3 SAMPLE OF TRANSITIONAL STAGE WRITING

There are four new methods of building students' spelling, punctuation, and capitalization skills. As you will read below, each has its advantages. You can decide which most adheres to your teaching style and to the instructional needs of your students. Many teachers combine the following approaches, and you may prefer to do so as well.

APPROACH 1: INVENTED SPELLING AND CREATIVE CONVENTIONS

By kindergarten, many children are using what Dyson and Genishi (1994) and others have labeled *invented spelling*. According to their research, students' invented spellings reflect these students' "current hypotheses about how our alphabetic writing system works" (p. 226). This means that they have the sounds in their head but may not be able to read or remember them. When students are free to spell and punctuate the way they think is right, especially when they are simultaneously taught phonemic awareness, they begin to initiate their own use of language principles (Juel, 1995; Fehring & Thomas, 1985). Without instruction, students' invented spellings are created because words are written the way they sound (*jress* for *dress* because *jr* and *dr* share the same point of articulation in the mouth), the way they look (*fro* for *for* because their visual memory recalled these three letters), or the way they make sense (*Wasapanataem* for *Once upon a time*) (Harste, Woodward, & Burke, 1984). Moreover, "it is important that students' invented spellings are valued and that they are interpreted as displays of these students' intelligence and emerging proficiencies. It is [also] clear that instruction in standard spelling can assist the developmental process, and that invented spellings change after exposure to spelling instruction" (Sowers, 1986, p. 246). Students who use invented spelling and creative writing conventions are not delayed in learning to traditionally spell, punctuate, or capitalize (Henderson, 1990; Gentry, 1987).

Research does suggest a number of techniques by which guided invented spelling can be carried out. For certain types of errors, it may be helpful to focus on phonemic awareness, helping children to divide problematic parts of spoken words into phonemes. For example, a child who spells *bread* as *bed* can be helped to analyze the /br/ cluster: /b/ followed by /r/. The child can be shown that each part of the cluster can be represented with a separate letter, yielding *br*. If the child then spells *bred*, the teacher might say that this is an excellent attempt, not mentioning at this time that the word actually contains an *a*.

Another way to guide invented spelling is to focus on reading. For instance, you can have the child read *bed* and help the child to realize that this printed word corresponds to *bed*, not *bread*. Confronted with the fact that they have spelled two different-sounding words the same, children sometimes change their spellings. Indeed, this happened about 40 percent of the time among the first-graders studied by Treiman (1991). This rate may be increased by teaching children how to use reading to check their spelling. Such an approach should help children learn to integrate reading and spelling, which are not always well connected in young children (Treiman, 1998).

You can also offer guidance, as well, on the use of orthographic and morphological spelling strategies. For example, a child who spells *can* as *ckan* can be shown known words that end with *ck* and words that have *ck* in the middle and can be led to the generalization that *ck* appears in these positions of words but not at the beginnings.

Thus, spelling instruction enhances students' abilities to read and write, create more accurate spellings on first attempts, read more unknown words, and hear and pronounce more words correctly in oral language activities (Block, 1996b; Mangieri & Block, 1999). Furthermore, when you allow your students to use invented spellings, their higher-order thinking about the content can be engaged without obstruction. Thus, if you authorize invented spelling (and permit creative use of other writing conventions) and teach students that different sounds are represented by different letter combinations, they learn that there are many orthographic and syntactic patterns in our language. You should also require, however, that students transpose their invented conventions to traditional forms when their writings are to be shared with others.

If you follow this approach, the 20 to 30 minutes a day that would have been traditionally spent on worksheet spelling drills are spent in real-world writing activities. In essence, students' writings become the textbook for spelling development. Similarly, students should develop their own lists of words that they want and need to spell. Evaluation of capitalization, punctuation, and spelling shifts from right–wrong answers on dictated tests to an analysis of correct use of spelling and writing conventions in students' compositions. Such analyses compute the percentage of invented words used and the quality of errors made (e.g., are errors becoming closer to traditional spellings, punctuation, and capitalization over time?). Such assessment is based on a thorough understanding of the developmental stages that students pass through in their spelling development. Once you have learned these stages, you can more rapidly build on students' present level of lexical mastery and assist their transport to traditional spelling, punctuation, and capitalization.

In summary, a child who has been encouraged to progress through the developmental stages of invented spelling and through the creative use of punctuation and capitalization is more likely to develop a deeper understanding of English orthography and writing principles than a child who lacks these constructive experiences:

> The composing of words according to their sounds . . . is the first step toward reading. Once the child has composed a word, he looks at it and tries to recognize it. The recognition is slow, for reading the word seems much harder than writing it. Often the child works it out sound by sound, the reverse of the process by which he wrote it, and then recognition dawns all at once. (Chomsky, 1976, p. 120)

Students' quality of writing also increases as they do not limit their expressions to their written vocabularies and they pen from imaginative thinking (Sowers, 1986). For example, a young girl in Sowers's study was excited as she read her story about the "froshus dobrmn pensr" (translation: ferocious doberman pinscher); her excitement would not have existed had she written only what she could spell ("bad dog").

APPROACH 2: MODIFIED TEXTBOOK APPROACH

In the past, textbook approaches for spelling, punctuation, and capitalization followed the same pattern: students were pretested over a set of words or rules, completed four days of drill and practice exercises, and took a posttest over the same words or rules. Students usually studied 36 units, which included the most frequently occurring words and punctuation and capitalization rules in our language. If all these exercises were completed, by the end of sixth grade, students would have been taught and tested over 97 percent of all words children and adults use in their writings, and all the rules that govern punctuation and capitalization (Wilde, 1989).

In the late 1940s Horn (1947) identified two strengths with this approach. The first is that the pretest helps students identify words they already know so they can study only those that are difficult for them. Because the average child knows how to spell 75 percent of the words at his or her grade level before studying them, there is no reason to teach the words already known (Hillerich, 1985). Through this pretest procedure, students can eliminate known words from their study list. The second strength is that students correct their own tests so they receive immediate feedback.

A weakness in this approach is that many students can score 100-percent correct on their weekly posttests and not transfer these correct spellings to their writing (Johnson, Langford, & Quorn, 1981; Treiman, 1998). A second difficulty is that many practice activities, although using words and rules in the unit, do not teach students how to spell, punctuate, and capitalize words when they compose. Teaching students to generate English language patterns has been found to be important in developing spelling skill (Graves, 1977; Bear & Templeton, 1999). Research also indicates that no more than 12 to 15 minutes a day should be spent in learning to spell. Additional time does not significantly increase spelling ability (Johnson, Langford, & Quorn, 1981; Mangieri & Block, 1999). Although recently published texts incorporate some of these research findings, the text you select should not ask students to do nonauthentic writing and spelling tasks.

If you modify a spelling textbook in the following ways, you can maximize its instructional strength.

1. Use more than one grade level from the series in your class.

2. Ask students to add words that they want to learn to their weekly lessons.

3. Ask students to learn words that they misspell in their own writing.

4. Teach words in thematic units so words you emphasize during your week's reading and oral language instruction are part of spelling instruction that week.

5. Have students with similar problems group themselves together and work on specific objectives using sample words from all grade-leveled textbooks together 4 days a week. On the fifth day, have students break into pairs to test each other and to look at all writing samples their partner wrote that week to see if the rules and words studied during the week transferred.

As an alternative, students can work at their own pace for 4 days a week, completing as many spelling units during the week as they are able. Then, on the fifth day, you can have students pair and test each other over individualized spelling lists. These lists are comprised of words that they have misspelled during the week's writings as well as in the spelling pattern lessons they have chosen to learn.

APPROACH 3: BASIC WORD LIST INSTRUCTION

Spellers are more accurate when they visualize alternatives rather than simply "thought" of them, concluded that visual information is used in the spelling process, not to generate alternatives but to choose among them (Kreinan & Gough, 1990; Tenney, 1990). For this reason, you can ask children to write a word and, if it doesn't "look" right, to rewrite it several times, being sure that they keep what they think looks right and to think of other possible spelling patterns that could make it look more correct.

This approach develops spelling skills by dividing the 3,000 most frequently occurring words of our language into lists (Hillerich, 1985). Each weekly list is introduced with a pretest that is immediately corrected by students. Then students list words they need to learn, and they keep records to measure their success. To begin this program, you can administer a test of basic English words to diagnose students' level of spelling ability. Those who correctly spell at least half the words on this pretest should be given more difficult words.

This approach requires about one hour a week of instruction. Once students spell all the words on the basic list correctly, they are ready to learn the 2,400 other most frequent words in our language (see Henderson [1990] for words grade-ranked by spelling patterns that can be used in this approach). When students master these lists, they can spell 98 percent of all the words they will ever write.

APPROACH 4: LEARNING TO SPELL DURING THE EDITING STAGE OF WRITING

This approach was used by Mr. Sullivan's class. Students learn to spell the words that they spelled incorrectly in their own writings. They also learn to spell other words that contain the same spelling pattern. This approach begins as students edit their writings, and they learn to spell at least one of the words they didn't know how to spell on their drafts. Students are taught the word patterns that they are not spelling correctly. (A list of the spelling patterns to use in this approach appeared in Chapter 5.) The fact that a student is inventing a pattern demonstrates that he or she is ready to learn its spelling. For example, if a student writes: "They mak the snak go in the lak," you could show the list of words with the *-ake* spelling pattern and ask the student to read each word. Then the student would return to the above sentence that he or she wrote and adjust the spelling. You could also teach spelling principles through minilessons. A sample follows:

Mr. Sullivan: You wrote everything about the trip to the cafeteria accurately. I also like that it is very descriptive. Catherine, you remembered to use periods throughout the book, and it's nice to see that. I'd like you to look at the word *said*. Say the letters you used to spell *said*.

Catherine: S . . . A . . . D.

Mr. Sullivan: Those are three of the letters in *said*. You are very, very close to spelling it 100-percent correct. What I'd like you to do right now is draw a line under said every time you see it on this copy of page 4 from *Dear Mr. Henshaw* that you are reading. Now, return to your writing. How do you spell *said*?

Let's see if you can use this approach to teach spelling. Study Susie's sample that follows, and describe a rule about spelling you would teach her:

I brok my ancl. I broke it when I was at mi mapl tre.

What would you teach Susie about spelling? When the editing approach is used, students who are not in conferences can meet in groups to increase spelling skills through the following activities:

1. *Disappearing Lists.* This activity was one section of a larger, experimental program called Success for All, created by Stevens, Madden, Slavin, and Farnish (1987). It begins with words students misspell in their writing. Pairs of students then test each other over their own personalized list of misspelled words. Words are taken off

Students enjoy and benefit from writing letters in plates of jello, pudding, or whipped cream. The use of tactile and kinesthetic senses enhances the ability to remember the individual letters in words.

the list when a student and that student's partner are convinced that the student can spell the word correctly. Students establish a standard to determine that a word can be spelled correctly (such as the word must be spelled correctly three times in a row in subsequent writings before it is removed from the spelling list).

2. *Wheel of Fortune Spelling.* In a recent research study, Hall and Cunningham (1988) used the Wheel of Fortune game to teach context and graphemic clues in spelling and reading. Words used in the game could be those on a wall chart in the room, words students select, or words from a content area of study. This game begins with four-member groups of students electing a moderator and three contestants. The moderator writes a cloze sentence on a sheet of paper, with the word to be spelled omitted from the sentence. Contestants spin a wheel for the amount of money each correct guess is worth. Contestants try to guess letters of the missing word until it is spelled correctly.

3. *Friday-Is-Game-Day.* On Friday, a gamelike activity is scheduled where individuals or teams earn points for correct spelling. Such activities include puzzles, spelling bingo, spelling bees, and having students write their words in pudding, whipped cream, or finger paint. To make spelling bees more valuable, instead of only one student from each team standing to spell a word, every team member uses an individual blackboard and writes the spelling of the word called. Individual student blackboards can be made from 8½- by 11-inch cardboard pieces that have been painted with blackboard paint, available at paint stores. Each team scores one point for each word spelled correctly by each member of the team.

4. *Look, Say, Cover, and Write.* In this activity, students look carefully at a word to memorize the spelling. In succession they then say the word aloud (or to themselves), cover it, and write the word from memory. Then, they remove their hand and check to see if their spelling was correct.

5. *Word Families.* Children learn word "families." They identify words that contain the same word part and that are related in meaning, such as words that contain the word *hand*. Students are given 2 days to collect as many words as they can find relative to their word family. Students share their words in a creative way, with the class. As demonstrated by Mr. Sullivan words with *hand* in them can be displayed on the outline of a hand, as shown in Figure 10.4. In their oral presentations students are required to ask questions about the related meanings of their spelling words—such as, "Why is it called a *hand*kerchief? under*hand*ed? *hand*y?" The day after Mr. Sullivan made this presentation, his students paired and their partner gave the spelling words they collected as a test.

6. *Discovering Famous Authors' Use of Conventions.* Basic punctuation and capitalization are traditionally introduced in first grade. After an initial explanation of these conventions, the most effective practice of their use occurs in editing groups, in the revision and editing steps. These sessions are effective because students want to communicate something, and they see the importance of using conventions to do so. As students progress, you can guide them to discover the more advanced rules (e.g., possessives, semicolons, dashes, and parentheses) by comparing the different punctuation styles of their favorite authors. Students can also use an editing checklist (see Figure 10.5) as they write to improve their awareness of correct punctuation and capitalization.

7. *Overcoming Types of Spelling Difficulties.* You may want to pause for a moment and review the chart of all developmental stages in the language arts (printed in Chapter 1). As you do so, you will notice how closely related the writing and spelling stages of development are. In spite of this, students can make random

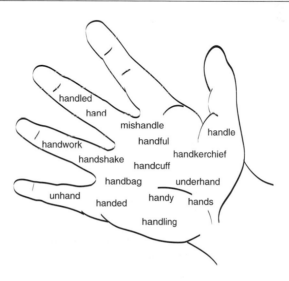

FIGURE 10.4 DEMONSTRATION OF MR. SULLIVAN'S LESSON ON HOW STUDENTS CAN USE THEIR KNOWLEDGE OF WORD FAMILIES TO IMPROVE THEIR SPELLING

EDITING CHECKLIST   NAME _____

AUTHOR _____ DATE _____

TITLE _____

_____ SPELLING   (It was a (speceD) shirt.)   *special*

(Watch for homonyms; (Wear) should I (where) it?)   *where*   *wear*

_____ CAPITALIZATION   (I looked good. let's go! I'm ready to visit doctor collins.)

(Watch for out of place capitals; We went to the School.)

_____ PUNCTUATION   (The sentences all end with punctuation marks⊙ I've checked for appropriate

use of commas∧ for example∧ in listing and for sentence clarity.

Apostrophes are used to show possession and as part of a contraction⊙)

_____ PARAGRAPH INDENTION   (¶ Another idea for.....)   *and that is the best...*

_____ MARGINS   (↱ then... and so...)

_____ COMPLETE SENTENCES   (Then∧ went home.)   *we*

_____ CLEAR MEANING   (They∧then went to MacDonalds after practice.)   *band*

_____ WHAT COULD MAKE THIS PAPER BETTER? _____

_____

_____

_____

_____

⬭	Spelling or word choice	⊙	Add period	¶	New paragraph
=	Capitalize	∧	Add comma	⌃	Insert
/	Don't capitalize	˅	Add apostrophe	ℓ	Delete

FIGURE 10.5 EDITING CHECKLIST

spelling errors or run into four types of difficulties. Specific instructional supports can be used to overcome the following causes of spelling difficulties.

Auditory Inattention.   Some writers cannot transpose individual sounds into letters. Their minds seem not to understand or attend to subtle differences between sounds. If auditory confusion is the cause of spelling difficulties, the words the student writes follow correct English spelling patterns but cannot be pronounced (e.g., *should* is written as "shoued").

Visual Inattention.   Students who have visual inattention hear sounds distinctly but cannot remember how to transpose these sounds into written words. The words they write may sound correct but do not contain correct English spelling patterns (*should* is written as "shhooood").

Spelling Rule Inattention.   Some students spell incorrectly because they **overextrapolate,** or violate the rules of English spelling patterns by applying a rule to a situation for which it is not valid. For example, they would overextrapolate the *-oo* sound and the ending sound of the past-tense ending morpheme *-ed* and would spell *should* as "shooled."

Homophones.   Some writers substitute a homophone for the word they intend to write. For instance, students who substitute *bear* for *bare* are either writing so rapidly that they are unaware of their error or neglecting to use meaning as a clue in spelling.

A first step to assist children with all these difficulties is to have them write notes to you (as opposed to asking you orally) for help in spelling out new words. These notes will demonstrate all the knowledge they have about the word. If you respond by asking them, "Why do you want to know how to spell [the word]?" students learn to spell the word correctly through your correctly spelled model (see Figure 10.6).

8. *Decorating Difficult Words.* Another effective method of instruction is to highlight the difficult sections of words with graphic symbols. These visual aids focus more attention on sections of words that are more complicated to spell, thus increasing their visual recall (Block, 1997). Mr. Sullivan used this instructional approach as shown in Figure 10.7.

HOW TO TEACH HANDWRITING

Handwriting instruction is important because "handwriting allows the student to see his own spirit in action" (Lehman, 1976, p. 2). In the recent past, the emphasis

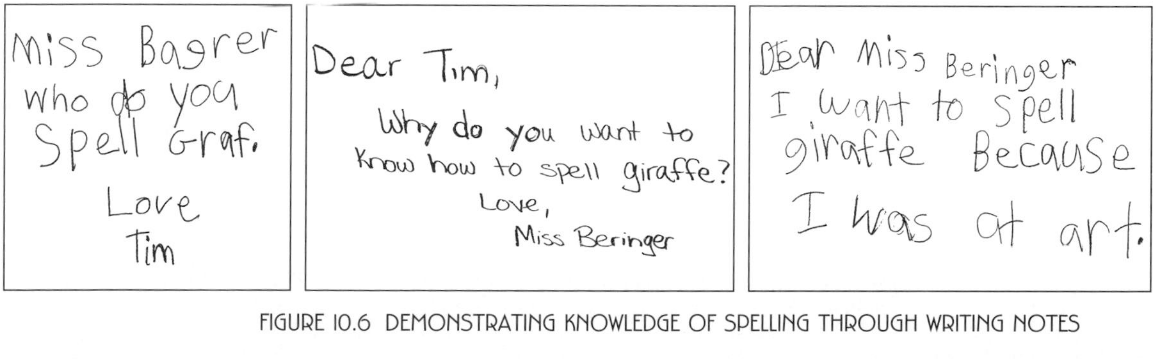

FIGURE 10.6 DEMONSTRATING KNOWLEDGE OF SPELLING THROUGH WRITING NOTES

1. Silent or confusing letters can be highlighted by pictures to aid decoding and spelling.

 The silent *u* becomes a shopping cart filled with items that you *buy* at the store.

people The silent *o* becomes the face of a person. *People* has the face of a person in it.

family It is hard to hear the *i* sound when *family* is pronounced. The *i* becomes a person in the family, and it is easier to remember.

World *World* is difficult to spell because the *er* sound is spelled *or.* The *o* becomes a globe of the world as a visual clue.

¢ent *Cent* and *sent*—which word refers to money? That's easy to remember when the *c* becomes a ¢ sign.

2. Writing scripts can be varied to convey the meanings of words. For example, students would write *holler, whisper, train, dancing,* and *doctor.*

3. Picture associations can also be used to help students learn letter patterns, such as a picture of a thumb, shoe, or church can be associated with *th, sh,* and *ch* to distinguish each from the others.

th		sh		ch		challenge	
wi	th	wi	sh	whi	ch	in	ch
tee	th	ca	sh	mu	ch	ba	th
pa	th	fi	sh	su	ch	ru	sh
		fre	sh			fla	sh
						di	sh

FIGURE 10.7 DECORATING DIFFICULT WORDS

Source: Example 2 adapted from "Sight Word Spelling Tricks," by C. E. Quinn, 1993, *Academic Therapy, 23*(3), p. 288.

on teaching handwriting was less than it should have been, and the following results occurred:

- 38 million letters are illegibly addressed each year, which costs the U.S. Postal Service $4 million annually.
- Poor handwriting costs American business $200 million a year.
- 40 percent of business executives say employee handwriting is getting worse.
- 58 percent of the information on hospital charts is illegible.

In spite of the greatly increased number of computers in use, the need for legible handwriting has not decreased but increased. For example, in 1992 U.S. consumers purchased 5 billion pens and pencils, which is double the number purchased in 1973 (Hackney, 1995).

You may be required to teach three types of handwriting:

Manuscript: discontinuous strokes

Cursive: flowing writing with continuous strokes

Italics: unconnected, but flowing strokes such as calligraphy

There are more than one hundred commercially prepared materials that teach penmanship. There are also four important principles that can make these programs successful:

1. As with all the language arts, you should integrate oral stimuli with the visual practice of writing letters. You describe how each letter is formed as you provide the visual stimuli by modeling how to make each letter. As students make the visual features of each letter, ask them to say the names of each letter stroke.

2. Do not force students into instruction too soon, and ensure that the following readiness skills are developed: muscle coordination, hand–eye coordination, ability to hold writing tools for long periods of time, and knowledge of allowing space between letters and words. It is also important to remember that without proper instruction, students often devise their own methods of writing, which leads to bad habits. These bad habits interfere with legibility and writing speed.

3. Research supports using discovery discussions to alter individual students' writing errors. Such instruction is more effective if students view and then replicate a model rather than trace difficult letters (see sample models in Figure 10.8). However, viewing and trying to copy a letter alone does not significantly change students' penmanship. Students need you to show them how to make each feature of troublesome letters, such as how to make the downstrokes, circles, and stems they contain (Peck, Askov, & Fairchild, 1980).

4. Erasers can be a problem for teachers and students. When students get in the habit of erasing, writing speed is slowed, and holes in their papers destroy meaning. To avoid these problems, you can demonstrate the process of crossing out errors instead.

MANUSCRIPT WRITING

Although several important readiness aspects of handwriting instruction occur in early childhood education programs, manuscript instruction traditionally begins in

FIGURE 10.8 HANDWRITING MODELS

From *Handwriting: Basic Skills and Applications* (p. 372) by W. B. Barbe, 1984, Columbus, OH: Zaner-Bloser. Copyright © 1984 Zaner-Bloser. Used by permission.

first grade. Because young students' small muscles are less well developed than those of older students, **manuscript handwriting,** which requires less small muscle coordination, may precede cursive writing instruction. Also, many first-grade students have trouble manipulating their writing utensils to make the angles required of cursive writing. However, researchers have found that giving first-graders giant pencils does not improve their penmanship. They prefer the smaller, "adult" writing utensils. In addition, first- and second-grade students tend to write longer stories if they use ballpoint or felt-tip pens instead of pencils (Askow & Peck, 1982). Another reason manuscript writing is often taught before cursive is that printed letters look like the typeset letters students read in books and thus are familiar (Askov & Peck, 1982; Duvall, 1986).

The first manuscript letters to teach are the lowercase letters because students use more of the muscle groups of the hand in their formation than in the formation of uppercase letters. Then, capitals should be taught one at a time and practiced as students learn to write their own and classmates' names. The suggested order to introduce manuscript letters starts with the easiest letters for first-grade students to write: *l, o, h, d, i, v,* and *x.* The most difficult letters for young students to write are *q, p, y, j, m, k, u, a,* and *g.* As late as age 9, many children continue to have difficulty in forming *r, u, b,* and *t.* Some students may require you to guide their hands when they are learning to write these letters.

The following activities are effective in teaching manuscript writing:

1. First, you say and then write a letter (with a crayon on paper or on the blackboard); students observe the process. Students need to see you demonstrate each letter stroke. You verbalize what you are doing and students verbalize after you. Students say the directions for making strokes as they write them. By talking aloud as they write, they see their creations, and strengthen their mental images. You should teach downstrokes, circle strokes, cross-strokes, and upstrokes in this order.

2. Students can trace letters (with the index finger) in the air several times before they pick up their pencils to write each one.

3. Students can practice penmanship at the chalkboard as the chalkboard affords freedom of movement; exercises larger arm and shoulder muscles, which aid students in developing eye–hand coordination; and provides a kinesthetic experience that speeds the learning of letter shapes (Collins, 1992c).

4. You can place a model of the alphabet on students' desks in a letter strip and use transparent notebook paper overlays, three-dimensional forms, clay or hand-held models, or onion-skinned overlay. After students have practiced one or more difficult letters, they can compare their letters to those on the model. When they judge that their letter forms are accurate, they can write a meaningful passage to communicate something important to someone else.

5. You can keep a jar of sharpened pencils (prepared by a student officer) and other writing utensils handy so students can experiment with new writing utensils. This variety of writing tools tends to sustain their interest in improving their penmanship.

CURSIVE HANDWRITING

Instruction in cursive handwriting usually begins in late second or early third grade, although it can begin earlier. In **cursive handwriting** instruction, the strokes of looping, retracing, rounding, and closing are taught separately. Students' most frequent errors in cursive writing are faulty endings, incorrect undercovers, mixed slants, failure to produce letters in the center of a word, incorrect formation of initial strokes, misformed capital letters, and inappropriate downstrokes.

Students can learn to write cursive more easily when they practice less complicated letters first. For example, have students write several short words with the same letter:

add, all, at, call, cup, cut, dad, did, do, got, go, had, hall, hid, hunt, it, lad, late, little, oat, old, pad, pat, pig, pill, tall, to, tooth, and up.

Once you have completed this lesson, you can help students recognize where most of their legibility errors occur in the above words (Hillerich, 1985). Students can also diagnose whether they have a problem with any of the following aspects of cursive writing through the activity described next.

1. Students can write the words *darling, good, guide,* and *adding.* Ask them to look at their words and determine whether their letters are closed at the top. If not, students can profit from practicing the circle stroke.

2. You can ask students to write *nothing, nautical, many,* and *number* and have them look at the letters *m* and *n.* Are their tops not rounded? If students do not like how these letters appear, they can profit from practicing rounded strokes.

3. Next, students can write the words *item, triangle,* and *time* and study the letters *t* and *i* to determine whether the two letters are the same size. If they are, students can benefit from practicing proper line length.

4. Students can also write the words *ladder, letter,* and *left.* They analyze whether there are loops on the letters *l* and *e.* If not, students can benefit from practicing the backstroke.

5. Last, pupils can write the words *umbrella, underwater,* and *runner.* They can study each letter to determine whether the tops of the *u* are not pointed. If not, students can improve their handwriting by practicing upstrokes and subsequent downstrokes.

The reasons that students have poor cursive penmanship stem from improper instruction, poor pencil grip, and incorrect posture. You can diagnose whether students are holding their pencils improperly and are sitting tall by watching them write. If they grip their writing utensils too tightly, the handwriting will be very dark, or writing will be slow. If students grip their utensils with proper tension, you should be able to take the pencils from their hands without having to pull hard.

Teaching the correct hand positions and pencil grips differs for left- and right-handed students.

Finally, students should have established a hand preference by first grade. If they have not, you should observe which hand they prefer for eating and playing catch on the playground and help them consistently use this hand each time they write. Similarly, if students in kindergarten do not believe they can write, you can demonstrate how drawing pictures, scribbling, writing random letters, writing traditional sentences in manuscript, and writing traditional sentences in cursive are all forms of writing and allow students to choose any one of them. Once kindergartners realize that they aren't expected to write words, most welcome the opportunity to scribble or draw as a means of writing (Friego, 1991).

TIPS FOR LEFT-HANDED WRITERS

Only 9.7 percent of girls and 12.5 percent of boys prefer to write with their left hands (Hawisher, 1987). You can help the left-handed students in your class overcome any self-consciousness they may feel by teaching them that hand preference makes no difference in their level of success in life. Writing with one's left hand is no different from choosing to eat *Cheerios* when their friends prefer *Captain Crunch*. You can also share a personal experience about a time when you were in a minority group, and what you learned from that experience. For older students, you can share names of highly successful left-handed people such as President Bush, President Ford, President Truman, Leonardo da Vinci, and Judy Garland who were also left-handed. You can also ask whether they know which teachers or administrators in their school are left-handed. Suggest that the reason they don't is that being right- or left-handed is inconsequential to a person's ability. You can also suggest that there are benefits to being in this smaller group of the population. For example, left-handed pitchers are rare and very valuable to major league baseball teams.

It is important to remember, however, that without your instruction, left-handed students may learn to adopt less effective writing positions. They may place their hand below the writing line or hook their hands over their pencils. You can alter these positions by teaching left-handed writers not to pull their arms toward their bodies as they write like right-handed writers, but to push their arms away from their bodies. They must also alter the way they grip their pencils, the position of the writing paper on their desks, and how they begin to form their letters. The difference in how they place their papers is shown in the previous photo. Left-handed writers should hold pencils an inch or more further back from the tip than right-handed writers. You must teach left-handed writers to place their paper properly, grip their pencil, and slant correctly. You can place a piece of masking tape on left-handed students' desks to mark the position where the upper-left corner of the paper should be placed each time students begin to write. The upper-right corner of the paper should be in line with the center of the student's body. Once students correctly position the paper a few times, you can remove the tape and have them determine their own paper position, as each may select a slightly variant position from this standard position. Once the student establishes a correct, personalized position, you can use tape to mark the upper-left corner for at least the next grading period, as shown in Figure 10.9.

Left-handed students should hold their writing instruments 1 to 1½ inches above the sharpened end. This position provides for better eye–hand coordination, which

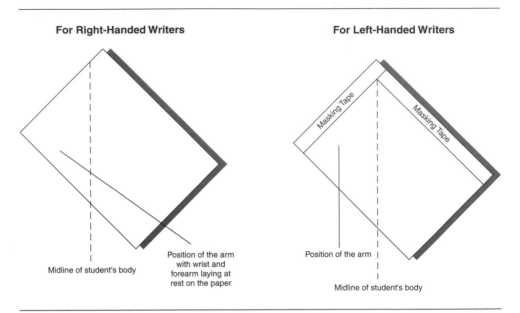

FIGURE 10.9 PROPER PAPER PLACEMENT FOR IMPROVED PENMANSHIP

Source: Adapted from *Fresh Look at Writing* (p. 301), by D. Graves, 1994, Portsmouth, NH: Heinemann.

is necessary to prevent hooking the wrist. If the pencil is held near the end, students tend to move the pencil point to see their words, which causes the wrist to hook. The best aid to assist students in remembering to hold the pencil up high is the "gripper." This is a triangular-shaped, soft, plastic ring that attaches to the pencil (available from Hoyle Products, Inc., 302 Orange Grove, P.O. Box 606, Fillmore, CA 93015).

Additional instructional strategies for left-handed students can be found on the website that accompanies this textbook and are described in the following list:

1. The blunt end of the pencil or pen should be directed back over the shoulder. The desk should be high enough for the child to see the pencil or pen as it touches the paper.

2. Each first attempt should be corrected as soon as it is made because learning to write in a right-handed system is difficult for left-handed students. By correcting first attempts, students avoid developing hand positions, postures, and grips that can make writing uncomfortable for them for the rest of their lives.

3. Ask students to write four sentences. Then make a tiny vertical line at the point where they place their pencil to begin each letter. Study these markings to analyze whether letter strokes are beginning at the proper slant for left-handed writers, which is through the slant of the pencil rather than the hand.

4. Demonstrate to students that each upward stroke pushes strokes rather than pulls strokes, which is the case for right-handed writers.

Ruben Cabral

I lerd that how to make my
lower case x in crsef. But I did not
just do it on paper I done it with
clay it was better becuse It isin't hard
I now I can write my x's bettes look?

x x x x x x x x x x x x x x x

FIGURE 10.10 ONE OF MR. SULLIVAN'S STUDENT'S SELF-ASSESSED HANDWRITING PRACTICE

5. Last, students should compare their writing samples to a handwriting model and identify one letter they wish to improve (see Figure 10.10).

Some students enjoy learning italics systems. You can use a calligraphy kit, for example, or invite someone to class to teach this form of writing to those who are interested. You can place a group of very good handwriters or gifted students in charge of engaging such a guest speaker. This group can select who will contact the guest, introduce the speaker, and write the follow-up thank-you note, in calligraphy of course!

SECTION 2   PUTTING THEORY INTO PRACTICE

Teaching Spelling, Writing Conventions, and Penmanship

In this section you will learn how to create daily lessons in which students use (1) children's literature and student compositions to master writing conventions; (2) word play and word patterning games to enhance their spelling abilities; and (3) "spelling demon" charts to overcome common spelling errors.

ACTIVITIES THAT TEACH WRITING CONVENTIONS

There are several lessons that improve students' penmanship and teach students about "spelling demons" and how to use better capitalization and punctuation.

LESSONS THAT IMPROVE STUDENTS' PENMANSHIP

Students benefit from practicing downstrokes (*i*), upstrokes (*t*), circles (*o*), and slants (*l*) in cursive writing. You can increase the enjoyment of such practice by telling a made-up story using students' names and descriptions of previous classroom events. Each time you say a student's name, everyone must write one row of the lowercase, cursive letter that corresponds to the capital letter that begins the name. Once everyone has finished the row of letters, you can continue the story.

As an aside, some students find it easier to make letters of proper size when you tell them that *a, c, e,* and *m* are "one-story letters." "Two-story letters" (such as *b, d, k,* and *l*) are introduced next; and, "basement letters" (such as *q, j, p,* and *y*) are introduced last. Table 10.1 can be used as a handwriting assessment.

TABLE 10.1 CLUES TO IMPROVE HANDWRITING

I. Rate the Quality of Your Handwriting

Excellent (1), Good (2), Average (3), Fair (4), Poor (5)

_____ Neatness

_____ Arrangement (margins, indentations)

_____ Legibility

II. Locate the Trouble Spots in Your Handwriting

Check (✔) one or two areas in which you need special practice:

_____ **Slant** (Do all your letters lean the same way? Are your down strokes really straight?)

_____ **Space** (Are the spaces between letters and words even?)

_____ **Size** (Are your tall letters *l, h, k, b,* and *f* about three times as tall as the small letters; the middle-sized letters *t, d, p* twice the height of small letters; and the lower loop letters one-half space below the writing line?)

_____ **Alignment** (Are all tall letters evenly tall; all small letters evenly small; and are all letters resting on the line?)

_____ **Line Quality** (Is the thickness of the lines in letters about the same throughout the page?)

_____ **Ending Strokes** (Are the endings without fancy swinging strokes, and are they long enough to guide the spacing between words?)

_____ **Letter Formation** (Are the loops open and equal in size? Are the hump letters *m, n, h, u* rounded? Are the letters *o, d, a, g, p, q* closed? Have you made long retraces in *t, d, p*? Are your capital letters well formed?)

_____ **Number Formation** (Do you use the correct form? Do you use the correct slant? Are the symbols well aligned?)

TEACHING "SPELLING DEMONS" AND WRITING CONVENTIONS

In this lesson students learn some of the most frequently misspelled words in our language. Once students are aware of types of errors they are likely to make in their work, you can help them overcome their problems by posting a spelling demons chart. Students add words to this chart that they misspell in their writing. The day before a test of the spelling demon words, the class can also create a mnemonic aid or clue to teach themselves how to spell the words from the demons chart. Charlene Peck has written a book entitled *Word Demons* that helps students master 86 spelling demons through a game she has devised. A second reference you may find useful in teaching spelling demons is *Graded and Classified Spelling Listed for Teachers* by Celeste Forbes. Both books are available through Educators Publishing Company in Cambridge, Massachusetts.

Hall and Cunningham (1988) suggest that students learn to use **configuration** to build spelling ability. Configuration is using the shape of the letters in a word to distinguish it from others, such as the versus that. As shown in Figure 10.11, when students have difficulty with a word, they spell it, cut around it, place it on the word wall, study the word's shape, and then test themselves on its spelling.

The following activities enable students to assess their growth in writing convention use.

1. Make a copy of one or two students' writing samples for the class. Omit the capital letters or punctuation marks relative to the concept you want to teach. As you

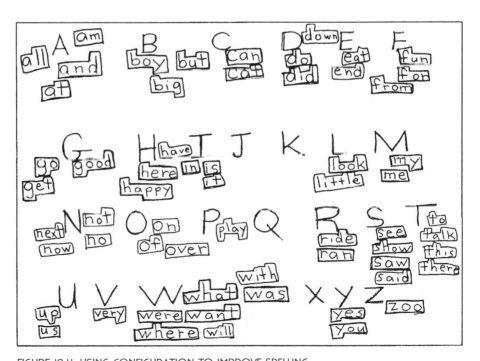

FIGURE 10.11 USING CONFIGURATION TO IMPROVE SPELLING

Source: From *Phonics They Use: Words for Reading and Writing* (p. 102), by P. M. Cunningham, 1991, New York: HarperCollins Publishers. Copyright © 1991 by HarperCollins Publishers. Reprinted by permission.

display this modified sample on the overhead projector, you and your students can discover together which capital letters or punctuation marks were omitted and how their addition enhances the message their classmate intended.

2. White out the punctuation marks and capital letters on cartoon strips and ask students to replace these marks and letters. Then they can compare their versions to the authors' originals.

3. Students can work in editing committees to develop charts with rules they've discovered that govern punctuation and capitalization. These charts can then be displayed at the editing center.

4. Students can explore how each punctuation mark began and report this information to classmates and younger students.

5. Victor Borge made a record called the *Audible Punctuation* system. He selected distinctive sounds to communicate each punctuation mark. Students learn the roles each mark plays because the sounds connote the meanings of the mark (e.g., the sound for period is a short plunk and a pause).

Whenever there is a need to correct students' errors, Graves (1994) suggests that you choose a few conventions or words that the student spelled correctly and say something like "I noticed that in the first four sentences you get the periods in just the right place [pointing to the period after the last word in the second sentence]. How did you know how to put this one here?" (Graves, 1994, p. 89). In this way, you can discern how much the student knows and then discuss how he or she can improve a few inaccurate sections of the writing.

INTEGRATING THE LANGUAGE ARTS

Building Punctuation and Capitalization Skills

Punctuation and capitalization should not be on the child's mind during the brainstorming and first draft stages of writing, but they should rise in importance during the editing and revising stages. To begin this lesson, you can provide an initial explanation of these conventions. Then students can either read their writings to another student, or several students can edit together. As students read their works aloud, readers and listeners can suggest punctuation according to what they hear. Books in Literature Card 23 are exceptionally good to read aloud for this purpose.

As students refer to and use the punctuation functions in the following lessons they discover the importance of correct punctuation in their writing. In addition, Literature Card 24 can be used to increase students' imagery as a tool in spelling as well as knowledge of writing conventions while reading about content familiar to their daily lives.

Myths, legends, folktales, and proverbs also develop writing abilities because they use a wide variety of punctuation tools. They are the oldest forms of storytelling, and have been handed down from generation to generation. Their purpose was to preserve a people's knowledge and truth in a form that demonstrated not only what had been accumulated and understood about life and living but also how to avoid pitfalls and dangers in life. These genres speak to our limitations as well as to our possibilities, and they speak with humor and enjoyment. The animal fable is one of the most

Literature Card 23

CHILDREN'S BOOKS THAT MODEL OR DESCRIBE PRINCIPLES OF SPELLING, PUNCTUATION, CAPITALIZATION, AND WORD ORIGINS

The following books and activities increase students' appropriate use of English conventions.

How Ships Play Cards: A Beginning Book of Homonyms by C. Basil, 1980 Morrow

Eight Ate: A Feast of Homonym Riddles by M. Terban, 1982 Clarion

The Story of the Dictionary by R. Kraske, 1975 Harcourt

101 Words and How They Began by A. Steckler, 1979 Doubleday

Last, First, Middle and Neck: All about Names by B. Hazen, 1979 Prentice-Hall

Words, English Roots, and How They Grew by G. Ernst, 1984 Scribner

Hannah Is a Palindrome by M. W. Skolsky, 1980 Harper & Row

Perplexing Puzzles and Tantalizing Teasers by M. Gardner, 1969 Simon & Schuster

Words by J. Sarnoff and R. Ruffins, 1990 Macmillan

Wonder in Words by M. Nurnberg, 1987 Harcourt Brace

Let's Look for Opposites by B. Gillham & S. Hulme, 1984 Coward-McCann

More Than One by J. Hoban, 1981 Greenwillow

Kitten Can by B. McMillan, 1984 Lee & Shepard Books

Andy, That's My Name by T. DePaola, 1991 Aladdin

The Word Book by G. Brandreth, 1988 Robson

The Mother Tongue: English & How It Got That Way by B. Bryson, 1990 Morrow

Dictionary of Idioms by L. Flavell & R. Flavell, 1992 Kyle Cathie

The Merriam-Webster New Book of Word Histories, 1991 Merriam-Webster

Answering Students' Questions about Words by G. Tompkins & D. Yaden, 1986 National Council of Teachers of English

An Avalanche of Anoraks by R. J. White, 1994 Crown

endearing of genres, partly because it teaches indirectly. Through this genre students learn strategies for overcoming human weaknesses without having to compromise their need for privacy. Just as we are somewhat blind to our own faults and have difficulty seeing ourselves as others see us, students can come to understand their shortcomings and overcome them through the genres of animal fables, myths, and legends.

Myths, fables, and legends are especially powerful in building students' spelling and capitalization. These genres introduce students to many Greek and Latin roots that dictate English spellings. Reading them helps students incorporate colons, semicolons, dashes, and quotation marks into their own writing more rapidly. They learn to use liberally a wide variety of punctuation as they model these genres in their writing.

Studies of historical fiction follow this genre nicely because students can see the past come to life, as demonstrated by one of Mr. Sullivan's colleagues, Ms. Brandt, in a unit at the end of this chapter. As children read historical fiction for enjoyment, they relive the past vicariously and explore the conflicts, joys, and despairs of people who lived before them. Historical fiction also provides a context to explore the human condition, and this is an important concern of many older elementary-aged children like Mr. Sullivan's seventh-graders (Hickman & Cullinan, 1989). They empathize with people in the past. They can also read about characters who exhibit strength in adversity, who can become their role models.

One member of a seventh grade community that studied myths stated: "I'm really glad we came together to talk about the different myths we were reading. I didn't realize before that

Literature Card 24

BOOKS WITH SURPRISE ENDINGS TO BUILD IMAGERY

Younger Readers

Miss Nelson Has a Field Day by H. Allard, 1985 Houghton Mifflin

Who Sank the Boat by P. Allen, 1989 Orchard

Clifford and the Grouchy Neighbors by N. Bridwell, 1990 Scholastic

The Velveteen Rabbit by M. Williams, 1984 Running Press

The Vanishing Pumpkin by T. de Paola, 1993 Putnam

Pleasant Dreams by A. B. Francis, 1983 Holt

Hugo and the Spacedog by L. Lorenz, 1991 Simon & Schuster

A Toad for Tuesday and other books by R. E. Erickson, New York: Lothrop

The Mysteries of Harris Burdick by Van Allsberg, 1984 Houghton

Snow Lion and other books by D. McPhail, 1989 Dutton

Oscar Mouse Finds a Home by M. Miller, 1985 New York: Dial

The Frog Who Drank the Waters of the World by P. Montgomery, 1983 Atheneum

Bert and the Missing Mop Mix-Up by S. Roberts, 1989 New York, Children's Television Workshop

The Principal's New Clothes by S. Calmenson, 1989 New York: Scholastic

Frog Medicine by M. Teague, 1991 New York: Scholastic

Dr. Desoto by W. Steig, 1983 New York: Scholastic

Something Special for Me by V. B. Williams, 1983 New York: Greenwillow

Older Readers

My Dog and the Knock Knock Mystery and other books by D. A. Adler, 1985 New York: Holiday

Arthur's April Fool by M. Brown, 1983 Little, Brown

Judge Benjamin: The Superdog Secret by McInerney, 1983 Holiday

The Lockkey Kids by S. Terris, 1986 Farrar, Straus & Giroux

The Mystery of the Smashing Glass by W. Arden, 1984 Random House

Christina's Ghost by B. R. Wright, 1987 Scholastic

The Castle of the Red Gorillas by W. Ecke, 1983 Prentice Hall

The Twiddle Twins' Haunted House by H. Goldsmith, 1989 Scholastic

The Borrowers by M. Norton, 1974 Caedmon

Tom's Midnight Garden by P. Pearce, 1984 Lippincott

The Revolt of the Teddy Bears by J. Duffy, 1985 Crown

A Wizard of Earthsea and other books by U. K. Le Guin, 1986 Chivers

World Famous Muriel and the Magic Mystery by Sue Alexander (5–8), 1990 Crowell

Coffin on a Case by Eve Bunting (10 and up), 1992 HarperCollins

Wake Me at Midnight by Barthe DeClements (8–12), 1991 Viking

Wild Geese by Ellis Dillon (10 and up), 1980 Simon & Schuster

Garbage Juice for Breakfast by Patricia Reilly Giff (6–9), 1989 Bantam

What's That Noise? by Mary Roennfeldt (3–6), 1985 W. Morrow

Nate the Great and the Halloween Hunt; Nate the Great and the Musical Note; Nate the Great and the Stolen Base; Nate the Great Goes Down in the Dumps by Marjorie Weinman Sharmat (6–9), 1984 Coward

The Hoax on You by Marilyn Singer (8–12), 1989 Harper

Encyclopedia Brown and the Case of the Disgusting Sneakers by Donald J. Sobol (7–12), 1984 Bantam

A Flight of Angels by Geoffrey Trease (9–13), 1989 Lerner

The Vandemark Mummy by Cynthia Voigt (10 and up), 1991 Atheneum

most of them were about struggles for power. It was neat to compare what power was to the Greeks in ancient times to what power means to us today. Things haven't really changed all that much. I liked writing about when I felt a sense of power in my life and when I didn't because I realized that I'm not so different from the other kids." (Wyshynski & Paulsen 1995, p. 263)

INSIDE CULTURALLY ENRICHED CLASSROOMS

Using Self-Stick Notes to Aid Students with Special Needs

To reduce the difficulty of spelling for some ESL children or students with learning differences you can write the Spanish word or a picture of the English word students are trying to read and spell below the English word. Then use self-stick notes to scaffold. Here is an example:

Day 1: You go to school.

(picture)

Day 2: You go to s   . [rest of word is covered with a self-stick note]

(picture)

Day 3: You go to school.

(cover the picture with a self-stick note)

If you teach bilingual students, Sally Mathenson-Mejia's (1989) article will be of interest. She describes six common spelling errors bilingual students make and methods to help them overcome them. Creating images to convey meanings of survival words is also helpful to English language learners. You can cover all but the beginning consonants and vowels of picturable nouns in big books and ask ESL and other students with special needs to use all the clues they see to deduce the word and its spelling. After they write what they believe the partially covered word to be, they can remove the self-stick note and judge the accuracy of their work.

RECOGNIZING AND REPORTING PROGRESS

Self-Assessments of Editing and Small-Group Discussions

Self-assessments are recommended because they enable students to evaluate the strategies that have been discussed.

Self-assessments are particularly valuable in the editing stages of writing and after group discussions have occurred. It is at these times when very specific objectives can be established to improve oral and written communications through direct actions before the next oral or written product is presented to others. Self-assessment also enables students to value, monitor, evaluate, and improve their own language and thinking. As Aristotle stated, "Each man judges well the things he knows, and of these he is a good judge" (*Ethics I*:3). Students know themselves better than any other subject. You can model ways in which students can write examples and rank their performances on that form.

Self-assessment can be used for more than written examinations. Students can also assess their oral performances during discovery discussions by either awarding points for the number of dimensions of a language arts competency that they demonstrated or giving themselves a global score for the quality of their total work. The following questions can assist students' self-assessments:

1. List or describe what you can do now when you read, write, speak, view, and so on that you could not do earlier in the year.

2. What are your best works during this grading period as a speaker, listener, reader, writer, speller, viewer, and thinker?

3. What are the most difficult concepts you have learned about (writing, spelling, reading, speaking, listening, viewing, thinking)? What did you do to learn it? What did this teach you about your learning styles and abilities? Why were these concepts difficult for you?

4. How have you changed as a reader, writer, speller, speaker, listener, thinker, or viewer? Give examples and work samples to support your answer.

5. What would you like to do better as a language user next grading period?

6. What do you do when you _____ (cite a specific objective taught during the grading period)?

7. What do you not understand about _____ and how could I help you?

8. Rate and defend how well you used your time and employed your study skills during this grading period.

Students can also complete self-assessments by providing annotations to attach to their report cards. In such annotations students also give themselves grades, after you explain the standards on which you will grade them. Examples of such report cards were presented by Judd (1989). Although most students grade themselves much like the actual grade they earn, self-assessments can serve as indicators of students' levels of self-esteem. One student (Brian) had a strong self-concept and teased in the assessment that he wrote of himself: "Brian is doing well in his assignments but he has not been doing many independent activities. He's doing better in his reading group and he's writing in his journal a lot. P.S. I love his jokes!" (Judd, 1989, p. 91). A spelling test that you can use as a teacher-graded or student-graded self-assessment appears in Figure 10.12. This assessment was created to diagnose students' grade level of spelling knowledge.

•●•

SECTION 3   TEACHERS AS CONTINUAL LEARNERS

Increasing Editing Abilities

In addition to the above methods, you can increase students' editing competencies through word patterns, spelling journals, and instruction that is taken into students' homes.

PROFESSIONAL DEVELOPMENT ACTIVITY

Teaching Word Patterns

Word patterns can be taught as a combination of word play and word pattern activities. The first type, Word Wizard, was developed by Culyer (1992). It is designed to improve students' spelling and can be used at two levels of difficulty. In the more

This spelling test was designed to place students in Dr. Fry's *Spelling Book;* however, it will give you a good idea of the spelling development of any student (child or adult). The levels are roughly grade levels. For example, students in an advantaged school should be able to spell all but 3 words in Level 1 at the end of the first grade; in a disadvantaged school, at the end of the second grade. *Directions:* Dictate the words and have the students write them. Say the word, use it in a sentence, say the word again (but not another time).

Directions for administering the spelling test:

1. Give each student a blank sheet of paper.

2. Starting with Level 1, dictate the words.

   a. Say the word

   b. Use the word in a sentence

   c. Say the word again (but not more than once)

3. Correct the test yourself or have students trade papers and correct. (If you have students correct each other's papers, be sure to spot check for accuracy of correction).

4. Any student missing 3 or more words at any level fails that level and should begin spelling instructions at that level.

SPELLING TEST—PRIMARY LEVELS

Suggested for Grades 1 through 3 and remedial elementary

LEVEL 1	LEVEL 2	LEVEL 3	LEVEL 4
1. and	9. small	17. foot	25. fellow
2. girl	10. off	18. break	26. strength
3. which	11. family	19. coat	27. shut
4. can	12. fly	20. loud	28. doubt
5. now	13. heavy	21. bottle	29. tea
6. book	14. over	22. laughed	30. secret
7. these	15. morning	23. service	31. dangerous
8. come	16. difference	24. shook	32. earn

SPELLING TEST—INTERMEDIATE LEVELS

Suggested for Grades 4 through 6 and remedial secondary

LEVEL 3	LEVEL 4	LEVEL 5	LEVEL 6
1. foot	9. fellow	17. film	25. basketball
2. break	10. strength	18. occupied	26. Iowa
3. coat	11. shut	19. gulf	27. anchor
4. loud	12. doubt	20. breeze	28. fuel
5. bottle	13. tea	21. dock	29. February
6. laughed	14. secret	22. store	30. prophet
7. service	15. dangerous	23. paw	31. cane
8. shook	16. earn	24. costume	32. division

FIGURE 10.12 SPELLING TEST TO DIAGNOSE STUDENTS' GRADE LEVEL OF SPELLING KNOWLEDGE

Adapted from *Spelling Book,* by E. Fry, 1996, Laguna Beach, CA: Laguna Beach Educational Books. (This book contains 3,000 instant words in rank order arranged in 195 spelling lessons with phonics for grades 1–6.)

difficult version, students are challenged by the Word Wizard to take two words and change one letter at a time in the first word until it becomes its antonym. For example, the Word Wizard could challenge first-grade students to change *cat* to *dog*. Students could do so by using the following sequence: *cat* to *hat* to *hot* to *hog* to *dog*. Another sequence they could use would be to change *cat* to *cot* to *dot* to *dog*. An easier way the Word Wizard can challenge students is to use a puzzle format where definitions are given beside the word in each sequence. By attaching meaning to the clues, students can more easily complete the sequence and mentally visualize the individual letters in the words to be spelled. The Word Wizard also builds metacognitive thinking and problem-solving abilities. A few sample items appear below. Many others that you can use are also available on the website that accompanies this textbook.

1. cat	2. lose	3. car	4. hate
hat	lone	bar	have
hot	line	ban	Dave
hog	fine	van	dove
dog	find		love

5. one	6. sick	7. dumb	8. push
ore	lick	dump	bush
are	lice	damp	bust
arm	mice	dame	best
aim	mile	dime	belt
dim	mill	dice	bell
Tim	will	rice	bull
tin	well	rise	pull
ten		wise	

Another word pattern lesson is to show how some word parts convey meaning and are spelled alike even when they sound different, such as *industry* and *industrial*. Nagy, Anderson, Schommer, Scott, and Stallman (1989) demonstrated that this is possible because these words are members of morphologically based word families. These morphemes dictate the spelling of derivational and inflectional words in their respective families. Learning to use these morphemes is important in leaning to spell. One method of helping students develop this ability is to give them a list of words, such as appears in the first and third columns below, and ask them to find other words that contain the same word part (examples appear in second and last columns).

photograph	photography	literate	literary
history	historical	culture	culturally
govern	governor	major	majority
microscope	microscopic		

When students are proficient with this strategy, you can help them understand the rationale behind silent consonants by using a procedure first reported by Donogue (1990). Give students the words in the first and third columns and ask them to think of related words in which the silent consonants are pronounced, such as those in the second and last columns.

bom*b*	bom*b*ard	sign	si*g*nal
sof*t*en	sof*t*	condem*n*	condem*n*ation
mus*c*le	mus*c*ular		

FOR YOUR JOURNAL

Spelling Journals

When students write regularly in their journals, they are simultaneously recording their knowledge of English orthography. For this reason, journals become an authentic writing activity for spelling instruction and assessment. When used for instruction, you can set aside one time a week in which students reread their journal entries to identify words they misspelled and to ask for words they would like to write but don't know how to spell. Most teachers find that selecting three to five words a week is valuable for students' growth. As demonstrated in Mr. Sullivan's class, some older students like Michael enjoy leading this activity (and with the help of a dictionary or thesaurus can locate almost all words that their peers desire). When words are identified, they are written in a special section of their writing journal entitled "Spelling Journal." Each word is listed and dated and spelling tests are given each week. At the end of the year, students can return to their spelling journals to realize how many words they learned to spell.

Journals can also be used to assess spelling. Students in kindergarten through third grade especially can count the number of words they wrote as well as the number of words spelled correctly from week to week; older students can count the number of words in their spelling journals and thematic units that they spelled correctly in their journals.

CONNECTING CLASSROOMS, PARENTS, AND COMMUNITIES

Taking Spelling into the Home

Many parents do not spell as well as they would like. For this reason, many language arts teachers select one difficult word for students to learn and teach to adults, and each week they have students create a mnemonic device that can help them learn that word. Students then explain to their parents how they learned to spell that word. In the process, parents learn to overcome that particular spelling demon themselves. After this activity has been in place for a few weeks, many parents send a word to school that they have difficulty spelling and ask for students' help in learning to spell that word. The following spelling demons are those that have been suggested by students and their parents for second through fifth grades. In addition, many teachers, like Mr. Sullivan, also ask parents to readminister at home on Wednesday evenings spelling tests that were given at school on the previous Fridays, as a review and reinforcement for students' retention. Spelling words are sent home and the test that parents administer is graded and signed by them. Some teachers also ask parents to require students to write a second word that was not studied at school but follows a spelling pattern that was taught (e.g., if *hat* was on the spelling list, students are asked to follow their spelling of *hat* with *cat,* which was not taught at school).

Second-Grade Spelling Demons

balloon	coming	lots	people	teacher
birthday	don't	much	pretty	that's
bought	every	name	Saturday	their
boys	father	nice	snowman	there
brother	friend	off	sometimes	train
brought	goes	once	store	very
children	likes	party	sure	white

Third-Grade Spelling Demons

afternoon	close	from	morning	today
again	cousin	getting	November	tomorrow
along	daddy	hello	now	vacation
answer	didn't	January	please	well
April	can't	know	received	write
arithmetic	fine	lessons	Sunday	writing
because	fourth	letter	teacher's	yours

Fourth-Grade Spelling Demons

all right	church	hide	meat	puts	Thursday
already	doctor	I'll	meet	quite	tonight
autumn	downstairs	isn't	met	reached	truly
been	earth	it's	mountains	sea	walked
bicycle	everyone	just	noise	soon	weather
cannot	half	laugh	ocean	spent	won
chose	haven't	legs	prince	though	

Fifth-Grade Spelling Demons

address	choose	language	quiet	shopping	they're
anyway	desert	lie	quit	sincerely	thinking
awful	different	neighbor	really	stationery	tooth
blow	fourteen	pieces	receiving	swimming	you're
chief	handkerchiefs	plain	schoolhouse	teaches	

• •

SUMMARY

This chapter presented several reasons why it is important to teach students spelling, writing conventions, and penmanship. There are four basic approaches to instruction: modified textbook, invented spelling, word lists, and editing committees. Several lessons were described that help students to improve their spelling and editing abilities. These included imagery, word pattern lessons, spelling journals, spelling demon charts, and word games. Several lessons were described that helped students to improve their penmanship and punctuation, such as reading aloud books from Literature Cards 23 and 24, auditory and visual clues, hand positioning, self-assessment activities, and writing in pudding and whipped cream. The next chapter will present ways in which language arts can extend and reinforce content learning.

HOW TO DO IT: USING WHAT YOU'VE LEARNED

The following opportunities enable you to reflect on and practice what you have learned.

ASSESSING YOUR LEARNING

1. Collect writing samples from students of the same age, preferably below third grade. Analyze those samples in two ways. First, identify the stage of spelling development that each sample indicates and state one instructional action you would take for each student. If you are not teaching, or cannot collect student writing samples, complete this analysis with the samples that appear in Figure 10.13. Once you've completed your analyses, share your answers with a partner. Check each other's thinking with the answers that their teachers' gave to these same questions in the Answer Key at the end of the book.

Second, use these same samples to diagnose something that each student needs to improve about his or her penmanship. Specify the instructional strategy you would use to overcome the difficulty. You can also check your answers against those given by their teachers in the Answer Key.

2. Outline the spelling program you will develop. Include a description of the class and grade level you teach (or are preparing to teach). Tell when and whether you will use textbooks in your spelling program. Describe two types of homework assignments you will give for spelling, punctuation, penmanship, and capitalization. Which, if any, of these assignments do you feel justified in giving to the whole class? Describe a type of homework assignment you would give to a student whose percentage of invented spellings is not decreasing.

3. Explain why it is so difficult to learn to spell and how spelling, reading, and writing are related. Select a book from Literature Card 23 or 24 and design a lesson to increase students' spelling awareness using that book.

4. How many of the following invented spellings can you recognize? Can you tell the stage of development each represents? After you have written each word correctly and identified its stage in students' spelling development (e.g., letter name stage), you can turn to the Answer Key at the back of the book to check your answer.

acl	revr	bothring	snrcls	youmembein	wereed
butrfli	next stordaber	yace dodl	alathawaup	vakumklenr	jimnozzme
mapl	lecdrek	ovr	rtst	filisdiler	plgavalegents

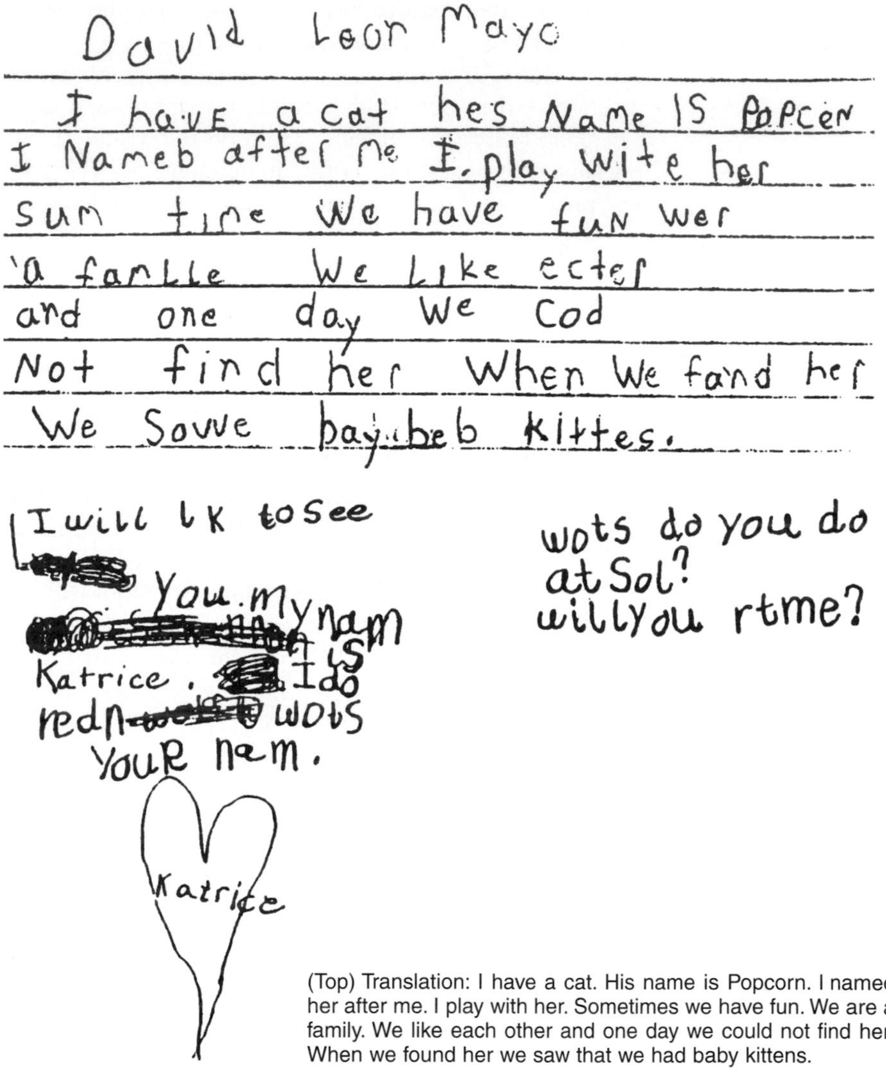

David Leon Mayo

I have a cat he's Name IS PoPceN
I Nameb affer me I play wite her
sum tine We have fun wer
'a fanlle We Like ecter
and one day We Cod
Not find her When We fand her
We Sowe bay·beb kittes.

I will lk tosee
~~You~~ You.mynam
~~~~ IS
Katrice. ~~~~ Ido
redn~~~~ wots
youR nem.

Katrice

wots do you do
at Sol?
willyou rtme?

(Top) Translation: I have a cat. His name is Popcorn. I named her after me. I play with her. Sometimes we have fun. We are a family. We like each other and one day we could not find her. When we found her we saw that we had baby kittens.

(Bottom) Translation: I will like to see you. My name is Katrice. I do reading. What is your name? What do you do at school? Will you write to me?

FIGURE 10.13 DIAGNOSING STUDENTS' SPELLING NEEDS

KEY TERMS EXERCISE

Below are the concepts introduced in this chapter. If you have learned a term, place a checkmark in the blank that precedes that term. If you are not sure of a definition of a term, increase your retention and return to reread its definition. If you have learned 15 of the terms in this chapter, you have constructed an understanding of a majority of the most important concepts that you need to develop your students' editing, spelling, and handwriting abilities.

_____ auditory inattention   (p. 430)

_____ authentic instruction   (p. 418)

_____ capitalization   (p. 422)

_____ configuration   (p. 441)

_____ correct spelling stage   (p. 422)

_____ cursive handwriting   (p. 433)

_____ guided invented spelling   (p. 418)

_____ homophones   (p. 431)

_____ invented spelling   (p. 422)

_____ italics   (p. 433)

_____ logographically   (p. 418)

_____ manuscript handwriting   (p. 433)

_____ penmanship   (p. 422)

_____ phonetic or letter name stage (p. 421)

_____ prealphabetic reading   (p. 418)

_____ precommunicative or prephonetic stage   (p. 420)

_____ punctuation   (p. 422)

_____ semiphonetic or early phonetic stage   (p. 420)

_____ spelling rule inattention (p. 431)

_____ traditional spelling   (p. 422)

_____ transitional stage   (p. 422)

_____ visual inattention   (p. 431)

FOR FUTURE REFERENCE

Books about Spelling, Handwriting, Punctuation, and Capitalization, or Seventh-Grade Students

Bean, W., & Bouffler, C. (1987). *Spell by writing.* Rozelle, Australia: Primary English Teaching Association.

Gentry, J. R. (1987). *Spel . . . is a four-letter word.* New York: Scholastic.

Gentry, J. R., & Gillet, J. W. (1992). *Teaching kids to spell.* Portsmouth, NH: Heinemann.

Gordon, K. E. (1984). *The transitive vampire: A handbook of grammar for the innocent, the eager, and the doomed.* New York: Times Books.

Hackney, C. S. (n.d.). *The left-handed child in a right-handed world.* Columbus, OH: Zaner-Bloser Handwriting.

Manning, M. M., & Manning, G. L. (1986). *Improving spelling in the middle grades* (2nd ed.). Washington, DC: National Education Association.

McAlexander, P. J., Dobie, A. B., & Gregg, N. (1992). *Beyond the "SP" label: Improving the spelling of learning disabled and basic writers.* Urbana, IL: NCTE.

Osborn, P. (1989). *How grammar works: A self-teaching guide.* New York: Wiley.

Powell, D., & Hornsby, D. (1993). *Learning phonics and spelling: In a whole language classroom.* New York: Scholastic.

Sassoon, R. (1983). *The practical guide to children's handwriting.* London: Thames and Hudson.

Welton, A. (1993). *Explorers and exploration: The best resources for grades 5 through 9.* Phoenix, AZ: Oryx.

Resources for Parents

Gentry, R. J. (1997). *My kid can't spell.* Portsmouth, NH: Heinemann.

Gentry, F. J. (1993). *Teaching kids to spell.* Portsmouth, NH: Heinemann.

Resources for Teachers

Bolton, F., & Snowball, D. (1993). *Ideas for spelling.* Portsmouth, NH: Heinemann.

Bolton, F., & Snowball, D. (1993). *Teaching spelling.* Portsmouth, NH: Heinemann.

Buchanan, E. (1989). *Spelling for whole language classrooms.* Winnipeg, Canada: Whole Language Consultants.

D'Nealian handwriting k–8. (1993). Glenview, IL: Scott Foresman.

Olsen, J. Z. (1991). *Cursive handwriting.* Potomac, MD: Author.

Olsen, J. Z. (1994). *Handwriting without tears.* Potomac, MD: Author.

THEMATIC UNIT: INTEGRATING LANGUAGE ARTS WITH SOCIAL STUDIES, NONFICTION, AND CHILDREN'S LITERATURE

Thematic Unit

This is the unit Ms. Brandt's seventh-graders most enjoyed during the year. As you read, you may want to list the opportunities students have to improve their editing, spelling, penmanship, and use of writing convention during their study.

Planning with Students

As this unit on the Holocaust begins, students can express their desired areas for study, and you can provide a list of events, people, and other nonfiction and fiction books for students to read and reference during the unit. Many excellent additional lesson plans concerning the Holocaust and facing history are ready for you to implement in your classroom as well by referencing the website that accompanies this book.

Generalizations

The Holocaust was a time in history when people of the Jewish faith, as well as others, were persecuted for their religious beliefs by the followers of Adolf Hitler. The story in *Number the Stars,* by Lois Lowry, occurs during this horrible time in history. Through reading this book and participating in the related activities, students become aware of the role that prejudice played during the Holocaust and how prejudice affects their lives today.

Objective

Through reading *Number the Stars,* students receive an overview of the events of the Holocaust and how it affected the people involved.

Content Area Concepts

Reading.   Students learn how authors create vivid characters through the descriptions of their actions and mannerisms.

Math.   (1) Large numbers are read by naming digits in consecutive places; (2) students measure distance between countries using a map scale; (3) recipes require precise measurements of volume; (4) star shapes can be constructed from circles; and (5) star shapes have lines of symmetry.

Science.   (1) The nerve endings in the nose help people distinguish between a wide range of smells; and (2) the earth's movement around the sun causes hours of daylight and darkness that vary with the seasons.

This unit was written by Meg Brandt, Hurst, Texas, Unit Plan: The Holocaust, Grades 4–7. Used by permission.

Social Studies.   (1) Symbols can be used on a map of Germany for locating the major concentration camps of the Holocaust; (2) a timeline can help students parallel events during the Holocaust and throughout *Number the Stars*; (3) students can use the dictionary to locate the meaning of *stereotype,* and to explore the concept through their own experiences; and (4) immigration brought each of us to America.

Physical Education.   Running strengthens endurance.

Language Arts.   A range of writing activities strengthen students' written communication.

Art.   Ideas and feelings about the Holocaust are expressed through drawing.

Music.   Ideas and feelings about the Holocaust are expressed through music.

Language Arts Strategies

You can use a combination of silent and oral reading with students as individuals, in small groups, and as a whole class in order to reveal each student's best learning strategy.

Resources

Nonfictional and fictional accounts that students can use in this unit are listed below.

Adler, D. A. (1987). *The number on my grandfather's arm.* New York: UAHC Press.

Bunting, B. (1989). *Terrible things: An allegory of the Holocaust.* New York: Simon & Schuster.

Chaikin, M. (1987). *A nightmare in history: The Holocaust 1933–1945.* New York: Houghton.

Frank, A. (1972). *Anne Frank—The diary of a young girl.* New York: Simon & Schuster.

Friedman, I. R. (1990). *The other victims: First person stories of non-Jews persecuted by the Nazis.* Boston: Houghton Mifflin.

Gray, R. D. (1983). *Hitler and the Germans.* Minnesota: Publications Company.

Greenburger, I. (1973). *A private treason: A German memoir.* Boston: Little, Brown.

Greene, Bette. (1973). *Summer of my German soldier.* New York: Dial.

Hersey, John. (1985). *Hiroshima.* New York: Random House.

Hurwitz, J. (1988). *Anne Frank—Life in hiding.* New York: Jewish Publication Society.

Kurzman, Dan. (1986). *Day of the bomb: Countdown to Hiroshima.* New York: McGraw-Hill.

Lowry, L. (1989). *Number the stars.* Boston: Houghton Mifflin.

Meltzer, M. (1976). *Never to forget—The Jews of the Holocaust.* New York: Harper Trophy.

Rogasky, Barbara. (1988). *Smoke and ashes: The story of the Holocaust.* New York: Holiday.

Rosenberg, M. B. (1994). *Hiding to survive.* New York: Clarion Books.

Stein, R. C. (1985). *World at war: Warsaw ghetto.* Chicago: Children's Press.

Process in Action

Suggested ideas for activities in content areas follow.

Reading

1. Read *Number the Stars,* by Lois Lowry. This can be done through a combination of individual reading by the students, the teacher reading aloud, and small group/paired reading;

2. Background of Hitler: Students locate a book on Hitler in the library and discuss what was found within groups, then share with the whole class.

3. Read Chapters 7, 8, and 9 ("Auschwitz-Birkenau," "Those on the Right," and "Those on the Left") from the book by Miriam Chaikin called *A Nightmare in History.* Have students write a poem or journal entry and describe how they might have felt in the situation described.

4. Characters are developed by their actions and speech. Students learn about character development by analyzing words that the author uses to describe individual characters. Your students can make character development webs that progress with the story (i.e., character traits are added to the web as new chapters are read).

5. Four or five students read different books by the same author. Have a panel discussion comparing the books in terms of author's emphasis, interest, and author's ability to develop memorable characters.

Science

1. Study the sense of smell and how smell plays a role in our everyday lives. This relates to the end of the book where the search dogs' sense of smell is manipulated to allow the escape of the Jews to Sweden (see pages 135–136).

2. In *Number the Stars,* many of the rescue efforts took place at night, with darkness being instrumental. Discover how the length of hours of daylight and of darkness vary from one day to the next for one week. Learn how this is caused by the position of the earth in relation to the sun as the seasons change. Ask students how the story might have varied at another time of the year.

Social Studies

1. Study the geography of Germany and the surrounding countries. Some major landmarks would be the concentration camps, Warsaw ghetto, and war headquarters.

2. Creating a timeline of events in the book as well as those of World War II will help students understand the time period involved. Then they can compare these

timelines to better understand how the events in the book correlate with other historical events in the world.

3. Students can learn the meaning of *stereotype* and how prejudice affects our attitudes toward others. Have students look up definitions of *stereotype* in several dictionaries then compare what they found in groups. The students can brainstorm different harmful biases that they know of and where they learned about them. Discuss why these biases exist and ways they might be eliminated from their lives.

4. Many different groups of people have made contributions to American society. Students can learn about these contributions by studying about immigration to the United States. This topic can be explored through a study of family history, focusing on each student's personal ancestry. Some students may not have access to much of their own history, so you could have them follow a historical figure or a classmate's history to help them understand immigration.

5. After learning more about their own personal histories, students can continue the study by writing an autobiography for an imaginary ancestor. Students should pick a time period and explain what daily life was like for that person. The children can describe one day or several days in the ancestor's life.

Physical Education

Students can participate in timed running to improve endurance and speed. Compare their time to how fast Anne Marie ran to catch the fishing boat. This activity should increase understanding and appreciation of Anne Marie's strength of character.

Art

1. Class mural: Use butcher paper to create a mural that depicts, in order, the major events found throughout the book. Students can work in groups, with each group selecting an event to illustrate.

2. Scrapbook: Students might enjoy choosing a character from the book and creating a scrapbook for that character. The scrapbook can include drawings to depict events in that character's life and journal entries that character might have written, and so forth.

Music

Write a song or ballad about the book or a character of choice (individually or in groups).

Other Special Activities

1. Field Trip: The Holocaust Center, 7900 Northhaven Rd., Dallas (Jewish Community Center), 214-750-4654. Reservations required for classes and guided tours, $1 per person. Hours: Mon.–Fri. 9:30–4:30, Sat. 12–4. Other such centers exist throughtout the United States, Canada, and Europe.

2. Arrange to have a survivor of the holocaust or a family member come to speak to your class. (This can be done through the Jewish Community Center in the area.)

Real-World Application

Request that students bring to class an item from home or draw a picture of something from their heritage that makes them unique. Discuss each person's strengths and contributions and how they can apply these in the world.

Promote total acceptance of each person in the classroom. After a few days, or a week, discuss how the class carried out the program. Students can respond with how they felt in an accepting atmosphere and how they were able to accept others.

Challenge the students to write letters to senators or members of the school board suggesting ways in which prejudice could be minimized in the community.

Reflections. Reflecting on the unit can give students a sense of closure and a beginning point for further study of the subject.

New Questions Raised. The students might come up with questions such as, "Could the Holocaust happen again? What can we do to prevent it? What other issue in history perplexes us? How could we learn more about it?"

New Insights. Stereotyping and prejudice do still exist in today's society; they did not disappear with the end of World War II.

New Powerful Language and Thinking Abilities Desired. Students should be able to understand how characters are developed by an author, orally describe the characters, and find comparisons between fictional characters and real people.

Summary Statements

There is often controversy surrounding the study of the Holocaust by young students, but it is generally agreed that most fourth-graders and older students should learn about this time in history. The more we educate about controversial issues, the more students can begin to form their own ideas and opinions. It is suggested that parents be contacted before this unit begins to let them know that their children will be dealing with difficult concepts and may need additional support during this study. It is my feeling that this topic not be avoided, and that, through sensitive and thorough planning, educators can teach it well.

The Center for Problem-Based Learning in Aurora, Illinois, teaches students how to infuse their language arts program with research and the resolution of community-based problems.

CHAPTER 11

INTEGRATING LANGUAGE ARTS ACROSS THE CURRICULUM

Michael reflected: "Ms. Morrison devoted the first three days of our eighth-grade language arts and social studies classes to talking about our lives. We started by telling about our recent summer vacations, our families, our future plans, our pets, our friends, and our fears. By the end of the week we were sharing our dreams and our aspirations. It was hard to believe how much we were willing to reveal in such a short time. She never pressured us to talk or asked us to elaborate. We actually began wanting to get to really know the people with which we would spend the rest of the year. We felt comfortable and loved. And it never failed to amaze us that she remembered these stories about our lives years later" (adapted from Peterson, 1992).

Michael continued, "I remember the day she asked if we wanted to join the Center for Problem-Based Learning. We were engaged in a problem-based learning group discussion. We had each read poetry, fiction, or nonfiction about environmental issues in our state. After we shared ideas about how we could help, she told us about problems that community leaders wanted our help in solving, and we selected ones that we wanted to explore. I choose to develop a new tourist guide for our city; Meisong and Juan selected the nuclear exposure problem and also designed a new symbol for the Chinese community. It showed the philosophy of Yin/Yang—the ideas of opposites and balances. We read more books and research reports than I'd ever read before! Our products were used by adults, and we really helped our city."

"Today the trend in some classrooms is to see reading and writing as tools for learning ... and to learn through [the language arts], to grow, change, and learn" (Harste, 1989, p. 19). This philosophy of integrating the language arts, fiction, nonfiction, poetry, and content area instruction has been judged to be one of the most important instructional advancements of the twentieth century (Cairney, 1990; Cox, Shanahan, & Sulzby, 1990; International Reading Association, 1999). In this chapter you will learn the benefits of this connection, including how students can learn to think like scientists, mathematicians, artists, historians, and public speakers. In doing so, many students come to assess their aptitudes and interests in future professions in a realistic fashion. They also perform authentic, content area speaking, listening, reading, and writing tasks in ways that will be required in the real world. By the end of the chapter, you will have the information to answer the following questions, which are based on the IRA, NCTE, NAEYC, TEKS, and other statewide and province-based standards for professional development:

1. What are the methods of integrating language arts and content area classes?

2. How can literature increase students' learning in science, math, social science, and the fine arts classes?

3. How can interdisciplinary studies, thematic units, and topic integration to increase students' learning?

4. How can students evaluate their learning through essays, authentic performances, mentoring, small-group assessments, and learning logs?

5. How can we increase students' understanding, application, and appreciation of media and processes related to the visual arts?

6. How can we increase students' understanding of the role of literature and the visual arts in relation to history, cultures, science, math, and the fine arts.

7. How can students collaborate with peers to use telecommunications and collaborative lessons as they investigate curriculum-related problems, issues, and information and to develop solutions or products for audiences outside the classroom.

• •

SECTION 1   THEORETICAL FOUNDATIONS

The Need to Integrate Language Arts Literature and Content Area Instruction

Including the language arts across the curriculum capitalizes on the natural link between language and thought. It also builds on the prior experiences pupils bring to school and excellerates students' drive to make sense of new information. When language arts and literature are included in content area instruction, students' attention shifts from the use of language as a means of displaying what has been learned to its use as a tool in the learning process itself. "This pedagogical shift from language as a product to be examined to language as an accompaniment to learning of all kinds is, as yet, occurring slowly. But, as theory, research, and practice indicate, the argument for such a shift is compelling" (Healy & Barr, 1991, p. 820).

There are several benefits. First, language aids learning, by providing regular occasions for students to discuss and write about new ideas that they encounter in all subjects. Instead of depending solely on teacher or text to point out the significance of new ideas, pupils who engage in regular uses of writing and talking in content area classes discover what meanings new ideas hold for them (Shanahan, 1997). For example, in order for pupils to develop lines of argument or to reflect on the causes of historical events, they must have an interested partner, usually the teacher, who encourages both their process of discovery and their application of new knowledge to situations that exist in our world today.

Second, integration enables content area instruction to become more student centered (Block, 1999b). Putting the learner in charge of his or her own translation of learning experiences is a radical departure from practices that encourage teacher-and-text-centered classrooms. Britton (1970) supported such a power shift more than 3 decades ago, arguing that it is not only possible but desirable in order to improve pupil achievement. Britton synthesized Vygotsky's and Bruner's theories for education and urged that schools should build on the inclination of human learners to use their verbal, reading, and writing skills for real, life-serving purposes. Moreover, when students read fiction, nonfiction, and poetry in their content area studies, two patterns emerge:

1. Generally, when given the choice, students opt to use tradebooks first, and find them more interesting, informative, and enjoyable than their textbooks.

2. Textbooks do not describe how authors obtained the information they used to construct their historical renditions, thus these books inhibit students' ability to make judgments about the reliability and validity of information and implied meanings in their texts (VanSledright, 1995).

Third, an integrated day in which students engage in intense participation builds denser background knowledge for topics and provides multisensory experiences that enable students to more easily transfer content to their lives (Crafton 1983; Beck & Dole, 1992). In addition, typically, textbooks do not allocate enough pages to specific subtopics to build students' in-depth understanding (McMahon, Goatley, and McGill-Franzen, 1999). Not only do textbooks, of necessity, cover many points briefly, but also they do not include in-depth examinations of culture, traditions, rationale, and emotions that underlay decisions surrounding historical events. When students read, discuss, listen, study, and write with tradebooks, fictional accounts, poetry, and current events literature, these voids are filled. Samples of children's literature that support content area instruction in history, social studies, science, and fine arts appear in Literature Cards 25–28.

Through integration, students read and write using many resources, and they discuss several perspectives. Such comparisons are less likely when textbooks are the sole reference during content instruction. Compounding the problem of limited coverage, transition words that show relationships between topics are included in few content area textbooks (Irvin, 1989; Beck & Dole, 1992). When other literature and students' writing are combined with texts, these connections become more explicit. Achievement on multiple choice and essay questions on content area material also increases significantly (Beck & McKeoun, 1994; Flood & Lapp, 1991). Moreover, assisting less able students to read tradebooks and children's literature for content area instructional purposes helps to increase their self-esteem because students feel smart when they read these books. **Tradebooks** are written using low-level vocabulary and easy readability levels that focus on a single content area subject only, such as trees, frogs, or the story of only one musician's life. Students can accumulate a lot more background about a subject because these books are understandable and captivating (Caswell & Duke, 1998). Using literature and tradebooks is also valuable because some students' personal and scholastic interests center on topics in social studies, science, math, and fine art. Allowing students, especially boys, to read extensively in their areas of interest motivates them to read and write because the specific topics in nonfictional content areas tend to be of greater interest

CHILDREN'S LITERATURE THAT ADDS TO STUDENTS' KNOWLEDGE OF HISTORY AND THE SOCIAL SCIENCES

Good Books with a Lot of Pictures

Ice Cream by W. Jasperson, 1989 Macmillan

Take a Walk in Their Shoes by G. T. Tuner, 1989 Cobblehill Books

A Country Far Away by N. Gray, 1989 Orchard

Eating the Plates by L. Penner, 1991 Macmillan

Weird Parents by A. Wood, 1990 Dial

Geography from A to Z by J. Knowlton 1998

Hello Amigos by T. Brown, 1986 Holt

Our Declaration of Independence by J. Schleifer, 1992 Millbrook Press

Our National Anthem by S. St. Pierre, 1992 Millbrook Press

Our National Holidays by K. Spies, 1992 Millbrook Press

They Had a Dream by J. Archer, 1993 Viking

John Brown by G. Everett, 1993 Rizzoli

Our Money by K. Spies, 1992 Millbrook Press

Ashanti to Zulu: African Traditions by M. Musgrove, 1976 Dial

Darkness and the Butterfly by A. Grifalconi, 1987 Little, Brown

The Girl Who Loved Wild Horses by P. Goble, 1993 Aladdin

Back Home by G. J. Pinkney, 1992 Dial

Osas' Pride by A. Grifalconi, 1993 Little, Brown

Rachel Parker, Kindergarten Show-Off by A. Martin, 1992 Holiday House

Good Books to Tell You a Lot about History and Social Studies

Our Constitution by L. Johnson, 1992 Millbrook

The Desert Is Theirs by B. Baylor, 1987 Aladdin

Imani's Gift at Kwanzaa by D. Burden-Palmon, 1993 Aladdin

My Name Is Maria Isabel by A. Ada, 1995 Aladdin

A Long Hard Journey by P. & F. McKissack, 1989 Walker

This Place Is Dry (series) by V. Cobb, 1989 Walker

When I First Came to This Land by O. Brand, 1965 Putnam

Cassie's Journey: Going West in the 1860's by B. Harvey, 1988 Holiday House

Follow the Drinking Gourd by J. Winter, 1988 Knopf

Hiroshima by L. Yep, 1995 Scholastic

Butterfly Boy by L. Yep, 1993 F, S, & G

Tar Beach by F. Ringgold, 1991 Crown

Faithful Elephants by Y. Tsuchiyo, 1988 Houghton Mifflin

Now Is Your Time! : The African-American Struggle for Freedom by W. D. Myers, 1991 HarperCollins

The Armadillo from Amarillo by L. Cherry, 1994 HarBrace

Good Books If You Are Just Beginning to Learn about History and Social Studies

Our National Symbols by L. C. Johnson, 1992 Millbrook Press

A Winter Walk by L. Barasch, 1993 Ticknor & Field

The Gift of the Sacred Dog by P. Goble, 1984 Aladdin

Charles Needs a Cloak by A. Turner, 1993 Macmillan

O Canada by T. Harrison, 1993 Ticknor & Fields

The Goat in the Rug by C. Blood and M. Link, 1990 Aladdin

The Milk Makers by G. Gibbons, 1985 Macmillan

Teammates by P. Golenbock, 1990 Harcourt Brace

Bright Fawn and Me by J. Leech & Z. Spencer, 1979 Crowell

Nettie's Trip South by A. Turner, 1987 Macmillan

Me and Willie and Pa by F. Monjo, 1973 Simon & Schuster

One Bad Thing about Father by F. Monjo, 1970 Harper & Row

Father of the Constitution: James Madison by K. Wilkie, 1963 Messner

Our Flag by E. Ayer, 1992 Millbrook Press

Letters from Rifka, 1992 Holt

Books That Have Several Chapters about History and Social Studies

Cowboy: An Album by L. Granfield, 1994 Ticknor & Field

The Black Press and the Struggle for Civil Rights by C. Senna, 1994 Franklin and Watts

Totem Pole by D. Hoyt-Goldsmith, 1990 Holiday House

Puerto Rico: An Unfinished Story by D. Hauptly, 1991 Atheneum

Talking Walls by M. Knight, 1992 Tilbury House

State Books—From Sea to Shining Sea by D. Fradin, 1992 Children's Press

Raney by C. Edgerton, 1985 Ballantine

The Russian Federation by D. Flint, 1992 Millbrook Press

Giant Animals by T. Maynard, 1995 Franklin Watt

The Underground Railroad by S. Cosner, 1991 Venture Books

Every Good-Bye Ain't Gone by I. Njeri, 1990 Random House

Pueblo Storyteller by D. Hoyt-Goldsmith, 1991 Holiday House

Down in the Piney Woods by E. F. Smothers, 1992 Knopf

The Riddle of the Rosetta Stone: Key to Ancient Egypt by J. Giblin, 1990 Crowell

For additional titles of fiction books suitable for use in the social studies classroom, see the website that accompanies this text and *American Historical Fiction and Biography for Children and Young People* by Hotchkiss, 1992.

CHILDREN'S LITERATURE THAT ADDS TO STUDENTS' KNOWLEDGE OF SCIENCE

Good Books with a Lot of Pictures

The Very Hungry Caterpillar by E. Carle, 1994 Putnam

The Very Busy Spider by E. Carle, 1989 Putnam

The Grouchy Ladybug by E. Carle, 1986 HarpC Child Books

Turtle in July by M. Singer, 1993 Macmillan

The X-Ray Picture Book of Dinosaurs and Other Prehistoric Creatures by K. Senior, 1995 Franklin Watts

Your Amazing Senses: 36 Games, Puzzles, and Quizzes That Show How Your Senses Work by R. & A. Van der Meer, 1987 Simon & Schuster

Smelling Things by A. Fowler, 1991 Children's Press

Cornelius by L. Lionni, 1983 Pantheon Books

Vegetables, Vegetables! by F. Robinson, 1994 Children's Press

Our Yard Is Full of Birds by A. Rockwell, 1992 Macmillan Child Group

Quiet by P. Parnall, 1989 Morrow

Tyrannosaurus Was a Beast by J. Prelutsky, 1992 Morrow

A Tree Is Nice by J. M. Udry, 1994 Scholastic

Knots on a Counting Rope by B. Martin Jr., & J. Archambault, 1993 Henry Holt & Co.

Mole's Hill: A Woodland Tale by L. Ehlert, 1994 HarBrace

Good Books to Tell You a Lot about the Subject

Growing Vegetable Soup by L. Ehlert, 1990 HarBrace

The Legend of the Bluebonnet by T. De Paola, 1983 G. P. Putnam's Sons

Corn—On and Off the Cob by A. Fowler, 1994 Children's Press

Now I Know (series) by S. Peters, 1997 Scholastic

Pets of the Presidents by J. Caulkins, 1992 Millbrook Press

Dinosaurs and More Dinosaurs by J. Craig, 1999 Scholastic

Carbohydrates by Dr. Alvin, R. & V. Silverstein, 1992 Millbrook Press

Fats by Dr. Alvin, R. & V. Silverstein, 1992 Millbrook Press

Proteins by Dr. Alvin, R. & V. Silverstein, 1992 Millbrook Press

Vitamins & Minerals by Dr. Alvin, R. & V. Silverstein, 1992 Millbrook

Exploring the World of Animals by P. Durant, 1995 Franklin Watts

Exploring the World of Astronomy by G. Burns, 1995 Franklin Watts

Exploring the World of Plants by P. Durant, 1995 Franklin Watts

Who's Sick Today? by P. Durant, 1997 Franklin Watts

Good Books If You Are Just Beginning to Learn about the Subject

Ducklings and Polliwogs by A. Rockwell, 1994 Macmillan Child Group

Hot and Cold by A. Fowler, 1994 Children's Press

Timelines Flight: Fliers and Flying Machines by D. Jeffries, 1991 Franklin Watts

Turkeys That Fly and Turkeys That Don't by A. Fowler, 1994 Children's Press

Mush by P. Seibert, 1992 Millbrook Press

How Does It Feel to Be Old? by N. Farber, 1988 Doubleday

Feathers by D. Patent, 1992 Dutton Child Books

The New Illustrated Dinosaur Dictionary by H. Sattler, 1990 Morrow

Dicovering Butterflies by D. Florian, 1990 Aladdin

The Rock by P. Parnall, 1991 Macmillan Child Group

Red Leaf, Yellow Leaf by L. Ehlert, 1991 HarBrace

The Great Kapok Tree: A Tale of the Amazon River Forest by L. Cherry, 1990 HarBrace

Our National Monuments by E. Ayer, 1992 Millbrook Press

Germs Make Me Sick by M. Berger, 1985 Crowell

Bird Watch by J. Yolen, 1990 Philomel/Putnam

The Witch's Eye by P. Naylor, 1998 Scholastic

Books That Have Several Chapters about the Subject

The Astronaut Training Book for Kids by K. Long, 1990 Lodestar Books

A Bird's Body and other books by J. Cole, 1982 Morrow

The Magic School Bus (series) by J. Cole, 1986 Scholastic

If You Lived on Mars by M. Berger, 1989 Lodestar Books

The Kingdom of Wolves by S. Barry, 1979 Putnam

Alligators, Raccoons, and Other Survivors: The Wildlife of the Future by B. Ford, 1981 Morrow

Machines That Think and Other Books by I. Asimov, 1984 Holt

Science Facts You Won't Believe by W. Gottlieb, 1983 Watts

Dinosaurs of North America by H. Sattler, 1981 Lothrop, Lee & Shepard

Jupiter by S. Simon, 1985 Morrow

Norby and Yobo's Great Adventure by J. & I. Asimov

The Big Stew by B. Shecter, 1999 Scholastic

The Banshee by K. Ackerman, 1999 Scholastic

The Tunnel by A. Browne, 1999 Scholastic

Outer Space and All That Junk by M. Gilden, 1999 Scholastic

Heartlight by T. A. Barron, 1999 Scholastic

The Midnight Horse by S. Fleischmann, 1999 Scholastic

Literature Card 27

INTEGRATING LANGUAGE ARTS INTO MATHEMATICS CURRICULUM

Good Books with a Lot of Pictures

Three Sides and the Round One by Friskey, 1975 Children's Press

My Very First Book of Shapes by E. Carle, 1970 Crowell

Adding Animals by Hawkins, 1997 Scholastic

Making Cents by E. Wilkensen, 1989 Little, Brown

A Chair for My Mother by V. Williams, 1983 Random House

Jumanji by C. Van Allsburg, 1981 Houghton Mifflin

The Toothpaste Millionaire by J. Merrill, 1972 Houghton Mifflin

26 Letters and 99 Cents by T. Hoban, 1987 Greenwillow

One, Two, Three to the Zoo by E. Carle, 1991 Picture Book Studio

Much Bigger Than Martin by S. Kellogg, 1976 Dial

Color Zoo by L. Ehlert, 1989 Lippincott

Willy Can Count by A. Rockwell, 1989 Arcade Publishers

How Many Feet in the Bed? by D. Hamm, 1991 Simon & Schuster

One Two, One Pair by B. McMillan, 1991 Scholastic

Waiting for Sunday by C. Blackburn, 1991 Scholastic

Good Books to Tell You a Lot about the Subject

Count Your Way Through India and other stories by J. Haskins, 1987–1990 Carolrhoda Books

All Shapes and Sizes by S. Hughes, 1986 Douglas & McIntyre

The Missing Piece by S. Silverstein, 1976 Harper & Row

What Is Symmetry? by M. & H. Sitomer, 1970 Crowell

What Do You Mean by Average? by E. James & C. Barkin, 1998 Scholastic

The Carrot Seed by R. Krauss, 1945 Harper & Row

The Half Birthday Party by C. Pomerantz, 1984 Clarion

Five Little Monkeys Jumping on the Bed by E. Christelow, 1989 Clarion

Mouse Count by E. Walsh, 1991 Harcourt Brace Jovanovich

This Old Man by C. Jones, 1990 Boston

Count on Your Fingers African Style by C. Zaslavsky, 1980 Crowell

Lines by P. Yenawine, 1991 Delacorte Press

The Book of Classic Board Games by S. Sackson, 1991 Klutz Press

Good Books If You Are Just Beginning to Learn about the Subject

One White Sail by S. Garne, 1992 Green Tiger Press

Shape Space by C. Falwell, 1992 Clarion

One Smiling Grandma: A Caribbean Counting Book by A. Linden, 1992 Dial

Eating Fractions by B. McMillan, 1991 Scholastic

Deep Down Underground by Oliver, 1993 Aladdin

Over in the Meadow by P. Galdone, 1986 Aladdin

Zero: Is It Something? Is It Nothing? by C. Zaslavsky, 1989 Franklin Watts

Ten Black Dots by D. Crews, 1986 Greenwillow

How Many Is a Million? by D. Schwartz, 1985 Lothrop, Lee & Shepard

The Hundred Penny Box by S. Mathis, 1975 Viking

Listen to a Shape by M. Brown, 1979 Franklin Watts

Moira's Birthday by R. Munsch, 1987 Annic

Fish Eyes: A Book You Can Count On by L. Ehlert, 1990 Harcourt Brace Jovanovich

Mushroom in the Rain by M. Ginsburg, 1974 Macmillan

Just a Mess by M. Mayer, 1987 Western

Books That Have Several Chapters about the Subject

Straight Lines, Parallel Lines, and Perpendicular Lines by M. Charosh, 1970 Crowell

Angles Are as Easy as Pie by R. Froman, 1997 Crowell

A Collection of Math Lessons from Grades 1–3 by M. Burns, 1988 Math Solutions Publication

Arithmetic Teacher (magazine)

Smart Spending: A Young Consumer's Guide by L. Schmitt, 1997 Scribner

Extra Cash for Kids by L. Belliston, K. Hanks, 1989 Wolgemuth & Hyatt

Esio Trot by R. Doahl, 1990 Viking

Where the Sidewalk Ends by Shel Silverstein, 1974 Harper & Row

The I Hate Mathematics! Book by M. Burns, 1975 Little, Brown

Sideways Arithmetic from Wayside School by L. Sachar, 1989 Scholastic

Ed Emberley's Picture Pie: A Circle Drawing Book by E. Emberley, 1984 Little, Brown

Making Cents: Every Kid's Guide to Money, How to Make It, What to Do with It by E. Wilkinson, 1989 Little, Brown

Clocks: Building and Experimenting with Model Timepieces by B. Zubrowski, 1988 Morrow

Literature Card 28

CHILDREN'S LITERATURE THAT ADDS TO STUDENTS' APPRECIATION OF THE FINE ARTS

Good Books with a Lot of Pictures

People at Work: Looking at Art by P. Conner, 1992 McElderry

The Pooh Sketchbook by E. H. Shepard, 1984 E. P. Dutton

Great Painters by P. Ventura, 1984 G. P. Putnam

Tuesday by D. Wiesner, 1991 Clarion

The Polar Express by C. Van Allsburg, 1985 Houghton Mifflin

Noah's Ark by P. Spier, 1977 Doubleday

I'm Dancing by A. McCarter and G. Reed, 1981 Charles Scribner

Free Fall by D. Weisner, 1980 Lothrop, Lee & Shephard

Teammates by P. Golenbock, 1990 Harcourt Brace Jovanovich

Possum Come a-Knockin by N. Van Laan, 1990 Alfred A. Knopf

Emma by W. Kesselman, 1980 Harper

No Good in Art by M. Cohen, 1980 Greenwillow

Draw Me a Star by E. Carle, 1992 Putnam

Mr. Panda's Painting by A. Rockwell, 1993 Macmillan

Good Books If You Are Just Beginning to Learn about Fine Arts Subjects

Pigs at Christmas by A. Dubanevich, 1990 Aladdin

I Am an Artist by P. Collins, 1992 Millbrook Press

Getting to Know the World's Greatest Artists (series) by M. Venezia, 1993 Children's Press

Getting to Know the World's Greatest Composers by M. Venezia, 1997 Scholastic

The Art School (series) by R. Smith, 1994 Dorling Kindersley

The Art Lesson by T. de Paola, 1989 G. P. Putnam

Fun with Paper by R. Supraner, 1981 Troll Associates

At Every Turn! It's Ballet by S. R. Sorine, 1981 Alfred A. Knopf

Song and Dance Man by K. Ackerman, 1988 Alfred A. Knopf

"Crayons" in Jack Prelutsky's *Read Aloud Rhymes for the Very Young* by M. Chute, 1986 Knopf

Good Books to Tell You a Lot about Fine Arts Subjects

Davinci by M. Venezia, 1989 Children's Press

Mary Cassatt by M. Venezia, 1989 Children's Press

Diego Rivera by M. Venezia, 1994 Children's Press

Francisco Goya by M. Venezia, 1991 Children's Press

Henri de Toulouse-Lautrec by M. Venezia, 1994 Children's Press

A Color Sampler by K. Westry, 1993 Ticknor & Fields

The Ways to Start a Day by B. Baylor, 1986 Aladdin

Lil' Sis and Uncle Willie: A Story Based on the Life and Paintings of William H. Johnson by G. Everett, 1991 Rizzoli International Publications

What Instrument Is This? by R. Hausherr, 1992 Scholastic

Let's Find the Big Idea by B. W. Carlson, 1982 Abingdon Press

How to Make Pop-Ups by J. Irvine, 1987 Morrow

Making Musical Things by A. Wiseman, 1979 Charles Scribner's Sons

"The Paint Box" in Scott Elledge's *Wider Than the Sky* by E. V. Rieu, 1990 Harper

The Art of Eric Carle by E. Carle, 1993 Picture Book Studio

The Joy of Drawing by B. Martin, 1993 Watson-Guptill

Books That Have Several Chapters about Fine Arts Subjects

Draw 50 Horses by L. Ames, 1984 Doubleday

Drawing from Nature by J. Arnmosky, 1982 Lothrop, Lee & Shepard

Drawing Dinosaurs & Other Prehistoric Animals by D. Bolognese, 1982 Franklin Watts

North American Indian Masks: Craft and Legend by F. Gates, 1982 Walker

Meet Matisse by N. Munthe, 1983 Little, Brown

Winslow Homer: The Gulf Stream by E. Goldstein, 1982 Garrard

The Magic of Color by H. Simon, 1981 Lothrop, Lee & Shepard

A Weekend with Matisse by F. Rodari, 1992 Rozzoli

A Weekend with Renoir by R. Skira-Venturi, 1992 Rozzoli

Michelangelo by R. MacNathan, 1993 Harry N. Abrams

Series TV: How a Television Show Is Made by M. Drucker & E. James, 1983 Clarion

The Sky Is Full of Song by L. B. Hopkins, 1983 Harper & Row

Jazz by L. Hughes, 1982 Franklin Watts

An Artist's Album by M. B. Goffstein, 1985 Harper

"Sister Ann" in *A Poem for a Pickle* by E. Merriam, 1989 Horrow

Teaching Drama to Young Children by M. Fox, 1986 Heinemann

than those in children's fictional literature (Duke, 2000). Therefore, content area knowledge and language arts skills increase simultaneously.

Fourth, integration of language arts instruction and content area topics should center on big ideas about our "human condition" (Bruner, 1998). Many teachers have voiced frustration that they have too many concepts to cover in too short a time. Studying one broad idea in the morning and afternoon can increase the amount of time you spend on single topics in language arts content area subject periods and the amount of time that students spend in sustained, reflective reading and writing during school hours. As a result, most students increase their higher-level thinking and enrich the depth of their writing and reading abilities. Also, in recent studies, researchers revealed that integrated instruction allows more dialog to occur. **Dialogical discourse** allows students to openly discuss and ask authentic, real-world questions that promote their own learning (Nystrand 1999).

Fifth, integration is not something that *you* plan and implement, but rather a process that occurs within learners. When curricular units are generated by the students, framed around broad, real-world current problems, and begin with students' interests, students can make connections between themselves, literacy, and the world. These connections can be spurred by the methods that are reported in this chapter. For example, Ms. Morrison and her eighth-grade students create their own ideas by integrating curriculum using the following method.

Ms. Morrison listens as students discuss the core of concepts that are to be introduced that week in either social studies, science, or math lessons. During this discussion, Ms. Morrison writes on the chalkboard the questions students ask that no one in the class can answer. For example, in the October unit, students were asking: "Why do immigrants come to the United States?" "What are living conditions like in other parts of the world?" "Is the American Dream concept still alive in the United States?" "Are immigrants who come to the United States today better off than the immigrants who came in the past?" "How can we create a society in which all people are valued equally?" With these questions in mind, students initiated an integrated study that lasted for 1 hour and 50 minutes because Ms. Morrison combined her language arts block with her social studies block.

Last, by integrating the curriculum, students can increase their understanding of themselves and the world around them. They do so because having a larger period of time to explore issues that are important to them develops their dispositions as learners. Curiosity, independence, responsibility, initiative, creativity, willingness to take risks, ability to ask questions, and desire to persevere have been demonstrated to increase significantly through such studies (Block, 1999; Dodge, 1994). When students acquire the skills they need to be successful learners, literacy and language, as well as mathematics thinking, scientific thinking, social inquiry, and the ability to express their ideas through language arts and technology, simultaneously develop. As a result, students function as contributing members of a community because they develop social skills and decision-making skills that benefit their own welfare as well as their classroom society and often society at large. When instruction becomes authentic in this way, students acquire information, satisfy their curiosity, and understand new vocabulary terms, all of which improve their writing as well (Harvey, 1998).

In summary, when authenticity reigns and topics are chosen by students, sincere questions and interests are spurred. Student research projects begin when real-world concerns are pursued. You can serve as their mentor by modeling how to read nonfictional texts, magazines, and tradebooks, and by sharing the information they contain. This will show students that you think studying both the language arts and the content areas is important (Harvey, 1998; Nystrand, 1999). With these benefits in mind, you can use the methods described next to integrate language arts and content instruction.

TYPES OF INTEGRATION

Integration can occur through thematic units, daily lesson plans, and topic integration methods.

Thematic units are illustrated at the end of even-numbered chapters in this textbook. They are usually completed in self-contained classrooms, and reading, writing, speaking, and listening skills are applied in the content area. Thematic units typically last for a week or longer and enable children to explore a topic in depth. Students often explore the topic by comparing multiple definitions; analyzing beneficial and detrimental outcomes relative to the topic; identifying past, present, and future applications to their lives; and reporting specific areas of personal interest. The most effective thematic units have four features: (1) themes are selected by students; (2) students' work culminates in a product or process that they present to people outside the classroom or can be used later in their lives; (3) students work concurrently on two subtopics so they can learn to think integratively; and (4) at least one of the subtopics selected by the class includes the examination of a current political, historical, economic, human, or environmental issue.

A description of how these five components would be evidenced in a thematic unit for older students appears in Figure 11.1. Topics in thematic units are broad-based rather than content-specific. For example, instead of younger students studying animals, a productive thematic unit would develop a theme around this topic such as, "How do living things adapt and change to survive and grow?"

In the unit depicted in Figure 11.1 students debated the "burn" policy of the national park system and created videotapes as well as poetry to support their positions. They read books and articles about the people, politics, and developments that were important in developing our first national parks. John Muir's *Yellowstone Park* was read aloud to provide background for students to choose an objective to pursue, which was to create a timeline to depict changes in national parks. Students also wrote poetry and reports (containing information from outside readings) to portray their predictions about the future of our national parks system. When this thematic unit was complete, students suggested other topics they wished to study. Motivation was high, and education was no longer viewed as the isolated study of bits and pieces of information. Across the curriculum, thematic studies became the way of learning students preferred.

Although thematic units contain the same components as daily lesson plans, each component takes one or more days to complete. For example, you can spend one day setting the objectives and allowing students to establish goals they wish to reach. You and your students can spend a day locating resources, such as those listed in the sample resource lists in Figure 11.2. Students can spend several days designing and writing projects and in-depth studies of a single topic, shown in the following

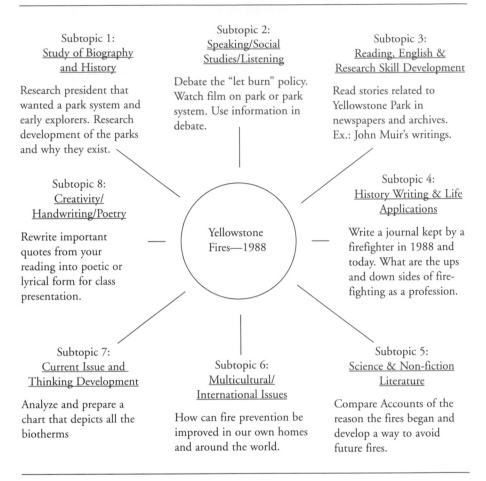

Subtopic 1:
Study of Biography
and History

Research president that
wanted a park system and
early explorers. Research
development of the parks
and why they exist.

Subtopic 2:
Speaking/Social
Studies/Listening

Debate the "let burn" policy.
Watch film on park or park
system. Use information in
debate.

Subtopic 3:
Reading, English &
Research Skill Development

Read stories related to
Yellowstone Park in
newspapers and archives.
Ex.: John Muir's writings.

Subtopic 8:
Creativity/
Handwriting/Poetry

Rewrite important
quotes from your
reading into poetic or
lyrical form for class
presentation.

Yellowstone
Fires—1988

Subtopic 4:
History Writing & Life
Applications

Write a journal kept by a
firefighter in 1988 and
today. What are the ups
and down sides of fire-
fighting as a profession.

Subtopic 7:
Current Issue and
Thinking Development

Analyze and prepare a
chart that depicts all the
biotherms

Subtopic 6:
Multicultural/
International Issues

How can fire prevention be
improved in our own homes
and around the world.

Subtopic 5:
Science & Non-fiction
Literature

Compare Accounts of the
reason the fires began and
develop a way to avoid
future fires.

FIGURE 11.1 THEMATIC UNIT ON THE YELLOWSTONE FIRES THAT MS. MORRISON'S
CLASS CREATED

example Ms. Morrison's class created to develop their awareness of and sensitivity
to other countries and cultural groups.

At the beginning of the year, Ms. Morrison's eighth-graders chose a country or
city for which they wanted to develop expertise. This choice became each students'
adopted "home" for a specified period of time. Their first integrative project was to
create or obtain a map depicting each student's new home. This map was displayed
and referenced throughout the unit so students increased their geographical knowledge. During the first half of the unit, students strengthened research skills as they
developed a scrapbook that described their adopted homes, including its art work;
collages of places and facts about it; newspaper clippings; magazine articles; travel
brochures; geographical information; and economic, social, and political facts. Each
student's scrapbook was uniquely crafted and was used as a tool to enhance his or

THEMATIC UNITS

BEARS *

BOOKS TO READ

ASK MR. BEAR,
by Marjorie Flack
CORDUROY and
A POCKET FOR CORDUROY,
by Don Freeman
POPPY THE PANDA,
by Dick Gackenbach
THE THREE BEARS,
by Paul Galdone
ALPHABEARS,
by Kathleen Hague
THE FORGOTTEN BEAR,
by Concuelo Jnerns
DO BABY BEARS SIT IN
CHAIRS?,
by Ethel & Leonard Kessler
BROWN BEAR, BROWN BEAR,
WHAT DO YOU SEE?,
by Bill Martin
BLUEBERRIES FOR SAL,
by Robert McCloskey
WINNIE THE POOH,
by A.A. Milne
LITTLE BEAR,
by Else Minarik
I'M TERRIFIC,
by Marjorie Sharmat
I'M GOING ON A BEAR HUNT,
by Sandra Sivulich
IRA SLEEPS OVER,
by Bernard Waber
THE BEAR & THE FLY
(wordless),
by Paula Winter

OTHER ACTIVITIES

BEAR FACTS (for discussion)

BEAR POEMS & SONGS

BEAR SNACKS (food tidbits)

BEAR BREAD

ADOPT A BEAR (journal records
activities the bear did that day)

PUPPET SHOWS (Goldilocks)

* June Brown, Southwest
Missouri State University

DINOSAURS *

BOOKS TO READ

MAKING SOFT DINOS,
by Linda Bourke
DIGGING UP DINOSAURS,
FOSSILS TELL OF LONG AGO and
MY VISIT TO THE DINOSAURS,
by Aliki Brandenberg
PATRICK'S DINOSAURS,
by Carol Carrick
THE MONSTERS WHO DIED,
by Vicki Cobb
DINOSAURS & BEASTS OF YORE,
by William Cole
DINOSAURS,
by Kathleen Daly
THE MACMILLAN BOOK OF
DINOSAURS AND OTHER
PREHISTORIC CREATURES,
by Mary Elting
DANNY AND THE DINOSAUR,
by Syd Hoff
DINOSAUR FUNBOOK,
by William Johnson
FLYING GIANTS OF LONG AGO
and
FLYING REPTILES IN THE AGE
OF DINOSAURS,
by John Kaufmann
THE TYRANNOSAURUS GAME,
by Steven Kroll
DINOSAURS,
by David Lambert
TIME EXPOSURE: A PHOTO-
GRAPHIC RECORD OF THE
DINOSAUR AGE,
by J. Burton
DINOSAURS: THE TERRIBLE
LIZARDS,
by R. Davidson
HOW TO KNOW DINOSAURS,
by C. Greene
THE WEB: WONDERFULLY
EXCITING BOOKS, VOL. II,
by J. Hickman & C. Huck
DINOSAURS OF NORTH AMERICA,
by H.R. Sattler
THE DINOSAURS,
by W. Service
* Kim Isaac, Sheila Pryor, and
Tammani Ramsy, Texas Christian
University, Fort Worth, Texas
* Sylvia Artmann, Dallas Baptist
University, Dallas, Texas

TEETH *

BOOKS TO READ

DR. DE SOTO,
by William Steig
LITTLE RABBIT'S LOST TOOTH,
by Lucy Bate
THE BEAR'S TOOTHACHE,
by David McPhail
ALBERT'S TOOTHACHE,
by Barbara Williams

OTHER ACTIVITIES

OUR TEETH STORIES, a class
book. Each child writes or
dictates a story about teeth
(a trip to the dentist, loosing
a tooth, what happens to teeth).

TOOTH SHAPED BOOK REPORTS

TOOTH BULLETIN BOARDS

SHOW AND TELL TEETH
(include animal teeth for
comparison).

INVITE A DENTIST TO CLASS

.

YOUR OWN IDEAS

FIGURE 11.2 SAMPLES OF THEMATIC UNITS FOR YOUNGER STUDENTS

her speaking and listening skills when presented to the class. Students also elected to participate in a poster contest. They prepared a poster and slogan that helped to sell their adopted homeland to the rest of the class. Students used persuasive language and factual information to present each adopted country in a positive light.

Part 2 of the unit involved student selections from the following options. Students elected to perform a role play concerning their country. The role play added to their study because students had to create real-world families, schools, interests, events, and activities that occurred in their homes. These elements had to have evolved from within the cultural parameters of their countries, based on students' growing awareness of how geography and culture impacted human behavior.

Additional information about constructing thematic units is available on the website that accompanies this textbook, and in *I've Got a Project* (by Geoff Ward); *Engaging Children's Minds: The Project Approach* (by Lillian Katz and Sylvia Chard); *Children's Literature: Springboard to Understanding the Developing World* (by Nancy Pollette); and in Valencia and Lipson (1998).

Topic integration is a second approach to integration and was developed by Beck (1980). It can be implemented in a self-contained classroom. Students' exploration of a topic begins with thinking about the relationship of that topic to other disciplines. Once students' questions are listed, groups or individuals select one they wish to answer. For example, Ms. Morrison's class chose a topic integration about the Civil War, and students examined the following questions involving various disciplines:

History: What was occurring at the time in Europe and Asia? Did the Civil War throw us behind these continents in the number of inventions?

Geography: What were the crucial states that led to secession?

Economics: What products and economic concerns contributed to the conflict between the North and South?

Math: What was the population of the United States? Compare it with that of the present.

Civics: What were the implications of the Civil War for civil rights, then and now?

Science: What were the influences and limitations of technology, compared with those of the present?

Industrial Arts: What tools and weapons were available? Compare with the present.

Home Economics: How might nutrition have influenced events in the war?

Language Arts: Who were some of the important people of the time? What did they contribute?

Music: What tunes were popular at the time? How did people listen to them? What instruments were most popular?

Art: What were the effects of the war on creative production? Which major artists were at work during this period?

When research to answer these questions was complete, students reported their findings to the class. Then they asked to complete a second topic integration study. They became interested in political elections and wanted to study the one they remembered best, the election of 1992. The questions that guided that study appears in Table 11.1.

TABLE 11.1 STUDY OF THE 1992 PRESIDENTIAL ELECTIONS WITH THE TOPIC INTEGRATION APPROACH

THE 1992 PRESIDENTIAL ELECTION

What would I like to know more about?

How can this relate to other content areas?

HISTORY	Who else was elected President in their 40s? How long has it been since a Democrat was in the office? (This could spin off to research on the ages of different presidents; finding out about different political parties; etc.)
GEOGRAPHY	What would it be like to move from Arkansas to Washington, DC? How far is it and how is it different? Where are all the places that President Clinton can travel now that he is President? (This could spin off into studying about cultures in various regions and their governments.)
MATH	How many more people voted for Clinton than for George Bush? How many people voted in my state? (This could lead into discussing how the voting system works and how votes are counted.)
SCIENCE	How do the machines operate that count the votes? How does the media get the news to us so quickly through radio and television? (This may lead into studying technology.)
LANGUAGE ARTS	Why did President Clinton choose Maya Angelou to read a poem at his Inauguration? What was the poem about?
MUSIC	Who taught President Clinton to play the saxophone?

INTEGRATING EACH DAY

Four activities can be used to integrate language arts and content area instruction in daily lessons: joining bits of information guides, idea maps, lesson agendas, and problem-based learning groups.

JOINING BITS OF INFORMATION GUIDES

A House for Hermit Crab

In this activity students select a theme that relates to their lives, a content area textbook, and at least two selections of literature and tradebooks (tradebooks from Literature Cards 25–28 can be read orally to the class to introduce topics). For example, Ms. Hulsey used this approach with her second-graders when she introduced a science unit on sea life from the textbook by reading Eric Carle's books, such as *A House for Hermit Crab,* and by planning a fieldtrip to the ocean. (*A House for Hermit Crab* describes a crab who is not really a hermit; he loves having others around him, and each of his neighbors performs an important function, e.g., the snails clean around him. When he locates a bigger shell, he moves in and invites sponges, a clown fish, sand dollars, and an electric eel to live near him.)

By reading this book aloud and asking students to note the research facts that Eric Carle listed on the inside front cover of *A House for Hermit Crab,* Ms. Hulsey helped students identify new vocabulary and subtopics of interest. Then they researched the subtopics of their choice to include more details in their writing. While they read, students also wrote facts that Carle included in his story or completed other objectives like the following:

- After the reading, students decided how each of Hermit Crab's neighbors might help him and created a persuasive invitation for another animal to join the hermit crab, as shown in Figure 11.3.

- Students read a second tradebook about an animal they chose and described how that animal benefited from befriending the hermit crab.

IDEA MAPS

In this activity every student reads a different tradebook and creates a semantic map or idea map to present to the class. Classmates take notes and add their own concepts to the map as they listen to their peers.

LESSON AGENDAS

This activity begins by introducing a new unit of study for which students have expressed interest. On this day students can select which pieces of information they want to learn, people responsible for obtaining each piece of information, and how

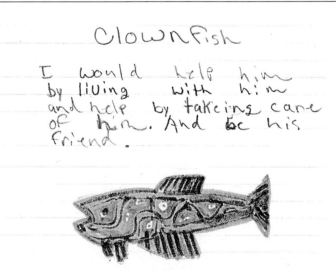

FIGURE 11.3 STUDENT EXAMPLE OF JOINING BITS OF INFORMATION GUIDE

much time they want to allocate to its study (Hagerty, 1990). A sample agenda form your class can use to record their plans is shown in Figure 11.4. The value of this type of integration is that students learn to initiate, take responsibility for, and plan the learning.

PROBLEM-BASED LEARNING GROUPS

Problem-based learning groups are either small groups of students or the whole class applying what they read to real-life situations. These groups focus on students generating creative ideas to solve problems in their lives or in their community. Problem-based learning began at the Center for Problem-Based Learning in Aurora, Illinois, and has been used in many school districts across the country. This format is similar to topic integration except that it can occur on a daily basis and end on that day, after students have had approximately 20 minutes to read about a subject. Alternatively, problem-based learning also can continue for several days.

Problem-based learning usually culminates with students contributing a product or an idea to a community agency that is facing a particular difficulty or issue at that present time in the students' lives. This format calls on a variety of learning strengths that each student can develop. It requires students to use a range of resources and provides opportunities for balancing student choice with your scaffolding. It offers an opportunity for students to address real issues of interest by engaging students to seek information from their community resources. Students can develop their own process of learning because no format for learning is available for them to follow.

| NAME OF GROUP _____ |
| DATE, PLACE, TIME _____ |
| AGENDA _____ |
| CONVENER _____ |
| RECORDER _____ |
| EVALUATOR _____ |
| SUMMARIZER _____ |

AGENDA ITEMS	PERSONS RESPONSIBLE	TIME ALLOTED

| NOTES: |
| |

FIGURE 11.4 SAMPLE AGENDA

•●•

SECTION 2   PUTTING THEORY INTO PRACTICE

Using Integration to Teach Students to Think More Like Scientists, Mathematicians, Social Scientists, and Fine Artists

Regardless of the approach selected for integrating your curriculum, the following activities assist students to learn more in specific content areas. Understanding language processes enables students to deduce how people within each discipline approach problems. Such knowledge can also help them select careers using this experiential information. Moreover, when students understand how differently content area experts use format, schema, and thinking approaches, they can better comprehend that discipline. They can also identify and appreciate the writing formats different content areas tend to follow, which increases reading comprehension. To develop this knowledge, you should collect as many tradebooks, texts, and reference books as possible relative to social science, science, mathematics, or fine art (see Literature Cards 25–28). Students can examine these books and make journal entries (in a learning log as described on pages 492–494) that evidence their understanding and appreciation of the following thinking and communication patterns.

Social Scientists Tend to Examine Primary Sources and Connect Them.   Social scientists question, infer, narrate, summarize, and declare. Social scientists also value information received through social interactions. They prioritize data according to national or social importance. You can test students' predilection to social science thinking patterns (as well as develop them) by creating language arts projects that answer questions relative to social issues. If they enjoy such projects (described below), and if they exert talents in completing them, careers in the social sciences, such as social work, teaching, history, and psychology, may be of interest to them.

- Volunteer to role play characters and events in a historical figure's life for a local drama society.
- Create a mural or a diorama of the life and times of a famous person to be displayed in a history classroom. (**Dioramas** are three-dimensional displays that recreate historical events.)
- Make a relief map of places important to a group of people to be displayed at a local supermarket. Synergetics (P.O. Box 84, E. Windsor Hill, CT 06028) has commercially prepared materials for such projects entitled *Joust for Fun* (the Middle Ages) and *Pioneer Skills* (American History). For example, *Joust for Fun* has 27 learning centers, 76 multidisciplinary activities, and culminates in a knighting ceremony with a medieval banquet. Similarly, *Pioneer Skills* contains 20 projects in which students practice survival skills.
- Evaluate multiple records of a historical or current social event to uncover hidden rationales for actions that were taken and share these in a letter to the editor of the local newspaper. "It's News to Me," Newsline Publications (P.O. Box 8114, Pittsburg, PA 15211, FAX 412-781-0595) has a unit available for classrooms in grades 3–13.
- Conduct a mock interview of a famous person for a schoolwide presentation on a day in history that relates to that person's life.

- Create a personal timeline for one's life that projects into the future and is stored for future reference in individual student journals. The sample in Figure 11.5 was developed after Ms. Morrison's eighth-graders read *The Hundred Penny Box*.

- Respond to an article. Students locate an editorial or critical article appearing in a U.S. publication that focuses on some aspect of a country. Students form groups, analyze the major arguments of the author, and make a chart or diagram that ranks these points and the evidence the author provides for each argument.

WRITING ACTIVITY

Create a personal timeline, telling important events for each year you've been alive.

RELATED BOOK

The Hundred Penny Box

PROCEDURE

PREWRITING:

1. Read and discuss the book with students. Focus attention on the fact that Aunt Dew had a special memory for each year of her life.
2. Ask students to think about each year of their lives and something special or significant that happened to them. Give them a prewriting timeline sheet and have them jot down events for each year of their lives. Have students take these sheets home and get help and suggestions from parents. (The prewriting sheet would simply list the years, from birth year to present, and leave space after each year for notes.)
3. Cut white drawing paper into approximately 3″ × 11″ strips. Give each student three strips. Students can tape the strips together and divide the resulting strip into equal-sized sections, one section for each year of their lives. For example:

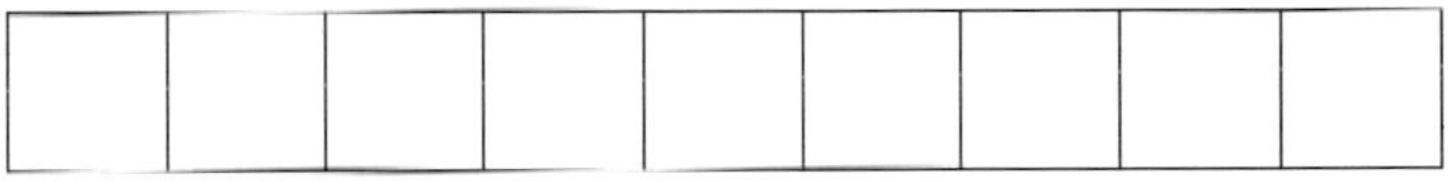

DRAFTING:

4. Have students design a timeline entry for each year of their lives. The entries should include the year, a written account of the event, and a photo or drawing which illustrates this event (when possible).

SHARING:

5. Have students share their timelines in small groups of 3–5 students. Post the timelines for further reading and sharing.

FIGURE 11.5 SAMPLE OF A PERSONAL TIMELINE WHICH IS USED TO TEACH STUDENTS HOW TO THINK AS IF THEY WERE SOCIAL SCIENTISTS

Created by Dr. Vicki Olson, 1996, professor at Augsburg College, MN. Used by permission.

Each student can then write his or her own persuasive response to the author's argument, supported by evidence and facts. Last, students sit on a discussion panel in which one student is mediator and the class is the audience. At this point, the chart or diagram defining the original author's argument is presented and each student displays his or her charted response (Fowler, 1992).

- Interior monologues or diaries. Students can examine an expressive picture or read about a person living in another country, complete research, and construct a diary or interior monologue based on that picture or reading. Interior monologues use the "I" voice to tell a story of a person's experiences, hopes, and fears. In doing an interior monologue, the student imagines how another person would tell his or her life story based on the evidence in photographs and research. Avery (1989) reports how she demonstrated interior monologues for her class by debuting a unit on historical China dressed and speaking as the Chinese emperor who created the Great Wall of China. Similarly, students' interior monologues can be used to introduce new topics in content area studies to the rest of the class.

- Create a message at least three paragraphs long that one character could give another character to explain or change the ending to a historical account. After students present their messages to the class, students state why this message is compatible with events of the time and could have occurred.

- Write a speech for the ceremony in which a main character in a current or past fictional or nonfictional book is presented an award. Share this presentation at a Rotary or Lions Club meeting in the city. This project can also be presented before younger classmates who admire each character. Once the descriptions have been written, they can be given to these younger classmates in oral or written form. For example, Ms. Morrison's class researched and pretended to be Abraham Lincoln and his advisors for fourth-graders who were studying the Civil War. They dressed up and described why he did not support slavery, why he declared war, and what it was like to be a leader during the Civil War.

- Students predict the future for a living person, where and with whom he or she will be in the future, and what will happen to this person 10 years from today. Then students compare their predictions with classmates.

Scientists in the Physical Sciences Analyze Problems, Observe, Classify, Hypothesize, and Verify More Than Other Professionals.   These researchers and artists also rely on information from sensory inputs, conduct field trips, cope with elements, and experiment with balance and design more than other professionals.

As Galileo is reported to have said in a town meeting in the early part of the nineteenth century: "That great book whichever lies before our gaze—I mean the universe—we cannot understand if we do not first learn the language and grasp the symbols in which it is written." A century later Mark Rafenstein (2000) continued this sentiment when he remarked: "The more words you know, the more powerfully you will think, and the more ideas you will invite to your mind." Today's challenge is to extend literacy to all aspects of scientific discovery. Doing so can occur in four ways.

First, we can teach science through literature tradebooks, expository nonfiction, and fictional writings. Students will be able to spend time, experience, and engage their prior knowledge in the steps and procedures of scientific inquiry, which are outlined in Figure 11.6. Text sets can be used to engage students' reading abilities

Why should we teach science in this manner?

Time

Early elementary education places heavy emphasis on reading and writing skills, which can leave little time for other subjects. Drawing out scientific meaning from literature helps the students to connect stories to subjects other than common reading skills.

Experience

Creating science activities from the content of stories shared in class helps make the piece of literature more real. By applying something occurring in a story to the students' lives, learning is more tangible and authentic.

Prior Knowledge

Science activities can be created using simple everyday objects. This approach helps students to think creatively about the world around them. Linking science with literature and everyday life allows students to connect prior knowledge to new ideas

What steps and procedures do the students follow?

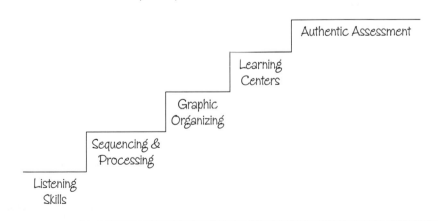

Authentic Assessment

Learning Centers

Graphic Organizing

Sequencing & Processing

Listening Skills

FIGURE 11.6 TEACHING SCIENCE THROUGH LITERATURE: EXAMINING THE SCIENCE OF EVERYDAY LIFE

Created by Antonio DeSapio, 2000, master of elementary education degree candidate at University of Notre Dame, South Bend, IN. Used by permission.

in exploring specific topics in science. These types of text sets range in readability levels from first grade through eighth grade and cover (1) properties of objects; (2) light, heat, and electricity; (3) the environment; (4) position and motion of objects; (5) weather; and (6) simple machines. (See Table 11.2 for examples.)

Second, students can better learn to use their visual arts skills, language arts skills, and scientific reasoning abilities when they follow a lesson that involves each of the steps of the scientific process. For example, you teach students to begin studying any subject by using their senses. Students should be informed by reading, speaking, listening, and visually observing. For the second step in the process, students group their observations according to specific properties that were salient to individual students and classify them. Then students estimate, measure, and explore some dimension of one of these properties. In the process of measuring, they collect, report, and interpret data. They investigate patterns and begin to hypothesize. They communicate the results of their work in reports, journals, graphs, and any technologically based displays. At the end of the process, they draw a scientific conclusion, deduce a cause-and-effect relationship, or infer a particular connection between elements in their study that they had not considered before. A lesson plan format for implementing this scientific process model for integrating language arts and science is found in Figure 11.7.

A third method is to subscribe to one or more of the scientific periodicals and popular magazines about science that students enjoy. These magazines are listed with

---

Students should be able to . . .

Science Process Skills
_____

Observe   use senses

_____

Classify   group according to properties

_____

Measure   use appropriate units of measurements; estimate

_____

Collect/Record/Interpret Data   look for patterns; leads to . . .

_____

Communicate   write reports; use journals; create graphs;
                                           research technology-based information

_____

Infer   draw conclusions; see causes and effects

FIGURE 11.7 A LESSON PLAN THAT INTEGRATES LANGUAGE ARTS AND SCIENCE BY IMPLEMENTING THE SCIENTIFIC PROCESS

Created by Caryn Ellison, 2000, gifted and talented teacher, Mishawaka, IN. Used by permission.

TABLE 11.2 TEXT SETS FOR INTEGRATING SCIENCE AND LANGUAGE ARTS

PROPERTIES OF OBJECTS*

Chromatography Garden
Planting a Rainbow
   by Lois Ehlert
Science Content: chromatography and the mixture of colors

Kente Chromatography
The Black Snowman
   by Phil Mendez
Science Content: the mixture of colors with the shade of black

Searching for Empty Space
Wilbur's Space Machine
   by Lorna Balian
Science Content: air, space, and gases

Glitter Wands
The Rainbow Fish
   by Marcus Pfister
Science Content: states of matter and density

Making Clouds and Rain
Bringing the Rain to Kapiti Plain
   by Verna Aardema
Science Content: weather, water cycle, and change of state

Weather Forecasters
The Rains Are Coming
   by Sanna Stanley
Science Content: weather and forces

Shrinky Plastic
George Shrinks
   by William Joyce
Science Content: temperature affecting matter

Growing Gators
Zack's Alligators
   by Shirley Mozelle
Science Content: physical changes and scientific experimentation

Iron for Breakfast
Gregory, the Terrible Eater
   by Mitchell Sharmat
Science Content: nutrition and magnetic properties of iron

Babushka's Eggs'periment
Rechenka's Eggs
   by Philomel Books
Science Content: egg dyeing and scientific experimentation

LIGHT, HEAT, AND ELECTRICITY*

Colors of the Rainbow
The River That Gave Gifts
   by Margo Humphrey
Science Content: rainbows and prisms

Whirling Colors
Carousel
   by Donald Crews
Science Content: light, vision, and properties of color

Chemiluminescence
Fireflies
   by Julie Brinckloe
Science Content: production of light and the effect of temperature on reactions

Are Mittens Warm?
Mama, Do You Love Me?
   by Barbara Joosse
Science Content: heat, insulation, and temperature

Is It Really Magic?
The Wartville Wizard
   by Don Madden
Science Content: static electricity

POSITION AND MOTION OF OBJECTS*

Keeping Your Balance
Mirette on the High Wire
   by Emily Arnold McCully
Science Content: balance, gravity, and engineering

Ramps and Cars
The Lazy Bear
   by Brian Wildsmith
Science Content: inclined planes, motion and gravity

Catch the Wind
Mirandy and Brother Wind
   by Patricia McKissack
Science Content: using wind to do work and forces

Folded Paper Kites
The Emperor and the Kite
   by Jane Yolen
Science Content: wind, kites, and aerodynamic forces

THE ENVIRONMENT†

The Empty Lot
   by Dale Fife
Science Content: examination of habitat

When the Woods Hum
   by Joanne Rider
Science Content: nature observation and identification

The Great Kapok Tree
   by Lynne Cherry
Science Content: rainforest habitats

Farewell to Shady Glade
   by Bill Peet
Science Content: nature observation and identification

Brother Eagle, Sister Sky
   by Chief Seattle
Science Content: reforestation and life cycles

WEATHER†

The Sun, the Wind and the Rain
   by Lisa Westburg Peters
Science Content: the effects of the elements

Hurricane
   by David Wiesner
Science Content: weather patterns around the globe

Ollie's Ski Trip
   by Elsa Beskow
Science Content: changing states, freezing and thawing

SIMPLE MACHINES†

The Magic School Bus at the Water Works
   by Joanna Cole
Science Content: the forces of water

The Neighborhood Trucker
   by Louise Borden
Science Content: mixtures of liquids and solids and changing states

Stay Away from the Junkyard!
   by Tricia Tusa
Science Content: mechanized parts and cause and effect

---

*Ideas taken from *Teaching Physical Science through Children's Literature,* by Susan E. Gertz, Dwight J. Portman and Mickey Sarquis, Terrific Science Press, 1996.

†From *Story Stretchers for the Primary Grades,* by Shirley Raines and Robert Canady, 1992.

TABLE 11.3 SCIENTIFIC MAGAZINES THAT STUDENTS ENJOY

Audubon Adventure
National Audubon Society
613 Riversville Rd.
Greenwich, CT 06830
(6 per year)

Chickadee
Young Naturalist Foundation
P.O. Box 11314
Des Moines, IA 50340
(10 per year)

The Curious Naturalist
Massachusetts Audubon Society
Lincoln, MA 01773
(4 per year)

Dolphin Log
Cousteau Society
8430 Santa Monica Blvd.
Los Angeles, CA 90069
(4 per year)

Electric Company
Children's Television
   Workshop
One Lincoln Plaza
New York, NY 10023
(10 per year)

Exploratorium Magazine
3601 Lyon St.
San Francisco, CA 94123
(4 per year)

Faces
Cobblestone Publishing, Inc.
20 Grove St.
Peterborough, NH 03458
(10 per year)

Junior Astronomer
Benjamin Adelman
4211 Coli Dr.
Silver Springs, MD 20906

Junior Natural History
American Museum of Natural
   History
New York, NY 10024
(Monthly)

Kind News
The Humane Society of the U.S.
2100 L St., NW
Washington, DC 20037
(5 per year)

My Weekly Reader
American Education Publications
Education Center
Columbus, OH 43216
(Weekly during the school year)

National Geographic World
National Geographic Society
17th and M St., NW
Washington, DC 20036
(Monthly)

Naturescope
National Wildlife Federation
1912 16th St., NW
Washington, DC 20036
(5 per year)

Odyssey
Kalmbach Publishing Co.
1027 North Seventh St.
Milwaukee, WI 53233
(Monthly)

Owl
Young Naturalist Foundation
P.O. Box 11314
Des Moines, IA 50304
(10 per year)

Ranger Rick
National Wildlife Federation
1412 16th St., NW
Washington, DC 20036
(Monthly)

Science World
Scholastic Magazines, Inc.
50 W. 44th St.
New York, NY 10036

Science Weekly
P.O. Box 70154
Washington, DC 20088
(18 per year)

Science News
Science Service, Inc.
1719 N Street, NW
Washington, DC 20036
(Weekly)

Science Activities
4000 Albemarle St., NW
Washington, DC 20016
(4 per year)

Scienceland
Scienceland, Inc.
501 Fifth Ave.
New York, NY 10017
(8 per year)

Space Science
Benjamin Adelman
4211 Colie Dr.
Silver Springs, MD 20906
(Monthly during the school year)

3-2-1 Contact
Children's Television Workshop
P.O. Box 2933
Boulder, CO 80322
(10 per year)

Wonderscience
American Chemical Society
P.O. Box 57136, West End Station
Washington, DC 20037
(4 per year)

Your Big Backyard
National Wildlife Federation
1412 16th St., NW
Washington, DC 20036
(Monthly)

Zoobooks
Wildlife Education, Ltd.
930 West Washington St.
San Diego, CA 92103

addresses in Table 11.3. Allowing children to explore scientific magazines at their leisure has been documented as the third most popular reading preference of sixth-grade students (Worthy, Moormon, & Turner, 1999). The popularity of scientific magazines as a preferred reading material for students was exceeded only by cartoons and comics, and storybooks or story collection text sets. Building on students' preferred reading interests and inclinations toward scientific magazines can enhance their knowledge of science and their use of reading as a valuable means of increasing scientific thinking.

Last, among the most valuable methods of integrating language arts and science is providing students with a list of websites as an initial starting point for productively searching for answers to penetrating questions that they generate themselves. A list of science websites that children have reported to enjoy appear in Table 11.4. Students will find not only the most current information on the Web, but also a wide variety of information. Because they can build scientific investigations on the latest knowledge, students can feel as if they are not only developing scientific skills, but also discovering areas that adults are simultaneously just beginning to explore. When students feel they are engaged in studies that are important to adults, the importance of their own work rises in their estimation. Exploring a scientific study of great interest builds students' self-confidence and their sense that they need to learn to read and write more effectively.

Mathematicians Tend to Think Sequentially More Than Other Professionals. Mathematicians depend on averaging, computing, rating, bidding, totaling, allocating, and estimating. By integrating the language arts with the following activities

TABLE 11.4 SCIENCE WORLD WIDE WEBSITES

www.nsta.org/	National Science Teachers Association
www.nsta.org/parents/	Help Your Child Explore Science
www.enc.org/	Eisenhower National Clearinghouse—Science
www.iste.org/	International Society for Technology in Education
www.ipl.org/	The Internet Public Library
www.ed.gov/	U.S. Department of Education
www.nasa.gov/	NASA Homepage
quest.arc.nasa.gov/	NASA K–12 Internet Initiative
www.spacelink.nasa.gov/index.html	NASA Spacelink
www.childrensmuseum.org/	The Children's Museum of Indy
www.msichicago.org/	Museum of Science and Industry—Chicago
www.exploratorium.edu./	Exploratorium Home Page—San Francisco
www.mamamedia.com/	Great Site for Kids
www.weather.com/twc/home page.twc	Weather Channel
www.rube-goldberg.com/	Rube Goldberg Website
madsci.wustl.edu/	Ask a Scientist
www.pbs.org/wgbh/nova/	NOVA Online
ericir.syr.edu/Projects/Newton/	Newton's Apple
www.beakman.com/	You Can with Beakman and Jax
www.janbrett.com/	Lots of Educational Activities
www.usc.edu/CMSI/CalifSF/	Science Fair Site

and reading the concept books in Table 11.5, students can use their language to assess their mathematical interests and talents.

- Students can create a classroom barter system. Students can determine the merits and disadvantages of bartering for modern businesses and use this experience to practice mathematical and monetary principles.

- Students can make recipes in class (e.g., using *Stone Soup*) and attend to measuring, fractions, and sequence. Also, students can end the eating experience with a 10-minute write about their self-assessed competencies and preferences for math.

- Older students can prepare graphs and charts and collect data for community agencies. Younger students enjoy graphing topics such as birth orders, favorite colors, types of pets, and favorite school subjects (Skolnick & Frazier, 1998).

- Students can ask questions about mathematics that spur students' curiosity. For example, after reading the book *How Much Is a Million?* (Schwartz, 1985), you can ask students whether they believe that it really takes 23 days and nights to count to a million, or whether it takes a billion goldfish to fill up the Super Bowl football stadium. When students become intrigued by topics like these, they often design their own experiments and explorations about mathematics. For example, Ms. Morrison's class averaged how many numbers students could count in a minute and then calculated how many numbers could be counted in a day. They were then able to reach a definitive answer to the question whether a million could be counted in 23 days (Whitin & Wilde, 1992).

- Students can create mathematical word problems for classmates from experiences in their lives. For example, Michael wrote: "I can buy a bag of Gummy Bears at the movies for $6.50. There are 100 pieces of candy in the bag. I can chew one piece for 15 seconds before it dissolves. I also like Milk Duds. I can buy a box of Milk Duds for $2.50. There are 25 pieces in the box. I can chew one piece for one minute before it dissolves. If I wanted to enjoy food for an entire movie that lasts 2 hours, how much of each would I have to buy, and which would be my most economical purchase?"

- Students should say the words for all the mathematical steps that they take in solving mathematical problems. Language can help them understand patterns that exist in math. By talking many hear the logic in the steps.

Scientists in the Fine Arts Tend to Observe and Appreciate Visual, Kinesthetic, and Auditory Dimensions of Learning More Than Other Scientists.   The importance of integrating the fine arts in a language arts program was stated by George Bernard Shaw. In his work he suggested that we use language to see ourselves and the arts to see our soul. He also went on to report that our physical survival doesn't seem to depend as much on our cognition as it does on our ability to develop and maintain our aesthetic dimensions of life (Sylvester, 1998).

Recently scientists have verified the value of integrating the fine arts and language development through brain research. Specifically they have identified fluctuations in the levels of serotonin released by neurotransmitters whenever students engage in motor or kinesthetic activity. Serotonin enhances relaxation and leaves students with a calm assurance that contributes subsequently to more verbal and cognitive control (Sylvester, 1998). Elevated serotonin levels are also associated with high self-esteem and social status.

TABLE 11.5 CHILDREN'S LITERATURE RELATING TO MATHEMATICAL CONCEPTS AND SKILLS

SORTING AND CLASSIFYING

Color Zoo	Lois Ehlert
Is It Red? Is It Yellow? Is It Blue?	Tana Hoban
Is It Rough? Is It Smooth? Is It Shiny?	Tana Hoban
Growing Colors	Bruce McMillan

POSITION AND SPATIAL SENSE

Sam Johnson and the Blue Ribbon Quilt	Lisa Cambell Ernst
The Village of Round and Square Houses	Ann Grifalconi
Rosie's Walk	Pat Hutchins

PATTERNS

Round Trip	Ann Jonas
Reflections	Ann Jonas
Ten Bears in My Bed	Stan Mack
Brown Bear, Brown Bear, What Do You See?	Bill Martin

COUNTING AND NUMBERS

One, Two, Three Going to Sea	Alain
One Bear All Alone	Caroline Bucknell
Count the Animals 1, 2, 3	Demi
Count and See	Tana Hoban
Who Wants One?	Mary Serfoza
One Sun, Two Eyes, and a Million Stars	Joanna and William Stobbs
One Wooly Wombat	Rod Trinca
1 Is One	Tasha Tudor
One Gorilla	A. Morozumi
The Right Number of Elephants	J. Sheppard
1 Is No Fun but 20 Is Plenty	Ilse-Margret Vogel
One Crow: A Counting Rhyme	Jim Aylesworth
Six Little Ducks	Chris Conover
Numbears: A Counting Book	Kathleen Hague
One, Two, Three, and Four. No More?	Catherine Gray
More Than One	Tana Hoban
Ten, Nine, Eight	Molly Bang
Two Ways to Count to Ten	Ruby Dee
Let's Look for Numbers	B. Gillham and S. Hulme
Seven Eggs	Meredith Hooper
Two, Four, Six, Eight	Ethel and Leonard Kessler
Numbers of Things	Helen Oxenbury
A Farmer's Dozen	Sandra Russell
Count on Your Fingers	Claudia Zalavsky

GRAPHING

Guess Who My Favorite Person Is?	Byrd Baylor
The Mysterious Tadpole	Steven Kellogg
Stone Soup	Marilyn Sapienza
Whose Shoes?	Brian Wildsmith

MEASUREMENT

Ten Beads Tall	Pam Adams
Goldilocks and the Three Bears	Jan Brett
The Chocolate Chip Cookie Contest	Barbara Douglas
The Biggest Nose	Kathy Caple
Inch by Inch	Leo Leonni
The Biggest House in the World	Leo Leonni
The Giant Jam Sandwich	John Vernon Lord
Goldilocks and the Three Bears	James Marshall

GEOMETRY

The Secret Birthday Message	Eric Carle
Ten Black Dots	Donald Crews
Picture Pie	Ed Emberley
The Most Wonderful Egg in the World	Helme Heine
Shapes and Things	Tana Hoban
Shapes, Shapes, Shapes	Tana Hoban
Circles, Triangles, and Squares	Tana Hoban
Shapes	Jan Pienkowski

ORDINAL NUMBERS

Too Many Eggs	M. Christina Butler
The Seven Chinese Brothers	Margaret Mahy
Owl Moon	Jane Yolen

TIME

Anno's Sundial	Mitsumasa Anno
The Grouchy Ladybug	Eric Carle
Let's Tell Time	Victor Fredrick
The Sun's Day	Mordicai Gerstein
Big Time Bears	Stephen Krensky
Time to . . .	Bruce McMillan
Monday I Was an Alligator	Susan Pearson
Time	Jan Pienkowski

MONEY

The Berenstein Bears' Trouble with Money	Stan and Jan Berenstein
A Quarter from the Tooth Fairy	Caren Holtzman
How Much Is That Guinea Pig in the Window	Joanne Rocklin
Caps for Sale	Esphyr Slobodkina
Alexander Who Used to Be Rich Last Sunday	Judith Viorst

FRACTIONS

Pezzettino	Leo Leonni
Gator Pie	Louise Mathews

PROBABILITY

Anno's Hat Tricks	M. Anno and A. Nozaki
Mouse Tales	Arnold Lobel
Sylvester and the Magic Pebble	William Steig
Elephant Buttons	N. Ueno
The Day That Henry Cleaned His Room	Sarah Wilson
Wacky Wednesday	T. Lesieg

ADDITION AND SUBTRACTION

The Shopping Basket	John Burningham
Rooster's off to See the World	Eric Carle
The Empty Pot	Demi
This Is the Bread I Baked for Ned	Crescent Dragonwater
Pondlarker	Fred Gwynne
Lon Po Po	Ed Young

Created by Jennifer M. Mullins, 2000, kindergarten teacher at St. Anthony's Elementary School, Robstown, TX. Used by permission.

An equal amount of research is being conducted on the power of music to improve language and brain development (Weinberger, 1998). Research has found that the brain honors music as much as it honors language. That is, children who are well equipped to understand music before they reach kindergarten have been found to develop more natural channels of communication and cognition. Learning music actually exercises the brain, not only by developing musical skills but by strengthening synapses between brain cells. As these synapses grow stronger, the human brain can process oral and written language more accurately and rapidly (Weinberger, 1998).

Third, participating in artistic activities has also been found to be stimulating for brain and language development. If you value verbal and visual modes of learning equally in your language arts program, not only will you accommodate diverse learning modalities, but also you will enable children to increase their neurological processing. Moreover, some students, if allowed, will make pictures before they begin writing. For example, Allison reported to her teacher: "I always do my pictures first because then I can get a good look at my pictures to help me with my describing words. If I wrote my words first, I wouldn't be able to see my describing words in my pictures" (adapted from Weinberger, 1998, p. 48). Thus, by inspiring children to travel through the colorful collages and images of nonfiction authors such as Leo Lionni, Ezra Jack Keats, and Joanna Cole, students begin to develop artistically as well as verbally. For each of these reasons, the following activities can be used to increase students' language and artistic abilities.

- You can use the thematic books in Literature Card 28 to enhance students' appreciation of the visual arts. Each book contains vivid pictures to assist students to develop their artistic and language abilities.

- You can recommend one of the books for parent use at home. These books advance the position that art is important in everyone's life. They are impressionable because they contain characters who are enjoying the fine arts early in their lives.

- By frequently guiding students through various museums, they can explore art and learn to appreciate it at a deeper level. A guide for such museum tours and books that prepare students for these trips are available on the website that accompanies this textbook.

- Many students appreciate the fact that they can bring their hobbies to school. Finding the time to incorporate them into the curriculum can be stressful for some teachers. Some teachers overcome this difficulty by embracing students' hobbies during the fine art periods at schools. Children can teach peers to enjoy their hobbies with verbal or written instructions and by sharing excerpts from books about their hobbies with others. Literature Card 29 lists hobby books that you can make available to students in a permanently operating hobby center in your room. Such a center can be opened when early finishers complete other activities.

INTEGRATING THE LANGUAGE ARTS IN CONTENT AREAS

Teaching Nonfiction

When students write fiction, they tend to include only action and plot elements. It is difficult to build students' abilities to write about characters, motives, emotions, reasoned judgments, and cause-and-effect relationships without instruction in

Literature Card 29

CHILDREN'S LITERATURE ABOUT HOBBIES THAT ADD TO STUDENTS' APPRECIATION OF THE FINE ARTS

Good Books with a Lot of Pictures about Hobbies

How to Run a Railroad: Everything You Need to Know about Model Trains and other books by H. Weiss, 1977 Crowell

Putting on a Play: A Guide to Writing and Producing Neighborhood Drama by S. & S. Judy, 1945 Scribner

How a Book Is Made by Aliki, 1986 Bantam

The River by D. Bellamy, 1988 Clarkson Potter

Things to Make and Do for Valentine's Day by T. DePaola, 1976 Franklin Watts

A Monkey Grows Up by R. G. Gelman, 1991 Scholastic

The Pottery Place by G. Gibbons, 1987 Harcourt Brace Jovanovich

Body Battles by R. G. Gelman, 1992 Scholastic

Trucks by G. Gibbons, 1981 Crowell

Make Your Own Animated Movies by Y. Anderson, 1991 Little, Brown

The Puffins Are Back by G. Gibbons, 1991 Holiday House

A Gallery of Games by C. Marchon-Arnaud, 1994 Ticknor & Fields

Good Books to Use for a Thematic Unit about Architecture and Building Objects as a Hobby for K–3

Toolbox by A. Rockwell, 1990 Macmillan Child Group

My Very First Book of Tools by E. Carle, 1986 HarpC Child Books

Saw, Hammer, and Paint: Woodworking and Finishing for Beginners by C. Meyer, 1999 Scholastic

The Way Things Work by D. Macaulay, 1988 Houghton Mifflin

The Village of Round and Square Houses by A. Grifalconi, 1986 Little, Brown

The Inside–Outside Book of New York City by R. Munro, 1985 Dodd, Mead

Archabet by B. Korab, 1985 National Trust for Historic Preservation

Round Buildings, Square Buildings, and Buildings That Wiggle Like a Fish by P. M. Isaacson, 1988 Knopf

Changes, Changes by P. Hutchins, 1971 Macmillan

Castle by D. Macaulay, 1977 Houghton Mifflin

Let There Be Light: A Book about Windows by J. Giblin, 1988 Crowell

A Short-Walk around the Pyramids and through the World of Art by P. M. Isaacson, 1993 Alfred A. Knopf

Eye's Delight: Poems of Art and Architecture by H. Plotz, 1983 Greenwillow

Super Structures by P. Nash, 1989 Garrett Ed. Corp

Good Books If You Are Just Beginning to Learn about a Particular Hobby

Fun with Hieroglyphs: From the Metropolitan Museum of Art by C. Roehrig, 1990 Viking

Super Word Find Fun by P. Brigandi & C. Lovitt, 1993 Scholastic

A Collage of Crafts by C. Guerrier, 1994 Ticknor & Fields

Mosaics with Natural Stones by W. Lauppi, 1974 Sterling

Batik and Tie Dyeing by C. & M. Yuian, 1974 Children's Press

Printing by H. Devonshire, 1988 Franklin Watts

Quilting as a Hobby by D. Brightbill, 1963 Bonanza

Indian Beadwork by Hofsinde, 1958 Morrow

More to Collect and Paint from Nature by J. Hawkinson, 1964 Whitman

Knitting by M. Phillips, 1977 Franklin Watts

Beginner's Guide to Photography by G. Laycock, 1998 Scholastic

Getting Started in Calligraphy by N. Baron, 1979 Sterling

Good Books to Use for a Thematic Unit about Architecture and Building Objects as a Hobby for 4–6

City: A Story of Roman Planning and Construction by D. Macaulay, 1974 Houghton Mifflin

Architecture: A Book of Projects for Young Adults by F. Wilson, 1968 Reinhold

Block City by R. L. Stevenson, 1988 Dutton

Architects Make Zigzags: Looking at Architecture from A to Z by D. Maddex, 1986 National Trust for Historic Preservation

Cathedral: A Story of Its Construction by D. Macaulay, 1973 Houghton Mifflin

Pyramid by D. Macaulay, 1975 Houghton Mifflin

Underground by D. Macaulay, 1976 Houghton Mifflin

Unbuilding by D. Macaulay, 1980 Houghton Mifflin

Ship by D. Macaulay, 1993 Houghton Mifflin

What It Feels Like to Be a Building by F. Wilson, 1988 National Trust for Historic Preservation

Super Wings: The Step by Step Airplane Book by P. Clemens & J. Delgado, 1992 Lowell House

Teacher Resources for Learning about Architecture

Encyclopedia of American Architecture by R. Packard, 1995 McGraw-Hill

People Who Live in Round Houses by C. Zaslavsky, in *Arithmetic Teacher,* 1989, 37: 18–21

nonfiction writing. Moreover, when you include instruction that increases students' ability to write nonfiction, they learn concept area subjects more effectively. As Graves (1999) stated: "A person learning history through the writing of nonfiction isn't going to accept simplistic explanations of events in the present or the past" (p. 48). Graves went on to state that without instruction in writing nonfiction, students are less skilled in reporting events in their own lives.

The following activities can assist you to develop students' abilities to write nonfiction. First, you can divide the periods that students would like to learn into ten year groupings. In this way, students can study one period in depth or explore an extraordinary event from that period that is of heightened interest to them. The resultant lexical density that is contained in what they read can assist them as they plan a report of what they learned. Of necessity, they will have to write more formal lexical items in their compositions than would occur in their fictional writings (Halliday, 1993). To illustrate, research has reported that items in nonfiction writing usually contain four to six clauses, more clauses per sentences, nominalizations, and noun phrases than do fictional writings. Such highly dense lexical structure is required of specialized language. It is necessary that the construction of communications of higher-level knowledge must be very specific (Unser, 1999).

Second, you can conduct a series of writing workshops. These would focus on distinct types of writing that advance nonfiction writing. For example, you can have a developing characters workshop, following these steps:

Step 1.   Do not use any student's name in this school in any nonfiction writing.

Step 2.   When you choose a historical fiction name, research the origin of that name.

Step 3.   Do research about real people from the period that you want to convey before writing about the characters.

Step 4.   Use the phone book and dictionaries to find names that reflect the period, as well as settings and locations in which your historical writings occur.

Step 5.   Write a few sentences about your character. Read the sentences. Classmates can ask four questions about this literary figure. Students' answers will provide the information you need to make your characters more complete.

Third, another method of teaching nonfiction is to encourage students to read biographies about famous people who exhibited qualities that they admire. The stories of past heroes and heroines can demonstrate how real people, with backgrounds similar to your students', overcame obstacles to succeed in making contributions to others.

Fourth, many nonfiction writers have proved to be elementary students' favorite authors. Students' reading and writing abilities grow when allowed to read several works from one of the following authors who have mastered the craft of nonfiction writing: Byron Barton, Melvin Berger, Joanna Cole, Tomie de Paola, Gail Gibbons, Patricia Lauer, Joann Ryder, and Milicient Selsam.

A fifth lesson is to teach students how to write nonfiction, stylistic features. There are five characteristics of nonfiction writing that help students to write and understand nonfiction after they read it. **Fonts** and **special effects,** including bulleting, subtitling, and listing, can be taught to enhance students' abilities to write descriptive data. **Signal words** can be taught to assist students' abilities to sequence ideas. These words include *such as, first, in conclusion, moreover.* You can teach students that these words alert their readers to halt and pay special attention to the information that is about to come and that the next words carry special significance in the mind of the author. Students can be taught to select **illustrations** and **photographs** to emphasize points in nonfiction writing. Students can also be taught to use **graphics** and be assigned to include at least one graphic, table, overlay, chart, or framed text that they make to enhance a nonfiction writing. This teaches students to learn other means of conveying important information. **Text organizers** teach students that prefaces, tables of contents, indexes, and appendices are valuable information sources in students' writings. You can challenge students to include them in their writings and point out how they help classmates locate important information that they want their peers to know (Harvey, 1998). Additionally, you can read nonfiction books aloud. Kobrin (1996) has a list of such books that have been used effectively with children of all ages.

Last, in many large cities, local newspapers publish booklets of additional classroom resources that they provide free for elementary and middle school teachers. For example, the staff of one large city newspaper located people in the community willing to pay for a year's newspaper subscription for classrooms. Through such programs, all students can have and read a newspaper of their own each day. Your newspaper may provide a service if you contact its public relations or education department.

INSIDE CULTURALLY ENRICHED CLASSROOMS

Mentoring and Gifted Students

Students from culturally diverse and advantaged backgrounds often benefit by learning about others who have backgrounds similar to their own. When this occurs, students receive mentoring. **Mentoring** is learning from a person whom one admires by watching, reading about, or hearing about their areas of expertise and your shared cultural perspective. The most obvious ways to encourage interaction between students and mentors is to invite to class people whom students admire or to take field trips to interview them about their use of language arts in their profession. Two equally attractive options follow.

1. You can provide opportunities for students to read autobiographies or biographies of famous children's authors and other figures from diverse cultures in *Writer's Voice* (Literacy Volunteers of New York City, Publishing Department, 121 Avenue of the Americas, New York, NY 10013), which features Bill Cosby, Carol Burnett, Kareem Abdul-Jabbar, and others; *Something About the Author: Autobiography Series; The Dictionary of Literary Biography: American Writers for Children Since 1960: Fiction; First Through Sixth Books of Junior Authors and Illustrators; Behind the Covers; Books Are by People: Interviews with 104 Authors and Illustrators of Books for Young Children; How Writers Write; How to Capture Live Authors and Bring Them to Your Schools; Something about the Author: Facts and Pictures about Authors and Illustrators of Books for Young People, Volumes 1–57; From Writers to Students: The Pleasures and Pains of Writing; The Pied Pipers: Interviews with the Influential Creators of Children's Literature;* and *Speaking for Ourselves: Autobiographical Sketches by Notable Authors of Books for Young Adults.*

2. Mentors can be peer tutors who befriend and share common aspirations with students. Clemens (1991, p. 74) discovered that one of the reasons why mentoring impacts multicultural students so much is that many benefit from "hands-on communication competencies to express and receive the information of greatest interest to them." Mentors promote such competencies by providing "big" words and goals that transform dreams into abilities. Mentors teach cooperation and diplomacy and, in the process, feel increased self-worth as they see what their ideas and work enable their partners to do and know. Mentors also learn that it is tough to be a good role model but that it is important to do so. They see their apprentice's behavior improve as a result. Mentors and apprentices can learn about responsibility and goal setting. For these reasons, many sixth- through eighth-graders improve their language arts abilities when they mentor younger schoolmates in components of the language arts.

In summary, it is important to address the special language needs of culturally diverse students. Mentors advance these students' confidence and skill in communication and thinking. Mentors can also increase students' abilities to build on the thoughts of others through attention to study and reference skills. Through mentoring, your language arts program can ably attend to students who are particularly susceptible to falling behind their peers. *Developing a Mentor Program* by Walter W. Haeger and John F. Feldhusen (1989, D.O.K. Publishers, East Aurora, NY 14052) is an excellent reference to consider in establishing such a program between students and adults.

RECOGNIZING AND REPORTING PROGRESS

Checklists and Group Assessments

Checklists are one of the best methods of evaluating information learned in language arts and content areas. They also can determine the degree to which the knowledge being assessed has depended on an advanced student's speaking, listening, reading, and writing skills.

A second type of assessment is a checklist that helps students determine how effective their reports, essays, and opinion papers are. These assessments isolate individual components of the language arts process that are demonstrated in a single work sample for content area and language arts.

For example, Michael wrote an opinion paper on reasons to control driving while drinking. His theme was that the government should pass tougher laws to punish people who drink while they drive. He gave three reasons for his opinion:

1. Many accidents are caused by drunk drivers.
2. Many accidents are caused by people who have been stopped many times for driving drunk.
3. Too many people drink and drive.

Samples of group assessments appear in Figures 11.8 and 11.9.

•●•

SECTION 3   TEACHERS AS CONTINUAL LEARNERS

Increasing Your Abilities to Integrate

Due to the power of integration to increase students' language abilities and content area knowledge, you will learn in this section of the chapter how to evaluate the degree

	Allison	Meisong	Juan	Michael
1. Calling attention to the difference between what someone said and what he/she meant	✓			
2. Basing a statement on some written source		✓		
3. Using an if–then statement ("But if we accept that, then. . . .")	✓		✓	
4. Encouraging someone else to express his/her ideas or add information	✓			
5. Asking for or offering a definition of a word or concept	✓			
6. Keeping the talk on topic ("But back to the question we started with. . . .")	✓			
7. Making a comment about the merits of a particular way of saying something ("I really like the way Mark said that—let's write that down.")				✓
8. Asking someone to repeat an idea to make it clearer	✓			

FIGURE 11.8 ASSESSMENT OF WRITTEN WORK THROUGH GROUP DISCUSSION

to which your classes are integrated, how well students use learning logs, as well as how to solicit parents' help in developing students' study skills at home and school.

PROFESSIONAL DEVELOPMENT ACTIVITY

Assessing Your Ability to Integrate

Many teachers monitor and evaluate their abilities to integrate the curriculum. The checklist shown in Table 11.6 is an assessment that can help you move toward a curriculum in which students process content more deeply and use their language arts competencies more ably. You can answer yes or no to the questions at the end of every year that you teach.

NAME _____   DATE _____

Answer the questions below without help from other group members.
Be sure to write what you think happened in the group.

Who was the group leader? _____
_____

What happened to make you think so? _____
_____

Why do you think this person became the group leader? _____
_____

Did anyone in the group try to control someone else? _____
_____

What did they do to make you think so? _____
_____

Why do you think they tried to control someone else? _____
_____

Did anyone seem to be controlled by the group or another group member? _____
_____

What happened to make you think so? _____
_____

Why do you think the person allowed himself or herself to be controlled? _____
_____
_____

FIGURE 11.9 ASSESSING GROUP WORK

FOR YOUR JOURNAL

Learning Logs

Learning logs are a type of journal writing in which students record, condense, summarize, and generalize what they have learned. It encourages students to monitor and evaluate what they are learning in content areas and to interpret new knowledge more reflectively. Learning logs also enable students to describe their learning process and how well they understood. A third use is to record data daily from content area activities to note changes in the process. Such journals are the clearest and most specific evidence of how much students learn each day in different subject areas because they write immediately after each learning experience (Bang-Jensen, 1995).

TABLE 11.6 CLIMBING THE LADDER TO EFFECTIVELY INTEGRATE THE LANGUAGE ARTS AND CONTENT AREA DISCIPLINES

	THIS YEAR	200_	200_	200_

1. Have your students had the opportunity to use topic integration, agendas, or joining bits of information approaches to content area instruction at least once this year?

2. Have you used a tradebook to introduce a new topic in a content area?

3. Have students created at least one idea map, spinoff writing, lesson agenda, report, diorama, or learning log this year?

4. Have you exposed students to the newspaper and incorporated it into at least two content area classes?

5. Did students ask to design their own thematic units at least once this year?

6. Are topics of study within content areas chosen by the students and you?

7. Are students finding that the end of one class period does not necessarily signal that they have to stop their work? Are they more frequently using two back-to-back classes to become intensely engaged in an integrative study that involves two or more subject areas?

8. Are students beginning to rework, write, or rehearse several times before they are satisfied that they have learned content area material thoroughly?

9. Are students asking fewer questions about what you expect, indicating that they are learning to set and meet more of their own objectives? Are you hearing fewer questions like "How long does the report have to be?" "Do we have to make a semantic map first?" "How many books do I have to read before I can write my report?"

10. When students need feedback, do they ask classmates to listen to their ideas and read their works?

11. Do you no longer wait until students have completed their content area assignments before you provide comments and assessments, and do you initiate conferences throughout students' creating process?

12. Has at least one class project been presented to the community or have students used their content knowledge to improve some part of their community, e.g., contributed to the school library, local newspaper, or PTA/PTO?

If you answered yes to all items you are an expert in integrating the curriculum! If you said yes to all but one, you are at a 92-percent level of integration. If you answered yes to 9 or 10 items (75% master), you can boost your students learning by incorporating methods from this chapter into your curriculum.

Learning logs can be implemented in many ways. In kindergarten classrooms in Ontario, Canada, for example, they are 10-page blank books in which teachers print *September 1997, October 1997,* and so on at the top of each page. At the end of each month each child draws, scribbles, or writes what they learned. Such learning logs make students' growth more visible to them and provides their teachers with evidence of their growing understanding of the world around them (Vasquez, 1993).

At higher grade levels, teachers ask students to make a spiral notebook into a learning log by dividing it into sections that denote the content areas or the interdisciplinary themes being studied. In these learning logs, students date every entry and use a ruler to draw straight lines between them. Some teachers ask students to make daily entries, and then to write conclusions about experiments and units on the last day. In these classrooms, learning logs become one performance measure of how much students have learned.

In other classes, entries are only made once a week or month. In such instances, learning logs are designed to increase students' abilities to summarize and integrate what they've learned. Ms. Morrison prefers that her eighth-graders make daily entries in their journals because she has witnessed how their writing and retention of content improves through this activity. She also reports that by October of each year students become engrossed in writing. They strive to recall all they have learned about a topic that day and to express what they learned very explicitly.

CONNECTING CLASSROOMS, PARENTS, AND COMMUNITIES

Parents Building Their Child's Study Skills

You may want to design your own parent skill forms. Such forms enable you to collect data beyond the classroom for which you can assess students' use of language arts and content area knowledge. Figure 11.10 is an example of how you can receive parents' input on study skills.

DEVELOPING TECHNOLOGICAL COMPETENCIES

Inkspot's Writer's Resource

Inkspot's Writer's Resource for young writers offers opportunities for adolescents to discuss in e-mail lists the writing ideas and approaches that are of interest to them. They can read articles by professional writers about their craft and also can attempt to publish their work at this site, although obviously very few works are accepted for publication here. There are also links to classified ads that can help them find ways to publish their work in print or on-line. In Inkspot's related Writing Genre's page, students can learn how to write mysteries, science fiction, drama, children's books, horror, and romance short stories and novels.

For example, the Biographer Maker gives students all the tools they need to write interesting biographies. Students are encouraged to raise important questions about the person they are studying. They are asked to research information about that person in books, electronic encyclopedias, and Internet sites. Finally, they are shown how to synthesize their material and organize their writing so that they can tell a good story. Links to lists of biographies are provided as examples for students to read.

| | **DEGREES OF SKILL** | | |
| | *Absent* | *Low* | *High* |

I. Special study–reading comprehension skills
   A. Ability to interpret graphic aids
      Can the student interpret these graphic aids?

	Absent	Low	High
1. maps			
2. globes			
3. graphs			
4. charts			
5. tables			
6. cartoons			
7. pictures			
8. diagrams			
9. other organizing or iconic aids			

   B. Ability to follow directions
      Can the student follow . . .

	Absent	Low	High
1. simple directions?			
2. a more complex set of directions?			

II. Information location skills
   A. Ability to vary rate of reading
      Can the student do the following?

	Absent	Low	High
1. scan			
2. skim			
3. read at slow rate for difficult materials			
4. read at average rate for reading level			

   B. Ability to locate information by use of book parts
      Can the student use book parts to identify the following information?

	Absent	Low	High
1. title			
2. author or editor			
3. publisher			
4. city of publication			
5. name of series			
6. edition			
7. copyright date			
8. date of publication			

FIGURE 11.10 STUDY SKILLS CHECKLIST   *(continued)*

Adapted from *Reading Skills Checklist,* by J. S. Rogers, 1984. Unpublished manuscript.

| | DEGREES OF SKILL | | |
| | *Absent* | *Low* | *High* |

Can the student quickly locate and
understand the function of the following
parts of a book?

1. preface
2. forward
3. introduction
4. table of contents
5. list of figures
6. chapter headings
7. subtitles

C. Ability to organize information
Can the student do the following?

1. take notes
2. note source of information
3. write a summary for a paragraph
4. write a summary for a short selection
5. write a summary integrating information from more than one source
6. write a summary for a longer selection

7. make graphic aids to summarize
   information
8. write an outline for a paragraph
9. write an outline for a short selection
10. write an outline for longer selections
11. write an outline integrating informa-
    tion from more than one source
12. use the outline to write a report or to
    make an oral report

FIGURE 11.10 (CONTINUED)

SUMMARY

This chapter described the rationale and benefits of integrating the language arts into content area instruction. Newspapers, magazines, and tradebooks were recommended to further students' learning of current, historical, mathematical, and scientific information. Similarly, students' learning can become more visible to themselves when they create idea maps, spin off writings, lesson agendas, reports, dioramas, and learning logs. Inkspots for Writers is a valuable technology tool to increase students' understanding of content area concepts, as matrices and checkpoint charts. Students can profit from being taught the processes of writing nonfiction. Students in culturally enriched classrooms benefit from finding mentors with shared academic interests and cultural backgrounds. To do so, students can read autobiographies and biographies about people they admire, listen to experts speak in their classes, and visit professionals at work.

You can increase your professional competencies by assessing how effectively you integrate language arts and content area instruction. Table 11.6 is designed to assist you in this assessment. In the next chapter, you will learn methods of increasing students' creativity and abilities to originate new ideas.

HOW TO DO IT: USING WHAT YOU'VE LEARNED

The following provide opportunities to reflect on and practice what you have learned.

ASSESSING YOUR LEARNING

1. You can ask local restaurants and businesses to display some of your students' content area reports. In contacting each business, you might ask them to display five of your students' best reports which have been typed and framed. You can change the reports once every grading period so the business has new information for their customers to read.

2. Combine one of the integrated approaches with the books listed in Literature Cards 25–29. In this combination, plan an integrated study around a theme. Members of your class can divide into grade-leveled groups with each group planning an integrated study of a different concept. In this way each group's integrated study is shared, and you have methods of building students' knowledge and communication skills for different themes and grade levels.

3. Choose one of the approaches to integration that you prefer. Design a one-week integration of language arts with content instruction. Incorporate into this plan one of the books from Literature Cards 25–29, and decide how it can introduce or enrich a content discipline for your students. Decide whether it should be read by all in conjunction with the textbook or used as a resource for selected students who want more information about its subject. How do you make that decision? Finally, design a one-week integration of language arts with content instruction.

4. Discuss the importance of student choice in each of the approaches to integration. With a group of elementary or middle school students, discuss methods of instruction they would like to add to their content areas that would entertain more of their interests and talents. Which of their ideas would you incorporate into your content area classes?

5. Combine what you learned in Chapter 2 with the information in this chapter and answer this question: In cross-age work, older students typically serve as tutors and younger students as novices who learn through inquiry and observation. What are the variety of roles younger students can assume in cross-aged learning situations to serve as teachers and active leaders for older classmates?

6. Students' interests and inquiries often extend beyond curriculum requirements. When integrating your curriculum, how can you use what you have learned in this chapter to balance the pull of discoveries by students and the push of curriculum requirements dictated by school district testing policies?

7. How can you ensure that students are involved in planning thematic unit and topic integration approaches to learning?

KEY TERMS EXERCISE

Below are the concepts introduced in this chapter. If you have learned a term, place a checkmark in the blank that precedes that term. If you are not sure of a definition, increase your retention by rereading its definition. If you have learned nine terms in this chapter, you have constructed an understanding of a majority of the most important concepts that you need to integrate language arts and content area instruction.

_____ dialogical discourse   (p. 468)

_____ dioramas   (p. 476)

_____ fonts and special effects   (p. 488)

_____ graphics   (p. 489)

_____ illustrations and photographs (p. 489)

_____ learning logs   (p. 492)

_____ mentoring   (p. 489)

_____ problem-based learning groups (p. 475)

_____ signed words   (p. 488)

_____ text organizers   (p. 489)

_____ topic integration   (p. 472)

_____ tradebooks   (p. 463)

FOR FUTURE REFERENCE

Books about Integration Across the Curriculum or Middle School Students

Apelman, M., & King, J. (1993). *Exploring everyday math: Ideas for students, teachers, and parents.* Portsmouth, NH: Heinemann.

Baker, A., & Baker, J. (1991). *Counting on a small planet: Activities for environmental mathematics.* Portsmouth, NH: Heinemann.

Baker, A., & Baker, J. (1991). *Mathematics in process.* Portsmouth, NH: Heinemann.

Baker, A., & Baker, J. (1991). *Maths in the mind: A process approach to mental strategies.* Portsmouth, NH: Heinemann

Baker, D., Semple, C., & Stead, T. (1990). *How big is the moon? Whole maths in action.* Portsmouth, NH: Heinemann.

Braddon, K. L., Hall, N. J., & Taylor, D. (1993). *Math through children's literature: Making the NCTM standards come alive.* Englewood, CO: Teacher Ideas Press/Libraries Unlimited.

Burk, D., Snider, A., & Symonds, P. (1992–1993). *Math excursions series.* Portsmouth, NH: Heinemann.

Burns, M. (1987–1990). *A collection of math lessons.* Sausalito, CA: Math Solutions Publications.

Burns, M. (1988, January). Beyond "the right answer" . . . Helping your students make sense out of MATH. *Learning, 23* 31–36.

Burns, M. (1992). *About teaching mathematics: A K–8 resource.* Sausalito, CA: Math Solutions Publications.

Participating in a classroom play enables students to experience the aesthetics of words.

CHAPTER 12

INCREASING CREATIVITY, POETIC AND DRAMATIC EXPRESSION ABILITIES, AND VISUAL ARTS SKILLS

"Creative thinking depends upon working at the edge more than the center of one's competence" (Perkins, 1984). Juan is working at a threshold of new, creative, expressive abilities. Today, he, Michael, and Allison are enacting the Chinese fairy tale *Wongatta and the Gentle Dragon*, which they wrote under Juan's mentoring. Juan is proud of his creation. His friends enjoyed the opportunity to exercise their creativity so productively. The play was a tremendous success!

People are born with a creative impulse. When we nurture it, the creative process can unite the affective and cognitive components of students' expression. In doing so, students can more vividly express what they feel so others can *know* and *feel* it. Another distinct benefit of the creative process is that many times students may not know where they are going with a thought or product, but if they are creating, usually they won't leave it. Thus, they sustain their engagement in language arts for longer periods of time.

As students integrate the language arts with content area knowledge, their depth of information and ability to exercise options, examine issues with diverging viewpoints and practice flexibility can increase significantly. These are important precursors to creative thinking. Students need your guidance, however, before they can consistently use these tools to create new solutions to real-world problems. This chapter can help you learn how language arts—particularly viewing, poetry, and drama—can promote students' imaginative language, creativity, and inventive expression and build their original ideas. You will also learn how authorial studies and bibliotherapy prompt students to make discoveries about themselves. By the end of this chapter, you will have answers to the following questions that represent the IRA, NCTE, NAEYC, and TEKS, as well as other statewide and province-based standards for professional development:

1. What skills comprise creativity and effective viewing abilities; why are they important, and how can they be developed in students?

2. What language arts lessons increase students' inventiveness?

3. How do you teach predictive thinking, brainstorming, and drama so students' viewing abilities and ingenuity expand?

4. Why is it important to develop students' poetic abilities?

5. How can you assess creativity?

6. How can you evaluate students' dramatic and poetic expressions?

7. What are the visual arts skills and how can they be taught?

SECTION 1   THEORETICAL FOUNDATIONS

Why Students Need to Develop Creative Thinking and Viewing Abilities

The driving force in writing, speaking, and viewing is called **voice**. Voice is the imprint of the uniqueness of ourselves in a communication. It requires discipline, instruction, craft, and creativity to develop fully.

Throughout history, educators have questioned why hands-on, creative learning activities decrease as students grow older. Research does not support this phenomenon. Wasserstein (1995) reported that, even throughout the middle school years, students at all levels of ability crave doing important work—work that involves their creativity. They seek opportunities to explore ideas for their own sake. For students to feel that their work is important, they need opportunities to invent solutions to real-world problems and to take the basics that they learn and move forward. Students of all ages trust their teachers. Those who "occupy students with trivial work violate their trust. Busywork destroys them" (Wasserstein, 1995, p. 43).

The cry for increased creative expression also rests on its impact on memory. When students invest their intense emotional intelligence into a creative expression, their long-term memory significantly increases (Jensen, 1998). Moreover, when students' creativity is ignited, the resultant emotions excite the brain's chemical system, which releases adrenaline. These chemicals fuse to build vivid memories, which turn learning into celebrative experiences. Such emotionally stimulated intelligences unconsciously unite the physical and mental systems until they activate a "powerful, multifaceted concentration to optimally organize a myriad of conscious and unconscious rational systems to solve challenges" (Sylvester, 1998, p. 35). Thus, developing students' creativity is the most reliable and effective means to ensure that this valuable learning tool is continually, automatically, and instantaneously available to them throughout their lives.

Before students can add emotion and creativity to their language arts and break with tradition, however, they must know the rules and the rationale behind them and know why they are choosing to move beyond and expand English language oral and written systems. Without this foundation what they create cannot have the force of tradition. Thus, without the knowledge discussed in Chapters 1–11 of this text, students cannot apply accurate knowledge and language arts tools to their creative communications. Without these tools, students' creativity can relate only on one level—an emotional one. In addition, practice using the creative tools described in this chapter tends to help students break down barriers of insecurity. This practice, coupled with hours and hours of working on basic components in reading, writing, speaking, listening, thinking, and viewing, may be all that is necessary for students' creativity to ignite.

ROLE OF CREATIVITY IN THE LANGUAGE ARTS

Creative artistry and **viewing** arise from a basic human need to express deep emotions and experiences. Creativity also leaves us significantly changed as it engages emotions and attention at an intense degree. Creativity unleashes deeper ways of expressing the human spirit. Since prehistoric times when people drew on the walls of their caves, the arts have told us who we are.

Creative people are always seeking new avenues of expression. They appreciate others' differences and perspectives and give credit to those having different visions. These people also have a great emotional outwardness. For students to increase creativity, however, they often have to break habits and change perspectives, explore silliness, seriously postpone judgment, explore logic, and allow things to happen. This process usually involves two stages: (1) inspiration, when a new suggestion enters the subconscious; and (2) the development and elaboration of that idea or inspiration. Both stages mature through instruction.

NEED FOR INSTRUCTION

There are several reasons why students need your help to learn to think creatively. First, creativity does not mature naturally without instruction. For instance, in a longitudinal study of kindergarten students, 84 percent ranked high in aptitude for creative thinking. By second grade, however, lacking instruction to expand this creative potential, only 10 percent sustained even a significant level of inventive capacity. It seems that unless we devote special attention to creativity in our language arts programs, most students cease their exploratory thinking processes. Most come to accept only one right answer and believe it is very easy to be wrong. Others believe that someone else knows all the answers and stop trying to find answers because they are valuable only if they fill someone else's (usually their teacher's) blanks. As Paul Messier, U.S. Department of Education, observed, before 5-year-old children go to school, when they want to cut a string, they cut it wherever they decide. After they come to school, however, they realize that there is only one middle. Thereafter, these same children work feverishly to cut each subsequent string exactly where all strings are supposed to be cut—in the middle (P. Messier, personal communication, July 19, 1996).

Second, instruction that increases creative thinking enables students to solve more complex problems in life. Through creative thinking students recognize the complexities and relationships between seemingly disparate ideas. Without this skill, many experiences outside school can convince them that answers to problems should be simple—that problems do not demand deep, creative reflection. For example, students see on television that "all you need is one grand shootout at the O.K. Corral at high noon and all this complex fuss that they have watched for three hours will be over," and so too should all problems be instantly and simply solved (Graves & Stuart, 1987, p. 23).

Third, your students need models of how to use creative thinking effectively. In their lives they often hear and see numerous examples of how language functions to criticize, protest, and punish. They have fewer exemplars, however, of its use to propagate ideas, establish long-term innovations, and project new visions. Because they have had infrequent experiences with creative thinking, students can assume that criticizing someone else's idea is a mature, "adult" way of thinking and communicating. The language lessons in this chapter, can teach students how to incubate ideas until they crystallize into workable plans of action. When students engage in this process, they also learn to express their emotional intelligences, access their imaginations, and complete positive mental images.

Last, developing students' creative thinking increases their pleasure in, and amount of, learning. As an example, one group of seventh-graders field-tested the problem-solving and decision-making activities that appear in Chapter 13. After 8 weeks of instruction, these students described how their future classes could be improved. Although they requested that schools continue to develop their decision-making and problem-solving abilities, they also wanted activities to develop their creativity. They wanted to enact situations in their lives about which they wished to gain more understanding. They wanted their "desks to be moved back so we can get involved in real life through hands-on thinking" (Collins, 1994).

ADVANTAGES OF INSTRUCTION

Creativity is the act of producing original ideas and products. Creativity springs from (a) seemingly simple and surprising events, (b) an ability to generate and recognize undervalued ideas, (c) not "joining the crowd," (d) redefining problems, (e) insights, (f) beliefs, (g) ambiguities, and (h) a willingness to excel and grow (Sternberg & Lubart, 1991). Although creativity has been a topic of interest to educational and psychological researchers for decades, knowledge about creativity has grown phenomenally in the last 40 years (Travis, 1992). For example, from 1855 to 1955 only 10 studies of creativity and its development were conducted in the world. From 1956 to 1966, 10 additional studies were completed. Now more than 250 studies are completed each year (see *Annual Review of Psychology*). The past void of knowledge explains why teachers did not focus on developing creative thinking.

Research indicates that creative people maintain high standards, accept uncertainty, and risk failure as a part of the process of reaching significant accomplishments. Highly creative individuals also approach what they perceive to be important aspects of their work with more intensity and engagement than less creative people (Sisk, 2000). Most exhibit an internalized license to challenge the conventional and to express their own insights frequently and fervently. For instance, Tesla, the inventor of the fluorescent light, the A.C. generator, and the Tesla coil, stated that he created images and language constantly to "project before my eyes a picture complete in every detail of a new machine I want to create." He tested devices mentally, by having them "run" for weeks, after which time he would examine them thoroughly for signs of wear "before he put his invention into oral and written words!" (Adams, 1986, p. 36).

Lacking similar opportunities, students cannot estimate the probable consequences of their creative actions. Without instruction through your language arts program, many may also continue to talk and think like their peers, and squelch their own creative ideas. Moreover, because creative ideas and acts are often imperfect, without your help, many cannot muster the courage to express themselves creatively. This fear of making a mistake can keep students from fashioning solutions and advancing their ideas through writing, speaking, and drawing, even into their adult years.

Before you implement the activities and lessons in this chapter, you and your students may enjoy assessing your present level of creativity. The Remote Associations Test (Mednick & Mednick, 1967) can be used as a pre- and posttest, but do not allow students to see correct answers until the posttest is taken. This tests for one type of creativity—aptness in making unique associations. Read (and ask your students to read) the three words in each line of the Remote Associations Test below and think of a fourth word that, when added to the beginning or end of each word, gives new meaning to each of the words in that line. (For example, if the word *bank* is added to *river, note,* and *blood,* new meanings emerge for all three words.) Now, write a fourth word that could change the meanings of the three words in each line below. Answer as many as you can in 3 minutes and then stop.

1. board	duck	dollar	+_____
2. file	head	toe	+_____
3. mark	fall	table	+_____
4. chicken	fever	butter	+_____
5. class	stage	soccer	+_____

A second aspect of creativity is pattern recognition. To test this component of creativity, unscramble as many of the following words as you can in 2 minutes.

Example: PPUPY = PUPPY	13. AEPHS
6. BEAHC	14. YPEON
7. ODELM	15. IETDR
8. NTRAI	16. AECRT
9. OESHR	17. PATOI
10. HROAC	18. RHTAE
11. CHARI	19. TANOG
12. UGARS	20. OBRAC

You should not check your answers until you have finished reading this chapter and learned how your and your students' ingenuity has matured as a result of reading and implementing the creativity building activities that are contained herein. When you retake the Remote Associations Test, time yourself for 3 minutes only; take the Word Patterning Test for 2 minutes; and then compare how much your creative abilities were enhanced by learning strategies in this chapter. If you answer 18 to 20 items correctly on your posttest, you are among the top 10 percent of creative people. If you score 13 to 17 items correctly, you are among the top 25 percent of adults in your ability to generate new ideas. If you answer 8 to 12 correctly, you are normal in your creative capacity. If you get fewer than 8 correct, you are below average, but you can change that. (For answers, see the Answer Key at the back of the book.)

SECTION 2   PUTTING THEORY INTO PRACTICE

How to Increase Students' Creativity and Viewing Abilities

Once students have taken the pretests on the previous page, you can teach several objectives designed to increase creative thinking, poetic and dramatic expression, and visual arts development. These instructional goals can be divided into three domains of creativity: thinking tools, generative processes, and innovative, insightful development.

- I. Creative Thinking Tools
  - A. SCRAMBLIN—the nine creative thinking processes
  - B. Estimating
  - C. Anticipating, forecasting, and predicting
  - D. Taking calculated risks
  - E. Brainstorming and synthesizing
- II. Generative Processes
  - A. Generating hypotheses
  - B. Planning—selecting strategies to reach a specific goal, create a product, or complete a process by organizing time, materials, and effort
  - C. Composing and building
- III. Innovative Thinking through Insight Development
  - A. Exploring a subject
  - B. Mulling over a subject
  - C. Making discoveries about form, rules, restrictions, values, and ideas

ACTIVITIES THAT DEVELOP CREATIVE THINKING TOOLS

Once you explain the above creativity domains and visual arts competencies, you can use the following activities to increase thinking and language tools that can be used throughout student's lives to overcome impasses. These are *brainstorming, consensus building, humor,* and *problem defining.* Brainstorming, brainwriting, consensus building, humor, and problem definition are activities that prepare students for such deeper applications of creative thought and visual arts skills, as described below.

BRAINSTORMING AND BRAINWRITING

Little Rabbit's Loose Tooth

Brainstorming is a thinking strategy to stimulate creativity by saying or writing as many ideas as come to mind about a topic. Brainstorming can be taught by presenting the guidelines in Figure 12.1. Preschool through second-grade students can practice brainstorming by sharing their predictions about the ending of a book. To do so, you can select a book to which students can easily relate, such as *Little Rabbit's Loose Tooth* by Lucy Bate, in which a rabbit has the dilemma of not knowing what to do with her tooth after it has been pulled. You ask students to pay attention to how their minds work as they think and share as many ideas as they can about what the rabbit could do. After ideas have been listed, you can discuss with students ways in which creative thinking is different from simply remembering.

1. *All ideas are welcomed.* No one says any idea is not good. No one needs to worry that their ideas are not good enough. All ideas help.

2. *Give as many ideas as you can.* The longer the list, the more likely it contains a number of workable ideas.

3. *Add to each other's ideas.* People can help each other.

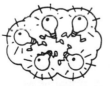

4. *Think of crazy and new ideas.* One idea can trigger a useful idea for someone else. Problems are often seen in new ways as a result of a new thought.

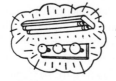

5. *Record each idea and combine ideas at the end.* After all ideas have been given, combine and select the best.

FIGURE 12.1 TEACHING STEPS IN BRAINSTORMING AND BRAINWRITING

You can continue this instruction by brainstorming the endings of the following books, which you can read aloud on consecutive days: *Animals Should Definitely Not Wear Clothing* (Jude Barrette); *The Very Busy Spider* (Eric Carle); *Little Polar Bear* (Hags de Beer); *The Day the Goose Got Loose* (Reeve Lindergh); *Oscar Mouse Finds a Home* (Moira Miller and Maria Majewska); *Obadiah Coffee and the Music Contest* (Valerie Poole); and *Stories to Solve* (George Shannon).

A lesson to develop the brainstorming skills of older students involves dividing the class into small groups of two or three students. Have students choose a topic, such as candy, fiber, or elephant. Each group can answer the following questions concerning the topic:

1. What is it like?
2. What are the kinds of it?
3. What is it a part of?
4. What are the parts of it?
5. What is it a stage of?
6. What are the stages of it?
7. What is it a product of?
8. What are the products of it?

All answers are acceptable. The purpose of the exercise is to develop older students' abilities to think about a topic from several different perspectives and visualize objects as completely as possible in their minds.

Students can also learn how brainstorming is used in the business world by reading current events in newspapers. Once students have used the process several times as a large class, you can ask them to brainstorm silently on their own for a few minutes before they meet in small groups. Then they can combine brainstorming ideas to reach solutions. You can end this lesson by inquiring why pausing before important meetings to perform a mental brainstorm can be a valuable tool for them to use as adults before they go to meetings scheduled at work.

Brainwriting is a modification of brainstorming (Rodriques, 1983). In brainwriting, students are divided into small groups. Each student writes his or her ideas about a topic on which they wish to compose. When someone comes to a lull in brainwriting about their own topic, that group member places his or her paper in the center of the table and takes another student's list, adding more ideas to that student's list. At the end of each brainwriting session, students reread their original brainwriting, along with the ideas classmates have added to their lists. Then they can begin their first drafts more creatively.

CONSENSUS BUILDING AND HUMOR

As your students feel more comfortable with brainstorming, you can model **consensus building,** which is the act of bringing all members of a group to agreement on a creative plan of action. The cardinal principle of consensus building is that group members continue to generate plausible alternatives until a plan is satisfactory to every member. Exercises for consensus building require group members to agree on a short list of alternatives derived from the longer brainstorming list. Students practice trying to reach consensus as one of their group members takes notes. Once agreement is reached, students list successful strategies they used to build consensus by referring to the notes this member took about the consensus process. Then they generate principles to follow in the future for situations in which a consensus must be reached.

Another creative thinking tool lesson is to introduce a study of humor, one of the purest forms of creativity. **Humor** is defined as a quality that appeals to a sense of the incongruous. Students who understand types of humor and incongruities not only expand their ability to express their own creative ideas, but recognize humorous interpretations of life more often than others. After you have introduced the following types of incongruities, you can ask students to point them out in future classes when they appear in student writings and literature. You may also teach minilessons so students learn how to talk so as to use the following forms of humor:

1. *Irony:* highlighting events that turn out the opposite from what is expected
2. *Word play:* using words in unusual or incorrect ways on purpose
3. *Contrast:* accenting differences between characters and events
4. *Just desserts:* creating unusual happenings in which wicked or foolish characters get what they deserve
5. *Exaggeration:* stretching the truth about someone or something
6. *Slapstick:* demonstrating very physical comedy, such as having objects collide in strange ways

Teaching students how to build consensus when they work in groups, as well as how to express humor during difficult times in their lives, are very important lessons. Their importance grows as technology becomes more prominent in managing lower-level thinking tasks. Our livelihood in the twenty-first century is increasingly based on the ability to work effectively with others and generate new ideas. Teaching students consensus building and humor skills can prepare them for a successful livelihood.

For these reasons, lessons in consensus building, humor-making, and the other activities in this chapter should start at a young age and continue through every grade level. At younger grade levels, I recommend that you start by teaching only one strategy at a time for about a 6-week period. For example, if you want to emphasize irony, watch for irony in books that you read, in discussions that you have, and in visual arts. Give several examples orally for about a 6-week period before you move on to a second strategy for understanding humor or for consensus building. In this way, students can gradually develop these skills and increase their creativity and ability to generate new ideas. Similarly, at the older grade levels, you can expand your curriculum by teaching students how to eliminate blocks to their creative thinking. Components of increased creativity, as well as diminished creativity, which can be modeled, taught, and demonstrated by older students, are described in Figure 12.2.

PROBLEM DEFINING

Problem defining is the process of moving from disarray to order (Sternberg & Lubart, 1991). Students who accurately define problems become significantly stronger thinkers, communicators, and appreciators of visual arts than students who

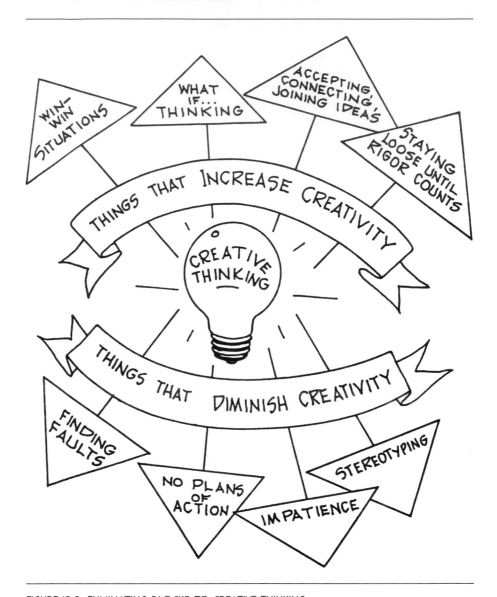

FIGURE 12.2 ELIMINATING BLOCKS TO CREATIVE THINKING

are not taught problem-defining skills (Collins, 1991a; Block, 1994). An effective instructional strategy to present problem defining is to *avoid* telling students what problem to solve. Rather, you can design a lesson that asks students to share aspects of human behavior that they want to better understand. At first students may not say anything because they may never have been asked to define problems for themselves. But if you wait, eventually one student will speak up, and then another. With the ice broken, more students become eager to contribute and to define a problem that they are curious to solve, such as: Why do parents make us dress up on special occasions? Why do some siblings fight a lot whereas others don't? And how do we choose our friends? With these problems defined you can introduce a discussion of blocks to creative thinking and how students can overcome them (see Figure 12.2).

In summary, creative thinking tools are the totality of thinking processes that produce original ideas and products. It often requires constructive risk-taking, brainstorming, comprehensive viewing, consensus building, humor, problem defining, and contemplative reflection.

The above activities students feel more comfortable with the spontaneity and irregular patterns with which creative ideas emerge. With this comfort level in place, students can develop generative processes so that their creativity becomes more permanent and a resilient state of mind. The following lessons build these processes.

LESSONS THAT EXPAND GENERATIVE THINKING PROCESSES

TEACHING CREATIVE DRAMATICS

Creative dramatics is the enactment of a story based on experiences, literature, history, current events, content area knowledge, and imagination (Wilhem, 1998; Noll, Kindahl, & Salazar, 1998; McMaster 1998). It is acting out and revealing one's imagination by becoming someone or something else. Creative dramatics uses creative expression, viewing, movement, and voice to enhance, extend, and deepen conceptual knowledge, and to empathize with characters. It allows students to learn physically, kinesthetically, mentally, and emotionally. In addition, it matures vocabulary, volume, tempo, pitch, and clarity in speech. Creative drama also integrates creativity, speaking, and listening with art. It can represent the human being's interpretation of life, expressed in a way that can be universally recognized and understood. At its best, creative drama can help students understand real-world conflicts and offer young players tastes of the magic and make-believe that imagination and the theater provide. Drama is also important in that it moves a private experience into a public domain, and enables learners to discuss and use new language forms.

> In other words, children are drawn to the dramatization activity for the same reason they are drawn to other forms of sociodramatic play: *to exercise some control over their lives, their wishes, and their destinies.* We have all heard of young children attempting to control play in the block corner, in the library area, while in line for the bathroom, and on the playground. Dramatization offers the child–author an opportunity to have the final say in a play situation, which is irresistible for most children. If classroom rules allow the author of the story to choose the cast, this furthers his or her influence over the action. The dramatization activity, therefore beyond any literary or literacy pretensions, presents a lesson in social interactions for the child. (Cooper, 1993, p. 71)

Creative drama also helps students:

Understand plot structure, character, objectives, and themes

Experience aesthetic appreciation for good literature

Express their learning through movement and voice

Learn the necessity of working together to create something of value

Find success and a place for themselves when they have difficulty in other subject areas

Enjoy and succeed together, which increases their self-confidence

Become thinking, feeling, and creative people more able to face life's challenges (McMaster, 1998; Noll, Lindahl, & Salazar, 1998; Wilhem, 1998)

As Davidson (1996, p. 71) cautions, however:

> Many times, when we are nervous about something, we try to sample it a small amount at a time. It may be tempting for teachers who are just beginning to support dramatic play to allow it for short periods at first. Resist this urge. It takes a while for dramatic play to get going. Leaving only a short time will not enable children to develop their play. If play periods are too short, children will have barely finished preparing for their plays when it is time to stop and clean up. After many such experiences, children may simply give up trying to engage their creativity.

Drama should be used in your language program because it is therapeutic; it enables students to assume responsibility for group decisions and is the most highly socialized art form (Lundsteen, 1989). Although much has been said about the creative and critical thinking abilities drama stimulates, of equal importance is the opportunity it affords students to feel and release emotions. Because of this, emphasis should be placed on the beauty of communicating, feeling, and thinking, with limited attention given to remembering every single word in a script (McClure, 1995). Creative dramatics can build on a continuum from interpretive to improvisational. The following activities provide a gradual progression that eases students into thinking dramatically. These lessons stretch generative, imaginative thinking through pretending, and visual arts skills through improvisations, role plays, and puppetry.

Improvisations.   Improvisations are the spontaneous acting out of an event. It matures students' abilities to visualize unknowns and break away from standard answers. Such abilities are important because they characterize adults who think beyond usual parameters and approach situations with unrestrained outlooks. Maurice Sendak (1989, p. 3) stated it well:

> The qualities that make for excellence in children's literature can be sweepingly summed up in a single word: imagination. And imagination as it relates to the child in my mind is synonymous with fantasy. Contrary to most of the propaganda in books for the young, childhood is only partly a time of innocence. It is, in my opinion, a time of seriousness, bewilderment, and a good deal of suffering. . . . Imagination for the child is a miraculous, free-wheeling device he uses to course his way through the problems of everyday life.

Providing opportunities for students to pretend to be fictional or historical characters they admire is a first step in developing imaginative thinking. To begin, students can play charades. Second, students can practice imaginative thinking by replicating in their minds the actions of a character in something they've read. To do so, they imagine events they did not read in which this character might have

played a role. Such pretending is based on interpretations and inferences of what is read. After they have invented their imaginary event, they can describe it orally, in writing, or through improvisations or charades. They defend with you the logic behind their improvisations before sharing them in class. A book that works well for subsequent improvisations is Judith Viorst's *If I Were in Charge of the World and Other Worries.* Through this book, students stimulate their imaginative thinking as they emulate the changes Viorst suggests and add their own.

Third, Ms. Phillips, Juan's, Meisong's, Michael's, and Allison's eighth-grade teacher extends the creativity of students in grades 4–8 in a new manner. Her students deeply enjoy this activity, and she encourages you to implement it in your class. In this new type of improvisations, students pretend that they are people involved in an important historical event. They reenact the event, adding details not present in material studied. Then they engage in in-depth research about one historical figure who was (or was not) a contemporary to the historical figure other classmates study. Next, they have pretend conversations between all their historical figures. They discuss their philosophies as related to problems other classmates submit. When these students ponder such "what if's" about life, they significantly augment their imaginative thinking because they answer from their characters' perspectives.

Role Playing.   Role playing is when students enact problematic events that could occur (Collins, 1991a; Block, 2000). You can reduce the risk-taking involved in role playing by first only pairing students. Pairs can then describe difficult situations they face, and role play solutions for each other. To increase compassion and empathy, students can reverse their roles and play one of their own adversaries. For example, they might enact a conversation between parents and a student, with the student playing the role of the parent. These reverse role plays enable students to see an opponent's point of view more clearly. To illustrate, Ms. Phillips asked Juan and her other middle school students to role play difficult interactions involving adults. She discovered that

> When students play their parents (in role playing), [students] reveal the lack of respect they feel. According to their rendition, parents fail to ask questions; instead they jump to some incorrect conclusions. Through my students' role plays I became a better parent and understood my own family better. As a teacher, role plays enlightened me to my students' important points of view concerning their needs (Phillips, personal communication, September 13, 1996).

Students can also role play a piece of literature from a villain's or a minor character's point of view. Role playing lessons can increase in difficulty when students (1) role play actual past events or readings, (2) move this enactment into a current setting that involves unresolved issues in our society, and (3) recast the events into a probable future setting. Computers can also assist students' scriptwriting. Play Write (IBM) is a software package that provides a format for puppet and play scripts. This software enables students to set up a professional script easily. Play Write also helps students understand spoken and written language. Moreover, Puppet Maker (IBM) and Puppet Plays (IBM) are software packages (among many others) that guide students to make their own puppets and provide hints for their own productions, as described below.

Puppetry.   Puppetry gives students a comfortable vehicle to project creative expressions, images, and imagination before others. Samples of puppets that are easy for students to make appear in Figure 12.3. To implement this lesson, allow students to select a personal situation, idea from literature, or current issue they wish to improve through their imaginative thinking. Then have them make their puppet of choice.

Pantomime.   Pantomime involves conveying meaning through facial expressions and body language. Young children can pretend to be kites flying on the breeze or a rubber band stretching. To present a pantomime, the children must think and talk about how characters or objects look (and feel and act), which involves in-depth thinking about the story. Whether watching or doing, children involved in pantomime enjoy the experience. They are focused on defining characteristics of a visual art form.

Choral Reading.   Choral reading begins by selecting a piece of prose or poetry that relates to a recent experience the class has had. This selection is divided into parts, and small groups of students read each part. Choral readings can also be completed as a whole-class unison reading by assigning pairs or groups of students to a specific part, or by asking groups of students to read in rounds. Before choral readings begin, students set a personal objective for their own speaking, reading, or thinking development. Then they evaluate their success. Choral reading allows children to experiment with different vocal inflections and increases their interpretive thinking and reading skills. See Table 12.1 for more information about how to teach choral reading.

Dance.   Dance is movement that contains a series of rhythmic and patterned bodily movements usually performed to music. It is something that is shared and understood around the world. The universality of dance and its themes can be demonstrated by showing films of dancing performed in different cultures and by asking students to practice the steps and rhythms.

Looking at other cultures can help students learn more about themselves and their own culture as well. Dance also provides opportunities to learn about and appreciate cultural diversity. Students of dance can develop skills in social relations by assuming the role of choreographer and creating dances for their classmates. By projecting their problems through dance, children may be able to work through some difficulties in their lives. The following recordings, films, and books enable students to dance to rhythms that are important in different cultures (collected and originally reported in Tiedt & Tiedt, 1995):

Authentic Afro-Rhythms. LP 6060, Kimbo Educational Products, P.O. Box 246, Deal, NJ 07723. Rhythms from Africa, Cuba, Haiti, Brazil, Trinidad, and Puerto Rico.

Authentic Indian Dances and Folklore. Kimbo Educational Products. Drumming and storytelling by Michigan Chippewa chiefs who narrate the history of their dances.

Authentic Music of the American Indians. Three records. Everest, Chesterfield Music Shops, Inc., 12 Warren St., New York, NY 10007.

Styrofoam Puppet

Cylinder Puppet

"For centuries, puppets have combined their magic with education." (Flower & Fortney, 1983)

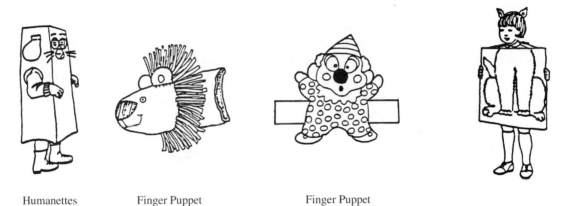

Humanettes

Finger Puppet
(from glove finger)

Finger Puppet
(with tabs)

Puppet Stages Students Can Make

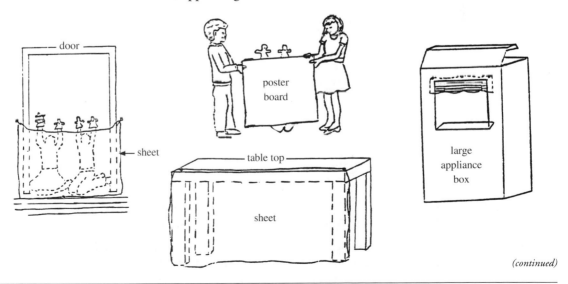

door

sheet

poster
board

table top

sheet

large
appliance
box

(continued)

FIGURE 12.3 PUPPETRY IN EDUCATION

Created by Stephanie Wells, 2000, master of education degree candidate at Texas Christian University, Fort Worth, TX. Used by permission.

Hand Puppets   Cloth Puppet   Rod Puppet

"Kids are born puppeteers. From the time they are old enough to sit up and carry on a simple conversation, you will find them inventing voices and personalities for every toy in their toy box: stuffed elephants who sing, action figures who dance, and dolls who hide in the dark." (Sherman, 1983)

"Puppets are useful in the classroom because they are fun—and they make learning fun. They are special little beings over whose lives even children can exercise control. Puppets are also magic. With strings, wires, rods, or a hand, they come to life and assume an independent personality." (Sherman, 1983)

Finger Puppets   Stick Puppets

"Puppetry, which is extremely popular with children today, is one of the oldest theatrical traditions and has endured throughout the ages." (Sherman, 1999)

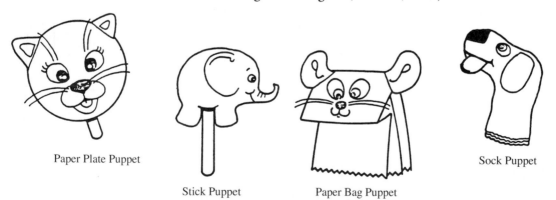

Paper Plate Puppet   Stick Puppet   Paper Bag Puppet   Sock Puppet

"Imaginative teachers all over the country are making puppets full partners in presenting lessons." (Flower & Fortney, 1983)

Adapted from *Puppets: Methods and Materials,* by C. Flower, and A. J. Fortney, 1983, Dairs Publications, Massachusetts; and "Talking Heads," by M. Sherman, *Family Fun Magazine,* 1999, at http://family.go.com.

FIGURE 12.3 (CONTINUED)

TABLE 12.1 HOW TO TEACH CHORAL READINGS

Choral reading is also called choral speaking, verse speaking, and unison speaking. Choral reading is the interpretation of poetry or prose by many voices speaking as one. It is best to allow developing readers to arrange the text into the type of speaking parts they desire.

BENEFITS OF CHORAL READING

- Develops an appreciation for reading and speaking as well as good literature
- Adds beauty and enjoyment to a speech and reading improvement program
- Encourages group participation and cooperation
- Reduces students' inhibitions of speaking before a group
- Increases developing readers' fluency

TYPES OF CHORAL READING

1. Unison Reading
All voices speak as one.

> Stop! Look! Listen!
> Before you cross the street.
> Use your eyes; use your ears;
> *Then* use your feet!
>
> —Anonymous

2. Line-a-Child or Sequence Reading
Each child reads at least one line. Readers must come in on time to prevent missing a beat.

> **This Little Cow**
>
> 1st Child: This little cow eats grass.
> 2nd Child: This little cow eats hay.
> 3rd Child: This little cow drinks water.
> 4th Child: This little cow runs away.
> 5th Child: This little cow does nothing
> All. But just lies down all day.
>
> —Mother Goose

3. Antiphonal Reading
The group is divided into two sections (girls/boys, etc.). Each group takes half the selection. A question–answer format or dialogue poetry is well suited to this arrangement.

> **Baa, Baa, Black Sheep**
>
> Group I: Baa, baa, black sheep,
> Have you any wool?
> Group II: Yes, sir; yes, sir.
> Three bags full.
>
> —Mother Goose

(continued)

TABLE 12.1 (CONTINUED)

4. Refrain Reading
Students have the responsibility for coming in on time and responding rythmically with the repetition of a word or phrase.

A Farmer Went Trotting

Teacher: A farmer went trotting upon his grey mare;
Class: Bumpety, bumpety, bump!
Teacher: With his daughter behind him so rosy and fair;
Class: Lumpety, lumpety, lump!

—Traditional

5. Three- or Four-Part Reading
Better suited for upper elementary grades, where voices can be classed as light or dark, or high, middle, and low. Each group is given a stanza.

The Gay Little Cricket

Group I: The gay little cricket is singing today,
All: "tee-dee, tee-dee, tee-dee!"
Group II: He rubs his wings, and he sings this way,
All: "tee-dee, tee-dee, tee-dee!"
Group III: He sings at work and he sings at play,
All: "tee-dee, tee-dee, tee-dee!"

SOURCES OF CHORAL READING LITERATURE

- *Sounds of Language Series* (1972) by Bill Martin & M. Brogan
- *Where the Sidewalk Ends* (1974) and *A Light in the Attic* (1981) by Shel Silverstein

---

The Lark in the Morning. Everest. Songs and dances from the Irish countryside.

The Real Flamenco. Everest. Songs and dances from Spain.

African Rhythms. Associated Films, Inc., 1621 Dragon St., Dallas, TX 75207. 13 minutes, color.

The Strollers. Associated Films. The Moiseyev Dance Company in a Russian folk dance. 6 minutes, color.

Dancer's World. Associated Films. Martha Graham discusses dancing as her students dance the emotions of hope, fear, joy, and love. 30 minutes.

International Folk Dancing, a book by Betty Casey. Doubleday, 1981. Includes directions and pictures of costumes that students can make.

TEACHING INNOVATIVE THINKING: THE SCRAMBLIN TECHNIQUE

To become innovative and ingenious, students must learn to "scramble" ideas, hence the title of the next lesson, **SCRAMBLIN**, which is the acronym for the nine processes of innovative thinking. You can teach these processes individually to students, even in nine separate lessons if you desire. Then you can introduce activities for students to self-initiate and practice these innovative thinking processes interactively. A description of these nine processes follows, as well as sample methods and examples for how to teach each process.

1. Substitute processes help students reach resolutions by expanding their repertoire of ideas and thinking patterns. A method of eliciting substitute thinking is to ask someone else's advice. In so doing, students become aware of alternative solutions and different ways of reasoning that they can apply to their situation. Another method is to consider how a person they admire would act in their situation. For example, if they are not doing well on their weekly math tests, they could ask three people who do well on their tests how they study and substitute these study habits for their own.

2. Combining is a process that helps students discover new ideas by combining two unlike objects, images, or events. For example, when students have a problem they can put unlike objects together to solve it like a reclining chair, which combines a stationary footstool with a stationary straight chair for comfort.

3. Rearranging is a process in which students change or reorder steps of a thinking process used for a previous solution or condition. Rearranging thinking is demonstrated in the following hypothetical situation: A student sits beside someone who talks all the time in science class. He feels as if he has tried *everything,* but that person keeps right on talking. He has tried not listening, telling the person not to talk, and asking the teacher if he could move. He could not be moved because the students sit in alphabetical order. By using rearranging thinking, students learn not to waste time trying to rearrange things they can't change, such as other people, their own (naturally friendly) nature, or a teacher's seating arrangement. Instead, they concentrate on what they can change. In this example the student discovered that he could change the direction in which the desks faced in the room. If the chairs in the room were rearranged, placing two rows at the back of the room and the remaining rows to the side by the windows, the class could remain in alphabetical order, but he would be across the room from the person disturbing him.

4. Adaptive thinking is a process in which students change a small detail about a first solution to improve it. For example, if a student wants to become a better basketball player, she can use adaptive thinking to reach this goal. She can begin by only shooting the shots that she knows she can make. She can then adapt the thinking slightly and add the new solution of practicing one new position shot, alone, each week. She can subsequently add several changes in simple steps, through adaptive thinking, until she is pleased with the results.

5. Minimizing improves an outcome by compacting, condensing, or simplifying it. This innovative process helps students identify dispensable elements. A method of initiating minimizing thinking is to teach students to ask themselves repeatedly, "What is something in this idea that I can simplify?"

6. Bigger thinking helps students innovate by adding parts. To develop this ability, have students think of ways to increase the size, strength, time, or frequency of actions to make them better. To magnify, students can write about an aspect of their problem to which they had not given adequate attention. This magnification can involve including additional facts and reflecting on opposing viewpoints of an issue, both of which take account of important information that could have been over-looked because of an initial, one-sided point of view. It is helpful if they ask the following questions as well: (a) What else might be happening? (b) What other things are possible? (c) What if _____? (d) What ideas can I get about _____ by thinking about _____?

7. Linking is based on the principle that the more responses produced, the greater the chances of reaching a satisfactory solution. If students have 20 ideas to choose from, they have a greater probability of having a quality idea than if they have only 2 ideas. They can initiate the linking thought process by asking themselves: (a) In what ways might I _____? (b) Make a list of things that _____. (c) How many different examples (reasons, solutions, etc.) can I think of?

8. Inventing makes students turn their thoughts upside down. Often inventors make special but extreme rearrangements. Students can turn ideas all around by becoming their own "devil's advocates" and thinking of reasons why an idea they value wouldn't work.

9. Newness is the process of developing new or novel responses. You can elicit new ideas by having students ask themselves: (a) What else, or what more? (b) What is a new, original way to _____? (c) Can I invent a new _____? (d) How can I change _____ to make _____?

Once students have been taught these SCRAMBLIN processes, they can create a thinking guide of their own to remind them of methods to initiate each of these generative processes. Then they can practice using these processes interactively by completing one of the following activities that Ms. Phillips and other teachers referred to in this textbook use to help their students solve problems.

1. Identify a situation at school that annoys you. Use SCRAMBLIN thinking process to suggest how to eliminate this annoyance.

2. Think of a time in the past when you wish you had used creative thinking. Describe that time in a short story. Only this time, change the ending by using the SCRAMBLIN processes. Describe what types of generative thinking you used to make this change.

3. Can you imagine a time in the near future when you could use innovative thinking? Describe why it could be necessary and how you would use it.

4. You have probably heard that too much of anything is not good. Use your innovative thinking to identify two situations in life for which thinking creatively could be detrimental rather than beneficial.

5. Your parents just told you that the family is going on a family vacation but the time conflicts with the most important party of the summer. What can you do?

6. Inventors take two objects and combine them to create solutions to problems (e.g., taking away the difficulty of not having space for a washer and dryer in small apartments by stacking them on top of one another. Think of an inconvenience in your life. Describe the process you would use to change it and the end product of

your inventive thinking. (See *Small Inventions That Make a Big Difference* by Donald Crump, National Geographic Publishers, 1984, for additional examples of inventions.)

7. Plan to improve something about your appearance or personality and describe the type of SCRAMBLIN thinking you did to make your change.

8. Think of the last time you felt as if you had tried everything, and everything failed. Knowing what you know now, what would you have done differently in that situation?

TEACHING STUDENTS HOW TO PREDICT

Perhaps one of the most important survival skills for this century is the ability to predict. **Predictive thinking** is gaining in importance because students must adapt quickly to change and to meet the challenge of new knowledge society increasingly amasses. Learning how to select among several outcomes from this mountain of information before they act can be taught in the following ways.

The Silver Whistle

You can tell students that they must learn to investigate all details, very carefully, before they predict. They are to consider what changes can occur in an environment, and how positively or negatively they affect the specific goals they want to reach. At this point in the lesson, older students can read *The Silver Whistle* and stop at several points to predict what Miguel is likely to do (or should do) next. Students can diagram the positive and negative effects of each action Miguel could take. Students can use these diagrams to explain to others why they made their predictions. After all students have explained their predictions, they can read the next section of the book to discover what action the author has Miguel take.

Younger students can be introduced to predictive thinking by describing how to attend to the positive and negative effects that details have on outcomes. You can teach that it is important to withhold judgment until they have explored enough details to obtain the maximum number of facts. Then you can ask them to predict the title and picture likely to be beneath the construction paper that you taped over the cover of a book that you read aloud to them. Once younger students complete this activity as a whole class, they can divide into three small groups for a second practice session. In this session, you can read a second book, but prevent students from seeing the pictures, the cover, or the title and do not read the ending. Next, you can ask one small group to predict the cover picture, one group to predict the title, and one group to predict the ending. Then, each group can show their prediction and explain the reasons for their prediction.

Following these activities, students can predict outcomes in their lives. They can begin by describing a past incident in the classroom and how one detail interacted with a second to produce the end result. Because these examples are based on events that actually happened, students have the experience to understand why these certain results occurred. Once students feel comfortable, they can elect to make creative and realistic predictions about events relative to their interests, such as sports, clothing trends, music, and technological advancements. Then they can justify their predictions by showing how alternative predictions are inconsistent with existing evidence.

Next, each student can make a prediction about something that is likely to occur by the end of the month in his or her life. This prediction can be sealed in a dated envelope, opened, and reviewed at the end of the month, after the event should have occurred. Last, students can elect to share the predictions they made in their envelopes and how they can improve their predictive thinking.

A more advanced activity challenges gifted students. They work in small groups to make predictions about future events at the end of each chapter in *Jumanji, Sixth Grade Secrets, Two Minute Mysteries, Stranger at Winfield House, The Tricksters, Fallen Angels, Call It Courage, Tuck Everlasting, Jane Eyre,* or *King Bidgood's in the Bathtub*. By the end of the second and subsequent chapters difficulty increases by having them also create proverbial or metaphorical sayings for their predictions. When each group finishes making predictions about their books, students write proverbs that state their opinion about the moral of the book.

INTEGRATING THE LANGUAGE ARTS

How to Cultivate Student Poets and Why It Is Important to Do So

A **poem** is defined as an arrangement of words in verse, expressing facts, ideas, or emotions in a style more concentrated, imaginative, and powerful than that of ordinary speech; some are in meter, some in free verse. Poetry is the only medium of written expression in which experience and emotions are captured simultaneously. Pinsky (2000) and McClure, Harrison, and Reed (1990) believe that people should hear fine poetry as well as attempt to write it because a poem read aloud unites cognitive and affective dimensions of the mind in new ways. You may never have created a truly beautiful poem yourself but you will have the opportunity to do so in For Your Journal (p. 536). Creating a beautiful poem enables you to show a model to students before you ask them to write poetically.

The information in this section of the chapter also acquaints you with several poetic forms and how to teach them to students. One of the most successful ways of doing so is to make "personal poetry collections." Then, on a regular basis, students can bind their favorite poems into a book. They can use their anthologies for choral readings, reader's theater, and/or partner readings. In addition, Literature Cards 30 and 31 contain books of poetry that you can read with your students. In addition to collecting their own poems (and those that they like from other poets), students can be taught to write and to appreciate the following poems, beginning with those that are of greatest interest to them: lyrics, narrative, free verse, diamante, cinquain, and Haiku. Lyric and narrative poems are poetry that usually tells a fictional (lyric or narrative) or nonfictional story (narrative) in more than four stanzas, which run several pages long (e.g., Edgar Allen Poe's *The Raven*). Other forms of poetry are described next.

Couplet.   A couplet is a two-line stanza that usually rhymes and contains the same number of syllables.

A Big Turtle
A big turtle sat on the end of a log,
Watching a tadpole turn into a frog. —Anonymous

Literature Card 30

POETRY TO BUILD STUDENTS' CREATIVITY AND VISUAL ARTS SKILLS

Good Books with a Lot of Pictures

Sing to the Sun by A. Bryan, 1992 HarperCollins

Joyful Noise: Poems for Two Voices by P. Fleischman, 1988 Harper & Row

Brown Bear, Brown Bear, What Do You See? by B. Martin Jr., 1983 Scholastic

Bunches & Bunches of Bunnies by L. Mathews, 1978 Scholastic

Catch Me and Kiss Me and Say It Again by C. Watson, 1978 Scholastic

Chicken Soup with Rice by M. Sendak, 1986 Scholastic

Each Peach Pear Plum by J. & A. Ahlberg, 1979 Viking

The Gingerbread Boy by P. Galdone, 1983 Harper

I Know an Old Lady Who Swallowed a Fly by N. B. Westcott, 1980 Dial

If All the Seas Were One Sea by J. Domanska, 1987 Dell

Jesse Bear, What Will You Wear? by N. W. Carlstrom, 1986 Doubleday

Mary Wore Her Red Dress & Henry Wore His Green Sneakers by M. Peek, 1988 Dell

On Market Street by P. Galdone, 1986a Dell

Polar Bear, Polar Bear, What Do You Hear? by B. Martin Jr., 1991 Scholastic

Three Little Kittens by P. Galdone, 1986b Dell

New Baby Calf by E. N. Chase Scholastic

Over in the Meadow: A Counting-Out Rhyme by O. A. Wadsworth & M. M. Rae, 1985 Greenwillow

I Am Phoenix: Poems for Two Voices by P. Fleischmann Harper & Row

Good Books to Tell You a Lot about the Subject

The Hopeful Trout, and Other Limericks by J. Ciardi, 1989 Houghton Mifflin

A Brighter Garden by E. Dickinson, 1990 Philomel

Always Wondering: Some Favorite Poems of Aileen Fisher by A. Fisher, 1991 HarperCollins

Grim and Ghastly Goings-On by F. Heide, 1992 Lothrop, Lee & Shepard

A Fine Fat Pig, and Other Animal Poems by M. Hoberman, 1991 HarperCollins

The Beasts of Bethlehem by X. Kennedy, 1992 Macmillan

Of Pelicans and Pussycats: Poems and Limmericks by E. Lear, 1990 Dial

The Animals: Selected Poems by M. Mado, 1992 McElderry

Bizarre Birds and Beasts by J. Marsh, 1991 Dial

The Singing Green: New and Selected Poems for All Seasons by E. Merriam, 1992 Morrow

The Butterfly Jar by J. Moss, 1989 Bantam Books

Something's Sleeping in the Hall by K. Kuskin

I Din Do Nuffin by J. Agard, 1983 Bodley Head

Good Books If You Are Just Beginning to Learn about the Subject

Mother Goose Rhymes by L. Obligado, 1990 Golden Press

Book of Nursery and Mother Goose Rhymes by M. DeAngeli, 1954 Doubleday

The Moon by R. Stevenson, Harper & Row

Shoes by E. Winthrop, 1986 Harper & Row

The Book of Pigericks by A. Lobel, 1983 Random House

Poems Children Will Sit Still For: A Selection for Favorite Nursery Rhymes by R. Caldecott

All the Colors of the Race by A. Adoff, 1992 Beech Tree Books

Blackberry Ink by E. Merriam, 1985 Morrow

If You Are a Hunter of Fossils by B. Baylor, 1980 Scribner

Poem Stew ed. by W. Cole, 1981 Lippincott

The Tamarindo Puppy and Other Poems by C. Pomerantz, 1980 Greenwillow

Peacock Pie: A Book of Rhymes by W. de la Mare, 1961 Knopf

Bear Hugs by K. Hague, 1989 Holt

Soap, Soup, and Other Verses by K. Kuskin, 1992 HarperCollins

A Hippopotamusn't and Other Animal Verses by P. Lewis, 1990 Dial

A Poem for Pickle: Funnybone Verse by E. Merriam, 1989 Morrow

Trees by H. Behn

Birches by R. Frost, 1988 Henry Holt

Books That Have Several Chapters about the Subject

Chocolate Dreams by A. Adoff, 1989 Lothrop, Lee & Shepard

Prayers from the Ark: Selected Poems by C. de Gasztold, 1992 Viking

Ghastlies, Goops, and Pincushions by X. Kennedy, 1989 Macmillan

Hey World, Here I Am! by J. Little, 1989 Harper & Row

Jane Yolen's Old McDonald Songbook by J. Yolen, 1994a

Tomie de Paola's Mother Goose by T. de Paola, 1985 Scholastic

Surprises by L. B. Hopkins, 1984 Scholastic

More Surprises by L. B. Hopkins, 1987 Scholastic

The Rose in My Garden by A. Lobel, 1984 Greenwillow

Seven Little Rabbits by J. Becker, 1985 HarperCollins

Singing Bee by J. Hart, 1982 Lothrop, Lee & Shephard

Spin a Soft Black Song by N. Givonnia, 1985 HarperCollins

A Swinger of Birches: Poems of Robert Frost for Young People by R. Frost, 1982 Stemmer House

Literature Card 31

BOOKS TO SPUR CURIOSITY AND CREATIVE THINKING

Good Books with a Lot of Pictures

Eureka! It's an Airplane! by J. Bendick, 1992 Millbrook Press

Eureka! It's an Automobile! by J. Bendick, 1992 Millbrook Press

Families: A Celebration of Diversity, Commitment and Love by A. Jenness, 1990 Houghton Mifflin

If You're Afraid of the Dark, Remember the Night Rainbow by C. Edens, 1992 Aladdin

Backyard Safaris by P. Busch, 1995 Aladdin

The Berenstain Bears in the Dark by S. & J. Berenstain, 1982 Random House

In the Castle of Cats by B. Boegehold, 1981 Unicorn Books

Coco Can't Wait by T. Gomi, 1984 William Morrow

Anna Banana and Me by L. Blegvad, 1987 Aladdin

The Grandpa Days by J. Blos, 1994 Aladdin

Handtalk Birthday: A Number and Story Book in Sign Language by R. Charlip & M. Beth, 1991 Aladdin

Everybody Needs a Rock by B. Baylor, 1985 Aladdin

Imaginary Gardens by C. Sullivan, 1989 Abrams

I Want to Learn to Fly by M. McGovern, 2000 Scholastic

Books for an Author Study about Eloise Greenfield and Gary Soto

Night on Neighborhood Street by E. Greenfield, 1991 Dial Books

Nathaniel Talking by E. Greenfield, 1989 Black Butterfly Children's Books

Under the Sunday Tree by E. Greenfield, 1988 HarperCollins

Daydreamers by E. Greenfield, 1981 Dial Books

Childtimes: A Three Generation Memoir, with Lessie Jones Little by E. Greenfield, 1979 Thomas Y. Crowell

Honey, I Love and Other Poems by E. Greenfield, 1978 Thomas Y. Crowell

Grandmama's Joy by E. Greenfield, 1980 HarperCollins

Grandpa's Face by E. Greenfield, 1988 Philomel

Talk about a Family by E. Greenfield, 1993 Harper

Neighborhood Odes by G. Soto, 1992 Harcourt Brace Jovanovich

Pacific Crossing by G. Soto, 1992 Harcourt Brace Jovanovich

The Shirt by G. Soto, 1992 Delacorte

Baseball in April & Other Stories by G. Soto, 1991 Harcourt Brace Jovanovich

Taking Sides by G. Soto, 1991 Harcourt Brace Jovanovich

A Fire in My Hands by G. Soto, 1990 Scholastic

Good Books If You Are Just Beginning to Learn about the Subject

All Creatures Great and Small by J. Herriot, 1973 G. K. Hall

Mrs. Frisby and the Rats of NIMH by R. O'Brien, 2000 Chivers

Dinosaur Detective 3: Bite Makes Right by B. B. Calhoun, 2000 General Publishing

Amazing Animals by G. Legg, 1994 Franklin Watts

The Girl Who Changed the World by D. Ephron, 1993 Ticknor & Fields

My Name Is Brian by J. Betancourt, 2000 Scholastic

Maizon at Blue Hill by J. Woodson, 1992 Delacorte

Mayfield Crossing by V. M. Nelson, 1993 Putnam

Jurassic Park by M. Crichton, 1990 Knopf

Chemistry for Every Kid: 101 Easy Experiments That Really Work by J. Van Cleare, 1989 John Wiley

Giants in the Earth by O. Rolvaag, 1991 HarperCollins

Saturnalia by P. Fleischman, 1990 HarperCollins

Ghost Train: A Spooky Hologram Book by S. Wyllie, 1999 Scholastic

Hear Your Heart and other books by P. Showers, 1999 Crowell

Books for an Author Study about Myra Cohn Livingston

My Head Is Red: And Other Riddle Rhymes, 1990 Holiday House

Dilly Dilly Piccalilli: Poems for the Very Young, 1989 Macmillan

Remembering and Other Poems, 1989 Macmillan

Up in the Air, 1989 Holiday House

Space Songs, 1988 Holiday House

There Was a Place, and Other Poems, 1988 Macmillan

Earth Songs, 1986 Holiday House

Higgledy-Piggledy: Verses and Pictures, 1986 Macmillan

Celebrations, 1985 Holiday House

Worlds I Know: And Other Poems, 1985 Atheneum

Monkey Puzzle, and Other Poems, 1984 Atheneum

No Way of Knowing: Dallas Poems, 1980 Atheneum

O Sliver of Liver and Other Poems, 1979 Atheneum

4-Way Stop, and Other Poems, 1974 Atheneum

If the Owl Calls Again: A Collection of Owl Poems, 1990 Macmillan

Triplet.   A triplet is a three-line stanza that usually rhymes.

Rain, Rain, Go Away
Rain, rain, go away.
Come again some other day.
Little Johnny wants to play. —Unknown

Quatrain.   A quatrain contains four lines of poetry with several ways to rhyme (popular framework for poetry). There are also *five-line verses* (besides limericks), *sestets* (six lines), *septets* (seven lines), and *octets* (eight lines). Each of these types of poetry can stand alone or become separate stanzas in a poem. For example, the couplet below was written as a poem in itself; the quatrain is a stanza in a longer poem.

Bladeskates glaze the sidewalk
Taking me fast as a hawk.

Rain comes down soft and steady,
Making the world heavy,
We put on our raincoats
And march with rain drops as our notes.

Limerick.   Limericks contain five lines of humorous or nonsense verse with an *aa bb a* rhyme scheme; that is, the first, second, and fifth lines rhyme, whereas the third and fourth rhyme with each other and are shorter than the other three. Younger students enjoy these especially when they describe animals, childhood experiences, or fantastic and strange happenings, such as:

There was an old man with a beard,
Who said, "It is just as I feared!—
Two Owls and a Hen,
Four Larks and a Wren,
Have all built their nests in my beard!"

Free Verse.   In the free verse the poet divides his or her lines according to the natural pauses in his or her thoughts and is not concerned with rhyme. This form allows children to express themselves more freely and make the pictures in their minds or their feelings and emotions into "word pictures."

Cinquain.   A cinquain (pronounced "sinkane") is a five-line poem. It assists students to choose more precise words that evoke the exact images they wish to represent. The cinquain pattern is one word naming the title in the first line; two words describing the title in the second line; three words expressing action in the third line; four words expressing a feeling in the fourth line; another word for the title in the fifth line. The following verse by Adelaide Crapsey is a cinquain written in 1914 during the last year of her life. Her brief word etchings are similar to the Japanese tanka and Haiku.

Clouds
Earth's roof
Moving grey mists
Gentle drips of rain
Overcast

Diamante.   Diamante (dee-ah-mahn´-tay) follows a diamond-shaped pattern that produces a seven-line poem following these specifications:

1 word:	subject noun	Winter
2 words:	adjectives	Cold windy
3 words:	participles (-ing, -ed)	Chattering my teeth
4 words:	noun related to subject	My frozen red hands
3 words:	participles	Slapping my face
2 words:	adjectives	Warming soothing
1 word:	noun (opposite of subject)	Heat

Haiku.   This form of Japanese poetry consists of 17 syllables. It is designed to link nature with humans. Its pattern is 5 syllables in the first line; 7 syllables in the second line; 5 syllables in the third line.

Green leafy branches
in the wind wave greetings to
the passing stranger

Format Poems.   This concept is usually used for younger children as an introduction to writing poetry.

I drew a _____.
I colored it _____.
The _____ I ever have seen.
The _____ was _____.
On _____ that was _____.
The _____ and _____ that I ever drew.
I drew what I thought was the _____.
I colored it _____.
Then my drawing was done.

Free-Form Poems.   Free-form poems describe something that is important to the author. They relate their thoughts, without concern for rhyme, the number of syllables per line, or the use of standard punctuation. e. e. cummings is the most popular contemporary poet who uses free-form poems. His poems are not written with capital letters and the lines may not move horizontally across the page. When Ms. Phillips showed e. e. cummings's work to the class, it ignited a vivid discussion about "what is poetry." Students also distinguished free-form poems from raps and graffiti.

Found Poetry.   In found poetry poets collect their favorite words and sentences from a book they have read and organize them so as to capture the emotions and meaning that the book held for them. It was also used in Ms. Phillips's class as a method of capturing important concepts from a unit of study. They wrote many lines from different poems and books in author studies. These poems captured the essence of the unit, an author's driving message, or the most distinguishing qualities in an author's writing style.

List Poems.   List poems usually follow a certain theme or idea and are often used to introduce students to methods for writing their own poems. For example, after reading Judy Viorst's poem *If I Were in Charge of the World,* Ms. Phillips's class enjoyed (as can students of all ages) writing their own poems modeled on the following list poem. In list poems students begin each line with the same phrase; in this case it is "If I were in charge of the world I would _____." To illustrate, Michael and Allison teamed up to write:

> If we were in charge of the world,
> We would be in charge of schools.
> There would be no violence, guns, or murder,
> There would be joy and laughter on every face,
> If we ruled the world; If we were in
> Charge of *all* the world.

Two other types of list poems are *"I wish" poems* and *"I like" poems.* These poems can be very effective for students attempting to write poetry for the first time. Each line begins with the same phrase (*I wish*) or word (*Red*) as illustrated by Meisong's *color poem* (which lists everything that is the same color in the student's life):

> **Red**
> Red is unlike other colors
> Red does not denote one concept
> Red is not like green for living
> Red is not like white for purity
> Red is not like blue for serenity
> Red is dynamic and bold as a nail color
> Red is solemn and reflective as a sunset
> Red is startling as a fireman

Other list poems, such as "If I could" and "I used to think _____ but now I know _____," can also be used as assessment tools for how much students have learned about a thematic unit, author study, or content area lesson.

Concrete Poetry.   Concrete poems form visual images. Examples are "The Sidewalk Racer" and "On the Skateboard" by Lillian Morrison. In these poems the poet arranges the words in the poem to match the shape of the subject (e.g., the shape of a skateboard), "just for fun." These poems build visual arts skills.

Ballad.   Older children can make use of a variety of other poetry formats, such as the ballad, which is a narrative poem whose stanzas read like a song. Ballads tell a story and were actually passed from generation to generation as songs. They are usually written in a group voice rather than in first person. Most ballads are written in quatrains and the second and fourth lines rhyme. Songwriters today, like Bob Dylan, still write ballads. Ms. Phillips's eighth-graders enjoyed writing ballads for social studies and history projects rather than writing reports as their end products.

POETRY LESSONS

In the For Your Journal activity (p. 536) you will have the opportunity to write one or more of these poems to express who you are and what you value. With your poem in hand, you will be ready to model for students how to write poetically. Seeing your written poem will give students confidence that they can write poetry as well. You can tell them from firsthand experience what they can expect to think and feel before, during, and after they create their poems. Examples of poetry lessons you can teach your students follow.

1. You can introduce a different type of poetry each day. Students can practice writing each type and decide which best matches the emotion they wish to express.

2. Write some cinquains on the board for your class. Discuss their pattern and characteristics. Write the pattern on the board so the class remembers it. It's not important at this time whether they follow the pattern exactly; the message they create is what is important. Let them see how a cinquain briefly expresses an idea that grows and expands in the mind of the reader. Then read some cinquains to the class. Let them listen and think about them. Ask for comments, then let them write more.

3. Exhibit a few choice Japanese prints. Create a central theme or scene on the bulletin board with Haikus the class made. Read a Haiku chosen by you or a child. Let the children offer their interpretations. What things come to mind when they hear the poem?

4. Older students can write stories and poems for first-graders. They will need to use a basic work list, such as the words from a first-grade reader or the basic sight words from Chapter 5, so their audience can read them. If students have trouble writing poems, their ideas may flow better if they realize the poems don't have to rhyme. At this point, you can share poems from Eve Merriam's *It Doesn't Always Have to Rhyme* or Shel Silverstein's *Where the Sidewalk Ends.* Books from Literature Card 30 can assist students to express their reactions poetically. Books from Literature Card 31 can also be used for many other activities in this chapter.

5. Parks and Parks (1992) and Craig (1992) recommend that you set poetry to music or let students use props to ignite their creative thinking. This activity assists students in understanding the rhythm and sounds within the English language. Words have rhythms and these rhythms inspire thought, which translates into meaning. Just as students learn how to read letters within words and words within sentences, they can learn how the modulation of sounds within the context of words and sentences in poetry affects meaning. They can use English language rhymes to translate meaning into speech better when music is coupled with poetry as they read it.

6. Once students have experienced success with poetry, Roskos (1992) recommends an activity called Free Response with a Sketch, which encourages generative processes while developing mental imagery. This lesson is composed of the following steps:

- Preselect pauses in the text. Make sure the pauses are judiciously spaced so that the reader has an opportunity to build up an adequate mental image.

- During each pause, ask the reader to jot responses to one or more of the following prompts (prompts may vary depending on the type of text and age of student):

    I see. . .
    I hear . . .
    I smell . . .
    I feel . . .

- After reading the selection, encourage students to develop a sketch or series of sketches that depicts their sensations and thoughts in connection with the text and that they would share with the author.

- Have the readers evaluate their sketches against the actual text, noting how the sketch captures the aesthetic feeling or gist of the selection.

- Provide an opportunity for sharing sketches through poetry as a means of retelling the text.

7. Students also enjoy learning how their favorite poets create poetry. Through a nearby university, you may be able to invite a professional poet to class or rent a video about a poet's life. This person can share the creative thought processes they use to germinate ideas and craft poems. Many poets report that their first thoughts emanate from (1) a fact or feeling they experience, (2) a melody they hear, (3) an image that takes shape in their mind, or (4) playing with sounds in words (Pinksy, 2000).

8. Once you have taught figurative language you can show how metaphors and similies make poems more intriguing and vivid. Once students discuss how poets use figurative language, they can experiment with its use.

9. You can locate picture-book poems and look at ways different artists illustrate them (e.g., compare Robert Frost's unillustrated poems in anthologies with *Stopping by Woods on a Snowy Evening* illustrated by Susan Jeffers, *Birches* illustrated by Ed Young, and *A Swinger of Birches: Poems of Robert Frost for Young People* illustrated by Peter Koeppen). See *Talking to the Sun: An Anthology of Poems for Young People* for other illustrated poetry and songs. You may also want to use *Go In and Out the Window: An Illustrated Songbook for Children* by the Metropolitan Museum of Art staff to view classical paintings from the Metropolitan collection chosen to illustrate favorite song poems; Susan Jeffers's illustrations for Henry Wadsworth Longfellow's *Hiawatha* and for Chief Seattle's letter in *Brother Eagle, Sister Sky;* and Byrd Baylor's poems about the Southwest illustrated in picture books by Peter Parnall (Cullinan, Scala, & Schroder, 1995).

10. You can model connections between poems and books. For example, when reading *Is Your Mama a Llama?* by Deborah Guarino, read "The Llama Who Had

No Pajama" by Mary Ann Hoberman. When reading *A Chair for My Mother* by Vera Williams, read poems from *Families* by Dorothy and Michael Strickland, as well as ones from *Fathers, Mothers, Sisters, Brothers* by Mary Ann Hoberman. When reading *The Little Fir Tree* by Margaret Wise Brown, read e. e. cummings's *Little Tree*. When reading Jean Little's book *Kate*, read the poem "Writers" from *Hey World, Here I Am!* also by Jean Little.

11. You can also have rhyming dictionaries available such as *Time to Rhyme* by Marvin Terban and *Talkaty Talker* by Molly Manley, both published by Wordsong/Boyds Mills Press in Honesdale, PA, and integrate poetry into content areas. Doing so enables students to more completely capture the mood of people at a historical event, for instance.

INSIDE CULTURALLY ENRICHED CLASSROOMS

Using Viewing to Increase Bilingual Students' Language Arts Abilities

Freeman and Freeman (1994) offer the following suggestions for developing the creativity, vocabulary, and viewing abilities of bilingual students. Videotapes in Spanish support various thematic studies (available through Madera Cinevideo, 525 East Yosemite Avenue, Madera, CA 93638). For example, a video of a museum display on dinosaurs is available in Spanish and English for elementary children. Such videos in Spanish serve as previews for a class field trip or as reviews for discussions after the trip. These excellent videos and the real experience at the museum provide the context Spanish-speaking students need to understand the same video in English, which is shown next.

Perhaps equally important to the video content is knowing that it was made in their native country. For example, Ms. Phillips used one video that began with a Mexican flag blowing in the wind. Juan, who seldom spoke up in class, showed that he immediately connected with the video by proudly announcing, "Mexico, eso es mi pais" ("Mexico, that is my country"). The next day Ms. Phillips showed the video *The Glass Blowers of Tonola* (Madera Cinevideo) in Spanish. When the narrator explained where this factory was located, Juan exclaimed, "That's the town where my dad was born!"

One school district has produced videos in Hmong based on big book stories, such as *The Little Red Hen* and *The Three Billy Goats Gruff.* In each video a Hmong-speaking narrator first provides background on the story. For example, *The Little Red Hen* video shows wheat growing and discusses in Hmong how the grain is separated and ground to make flour. Then the scene shifts to a bakery to show the steps in making bread. *The Three Billy Goats Gruff* video begins at the zoo with a close-up look at goats. The film then moves to different kinds of bridges with a discussion of what one normally sees under them. Each tape ends with a reading of the story in Hmong as the pages of the big book are shown. These videos help prepare Hmong-speaking students to participate when the teacher later reads the same books in English (Freeman & Freeman, 1992, pp. 191–192).

In addition, after a celebrative experience at school, a member of the school staff who speaks the first language of bilingual students can respond to it (and then write about it in a book) in that first language, which can be referenced in future years when other students share similar events schoolwide. Such a person could also show bilingual students how to express their feelings and thoughts creatively through poetry or drama. For example, Ms. Phillips invited her principal to class on the day she introduced list poems. Her principal, Mr. Hernandez, demonstrated an "I wish" poem in Spanish. When he had finished, Juan wrote an "I wish" poem because he was so motivated; it was the first poetry that Juan had ever written.

Viewing can also be used to inform students about aspects of their culture. For example, many cable channels broadcast "Know Your Heritage," which reports aspects of African-American and other cultural heritages in a game show format. For more information about this broadcast, you can contact Donald Jackson, Central City Marketing Inc., 1716 South Michigan Ave., Chicago, IL 60616.

In summary, "the world of just text is irrevocably dead." Allen De Bevoise, one of the country's leading innovators in interactive technology, made this statement in reference to images being of equal importance as words. Visual images are fast becoming the focus of enormous attention because of their inherent power to communicate. "We are in a new age where the image can now be central, thanks to technology in large part. Images are all around us," explains De Bevoise. "Today, they have the potential to be as fundamental to education as words and numbers, adding significantly to the excitement, depth and relevance of what and how children learn" (1995, p. 4).

The argument goes beyond how images are used in education, according to Emmy Award–winning children's television producer Cecily Truett. She believes images can present confusing, somewhat subjective experiences to viewers who lack the instruction to help guide them to accurate interpretations. "Children need tools with which to contextualize these images . . . art making, art criticism, and art history and aesthetics are critical tools for today's educators. These tools must translate to skills, critical skills that human beings must have to navigate their way through the new media universe." Truett underscores the importance of language arts education in interpreting these images: "Without [instruction] our children are going to be at sea in a storm of media images without the critical skills they need to digest, deconstruct, analyze, and make final judgments about how image experiences are relevant to their own lives" (Truett, personal communication, December 12, 1994).

RECOGNIZING AND REPORTING PROGRESS

Assessing Creativity and Viewing Competencies

There are several standardized tests that assess students' creative communication abilities and viewing competencies. These can be ordered through universities. You can also assess students' growth in creativity and visual arts skills by asking them to collect representative work samples that reflect their growth over a specified period of time. For example, students could

- Collect and write a total of 20 poems
- Keep five samples of their creativity and/or analyses of visual artistry

- Complete a critic's job sheet for movies and television shows
- Complete the sample drama assessment form in Figure 12.4.

Another important assessment activity is storytelling. You can ask students to create a story relative to content material that they have studied or language arts lessons that you have developed. Storytelling is a valuable evaluation tool because it accesses multiple intelligence and expresses knowledge gains in both parts and wholes. Storytelling enables students to put semantic information into a format that retrieves an entire idea with its bounded details, simultaneously (Caine & Caine, 1994). In

---

NAME: _____   PERIOD BEGINNING: _____   ENDING: _____

FOCUS: _____

(1—LOWEST; 5—HIGHEST)

	FIRST OBSERVATION	SECOND OBSERVATION	THIRD OBSERVATION
Is able to use body effectively to show ideas, feelings, imitative action	1 2 3 4 5	1 2 3 4 5	1 2 3 4 5
Uses sensory recall to guide pantomime	1 2 3 4 5	1 2 3 4 5	1 2 3 4 5
Demonstrates understanding of spatial perception in			
(1) self-space	1 2 3 4 5	1 2 3 4 5	1 2 3 4 5
(2) shared space	1 2 3 4 5	1 2 3 4 5	1 2 3 4 5
(3) larger space	1 2 3 4 5	1 2 3 4 5	1 2 3 4 5
Can control body movement in terms of			
(1) tempo (fast, medium, slow)	1 2 3 4 5	1 2 3 4 5	1 2 3 4 5
(2) feelings	1 2 3 4 5	1 2 3 4 5	1 2 3 4 5
(3) roles	1 2 3 4 5	1 2 3 4 5	1 2 3 4 5
Listens to			
(1) follow directions	1 2 3 4 5	1 2 3 4 5	1 2 3 4 5
(2) show respect	1 2 3 4 5	1 2 3 4 5	1 2 3 4 5
Is willing to try new things	1 2 3 4 5	1 2 3 4 5	1 2 3 4 5
Shows original thought and imaginative expression	1 2 3 4 5	1 2 3 4 5	1 2 3 4 5

Comments (note areas of most improvement or greatest strengths and any problem areas):

_____

FIGURE 12.4 CREATIVE DRAMA PROGRESS CHART: EXAMPLE OF HOW TO GRADE PROCESSES AND PRODUCTS OF CREATIVITY AND VISUAL ARTS ABILITIES

Source: From *Creative Drama in the Classroom/Grades 4–6* (p. 49) by J. Cottrell, 1987, Lincolnwood, IL: National Textbook Co. Used by permission.

addition, storytelling enables students to recall information more effectively because the process engages their emotional memory. This emotional intelligence is tapped by the conflict or plot of the story that they create. In addition, because storytelling involves creative aspects, students invest their ability to analyze and express visual artistry when involved in this type of assessment. Last, students employ episodic memory to locate, recall, and present each aspect of the story they create, an ability that is well developed in many minority cultures. Finally, you can begin this evaluation by asking pupils to "Tell me all you have learned as if it was a story that others could read."

SECTION 3   TEACHERS AS CONTINUAL LEARNERS

Increasing Students' Creativity

In this section you will read about three of the most important competencies you can develop to increase students' abilities to think creatively and view analytically and aesthetically: conducting readers' theatres, keeping poetry journals, and providing resources to develop creativity at home.

PROFESSIONAL DEVELOPMENT ACTIVITY

How to Conduct Readers' Theatre

Several research studies have been conducted to demonstrate the effectiveness of **readers' theatre.** Readers' theatre is a form of drama in which participants read aloud from scripts and convey ideas and emotions through vocal expressions and sometimes props. In Readers' theatre stories (scripts) are read in front of the class. Readers never memorize their lines in readers' theatre. All "actor–readers" are on the stage at all times. Readers not involved in a particular scene face away from the audience. Turning to face the audience marks their entrance. Costuming and staging are simple. The objective of costumes, props, and staging are to suggest, not to replicate, reality. Thus, in a readers' theatre of *Three Little Pigs,* only a stock puppet would be held to represent each character. The steps to follow in presenting a readers' theatre appear in Figure 12.5.

The benefits of readers' theatre include students feeling as if they are part of the story itself, which motivates them to reread more (Wolf, 1998). Second, readers' theatre has been demonstrated to improve reading fluency, especially for students who need practice eliminating hesitancies in their speech (Martinez, Roser, & Strecker, 1999). Third, readers' theatre also can build on students' love of series books or text sets. Once they have read several books by the same author, or on the same topic, they gain confidence that they can create their own readers' theatre. Doing so develops their creativity at the same time they develop their reading abilities. In addition, you can make several books and websites available to students. Either you or students can use these resources to develop a readers' theatre. The

How to Do Readers' Theatre

Step 1: Choose a favorite book that you would like to turn into a Readers' Theatre.

Step 2: Decide what events and characters in your book you would like to play.

Step 3: Determine what message you would like your audience to receive and decide how to convey it using only words.

Step 4: Obtain teacher approval for the play and add teacher's changes as necessary.

Step 5: Make one costume item to wear, for example, a glove or name tag.

Step 6: Practice the play. All backs face the audience, unless you are reading.

Step 7: Invite whomever you want to the live performance. Add music to the script.

Step 8: Perform in front of a live audience.

Benefits

Readers' Theatre is great because it lets all students participate. It helps students gain confidence speaking in front of audiences. Students enjoy participating, and their listening abilities increase as well as their accuracy, rate, phrasing, and expressiveness.

FIGURE 12.5 HOW TO DO READERS' THEATRE

Created by Andrea Bueno, 2000, elementary teacher at All Saints Elementary School, Kansas City, KS. Used by permission.

following publishers and the books in Literature Card 32 provide excellent scripts for readers' theatre.

1. D.O.K. Publishers, P.O. Box 605, East Aurora, NY 14052—distributes low-cost scripted readers' theatre for grades K–2 and 3–9.

Literature Card 32

BOOKS THAT STUDENTS ENJOY WRITING AS SCRIPTS FOR READERS' THEATRE

Easy Books

A Bear for Miguel by E. M. Alphin, 1996 HarperCollins
The Golly Sisters Ride Again by B. Byars, 1994 HarperCollins
My Brother by B. Byars, 1996 Viking
Ant Plays Bear by B. Byars, 1997 Viking
Are You My Mother? by P. D. Eastman, 1960 Random House
Hattie and the Fox by M. Fox, 1987 Bradbury
Whose Mouse Are You? by R. Kraus, 1970 Aladdin
Fox in Love by E. Marshall, 1994 Puffin
Three by the Sea by E. Marshall, 1981 Puffin
Three up a Tree by E. Marshall, 1986 Puffin
Fox on Stage by J. Marshall, 1993 Puffin
Little Bear by E. H. Minarik, 1957 Harper & Row
Morris the Moose by B. Wiseman, 1959 HarperTrophy

Books for Average Readers

Arthur Babysits by M. Brown, 1992 Little, Brown
Arthur Meets the President by M. Brown, 1991 Little, Brown
Emily and Alice by J. Champion, 1993 Harcourt Brace

Emily and Alice Again by J. Champion, 1995 Harcourt Brace
I Am the Dog, I Am the Cat by D. Hall, 1994 Dial
Tell Me a Story by A. Johnson, 1989 Orchard
Wings: A Tale of Two Chickens by J. Marshall, 1986 Viking
The Salamander Room by A. Mazer, 1991 Knopf
King of the Playground by P. R. Naylor, 1992 Atheneum
There's a Dragon About: A Winter's Revel by R. Schotter & R. Schotter, 1994 Orchard
Tops and Bottoms by J. Stevens, 1995 Harcourt Brace
The Horrible Holidays by A. Wood, 1988 Dial

Challenging Books

Moon Rope/Un Lazo a la Luna by L. Ehlert, 1992 Harcourt Brace Jovanovich
Cinderella by B. Karlin, 1992 Little, Brown
Anansi Goes Fishing by E. A. Kimmel, 1992 Holiday House
Anansi and the Talking Melon by E. A. Kimmel, 1994 Holiday House

Adapted from literature cited in "I Never Thought I Could Be a Star: A Readers Theatre Ticket to Fluency," by M. Martinez, N. L. Roser, & S. Strecker, 1998, *The Reading Teacher, 52*(4), 332.

2. Institute for Readers' Theatre, P.O. Box 17193, San Diego, CA 92117—provides scripts and information about production.

3. Shirley Sloyer's book, *Readers' Theatre: Story Dramatization in the Classroom* (National Council of Teachers of English, 1982) and Carolyn Feller Bauer's book, *Presenting Readers' Theatre,* are handbooks of techniques that include suggestions for materials to use in readers' theatre.

4. Readers' Theatre Script Service, P.O. Box 178333, San Diego, CA 92117—produces kits with parts written for different reading difficulty levels; (619) 961–8778.

5. The Economy Company, 1901 N. Walnut, Oklahoma City, OK 73125—produces kits with parts written for different reading difficulty levels.

6. *Reader's Theatre* by C. Georges and C. Cornett, Buffalo, NY, D.O.K. Publishers, 1990—contains 30 readers' theatres of various size casts.

7. *The Readers' Theatre* series of plays published by Curriculum Association.

8. *The Missing Prince, and Other Primary Plays for Oral Reading* by Ann R. Talbot.

9. *The Lost Cat, and Other Primary Plays for Oral Reading* by Ann R. Talbot.

FOR YOUR JOURNAL

Beginning Poetry Journals

Once you experience the creativity that poetry helps to release, you'll have an expressive tool few possess. If you lack confidence that you can become a poet, select an important value in your life and one or more of the poetic formats in this chapter that appeal to you. Write one or more poems that express your values. These can become models for your students, who can keep a "poetry journal" where they recopy favorite poems they read as well as those they write.

Describe the benefits you experienced from keeping a poetry log in your journal. Share your poems with your students. If you aren't teaching, write a poem and then set a goal to develop your creativity this week, using one of the strategies in this chapter. Reassess your creativity gains at the end of the week.

CONNECTING CLASSROOMS, PARENTS, AND COMMUNITIES

Providing Resources for Creativity

Many community functions require that parents locate poetry and plays for children to recite and enact on special occasions. The following are favorite videos, pedagogical books, and anthologies of poetry and drama that you can recommend to parents and use in your classroom.

POETRY

Multimedia

Poetry Please! is a 13-tape (15 minutes each) video series in which three mice puppets interact with a poet and in the process learn what poetry is. *Poetry Please!* is published by TV Ontario (143 W. Franklin Street, Suite 206, Chapel Hill, NC 27514).

Poetry Works is a kit of 75 posters and an idea book for kindergarten through third grade. *Poetry Works* is published by Modern Curriculum Press (13900 Prospect Road, Cleveland, OH 44136).

Handbook of Poetic Forms and *Poetic Forms: 10 Audio Programs* by Ron Padgett, available from Teachers and Writers Collaborative (5 Union Square West, New York, NY 10003).

Langston Hughes Curriculum Packet: Dig and Be Dug in Return, by Susan Danielson, Oral History Program, 5006 N.E. Mallory, Portland, Oregon.

Books about Teaching Poetry

Astro Poetry: Students Working As Poets by William Rakauskas and *Producing Award-Winning Student Poets: Tips from Successful Teachers* are available from the Illinois Association of Teachers of English.

Wishes, Lies, & Dreams: Teaching Children to Write Poetry and *Rose Where Did You Get That Red?* by Kenneth Koch, and *Teaching Great Poetry to Children* and *Sleeping on the Wing: An Anthology of Modern Poetry with Essays on Reading and Writing* by Kenneth Koch and Kate Farrell are available from Teachers and Writers Collaborative, 5 Union Square West, New York, NY 10003.

The Haiku Handbook: How to Write, Share, and Teach Haiku by William J. Higginson, with Penny Harter, available from Teachers and Writers Collaborative.

The following popular books about teaching poetry are usually available in city libraries.

Moving Window: Evaluating the Poetry Children Write by Jack Collom

Using Poetry to Teach Reading and Language Arts by Richard J. Smith

It Doesn't Always Have to Rhyme by Eve Merriam

Books of Poetry

Don't You Turn Back by Langston Hughes

If I Were in Charge of the World, and Other Worries by Judith Viorst

Poetry for Poetry Haters by Jane Moyer

Where the Sidewalk Ends by Shel Silverstein

Time for Poetry by May Hill Arbuthnot

O Sliver of Liver, and Other Poems by Myra Cohn Livingston

Morning, Noon, and Nighttime, Too by Lee Bennett Hopkins

Let's Marry, Said the Cherry, and Other Nonsense Poems by N. M. Bodecker

The Rose on My Cake by Karla Kuskin

Eats by Arnold Adoff

Reflections on a Gift of Watermelon Pickles by Steven Dunning

Plays

Holidays on Stage by Virginia Bradley, Dodd, Mead and Company, New York, 1981 (original plays for holidays)

Skits and Spoofs for Young Actors by Val R. Cheatham, Plays, Inc., Boston, 1977 (one act, royalty-free plays, skits, and spoofs for the amateur stage)

Easy Plays for Preschoolers to Third Graders by Amorie Havilan and Lyn Smith, Quail Ridge Press, 1985 (a collection of 12 plays for various holidays, which can be read as stories, performed as monologues with pantomime, or presented as plays)

Plays Children Love: A Treasury of Contemporary and Classical Plays for Children edited by C. A. Jennings and A. Harris, Doubleday, 1981

Plays from African Folktales by C. Korty, Scribner, 1975

SUMMARY

This chapter discussed the value of developing students' creativity and viewing abilities. Several methods of increasing these skills were explained, including SCRAMBLIN, drama, poetry, and readers' theatres. As children hear and read great quantities of poetry, they become more discerning about poetic elements, topics, and styles, and feel the many moods of poetry. Reading and discussing outstanding poetry also enables children to develop an appreciation for quality writing, as do the other activities in this chapter. Creativity and critical viewing abilities develop slowly. They are the result of careful instruction and many experiences with these processes over a period of years. Children who are fortunate enough to have developed a high level of creativity will be the richer for it. Those of us who work with children have both the opportunity and the responsibility to enrich their lives by developing their creativity in poetic and theatrical expressions and viewing skills.

In the next chapter, you will learn how fiction, nonfiction, and your language arts program can increase students' thinking abilities and multicultural understanding.

HOW TO DO IT: USING WHAT YOU'VE LEARNED

The following provide opportunities to reflect on and practice what you have learned.

ASSESSING YOUR LEARNING

1. Posttest your level of creative thinking. Return to page 505 and take the Remote Associations and Pattern Recognition Tests. Has your reading of information concerning creative thinking increased your creative abilities? Administer these tests to your students before and after they have completed several activities in this chapter. How do their pre- and posttest scores compare?

2. Begin a collection of student and adult poems to display as models for your students. Devise a plan for collecting these samples. Make large decorative charts depicting the formulas of poetry types discussed in this chapter to display in your class during poetry studies like those presented on pages 522–528.

3. If you are teaching, you may ask a group of students to lead the class in making puppets and puppet plays. If you are not yet teaching, decide on and defend the proportion of time you will spend in developing students' creativity. Should this proportion vary by grade levels? Why or why not? What are the differences between prose, poetry, and plays as far as the types of generative processes that they stimulate?

4. Invite groups of students to study their favorite authors or poets and create a readers' theatre. Allow 3 weeks for students to read about their authors and write a readers' theatre they can lead. During this time, every student must read (or have read to them) at least two books about the topic to be enacted.

5. Plan a poetry study similar to the one Ms. Phillips used (pages 530–531) to last 2 weeks. Select poems and prepare classroom displays in chart form or on overhead transparencies for this unit. Ask a group of students to write at least three different types of poems as the first entries in their poetry journals. Assess what you and they learn from this experience.

KEY TERMS EXERCISE

Below are the concepts introduced in this chapter. If you have learned a term, place a checkmark in the blank that precedes that term. If you are not sure of the definition of a term, increase your retention and return to reread its definition. If you have learned 20 of the terms in this chapter, you have constructed an understanding of a majority of the most important concepts that you need to increase your students' creativity, poetic and dramatic expression abilities, and visual arts skills.

_____ ballad   (p. 527)

_____ brainstorming   (p. 507)

_____ brainwriting   (p. 508)

_____ choral reading   (p. 514)

_____ concrete poetry   (p. 527)

_____ consensus building   (p. 508)

_____ creative artistry   (p. 503)

_____ creative dramatics   (p. 511)

_____ creativity   (p. 504)

_____ dance   (p. 514)

_____ found poetry   (p. 506)

_____ free-form poems   (p. 526)

_____ humor   (p. 509)

_____ improvisations   (p. 512)

_____ list poems   (p. 527)

_____ pantomime   (p. 514)

_____ poem   (p. 522)

_____ predictive thinking   (p. 521)

_____ problem defining   (p. 509)

_____ puppetry   (p. 514)

_____ readers' theatre   (p. 533)

_____ role playing   (p. 513)

_____ SCRAMBLIN   (p. 518)

_____ viewing   (p. 503)

_____ voice   (p. 502)

FOR FUTURE REFERENCE

*Books about Poetry, Creativity, Drama, and Viewing Competencies
and Middle School Students*

Allen, E. G., & Wright, J. P. (1978, February). Just for fun: A creative dramatics learning center. *Childhood Education, 43,* 169–175.

Brewer, C., & Campbell, D. G. (1991). *Rhythms of learning: Creative tools for developing lifelong skills.* Tucson: Zephyr Press.

Graves, D. (1992). *Explore poetry: The reading/writing teacher's companion.* Portsmouth, NH: Heinemann.

Heard, G. (1989). *For the good of the earth and sun: Teaching poetry.* Portsmouth, NH: Heinemann.

Hopkins, L. B. (1987). *Pass the poetry please.* New York: HarperCollins.

Larrick, N. (1991). *Let's do a poem: Introducing poetry to children through listening, singing, chanting, impromptu, choral reading, body movement, dance, and dramatization.* New York: Delacorte.

Last, E. (Ed.). (1990). *A guide to curriculum planning in classroom drama and theatre.* Madison: Wisconsin Department of Public Instruction.

McCaslin, N. (1986). *Children and drama.* New York: Longman.

McCaslin, N. (1987). *Children and drama in the primary grades. A handbook for teachers.* New York: Longman.

McClure, A., Harrison, P., & Reed, S. (1990). *Sunrises and songs: Reading and writing poetry in the elementary classroom.* Portsmouth, NH: Heinemann.

Martinez, M. (1993). Motivating dramatic story reenactments. *The Reading Teacher, 46* (8), 682–688.

Nix, K. (1987). On producing brand-new book lovers. *Children's Literature Association Quarterly, 12*(3), 131–134.

Additional Books for Teachers

Plays and Poetry

African Americans who made a difference, coordinated by Liza Charlesworth. 128p.

Famous Americans: 22 short plays for the classroom, coordinated by Liza Charlesworth. 200p.

15 easy folktale fingerplays, by Bill Bordh. 80p.

Greek myths: 8 short plays for the classroom, by John Rearick. 88p.

Instant activities for poetry that kids really love! edited by Linda Ward Beech. 72p.

Favorite poetry lessons: A poet's great lessons for teaching free verse, rhyming list poems, synonym poems, clerihews, wish poems, letter poems, persona poems, and more, by Paul Janeczko, 96p.

25 just-right plays for emergent readers: Reproducible, thematic, with cross-curricular extension activities, by Carol Pugliano. 64p.

Quick poetry activities you can really do, by Jacqueline Sweeney. 112p.

Teaching poetry: Yes you can! by Jacqueline Sweeney. 120p.

10 American history plays for the classroom, by Sarah Glasscock. 96p.

10 women who helped shape America: Short plays for the classroom, by Sarah Classcock. 96p.

Thematic poems, songs, and fingerplays: 45 irresistible rhymes and activities to build literacy, by Meish Goldish. 96p.

Mystery plays: 8 plays for the classroom based on stories by famous writers, by Tom Conklin. 80p.

Plays around the year: More than 20 thematic plays for the classroom, coordinated by Liza Charlesworth. 200p.

Plays about the presidents: Short classroom plays, background information, and activities about 12 influential presidents, by Timothy Nolan. 128p.

A poem a day: More than 200 cross-curricular poems that teach and delight, by Helen H. Moore. 136p.

Poems just for us! 50 read-aloud poems with cross-curricular activities for young learners, by Bobbi Katz. 96p.

Poetry place anthology. 192p.

Origami

Araki, C. (1965). *Origami in the classroom.* Charles E. Tuttle Co.

Bang, M. (1985). *The paper crane.* Greenwillow Books.

Coerr, E. (1977). *Sadako.* G. P. Putnam's Sons.

Harbin, R. (1974). *Origami.* Hamlyn.

Harbin, R. (1971). *Secrets of origami.* Oldbourne Book Co.

Kroll, V. (1994). *Pink paper swans.* Eerdmans.

Hawcock, D. (1987). *Art from paper.* Crescent Books.

Nakano. (1985). *Easy origami.* Viking Kestrel.

Internet Resources to Enhance Students' Creativity and Visual Arts Skills

www.creativedrama.com/search.htm

Teachers can find creative drama, classroom ideas, theater games, books, and Internet links at this website.

www.falcon.jmu.edu/~ramseyil/drama.htn

This website provides numerous links for students to explore drama on the Internet.

Teachers Online: The Storytelling Home Page   www.members.aol.com/storypage

This website provides resources for storytelling and puppetry, including online sources of stories.

Students Online: Stage Hands Puppets Activity Page
    www.fox.nstn.ca/~puppets/vent.html

This website publishes puppet plays and drawings of puppets and sets by and for children; users can download patterns and ideas for puppetmaking (e.g., origami stick puppets) and send e-mail questions.

Our Poetry Imaginations: Mrs. Jones' Second-Grade Poetry Collection
    www.frii.com/~darhodes/

This delightful poetry page illustrates how to enable grade 2 students to compose free verse poems by going through a four-step composition process.

Poetry Post   www.mecca.org/~graham/Poetry_Post.html

Grahamwood Elementary School's grades 5 and 6 gifted students have created a site where visitors can read poems from students around the world and then post their own poems to add to the collection.

THEMATIC UNIT: TEACHING POETRY[1]

This unit is about teaching poetry to students. As you read, you might think about which additional activities from this chapter you would add to this unit and why.

Objectives

1. Learners will appreciate different types of poetry through reading, listening, writing, and performing.
2. Learners will express their feelings through writing their own poetry.
3. Learners will explore classic forms of poetry through class discussions, small groups, peer discussions, or conferences.

Process in Action.   Students can participate in class and group discussions about poetry read aloud in class. They can develop a poetry folder or journal in which they can express their ideas, concerns, and preferences. These entries can then be discussed with you during discovery discussions. Students may create poems in groups, pairs, or individually.

Integration of the Language Arts.   Students can read aloud to the class or small groups their favorite poems of the week. They may write their own if they wish. They should be encouraged to take risks and examine new ideas. Their feelings and emotions can be portrayed in their poetry. You may foster viewing and thinking skills through think-alouds performed before the class. You can also develop mini-lessons to teach the different technical terms of poetry.

Personalizing Instruction.   Students are introduced to poetry from many ethnic backgrounds and cultures. These cultures are represented in the class and school libraries, and you can read aloud from these books. Different cultures represented by students in the classroom aid in appreciating the multiculturalism of our society. Students should be encouraged to share nursery rhymes, songs, and poetry from their different cultures. By studying poetry from various cultures, themes can be integrated across the curriculum and serve as excellent resources for history and social studies.

Removing Obstacles for All Students.   Students are grouped according to their language arts strengths. They receive a poem to read and discuss in these groups. They work together to discover the meaning of the poem. This builds on each child's individual strengths. Some students also enjoy writing "silly songs, haiku, and rhyming poems. Instructions for writing these forms appear in Figure 12.6.

Real-World Applications.   Students are encouraged to participate in the State Poetry Society and the Poetry Society of America. They share the poetry produced inside and outside this classroom, giving them a feeling of contribution to the field

---

[1]This unit was written by Natalie Phillips, a middle school teacher in Houston, Texas.

Silly Songs

The Eency Weency Rattler
Was hiding in a spout.
Out came the farmer and scared the rattler out.
Out came the momma and bit him on the shin
And the Eency Weency Rattler
Is in the spout again.

The Eency Weency Rattler
Crawled in a lady's shoe.
The lady took a peek and the rattler hollered,
"BOO!"
After all the screaming the rattler had a grin
And the Eency Weency Rattler
Hid in the spout again.

Now it's your turn to write a silly song. You can use the "Itsy, Bitsy Spider" or any other silly song you already know. Remember to use your imagination, be creative, and have fun!

Steps to get you started

_____ Step 1: Think of a song.

_____ Step 2: Think of a different animal and change the words.

_____ Step 3: Write the song.

_____ Step 4: Illustrate the song with a picture.

_____ Step 5: Sing your song to a friend.

(continued)

FIGURE 12.6 HOW STUDENTS CAN USE SONGS TO WRITE THEIR OWN POETRY

Created by Katie Bennett, 2000, second-grade teacher at Holy Rosary, Shreveport, LA; and Jennifer Viessman, 2000, third-grade teacher at St. John's, Shreveport, LA. Used by permission.

HAIKU

I saw a rainbow
It is very beautiful
Then it went away

_____ Step 1: Pick a topic. rainbow

_____ Step 2: Brainstorm descriptive words. _colorful, bright, arched, misty, beautiful, hopeful, cheerful, high_

_____ Step 3: Write a phrase with exactly 5 syllables. _the cheerful rainbow_

_____ Step 4: Write a phrase with exactly 7 syllables. _so bright and high in the sky_

_____ Step 5: Write a phrase with exactly 5 syllables. _misty and hopeful_

_____ Step 6: Put the three phrases together and illustrate. _The cheerful rainbow_
So bright and high in the sky
Misty and hopeful

Rhyming Poems

If I Were a Frog . . .

I wish I were a bright green frog.
I'd sleep each day on a sunny log.
And for a snack I'd eat a fly
Whenever one came buzzing by.

I'd leap, then swim in a pretty lake,
And do frog things, for goodness sake.
It would be great but I suppose
That I would miss Spaghettios!®

Rhyming is easy! All you need is

1) a thought or idea
2) some good rhyming words to use at the end of lines
3) your imagination

Here are some of the -oon rhyming words to get you started.

afternoon	croon	high noon	new moon	silver spoon
attune	doubloon	honeymoon	noon	soon
baboon	dragoon	June	octoroon	spoon
balloon	dune	lagoon	pantaloon	strewn
bassoon	forenoon	loon	platoon	tablespoon
boon	full moon	lune	prune	teaspoon
brigadoon	goon	macaroon	raccoon	tycoon
buffoon	half moon	maroon	Rangoon	tribune
cartoon	harpoon	monsoon	saloon	tune
cocoon	harvest moon	moon	sand dune	typhoon

FIGURE 12.6 (CONTINUED)

of poetry. They may read their own poetry in class, to other teachers, and to their parents. (I mounted a large pocket chart in my room that had laminated copies of my 30 favorite poems. Students were to copy their favorites into their notebooks. Each time they did so, they had to add another poem that they valued to the chart. This poem could be written by that student or any other poet. By the end of the year, 300 poems were on display.)

By capitalizing on the diversity of a multicultural classroom, teachers can provide an environment for students to develop their social skills and increase their abilities to communicate with others who have different backgrounds and perspectives.

CHAPTER 13[1]

INCREASING STUDENTS' THINKING AND MULTICULTURAL UNDERSTANDING THROUGH THE LANGUAGE ARTS PROGRAM

Miguel and Joshua (Juan's younger twin brothers) enjoy their class and Ms. Predo very much. In their room, 22 students in grades 5, 6, and 7 work together as a community of learners for three years. Everyone learns from one another in a nurturing atmosphere that is similar to a family structure. Instruction is student-centered and individualized because all know each other's strengths and needs. Language arts instruction in this community, unlike single-aged classes, in is based on more peer modeling, paired scaffolding, and mentor relationships. Higher-level thinking and problem solving are developed more through person center, printed thinking guides, mini-lessons provided by peers, and daily, peer led discovery discussions. Developmentally appropriate lessons are often arranged in thematic units focused on problems students bring to school. These lessons occur in small clusters of students who group themselves around subtopics of interest.

As Siegel (1995) stated: "Children need assignments in multilogical issues. They need to discover opposing points of view in nonthreatening situations. They do this best when they learn how to role play the thinking of others, advance conclusions other than their own, and construct reasons to support them" (p. 5). In Ms. Predo's class the older students are adept at pointing out inconsistencies, and the younger ones are challenged to construct reasons to support their conclusions.

Today, Ms. Predo reports that librarians conducted a survey of adults to discover 25 books that have shaped their lives: The Adventures of Huckleberry Finn by Mark Twain; Atlas Shrugged by Ayn Rand; The Autobiography of Malcolm X; the Bible; The Catcher in the Rye by J. D. Salinger; Charlotte's Web by E. B. White; Democracy in America by Alexis de Tocqueville; The Diary of a Young Girl by Anne Frank; Gone With the Wind by Margaret Mitchell; The Gulag Archipelago by

---

[1]Research for the multilingual discussion in this chapter was completed by Ms. Nidia Prego, a bilingual elementary teacher who has taught in the United States and Costa Rica.

Alexander Solzhenitsyn; <u>Hiroshima</u> by John Hersey; <u>How to Win Friends and Influence People</u> by Dale Carnegie; <u>I, Claudius</u> by Robert Graves; <u>Invisible Man</u> by Ralph Ellison; <u>The Little Prince</u> by Antoine de Saint Exupery; <u>The Lord of the Rings</u> by J. R. R. Tolkien; <u>1984</u> by George Orwell; <u>Charlotte's Web</u> by E. B. White; <u>The Secret Garden</u> by Frances Hodgson Burnett; <u>Silent Spring</u> by Rachel Carson; <u>To Kill a Mockingbird</u> by Harper Lee; <u>Treasure Island</u> by Robert Louis Stevenson; <u>Walden</u> by Henry David Thoreau; and <u>War and Peace</u> by Leo Tolstoy (<u>Reading Today</u>, Dec. 1994–Jan. 1995). As she holds up each book, but one, she describes the story. The book she does not describe is <u>Roots</u> by Alex Haley, which she begins reading aloud instead.

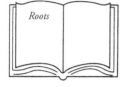

At the end of the first chapter, she asks students to propose reasons why this book had changed lives. Each group kept reading the book for the rest of the week and presented their reasons and justifications for the book's acclaim at the end of the week. The unit at the end of the Chapter 14, "I Dare to Dream" had begun.

"Students must learn to identify problems in, and reason effectively with, printed information throughout life" (Escalante, 1995, p. 3). Beck adds,

> Language arts is the perfect vehicle for developing higher-order thinking because literature—perhaps more than any other source of information—provides powerful models of problem-solving processes. It is full of characters who engage in effective and ineffective attempts at solving problems, who use incisive or fuzzy reasoning, and who rely on adequate or inadequate evidence—What is needed is to move the activities that involve higher-order thinking into the core of our lessons, to move our concern toward developing higher-level thinking into the mainstream of instruction. (1989, pp. 680, 682)

One purpose of this chapter is to demonstrate ways your language arts program can increase critical thinking and multicultural understanding. You will learn how your student-centered instruction can shift from teaching students about things to showing them how to form ideas, resolve conflicts, embrace ambiguity, engage in self-critiques, and capitalize on their rich cultural and language backgrounds. Doing so increases their abilities to communicate with those who have different perspectives. Such knowledge is increasingly important as students prepare to live in an increasingly multicultural world and pursue multicultural and multilingual opportunities.

A second purpose of this chapter is to help students from diverse language and cultural backgrounds use their rich cultural and social knowledge to advance along the language continuum. In classrooms where many cultures are represented, students have the added opportunity of exploring various multicultural perspectives through firsthand experience, and of developing interconnections between their culture's past traditions and current world issues. By the end of the chapter you will also have answers to the following questions, which represent IRA, NCTE, NAEYC, TEKS, and other statewide and province-based standards for professional development:

1. What cultural variables affect students' language arts abilities?
2. What social variables affect language arts success?

3. What instructional supports reinforce students' cultural and social understanding and language strengths?
4. What activities address the needs of English language learners?
5. How can the language arts needs of urban, rural, migrant, and immigrant students be effectively addressed in self-contained classrooms?
6. How can language arts instruction increase students' thinking abilities?
7. How can expert prompting in computer technology advance students' language development and multicultural understanding?
8. How can you integrate autobiographies and biographies into the language arts program to increase students' thinking and multicultural understanding?

SECTION 1   THEORETICAL FOUNDATIONS

Students Need to Think Critically with a Multicultural Sensitivity

"The principal goal of education is to create men who are capable of doing new things, not simply of repeating what other generations have done— men who are creative, inventive discoverers. The second goal of education is to form minds which can be critical, can verify, and not accept everything they are offered."

—Jean Piaget

Research indicates that the information and lessons in this chapter not only strengthen students' cognitive and scholastic achievements but also positively affect their self-esteem (Block & Mangieri, 1996; Block, 2000; Collins, 1992b; Jensen, 1998). Although no one can accurately predict the problems youths will face as adults, we do know that teaching them to use language arts to advance their thinking abilities and multicultural understanding can increase their problem-solving abilities throughout their lives. Such instruction can also enable many to conquer new challenges and open new doors of opportunity. Edward deBono, one of the leaders in thinking development stated:

> Sooner or later people are going to start thinking for themselves. There is no way of stopping them except with a powerful party line which preempts this activity. It may be better to learn to think in an open fashion rather than let thinking be only an expression of emotional discontent. . . . Why is it assumed that children will be against something as soon as they start to think about it. . . . The opposite seems to be the case; when children did think about some aspect of society, they often came to appreciate why things had to be done in a certain way. (1993, pp. 3, 4)

The type of complex communication abilities to be discussed in this chapter are most often categorized as critical thinking; problem solving; and high-level, reflective communications. In analyzing various definitions of language arts abilities, common characteristics appear (Beyer, 1993; Block, 2000; Costa, 2000; Jensen, 1998).

Recent studies report a similar relationship between home and cultural factors on oral and written language (Nieto, 1999; Genishi, 1992; Heath, 1983; Vygotsky, 1978). To illustrate, Heath's study of children from three communities and cultures revealed distinctly different attitudes toward written language. Children of Gateway (African and Anglo American families constituting the mainstream community) received an early initiation to books, written and oral narratives, book-reading behaviors, and questioning routines. Parents from Roadville (an Anglo American mill community) expected their children to learn alphabet letters through workbooklike activities. Stories were to convey moral messages. Trackton children, on the other hand, lived in a highly oral African American mill community where storytelling and verbal attention-getting skills were prized. Few children read or wrote prior to entering school, nor were they praised in general by parents for doing so. Because cultural, social, and second-language factors also shape students' assumptions about language processes, educators have increased their attention to these influences during instruction.

Culture can be defined as the "shared beliefs, values, and patterns of behavior that define a group, and that are required for group membership" (Peregoy & Owen, 1993). **Socioeconomic** cultural backgrounds are aspects of one's social condition that affect language as human beings interact with one another, including the management of income, expenditures, production, distribution, and consumption of wealth. At the community and family level, **sociocultural** influences on language include (1) spoken home language; (2) values, beliefs, and goals; (3) religion; (4) cultural traditions and experiences; (5) students' ways of responding to adults and displaying politeness; (6) use of language arts resources and time spent in language arts activities; (7) historical background; (8) children's perceptions of their teachers; (9) the importance placed on reading ability; (10) how children should behave when adults are speaking; (11) the amount of competition or cooperation displayed to peers; and (12) the amount of control children should exercise over their own destinies (Moll, 1999; Reyhner & Garcia, 1989).

Cultural discontinuity describes an internal conflict students experience when a disparity occurs between cultural values and activities concerning language at home and those practiced at school. For example, in some cultural groups, parents and teachers expect a literal account of what students remember when they speak; other cultural groups expect students to explain the reasons why things occurred, and others encourage a child to embellish a story by "making up" people and actions that were not part of the actual story. When home cultural practices and values are incorporated into your classroom, less cultural discontinuity occurs (Nieto, 1999; Moll, 1999). When you encourage readers and writers to value their cultures and the richness of their own languages, you help students achieve even higher levels of language arts success (O'Neill, 1991; Heath, 1983; Cazden, 1994). As John O'Neill stated, when you consider such variables, your teaching is more likely to provide the multiple supports to language arts that most multicultural and multilingual students need:

> Johnny can't read because he needs glasses and breakfast and encouragement from his absent father; Maria doesn't pay attention [during reading instruction] because she doesn't understand English and she's worried about her mother's drinking and she's tired from trying to sleep in her car. Dick is flunking because he's frequently absent. His mother doesn't get him to school

because she's depressed because she lost her job. She missed too much work because she was sick and could not afford medical care. Jimmy couldn't stay awake in class and didn't turn in his homework because he worked eight hours the night before at his part-time job at the mall; he's saving to upgrade his car stereo and needs another $400 for the limo, hotel room, and "entertainment" at the Senior Prom. (O'Neill, 1991, p. 6).

APPROACHES TO BUILD MULTICULTURAL SENSITIVITY THROUGH THE LANGUAGE ARTS

There are four approaches to language arts instruction, which include a multicultural perspective and eliminate cultural discontinuity for students (Banks, 1988; Rasinski & Padak, 1990; Au, 1993).

The **contributions approach** includes lessons and multicultural literature in which students are challenged to make contributions to others using language arts in a culturally based manner, and to examine the contributions that others from their culture have made to society in the past. In this approach lessons move beyond merely learning about various holidays and leaders from different cultures to developing students' deeper understanding of their own and others' cultural diversities (including gaining information about the 12 sociocultural influences listed on the previous page).

The **additive approach** uses multicultural literature in the existing curriculum (Rasinski & Padak, 1990). In this approach all units in language arts classes include multicultural books. A book is read aloud to students and studied because it is a powerful, well-written book that students can enjoy and grow from, and because it accurately depicts a cultural value that one or more students in the class share.

In the **transformation approach** historical and contemporary issues of interest and importance to students are studied. These issues become a part of the language arts curriculum, and they are studied from various cultural viewpoints. In this approach, students read and discuss books that describe events in history from several points of view. For example, students from Anglo American and Native American cultures could read and interpret *Columbus* by Martin Labur (1994) and *Encounters* by Patricia Yolen (1994). *Everybody Cooks Rice* by Dooby (1991) could be read and responses could include common and distinctive features of families from diverse cultures.

In the **social issues approach** students identify important social issues and use their language arts abilities and their diverse cultural perspectives and strengths to solve them. The following recommendations are offered to implement a multicultural climate that embraces sociocultural richness and personalizes instruction that capitalizes on students' strengths. However, because no one can be described only by cultural heritage, none of us possess all the attributes of every member of our cultural heritage. Therefore, the purpose of presenting the following research findings is to identify specific language situations in which cultural differences of some students may require adapted instruction. These situations involve times when confrontation emerges, when cooperation and competition exist, and when deadlines or questions are posed. First, many students of European descent confront a problem directly whereas in some cultures, such as Asian American ones, direct confrontation is avoided as much as possible. Similarly, students from various cultures may not express displeasure directly but may employ a go-between to speak for them. Such students also feel uncomfortable expressing another point of view during language arts discussions. You can help these students find ways to express themselves through the activities described later in this chapter.

Second, students are expected to be cooperative, but many cultural groups do not cooperate on tasks that compromise their own principles or conflicts with their sense that they should be working individually rather than cooperatively. Highly successful language arts teachers are sensitive to these feelings and give a variety of options so students can use familiar circumstances and gradually move on to more challenging tasks in which cooperative work is necessary and can be appreciated by all.

In like manner, competition is alien to many cultural groups, although it is highly valued in the European American culture. For example, many Southeast Asians feel a strong sense of community that inhibits the desire to win at the expense of others. Similarly, many Hispanic Americans are group oriented and may not wish to be singled out. Many Native American children also value getting along in the group more than winning. Many of these students can have difficulty participating in language games and competitive activities that have negative consequences. Their culture's conceptions of time and harmony with nature may also lead to a pace of performing tasks that some teachers view as reluctance or nonengagement. If you use your own cultural lenses to interpret this behavior, you may believe that these students are not motivated, or that they don't take responsibility for their own learning (Gay, 1995), when it is the parameters of the task that they are rejecting. In essence, pupils should not be rejected or frowned upon for not becoming motivated by competition.

Third, collaboration between students is often called cheating, but many groups value sharing more than individual success. If students with these cultural views are allowed to work in team activities, they can exercise personal learning preferences to collaborate and share.

Fourth, in a multicultural classroom, some students may not volunteer to participate, may talk at the same time as the teacher, or may try to answer every question themselves. These students have very different ideas about taking turns. If you provide opportunities for all turn-taking options, you can enable quieter students to be represented by more dominant students through pairings and responding as duos in writing.

Fifth, students from various cultures may have been taught only by rote memorization prior to your class and may have trouble adjusting to sharing information, developing independence, and communicating in a group situation. You can help by assigning different tasks to every member and carefully explaining their roles. Similarly, punctuality is not a commonly shared value in all cultures. Some students may need explicit instructions about due dates emphasizing that specific deadlines are not just approximations or suggestions.

European Americans are expected to ask questions to show that they are involved with learning, whereas in other cultures (like Southeast Asia) if students ask questions, they are considered rude. In these cultures, teachers impart wisdom and students listen without expressing opinions. You can accomodate these students by using strategies such as discovery discussions and paired learning so all students can be involved without being singled out. Another important aspect of the multicultural classroom is language, which has been called the "carrier of the culture." For many students, their first language is the heart of their identity. They learn through their language; that's how they put words to thoughts. You have the responsibility to bring these pupils' languages into the classroom, to acknowledge their importance, and to value their ability to speak two languages. Many books are written in languages that students of all language groups can enjoy.

Such books, listed on the literature cards in this chapter, have been described by Violet Harris (1993) as stories from the source; told from an ethnic perspective; placed within the context of ethnic life; and reflective of a particular group's language, culture, and beliefs. She encourages teachers to use these rich language arts resources, such as Virginia Driving Hawk Sneve's portrayal of the Native American life she has known (e.g., *Dancing Teepees,* 1989) and Angela Johnson's depiction of African American children engaged in daily family life activities (e.g., *The Leaving Morning,* 1992). Harris urges us to become familiar with multiethnic children's literature, to share it liberally with children, and to develop long-range purchasing plans to ensure its presence in their lives. Similarly, students learning English as a second language need books with lots of repetition and patterns, and often enjoy teaching peers to count and give greetings in their own native languages.

AFRICAN AMERICAN CULTURE

For some African American students, the following instructional adaptations may strengthen their self-initiated use of language arts for their own pleasure and growth. As a generalization, many students in this culture value fairness; people, especially kinship, approximations more than precision; spontaneity more than generating backup plans; completing a process more than creating a perfect end product; intuitive learning and nonverbal behavior more than linear, analytic thinking and precise language; and exaggerating stories more than reporting factual accounts (Cazden, 1993; Heath, 1983; Hillard, 1989).

Some pupils with these cultural values may engage in verbal interactions more frequently within teacher-absent peer groups than when teachers are members of the group. Their conversations with you are often characterized by simple language, devoid of the nuances and connotations that are one of their language strengths (Cazden, 1993; Purcell-Gates, 1991). Many African American students do not make continuous eye contact with their teachers. They often look around the room as they talk because they value others' appreciation of their vivid expressions and gestures (Banks & Banks, 1993). Such cultural differences in speaking and listening styles could lead to misunderstandings. For example, many African Americans do not nod their heads and make responses such as "um-hmm" when listening to their teachers. As a result, some teachers think these students do not understand, so they persist in explaining and reexplaining the same point. In turn, these students interpret their teachers' tendency to dwell on the same point as "talking down" to them and become insulted (Ladson-Billings, 1995; Dyson, 1999).

Similarly, some African Americans learn globally; that is, they don't learn language arts well when information is presented piecemeal. They prefer to see an entire process in action. They also process information verbally; information may not be "real" to them until they respond verbally. They also enjoy responding verbally

Literature Card 33

CHILDREN'S LITERATURE THAT PORTRAYS AFRICAN AMERICAN CULTURES

Adler, D. (1989). *Jackie Robinson.* New York: Holiday House.

Adoff, A. (1968). *I am the darker brother.* New York: Macmillan.

Adoff, A. (1970). *Malcolm X.* New York: Crowell.

Cameron, A. (1981). *The stories Julian tells.* New York: Pantheon.

Clifton, L. (1979). *The lucky stone.* New York: Dell.

Giovanni, N. (1985). *Spin a soft black song.* New York: Farrar, Straus & Giroux.

Greenfield, E. (1973). *Rosa Parks.* New York: Crowell.

Greenfield, E. (1977). *Mary McLeod Bethune.* New York: Crowell.

Greenfield, E. (1988). *Under the Sunday tree.* New York: Harper & Row.

Greenfield, E. (1989). *Nathaniel talking.* New York: Black Butterfly.

Guy, R. (1973). *The friends.* New York: Bantam.

Hamilton, V. (1967). *Zeely.* New York: Macmillan.

Hamilton, V. (1968). *The house of Dies Drear.* New York: Macmillan.

Hamilton, V. (1971). *The planet of Junior Brown.* New York: Macmillan.

Hamilton, V. (1974). *M. C. Higgins, the great.* New York: Macmillan.

Hamilton, V. (1983). *Willie Bea and the time the Martians landed.* New York: Greenwillow.

Hamilton, V. (1985). *The people could fly.* New York: Knopf.

Hamilton, V. (1988). *Anthony Burns: The defeat and triumph of a fugitive slave.* New York: Knopf.

Hamilton, V. (1988). *In the beginning: Creation stories from around the world.* San Diego, CA: Harcourt Brace Jovanovich.

Hamilton, V. (1990). *Cousins.* New York: Philomel.

Johnson, A. (1990). *When I am old with you.* New York: Orchard.

Jones, R. (1991). *Matthew and Tilly.* New York: Dutton.

Langstaff, J. (1987). *What a morning! The Christmas story in black spirituals.* New York: Macmillan.

Keats, E. J. (1964). *Whistle for Willie.* New York: Viking.

Keats, E. J. (1967). *Peter's chair.* New York: Harper.

Lewin, H. (1981). *Jafta.* Minneapolis, MN: Carolrhoda.

Mathis, S. (1971). *Sidewalk story.* New York: Puffin.

McKissack, P. (1986). *Flossi and the fox.* New York: Dial.

McKissack, P. (1988). *Mirandy and brother wind.* New York: Knopf.

McKissack, P. (1989). *Nettie Jo's friends.* New York: Knopf.

Mollel, T. (1991). *The orphan boy.* New York: Clarion.

Monjo, F. N. (1970). *The drinking gourd.* New York: Harper.

Ringgold, F. (1991). *Tar beach.* New York: Crown.

San Souci, R. (1989). *The talking eggs.* New York: Dial.

Schroeder, A. (1989). *Ragtime Tumpie.* Boston: Joy Street. (1989). Boston: Little, Brown

Shelby, A. (1990). *We keep a store.* New York: Orchard.

Steptoe, J. (1969). *Stevie.* New York: Harper.

Steptoe, J. (1980). *My daddy is a monster . . . sometimes.* New York: Lippincott.

Steptoe, J. (1987). *Mufaro's beautiful daughters.* New York: Lothrop, Lee & Shepard.

Steptoe, J. (1988). *Baby says.* New York: Lothrop, Lee & Shepard.

Wahl, J. (1991). *Tailypo!* New York: Holt.

Walters, M. P. (1986). *Justin and the best biscuits in the world.* New York: Lothrop, Lee & Shepard.

Yarbrough, C. (1979). *Cornrows.* New York: Coward-McCann.

Yarbrough, C. (1989). *Shimmershine queen.* New York. Putnam.

and spontaneously to speakers. This can be disconcerting to teachers who like quiet when they talk.

HISPANIC CULTURAL GROUPS

According to data from the 1980 and 1990 census, by 2030 Hispanics will become the largest minority group in the United States. Because past educators were not as skilled in using Hispanic students' strengths to increase their values for and abilities in language arts, in 1990 only 60 percent of that cultural group graduated from high school; one in three were retained at least once in their school careers, and seven out of ten were placed in segregated classes, which was up from the 56 percent of such placements in the 1950s (Garcia, 1991). In this section, you can learn how to create language arts instruction that builds on these students' cultural strengths.

Although Hispanic Americans include the widest variety of cultural groups with distinct national origin, socioeconomic status, and cultural background, individual experiences vary greatly depending on origin of the family, occupation, and where they live. The most appropriate label for this group may be an *ethnolinguistic,* to reflect the fact that some people who identify with the culture do not speak Spanish. The label *Latino* includes people who come from different countries and speak different varieties of Spanish. Today, people from communities with roots dating back to the settlement of California in the 1700s likely feel that they have little in common with recent immigrants from El Salvador. Thus, as Tiedt and Tiedt (1995) state:

> It is not surprising, then, that there is much confusion over how to determine who is a member of this minority (Spanish-sounding last name, lack of knowledge of English, or birth in a Spanish-speaking country are some of the criteria that have been suggested) or what label to use to identify people (Latino, Hispanic, and Chicano have been some of the options). The Latino students that you have in the classroom may have lived in this country for a generation, immigrated from Mexico leaving many relatives still there, or arrived as war refugees with no option but permanent settlement in this country. These origins affect the extent to which the students have already learned English and also the family's desire to maintain Spanish at home. (p. 177)

In an ethnographic study of a Californian high school located in an agricultural–suburban community, Matute-Bianchi (1986) found that approximately half of the Mexican-descent students rejected behavioral and instructional patterns of traditional instruction, such as participating in class discussions, carrying books from class to class, asking teachers for help in front of peers, and making it obvious that they were expending effort to do well in school. In these students' minds, it was not possible to participate in both the dominant school culture and their own Chicano culture.

> To cross these cultural boundaries means denying one's identity as a Chicano and is viewed as incompatible with maintaining the integrity of a Chicano identity. Hence, school policies and practices are viewed as forces to be resisted, subverted, undermined, challenged, and opposed. Often the opposition takes the form of mental withdrawal, in which the students find themselves alienated from the academic content of the school curriculum and the effort required to master it. (Matute-Bianchi, p. 255)

Most Hispanics place a high value on family unity and community bonding, which often creates conflicts for students who are asked to develop their identity, individuality, and self-awareness during the school day (Neitro, 1999; Moll, 1999). A second conflict arises when children give or receive sympathetic aid from a classmate or express repeated requests for guidance and direction from teachers. This cultural characteristic of mutual dependence and cooperative achievement contrasts

---

Literature Card 34

CHILDREN'S LITERATURE THAT REPRESENTS HISPANIC CULTURES

Primary

Baylor, B. (1963). *Amigo.* New York: Macmillan.

Belpre, P. (1960). *Perez and Martina.* New York: Warne.

Belpre, P. (1965). *Dance of the animals.* New York: Warne.

Belpre, P. (1969). *Santiago.* New York: Warne.

Belpre, P. (1973). *Once in Puerto Rico.* New York: Warne.

Brown, T. (1986). *Hello amigos!* New York: Holt.

Delacre, L. (1989). *Arroz con leche.* New York: Scholastic.

Delacre, L. (1990). *Las Navidads.* New York: Scholastic.

dePaola, T. (1980). *The lady of Guadalupe.* New York: Holiday.

Dorros, A. (1991). *Tonight is carnaval.* New York: Dutton.

Martel, C. (1976). *Yagua days.* New York: Dial.

Rohmer, H. (1989). *Uncle Nacho's hat.* Emeryville, CA: Children's Book Press.

Intermediate

Cameron, A. (1988). *The most beautiful place in the world.* New York: Knopf.

Maestas, J. G., & Anaya, R. A. (1980). *Cuentos! Tales from the Hispanic Southwest.* New York: Knopf.

Meltzer, M. (1982). *Hispanic Americans.* New York: Crowell.

Mohl, N. (1977). *In Nueva York.* New York: Dell.

Mohl, N. (1979). *Felita.* New York: Dial.

Mohl, N. (1986). *Going home.* New York: Dial.

Soto, G. (1990). *Baseball in April and other stories.* San Diego, CA: Harcourt Brace Jovanovich.

Soto, G. (1991). *Taking sides.* San Diego, CA: Harcourt Brace Jovanovich.

Thomas, P. (1978). *Stories from el barrio.* New York: Knopf.

---

with the individual critical and creative responses emphasized in many classrooms. These values can surface in subtle ways, such as showing respect for an adult who is correcting your behavior by looking down and not making eye contact.

Ruez (1993) has identified classroom features that contribute to success for students of Hispanic descent: an emphasis on oral and written English; a setting of informal and familylike small-group projects and learning centers; and student-initiated topics for thematic units. Teachers *rarely* worked with groups larger than eight. Most of the time the teacher traveled about the room assisting individuals. Large-group instruction was usually confined to start-up activities at the beginning of the day. Thematic unit topics were selected by students. For example, early in the year Ms. Predo asked: "What do you want to learn?" When students agreed on a topic, Juan said "I want to learn about the chemicals (pesticides) that my father works with that are making my little brother sick." Teachers and students made a list of questions and specific learning goals. Over the next few weeks, these classrooms organized reading, writing, research, science, math, and social studies assignments that addressed these learning goals in an integrated fashion.

NATIVE AMERICANS

Native Americans have the highest dropout rates in the nation. Unfortunately, they also receive the least amount of instruction that capitalizes on their cultural strengths (McCarty, 1993). As a general rule, nature is held in high regard in the

Native American culture, and time is often of secondary importance to the activity in which they are engaged. As a result, many students from this culture conceive of time in large blocks—such as morning, afternoon, and evening. Because of this, they may not understand the importance of completing assignments within a 50-minute period. In addition, for many Navajo students, working in heterogeneous groups is against cultural values, and same-sex groups are preferred.

Moreover, for students whose primary language is the tribal speech, bilingual approaches presented throughout this book are successful. Including units with the Native American literature presented in Literature Card 35 benefits students by expanding their respect for the diversity among Native Americans. Enabling Native Americans to use poetic expression in their writing, and to experiment with multiple genres can capture their cultural value for intuitive knowledge. An example of Ms. Predo's students' summation of a thematic unit on Tomie dePaola's *The Legend of the Indian Paintbrush* appears in Figure 13.1.

Using drama is an effective strategy to increase comprehension and affective responses to language arts for students, but whereas acting appeals to African American and Hispanic American students, many Native Americans prefer to write the scripts and to do so individually. This process expands Native American readers' knowledge of traditional English prose, plot structure, and methods of developing characterization better than direct instruction in story grammar.

Literature Card 35

CHILDREN'S LITERATURE THAT PORTRAYS THE NATIVE AMERICAN CULTURES

Prepared by Peggy K. Ford and Susan L. Ford Carr
Tarrant County Junior College

Aaseng, N. (1992). *Navajo code talkers.* Walker. [Navajo].

Adler, D. (1993). *A picture book of Sitting Bull.* Holiday. [Hunkpapa Sioux].

Ancona, G. (1993). *Powwow.* Harcourt Brace. [Native American].

Ata, T. (1989). *Baby rattlesnake.* Children's Book Press. [Chickasaw].

Becker, J. (1994/1974). *Seven little rabbits.* Walker. [Native American].

Begay, S. (1992). *Maii and Cousin Horned Toad.* Scholastic. [Navajo].

Bierhorst, J. (1982). *The whistling skeleton: American Indian Tales of the Supernatural.* Four Winds. [Pawnee, Blackfoot, and Cheyenne].

Blumberg, R. (1987). *The incredible journey of Lewis and Clark.* Lothrop, Lee & Shepard. [Native American].

Bruchac, J. (1993). *Fox song.* Philomel. [Abenaki].

Clark, A. N. (1991/1941). *In my mother's house.* Viking. [Tesuque Pueblo].

Cohen, C. L. (1988). *The mud pony.* Illustrated by Shonto Begay. Scholastic. [Skid/Pawnee].

Cohlene, T. (1990). *Quillworker: A Cheyenne legend.* Watermill. [Cheyenne].

de Brebeuf, F. J. (1990). *The Huron carol.* Illustrated by Frances Tyrrell. Dutton. [Huron].

DeFelice, C. (1990). *Weasel.* Macmillan. [Shawnee].

dePaola, T. (1983). *The legend of the bluebonnet.* Putnam. [Comanche].

dePaola, T. (1988). *The legend of the Indian paintbrush.* Putnam. [Plains].

Dubois, M. L. (1994). *Abenaki captive.* Carolrhoda. [Abenaki].

Ekoomiak, N. (1990). *Arctic memories.* Holt. [Inuit Eskimo].

Esbensen, B. J. (1989). *Ladder to the sky.* Little, Brown. [Anishinabe/Ojibway].

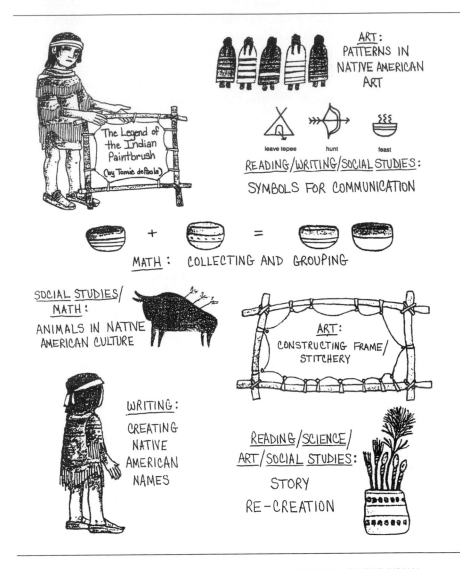

FIGURE 13.1 SEMANTIC MAP OF A THEMATIC UNIT FOR <u>THE LEGEND OF THE INDIAN PAINTBRUSH</u> BY TOMIE DEPAOLA

Created by Lauren Hauchen, second-grade teacher, Fort Worth, TX, 2000. Used by permission.

Moreover, because English-language authors portray story characters through subtle as well as explicit means, it is sometimes difficult for Native American students to recognize how characterization evolves. When you conduct a think-aloud based on an excerpt about a character from a book, they benefit from demonstrations of how descriptions, actions, conversations, and thoughts reveal characters. Native American students also profit from transforming traditional folktales, fairy tales, and fables from their culture into contemporary American life because legends are prevalent in their culture. Transformations can include altering the story's style, details, main events, setting, point of view, and characters' occupations to modernize the moral. Before they begin, you can present several models by sharing traditional stories and their modern transformations, such as *Cinderella* and *Princess Smartypants* and *The Three Little Pigs* and *The True Story of the Three Little Pigs.* Then you can ask Native American pupils to draft their initial ideas alone; critique and synthesize in group discussions; and script their concluding work as a drama that others can enact before the class. After they present the drama, the audience can identify the original folktale from which the script emerged. The books listed on Literature Card 11, in Chapter 4, are excellent for this purpose.

ASIAN AMERICANS

Like Hispanics and Native Americans, Asian Americans comprise many distinct cultures. As a group, Asian Americans value education for self-improvement, developing self-esteem, and enhancing family honor. They also view learning and the language arts as a powerful tool in overcoming occupational discrimination. An Asian proverb illustrates: "There is nothing without education. Education is more important than money." In interviews, 100 percent of East Asian parents (compared to 48 percent of Anglo parents) stated that a grade of "C" was unacceptable for their children (Fu, 1995; Yao, 1991). As a result of this parental expectation, Asian students (as measured on achievement tests and report cards) exceed those of all other cultural groups in academic performances (Schneider & Yongsook, 1991).

Moreover, many Asian Americans believe that asking teachers (or speakers) questions shows a lack of respect by implying that they did not adequately explain the topic (Fu, 1995). For immigrant students, language problems as well as lack of access to individualized teacher assistance can create tremendous strain. For instance, Chieu Huynh, a recently arrived Vietnamese student, describes having to compete with classmates for scarce teacher time.

Interviewer: Do you ask for help?

Chieu: I try to see the teacher, but there are so many people. Every problem is hard to understand, so I can't ask about every single problem. There's so many people in line. There's only one teacher. I don't get my turn, so I don't go in. So I get further and further behind. I can't catch up (Phelan, Yu, & Davidson, 1994, p. 428).

Children's literature that portrays the Asian culture appears in Literature Card 36.

STUDENTS FROM URBAN CULTURES

Distinct socially related attributes of urban city youth have been identified. Freire (1995) distinguishes this population as the "underserved." Regardless of their cultural heritage, students raised in crowded inner cities profit from school experiences in which they use (a) their imaginations, (b) performance-based activities, (c) their abilities to work with others, (d) oral skills, and (e) gamelike structures (Dyson, 1999; Haberman, 1995). As Zarnowski (1991) discovered in an interview with Nicholasa Mohl, a Puerto Rican American children's author who reports her own experiences of living in New York City's barrio (Spanish Harlem), the Bronx, and

Literature Card 36

CHILDREN'S LITERATURE THAT REPRESENTS ASIAN CULTURES

Grades K–2

Boholm-Olsson, E. (1988). *Tuan.* New York: Farrar.

Friedman, I. R. (1984). *How my parents learned to eat.* Boston: Houghton.

Hodges, M. (Reteller). (1964). *The wave.* Boston: Houghton Mifflin.

Levinson, R. (1988). *Our home is the sea.* New York: Dutton.

Mosel, A. (1972). *The funny little woman.* New York: Dutton.

Sakade, F. (1958). *Japanese children's favorite stories.* New York: Tuttle.

Yashima, T. (1955). *Crow boy.* New York: Viking.

Grades 3–4

Bunting, E. (1982). *The happy funeral.* New York: Harper.

Chang, H. (1988). *Mary Lewis, and the frogs.* New York: Crown.

Clark, A. N. (1979). *In the land of small dragon.* New York: Viking.

Coerr, E. (1977). *Sadako and the thousand paper cranes.* New York: Putnam.

Coutant, H. (1974). *First snow.* New York: Knopf.

Ishii, M. (1987). *The tongue-cut sparrow.* New York: Lodestar.

Louie, A.-L. (1982). *Yeh-Shen.* New York: Philomel.

Luenn, N. (1982). *The dragon kite.* New York: Harcourt Brace Jovanovich.

Pratt, D., & Kuls, E. (1967). *Magic animals of Japan.* New York: Parnassus.

Vuong, L. D. (Reteller). (1982). *The brocaded slipper.* Reading, MA: Addison-Wesley.

Yagawa, S. (1981). *The crane wife.* New York: Morrow.

Yolen, J. (1967). *The emperor and the kite.* New York: World.

Grades 5–6

Huynh, Q. N. (1982). *The land I lost: Adventures of a boy in Vietnam.* New York: Harper.

Johnson, A. (1990). *The leaving morning.* New York: Putnam.

Lehrman, R. (1994). *Separations.* New York: Viking.

the Lower East Side, Mohl attributes her adult success with language arts to the nurturing power of her imagination:

> From the moment my mother handed me some scrap paper, a pencil, and a few crayons, I discovered that by making pictures and writing letters I could create my own world . . . like "magic." In the small crowded apartment I shared with my large family, making "magic" permitted me all the space, freedom, and adventure that my imagination could handle [and my crowded environment could not have given me without the language arts]. (Nakamura, 1989, p. 185)

When students read books on Literature Card 36, in which urban figures are central characters, they can discuss which part of their own experiences are universal, and which are unique to urban life.

Haberman (1995), Brookhart and Rusnak (1993), and Compton-Lilly (2000) have identified characteristics of star teachers for populations in urban areas who are underserved. These characteristics are described in Table 13.1. As an example, Brookhart and Rusnak's study (1993) describes the way one of these effective urban teachers opens one of her lessons:

> I give them a little scenario in the beginning saying when you criticize someone's poem you're not criticizing them. You're just looking at their work. Sometimes kids can get very unhappy, "He doesn't like my poem, he doesn't like me." We talk about that before I ever let them sit down in groups. . . . You have to create an atmosphere where they trust you and they really want to learn, and that takes a long time . . . [I tell them] that there is a difference between saying, "Be quiet, please," and "Shut up." I don't use "shut ups"; they don't use "shut ups." (p. 24)

TABLE 13.1 STAR TEACHERS OF THE UNDERSERVED

- They tend to be nonjudgmental. As they interact with children and adults in schools, their first thought is not to decide the goodness or badness of things but to understand events and communications.

- They are not moralistic. They don't believe that preaching is teaching.

- They are not easily shocked even by horrific events. They tend to ask themselves, "What can I do about this?" and if they think they can help, they do; otherwise, they get on with their work and their lives.

- They not only listen, they hear. They not only hear, they seek to understand. They regard listening to children, parents, or anyone involved in the school community as a potential source of useful information.

- They recognize they have feelings of hate, prejudice, and bias and strive to overcome them.

- They do not see themselves as saviors who have come to save their schools. They don't really expect their schools to change much.

- They do not see themselves as being alone. They network.

- They see themselves as "winning" even though they know their total influence on their students is much less than that of the total society, neighborhood, or gang.

- They enjoy their interactions with children and youth so much they are willing to put up with irrational demands of the school system.

- They think their primary impact on their students is making them more humane and less frustrated, or raising their self-esteem.

- They derive all types of satisfactions and meet all kinds of needs by teaching children or youth in poverty. The one exception is power. They meet no power needs whatever by functioning as teachers.

Results from other recent studies (Graham & Block, 1994) support the need to complete detailed planning and explicit instruction for inner-city students. Students who live in urban settings appear to advance their language arts when lessons include clear objectives and procedures, and tie the activities to their lives through in-class discussions, modeling, and simulations.

STUDENTS FROM RURAL, MIGRANT, AND RECENT IMMIGRANT CULTURES

In 1986, the poverty rate was 50 percent higher in rural than in metropolitan counties. This rate remained higher, rose more rapidly, and fell more slowly than the metropolitan rate (De Young & Lawrence, 1995). Moreover, among rural populations, migrant workers, and recent immigrant populations, displaced workers were unemployed 50 percent longer than urban workers, and when they did return to work, they were more likely to take pay cuts and lose insurance benefits (Stern, 1994). When rural children grow up in communities in which physical labor and government assistance are the predominant sources of adult income, building reader's and writers' aspirations to increase their language arts abilities is difficult. They often have fewer selections of quality literature to choose from, fewer models of language arts being used to improve lives, and less parental support to reach the highest level of language arts than their urban counterparts.

The PACERS (Program for Academic and Cultural Enhancement of Rural Schools, University of Alabama) is being used from Alabama's Appalachia to the Black Belt to the Wiregrass. In this program, students serve their own communities. They read so as to write community surveys, newspaper stories, history projects, and photographic documentation for the community's newspaper, city government, and other agencies in need of personnel to improve the community. A second component enables pupils to build parks, put on plays, and perform musical programs to add to the beauty and entertainment opportunities for the community (Haas & Lambert, 1995).

The second program is REAL Enterprises (Rural Entrepreneurship through Action Learning). This project began, and is used most widely, in South Georgia where predominantly African American, low-income students research, plan, set up, and operate businesses in their communities in cooperation with high schools and community colleges. The businesses that are presently designed and operated by students include stores selling comic books, used books, and magazines; T-shirt printing operations; gift shops; and craft studios. Students are not the only beneficiaries because community members have new goods and services that were not available before. A closer bond between students, teachers, community, and school is the result. More than 500 community leaders serve as a community support team for REAL and the schools (Haas & Lambert, 1995).

MEETING THE NEEDS OF ENGLISH LANGUAGE LEARNERS

The opportunity to teach students who are learning English as another language is becoming more common in the United States and Canada. Estimates indicate that in the United States alone approximately 3.4 million students have limited English proficiency (The Condition of Bilingual Education in the Nation, 1991). To cite one example, the Los Angeles Unified School District has 77 major languages and dialects of students who require adapted instruction in the language arts (Ross, 1995).

The most recent term for students who are not native English speakers is *English language learners*. Within this population, students who are not yet sufficiently fluent in English to use it solely to perform academic tasks are often referred to as *limited English proficient* (LEP) or *potentially English proficient* (PEP) students (Freeman & Freeman, 1992) or *readers and writers of English as another language* (REAL) (Rigg & Allen, 1989). Also, within the population of English language learners are **bilingual** students or children who speak both their native language and English fluently.

The diversities that exist between and among multilanguage students bring important obligations and opportunities to your language arts program. A first step is to incorporate the special talents children develop through their culture into the language arts lesson plans. For example, Ms. Predo's class was comprised of more than 80 percent multicultural and multilingual students. These middle school students could not comprehend stories at a second-grade readability level, but they wanted to mentor second-graders. Through gestures and dialect, in one minute, Juan accomplished more than 9 months of instruction could have done. Ms. Predo incorporated his value to take care of younger siblings into her language arts program. The following is Ms. Predo's description of what Juan did.

The Steadfast Soldier

Juan won the leading role in "The Steadfast Soldier," a play the class wrote. He and 12 of the 18 other class members completely rewrote the plot of this story to match messages they wanted to convey about their culture to these students' younger siblings. Using his unique abilities to respond to present conditions more rapidly than other culturally influenced students could, Juan realized that at the climax of the play every child was completely engrossed, all eyes were on him, and every child awaited the main character's next words. At this moment, Juan spontaneously deviated from the script, stepped forward, as if to leave the stage and become himself rather than the steadfast tin soldier, and said: "I want you to know something really important before I tell you the end of this story. If I hadn't learned to read English this year, I would not be able to be this actor and it really is fun to act today. You must learn to read this year, for me. If you will do that for me, say 'Yes!' " All the children responded loudly. Then, he quickly turned to Ms. Predo and said: "Can I come back in 2 months and have everyone here read to me so I can be sure they know how?" She said yes. Juan jumped back in the cast; said the closing lines of the play; came back in 2 months; and heard *every* child read a book that they had selected.

The lessons in this chapter can enable students to learn to think and communicate ideas that may be in opposition to others. Some may require extra modeling from you before they venture to express their opinions. Such models and lessons, described next, occur more naturally in student-centered language arts programs that adhere to the principles stated in the first section of this chapter.

SECTION 2 PUTTING THEORY INTO PRACTICE

Teaching Students How to Think at a High Level and How to Increase Their Multicultural Understanding

This section of the chapter introduces elements of critical thinking processes, as well as lessons that develop them. You can introduce higher-level thinking and communication abilities in several ways. When Ms. Predo applied these methods in her class, Michael described how they helped him:

> When I look back [over Ms. Predo's lessons], I see how much they helped me. My poems used to be very basic in the beginning; they were all rhymed haiku because that was all I knew about.

Then I [did as Ms. Predo taught me and] experimented with going along with my feelings and ideas . . . don't kill yourself going over the rhymes, go with what you feel. I did that for 2 months. Then I started compacting them, shortening them to make deeper meaning. I could see that it would make more of a point if I washed out the *the*s and *and*s and *if*s. Now that I have learned the lessons about thinking processes, I am working on something different—the morals. If one day my mom's car broke down, I might write that night about how a fish got caught or the feeling of not being able to swim. Now I am not trying to write how I feel only, but metaphors too! (Wolf, 1989, p. 38)

DIMENSION 1: BASIC THINKING SKILLS

The Dimension 1 thinking skills include the ability to translate, relate, and order sensory, literary, and visual input. The specific abilities you can teach are: (1) using, rehearsing, and repeating mnemonic lists (e.g., memory aids, imagery, semantic maps, examples); (2) using synonyms and examples; and (3) condensing, summarizing, and revising. Through your modeling, students can learn to evaluate facts, draw conclusions, reason about a conclusion's attractiveness, and reflect on what is true or best. In essence, you can teach them to distinguish what they know from what they merely suspect to be true.

You can also teach students to accept and reject incoming information by asking questions of those who think differently from themselves. This requirement helps students realize that others know things that they don't, and that together they can work interdependently to create new knowledge. In addition, you can teach condensing, summarizing, expanding, and revising by selecting two types of literature on the same topic.

Students also can assist other students to develop these thinking abilities by discussing the similarities and differences between two authors' writing styles. You can emphasize the importance of these skills by stating: "I know that sometimes you may think that it takes too much time to stop and compare things. When I go to the grocery store and if I'm in a hurry, then I don't compare prices to find out which one is the cheapest and I end up spending more money than I should. But when I go and take my time, I compare items and prices and this saves me a lot of money. Throughout life it will be important for you to learn to compare."

Then you can introduce the Venn diagram in Figure 13.2. This thinking tool can help students discover the similarities and differences between an orange and an apple that you place on each small group's table. As each student suggests how the fruits are alike, you can ask them to do a think-aloud about the thought processes they used to detect the similarity. (For example, perhaps many will say that their senses assisted in recognizing common features.) Then you can teach that comparing things means to look carefully at each part of objects, ideas, or events to determine parts that are similar to other objects, ideas, or events. By taking time to observe these relationships, students can learn and remember new information better.

After completing one large Venn diagram as a class, students can choose one of the following activities to apply the diagram independently:

1. Select two books by Dr. Seuss. Look at each book and tell how they are alike and how they are different. Write similarities and differences on the Venn diagram in Figure 13.2.

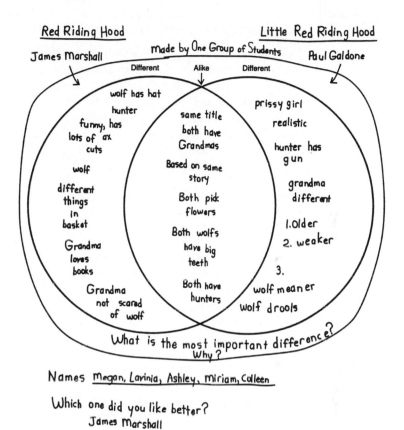

NAME _____ DATE _____

I'm confused about _____

<u>Red Riding Hood</u>   <u>Little Red Riding Hood</u>

James Marshall   Made by One Group of Students   Paul Galdone

Different   Alike   Different

wolf has hat
hunter
funny, has
lots of ax
cuts

wolf

different
things
in
basket

Grandma
loves
books

Grandma
not scared
of wolf

same title
both have
Grandmas

Based on same
story

Both pick
flowers

Both wolfs
have big
teeth

Both have
hunters

prissy girl
realistic

hunter has
gun

grandma
different

1. older
2. weaker

3.

wolf meaner
wolf drools

What is the most important difference?
Why?

Names <u>Megan, Lavinia, Ashley, Miriam, Colleen</u>

Which one did you like better?
James Marshall

Why? because it was funny

FIGURE 13.2 COMPARING AND CONTRASTING LESSON: AN EXAMPLE FROM MS. PREDO'S CLASS

2. Go to the book center and pick any two books with a partner. Take these books to the listening center and record on the tape recorder how they are alike and how they are different.

3. Choose two favorite sports, television, or movie stars. Record how these two superstars are alike and different on a Venn diagram.

You can challenge students to rethink and reformulate the comparing process by leading a discussion on how this type of thinking can increase their abilities to relate more positively with others in the future. Students can also compare the qualities of villains portrayed in literature (e.g., the foxes in *The Amazing Bone* by William

Sylvester and the Magic Pebble

Steig and *Sylvester and the Magic Pebble*), and compare television sitcoms with reality. Such comparisons help students understand the complex relationship between fact and fantasy and life and the entertainment industry.

DIMENSION 2: ESSENTIAL THINKING PROCESSES

Dimension 2 includes processes such as detecting patterns and principles; inferring next events, causation, theme, and/or purpose; translating and interpreting; and noting inconsistencies as well as reasons why they exist. You can teach students these components through the following activities.

You can ask students to organize information, label it, and combine it with two or more sets of facts to create an example. For example, you can list the following words on the board and ask what could be a next set of words:

ate	bite
cake	ice
eight	

Students should give a word with long /a/ sound as all words in the first column are illustrations of the concept of ways to spell the long /a/ sound. More able students can suggest a word with the long /i/ sound for column two, such as *eye* or *I*.

You can teach students to **judge credibility** by describing the guidelines in Figure 13.3. As each is presented, you can ask students to cite examples of when they used one of these guidelines effectively to judge credibility. The lesson proceeds by providing the following examples of when students can use the guidelines in Figure 13.3. You can say, "One way you can use these guidelines in real life is when two friends have conflicting stories and ask you to help resolve their differences. You will also find this skill helpful when people present information you know nothing about. When you become an adult, you may be called to serve on a jury. Using the information in Figure 13.3 will be important then and in your daily life." Students can then meet in small groups and use Figure 13.3 to determine the verdict in three stories from the books *You Be the Jury* and *You Be the Jury II*. As they read they can also record points in the story where the credibility of sources was indicated.

You Be the Jury

In addition, students who have limited English can learn the thinking skills in Dimensions 1 and 2 by putting objects into categories and describing the thought process they used to do so. Then you can present other objects and ask, "What would you have to do to categorize this?" Moreover, many can often learn how to summarize faster if they are allowed to write a summary of what they themselves wrote rather than what they read from books.

DIMENSION 3: DECISION MAKING

Making effective decisions involves selecting from two or more competing alternatives. You can teach students that there are several components in making effective decisions: (1) anticipating the consequences of alternative actions before taking a stand, (2) using outside resources and soliciting advice from other people, (3) having a positive attitude and being fair to all sides, (4) seeking truth and objective

FIGURE 13.3 TEACHING STUDENTS TO JUDGE CREDIBILITY

evidence, (5) listening to various points of view, (6) recognizing propaganda and inconsistent application of standards, and (7) considering the well-being of those affected by decisions. Activities that build decision-making abilities follow.

You can strengthen students' decision-making processes by introducing the sub-components described above. You can ask students to write about a decision they do not know how to make; they follow steps 1 through 7 above and make their decision. Next, you can have students report aspects of the decision-making steps that were most beneficial to them. For example, Ms. Predo read *The Giving Tree* by Shel Silverstein, and students applied the components of effective decision making to reach a decision that the tree and man could have made to improve the outcome. Meisong wrote: "The man could have planted a tree next to the tree. The tree could have watched it grow and when it grew then they could have visited with each other."

You can teach students how to listen to various points of view. Students can demonstrate their use of these competencies in writing by completing a point-counterpoint

The Giving Tree

story. After writing such stories, students can analyze how they made their decisions and how they can better study opposing sides of issues in real life. Figure 13.4 is an example of such a point-counterpoint activity that Ms. Predo's class completed using *Jack and the Beanstalk*. In this activity, Juan gave alternative reasons for Jack's decision to climb the beanstalk.

You can also teach students how to use decision-making tools such as the **Weighted Characteristics Test** shown in Figure 13.5. You can dispel students' misconceptions about the difficulty of this lesson by stating that the ability to make decisions is not as difficult to develop as they might expect, and that this tool can be used to improve the quality of their thought and communication processes. For example, you might say, "Because you will be in situations throughout your life where you have to make choices, you will profit by using the Weighted Characteristics Test. It enables you to see both sides of the problem more clearly before you select an action that is best for you."

Then you can inspire students' thinking by asking them to recall a time in their lives when they had to make a very important decision. Next, you can present Figure 13.5 and say:

"The Weighted Characteristics Test was invented by Benjamin Franklin. Look at the figure. Whenever you have to make a difficult decision you can list the arguments on different sides of the balance scale, just as Juan did to decide if he would play football in high school. Below each choice, list every possible negative and positive consequence that could arise if you selected that choice. Once you've listed all the consequences, count the total for both sides of the scale. For example, if the right side of the scale had five consequences and the left side had five, you would have a total of ten consequences. You would then use the total number 10 to weigh each consequence. You would assign a 10 to the most important consequence, in your

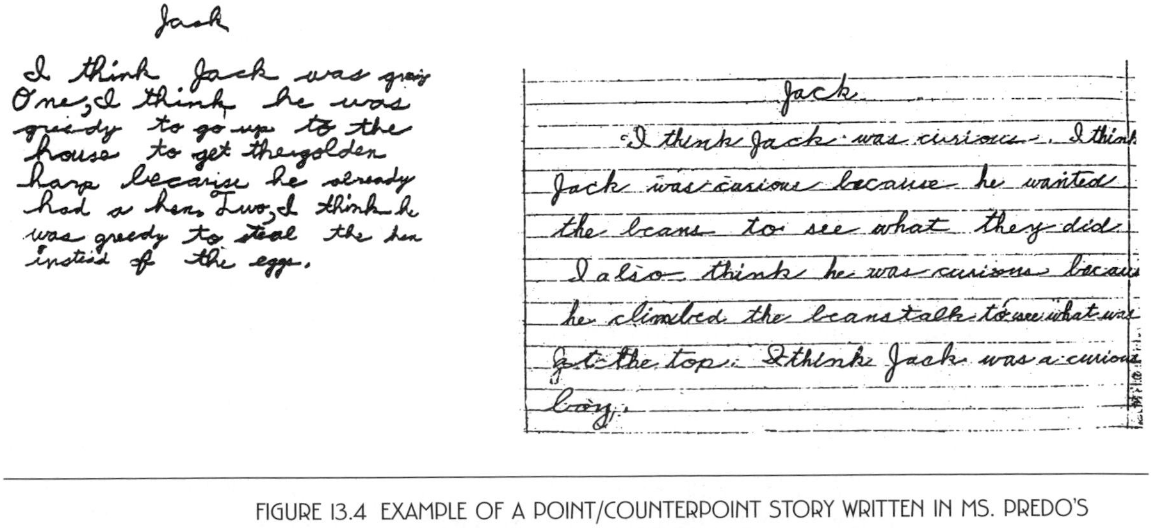

FIGURE 13.4 EXAMPLE OF A POINT/COUNTERPOINT STORY WRITTEN IN MS. PREDO'S CLASS TO PRACTICE GENERATING ALTERNATIVES BEFORE MAKING DECISIONS

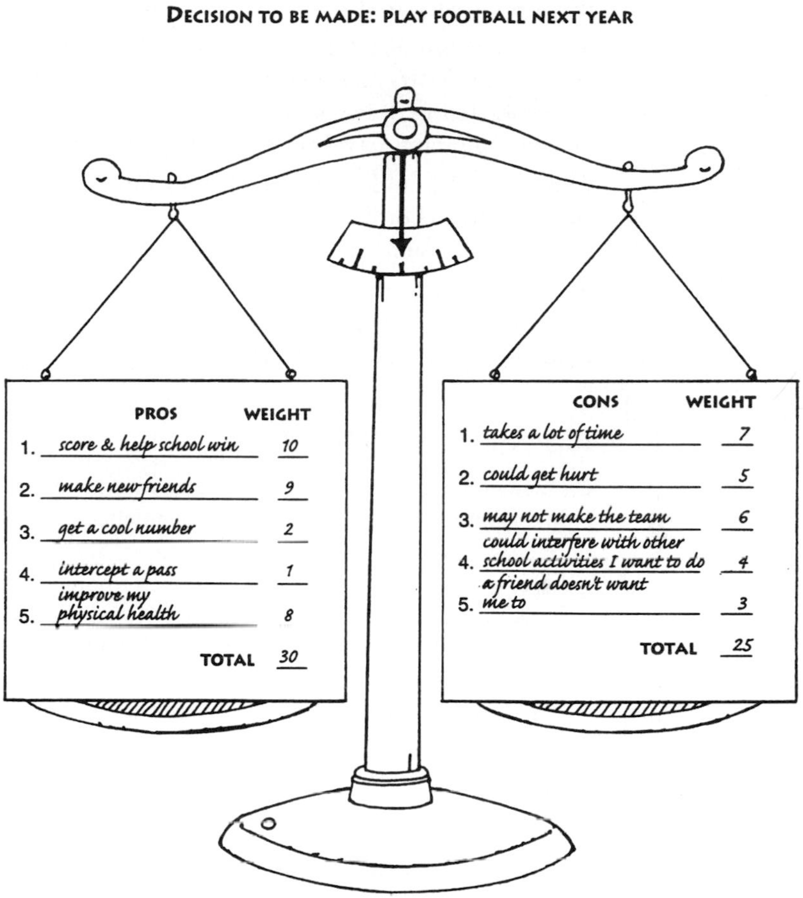

DECISION TO BE MADE: PLAY FOOTBALL NEXT YEAR

PROS	WEIGHT
1. score & help school win	10
2. make new friends	9
3. get a cool number	2
4. intercept a pass	1
5. improve my physical health	8
TOTAL	**30**

CONS	WEIGHT
1. takes a lot of time	7
2. could get hurt	5
3. may not make the team	6
4. could interfere with other school activities I want to do	4
5. a friend doesn't want me to	3
TOTAL	**25**

FIGURE 13.5 THE WEIGHTED CHARACTERISTICS TEST (AN EXAMPLE FROM MS. PREDO'S CLASS)

opinion. It can be a positive consequence that you really want to occur or it can be a negative consequence that you really want to avoid. The second most important consequence receives a weight of 9 and so on. Once all consequences are weighted, you can total both sides of the scale. The solution with the highest number of points is likely to be the decision that is best for you at that point in time using all the information that is available.

You can also integrate these lessons across the curriculum through the following activities.

1. *Social Studies:* Ask students to identify a problem that exists in their school or community and use the Weighted Characteristics Test to develop a possible solution.

2. *Current Issues and Personal Decisions:* Have students pretend that they had a fight with a friend and they can't decide if they should (a) apologize and explain their side again; (b) go up and talk to their friend and pretend nothing happened; or (c) ignore their friend until he or she comes to them. What should they do and why? How did they decide what to do?

3. *Mathematics:* Read the books *If You Had a Million Dollars* by David Schwartz, and *A Chair for My Mother* by Vera Williams. Have students use the Weighted Characteristics Test to decide how to spend some money that either the class has earned on a group project or money they have earned individually.

4. *Science:* Ask students to complete a journal entry about Thomas Edison or a scientist of their choice. As they study the scientist, have them seek to discover how they made decisions and if they used the Weighted Characteristics Test.

5. *Fine Arts:* Have students read books such as *Great Painters* by Piero Ventura, *An Artist* by M. B. Goffstein, and *Marc Chagall* by M. B. Goffstein. Then ask students to identify how these people made decisions.

DIMENSION 4: PROBLEM SOLVING

Problem-solving thinking involves (1) analyzing and resolving perplexing and difficult situations, (2) assessing the reasonableness and quality of ideas, (3) rejecting poor reasoning, (4) explaining assumptions, and (5) using problem-solving strategies. The following activities build the components of problem-solving thinking. After these strategies have been taught, students can hold a trial and videotape it to analyze aspects of their thinking that had the most positive impact on solving the problems.

Similarly, you can teach the problem-solving tools described in Table 13.2. Once students feel comfortable with these tools, they can select two that they will use in their lives when problems arise. Books that work well in teaching these problem-solving tools are *You Be the Jury; You Be the Jury II; The First Woman Doctor; Frederick Douglass Fights for Freedom; John F. Kennedy: America's 35th President; The Unfinished Stories for Facilitating Decision Making in the Elementary Classroom* (NEA Professional Library, P.O. Box 509, West Haven, CT 06516); and *Options: A Guide to Creative Decision Making* by Dianne Draze (Dandy Lion Publications, P.O. Box 190, San Luis Obispo, CA 93406).

Students from different cultural backgrounds need to be guided to see that many options are at their disposal for problem solving. By practicing more than one strategy (under your guidance) when they are perplexed, they can more quickly learn to correct their own problems. You can teach them to practice more than one strategy before asking for your help. This action can simultaneously increase their chances for success while building their self-esteem.

DIMENSION 5: DEVELOPING STUDENTS' METACOGNITIVE THINKING ABILITIES

Metacognitive thinking involves three components: self-knowledge, self-appraisal, and self-regulation (Paris, Lipson, & Wixson, 1983). Students can learn *not* to (1) simply agree or disagree; (2) accept or reject conclusions on the basis of egocentric attachment or excessive desire; and (3) assume that they are wrong if their reasons deviate from others'. Students can learn to self-regulate by using strategies that

TABLE 13.2 PROBLEM-SOLVING STRATEGIES

The following are strategies that increase students' problem-solving abilities.

MEANS–END ANALYSIS	Method of moving through problem space in which differences between present state and goal state are examined (e.g., when adjusting the TV screeen, instead of just turning knobs, you evaluate the present state— whether the color is too bright or horizontal lines are interfering—which determines your adjustment)
TRIAL AND ERROR	Method of making moves or decisions until your goal state is reached or you give up (e.g., rat in the maze)
HILL CLIMBING	Method that assumes you always know at what stage you are in a process and take action based on your position (e.g., doctor determines optimal dosage of a drug by increasing or decreasing the dose until patient's health is observed to be progressing)
ANALOGIES	Method in which analogies or comparisons are made between the problem and personal experienccs and problems in other domains (e.g., Alexander Graham Bell compared the membranes that operate the bones in the ear to the material he used to move a piece of steel, which resulted in the creation of the telephone)
BRAINSTORMING	Method in which a large number of solutions are produced by brainstorming the topic; imagination and creativity are promoted and no idea is criticized; solutions are evaluated to find one that solves the problem despite current restrictions
FORWARD INFERENCING	Method in which conclusions are drawn based on given information (e.g., students are asked to read a paragraph in the middle of a book and then write about what they think happens prior to and after the passage they read)
BACKWARD REASONING	Method in which visualizing the conclusion is easy but getting to it is not (e.g., mazes children complete to get from a starting point to an end point; children tend to start at the end point to get to the starting point)
LEARNING HOW TO MAKE REPEATED MINOR CORRECTIONS	Method of learning to make mid-course minor corrections in order to reach the ultimate goal
HINTS	Method in which additional information comes to light after an individual has begun to work on a problem. Hints can provide important information for solving the problem and sometimes change the way it is approached.
SPLIT-HALF	Method of selecting a solution based on a sequentially organized set of possible solutions (e.g., the first step in searching for the clog is separating the pipe halfway between where it is connected to your sink and where it meets the street; the second step is to determine which half contains the clog by observing whether the water is running freely at this point; if not, the third step is to locate the stoppage by examining the midpoint between the sink and the breakage; steps continue using this split-half method until you find the stoppage)

(continued)

TABLE 13.2 (CONTINUED)

STORYTELLING	Method of using past real-life stories to shed light on new problems
VISUALIZATIONS	Method in which a successful solution is visualized as if one lived in a perfect world; steps toward realizing this ideal help clarify the goal
RESTATE THE PROBLEM	Method of reframing a problem, particularly useful for solving ill-defined problems (e.g., to solve the problem of how to save money, you may decide to eat peanut butter sandwiches instead of going out to eat; however, if you restate the problem as how to have more money, you may decide to find a better paying job, which will enable you not only to have more money but to save more as well)
SELECT ONLY RELEVANT INFORMATION	Method in which irrelevant or misleading information is filtered out, allowing one to focus on only useful information to solve a problem
CONSULT EXPERTS	Method in which experts are enlisted to help solve the problem (e.g., hiring an accountant during tax season)

These strategies may work in isolation, but often the best strategy for solving a problem is to use a combination of several of the above.

"repair" their thinking and to overcome barriers that interfere with their talents and goals. Social interactions can assist students to develop these metacognitive processes.

One lesson that builds metacognition is called You Be the Counselor. It builds metacognition by enabling students to walk in another person's shoes. Its purpose is to help students understand reasons for their beliefs. In this lesson, you can teach the following metacognitive processes before students read: "To assist others you must know a lot about yourself and the other person. You must also pay attention to why you and they behave the way you do; you must understand which strengths and weaknesses in your and the other person's personalities led to the situation you and they face; you should separate facts from your assumptions and beliefs; and you must question facts, beliefs, and assumptions that others present that do not match what is expected or normal."

Next, you can have students select a book in which characters conflict (such as the story of *The Three Little Pigs*), and in which the author's metacognitions favor one side (e.g., the story of the three little pigs is told from the pigs' point of view). Students can then use the metacognitive process you taught and write the likely metacognitions of the opposing character (the wolf).

Once students finish these metacognitive reports, they can be interviewed as if they were the opposing character. For example, Ms. Predo's class chose *The Three Little Pigs,* and students became the wolf they created. They were asked, "What will you do if the jury decides to place you on probation for harassing the pigs and for breaking and entering?" (Responses to this question in Ms. Predo's class included "I will rebuild the three pigs' houses," "I will buy the material for them," and "I really didn't eat any of them, and actually the pigs learned a lesson about how to build their houses on account of me.") "What will you think and how will you respond if the city decides to give you a medal for reforming and rebuilding the pigs' houses?" and "Why did you blow down the pigs' houses if you weren't intending to eat them?" (One "wolf" answered by stating: "I thought it was unnatural for pigs to have houses.")

Dimension 6 is creative thinking, and methods of developing it were presented in Chapter 12.

DIMENSION 7: THINKING MORE EFFECTIVELY IN GROUPS

Students who think effectively in groups understand and depend on the nature of thinking as it evolves in group settings. These abilities include mentoring, networking, understanding the difference between winning and being right, setting challenging goals with others, using diverse talents collaboratively, exercising reciprocity, eliminating blocks to group productivity, listening carefully to others' ideas, asking better questions, and being sensitive to others' needs. The following activities can develop students' group work skills.

Four-member groups can read copies of the same selection of children's literature. Each member is assigned a different purpose: One student reads and evaluates the quality of thinking or writing in the story; a second analyzes the main character's problem-solving strategies; a third ties story events to the modern world, projecting when such events might occur in the future; and a fourth studies how new characters increase or decrease their trustworthiness, and they recommend ideas to classmates as to how they can successfully extend their trust to others. Each person shares what they learned with their group. Once groups are finished, they evaluate their group thinking skills, using a group assessment form from Chapter 12.

A second activity to build group thinking processes is to teach students to make statements of appreciation and give compliments. In this lesson, students are taught to offer the following statements when they work in groups: "I liked it when . . ."; "I felt good when you . . ."; "I admired you for . . .". The second step is to ask students to set the goal of making at least one statement of appreciation to each member of their group.

The third activity teaches students to overcome peer pressure by learning about famous people in history who faced serious peer pressure (Myers, 1992). You can begin by introducing the books *Hey, Al* by Arthur Yorinks and *Gee, Wiz* by Linda Allison. Students analyze how characters in these books tried to discourage others. They can complete a chart with the headings: *Peer Pressure and Its Consequences*. Then, students can list strategies other historical and fictitious figures used to overcome peer pressure by reading one of the following books: *Meaning Well* by Sheila Cole; *The Glass Pipe* by Robert Coles; *Amelia Quackenbush* by Sharloya Gold; *Trapped* by Roderic Jeffries; *Pickpocket Run* by Annabel and Edgar Johnson; *Cross-Country Runner* by Leon McClinton; *Edgar Allen* by John Neufeld; *The Girl from Nowhere* by Hertha Von Bebhardt; and "The Eye of Conscience" in *Perspectives* by Harcourt Brace Jovanovich, pp. 92–101. After reading, they can answer these questions:

1. How might things have been different if the people you read about had not used a strategy to overcome peer pressure?

2. What are some options the characters overlooked?

3. How will you respond if facing a similar situation?

Once students learn group work skills, they can begin to collaborate and build consensus, perhaps first in pairs, next in groups of four, and later in larger groups. Older students can teach younger ones these group strategies by preparing an oral presentation with a visual aid, such as a bulletin board. Such mentoring experiences build confidence and sensitivity.

The Bear and the Crow

Students can also divide into groups and read "The Bear and the Crow" from *Fables* by Arnold Lobel, and discuss their values about wearing the "right" clothes and being "in style." They can answer the questions, "Who influences my decisions concerning what clothes I wear?" and "What are the consequences of my decisions?"

You can also teach students how to negotiate. Books that depict a wide range of cultural differences and negotiations that are made between various characters introduce this unit well. Samples of such books are

1. *Ishi. Last of His Tribe* by Theodora Kroeber, 1995, Houghton/Parnassus Press, Boston (story of the last survivor of the Yahi Indian tribe)

2. *Journey to Washington* by Daniel K. Inouye, with Lawrence Elliott, 1995, Prentice Hall, Englewood Cliffs, NJ (autobiography of the first Japanese American to be elected to Congress)

3. *The Story of My Life* by Helen Keller, 1959, Doubleday, New York (Helen Keller's early life and education)

4. *Martin Luther King, Jr.* by Jaqueline Harris, 1993, Watts, New York (overview of the historic achievements of the civil rights movement and Dr. King)

5. *My Family and Other Animals* by Gerald Durrell, 1994, Penguin Books, New York (the story of this British zoologist's boyhood five years on an island with his family)

6. *Just One Friend* by Lynn Hall, 1995, Scribners, New York (how a 16-year-old girl with learning difficulties deals with the loss of her best friend)

7. *All Creatures Great and Small* by James Herriot, 1990, St. Martin's Press, New York (the author's life as a young veterinarian)

8. *The Dog Who Wouldn't Be* by Farley Mowat, 1995, Little, Brown, New York (a dog's adventure)

9. *Abe Lincoln Grows Up* by Carl Sandburg, 1989, Harcourt Brace Jovanovich, San Diego (Lincoln's early years up to age 19)

10. *Amos Fortune, Free Man* by Elizabeth Yates, 1970, E. P. Dutton, New York (biography of a slave from life in Africa to the United States)

Finally, students can cite examples from their personal experiences in which they have witnessed the positive effects of some of these negotiating strategies. You can also have students videotape one of their small-group meetings in a content area before and after this lesson and see if their negotiating skills improved.

DIMENSION 8: ABILITY TO THINK EFFECTIVELY WHEN ALONE

People differ in their willingness to pursue and hold on to the power of their own ideas. You can increase students' willingness to "hold on" to such inventions by increasing the quality of thinking they do when working alone, such as being responsible for goals they set and directions that they establish. As Elbow (1981) stated: "The mark of the person who can actually make *progress* in thinking—who can sit down at 8:30 with one set of ideas and stand up at 11:00 with better ideas—is a willingness to notice and listen to those inconvenient little details, those annoying loose ends, those embarrassments or puzzles, instead of impatiently sweeping them under the rug" (p. 131). The components of these thinking processes that you can teach are how to set personal priorities, improve marginal performance, stimulate intellectual curiosity, and present ideas clearly.

You can model how to do each of these thinking processes by describing and showing samples of the work of past students who were successful in completing self-initiated projects. You can also have students practice establishing weekly priorities for 3 weeks, and making journal entries each Friday about their growth in thinking when working alone. Students can also set new goals for reading, writing, and working alone during the coming week.

A second lesson is designed to increase students' reflection. Students can read a first-person narrative from books such as *Growing Up Adopted; Anne Frank: The Diary of a Young Girl; If This Is Love, I'll Take Spaghetti; My Side of the Mountain; Boris; Little House in the Big Woods; A Year in the Life of Rosie Bernard; Roller Skates; Thimble Summer; All It Takes Is Practice; On the Frontier with Mr. Audubon; Self-Portrait: Margot Zemach; Me and Willie and Pa; The Story of Abraham Lincoln and his Son Todd;* and

Poor Richard in France. Students are not to see the title or any pictures as they read and figure out who the first-person narrator is. They can tell you and indicate the point in the story where they made an identification. Students can also write the rationale for their reasoning and continue to read the remainder of the selection. They may change their minds at any time. With each change, students can describe weaknesses in their first reasoning process. After all have finished, the first students to identify the narrator correctly can explain the thinking processes they used to classmates. Students can then make a journal entry to describe occasions in their life when they can increase their reflectivity by suspending judgments and attending to details.

You can punctuate the importance of learning these abilities by telling students that The Power of Positive Students Program reports that 87 percent of people do not have goals. Of the 13 percent that set goals, only 3 percent write them down. These 3 percent of our population accomplish 50 to 125 times more than others. You can teach students to establish goals by asking them to set two for the coming week, with a plan of action and a target date for each. They can use a table like the following, to do so.

MY PERSONAL AND SCHOOL GOALS (AND PLANS OF ACTION) ARE:	TARGET DATE
1. _____	_____
_____	
2. _____	_____
_____	

A last activity is to help students analyze what they can do to become more successful and creative group leaders. Students can identify five people they judge to possess exceptional skill in these areas. They can interview these people and condense their strategies to one sheet, such as that prepared by Ms. Predo's class in Figure 13.6.

INTEGRATING THE LANGUAGE ARTS THROUGH AUTOBIOGRAPHIES AND BIOGRAPHIES

So far, in this chapter, you have learned strategies and activities that enhance students' thinking skills, cognitive processes, decision making, problem solving, group work skills, and strategies for working alone, which in turn can improve their abilities to understand those from different backgrounds and perspectives. You have also discovered that students' first step toward critical thinking is observing your modeling followed by instruction in quality thinking. In this section you can learn how the study of autobiographies and biographies enhances students' development in many of these competencies.

When students are introduced to good biographies and autobiographies, they often "feel as if the biographical [person] has become their personal friend. These children can carry with them into adulthood a love of nonfiction that portrays the lives of interesting people with whom they can identify and from whom they can learn. Biography also offers children not only the high adventure and engrossing drama that fiction supplies, but also the special satisfaction of knowing that the people and events described are 'really real' " (Norton, 1995b, p. 646).

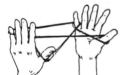

1. Assume responsibility
2. Have high expectations for self and others
3. Express themselves concisely and fluently
4. Foresee consequences and implications of decisions
5. Exercise good judgment in decision making
6. Are liked by peers
7. Are self-confident
8. Are organized

1. Are determined to succeed
2. Overcome obstacles
3. Enjoy competition
4. Are honest
5. Possess much talent or ability
6. Set goals
7. Work consistently toward a goal
8. Are motivated to be the best

1. Think independently
2. Exhibit original thinking in oral and written expression
3. Come up with several solutions to problems
4. Possess a sense of humor
5. Create and invent
6. Improve often
7. Are challenged by creative tasks
8. Do not mind being different from the crowd

FIGURE 13.6 CHARACTERISTICS OF LEADERS, WINNERS, AND CREATIVE THINKERS

Biographies and autobiographies can teach students about brave men and women from cultures like theirs who have conquered, explored, fought discrimination, and changed their own or others' lives through perseverance and inventions. **Autobiographies** are stories of a person's life written by that person. **Biographies** are stories written about a person's life by someone other than that person. Literature Card 37 contains a list of autobiographies and biographies that students have enjoyed. Students can enjoy and profit from thematic units that employ these books (as shown at the end of Chapter 14).

Students can analyze the characteristics of the person featured in the autobiography or biography they read and compare these characteristics to their own personalities

Literature Card 37

AUTOBIOGRAPHIES AND BIOGRAPHIES THAT BUILD CRITICAL THINKING AND MULTICULTURAL UNDERSTANDING

The following books can be used in a unit to build students' critical thinking and understanding of autobiographical and biographical genres. They can be used to build students' abilities to write an autobiography and/or biography, to identify with characters they admire, as well as to increase metacognitive, plausible, and predictive thinking.

Sports Legends (Series), 1990 New York: Crestwood House Publishers

American Women of Achievement (Series), 1992 New York: Chelsea House Publishers

Stories of the Poets by S. Mee, 1995 New York: Harper

Lives of the Artists (Series) by M. B. Goffstein, 1990 New York: Macmillan

Picture Book of Martin Luther King (Series) by D. A. Adler, 1993 New York: Simon & Schuster

Charlie Brown, Snoopy and Me: And All the Other Peanuts Characters by Charles Schultz, 1992 New York: Macmillan

My Life with the Chimpanzees by Jane Goodall, 1994 New York: Viking

Pocahontas and the Strangers by C. R. Bulla, 1994 New York: Harper

The Story of Thomas Alva Edison, Inventor: The Wizard of Menlo Park by M. Davidson, 1993 New York: Dial

Stealing Home: The Story of Jackie Robinson by B. Denenberg, 1994 New York: Scholastic

World Leaders—Past and Present (Series), 1992 New York: Chelsea House Publishers

Black Americans of Achievement (Series), 1993 New York: Chelsea House Publishers

The Double Life of Pocahontas, 1989 New York: Penguin, and other books by Jean Fritz

Heroes (Series) by M. Billings and B. Billings, 1989 New York: Scholastic

Writers' Voices and *New Writers' Voices* (Series) published 1989 New York: Literacy Volunteers of New York

Laura Ingalls Wilder by P. R. Giff, 1990 New York: Macmillan

The First Women Doctors by R. Baker, 1992 New York: Simon & Schuster

The Story of My Life by Helen Keller, 1956 New York: Harcourt

Harry Houdini: Master of Magic by R. Kraske, 1987 New York: Holt

Sole Survivor by R. L. McCunn, 1991 New York: Viking

The Death of Lincoln by L. Hayman, 1990 New York: Greenwillow

A Man Named Thoreau by R. Burleigh, 1995 New York: Simon & Schuster

---

using a matrix, semantic map, or chart. Then they can write or discuss what it would have been like to be the famous person's best friend. Each student can identify activities the two might enjoy in the student's community and write an analysis of what they think made the person successful.

American Surnames

This lesson can culminate with students writing their own autobiography. They can begin by studying the history of their name, through conferences with parents and nonfiction books such as *Baby Names from Around the World* by Maxine Fields (Pocket Books, 1985); *American Surnames* by Elsdon C. Smith (Chilton Book Company, 1969); or *American Given Names* by George R. Stewart (Oxford University Press, 1979). Students can then focus on what they judge to be their strengths of character. Next, students can pair with a friend to write biographies of each other without consulting one another. Afterward students can compare their autobiographies to the biography their partners wrote about them. They can explain why differences in perceptions and self-perceptions exist, and report the differences between autobiographical and biographical genre that they have learned. They can also describe the metacognitive thinking processes that this activity helped them develop.

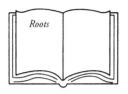

Additional references for autobiographies are *Exploring the Lives of Gifted People* by Kathy Balsamo (Good Apple, 1987); *Learning from the Lives of Amazing People* by J. Gudeman (Good Apple, 1988); and six series from Scholastic entitled *Champions of Change, Spotlight on TV Stars, Spotlight on Movie Stars, Spotlight on Sports Stars, Superstars,* and *Superstars in Action.* An example of how to teach autobiographies and biographies appears in Chapter 14. This unit was created by Juan and his classmates to learn more about Alex Haley, the author of *Roots.*

INSIDE CULTURALLY ENRICHED CLASSROOMS

Activities That Strengthen Multicultural Learning

You can employ several activities to strengthen the language arts' abilities of students from a wide variety of multicultural backgrounds. They are divided into different seasons of the school year.

OPENING OF SCHOOL ACTIVITIES

On the first day of school you can collect information about students' birthdays, as well as dates of celebrations that occur in their families and record them on the classroom calendar. In the week that precedes a special culturally based celebration or birthday of a student, you can ask that student to write about it and share that information with the class. In addition, based on the information you receive from the attitude and interest surveys in Chapter 2, you can place students in culturally homogeneous or heterogeneous groups to discuss a topic of interest. During the second week of school, students can invite their parents or other adults from their neighborhoods to school or interview them about a specific culturally relevant topic of each group's interest. During the third week, students can select a few adults to invite to school to describe their culturally diverse experiences with, and uses of, the language arts.

Regardless of the interest areas students list, your selection of a specific area within that broader interest can enlarge the value of the study by eliciting students' culturally and socially related questions about all topics. For example, Ms. Predo's students wanted to learn about occupations, and many of them came from Mexican American families whose members were involved in carpentry, roofing, masonry, house painting, architecture, and landscaping. Thus, Ms. Predo began the next week's language arts activities by asking students questions about family members' occupations that they would like to explore and whether students with similar questions would like to work together. She also asked them to describe ways in which they would like to share their findings and to name a day on which this could occur. Their decisions provided her with additional information concerning her self-efficacy and learning style preferences as well as how much time they preferred to invest in learning new information.

In the process of spending 4 or 5 days studying various areas of interest, students can engage in studying biographies from their culture who were successful in their interest area. You can make books about the following leaders available for students' selection: Hank Aaron, Seiji Ozawa, Lee Trevino, Bill Cosby, Jesse Owens, Leonard Bernstein, Michael Jordan, Woody Allen, Whitney Houston, Jim Thorpe, Arna Bontemps, Marguerite de Angeli, Natashema Mohl, Mabel Leigh Hunt, John Tunis, Dorothy Sterling, M. O'Moran, Eloise Jarvis McGraw, Elise Greenfield, Laura Armer, Scott O'Dell, Ann Nolan Clark, Virginia Sorensen, Ellis Credle, Jesse Stuart, Caesar Chavez, Dolores Huerta, and Gary Soto.

While students are working in interest groups for 3 to 8 days, you are collecting more information on an individual basis using the observation guides in Chapters 2 and 3 so that you can design personalized instruction. In the process, you can also ask students to share "tricks" that they have invented to help them become better readers and writers. Descriptions of these strategies are additional clues to the learning style preferences of individual students.

Immediately following this unit, you can ask students to discuss quotations or proverbs their family says to each other, such as "Two wrongs don't make a right" or "Early to bed, early to rise; makes a man healthy, wealthy, and wise." Depending on the language arts needs of your students, they can either copy their favorite from the board, discuss meanings behind their favorites, or select one to three sayings and create an original story that illustrates the single or combined message.

MID-YEAR ACTIVITIES

Students can create books to express their own ideas or feelings using one of the types described in Chapter 9. In their simplest form, multicultural and multilingual students can make **"I" books** in which they describe themselves, either by drawing four pictures on a page divided into four squares (as shown in Figure 13.7) or by writing the words they want with your or a classmate's assistance.

Second, according to the schedules presented in Chapter 2, Fridays should become special days for multicultural and multilingual students. Friday's schedule should set aside time to celebrate the special successes that each student has attained. One activity to accomplish this goal is Student of the Week day. Some Fridays can be reserved for a particular student's special day. Parents are notified ahead of time so you can secure items for the child's bulletin board, thus making a home-to-school connection. Also, on this Friday, all the students in the class write a note to the Student of the Week's parent(s). Have them describe something they appreciate about the child, something they do well, or something they did in class that was valuable to the class. You can proofread each, copy them in a publishable form, and send them home to the selected child's parent(s). On the following Friday, right before the next Student of the Week is announced, the outgoing student of the week can talk about him- or herself, read a portion of a favorite book to the class, tell important things they appreciated about how they were treated during the week, or discuss what is important to them about school and language arts.

Many multicultural and multilingual students also enjoy reading and writing with bilingual or older same-culture students and adult volunteers. Through such conversations, discovery discussions, play, scaffolding, and mentoring language arts abilities can increase. Books printed in Spanish and English for such instruction appear in Literature Card 38. A sample of how to create your own translations (such

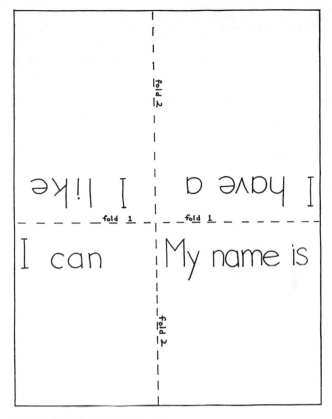

FIGURE 13.7 "I" BOOK PATTERN

as "Twinkle, Twinkle Little Star") appears in Figure 13.8. You can also explore several cultures by using the units depicted in Figure 13.9.

In summary, as the review of literature and activities in this section of the chapter demonstrate, considerable evidence exists that students from different cultural and social groups learn differently. Their approaches to language arts differ in cognition, personality, and perception. The knowledge gained from this chapter can help prevent you from inadvertently causing students to respond negatively to the language arts merely because their cultural values and background experiences conflict with or don't relate to the instruction you delivered. The knowledge in this chapter, however, provides relevant, stimulating, and unrestraining language arts experiences for your students.

RECOGNIZING AND REPORTING PROGRESS

Culturally Biased Tests

Earlier in the chapter the point was made that multicultural and multilingual students face difficulties when taking tests. You may want to take the culturally biased

Literature Card 38

CHILDREN'S LITERATURE PRINTED IN SPANISH AND ENGLISH

An ABC in English and Spanish by R. Tallon

Idalia's Project ABC—Proyecto ABC: An Urban Alphabet Book in English and Spanish by Idalia Rosario

Harry y el Terrible Quiensabeque (Harry and the Terrible Whatzit) by D. Gackenbach

Gato y Perro (Cat and Dog) by E. H. Minarik

Como Crecen los Perritos (How Puppies Grow) by M. E. Selsam

Fievel y el Nuevo Mundo (An American Tail) by Judy Freudberg

La Gallinita Roja (The Little Red Hen) by L. McQueen

Arroz con Leche (Popular Songs and Rhymes from Latin America) by L. Delacre

El Premio del Cuco (The Cuckoo's Reward) by Kouzel

El Pirata sin Cabeza (The Headless Pirate) and other books by Rohmer and Anchondo

Cuento de un Cocodrilo (A Crocodile's Tale) by Aruego and Aruego

Clifford el Gran Perro Colorado (Clifford the Big Red Dog) by N. Bridwell

El Sandwich Mas Grande, Jamas (The Biggest Sandwich Ever) by R. G. Gelman

Los Dinosaurios Gigantes (Giant Dinosaurs) by E. Rowe

Pollita Chiquita (Henny Penny) by Zimmerman

Donde Esta Wally? (Where's Waldo?) by Handford

La Historia de la Polliat (Little Chick's Story) by M. Kwitz

Mi Mama, la Cartera (My Mother, the Mail Carrier) by I. Maury

Los Espiritus de Mi Tia Otilia (My Aunt Otilia's Spirits) by R. Garcia

Ah! Belle Cite! (A Beautiful City ABC) by Poulin

Como Es la Tierra (What the Earth is Like) by Parker

El Espacia: Estrellas, Planetas y Naves Espaciales (Space, Stars, Planets and Space Ships) by Becklake

Como Ha Vivido la Humanidad (How Humanity Has Lived) by Anne Millard

Mitos, Heroes y Monstruos de la Espana Antigua (Myths, Heroes and Monsters of Ancient Spain) by Pollux Hernunes

De la Oruga a la Mariposa (From the Caterpillar to the Butterfly) by Paul Whalley

Pinatas and Paper Flowers: Holidays for the Americas in English and Spanish by Alma Flor (Spanish version by Lila Perl)

El Arbol (The Tree) by D. Burnie

Maravillas del Mundo (Wonders of the World) by Giovanni Caselli

El Rio y la Laguna (The River and the Pond) by Steve Parker

La Meteorlogia, el Tiempo y las Estaciones (Meteorology, Weather and the Seasons) by Pierre Kohler

El Pajaro y su Nino (The Bird and Its Child) by David Burnie

test in Table 13.3 on page 586 to experience how difficult it is to score well on a test of content outside of your cultural knowledge. Once you are finished, you can compare your answers to the Answer Key at the back of the book. As you take the test, notice your feelings and monitor your self-esteem. Similar feelings of frustration and futility are often experienced by students whose teachers' assessments are insensitive to their cultural and linguistic differences.

SECTION 3   TEACHERS AS CONTINUAL LEARNERS

Reaching the Underserved

In addition to the above activities, you can secure special resources that increase the learning of underserved populations, and use think pads, diary journals, and bibliotherapy to assist students from diverse cultures.

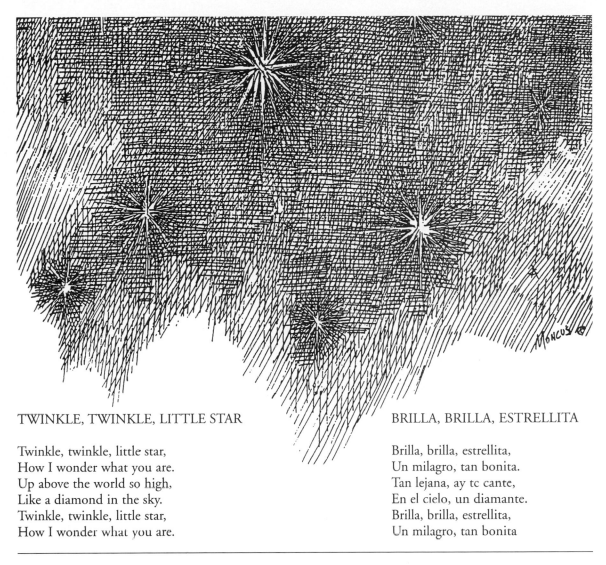

TWINKLE, TWINKLE, LITTLE STAR

Twinkle, twinkle, little star,
How I wonder what you are.
Up above the world so high,
Like a diamond in the sky.
Twinkle, twinkle, little star,
How I wonder what you are.

BRILLA, BRILLA, ESTRELLITA

Brilla, brilla, estrellita,
Un milagro, tan bonita.
Tan lejana, ay tc cante,
En el cielo, un diamante.
Brilla, brilla, estrellita,
Un milagro, tan bonita

FIGURE 13.8 SAMPLE TO TEACH STUDENTS TO READ SPANISH–ENGLISH BOOKS IN PAIRS

PROFESSIONAL DEVELOPMENT ACTIVITY

Securing Additional Resources

Subscribing to professional journals is an important way to upgrade your teaching abilities. Encouraging students to join book clubs helps them strengthen their reading abilities. The following are lists of professional journals to which you can subscribe and a list of children's book clubs. These book clubs charge reduced prices for paperback versions of children's literature. When students order books, you receive bonus points toward free books that are mailed to the school and can be placed in your classroom library.

INTRODUCTION

The world that we live in is filled with an array of people, cultures, and traditions. Although sometimes we may not take notice of the differences around us, it is important to understand and recognize the beauty of every group of people. The advantage of diversity in our lives is the unique perspectives and cultural awareness that it lends to each family, region, and personality. This unit can help us to understand the diversity that exists all around us and appreciate what each group has to give.

AFRICAN/AFRICAN AMERICAN

A Is for Africa by Ifeoma Onyefulu
Annie's Gifts by Angela Shelf Medearis
Aunt Harriet's Underground Railroad in the Sky by Faith Ringgold
Boundless Grace: Sequel to Amazing Grace by Mary Hoffman
Back Home by Gloria Jean Pinkney
Chicken Sunday by Patricia Polacco
The River That Gave Gifts by Margo Humphrey
Seven Candles for Kwanzaa by Andrea Davis Pinkney
The Story of Ruby Bridges by Robert Coles
Sweet Clara and the Freedom Quilt by Deborah Hopkinson
Two Mrs. Gibsons by Toyomi Igus
Where Are You Going Manyoni? by Catherine Stock
White Socks Only by Evelyn Coleman
Her Stories: African American Folktales, Fairy Tales, and True Tales by Virginia Hamilton
Hold Fast to Dreams by Andrea Davis Pinkey
The Friendship and the Gold Cadillac by Mildred D. Taylor
Kwanzaa: A Family Affair by Mildred Pitts Walter

OTHER ACTIVITIES

Naming ceremony activity
Write own folk tale
Music (for discussion, listening)
Tribes/language (for discussion)
Art—make own masks
Slavery, segregation, geography (discussion)

ASIAN/ASIAN AMERICAN

The Bracelet by Yoshida Uchida
Cleversticks by Bernard Ashley
Dumpling Soup by Jana Kim Rattigan
Grandfather's Journey by Allen Say
The Greedy Man in the Moon retold by Rick Rossiter
The Last Dragon by Susan Miho Nunes
The Lotus Seed by Sherry Garland
Luka's Quilt by Georgia Guback
Mama Bear by Chyng Feng Sun
Tree of Cranes by Allen Say
Yang the Third and Her Impossible Family by Lensey Namioka
Believers in America by Steven Izuki
Chinese New Year by Dianne M. MacMillan
Tiger in the Mountain Pass by Jinye Lorenz
Change by Jinye Lorenz
The Moon Lady by Amy Tan
The Abacus Contest by Priscilla Wu
Moontellers by Lynn Moroney
West Coast Chinese Boy by Sing Lim
The Best Older Sister by Sook Nyul Choi

OTHER ACTIVITIES

Asian poetry (write own poems)
Tai Chi (in class activity)
Kabuki Theater (video, in class discussion)
Oragami
Holidays/special occasions
Art—painting natural scenes
Food (in class)

FIGURE 13.9 MULTICULTURAL UNIT: CULTURE AND TRADITIONS

All sources taken from www.cofbooks.com/cof-4-6-b.html, www.gallaudet.edu/~ghware/nat.html, and www.hachai.com/.

HISPANIC/HISPANIC AMERICAN

Abuela's Weave by Omar S. Castaneda
Fiesta! by Ginger Foglesong Guy
Hooray, a Piñata! by Elisa Kleven
In My Family/En Mi Familia by Carmen Lomas Garza
Isla by Arthur Dorros
Jalapeño Bagels by Natasha Wing
Lights on the River by Jane Resh Thomas
The Little Painter of Sabana Grande by Patricia Maloney Markun
The Old Man and His Door by Gary Soto
Saturday Sancocho by Leyla Toffes
Too Many Tamales by Gary Soto
Latino Rainbow by Carlos Cumpión
The Ice Dove and Other Stories by Diane de Anda
Fitting In by Anil Bernardo
Maria by Theodore Taylor
Watch Out for Clever Women! told by Joe Hayes
Crazy Weekend by Virginia Hamilton
In Nueva York by Nicholasa Mohr
Felita by Nicholasa Mohr
Going Home by Nicholasa Mohr
Baseball in April and Other Stories by Gary Soto

OTHER ACTIVITIES

Traditions (in class discussion)
Family (discussion on importance)
Food (in class activity)
Art—piñatas
Language
Culture
Music

NATIVE AMERICAN

Brave as a Mountain Lion by Ann Herbert Scott
Brother Eagle by Sister Sky
Dragonfly's Tale by Kristina Rodanas
Dreamcatcher by Audrey Osofsky
Dreamplace by Geaorge Elta Lyon
The First Strawberries, a Cherokee Story retold by Joseph Bruchac
Giving Thanks: A Native American Good Morning Message by Chief Jake Swamp
Gluskabe and the Four Wishes by Joseph Bruchac
Mystery of Navajo Moon by Timothy Green
The Rough-Face Girl by Rafe Martin
Ten Little Rabbits by Virginia Grossman
Children of the Longhouse by Joseph Bruchac
Cloudwalker: Contemporary Native American Stories by Joel Monture
Iroquois Stories: Heroes and Heroines, Monsters and Magic by Joseph Bruchac
Less Than Half, More Than Whole by Kathleen and Michael Lacapa
We Are Mesquakie, We Are One by Hadley Irwin
Songs of Our Ancestors by Mark Turcotte
The Day of the Ogre Kachinas by Peggy D. Spence
Dog People by Joseph Bruchac
Turquoise Boy by Terri Cohlene
Songs from the Loom by Monty Roessel
Daughter of Suqua by Diana Johnston

OTHER ACTIVITIES

Creation stories (read and write own)
Culture
Traditions
Reservations (class discussion)
History/geography
Art—dreamcatcher, pottery
*Guest speaker

JEWISH/JEWISH AMERICAN

Danilel's Story by Carol Matas
The Grey Striped Shirt by Jaqueline Jules
Jewish Holidays in the Fall by Dianne M. MacMillan
The Story of Passover by Norma Simon
The Christmas Menorahs by Janice Cohn
We Celebrate Hanukkah by Susan Hughs
Nine Spoons by Marci Stillerman
The Lost and Found Wallet by Mayer Bendet
The Marvelous Mix-Up and Other Tales of Reb Sholem by Ruchama King Feuerman
One-of-a-Kind Yanky and Other Stories by Pia Wolcowitz
The Great Potato Plan by Joy Nelkin Weider
The Kingston Castle by Ruth Abrahamson
The Story Hour: Volumes 1 and 2 by David S. Pope
The Three Gifts and Other Stories by David S. Pope
Yitzy and G.O.L.E.M. by Shalom Cohen

OTHER ACTIVITIES

Religion (discussion in class)
Holidays
Journal activity
Holocaust
Art—create information cards on Jewish religion and special occasions
History
*Introduction to final project
Design a theme park that has culture-based "rides." Each ride has an explanation of the group represented and some aspect of their culture (much like a Disney World "park").

FIGURE 13.9 (CONTINUED)

TABLE 13.3 AN EXAMPLE OF A CULTURALLY BIASED INTELLIGENCE TEST

NAME _____

I. Completion
Fill in the blank space with the correct word or words.

    1. Wow! Did you see Bob Gibson _____ the ball?
    a) throw   b) toss   c) chuck

II. True or False
Mark *T* or *F* after each sentence.

    2. A hog is a hustler. _____

    3. A chine is an automobile. _____

    4. A capping dude is a fellow who never complains and is very easy-going. _____

    5. A prat is some sort of a con game. _____

III. Multiple Choice

    6. When a person speaks of *Hat'n up* he means
    a) clothing   b) idea   c) moving on

    7. The best definition of *roul* is
    a) something loud and emotional
    b) transposing the effects of pain and sorrow into something beautiful
    c) the spiritual as opposed to the secular

    8. If a person says he is going to *Pull his coat off to it,* he means
    a) that he wants to start a fight
    b) he wants to have respect
    c) explain something thoroughly

    9. If a person says she's going to *Lay her purse upside yo' head,* she means
    a) she is going to clobber you
    b) she is going to give you some money
    c) she is going to let you see for yourself that she has no money

    10. If a person is going to get his *fro blown dry,* you know he doesn't have
    a) a car   b) a thirst   c) a conk

Source: Adapted from *Black Language,* by R. H. Bentley and S. D. Crawford, 2000. Unpublished manuscript; and from *Turning on Learning: Five Approaches for Multicultural Teaching Plans for Race, Class, Gender and Disability,* by B. H. Suzuki, 2000. Unpublished manuscript.

PROFESSIONAL JOURNALS

1. Journals for New Teachers

   New Teacher Advocate
   Kappa Delta Pi
   P.O. Box A
   West Lafayette, IN 47906-0576
   (a journal devoted to literacy and
   content area discipline issues that
   face first-year teachers)

2. Journals for Elementary Teachers

   The Reading Teacher
   International Reading Association
   800 Barksdale Road
   P.O. Box 8139
   Newark, DE 19711

   Language Arts
   National Council of Teachers
   of English
   1111 Kenyon Road
   Urbana, IL 61801

   Booklist
   c/o American Library Association
   50 East Huron Street
   Chicago, IL 60611

   CBC Features
   c/o The Children's Book Council
   67 Irving Place
   New York, NY 10003

   Journal of Youth Services in Libraries
   c/o American Library Association
   50 East Huron Street
   Chicago, IL 60611

   The Horn Book Magazine
   Park Square Building
   31 St. James Avenue
   Boston, MA 02116

   The New Advocate
   Christopher-Gordon Publishers, Inc.
   P.O. Box 809
   Needham Heights, MA 02194-0006

   Primary Voices K–6
   National Council of Teachers
   of English
   1111 Kenyon Road
   Urbana, IL 61801

3. Journals for Middle School,
   Secondary School, and Adult
   School Teachers

   Journal of Reading
   International Reading Association
   800 Barksdale Road
   P.O. Box 8139
   Newark, DE 19711

   School Library Journal
   P.O. Box 1978
   Marion, OH 43305-1978

   The ALAN Review
   c/o National Council of Teachers
   of English
   1111 Kenyon Road
   Urbana, IL 61801

   The Bulletin
   c/o National Council of Teachers
   of English
   1111 Kenyon Road
   Urbana, IL 61801

4. Journals for Language Arts Teachers
   of All Levels

   *Exploring the United States through
   Literature*
   Oryx Press
   4041 North Central Avenue,
   Suite 700
   Phoenix, AZ 85012-3397
   (7-volume series of resources for
   teachers and librarians that provide
   sources of literature and authors
   for the region in which students
   live)

   Teaching Exceptional Children
   The Council for Exceptional
   Children
   1920 Association Drive
   Reston, VA 22091

   *RASE: Remedial and Special
   Education*
   5341 Industrial Oaks Boulevard
   Austin, TX 78735

Learning Disability Quarterly
c/o The Council for Learning
Disabilities

P.O. Box 40303
Overland Park, KS 66204

CHILDREN'S BOOK CLUBS

Scholastic Book Clubs
P.O. Box 7500
Jefferson City, MO 65102-9981
800-724-2424
(Scholastic has five clubs: Firefly
[pre-K], See Saw [K–1], Lucky
[2–3], Arrow [4–6], and Tab [7–9
and up].)

Troll Book Clubs
2 Lethbridge Plaza
Mahwah, NJ 07430
800-541-1097

(Troll has five clubs: Troll Pre-K/K
[preschool–K], Troll 1 [K–1],
Troll 2 [2–3], Troll 3 [4–6], and
Troll 4 High Tops [6–9].)

Trumpet Book Clubs
P.O. Box 605
Homes, PA 19043-9865
800-826-0110
(Trumpet has three clubs: Early
Years [preK–K], Primary Years
[1–3], and Middle Years [4–6].)

PACIFIC AND MULTICULTURAL LITERATURE INTERNET RESOURCES*

Guam and Micronesian Literature

Legends of Guam Part 1—read several of Guam's most well-known legends, ns.gov.gu/legends.html

Legends of Guam Part 2—more Guam legends, guam.org.gu/hemplo

Multicultural Sites

Multicultural Pavilion—Excellent source on multicultural education, with multicultural literature links at Multicultural Paths-Other Sites, curry.edschool. virginia.edu/go/multicultural

Kay Vandergrift's Children's Literature Page—Another strong resource on children's literature. Includes a section on gender and culture, with links to websites, www.scils.rutgers.edu/special/kay/culture.html

Tales of Wonder: Folk and Fairytales from around the World—Online full text versions of folk and fairy tales, members.xoom.com/darsie/tales/index.html

At Home with Multicultural Adolescent Literature—borg.lib.vt.edu/ejournals/ ALAN/fall95/Ericson.html

Dietrich, D. & Ralph, K. S. Crossing borders: Multicultural literature in the classroom. *Journal of Education Issues of Language Minority Students, 15,* Winter 1995. Boise State University, www.nebe.gwv.edu/miscpubs/jeilms/vol15/crossing.htm

---

*These websites were recommended in "Exploring Literacy on the Internet," by B. Dalton, 2000, *The Reading Teacher, 53*(8), p. 691.

Walk a Mile in My Shoes—Multicultural Curriculum Resources, http://www.wmht.org/trail/explor02.htm

Asian Pacific Island Resources, www-bcf.usc.edu/~cmmr/Asian.html

Clearinghouse for Multicultural Bilingual Education. Picture books/Young reader-Asian Pacific, www.weber.edu/MBE/Htmls/MBE-Books-PBYR-Asian.html

Folk and Fairy Tale website links by D. K. Ashelman. A collection of electronic texts, as well as links to other folklore websites, www.pitt.edu/~dash/folklinks.html

General Literature Sites

David K. Brown's CLWG: Children's Literature Web Guide. Extensive literature resources, www.acs.ucalgary.ca/~dkbrown

Carol Hurst's Children's Literature website. Extensive literature resources, www.carolhurst.com

Guam and Micronesia Websites

Government of Guam Home Page—an excellent starting place to learn about Guam, www.gov.gu

Official page of the Federated States of Micronesia, with links to Yap, Pohnpei, Kosrae, and Chuuk, www.visit-fsm.org

Republic of the Marshall Islands—official government page, www.rmiembassyus.org

Bikini Atoll, Marshall Islands—a very interesting site about this island, www.bikiniatoll.com

Republic of Palau—welcome page, www.visit-Palau.com

Guam Council of the International Reading Association, www.read.guam.org

Pacific Websites

Michael's Pacific Sites—my favorite source for Pacific sites, www2.hawaii.edu/~ogden/piir

Pacific Resources for Education and Learning (PREL)—educational issues in the Pacific and related resource links, w3.prel.hawaii.edu

Pac-Lit website, www.uog.edu/coe/paclit/index.html

FOR YOUR JOURNAL

Think Pads and Diaries

Keeping journals is one of the most valuable ways for recording reflections. **Think pad journals,** or diaries, provide a place where students can release emotions calmly and write about feelings before they take action. Students can also write about a personal dilemma and compare how writing down their thoughts (with the aid of a think pad journal) increased their ability to solve problems. As demonstrated by

Literature Card 39

LITERATURE THAT DESCRIBES THE DIFFICULTIES AND JOYS IN EVERYDAY LIFE

The numbers in the parentheses are the age levels for which each book is recommended.

Story Hour—-Starring Megan! by Julie Brillhart (4–7), 1992 Morton Grove, IL: Whitman

No Nap by Eve Bunting (2–6), 1989 New York: Clarion Books

Bingo Brown's Guide to Romance by Betsy Byars (10–13), 1992 New York: Puffin Books

Wanted . . . Mud Blossom by Betsy Byars (8–12), 1991 Bodley Head

The Snow Speaks by Nancy White Carlstrom (6–10), 1992 Boston: Little, Brown

Mr. Jordan in the Park by Laura Jane Coats (4–8)

Texas Star by Barbara Hancock Cole (4–7), 1990 New York: Orchard Books

White Snow, Blue Feather by Julie Downing (2–6), 1989 New York: Bradbury Books

Monsters by Russell Hoban (6–9), 1989 New York: Scholastic

Crane's Rebound by Alison Jackson (8 and up), 1993 New York: Pocket Books

Do Like Kyla by Angela Johnson (4–7), 1994 New York: Scholastic

How Pizza Came to Queens by Dayal Kaur Khalsa (6–9), 1996 New York: C. Potter

Frannie's Fruits by Leslie Kimmelman (5–7), 1989 New York: Scholastic

Amy Elizabeth Explores Bloomingdale's by E. L. Konigsburg (4–8), 1989 New York: Atheneum

Snow Day by Betsy Maestro (4–8), 1989 New York: Scholastic

Newfound by Jim Wayne Miller (12 and up), 1989 New York: Orchard Books

Josie Smith by Magdalen Nabb (6–8), 1995 London: Collins Childrens

The Winter Room by Gary Paulsen (11 and up), 1996 New York: Bantam Doubleday Dell Books for Young Readers

The Wise Woman and Her Secret by Eve Merriam (6–10), 1991 New York: Simon & Schuster

Appalachia: The Voices of Sleeping Birds by Cynthia Rylant (5 and up), 1993 New York: Trumpet Club

Dear Dad, Love Laurie by Susan Beth Pfeffer (8–12), 1989 New York: Scholastic

The Leaving, and Other Stories by Budge Wilson (11 and up), 1993, 1990 New York: Scholastic

Just Like Max by Karen Ackerman (4–8), 1990 New Jersey: Knopf by Random House

Song and Dance Man by Karen Ackerman (all ages), 1989 New York: Scholastic

A Visit with Great-Grandma by Sharon Hart Addy (4–8), 1989 Whitman

One Sister Too Many by C. S. Adler (10–12), 1991 New York: Aladdin

Stina by Lena Anderson (4–8), 1990 New York: Greenwillow

Stina's Visit by Lena Anderson (4–8), 1991 New York: Greenwillow

Mom Is Dating Weird Wayne by Mary Jane Auch (8–12), 1991 New York: Bantam Skylark

Willie's Not the Hugging Kind by Joyce Durham Barrett (5–8), 1991 New York: HarperCollins

The Outside Child by Nina Bawden (9–12), 1994 New York: Puffin Books

The Perfect Spot by Robert J. Blake (4 and up), 1992 New York: Philomel Books

The Grandpa Days by Joan W. Blos (3–7), 1989 New York: Simon & Schuster

The Wooden Doll by Susan Bonners (5–8), 1991 New York: Lee & Shepard Books

Allison and Meisong in Chapter 2, when students share children's literature or their own writing in an author's chair, classmates' listening and vocabulary abilities can increase, especially when you begin these sessions by making comments such as the following: "Allison is going to read a book she really likes. During her reading, our job is to use our think pads to listen so well that we can see how many of the author's words we can write and learn. Next, we'll discuss what we really liked in the book and the connections it made to our lives."

CONNECTING CLASSROOMS, PARENTS, AND COMMUNITIES

Bibliotherapy

Bibliotherapy is the use of books to influence a student's total development; a process of interaction between the reader and literature used for personality assessment, problem solving, adjustment, and growth. Bibliotherapy includes reading materials that can have a therapeutic effect on mental or physical ills of a reader. Bibliotherapy also helps students gain greater insight into their problems, focus attention outside themselves, and realize that they are not alone in having a problem. It helps students share their problems with others; gives students new insights into alternative solutions; and shows how others encounter anxieties, frustrations, hopes, disappointments, failures, and successes.

Bibliotherapy can be used in conjunction with journal writing to prevent difficult situations from becoming big problems. To combine bibliotherapy and journal writing, the following guidelines will be helpful. Plan carefully before implementing a bibliotherapy activity for the class or an individual student. Before introducing the topic, explain the benefits of bibliotherapy to the class as well as how it is implemented during the journal-writing time of the day. Select five books about different topics and mark passages from each that you can read aloud to stimulate discussion. Then you can lead students through a series of questions that (1) draw them into the main character's situation; (2) direct them to examine the actions the character took to overcome the problem; and (3) apply the story to problems that occur in their daily lives.

After bibliotherapy has been defined, students spend the first journal-writing session writing about difficult situations they face. You can either read the journals and help students use bibliotherapy to overcome one of these situations or establish a bibliotherapy unit in which students spend several days reading books in which fictional and nonfictional characters face one or more of the difficulties students face. When each book is finished, students write in their journals the feelings and insights the book helped them apply to their own lives. You can also involve parents in the bibliotherapy process, if you desire, by allowing students to select two or three books they wish to take home and discuss with their parents.

Sudden behavior changes could signal that a problem exists outside of the classroom. In such cases, you can engage a student in the bibliotherapeutic process by selecting a book together. I recommend providing at least two books about the area of interest from which the student can choose. You may also wish to establish a permanent bibliotherapy section in your classroom library (Coleman, 1992). Such a section can enable students to discover books that deal with problems they face. Another advantage of a bibliotherapy section is that several students can choose to read different books on the same problem and meet in response groups to evaluate how successfully the people in each book resolved the problem. In this system, students can also use journals to record the groups' discussions. A recorder for the group writes a summary of their evaluations, places it on one of the bookmarkers described in Chapter 9 and then inserts it in the book for classmates' future reference. In addition, it is valuable for you to read a book and write a response in your journal. In this way you can provide a model when you introduce bibliotherapy to your students. Again, books to use for bibliotherapy are listed throughout this book.

DEVELOPING TECHNOLOGICAL COMPETENCIES

Online Computer Coaches

Several universities and computer scientists are developing intelligent coaches on computers (Lesgoald, 2000; Molnar, 1999; Cognition and Technology Group at Vanderbilt, 2000). These coaches provide methods experts use to solve a problem after a student selects an incorrect solution to that problem. Once a student clicks on a particular element in the problem, a menu appears. Clicking on one of the questions in the menu produces an answer to that question. Alternatively, the computer coach will tell students what to do next if they have not selected a question they want answered. An example of these coaching tools appears in Figure 13.10.

SUMMARY

Many multicultural and multilingual students do not reach their potential without your planned interventions and cultural sensitivity. Failure to master English can result in decreased participation in their communities and will likely reduce their life choices. This chapter has examined the cultural characteristics of various types of students. Educators agree that these students process information differently, in ways that in many cases are in direct opposition to previous classroom structures in

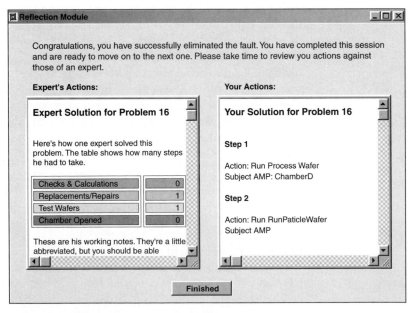

FIGURE 13.10 NEW ADVANCEMENTS IN COMPUTER TECHNOLOGY

From *Using Expert Tutors as Computer Coaches,* by A. Lesgold, 1999 April. Paper presented at the annual meeting of the American Educational Research Association, Ontario, Canada. Used by permission.

which they were asked to speak, read, and write. As you have learned, teaching higher levels of thinking is among the most important tasks in education. Reinforcing cultural strengths often allows students the freedom to alter their preconceived notions about themselves, as well as others' cultures. Several activities to enhance higher-level thinking and multicultural understanding are "I" books, thinking pads, and bibliotherapy. In the next chapter, you will learn how to select assessments that are the best indicators that students are achieving at their highest levels of competence.

HOW TO DO IT: USING WHAT YOU'VE LEARNED

The following provide opportunities to reflect on and practice what you have learned.

ASSESSING YOUR LEARNING

1. African American students tend to make more episodic than topic-centered responses during language arts conversations. They also talk about topics out of the sequence in which they were introduced. Being aware of the value these personally embellished statements hold for students, how will you respond to their extraneous comments?

2. You can keep a journal of your teaching behaviors for a specific type of culturally or linguistically different student or group of students for 2 weeks. In your entries, focus on what you do, when you do it, and how you "teach the whole student." At the end of the period, analyze your entries to determine how your instructional behaviors represent the descriptions reflected in this chapter and are responsive to these students' special needs. How can you modify your teaching style to correct any insensitivities or ineffective methods employed?

3. You can have your students read several different ethnic groups' accounts of an event or incident. After they do, have them give reasons for their interpretations and explore how their own ethnic identities, cultural backgrounds, and personal characteristics contributed to their reasoning.

4. If you are teaching, select one activity from each dimension of thinking and teach it to your students. Ask them to assess what they've learned as you also analyze their strengths. If you are not teaching, prepare one lesson from a dimension of thinking by reading the literature that accompanies it and write lessons for the grade level you prefer to teach.

KEY TERMS EXERCISE

Below are the concepts introduced in this chapter. If you have learned the definition of a term, place a checkmark in the blank that precedes that term. If you are not sure of a definition, increase your retention and return to reread its definition. If you have learned 10 of the terms in this chapter, you have constructed an understanding of a majority of the most important concepts that you need to increase your students' higher-level thinking and multicultural sensitivity.

_____ additive approach   (p. 551)

_____ autobiographies   (p. 577)

_____ bibliotherapy   (p. 591)

_____ biographies   (p. 577)

_____ cultural discontinuity   (p. 550)

_____ culture   (p. 550)

_____ contributions approach (p. 551)

_____ "I" books   (p. 580)

_____ judge credibility   (p. 566)

_____ social issues approach   (p. 551)

_____ sociocultural   (p. 550)

_____ socioeconomic   (p. 550)

_____ think pad journals   (p. 589)

_____ transformation approach (p. 551)

_____ Weighted Characteristics Test (p. 568)

FOR FUTURE REFERENCE

Books about Higher-Level Thinking and Multicultural Understanding

The following references can increase your students', their parents', and your knowledge about specific cultures.

Southeast Asian Refugee Youth: An Annotated Bibliography
Southeast Asian Refugee Studies Project
Center for Urban and Regional Affairs
University of Minnesota
Minneapolis, MN

Los Angeles County Public Ethnic Resource Centers: The American Indian, Asian Pacific, African American, Chicano
Los Angeles County Public Library. ERIC ED 298 962.

Vietnamese Culture Kit by Thanhliem Nguyen
Iowa State University of Science and Technology
Research Institute for Studies in Education. ERIC ED 149 602. Ames, IA.

A Manual for Teachers of Indochinese Students
Intercultural Development Research Association
San Antonio, TX. ERIC ED 205 663

Some Hints to Work with Vietnamese Students
Arizona State Department of Education
Phoenix, AZ. ERIC ED 133 383

Teaching Multicultural Literature in Grades K–8
Edited by Violet J. Harris
Christopher Gordon, Norwood, MA

Multicultural Review (A journal with reviews of multicultural children's literature "dedicated to a better understanding of ethnic, racial and religious diversity")
Greenwood Publishing Group
88 Post Road West
P.O. Box 5007
Westport, CT 06881-5007

Multicultural Publishers Exchange
   (Publisher of books by and about people of color)
   Box 9869
   Madison, WI 53715
   1-800-558-2110

Hispanic Books Distributor
   1665 W. Grant Road
   Tucson, AZ 85745
   (Selections are evaluated according to subject matter, literary quality, and format, with publications ranging from preschoolers to middle school readers, as well as resource books. Also has a *Hispanic Books Bulletin* to which you can subscribe.)

The Kiosk
   19223 DeHavilland Dr.
   Saratoga, CA 95070
   (408) 996-0667
   (Publishes games, posters, diplomas, bookmarks, and stationery in several languages)

Mariuccia Ioconi Book Imports
   1110 Mariposa
   San Francisco, CA 94107
   (415) 285-7393
   (Publishes Spanish-language records and books for children, including a "big book" series)

Santillana Publishing Company
   901 W. Walnut Street
   Compton, CA 90220
   1-800-245-8584

World Wide Games
   Exceptional handcrafted games
   Colchester, CT 06415
   (A selection of authentic games from around the world)

National Association for Bilingual Education (NABE)
   1220 L Street NW, Suite 605
   Washington, DC 20005

National Association for Multicultural Education (NAME)
   261 Bluemont Hall
   Kansas State University
   Manhattan, KS 66505

Center for Applied Linguistics
   Publication Program
   1611 North Kent Street
   Arlington, VA 22209

Center for Southeast Asia
   260 Stephens Hall
   University of California at Berkeley
   Berkeley, CA 94270

Indochinese Materials Center
    U.S. Department of Education, Region VII
    601 East 12th Street
    Kansas City, MO 64106

JACP, Inc.
    414 East Third Street
    San Mateo, CA 94401

Southeast Asian Learning Project
    Long Beach Unified School District
    701 Locust Avenue
    Long Beach, CA 90813

Teachers of English to Speakers of Other Languages
    School of Languages and Linguistics
    Georgetown University
    Washington, DC 20009

African Imprints Library Services
    410 West Falmouth Highway
    Box 350
    West Falmouth, MA 02574
    (Provides recent children's books available from twenty African nations)

Farrar, Straus, and Giroux
    19 Union Square West
    New York, NY 10003
    (Specializes in Swedish literature)

Kane/Miller Book Publishers
    P.O. Box 529
    Brooklyn, NY 11231-0005
    ("Cranky Nell" imprint)

Lerner Publications Company/Carolrhoda Books
    241 First Avenue North
    Minneapolis, MN 55401

Picture Book Studio
    P.O. Box 9139
    10 Central Street
    Saxonville, MA 01701

Tundra Books of Northern New York
    Box 1030
    Plattsburgh, NY 12901
    (Specializes in Canadian, French/English bilingual books for children)

Wellington Publishing Company
    P.O. Box 14877
    Chicago, IL 60614

Aims International Books, Inc.
  3216 Montana Avenue
  P.O. Box 11496
  Cincinnati, OH 45211
  (Spanish books)

Bilingual Publications Co.
  1966 Broadway
  New York, NY 10023
  (Spanish books)

Hispanic Book Distributors, Inc.
  1665 West Grant Road
  Tucson, AZ 85745

Iaconi Book Imports
  300 Pennsylvania Avenue
  San Francisco, CA 94107
  (Spanish books)

Lectorum Publications, Inc.
  137 West 14th Street,
  New York, NY 10011
  (Spanish books)

Hispanic Literature

Mohl, N. (1973). *Nilda.* New York: Harper. [Paperback reprints of all of Mohl's books are available through Arte Publico, in Houston, TX.]

Mohl, N. (1975). *El Bronx remembered.* New York: Harper.

Mohl, N. (1977). *In Nueva York.* New York: Dial.

Mohl, N. (1979). *Felita.* New York: Dial.

Mohl, N. (1985). *Rituals of survival: A woman's portfolio.* Houston, TX: Arte Publico.

Mohl, N. (1986). *Going home.* New York: Dial.

Multicultural Children's Literature

American Indian stories. (1991). New York: Raintree.

Anderson, D. (1988). *The Spanish armada.* New York: Hampstead.

Anno, M. (1975). *Anno's counting book.* New York: Crowell.

Aoki, E. M. (1981). "Are you Chinese? Are you Japanese? Or are you just a mixed-up kid?" Using Asian American children's literature. *The Reading Teacher, 34,* 382–385.

Banchek, L. (1978). *Snake in, snake out.* New York: Crowell.

Bell-Villada, G. H. (1990). *Garcia Marquez: The man and his work.* Chapel Hill, NC: University of North Carolina Press.

Beller, J. (1984). *A-B-C-ing: An action alphabet.* New York: Crown.

Burningham, J. (1969). *Seasons.* Indianapolis: Dobbs-Merrill. (See also *Sniff, Shout,* and other books about sounds by the author.)

Buttlar, L., & Lubomyr, W. (1977). *Building ethnic collections: An annotated guide for school media centers and public libraries.* Littleton, CO: Libraries Unlimited.

Cannon, A. E. (1990). *The shadow brothers.* New York: Delacorte.

Carlson, R. K. (1972). *Emerging humanity: Multiethnic literature for children and adolescents.* Dubuque, IA: Wm. C. Brown.

China and *Japan.* (1991). New York: Raintree.

Cofer, J. O. (1990). *Silent dancing: A partial remembrance of a Puerto Rican childhood.* Houston, TX: Arte Publico Press.

Carle, E. (1974). *My very first book of colors.* New York: Crowell. (See other concept books by same author.)

Conatty, M. (1987). *The armada.* New York: Warwick.

Cox, J., & Wallis, B. S. (1982). Books for the Cajun child: Lagniappe or a little something extra for multicultural teaching. *The Reading Teacher, 36,* 263–266.

Books in Spanish for Young Readers

Aula: Enciclopedia del estudiante (Aula: Students' encyclopedia). (1988). Translated by Javier Gomez. Barcelona: Editorial Planeta-De Agostini. ISBN 84-395-0802-6. 10 volumes. Grades 5–9. The purpose of this series is to interest young readers in the world in which they live. All titles include many illustrations and brief, easy-to-read descriptions. (Grades 5–8).

Becklake, Sue. (2000). *El espacia: Estrellas, planetas y naves espaciales (Space: stars, planets and space ships).* London: Dorling, Kindersley. ISBN 84-7655-560-1.

Caselli, Giovanni. (1992). *Maravillas del mundo (Wonders of the world).* Barcelona: Plaza Joven-Circulo. ISBN 84-7655-559-8.

Millard, Anne. (1992). *Como ha vivido la humanidad (How has humanity lived).* Barcelona: Plaza Joven-Circulo. ISBN 84-7655-639-X.

Parker, Steve. (2000). *Como es la tierra (How is the earth).* Translated by Fernando Cano. San Francisco: Scholastic. ISBN 84-7655-638-1. This series of books introduces young readers to astronomy, space and space exploration, the history of man and civilization, life in the oceans and seas, the effect of seasons on the earth, and volcanoes and mountains. Grades 4–7.

    Elcielo (The sky). (2000). New York: Scholastic. ISBN 84-7417-086-9.

    En el aire y en el espacia (In the air and in space). (2000). New York: Scholastic. ISBN 84-7417-084-2.

    Los hombres y lan civilizacion (Men and civilization). (2000). New York: Scholastic. ISBN 84-7417-091-5.

    Los mare y los oceanos (Seas and oceans). (2000). New York: Scholastic. ISBN 84-7417-087-7.

    Los paisajes y las estaciones (Landscapes and seasons). (1988). Madrid: Javier Vergara. ISBN 84-7417-085-1.

    Los volcanes y las montanas (Volcanoes and mountains). (1989). Madrid: Javier Vergara. ISBN 84-7417-089-3.

Hernunes, Pollux. (1989). *Mitos, heroes y monstruos de la Espana antigua (Myths, heroes and monsters of ancient Spain).* Madrid: Anaya. ISBN 84-7525-496-9. Grades 8 & up.

Kohler, Pierre. (1988). *La meteorologia, el tiempo y las estraciones (Meteorology, weather and the seasons).* Translated by Matia Puncel. Madrid: Edicones SM. ISBN 84-348-2572-4. Grades 5–9. This series of books introduces young readers to trees, birds, rivers and ponds, and butterflies. It contains close-up photographs, charts and drawings in color, and brief, clear descriptions. Grades 4–8.

Burnie, David. (1992). *El arbol (Tree).* Madrid: Santillana, Altea. ISBN 84-372-3708-4.

Burnie, David. (1992). *El pajaro y su nido (Bird).* Madrid: Altea. ISBN 84-372-2710-6.

Parker, Steve. (1992). *El rio y la laguna (Pond and river).* Madrid: Santillana, Altea. ISBN 84-372-2707-6.

Whalley, Paul. (1992). *De la oruga a la mariposa (Butterfly).* Madrid: Santillana, Altea. ISBN 84-372-2709-6.

Debates are an effective language arts activity that can be used for performance assessment.

CHAPTER 14

ASSESSMENT AND GRADING OPTIONS IN THE LANGUAGE ARTS PROGRAM

Mr. Markham completed his evaluation of the cumulative language arts program of Juan, Michael, Allison, and Meisong from preschool through eighth grade. In the process he realized that few of their assessments included self-evaluations, and throughout the years students had rarely recorded the reasons for their answers. He vowed to serve on the Portfolio Assessment Committee for his school district in the coming school year to correct this deficit in their language arts assessment processes.

Other problems also existed. The school board was demanding more frequent testing of students. Unfortunately, the only type of assessments they were familiar with were standardized achievement tests. School board members wanted to evaluate how well students were doing in reading and writing before third grade. Teachers disagreed. Mr. Markham wanted to educate the school board and parents about performance-based assessments.

Teachers in Mr. Markham's district also wanted to build more assessments into the instructional process, to include students in their parent-teacher conferences, and to demonstrate how much students' self-initiated use of the language arts had increased. These measures, coupled with a new narrative report card, would strengthen their ability to document the goals of their language arts program and the progress of individual students. Mr. Markham was certain that such a diversified and authentically based assessment program would ensure that no student could "slip through the cracks" in their school district. It would also enable teachers and administrators to describe to leaders more completely all dimensions of growth that students were attaining through the language arts curriculum.

We are at a crossroads in language arts assessments. The forms and products of student communication are being critiqued in unprecedented ways by a wide range of concerned people—psychometricians (e.g., Linn, Baker, & Dunbar, 1991; Shephard,

1991; Tierney, 1998), policy makers (e.g., Darling-Hammond, 1991; Smith, 1991), test publishers (e.g., Kean, 1992), language arts researchers (e.g., Calfee & Heibert, 1991; Valencia & Pearson, 1987), and classroom teachers (e.g., Howard, 1990). Standardized tests are limited in their ability to provide information on which to base decisions about individual student instruction and diagnoses (Wixon, Valencia, & Lipson, 1994). We are also "only beginning to realize the significance of perspectivism, of the rejection of objectivism, of fixed authorities, of standards residing in some higher realm—standards that apply to everyone and everything" on measurement errors and test anxiety for students (Dyson & Genishi, 1994, p. 12).

At the same time, there is enthusiasm for alternative assessment options such as portfolios; embedded assessments; self-assessments; benchmarks; observations; interviews; and networkable, interactive, technology-driven assessments. Such alternative forms of assessment have also been called (a) *authentic assessments* because they evaluate students in the process of performing language tasks that they do outside the classroom (Wiggings, 1989); (b) *performance assessments* because the evaluation occurs while students are engaged in the act of completing a communication (Stiggins & Bridgeford, 1985), or (c) *dynamic assessments* in that tests call on an interactive application of several communication and thinking processes simultaneously. These are designed to document students' communication history and to ensure that they participate in establishing their future goals. Unless assessment provides these vantage points, students have only their present performance as the single gauge of their competence.

There have been recent calls to reform the general purposes, policies, and procedures of standardized testing in the language arts (Gomez, Graue, & Bloch, 1991; Madaus & O'Dwyer, 1999). This new era rests on recent research reported in this section of the chapter. When you have finished this chapter, you can set your assessment guidelines, use new knowledge about assessment issues and tools in your instructional program, and develop documents that provide complete literacy descriptions for all students. By the end of the chapter you also will have answers to the following questions relative to IRA, NCTE, NAEYC, TEKS, and other statewide and province-based standards for professional development:

1. How are language arts assessments and grading practices changing? Why are they changing?
2. What are the best evaluation instruments to measure your students' success in reading, writing, grammar, spelling, speaking, listening, and thinking in an integrative, student-centered manner?
3. How do portfolios, anecdotal records, checklists, rating scales, student self-assessments, conferences, interviews, and group evaluations document students' learning products, and language and thinking processes?
4. What are the best methods to grade language arts products and processes?
5. What types of weekly language arts assessments are available?

•●•

SECTION 1 THEORETICAL FOUNDATIONS

Students' Assessment Needs

Language arts assessments can be made through several measurement tools, weekly assessments, assigned grades, and annual language arts program evaluations. It may take a full year of experimenting with the evaluation systems in this chapter before you discover the best adaptations for your students. Your pioneering experimentation will be worth the effort, as three teachers in Paradise's (1991) study reported. Through developing a new assessment program, these teachers grew to know their students better and helped them reach higher communication goals than they had ever reached before.

Many school districts are developing assessments to replace paper-and-pencil language arts tests. These districts are constructing computer-based tests, videotaped evaluations, student-selected samples of in-class products, conference records, and students' self-assessments for judging the quality of their language abilities (Valeri-Gold, Olson, & Deming, 1991–1992).

In some districts, site-based managers may also ask you to assess students with a **standardized test,** a test whose results are tabulated from criteria designed to compare students' performances one to the other. Standardized tests differ from tests you make because they compare large groups of students. They are either norm-referenced or criterion-referenced. Standardized tests are usually machine scorable instruments with scores reported in **norms,** which are average performances as well as degrees of deviation above and below the average of a nationally based population sample, and **percentiles,** which indicate how one student scores in relation to 90 other students. For example, a student who scored in the 97th percentile scored higher than 96 percent of the students in the normative sample population on which the test was field-tested.

Standardized tests also report **stanines,** which are scores that range from 1 to 9 so that one-tenth of students' scores represent one stanine. Stanine 1 designates the lowest 10 percent of student scores; stanine 9 represents the highest 10 percent of student scores. Standardized test scores are also reported in **grade equivalencies,** which indicate whether the performance of a student is equal to the average score of students in a specific grade. For example, if a fifth-grade student scores an 8.5 grade equivalency on a word recognition test, it means that this student scored as many words correctly as the average student in the fifth month of the eighth grade. It does not mean that this student should be in the eighth grade. Some of the most widely used standardized tests appear in Table 14.1.

Criterion-referenced tests, on the other hand, are scored by totaling the number of items scored correctly. A score of 80 percent means that a student mastered 80 percent of the instructional objectives assessed by that testing instrument. The student is not compared to anyone else, and in most schools all students are expected to reach a level of 75 to 80 percent proficiency on such tests. Reaching this level is judged as achieving satisfactory progress in the objectives measured.

TABLE 14.1 STANDARDIZED TESTS TO ASSESS THE LANGUAGE ARTS

TEST	APPROPRIATE LEVELS	SUBTEST SCORES
ORAL READING		
Gray Oral Reading Test, Revised	Grades 1–12	Oral reading quotient, passage score, comprehension score
Slosson Oral Reading Test, Revised	Grades 1–8 and high school	Reading level
DIAGNOSTIC READING		
Diagnostic Reading Scales	Grades 1–6	Independent instruction, frustration levels, eight phonic tests
Durrell Analysis of Reading Difficulty	Grades 1–6	Oral reading, silent reading, listening, flash words, word analysis, spelling, handwriting, visual memory, hearing sounds
Formal Reading Inventory	Grades 1–12	Standard scores, percentile ranks
Test of Early Reading Ability, 2nd ed.	Ages 3.0 to 9.11	Total score
Tests of Language Development, 2nd ed.	Ages 4.0 to 12.11	Twelve tests of oral language concepts
Test of Written Language, 2nd ed.	Ages 7.0 to 17.11	Nine subtests of written language concepts
INTELLIGENCE		
Peabody Picture Vocabulary Test, Revised	Ages 2.6 to 18	IQ, mental age
Slosson Intelligence Test, Revised	Ages 4 and above	IQ, mental age
Test of Nonverbal Intelligence	Ages 5 to adult	IQ, mental age
EMERGENT LITERACY		
An Observational Survey of Early Literacy Achievement	K–1	Oral reading, letter identification, concepts about print, sight-word recognition, writing vocabulary, hearing and recording sounds in words
SURVEY TESTS		
Boehm Test of Basic Concepts, Revised	Grades K–2	Total score of concept knowledge
Gates-MacGinitie Reading Tests	Grades K–12	Vocabulary, comprehension, total
DIAGNOSTIC READING TESTS		
MAT6 Reading Diagnostic Tests	Grades K.5–9.9	Varies with form—visual discrimination, auditory discrimination, sight vocabulary, reading comprehension, rate of comprehension
Stanford Diagnostic Reading Test	Grades 1.5–13.0	Varies with form—phonetic analysis, vocabulary, comprehension, and scanning
Test of Reading Comprehension	Ages 7.0 to 7.11	General reading comprehension core, general vocabulary, syntactic similarities, paragraph reading, sentence sequencing

Adapted from Chapter 3: "Formal Assessment Procedures," (p. 79) in *Assessing & Guiding Reading Instruction,* by M. D. Collins and E. H. Cheek Jr., 1999, New York: McGraw-Hill.

ISSUES IN TEST ASSESSMENT

Within the last 10 years, standardized tests of language arts have been criticized, and they are being revised (Tierney, 1999). Standards for the Assessment of Reading and Writing (1994) summarized these critiques when they stated that standardized tests of the past (1) did not promote student learning; (2) were poor predictors and indices of individual student performances; (3) contained content mismatched to individual teachers' classroom curriculum; (4) restricted the amount, depth, and breadth of material students were taught; (5) labeled students and placed them in programs beneath their capabilities; (6) were culturally and socially biased; and (7) measured superficial, nonauthentic, and limited ranges of students' knowledge. Moreover, there is growing impatience with student assessments that require and measure recall without assessing the thinking processes, creativity, and self-knowledge students use to answer questions and solve problems, as shown in Table 14.2.

Wolf et al. (1991) argue that future language arts assessments must be guided by a sense for the intent and meaning that develops over the long run of a discourse: "to write or speak is to produce—to have ideas, to map them into chosen words, and to reflect on the power and accuracy of what you have produced . . . standard achievement tests offer no way to sample the wondering, investigation, data collection, or reflection that are essential to serious work well done" (p. 45).

On the other hand, Wolf et al. (1991) cautioned, "If the current interest in alternatives to standardized testing is to be anything but this decade's flurry, we have to be as tough-minded in designing new options as we are in critiquing available testing. Unless we analyze the workings of these alternatives and design them carefully, we may end up with a different, but perhaps no less blunt, set of assessment instruments" (p. 60). Educators are still exploring ways in which these types of assessments can be used to meet the demands of institutional and national accountability. With these issues in mind, and by following the nine principles that follow, you can begin to create better assessment tools for your students.

STANDARDS FOR THE ASSESSMENT OF LANGUAGE ARTS

To address these ends the International Reading Association and National Council of Teachers of English prepared a position statement entitled "Standards for the Assessment of Reading and Writing" (IRA and NCTE Joint Task Force on Assessment, 1994). These standards, summarized in Table 14.2, are described below.

Principle 1: Your assessments should become more authentic. Authentic assessment is evaluation that is expressed in discourse, conversations, performances, and products that make reasonably complete, integrated statements, and that reflect students' production of in-depth knowledge (Newmann, 1991). Assessments can use tasks, text materials, and contexts that students engage in outside of school. The focus of your assessments is to prepare students to be learners and performers in varying types of learning and working responsibilities they must assume throughout their lives.

You must also include more than paper-and-pencil tests. Few assessments that expand thinking and integrate the language arts are possible when paper-and-pencil tests are the only evaluations used in your student communication center. More and more teachers are using oral, listening, and performance-based activities to assess language.

TABLE 14.2 A SET OF CONTRASTS BETWEEN TWO VIEWS

NEW VIEWS OF THE READING PROCESS TELL US THAT . . .	YET WHEN WE ASSESS READING COMPREHENSION, WE . . .
Prior knowledge is an important determinant of reading comprehension.	Mask any relationship between prior knowledge and reading comprehension by using lots of short passages on lots of topics.
A complete story or text has structural and topical integrity.	Use short texts that seldom approximate the structural and topical integrity of an authentic text.
Inference is an essential part of the process of comprehending units as small as sentences.	Rely on literal comprehension test items.
The diversity in prior knowledge across individuals as well as the varied causal relations in human experiences invite many possible inferences to fit a text or question.	Use multiple choice items with only one correct answer, even when many of the responses might, under certain conditions, be plausible.
The ability to vary reading strategies to fit the text and the situation is one hallmark of an expert reader.	Seldom assess how and when students vary the strategies they use during normal reading, studying, or when the going gets tough.
The ability to synthesize information from various parts of the text and different texts is hallmark of an expert reader.	Rarely go beyond finding the main ideas of a paragraph or passage.
The ability to ask good questions of text, as well as to answer them, is hallmark of an expert reader.	Seldom ask students to create or select questions about a selection they may have just read.
All aspects of a reader's experience, including habits that arise from school and home, influence reading comprehension.	Rarely view information on reading habits and attitudes as being important information about performance.
Reading involves the orchestration of many skills that complement one another in a variety of ways.	Use tests that fragment reading into isolated skills and report performance on each.
Skilled readers are fluent; their word identification is sufficiently automatic to allow most cognitive resources to be used for comprehension.	Rarely consider fluency as index of skilled reading.
Learning from text involves the restructuring, application, and flexible use of knowledge in new situations.	Often ask readers to respond to the text's declarative knowledge rather than to apply it to near and far transfer tasks.

Source: From "Reading Assessment: Time for a Change," by S. W. Valencia and P. D. Pearson, 1987, *The Reading Teacher, 40*(8), pp. 726–732. Reprinted with permission of Sheila Valencia and the International Reading Association. Copyright © 1987 by the International Reading Association. All rights reserved.

Principle 2: Your tests should cover a wider range of abilities and talents than in the past. Most former language assessments focused almost exclusively on measuring language activities that occur only in the prefrontal cortex—that is, on students' verbal–linguistic knowledge, their abilities to be logical with and manipulate printed words

(Tierney, 1999). In the future, students' talents in auditory, kinesthetic, intrapersonal, interpersonal, gestalt visual, and auditory dimensions of communication and contemplation must become part of their literary profile. When these talents are assessed, such evaluations enable students to use their skills in visual–spatial, bodily–kinesthetic, musical–rhythmical, interpersonal–intrapersonal, logical–mathematical, and verbal–linguistic communication modalities, illustrated in Table 14.3 (Gardner & Hatch, 1989).

Principle 3: You should no longer measure isolated language and thinking skills; rather, you must assess several student competencies simultaneously as these abilities work interactively to reach a measurable end product or process. Such tests also document students' planning abilities, and are essential if you are to obtain a complete picture of each student's capabilities. The need for this type of assessment was expressed as early as 1915 by William James, a father in educational reform:

> No elementary measurement, capable of being performed in a laboratory, can throw light on the actual efficiency of the subject; for the vital thing about him, his emotional and moral energy and doggedness, can be measured by no single experiment, and becomes known only by the total results in the long run. . . . Be patient, then, and sympathetic with the type of mind that cuts a poor figure in examination. It may, in the long examination which life sets us, come out in the end in better shape than the glib and ready reproducer, its passions being deeper, its purposes more worthy, its combining power less commonplace, and its total mental output consequently more important. (1915, pp. 135–136)

Principle 4: Your assessments should be less teacher-directed and provide for collaborative reflections between you and your students, as well as parents in some instances. Your assessments must be comprised of more student self-assessments than in the past. Students need the confidence and successful experiences of evaluating their own learning to be most successful in life. One of your assessment goals should be to help them internalize high standards and develop valid criteria for judging the quality of their work. As Levi (1990) stated, you can help students develop self-evaluative strategies, see their own possibilities, and articulate their goals for their coming month's work. In doing so, you and they articulate targets for short and long periods of work, and fashion instructional and assessment instruments together.

Students hone their evaluative thinking through your guided practice in producing original conversations and writings for assessment and through repairing and building performances assessed with you. Such disciplined self-inquiry consists of three features: (1) self-selected use of students' own knowledge bases, (2) in-depth demonstrations (rather than superficial, rote application) of information they have learned, and (3) production of new understandings in real, integrated forms that have intrinsic value to the students themselves (Tierney, 1999). Self-assessment also affords opportunity for students to ask for and count on the help of others in collaborative evaluations, which occurs more and more frequently as they enter adult life.

As more and more teachers are guiding students to become "coresponsible" for and "co-owners" of their learning, more parents are becoming an important component in the assessment process. They provide distinctive information about their children's literary performances. As a matter of fact, the State Department of Education in Vermont includes a community component in its language arts assessment

TABLE 14.3 MULTIPLE INTELLIGENCE ASSESSMENT MENU

VERBAL–LINGUISTIC INTELLIGENCE *(Language Arts-Based Assessment Instruments)*	LOGICAL–MATHEMATICAL INTELLIGENCE *(Cognitive Patterns-Based Assessment Instruments)*	VISUAL–SPATIAL INTELLIGENCE *(Imaginal-Based Assessment Instruments)*	BODILY–KINESTHETIC INTELLIGENCE *(Performance-Based Assessment Instruments)*
• written essays • vocabulary quizzes • recall of verbal information • audiocassette recordings • poetry writing • linguistic humor • formal speech • cognitive debates • listening and reporting • learning logs and journals	• cognitive organizers • higher-order reasoning • pattern games • outlining • logic and rationality exercises • mental menus and formulas • deductive reasoning • inductive reasoning • calculation processes • logical analysis and critique	• murals and montages • graphic representation and visual illustrating • visualization and imagination • reading, understanding, and creating maps • flowcharts and graphs • sculpting and building • imaginary conversations • mind mapping • video recording and photography • manipulative demonstrations	• lab experiments • dramatization • original and classical dance • charades and mimes • impersonations • human tableaux • invention projects • physical exercise routines and games • skill demonstrations • illustrations using body language and gestures

MUSICAL–RHYTHMIC INTELLIGENCE *(Auditory-Based Assessment Instruments)*	INTERPERSONAL INTELLIGENCE *(Relational-Based Assessment Instruments)*	INTRAPERSONAL INTELLIGENCE *(Psychological-Based Assessment Instruments)*
• creating concept songs and raps • illustrating with sound • discerning rhythmic patterns • composing music • linking music and rhythm with concepts • orchestrating music • creating percussion patterns • recognizing tonal patterns and quality • analyzing musical structure • reproducing musical and rhythmic patterns	• group jigsaws • explaining to or teaching another • think-pair-share • round-robin • giving and receiving feedback • interviews, questionnaires, and people searches • empathic processing • random group quizzes • assess your teammates • test, coach, and retest	• autobiographical reporting • personal application scenarios • metacognitive surveys and questionnaires • higher-order questions and answers • concentration tests • feelings, diaries, and logs • personal projection • self-identification reporting • personal history correlation • personal priorities and goals

Source: From *Multiple Intelligence Approaches to Assessment,* by D. Lazear, 1999, Tucson, AZ: Zephyr Press. Copyright © 1999. Permission to publish granted by Zephyr Press, P.O. Box 6606, Tucson, AZ 85728-6006.

program. It asks schools to host assessment-report nights for citizens in the school neighborhood to describe the language and thinking strengths and weaknesses that they have observed in the youth in their neighborhood (Allen, 1991).

Principle 5: Your assessment should demonstrate where students are in their educational development and not where they are in comparison to a constantly changing peer population. Student growth is measured by their progress since their last assessment. You assess them on how adeptly they are striving toward goals that you and they collaboratively established (Standards for the English Language Arts, 1996).

Principle 6: You should make planned and unplanned assessments. More and more of the evaluative component of the language arts program must be made during, rather than after, instruction. Such assessments can document impromptu insights students have, how they transfer previous instruction to novel events, and how well they demonstrate a new communicative talent or skill for the first time. You can develop charts, inventories, and checklists that record moments in your classroom community when individual members and groups demonstrate communication and thinking competencies at times when you had not planned to assess them. You can also use eight types of planned assessments, to be described in the next section of this chapter. You can schedule them systematically so that you measure students' communication abilities approximately once a week.

Principle 7: New forms of statewide and national standardized testing are likely to continue and must be one component in your language arts program. Statewide and national norm-referenced testing is likely to be the primary tool by which your school's total language program (kindergarten through twelfth grade) will be measured. Your program must likely meet statewide, national, and international standards. In 1993, for example, each state had the option to participate in a new standardized test designed to rank state performances in language arts to international performances.

Principle 8: You will no longer view overnight grading as the most effective form of immediate feedback. Presently many good teachers translate *immediate feedback* to mean quick, overnight turnaround in grading written papers. Unfortunately, recent research suggests that nightly grading of daily papers not only violates some of the principles of best assessment presented above, but does not provide immediate enough feedback to students so that they can erase learning errors permanently. Moreover, it may be impossible for you to accurately grade even one set of written work overnight. That is, if you have 25 students, you can only spend a total of 7½ minutes per paper reading, grading, writing commentary, and recording a grade if you are to finish the set in 3 hours and 20 minutes! Even if you could complete such a feat every night for 170 days a year without illness or burnout, Linden and Wehimbey (1990) found that many students do not know how to transfer your comments and grades to the new piece of work that they do in class the next day. Most students are left to make their own inferences about how the errors you marked should be corrected in new contexts. In addition, many students make the wrong inference about their grade. If they receive a "good grade," many are relieved and believe that they pleased you. They hope they are able, or lucky enough, to do so again. If they receive a "bad grade," many feel they are not smart and that they have disappointed and displeased you. Neither interpretation builds students' risk-taking behavior, confidence, self-assessment abilities, or thinking and language competencies.

The more effective system of providing immediate feedback is to disassociate it from assessment. You can give more immediate and effective feedback by providing detailed guidance on students' performances as they occur in class. This feedback enables students to correct the concept while it is forming, through the suggestions and strategies you offer in the immediately relevant context in which they are working. Such feedback is as close as possible to the point in time and the learning context in which the communication is made to effect lasting change for the student (Campione & Brown, 1993; Linden & Whimbey, 1990). Such immediate feedback enables a student to make a correction as soon as possible after a trial so the student's full attention is centered on the concept. For example, an incorrect verb is written as you are watching the child write a sentence; you discuss a more appropriate alternative, watch the child write it, ask the child to read the altered sentence aloud, and then ask, "How does this verb make your communication clearer?"

In brief, a comprehensive language arts evaluation provides a complete literacy description of each student's strengths and goals for improvement in speaking, listening, reading, writing, and thinking. Norm-referenced and criterion-referenced standardized tests must likely be one component of your language arts program. Several changes are occurring in language arts assessment. Among them are fewer paper-and-pencil tests and measuring language as students use it in the classroom. Students should learn to assess themselves. Ways in which this can be accomplished are with the assessment tools described in the next section of this chapter: anecdotal records, portfolios, self-assessments, group work grades, rating scales, journals, retellings, debates, and outside evaluators. These can be administered on a weekly basis, as described in a subsequent section of this chapter.

•-•

SECTION 2   PUTTING THEORY INTO PRACTICE

New Assessment Tools

There are eight new language arts assessments. As you read each description, you may profit from placing a checkmark next to the form of assessment you prefer. After this section, you will have the opportunity to merge tools you selected into a full year's evaluation program.

ANECDOTAL RECORDS AND PERFORMANCE-BASED ASSESSMENTS

As described in Chapter 3, anecdotal records are handwritten notes of student, small group, and class actions that indicate progress in communication and thinking. Although teachers for many years have made mental anecdotal records to guide their next day's instruction, more and more language arts teachers are using a written, anecdotal record-keeping system to document their students' language progress. The first step in devising an anecdotal record-keeping system is to select a form that is comfortable for you. Some teachers carry a clipboard throughout the day, and make notes about important occurrences constantly. Others use a spiral notebook, individual student notecards, or separate file folders to record information on different students at the end of each day. Others set aside a specific time at the end of the week to make anecdotal notes; and a few educators establish different categories of anecdotes and record information in each category on a different day.

PORTFOLIOS

Portfolio assessment is a chronologically sequenced collection of students' work that represents their ability to make high-level decisions; compare single entries of their work; and produce, perceive, and reflect on their language and thinking competencies. The portfolio focuses on the student's growth over time, measures student effort, experimentation, and the learning process and products. Portfolios can become student–teacher–parent collaborative assessments, in which students select entries. Students can express their opinions about what they want to include in their portfolios and how they want to measure their learning trails during each subsequent portfolio conference. As Fuhler (1990) reported, student involvement heightens their awareness that their efforts play a significant role in their level of success and that their opinions are valid. Samples of the types of items that can be included appear in Figure 14.1.

As Shanahan (1991) states "portfolio assessment positions students to learn about themselves at the same time as it places teachers in the position of being an assessment coach" (p. 105). Your students and you assess the connections between samples, patterns of growth, and ability of students to plan their new thinking and learning trails. If your school district does not have a portfolio program in which portfolios are passed from one grade-level teacher to the next, you can follow these procedures to begin such a program for your class or school.

1. Designate a spot and a filing system where portfolios will be placed. This location should be accessible to students so they can store their work easily. Students will cull samples in their portfolios, and select their best at least once each grading period.

2. Decide when portfolio conferences will be held and the dimensions of literacy to be assessed during each conference.

3. Write a letter to parents to describe the portfolio program. In this letter, describe how the portfolio will be linked with other types of language arts assessments and why some student work samples are being reserved for the portfolio and not sent home each week.

4. Introduce portfolio assessment to your class by showing portfolios from former students or one you made of your work. Also describe (and show) how artists, models, writers, and other communication artists use portfolios in their careers (Farr & Tone, 1994).

5. Make several options available as to the types of containers students can use for portfolios, including artist's folders, pocket notebooks, manilla folders, and compendium folders (NEA, 1993).

6. Explain that portfolios contain two types of documentation to ensure consistency from one student to another. The first documents are required work samples

❖ Ideas for the Collection Portfolio ❖

- Writing samples
  - *A writing process "package" showing an assignment taken from rough draft through the editing and revision process to the final polished draft*
  - *Writing samples showing different parts of the process*
  - *Writing prompts and rubrics associated with samples*
  - *Writing done for content areas such as social studies or science*
  - *Writing inventory or checklist* — *Writing samples reflecting different genres*
  - *Research reports* — *Journal or learning log entries (photocopies)*
  - *Interview notes*
- Reading inventories or checklists
- Responses to reading
  - *Book reports/reviews* — *Open-ended questions with scoring rubrics*
- Tape recordings of oral reading
- Photographs of projects and activities
- Video tapes of skits, activities, etc.
- Mathematics checklist and mathematics problem-solving samples
- Introductory note to potential audience
  - *Parents* — *Guests*
  - *Interested educators* — *Explanations of criteria for selection*

❖ Ideas for the Showcase Portfolio ❖

- A selection of items from the Collection Portfolio showing:
  - *Best work* — *Growth over time*
- Student's reflections on selections or general progress
- The self-esteem folder
  - *Memorabilia* — *Awards*
  - *Newspaper clippings and photos* — *Snapshots*
  - *Team photos* — *Playbills*

❖ Ideas for the Teacher/Student Assessment Portfolio ❖

- Photocopies of material from the Showcase Portfolio
- Anecdotal records
- Conference records
- Interest inventories
- Teacher-made tests
  - *Unit tests* — *District test scores*
  - *Open-ended tests* — *Standardized test scores*
- Student evaluations of teacher

❖ Ideas for the Teacher Resource Portfolio ❖

- References to passages in books
- Student evaluations of teacher
- Notes from peer coaching

- Articles from education magazines and journals
- Notes from education classes and in-services
- Copies of administrative evaluations

FIGURE 14.1 WHAT CAN STUDENTS PUT IN THEIR PORTFOLIOS?

that meet criteria you and they set. These documents accompany student narratives that describe why the student judged each work sample to demonstrate a new language growth. The second documents are those that you and the class agree represent the learning objectives specified for the grading period. All class members will have one document for each learning objective. Therefore, in this system, half of each portfolio is personalized to each student's learning history and individual goals. The second half records each student's completion of goals the class established (Bergeron, Werruth, & Hammer, 1997).

7. Students create a table of contents for their portfolio and attach it to the front cover. A sample appears in Table 14.4. An alternative table of contents lists "skills I can use and things I want to learn," as well as the title and date of entry for each item in the portfolio:

Skills I Can Use and Things I Want to Learn	Items in My Portfolio	Date Entered
1. _____	1. _____	_____
2. _____	2. _____	_____
3. _____	3. _____	_____

TABLE 14.4 EXAMPLE OF THE INTRODUCTORY PAGES IN STUDENTS'
PORTFOLIOS: A PORTFOLIO INVENTORY SHEET

Name: _____

1. Cursive Handwriting Sample

   _____ Sept.   _____ Jan.

   _____ Oct.   _____ Feb.

2. Writing Samples

   _____ Narrative

   _____ Expository

      _____ Descriptive

      _____ Explanatory

      _____ Persuasive

   _____ Poetic

3. Journals

   _____ Dialogue

   _____ Literature Responses

4. Social Studies Informational Reports

   _____ Questioning Strategies

   _____ Research

5. Science Writing

   _____ Written "Observations"

   _____ Data Collection

6. Mathematical Sample

7. Fine Arts Sample

8. Spelling Assessment

Checklists

_____ Reflective Work Habits Survey

_____ Personal Interests Survey

_____ Books Read for Class

_____ Books Read Independently

_____ Books Read This Grading Period:

_____

_____

TABLE 14.5 INSTRUCTIONS TO PARENTS ABOUT "FRIDAY FOLDERS"
(PORTFOLIOS TAKEN HOME EVERY WEEK)

Dear Parents,

This is your child's Friday Folder. The Friday Folder contains your child's
school work and will come home every two weeks for your viewing pleasure.
This folder also contains a letter to you from your child describing recent
learnings and activities. The Friday Folder needs to be returned to school on
Monday with work intact. The reasons for work coming back are threefold.
First, some of the work is still in progress. Second, your child will be taking
time to reflect on his/her work and to set future learning goals. Finally, your
child will also be selecting several pieces from the Friday Folder to keep in
his/her classroom portfolio.

The classroom portfolio is an organizational tool for me, you, and your child
to be able to view growth in all areas throughout the entire year. The portfolio
will contain pieces that are significant to your child, either because the pieces
showed improvement or the child viewed them to be his or her "best." Each
piece in the portfolio will be described and be accompanied by a self-reflection.
Your child may take his/her portfolio home at the end of the year. Please send
your comment below.

Mr. Markham

---

8. You can allow parents to assist their children to select their best work to include
in the portfolio (see Table 14.5).

9. Portfolios can be graded in several ways. (See Figure 14.2 for a sample portfolio
assessment form.)

  a. As noted above, at the end of each grading period, students sort through their
     documents and select those they wish to include. They then state why they
     chose each piece, what it demonstrates that they learned, and their future goals
     relative to each document. Students can also develop a self-evaluation report
     that they submit to the teacher during the portfolio assessment conference.

  b. Evaluation can be on the basis of only one or two pieces among the several
     that are stored in the portfolio that each student submits (Shuman, 1991).

  c. You can use published, standardized portfolio programs and the assessment
     criteria they provide. Such commercially prepared portfolios include *The
     Riverside Integrated Literature and Language Arts Portfolio; Psychological Corpo-
     ration's Integrated Language Arts Portfolio;* and portfolios published by Silver-
     Burdett and Ginn, D.C. Heath, Harcourt Brace and Jovanovich, and Scott
     Foresman. In addition, Portfolio Assessment Clearinghouse is now publishing
     a bulletin entitled "Portfolio News" to help you keep abreast of advancements
     in portfolio assessment.

Name _____ Date _____

Points

I. Process evaluation (20 points) Rate each area.
   A. Sharing artifacts and reflections with peers. (5 or 10 points)   _____
   B. Submitting portfolio for two interim reviews. (5 or 10 points)   _____

                                                    Total _____

II. Product evaluation (30 points)
   A. Aspects of the portfolio (8 points). Rate each area for 1 or 0 points.
      1. Literacy autobiography (1 point)   _____
      2. Reading for different purposes (1 point)   _____
      3. Writing for different purposes (1 point)   _____
      4. All stages of writing process (1 point)   _____
      5. Use of word processing system (1 point)   _____
      6. Oral interpretation of children's literature (1 point)   _____
      7. Significance of role models (1 point)   _____
      8. Talking and listening for different purposes (1 point)   _____

                                                      Total _____

   B. Reflections on artifacts (12 points). Choose one.
     ➤ All reflections are substantive and well composed. (12 points)
     ➤ Most reflections are substantive and well composed. (9 points)
     ➤ Some reflections are substantive and well composed. (6 points)
     ➤ Few reflections are substantive and well composed. (3 points)

                                                      Total _____

   C. Summative reflective piece (10 points). Choose one to represent
      your evaluation of (a) what you learned about your own literacy,
      (b) how your literacy experiences might affect your teaching of literacy,
      and (c) personal literacy goals and plan of action.
     ➤ Each of the three areas is adequately elaborated, and the writing
       is carefully composed. (10 points)
     ➤ Each area is addressed in carefully composed writing. Two areas
       are adequately elaborated; one area needs further development.
     ➤ Each area is addressed. The writing style is adequate. Two areas
       need further elaboration. (6 points)
     ➤ Each area is addressed. The writing style is adequate, but all
       three areas need further elaboration. (4 points)
     ➤ One or more areas are not addressed. Writing style is not
       satisfactory. (2 points)

                                                      Total _____
                                         Grand total _____

Points possible = 50

FIGURE 14.2 CRITERIA FOR EVALUATING A LITERACY PORTFOLIO

Source: Adapted from "Evaluating Literacy Portfolios," by R. Wagner, 1994, *The Reading Teacher, 47*(5).

      d. You can evaluate portfolios by awarding points in more than one category of
      growth. For example, students and you can agree to grade portfolios on three
      criteria: degree of document variety (receiving from 1 to 5 points of weight);

demonstrations of five major objectives taught during the grading period (receiving from 1 to 5 points of weight); and level of unique expressions of individual students' creativity, initiative, oral communication skill, group work competencies, and student-selected goal (receiving from 1 to 5 points of weight). Total points earned could then be multiplied by 6.67 to determine a portfolio grade on a 100-point scale.

e. Parents can be involved in assessing portfolios. They can make written comments to the student and teacher, review portfolios during parent conferences with teachers or at parents' nights at the school; or complete suggestions for follow-up activities that can be carried out at home after a portfolio has been graded by you and the student in a collaborative conference.

STUDENT SELF-ASSESSMENT

Self-assessments are opportunities for students to value, monitor, evaluate, and improve their own language and thinking skills. As Aristotle stated, "each man judges well the things he knows, and of these he is a good judge"(*Ethics* I:3). You begin this assessment system by selecting or adapting a self-assessment form like the one in Figure 14.3. You then complete a model form, as if you were a student and illustrate how students can complete their self-assessment in the grading period specified.

In addition to the completion of written forms, students can assess their performances during evaluation interviews and conferences. Such assessments either award points for the number of questions completed or determine a global score for the quality of the answers. A list of example interview questions follow:

1. List or describe what you can do now that you could not do earlier in the year.

2. What are your best works as a speaker, listener, reader, writer, and thinker? Why?

3. What were the most difficult concepts you learned about writing, reading, speaking, listening, and thinking? Why were these difficult for you?

4. How have you changed as a reader, writer, speaker, listener, and thinker?

5. What would you like to do better as a reader, writer, speaker, listener, and thinker?

6. What do you do when you _____ [a specific objective taught during the grading period]?

7. Of the reading, writing, speaking, listening, and thinking activities that we have done lately, in which are you most confident?

8. What do you still not understand, and how can I help you understand it?

9. Rate and defend how well you used your time [how well you learned] this grading period.

10. What do I need to ask you for you to best demonstrate how much you've learned?

Students can also complete annotations that are attached to their report cards. In such annotations students grade themselves after you explain the standards by which you will grade them. An example of a student self-assessment created in Lotus is shown in Figure 14.4.

Name: _____ My Reading Record				
Date Started	Title	Author	Date Completed	Rating
				★ ★ ★ ★ ★
				★ ★ ★ ★ ★
				★ ★ ★ ★ ★
				★ ★ ★ ★ ★
				★ ★ ★ ★ ★
				★ ★ ★ ★ ★
				★ ★ ★ ★ ★
				★ ★ ★ ★ ★
				★ ★ ★ ★ ★
				★ ★ ★ ★ ★
				★ ★ ★ ★ ★
				★ ★ ★ ★ ★
				★ ★ ★ ★ ★
				★ ★ ★ ★ ★

FIGURE 14.3 SAMPLE SELF-ASSESSMENT FORM

Created by Julie DiBona, 1999, master of education degree candidate at University of Notre Dame, South-bend, IN. Used by permission.

EVALUATING GROUP PROJECTS, GROUP DISCUSSIONS, AND PAIRED ASSIGNMENTS

Group grades can serve as individual member grades, total group grades, improvement scores, or as combined grades. The most frequently used assessments of group work include video and audio pre- and posttest replays, video and audio analyses, group self-assessments, and teacher-graded group work.

Paired learning sessions can be assessed through checklists and interviews completed by partners, using questions such as the following:

1. What do you want to tell me about what you've learned relative to _____ _____?

2. What was your favorite part?

3. What was the purpose of _____?

4. What was difficult about _____?

Partners can also tell each other something they do well. Other types of paired assessments are long-term. For example, as you may recall, Ms. Stone's fifth-graders participated in a cross-aged project with kindergarten children. The grade they received on the project came from the two books they completed at the end of the year. The first, *The Favorite Books of Kindergarten Students at Our Elementary School;* was written for parents of kindergarten students; the second, *How to Be a Good Tutor,* was written for students and parents. Both were placed in the school library.

RATING SCALES

Rating scales are charts that indicate the degree to which specific skills or qualities have been achieved. Rating scales can be used as self-assessment instruments or as teacher-made tests. Figure 14.4 is an example of a rating scale for writing.

Date: _____

Student's Name: _____   Grading Period:
                                             1   2   3   4   5   6
                                             (circle one)

I. Name four ways the quality of your reading and writing has improved in your journal entries in the past six weeks.

II. Name four ways that thoughts about what you have read were used in your journal entries in the past six weeks.

III. How have you improved your ability to express your opinions, emotions, ideas, and experiences in your journal entries in the past six weeks?

IV. How have you met our previously set goals? How have you achieved the goals we set during our last conference?

FIGURE 14.4 GRADING JOURNALS THROUGH STUDENT SELF-ASSESSMENTS

ASSESSING THE INTEGRATION OF LANGUAGE ARTS AND THINKING

About mid-year, you should evaluate the integration of language arts and thinking strategies in your class. For example, you can give a student (or group of students) a body of information and a simulated problem to solve. Then you state the criteria on which their work will be graded. A second option is to ask students to provide three or more examples of their mastery of different language arts concepts in relation to a single topic. To illustrate, students can be divided into three groups, each of which is to prepare a written, oral, and thinking skill presentation relative to a body of knowledge on which they will be assessed.

A third option is to give more than one grade to a performance or assign points to its parts. For example, distinct assessments can be made of students' (1) preparation, (2) overall content, (3) presentation quality, and (4) documented language arts and thinking objectives learned.

Performance Assessment Covering Content Area Unit

1. Completed learning log	1–5 points
2. Read five informational books on the topic	1–5 points
3. Helped the group to make a record and used one of the problem-solving strategies learned this grading period	1–15 points
4. Communicated effectively in the group presentation	1–15 points
5. Made an original contribution to the class's body of knowledge	1–15 points
6. Written project was accurate and skillfully prepared using objectives learned during this grading period	1–15 points
7. Group work skills improved	1–10 points
8. Documented insights gained in communication and thinking abilities since last project grade	1–20 points
	0–100 points

GRADING JOURNALS AND OTHER WRITINGS

Journals can be graded holistically (based on overall impression of effectiveness in communication), by primary process assessment (focused on individual aspects of writing), or through a rubric (series of quality indicators). Each of these types adhere to the principle that the assessment of student writing emphasizes the worth of each student's effort and growth and that every author has room for improvement. Because journal writings are usually personal expressions in which students take a risk to express their thoughts, acceptance and appreciation of these expressions should be evident in the evaluations. For this reason, journal assessment must be planned as carefully as the instructional objectives they are designed to achieve.

The first step in journal evaluation is to make the assessment criteria clear before students begin to write. For example, you can test different strengths at separate evaluation periods in the year. When assessments are made in this way, five aspects can be assessed:

1. *Thought:* Rate the quality of thinking that underlies the ideas. How rich are the ideas? Are any unique? Do the ideas evidence critical thinking and/or logical ordering?

2. *Authenticity:* Is the writing sincere? Does it represent a genuine (or convincing) experience? Do you hear the "voice" of the writer? Do readers become involved and can they relate the messages to their personal experiences easily?

3. *Power:* Is the language effective? Is the density, clarity, and breadth of word choice and writing style increasing?

4. *Growth:* Has the student improved since the last grading period, and to what degree? Is the student taking risks? Is the student writing longer and more varied genres?

5. *Conventions:* Does the student use effective grammar, standards of usage, spelling, punctuation, and capitalization?

Self-evaluations of journals can be combined with your evaluation, with one method of doing so shown in Figures 14.4 and 14.5. After students have answered the four questions in Figure 14.4, award points for the number of journal entries made: 1 to 3 points per journal entry for the correct use of writing conventions, 1 to 3 points per selection for quality of writing in that the student used new objectives learned during this grading period, and 1 to 16 points as a response to the quality of the student's self-assessment, completed in Figure 14.5. As you read each journal, you can search for and note what each student is ready next to learn to become a more effective writer. These notes can be written at the bottom of Figure 14.5 and taken to your student–teacher conference. At that time you and the student can establish new objectives for the next grading period.

RETELLINGS AND DEBATES

Retellings can become valuable assessment tools. During retelling you can analyze a student's free recall of an event; specific communication or thinking objectives; or reading, listening, and writing experiences. Criteria include types of inference that the student evidenced, parts of the event that were most vividly remembered and reasons why, and what the retelling demonstrated about the student's growth as a communicator and thinker.

Similarly, evaluations of debate performances can measure these attributes as well. All members of the class can award up to 5 points per speaker in debate teams, and debaters can review peers' evaluations to improve their speaking abilities. Students can also assess themselves by awarding points after a retelling or a debate. And

Student Name: _____

Criteria: _____

Date: _____
Grading Period:
1   2   3   4   5   6
(circle one)

A. Quantity: 12 journal entries
   (2 per week) required
   each 6 weeks (one
   point per entry)

12%

_____

B. Correct Use of Writing Conventions (1–3 points per
   selection for grading period)
   1. Mechanics—Grammar
   2. Spelling/Punctuation/
     Capitalization
   3. Sentence Formation
     36 points—above average
     24 points—average
     12 points—below average

36%

_____

C. Quality: Using previously
   stated objectives
   1. Completely address the
     objectives learned this
     grading period (1–3 points
     per selection)
   2. Quality and richness of
     language (1–3 points per
     selection)
   3. Express opinions, ideas,
     feelings (1–3 points per
     selection)

36% (36 points
maximum)

_____

D. Grade on Self-Evaluation
   (4 parts of 1–4 points each
   from student self-evaluation
   form)

16% (16 points
maximum)

_____

TOTAL POINTS
EARNED

_____

TEACHER & STUDENT CONFERENCE COMMENTS:
(Set goals for next grading period.)

FIGURE 14.5 FORM FOR TEACHERS TO GRADE STUDENTS' JOURNALS

you can assess students' retellings, debates, and other speeches, and change the directions section to include more advanced communication objectives as students'
abilities increase during the year using assessment forms shown in Chapters 3 and 4.

CASE STUDIES

Special needs students profit from individual case-study assessments. These assessments are usually completed in collaboration with the student, student's parent, and other professionals in your building who work with the student. The case study contains very specific weekly goals in each of the language arts, as well as targeted objectives for thinking development. Case studies are analyzed by professionals alone and then in consultation with the student.

SINGLE OR MULTIPLE OUTSIDE EVALUATORS

Your language arts program and students can benefit from outside evaluations of their work. Evaluations can be of single samples or of works in progress, as evaluators observe the class engaged in normal activities.

TRANSFERRING PRACTICES INTO GRADING PERIODS

Your language arts assessment program can be divided into six grading periods, with one assessment tool implemented each week. In this program, you will record one language arts grade per week, which is required in many states.

First Grading Period.   The focus of the first grading period is to teach students how to use each type of evaluation tool. You will also collect benchmark data for end-of-year comparisons. Assessments to be obtained during the first grading period follow:

Week 1. Describe the anecdotal record-keeping system you have designed. Collect one benchmark anecdotal record for the class as a whole and one for each individual student.

Week 2. Describe the portfolio system you created for your room or that is used throughout the school. Create individual student portfolios, and allow students to select their first sample from their first 2 weeks' work. This choice is graded and also becomes the benchmark to which students compare end-of-year samples.

Week 3. Describe the system the class will follow to write in and evaluate their journals. A benchmark entry is made in the journal and the grading system is modeled and implemented.

Week 4. Describe retellings, debates, oral and listening assessments, performance assessments, and rating scales. You and students develop objectives for the remaining 2 weeks in language arts and dimensions of thinking, and select one of these forms of assessment to evaluate these objectives. In your discussion, provide evidence of students' first-week levels of performance in speaking, reading, writing, listening, thinking processes, decision making, problem solving, creativity, metacognitions, group skills, and abilities to work alone that you obtained from the diagnostic activities in Chapter 2 and from the first 3 weeks' evaluations described above.

Week 5. Explain the process and purposes of self-assessment. Students complete the first self-assessments in communication and thinking competencies. You and your students either decide to design your own self-assessments or to select from three that you provide.

Week 6. Select portfolio entries, hold conferences, and take (and graded if desired) the second portfolio sample. Grade the evaluation form selected during the fourth week of the period.

Second Grading Period (weeks 7–12 of the school year). The focus of the second grading period is to document students' rates of growth in each language art and to compare their present performances with their own performance-based learning history, which is evidenced in works since the first week of school or through references to prior years' performances and portfolios from past years, if available. Standardized tests are often administered during this grading period.

Week 7. Students compare the new anecdotal entry you make this week for the class and each student to the record you made 5 weeks ago. Students discuss their growth and set a new goal for this grading period.

Week 8. Conduct conferences for the purpose of awarding grades concerning specific competencies in language arts and thinking development.

Week 9. Grade journal entries.

Week 10. Describe the purposes of and the types of group work skill assessments you and students can use. Collect a benchmark sample and grade it using this instrument. Students select the instrument from the choices you provide.

Week 11. Begin case studies for special needs students, and collect benchmark data in collaboration with these students. Students who are not involved in creation of case studies complete a self-assessment of this grading period's work, compared to the last grading period.

Week 12. Assess portfolios and journals; hold individual student conferences.

Third Grading Period (weeks 13–18 of the school year). The focus of this grading period is to (1) build students' goal-setting abilities; (2) help them understand the trail of progress they have accomplished in half a year; and (3) help them increase their learning successes in the second half of the year.

Week 13. Analyze the anecdotal records from the first 13 weeks of school for two patterns of strength per student, and for the class as a whole. Students improve the anecdotal record-keeping system and establish a new objective for their growth during this grading period. Students also evaluate their own language arts abilities and make suggestions to improve them.

Week 14. All members of the student-centered community establish objectives for this grading period. Students also select an appropriate assessment for these objectives, such as retellings, debates, oral or listening assessments, group work skill assessments, or rating scales. Begin the selected assessment.

Week 15. Analyze journals for breadth and depth of communication and thinking strengths.

Week 16. Explain integrated assessments and take a benchmark assessment of students' abilities to integrate the language arts into content area instruction.

Week 17. Invite an external evaluator to class to assess communication and thinking competencies; share videotaped analyses of the class with students as the evaluator explains the growth noted.

Week 18. Hold mid-year portfolio and journal conferences, and encourage risk-taking to expand communication and thinking competencies during the last half of the year.

Fourth Grading Period (weeks 19–24 of the school year).   The focus of this grading period is to award points on the basis of students' abilities to become more responsible for their own learning. Some grades are based on students' abilities to set and implement their learning goals.

Week 19. Take anecdotal records; students reflect on all anecdotal records that have been collected concerning their work throughout the year. Students set a goal to reach by the end of the year; they develop a plan of action and a method by which they want to be assessed.

Week 20. Students self-assess their journals. Points are awarded for students' abilities to set and reach new goals in their writing abilities by the last week of this recording period.

Week 21. Invite parents to participate in the evaluation process, using a system that you and students create.

Week 22. Explain the purposes of paired assessment. Explain, administer, and grade a paired activity.

Week 23. Take the second integrated assessment.

Week 24. Grade portfolios and journals. Hold individual conferences.

Fifth Grading Period (weeks 25–30 of the school year).   The focus of this grading period is on developing students' abilities to design goals, methods, and evaluations that meet specific communications and thinking needs that they identify.

Week 25. Examine anecdotal records. Students set a 6- to 12-week plan of action to improve in two communication and thinking competencies. Points are awarded for the identification of individual needs, problem-solving skill, and the success of the plan created.

Week 26. A second outside evaluator provides information to you concerning specific objectives students have set for themselves. You and the outside evaluator consult to determine suggestions for individual student's improvement.

Week 27. Journals become learning logs to document learning styles. Students self-assess one aspect of communication or thinking competence they have learned to date.

Week 28. Assess a retelling, debate, or other speaking or listening activity.

Week 29. Make the third integrated assessment.

Week 30. Grade portfolios and journals and hold conferences. Portfolios are graded based on students' ability to take risks and reach goals in each of the language arts and thinking competencies.

Sixth Grading Period (weeks 31–36 of the school year).   The focus of this grading period is to celebrate accomplishments! Students compare first 6-week benchmarks to works completed during this grading period. A second, and equally important, purpose of this recording period is for students to design their own program for continued growth throughout the summer.

Week 31. Students record their own anecdotal records and use their analysis of their year's record to prepare their "summer learning plan."

Week 32. Collect taped readings as posttests of those administered during the first 6 weeks. Students listen to their first of the year's reading and last 6 week's reading and make analyses. Students also plan the way their reading, listening, speaking, writing, and thinking will be assessed this week.

Week 33. Grade journals. Students celebrate their trail of growth in writing ability for the year. They design the last goals for their journals and how their journals will be continued throughout the summer.

Week 34. Make the last integrated assessment and compare it to previous ones. Although acclaim is given for superior performances, every student is praised for at least one area of learning.

Week 35. Give a group or paired grade for a debate, dramatic performance, or discussion. Award oral improvement points. Pay tribute to each student for an area of most improvement in speaking, listening, and/or thinking ability.

Week 36. Teachers, students, and parents assess portfolios and journals. Students contribute something of value to the school on an individual basis or as a class.

INTEGRATING THE LANGUAGE ARTS

Completing Comprehensive Literacy Assessment

Students can complete documents that demonstrate their breadth and depth of literacy by using the sample assessment tools illustrated in this textbook. Popular authors and books you can recommend to middle school students appear in Literature Card 40. These books can become the content about which students' high-level thinking and language arts abilities can be assessed through a wide variety of oral, written, poetic, dramatic, or group responses.

INSIDE CULTURALLY ENRICHED CLASSROOMS

Assessing Multiple Intelligences

Students deserve opportunities to be evaluated in their best light. Hispanic children are able to express what they comprehended better through interviews than through standardized or teacher-made multiple choice tests. Similarly, minority culture children enrolled in the same classrooms as majority culture children (and of the same socioeconomic level) often not only know less about the range of topics included on standardized tests but also are unaccustomed to making the types of inferences needed to answer such scripturally implicit questions. Many low- and average-scoring

Literature Card 40

POPULAR AUTHORS FOR MIDDLE SCHOOL STUDENTS

Richard Adams	Barbara Corcoran	Madeleine L'Engle	Ellen Raskin
Lloyd Alexander	Robert Cormier	Ursula LeQuin	Wilson Rauls
Mildren Ames	Paula Danziger	Robert Lipsyte	Willo Davis Roberts
Judi Angell	Lois Duncan	Lois Lowry	Zilpha Snyder
Peter Beagle	Paul Gallico	Margaret Mahy	Mary Stewart
Jay Bennett	Jean George	Ann M. Martin	Mildred Taylor
T. Ernesto Bethancourt	Barbara Girion	Harry Mazer	Theodore Taylor
Judy Blume	Bette Greene	Norma Fox Mazer	Crystal Thrasher
Frank Bonham	Lynn Hall	Jean Lowery Nixon	Stephanie Tolan
Betsy Byars	Harry Harrison	Scott O'Dell	Julian Thompson
Eleanor Cameron	S. E. Hinton	Zibby O'Neal	J. R. R. Tolkien
Joy Chant	Isabelle Holland	Katherine Patterson	Rosemary Wells
Agatha Christie	Irene Hunt	Richard Peck	Robert Westall
John Christopher	Judith Kerr	Robert N. Peck	Leonard Wibberley
Patricia Clapp	M. E. Kerr	Susan Beth Pfeffer	Paul Zindel
Ellen Conford	Gordon Korman	D. M. Pinkwater	
Susan Cooper	Jim Kjelgaard	Kin Platt	

students who do not have abundant verbal–linguistic intellectual strengths tend to rely solely on literal interpretations on paper-and-pencil tests. Moreover, many Hispanic students require more time to finish tests than majority culture students.

Other students from diverse background experiences and learning preferences can also profit from having the opportunity to be evaluated on one or more of the multiple intelligence assessment options listed in Tables 14.3 and 14.6. These options enable them to exhibit their greatest language strengths.

RECOGNIZING AND REPORTING PROGRESS

An Overview of Assessment

The components of the assessment process and the strategies shown in Table 14.6 may be used in parent–teacher conferences and with colleagues to describe the type of assessment you use to evaluate your students.

WAYS OF GATHERING ASSESSMENT INFORMATION

1. *Formal Tests.* There are two types:
   a. Standardized tests compare the student's performance with that of other students of comparable age and grade levels.

TABLE 14.6 ASSESSMENT STRATEGIES

BUILDING BACKGROUND	READING THE LITERATURE	RESPONDING TO LITERATURE	DEVELOPING STRATEGIES AND SKILLS
quick write	guided reading	story frame	journal pages
think-pair-share	monitoring comprehension sheet	monitoring comprehension sheet	writing samples
story mapping			student resource pages
prediction chart	oral reading	literature log	discussions
knowledge chart	teacher observation	teacher conferences (individual, small group, casual)	self-evaluation
graphic organizer	audiotaping of oral reading		peer evaluation
teacher observation		discussing and sharing	monitoring comprehension sheet
student resource book	shared reading		
	discussions	peer response group	student modeling
discussions	cooperative reading	journal pages	teacher observation
brainstorming	reading notes in journal	story retellings	teacher conferences
word web		story summary	
	use of strategies	character map	
	checklists	Venn diagram	
		dramatic activities	
		story pyramid	
		writing samples	

Source: Adapted from *Assessing Cognitive Behavior: An Integrative Approach* (p. 231), by D. Meichenbaum, J. Rothlein, and R. Fredericks, 1995, New York: Plenum.

b. Criterion-referenced tests determine directly if the student has mastered specific reading skills.

2. *Informal Tests.* These include teacher-made tests and other nonstandard measures. Informal tests permit the teacher to gather information in an unconstrained and relaxed manner.

3. *Interviews.* Interviews involve discussions with parents, teachers, or the student. The purpose of the interview is to gain a more comprehensive picture of the student's attitudes, abilities, behaviors, and reading habits.

4. *Reports from Related Professionals.* Useful information from other professionals may come from sources such as medical, psychological, or speech and language reports.

5. *Cumulative Records.* These provide the teacher with an overview of a student's school history. They contain attendance reports, changes of schools, report card grades over the years, grade repetitions, age of beginning school, and so on.

6. *Observations.* Teachers should observe students in a variety of settings to gain important assessment information.

7. *Sample Teaching Lessons.* This method uses work samples (or diagnostic teaching) in which students are given an instructional task for the purpose of gathering diagnostic information. The teacher gains valuable information about the student's likelihood of success using a particular strategy by actually trying out an instructional technique during the diagnostic period.

THE LANGUAGE ARTS DIAGNOSTIC PROCESS

Phases of the Process

The exact sequence of the diagnostic process may vary because the diagnosis varies with each student. Sometimes several phases are accomplished simultaneously. Occasionally, you must go back to an earlier phase. However, there is general agreement that a reading diagnosis proceeds from more general to more specific concerns.

1. *Determining the Existence of a Reading Problem.* Objective evidence is needed to substantiate the existence of a reading disability.

2. *Investigating Correlates of Reading Disability.* Reading disabilities are often accompanied by related problems known as correlates. Correlates of reading disability are nonreading factors that may impinge on learning to read. These include environmental, emotional, physical, intellectual, and language factors. Teachers should be cautious about interpreting a correlate as the cause of a reading problem.

3. *General Reading Diagnosis: Determining the Reading Level and the General Areas of Reading Difficulties.* When gathering this information, it is important to remember that the student's reading level may vary depending on factors such as interest and background for the text being read and the content in which the reading takes place.

4. *Specific Reading Diagnosis: Determining Specific Reading Strengths and Weaknesses.* This phase involves the detailed analysis of the student's reading abilities. To gather this information the teacher assesses the precise abilities and needs in word recognition and analyzes the strategies the student is using to recognize words. Emphasis should be placed on tasks that are similar to those done in the classroom because the aim is to help the student succeed in the regular classroom situation.

5. *Developing a Teaching Plan.* This should include the areas of reading to be taught; the appropriate level of reading for instruction; the materials to be used for teaching; the instructional methods; and time, frequency, and duration of instruction.

6. *Using Diagnostic Teaching to Monitor Ongoing Needs.* Teachers should remain sensitive to changing needs even after the formal diagnosis is concluded. If a student's response to teaching indicates that an instructional strategy is not effective, the teacher should change the instructional plans.

THE LANGUAGE ARTS DIAGNOSIS

Some general principles

1. The diagnosis is a decision-making process.

2. The diagnosis evaluates the student objectively.

3. The diagnosis considers the whole individual.

4. Diagnosis, instruction, and remediation are a continuous process.

SECTION 3 TEACHERS AS CONTINUAL LEARNERS

Improving Assessment Competencies

Throughout this textbook you have developed several language arts competencies. This section is about an assessment that can be used to evaluate your language arts program, grade journals, and videotape your classroom for instruction and assessment.

PROFESSIONAL DEVELOPMENT ACTIVITY

Mid-Year and End-of-Year Language Arts Program Evaluation

At mid-year and at the end of the year, assess your language arts program. Before you do so, on the last day before winter and summer vacation, ask students to submit written suggestions for classroom improvement. Students can cite the rationale and methods for making the changes they suggest. You can also ask what they would like to learn that they have not yet learned, and how they would like to learn it. After reading these suggestions, you can complete the following evaluation before you leave for winter or summer vacation. Commit to yourself that you will not turn off your classroom lights or leave for your vacation until you complete the following assessment of your language arts program. If your answer to any of the following questions is yes, you can spend the vacation period devising a plan to alter your program.

1. Have you unintentionally implemented a practice or schedule that doesn't create language learning (e.g., you have trouble disciplining students so you play records they bring to school and allow them to sing if they "behave" all week. Although reading lyrics can build reading vocabularies, singing random songs, unrelated to instructional goals, is not within your master language arts plan. You can profit by improving your time and classroom management skills and eliminating this Friday Reward because it does not help your students grow).

2. Are any of the students in your room not yet taking risks? Looking at each desk in the room, picture an incident in which that child initiated a challenging language and thinking task for him- or herself. If you can't picture one, write that child's name on a piece of paper. Think about activities and grouping systems you can implement in January (or next year) to help that child (or children like him or her) become a more active, self-directed learner.

3. Recount the last week of instruction. As you picture each day's activities, were there any assignments in which students spoke, read, wrote, listened, created, or

thought in ways they do not in the real world. What can you do to change these activities?

4. Look around the room to see if your instruction is student centered. Count the number of items you asked students to perform and the number of times students asked you to do a special project they wanted. How can you improve the ratio between these two numbers?

5. Have you avoided teaching a difficult concept? Do you have a student, colleague, or a parent-aide who could assist in making that instruction possible? How can you plan for it over the winter or summer vacation?

6. Have you subconsciously negotiated something with your students that doesn't build their language and thinking? For example, do they know that you really don't like for them to ask questions? Do they know they should agree with your points rather than disagree? Do they know that if they are quiet and just write the full period that you will praise their writings even if these writings aren't good quality?

7. What have you done a better job teaching thus far this year than ever before? If so, why and how do you plan to further improve? If not, what can you change?

8. What have your students done better than any other group has ever done before?

9. Is something difficult or uncomfortable for you in the way you relate to a student? Can finding something that the student does well or can do to help you and the class strengthen the bond between you and this student? What is your first idea to change this difficult relationship? What can you do to accomplish it over the winter or summer vacation?

10. Are you taking more papers home to grade than you'd like? How can you alter this practice?

11. Have your students become lax in using effective classroom rules and procedures? Do they need to practice such things as moving from center to center in the room, working effectively in centers, throwing away trash, or sharpening pencils and leaving the room without disturbing others? Do you need to ask them questions about disruptive scenarios, such as "What if I'm conferring with a student and you need something, what do you do?"

12. Have you found yourself beginning class discussions without spending time preparing a variety of respondent-centered questions in advance? (See Chapter 3 if you need to improve your questioning skills.)

13. Would you like more of your discussion periods to begin with questions students ask?

14. Would you like to say the following more frequently in your class: "Tell me another interpretation," "What do you think another reason might be?" "I'd like to hear two viewpoints," "I prefer that you think a moment before you respond to the next issue"?

15. Is the teacher–student–teacher turn-taking cycle evident in your room? Are you restating student responses, answering students' questions without using deliberate silence or answering with another question? Do you want to increase the times you model how to ask questions for clarification?

16. Do you want to increase the number of times students make connections between concepts under discussion and information from their lives and previous discussions?

17. Do you want to increase the number of strategies you use to respond to students' incorrect answers by giving a relevant prompt, paraphrasing, or giving an example or nonexample; or by saying "Think again," "Tell us your thinking," "Remember that—I'm going to return to you again today for that information," or "That would have been correct if . . ."?

18. Do you want to hold more exploratory, fishbowl, integrative, and paired discussions in your class?

19. Do you want to improve the *Individual Students' Oral Language Needs Monitor,* diagnostic instruments in Chapter 3, or any evaluation or instructional tools used this year?

20. Your own question for this year is _____

_____

FOR YOUR JOURNAL

Grading Journals

Review all the journal entries that you have made in the course of reading this textbook. Grade your journal using all the information you have learned about assessment. What did this experience do to improve your ability to grade your students' journals? What grade did you give yourself and why? You can also adapt the grading system in Figures 14.4 and 14.5.

CONNECTING CLASSROOMS, PARENTS, AND COMMUNITIES

Tools for Continual Professional Development

There are many tools you can use to assist in your continuous growth as an educator. Parents, students, and community members can become important partners in this process. For example, the following is a form you can use to assess the videotapes you make of yourself teaching your students. You can improve as a teacher if you videotape yourself for 15 minutes each year. If you store these segments on the same tape, you can also view how you improve from year to year.

FORM TO BE MAILED TO PARENTS PRIOR TO VIDEOTAPING

I would appreciate your granting me permission to videotape a segment of a lesson I will teach next week. The purpose of this tape is for me to assess my instruction. It will not be used to assess your child in any way. He or she will not be identified individually and may not be in the tape. The central focus will be on the actions I am taking. I videotape myself each year to identify improvements I can make. If you grant permission, please sign below.

Signature _____   Date _____

VIDEOTAPE ANALYSIS

You can complete the following assessment after viewing each of your videotapes.

Date _____   Grade Level _____   Subject _____

My goal for improvement is:

What was one of the greatest instructional strengths I gained since my last videotaping?

What were the most distracting elements in my teaching style, delivery, lesson format, or content that I want to eliminate before my next videotaping? How will I eliminate them?

How could I improve my presentation style and interactions with students?

    a. voice, tone, pitch, melody, speed, eliminate crutch words

    b. body movements, mannerisms, gesturing, posture

    c. eye contact

    d. other:

Did I implement the principles of effective language arts instruction stated in Chapter 1?

SUMMARY

This chapter presented several principles for effective language arts assessment. It also described new methods of assessment as well as how to integrate grading into your instruction. Specific attention was also given to ways in which you can evaluate your language arts program, students' journals, and yourself. By completing the mid-year and end-of-year assessment, asking students to evaluate the language arts program, and videotaping yourself once a year, your language arts program can continue to meet more of your students' needs with every succeeding year.

HOW TO DO IT: USING WHAT YOU'VE LEARNED

The following provide opportunities to reflect on and practice what you have learned.

ASSESSING YOUR LEARNING

1. At the Annual Meeting of the National Reading Conference, Dr. Arthur Applebee stated that future language arts teachers should not allow "eclecticism to run wild." What can you do to prevent this from occurring in your classroom?

2. Professor Elizabeth Parillo (1991) stated: "I like questions now even better than answers"; basketball coach John Wooden stated: "It's what you learn after you know it all that counts." What is your response to these statements? How can they be used as gauges for assessing your students?

3. Ms. Sara Day, an elementary school teacher, implemented an idea to advance language arts instruction in her school: "If I have an idea that works well, I write it up in a little note and post it in the lounge. That way, I'm not pushy or 'braggy,' but I can help my other language arts teachers." What can you do to help your colleagues?

4. As we stated in Chapter 1, you must begin with an ideal and end with an ideal. Reflect on how your philosophy of instruction and evaluation has changed in the course of reading this book. Note five changes in the ideal language arts program you now wish to establish.

KEY TERMS EXERCISE

Below are the concepts introduced in this chapter. If you have learned the definition of a term, place a checkmark in the blank that precedes that term. If you are not sure of a definition, increase your retention and return to reread its definition. If you have learned three of the terms in this chapter, you have constructed an understanding of a majority of the most important concepts that you need to assess your students' growth in language arts abilities.

_____ grade equivalencies (p. 603)	_____ rating scales (p. 618)
_____ norms (p. 603)	_____ standardized test (p. 603)
_____ percentiles (p. 603)	_____ stanines (p. 603)

FOR FUTURE REFERENCE

Books to Increase Your Knowledge of Assessing Language Arts Abilities

Anthony, R. J., Johnson, T. D., Mickleson, N. L., & Preece, A. (1991). *Evaluating literacy: A perspective for change.* Portsmouth, NH: Heinemann.

Applebee, A. N., & Langer, J. A. (1983). Instructional scaffolding: Reading and writing as natural language activities. In J. M. Jensen (Ed.), *Composing and comprehending* (pp. 183–190). Urbana, IL: ERIC Clearinghouse on Reading and Communication Skills and National Conference on Research in English.

Au, K. H., Scheu, J. A., Kawakami, A. J., & Herman, P. A. (1990). Assessment and accountability in a whole literacy curriculum. *The Reading Teacher, 43*(8), 574–578.

Bouffler, C. (Ed.). (1992). *Literacy evaluation issues and practicalities.* Gainsville, New South Wales, Australia: Primary English Teaching Association.

Calfee, R. C. (1992). Authentic assessment of reading and writing in the elementary classroom. In M. J. Dreher & W. H. Slater (Eds.), *Elementary school literacy: Critical issues.* Norwood, MA: Christopher-Gordon.

Campione, J. C., & Brown, A. L. (1985). *Dynamic assessment: One approach and some initial data.* (Tech. Rep. No. 361). Urbana: University of Illinois, Center for the Study of Reading.

Clark, C. H. (1982). Assessing free recall. *The Reading Teacher, 35*(6), 434–439.

Clay, M. M. (1985). *The early detection of reading difficulties.* (3rd ed.). Portsmouth, NH: Heinemann.

Cleland, J. V. (1999). We can charts: Building blocks for student-led conferences. *The Reading Teacher, 52*(6), 588–595.

Cohen, L. (1999). The power of portfolios. *Scholastic Early Childhood Today, 13*(1), 23–29.

Courtney, A. M., & Abodeeb, T. L. (1999). Diagnostic–reflective portfolios. *The Reading Teacher, 52*(8), 708–714.

Falk, B. (1998). Testing the way children learn: Principles for valid literacy assessments. *Language Arts, 76*(1), 57–66.

Gillet, J. W., & Temple, C. (1990). *Understanding reading problems: Assessment and instruction.* (3rd ed.). Glenview, IL: Scott Foresman.

Glazer, S. M., & Browing, C. S. (1993). *Portfolios and beyond: Collaborative assessment in reading and writing.* Norwood, MA: Christopher Gordon.

Gronlund, G. (1998). Portfolios as an assessment tool: Is collection of work enough? *Young Children, 53*(1), 4–10.

Jones, J. (2000). Early childhood assessment. *Scholastic Early Childhood Today, 13*(1), 30.

Popham, W. J. (1999). Why standardized tests don't measure educational quality. *Educational Leadership, 56*(1), 8–16.

Potter, E. F. (1999). What should I put in my portfolio? Supporting young children's goals and evaluations. *Childhood Education, 75*(4), 210–214.

Smith, S. S. (1999). Reforming the kindergarten round-up. *Educational Leadership, 56*(1), 39–44.

THEMATIC UNIT: DARE TO DREAM[1]

This unit demonstrates how new assessment strategies can be integrated into language arts instruction. As you read the unit, you can list the principles of effective assessment that were used in it.

Generalization

Students can value the ability of others to have dreams and make them come true. At the same time, they can define their own personal dreams and learn how to realize them.

Objectives

1. Read about different characters that have successfully made a dream become a reality.
   Reading Strategy: Simultaneously develop decoding and comprehension abilities

2. Interview someone they admire and ask about their accomplishments or how they were able to make a dream become a reality.
   Writing Strategy: How to write questions
   Listening Strategy: How to take notes

3. Define what makes a good storyteller and share a story of someone's success with others.
   Speaking Strategy: Ability to speak in front of class
   Reading Strategy: Read out loud with proper intonation, and so forth

4. Verbalize their dreams or goals in a clear, concise fashion and think through possible ways of successfully reaching their goals.
   Thinking Strategy: Metacognition and abilities to work alone
   Writing Strategy: Writing goals and developing goal-setting strategies

Resources

Alexander, L. (1992). *The fortune-tellers.* Illus. by T. S. Hyman. New York: Dutton.

Hopkins, D. (1993). *Sweet Clara and the freedom quilt.* Illus. by J. Ransome. New York: Alfred A. Knopf.

Mitchell, M. K. (1993.) *Uncle Jed's barbershop.* Illus. by J. Ransome. New York: Simon & Schuster.

Pinkney, G. J. (1994). *The Sunday outing.* Illus. by J. Pinkney. New York: Dial.

---

[1]This unit was written by Ms. Nidia Predo, teacher in San José, Costa Rica.

Process in Action

1. You can read *The Fortune-Tellers* out loud to class. Then, you can hold a class discussion on how people have dreams and how these became a reality.

2. Based on *The Fortune-Tellers,* brainstorm on what characteristics make a story fun to hear read out loud and what traits a good storyteller possesses.

3. From the books made available in class (on dreams and making them come true), or by soliciting the librarian's aid, ask students to select one book to share with the class. This book can be read out loud or retold to the class.

4. Have students choose a person they admire because of something they have accomplished (a dream made reality) and interview them. They could write possible questions and have a friend revise and edit them.

5. If the person they admire is a historical figure, they could read autobiographies and biographies about them.

6. Ask students to share their findings with others by writing about this person or historical figure and including a short biographical sketch of them in a class "book" entitled *Dare to Dream.*

7. Then you can ask students to read *Uncle Jed's Barbershop* with a partner. This can be a decoding words practice in which the partners work together to determine what decoding strategy they can use. They can refer to the Thinking Aid of Decoding Strategies if they desire. After they have finished, students can write about what they learned to improve their decoding abilities. Selected pairs could read and discuss these before the group. While students work, you can move from pair to pair performing think-alouds to model decoding strategies for difficult words.

8. You can have small groups (no more than five students) choose a historical figure (or a contemporary person) and share with others how this person was able to make a difference in their community by daring to dream. Possible ways of sharing include panel presentations, readers' theatre, short skit, dance, song, and posterboard presentation. A student script can recreate famous people's lives, such as the saga of Rosa Parks.

Recognizing and Reporting Progress

You can determine if progress has been made by individual students and by the class as a whole by making checklists that the class compiles, such as the one created for effective storytelling in Chapter 3. Once students share with the class, you as well as their peers can fill out the checklist and provide feedback.

Reflections

Students can make extensive use of problem-solving journals in this unit. In these they can discuss what the different stories made them think about and their own personal goals. If these goals are to be reached, students must define what abilities they need and how they can begin working on achieving these goals. The following poem was selected as a favorite by my students.

Dreams

Hold fast to dreams
For if dreams die
Life is a broken-winged bird
That cannot fly.

Hold fast to dreams
For when dreams go
Life is a barren field
Frozen with snow.

—Langston Hughes, from *Selected Poems*

APPENDIX

CORRELATING THE OBJECTIVES OF TEXAS ESSENTIAL KNOWLEDGE AND SKILLS (TEKS) WITH STATE-MANDATED, PROVINCE-BASED CURRICULA

In the past five years, many states, provinces, and countries have created government-mandated curriculum for grades K–8. *Teaching the Language Arts,* Third Edition, was written to develop teachers' competencies in these important curricular domains. State-mandated curricula from numerous locations, including Texas, Kentucky, Connecticut, New York, New Jersey, Nevada, Missouri, Georgia, California, Nebraska, Oklahoma, Wisconsin, Indiana, three Canadian provinces, Australia, New Zealand, England, and The Netherlands, were studied before this textbook was written. Every chapter was constructed to provide teachers with (1) the research base on which individual language arts curriculum were developed; (2) a variety of instructional approaches that educators can implement at primary, intermediate, and middle school levels to develop these language arts competencies with the students under their care; (3) activities that have proven successful in addressing the specific curriculum objectives that are likely to appear in a government-mandated language arts curriculum; and (4) alternative forms of informal and formal assessment of students' skills in each of the language arts.

This textbook was designed so that preservice and inservice teachers can reference it frequently throughout their teaching careers. In doing so, they can expand the educational opportunities of their students in the exact curricular areas that their departments of education expect. The purpose of this Appendix is to demonstrate how *Teaching the Language Arts,* Third Edition, addresses teachers' educational needs in state-mandated curricula. It is based on the Texas Essential Knowledge and Skills (TEKS) curricular goals for the state of Texas. In July 1997, the State Board of Education adopted TEKS as a new, state-mandated curriculum. Beginning with the 1998–1999 school year, all publicly supported school districts in the state of Texas were required to use TEKS as the basis for their classroom instruction in language arts, as well as other content areas. The TEKS for each subject and grade in the language arts curriculum included a broad "knowledge and skills" statement that described what students should learn within that particular language arts domain. Under each knowledge and skills statement was a list of specific "student expectations" that outlined what students, at that grade level, should be able to do to demonstrate their competence in that domain.

The purpose of TEKS is to designate specific student expectations for each subject and grade level. Expressing the specific expectations of the TEKS in terminology that correlated with the specific skill to be assessed on the state-mandated criterion-referenced test (TAAS) reinforced the link between the Texas student-assessment program and the state-mandated curriculum. Similar curricula, tests, and correlations exist in many other educational communities around the world.

How are the TEKS (and other state-mandated) objectives addressed in *Teaching the Language Arts,* Third Edition? At each chapter opening, a list of specific goals for that particular chapter were presented in a language similar to that used in TEKS and other statewide curricula. Readers can reference the introductory section of each chapter to ascertain which discussions correlate with the objectives that individual educators want to address to meet their students' needs. Every TEKS objective (and those of most state-mandated curricula) can be located in this way. After a specific objective has been identified, the discussions in that chapter can be studied to advance the educator's knowledge concerning research, implementation, and assessment of that objective for students at their specific grade level.

For instance, Chapters 6 and 7 were written to address the "knowledge, skills, and expectations" of TEKS (and other state-mandated curricula) relative to the Reading Comprehension Domain. Within this TEKS domain, 6 objectives, 12 knowledge and skills goals, and 19 student expectations were cited for fifth-grade teachers' mastery. The content and number of skills in this domain are similar for each grade K–8. The information that fifth-grade teachers need to increase students' abilities in each of the following objectives described in the TEKS for grade 5 can be obtained by studying the content in Chapters 6 and 7 of this textbook. Each of the other domains of TEKS (and other state-mandated curricula) is addressed in a similar, targeted manner. The goal is for all teachers to receive the depth and breadth of competencies needed to move from state to state, and from pupil to pupil, so that they are in command of the responsibilities for teaching those in their charge.

The following correlation relates Chapters 6 and 7 of *Teaching the Language Arts,* Third Edition, to the TEKS Reading Comprehension Domain, grade 5.

TEKS Objective 5.9: Reading/Vocabulary Development: The student acquires an extensive vocabulary through reading and systematic word study (see pages 212–217).

TEKS Objective 5.10: Reading Comprehension: The student comprehends selections using a variety of strategies (see pages 202–224).

TEKS Objective 5.12: Reading/Text Structures/Literary Concepts: The student analyzes the characteristics of (genres) (see pages 296–301).

TEKS Objective 5.13: Reading/Inquiry/Research: The student inquires and conducts research using a variety of sources (see pages 248–251).

TEKS Objective 5.10: Reading Comprehension/Summarization: The student comprehends selections using a variety of strategies to determine main ideas and how those ideas are supported with details; and paraphrases and summarizes text to recall, inform, or organize ideas (see pages 302–314).

TEKS Objective 5.10: Reading Comprehension/Relationships: The student comprehends selections using a variety of strategies to analyze structure and progression of ideas, such as cause and effect or chronology to locate and recall information (see pages 301–316, 348–353, and 382–384).

TEKS Objective 5.11: Reading/Literary Response: The student expresses and supports responses to various types of texts (see pages 251–258).

TEKS Objective 5.10: Reading Comprehension/Inferences: The student comprehends selections using a variety of strategies to draw inferences (see pages 306–313).

TEKS Objective 5.12: Reading/Text Structures/Literary Concepts: The student analyzes the characteristics of characters, including their traits, motivations, conflicts, points of view, relationships, and changes they undergo, story plot, setting, and problem resolution (see pages 315–316, 405–407, and 322–325).

TEKS Objective 5.13: Reading/Inquiry/Research: The student inquires and conducts research using multiple sources, including graphic sources of information, to interpret and draw conclusions from information gathered (see pages 494–496).

TEKS Objective 5.10: Reading Comprehension: The student learns to distinguish points of view, propaganda, and statements of fact and opinion in a variety of written texts (see pages 549–562 and 163–167).

TEKS Objective 5.12: Reading/Text Structures/Literary Concepts: The student analyzes the characteristics used to produce texts with different purposes, such as to inform, influence, express, or entertain, and describes how the author's perspective or point of view affects the text (see pages 333–354).

ANSWER KEY

CHAPTER 1

1. Answers to Table 1.1: "Do You Employ Principles from Constructivistic, Psycholinguistic, and Sociolinguistic Theories in Your Language Arts Program?" To have employed every cognitive, psycholinguistic, and sociolinguistic principle, you should have checked *yes* to questions 1–19 and *no* to question 20.

1. Constructivistic	6. Sociolinguistic	11. Sociolinguistic	16. Sociolinguistic
2. Psycholinguistic	7. Constructivistic	12. Sociolinguistic	17. Constructivistic
3. Psycholinguistic	8. Constructivistic	13. Constructivistic	18. Constructivistic
4. Psycholinguistic	9. Psycholinguistic	14. Psycholinguistic	19. Psycholinguistic
5. Sociolinguistic	10. Constructivistic	15. Sociolinguistic	20. Psycholinguistic

There are seven Constructivistic items; seven Psycholinguistic items; and six Sociolinguistic items. To determine the percentage of your philosophy that contains constructivistic, psycholinguistic, and sociolinguistic principles, divide your correct answers for each category by the total items in each category. For example, if you have six of the seven Constructivistic items, you have a classroom that is based on 86 percent of the constructivistic learning principles.

CHAPTER 4

1. The answer to Figure 4.4 is *puppy.*

2. The answer to "Using What You've Learned" Number 4: Ms. Stone asked Santiago to show her what a diario was. It was his journal. Santiago wanted to write a purpose-posing entry. Ms. Stone also asked Santiago to teach the class the word *diario.* These two actions showed Ms. Stone's value of Santiago's first language. As a result, Santiago began asking more questions (with less intimidation) as he listened and read for the rest of the school year.

CHAPTER 5

1. The answer to "Using What You've Learned" Number 6 is semantic context clues and the word's configuration. Ms. Hulsey built on this strength and used cards with partners and "What to Do When I Don't Know a Word" because she wanted to expand this decoding base.

2. Answers to Table 5.4 follow.

PHONICS EVALUATION ANSWER KEY

Phonemic Awareness

1. d   2. e

Long Vowel Sounds

3. c   4. d   5. a   6. c   7. b

Short Vowel Sounds

8. st*a*mp   10. tr*u*ck   12. h*u*mble   14. b*u*tter   16. cr*e*pt
9. p*o*pped   11. d*i*mple   13. *i*ntern   15. c*o*tton   17. g*a*mble

Sandwich Words

18. long *a* sound
19. long *o* sound
20. long *e* sound

Layer Cake Words

21. *a-e:* pane, sale, crate
22. *i-e:* slide, price
23. *o-e:* broke, pole
24. *u-e:* huge

Digraphs

25. phase—*ph*, charge—*ch*, rough—*gh*, throw—*th*, which—*ch*, enough—*gh*

Consonant Blends

26. *bl*anket, *pl*ow, *str*ange, *pr*ogram, *cl*ock, *st*andard, *spr*ain, *tr*auma, *dr*aw, *sm*ash, *fl*ock, *dr*ake

Diphthongs

27. Couch—*ou*, convoy—*oy*, spoil—*oi*, fowl—*ow*, crew—*ew*

CHAPTER 8

1. The answer to "Using What You've Learned" Number 5: Ms. Billick used a discovery discussion to teach how to eliminate words that are used repeatedly, how to use figurative language, and how to employ sentence combining approaches to strengthen written communication. At the end of this discovery discussion, Brooke revised her writing as follows:

    "Brooke was born on January 2nd eleven years ago. Although she has four siblings, she only lives with her older sister, Cara, because her stepbrothers live with her father. Mike and Scott are 14 years old and are twins. At home, Brooke enjoys playing with her friends and her two cats, Tiffany and Patches. Some of her favorite things are baseball, pizzas, and the color green."

2. The answer to "Using What You've Learned" Number 7: It would have been easy for the teacher to criticize the student's writing and to jump into a teaching segment about sentence fragments and how to write proper sentences. However, instead she complimented the improvement the student had made. She said that the sentence was wonderful. She also asked the student to write another sentence to tell the class more about it. If sentence fragments continue even after the student is writing longer pieces, teaching a lesson at students' request, about eliminating sentence fragments is proper. At this point in the student's development, providing immediate, specific feedback and encouraging more writing was the best course of action.

CHAPTER 9

1. The answer for p. 359: Teach the silent *le* rule at the end of words (and other patterns such as *ble* and *te*) because Susie is spelling *ancl* for *ankle* and *mapl* for *maple*. *My* was spelled correctly once, but *mi* another time.

2. Answer for "Using What You've Learned" Number 1: In Figure 9.11 both students are in the transitional stage of spelling development. The activities chosen for David were the Word Parts Sort Activities, such as the X Files Sorts game Michael invented, and asking David to write 10 words with the *corn* pattern, *some* pattern, *are* pattern, fam*ily* pattern, *each* pattern, *other* pattern, *found* pattern, *saw* pattern, and b*aby* pattern. The aspect of David's handwriting that his teacher taught him was size so that all his lowercase letters would be the same size and all his uppercase letters would be the same size. Katrice was in the phonetic and letter name stage of spelling development. Using books in Literature Card 24 her teacher provided overlays in which Katrice underlined the words *like, name, reading, what, school, write,* and *to.* Then her teacher asked Katrice to rewrite a note using as many of the new spellings she had learned as she could. She worked on handwriting activity for spacing. She taught Katrice to move her pencil over one pencil width between each word.

CHAPTER 10

1. Answers to invented spellings on p. 451 are ankle, bothering, butterfly, Yankee Doodle, maple, over, river, Santa Claus, next-door neighbor, all the way up, electric, artist, human being, worried, vacuum cleaner, Jim knows me, Phyllis Diller, pledge of allegiance.

CHAPTER 11

1. Answer key for the "Remote Association and Pattern Recognition Test":

1. bill	6. beach	11. chair	16. trace, crate
2. nail	7. model	12. sugar	17. patio
3. water	8. train	13. phase, shape	18. heart, earth, hater
4. yellow (or fly)	9. shore, horse	14. peony	19. tango
5. coach	10. roach	15. tired, tried	20. cobra, carbo

CHAPTER 13

1. Answer to "Using What You've Learned" Number 2: Moll (1992) provided this example of a classroom teacher who was describing the Hispanic culture. The activity being described was selecting a book and then teaching three vocabulary words to students that they wanted to learn.

2. Answers to Table 13.3

Completions:	Multiple Choice:
1. c	6. b
True and False:	7. a
2. F	8. c
3. F	9. a
4. T	10. b
5. T	

REFERENCES

Adams, M. J. (1990). *Beginning to read: Thinking and learning about print.* Cambridge, MA: MIT Press.

Adams, M. J. (1991). Beginning to read: A critique by literacy professionals and a response by Marilyn Jager Adams. *The Reading Teacher, 44*(6) 370–396.

Agnew, P. W., Kellerman, A. S., & Meyer, J. (1991). *Multimedia in the classroom.* Boston: Allyn & Bacon.

Allen, R. V. & Allen, C. (1976). *Language experiences in reading.* Chicago: Encyclopedia Britannica.

Allen, V. G. (1994). Selecting materials for the reading instruction of ESL children. In K. Spangenberg-Usbschat (Ed.), *Kids come in all languages: Reading instruction for ESL students* (pp. 108–134). Newark, DE: International Reading Association.

Allington, R. (1980). Teacher interruption in behaviors during primary grade oral reading. *Journal of Educational Psychology, 72,* 371–377.

Allington, R. (1984). Oral reading. In P. D. Pearson (Ed.), *Handbook of reading research* (pp. 829–864). White Plains, NY: Longman.

Allington, R. (1993). Michael doesn't go down the hall anymore. *The Reading Teacher, 46*(7), 602–604.

Allington, R. (1995). Inclusion: What we know and don't know. Paper presented at the annual meeting of the International Reading Association, Anaheim, CA.

Allington, R. & McGill-Franzen, A. (1989). School response to reading failure. *Elementary School Journal, 89,* 529–542.

Allington, R. L. (1994). The schools we have. The schools we need. *The Reading Teacher, 48*(1), 14–29.

Allington, R. L. & Cunningham, P. M. (1996). *Schools that work: Where all children read and write.* New York: HarperCollins.

Allison, L. & Weston, M. (1993). *Wordsaroni, word play for you and your preschooler.* Boston: Little, Brown.

Altweger, B. & Ivener, B. L. (1994). Self-esteem: Access to literacy in multicultural and multilingual classrooms. In K. Spangenberg-Urbschat (Ed.), *Kids come in all languages: Reading instruction for ESL students* (pp. 65–81). Newark, DE: International Reading Association.

Anderson, J. R. (1985). *Cognitive psychology and its implications* (2nd ed.). New York: W. H. Freeman and Company.

Anderson, R. (1985). Comments on *Becoming a nation of readers. Annual Review of Psychology.* 1985. Washington, DC: U.S. Department of Education, National Institute of Education.

Anderson, R. C. & Pearson, P. D. (1984). A schema-theoretic view of basis process in reading comprehension. In P. D. Pearson (Ed.), *Handbook of reading research* (pp. 255–292). New York: Longman.

Applebee, A. (1991, December). The future of literature instruction: Survey of effective teachers. Paper presented at the annual meeting of the National Reading Conference, Austin, TX.

Applebee, A. (1993). *Literature in the secondary school.* Urbana, IL: National Council of Teachers of English.

Applebee, A. (1999). Teachers' and students' perceptions of language arts goals. *Research in the Teaching of English, 33*(2), 293–317.

Applebee, A., Langer, J., & Mullis, A. (1988). *Report on the national assessment of educational progress.* Princeton, NJ: Educational Testing Service.

Askov, E. N. & Peck, M. (1982). Handwriting. In H. E. Mitzel, B. Hardin, & W. Rabinowitz (Eds.), *Encyclopedia of Educational Research* (5th ed.). New York: The Free Press.

Atwell, N. (1984). Writing and reading literature from the inside out. *Language Arts, 61*(3) 240–252.

Atwell, N. (1995). Writing to learn in an elementary school. Clemson University, SC: Bread Loaf Grant.

Au, K. H. (1993). *Literacy instruction in multicultural settings.* San Diego, CA: Harcourt Brace College.

Avery, D. (1993). *And with a light touch.* Portsmouth, NH: Heinemann.

Baker, L. & Brown, A. L. (1984). Metacognitive skills and reading. In P. D. Pearson (Ed.), *Handbook of Reading Research* (pp. 491–572). New York: Longman.

Bandura, A. & Schunk, D. H. (1981). Cultivating competence, self-efficacy, and intrinsic interest through proximal self-motivation. *Journal of Personality and Social Psychology, 41,* 586–598.

Bang-Jensen, V. (1995). The forgotten fourth and fifth: Views of what upper elementary students are doing in developmentally appropriate classrooms. Unpublished raw data.

Banks, J. A. (1988). *Multiethnic education: Theory and practice.* Boston: Allyn & Bacon.

Banks, J. A. & Banks, C. A. M. (Eds.). (1993). *Multicultural education: Issues and perspectives.* Boston: Allyn & Bacon.

Baratz, F. & Shuy, J. (1969). *Teaching black children to read.* Washington, DC: Center for Applied Linguistics.

Barclay, K. (1992). Six ways lyrics assist students to improve their literacy. Unpublished manuscript. Macomb, IL: Western Illinois University.

Barker, G. & Graham, S. (1987). Developmental study of praise and blame as attributional cues. *Journal of Educational Psychology, 78,* 62–66.

Barkowski, J. & Carr, M. (1987). Metamemory in gifted children. *Gifted Child Quarterly, 31*(1), 40–44.

Barnes, D. (1975). *From communication to curriculuum.* New York: Penguin Books.

Barry, A. L. (1998). Hispanic representation in literature for children and young adults. *Journal of Adolescent and Adult Literacy, 30,* 630–632.

Barton, B. (1986). *Tell me another: Storytelling and reading aloud at home, at school and in the community.* Portsmouth, NH: Heinemann.

Baum, S. M., Renzulli, J. S. & Hebert, T. P. (1994). Reversing underachievement: Stories of success. *Educational Leadership, 52*(5), 48–52.

Baumann, J. F., Hoffman, J. V., Moon, J., & Duffy-Hester, A. M. (1998). Where are teachers' voices in the phonics/whole language debate? Results from a survey of U.S. elementary classroom teachers. *The Reading Teacher, 51*(8), 636–650.

Baumann, J. F., Seifert-Kessell, N., & Jones, L. A. (1992). Effect of "Think-Aloud" instruction on elementary students' comprehension monitoring abilities. *Journal of Reading Abilities, XXIV* (2), 143–172.

Beal, C. R. (1990, August). Development of knowledge about the role of inference in text comprehension. *Child Development, 61*(5), 101–113.

Bear, D. R. & Templeton, S. (1998). Explorations in developmental spelling: Foundations for learning and teaching phonics, spelling, and vocabulary. *The Reading Teacher, 52*(3), 222–242.

Beck, I. (1989). Reading and reasoning. *The Reading Teacher, 42*(9), 676–684.

Beck I. & Dole, J. (1992). Reading and thinking with history and science text. In C. Collins & J. Mangieri (Eds.), *Thinking development: An agenda for the twenty-first century* (pp. 173–185). Hillsdale, NJ: Lawrence Erlbaum.

Beck, K. & McKeoun, M. (1994). Knowledge, compliance, and attitudes of teachers toward mandatory child abuse reporting in British Columbia. *Canadian Journal of Education, 19*(1), 15–29.

Beentjes, R. & Van Den Voort, J. (1988). *Caption vision.* (Research Report No. 213). New York: Center for Visual Acuity.

Bell, N., Grossen, M., & Perret-Clermon, A. (1985). Sociocognitive conflict and intellectual growth. In M. W. Berkowitz (Ed.), *Peer conflict and psychological growth, new directions for child development* (Vol. 29, pp. 41–54). San Francisco: Jossey-Bass.

Bellance, J. & Fogarty, R. (1990). *Blueprints for thinking in the cooperative classroom.* Palatine, IL: Skylight.

Berghoff, B. & Egawa, K. (1991). No more "rocks": Grouping to give students control of their learning. *The Reading Teacher, 44*(8), 536–542.

Berliner, D. (1994). Expertise. In J. Mangieri & C. Block (Eds.), *Creating powerful thinking in teachers and students* (pp. 443–452). Fort Worth, TX: Harcourt Brace College.

Berliner, D. C. & Tikunoff, W. J. (1976). The California beginning teacher evaluation study: Overview of the ethnographic study. *Journal of Teacher Education, 27,* 24–30.

Berninger, D. & Abbot, B. (2000). A multiple connections approach to early intervention for spelling problems: Integrating instructional, learner, and stimulus variables. *Journal of Educational Psychology, 93*(6), 622–634.

Beyer, B. (1987). *Practical strategies for the teaching of thinking.* Boston: Allyn & Bacon.

Beyer, P. K. (1988). *Developing a thinking skills program.* Boston: Allyn & Bacon.

Bitton, J. (1966). Literature as experience. Speech at Dartmouth Conference, Dartmouth, NH.

Blatner, A. & Blatner, A. (1988). *The art of play.* New York: Human Sciences Press.

Block, C. (1990). *SSE and adolescents, 45 minutes of silent reading.* Fort Worth: Texas Christian University.

Block, C. (1993). History of reading instruction. In C. Collins Block (Ed.), *Teaching the language arts: Annotated instructors edition* (pp. 111–117). Boston: Allyn & Bacon.

Block, C. (1994). Developing problem-solving abilities. In J. Mangieri & C. Block (Eds.), *Creating powerful thinking in teachers and students* (pp. 244–261). Fort Worth, TX: Harcourt Brace.

Block, C. (1995). A new lesson plan that builds reading and thinking ability. *Elementary School Journal, 93*(3), 132–145.

Block, C. (2001). *Teaching reading comprehension.* Boston: Allyn & Bacon.

Block, C. & Mangieri, J. (1994). *Creating powerful thinking in teachers and students.* Fort Worth, TX: Harcourt Brace College.

Block, C. & Mangieri, J. (1995a&b, 1996) *Reason to read: Thinking strategies for life through literature, Volumes 1–3.* Menlo Park, CA: Addison.

Block, C. & Zinke, J. (1995). *Creating a cultural enriched curriculum for k–6.* Boston: Allyn & Bacon.

Bloom, B. (1956). *Taxonomy of cognitive abilities.* New York: Harper & Row.

Bloome, D. (1986a). Building literacy and the classroom community. *Theory into Practice, 15,* 71–76.

Bloome, D. (1986b). Reading as a social process in a middle school classroom. In D. Bloome (Ed.), *Literacy and schooling* (pp. 123–149). Norwood, NJ: Ablex.

Bloomfield, L. (1933). *Language.* New York: Holt, Rinehart & Winston.

Blout, N. (1973). Research on teaching literature, language and composition. In R. Travers (Ed.), *Second handbook of research on teaching* (2nd ed., pp. 692–744). Chicago: Rand McNally.

Boomer, G. (1984, October). Literacy, power, and the community. *Language Arts, 61,* 575–584.

Booth, W. (1989). *The rhetoric of fiction.* Chicago: University of Chicago Press.

Borick, G. (1979). Implications for developing teacher competencies from processes and procedure research. *Journal of Teacher Education, 30,* 77–86.

Bracey, G. (1995). The assess or assessed: A "Revolutionist" looks at a critique of the Sandia Report. *Journal of Educational Research, 88*(3), 136–144.

Braumann, J. F., Hooten, H., & White, P. (1999). Teaching comprehension through literature: A teacher–research project to develop fifth graders' reading strategies and motivation. *The Reading Teacher, 53*(1), 31–35.

Brewer, T. (1995). Sequential learning in art. *Art Education, 48*(1), 656–672.

Bridwell, L. S. (1980). Revising strategies in twelfth grade students' transactional writing. *Research in the Teaching of English, 14,* 197–222.

Brike, K. (1991). A fantastic flying journey—through literature. *Language Arts, 68,* 568–573.

Britton, J. (1970). *Language and learning.* Harmondsworth, UK: Penguin.

Britton, J. (1975). *The development of writing abilities* (pp. 11–18). London: Macmillan.

Brookhart, S. & Rusnak, T. (1993). A pedogogy of enrichment not poverty. *Journal of Teacher Education, 44*(1), 17–26.

Brooks, J. G. & Brooks, M. G. (1993). *In search of understanding.* Alexandria, VA: Association for Supervision and Curriculum Development.

Brophy, J. (1988). Educating teachers about managing classrooms and students. *Teaching and Teachers Education, 4*(1), 1–18.

Brophy, J. (1994). Trends in research on teaching. *Midwestern Educational Researcher, 7*(1), 29–39.

Broudy, H. S. (1987). *The role of imagery in learning.* Washington, DC: The Getty Center for Education in the Arts.

Brown, A. & Campione, J. (1986). Interactive learning environment and the teaching of science and mathematics. In M. Gardner & T. Hatcher (Eds.), *Toward a scientific practice of science education* (pp. 401–410). New York: John Wiley & Sons.

Brown, A. L. (1980). Metacognitive development and reading. In R. J. Spiro, B. C. Bruce, & W. F. Brewer (Eds.), *Theoretical issues in reading comprehension* (pp. 453–481). Hillsdale, NJ: Erlbaum.

Brown, A. L. & Palincsar, A. S. (1990). Reciprocal teaching of comprehension strategies. A natural history of one program for enhancing learning. In J. G. Borkowski & J. D. Day (Eds.), *Intelligence and cognition in special children: Comparative studies of giftedness, mental retardation, and learning disabilities* (pp. 79–93). New York: Ablex.

Brown, C. L. & Tomlinsen, C. M. (1993). *Essentials of children's literature.* Fort Worth, TX: Harcourt Brace.

Bruner, J. (1985). Models of the learner. *Educational Research, 14*(6), 5–8.

Bruner, J. (1986). *Actual minds, possible worlds.* Cambridge, MA: Harvard University Press.

Bruner, J. (1990). *Arts of meaning.* Cambridge, MA: Harvard University Press.

Bruner, J. (1998). The human condition. Paper presented at the annual meeting of the American Psychological Association, Boston.

Burley-Allen, M. (1982). *Listening: The forgotten skills.* New York: Wiley.

Burns, B. (1998). Changing the classroom with literature circles. *Journal of Adolescent Adult Literacy, 41*(2), 124–127.

Caine, J. & Caine, T. (1994). Instructional applications of brain research. In MariLee Sprenger (Ed.), *Learning and memory: The brain in action* (pp. 169–179). Alexandria, VA: Association for Supervisor and Curriculum Development.

Cairney, T. (1990). *Other worlds: The endless possibilities of literature.* Portsmouth, NH: Heinemann.

Calfee, R. (1994). Teaching advanced skills to at-risk students. In D. Mangieri & C. Block (Eds.), *Creating powerful thinking in teachers and students* (pp. 146–172). Fort Worth, TX: Harcourt Brace College.

Calkins, L. M. (1983). *Lessons from a child.* Portsmouth, NH: Heinemann.

Calkins, L. M. (1986). *The art of teaching writing.* Portsmouth, NH: Heinemann.

Calkins, L. M. (1991). *Living between the lines.* Portsmouth, NH: Heinemann.

Calkins, L. M. (1994). *The art of teaching writing* (2nd ed.). Portsmouth, NH: Heinemann.

Campbell, F. & Ramey, C. (1995). Cognitive and school outcomes for high-risk African-American students at middle adolescence. *American Educational Research Journal, 32*(4), 743–772.

Canney, G. F., Kennedy, T. J., Schroeder, M., & Miles, S. (1999). Instructional strategies for k–12 limited English proficiency (LEP) students in the regular classroom. *The Reading Teacher, 52*(5), 540–549.

Carr, E. & Ogle, D. (1987). K-W-L plus: A strategy for comprehension and summarization. *Journal of Reading, 30,* 626–631.

Carver, R. P. (1998). *Can all of the variance in word identification be explained by cipher knowledge and lexical knowledge?* (Handout). Austin, TX: National Reading Conference.

Cassady, J. H. (1998). Wordless books: No-risk tools for inclusive middle-grade classrooms. *Journal of Adolescent and Adult Literacy, 42,* 428–430.

Castello, R. (1976). Listening guide—A first step toward notetaking and listening skills. *Journal of Reading, 19*(4), 289–290.

Caswell, L. J. & Duke, N. K. (1998). Nonnarrative as a catalyst for literacy development. *Language Arts, 75*(2), 108–117.

Cavanaugh, M. R. & Mlynarczyk, R. W. (1999). Review. Conversations of the mind: The uses of journal writing for second-language learners. *Journal of Adolescent and Adult Literacy, 43,* 82–95.

Cazden, C. (1993). *Whole language plus.* Portsmouth, NH: Heinemann.

Cazden, C. B. (1990). Differential treatment in New Zealand: Reflections on research in minority education. *Teaching and Teacher Education, 6*(4), 291–303.

Cecil, N. L. (1989). *Freedom fighters: Affective teaching of the language arts.* Salem, WI: Sheffield.

Center for Study of Improvement in Writing. (1998). Center report on literacy achievement. New York: Author.

Chall, J. S. (1983, 1993). *Stages of reading development.* New York: McGraw-Hill.

Chall, J. S., Jacobs, V. A., & Baldwin, L. E. (1990). *The reading crisis: Why poor children fall behind.* Cambridge, MA: Harvard University Press.

Chamot, A. U. & O'Malley, J. M. (1994). *A cognitive academic language learning approach: An ESL content based curriculum* (2nd ed.). Rosaylyn, VA: National Clearinghouse for Bilingual Education.

Chase, P. (1995). A harvest of learning for a multiage class. *Educational Leadership, 77*(1), 51–58.

Chatton, B. (1993). *Using poetry across the curriculum: A whole language approach.* Phoenix, AZ: Oryx Press.

Children's Book Council. (1995). *More kids' favorite books.* New York: International Reading Association.

Chomsky, C. (1969). *The aquisition of syntax in children* (pp. 5–10). Cambridge, England: Cambridge.

Chomsky, N. (1975). *Reflections on language.* New York: Random House.

Chomsky, N. (1976). After decoding: What? *Language Arts, 53,* 288–296.

Christenbury, L. & Kelly, P. (1983). *Questioning: A path for critical thinking.* Urbana, IL: National Council of Teachers of English.

Cianciolo, P. (1982). Responding to literature as a work of art. *Language Arts, 59,* 259–264.

Clark, D. (1988). *Dyslexia: Theory and practice of remedial instruction.* Parkton, MD: York Press.

Clarke, L. K. (1988). Invented versus traditional spelling in first graders' writings: Effects on learning to spell and read.

Research in the Teaching of English, 22, 281–309.

Clark, M. A. (1979). Reading in Spanish and English: Evidence from adult ESL students. *Language Learning, 29,* 121–150.

Clay, M. M. (1975). *What did I write?: Beginning writing behavior.* Auckland, New Zealand: Heinemann.

Clay, M. M. (1979). *Observing young readers.* Portsmouth, NH: Heinemann.

Clay, M. M. (1991). *Becoming literate: The construction of inner control.* Auckland, New Zealand: Heinemann.

Clay, M. M. (1993a). *An observation survey of early literacy achievement.* Portsmouth, NH: Heinemann.

Clay, M. M. (1993b). *Reading recovery: A guide for teachers in training.* Portsmouth, NH: Heinemann.

Clay, M. M. (1995). Preface. In R. Ruddell & M. Ruddell, *Theoretical models and process of reading* (5th ed.). Newark, DE: International Reading Association.

Clay, M. M. (1998). *By different paths to common outcomes.* York, ME: Stenhouse.

Clymer, T. (1996). The utility of phonic generalizations in the primary grades. *The Reading Teacher, 50*(3), 182–187.

Cody, D. (1985). Dealing with dyslexia. *Sky Magazine, 24,* 24.

Cole, M. & Griffin, P. (1987). *Contextual factors in education.* Madison, WI: Wisconsin Center for Educational Research.

Coleman, S. (1992). Bibliotherapeutic section in the library. Unpublished manuscript. Fort Worth, TX: Texas Christian University.

Collier, V. P. (1987). Age and rate of acquisition of second language for academic purposes. *TESOL Quarterly, 21,* 617–640.

Collins, C. (1987). *Time management for teachers.* Englewood Cliffs, NJ: Prentice Hall.

Collins, C. (1988). Principals: Taking the lead in thinking skills development. *Reach: Volume III* (pp. 17–34). Austin, TX: Texas Education Agency.

Collins, C. (1989a). Increasing thinking ability through middle school reading instruction. Paper presented at a meeting of the National Reading Conference.

Collins, C. (1989b). *Bring out the talents and oral expression skills of shy students.* Fort Worth, TX: Educational Research Dissertation.

Collins, C. (1990). Strategies for active engagement: Vignettes that build a questioning mind. Paper presented at the annual meeting of the International Reading Association, Atlanta, GA.

Collins, C. (1991a). Diary of daily events in a non-segregated African-American school. Unpublished manuscript. Fort Worth, TX: Texas Christian University.

Collins, C. (1991b). Audiotaped transcript of Tracy Boyd's tutoring session. Fort Worth, TX: Texas Christian University.

Collins, C. (1992a). *126 strategies that build the language arts.* Boston: Allyn & Bacon.

Collins, C. (1992b). Improving reading and thinking: From teaching or not teaching skills to interactive interventions. In M. Pressley, K. Harris, & I. Guthrie (Eds.), *Promoting academic competence and literacy in schools* (pp. 149–167). San Diego: Academic Press.

Collins, C. (1992c). Thinking development through intervention: Middle school students come of age. In C. Collins & J. Mangieri (Eds.), *Thinking development: An agenda for the twenty-first century* (pp. 121–135). Hillsdale, NJ: Erlbaum.

Collins, C. & Mangieri, J. (Eds.). (1992). *Teaching thinking.* Hillsdale, NJ: Erlbaum.

Compton-Lilly, C. (2000). Stereotypes about challenging urban parents. *Language Arts, 77*(5), 420–427.

Cooper, H., Valentine, J. C., Nye, B., & Lindsay, J. J. (1999). Phonological awareness as a precursor for second grade literacy success. *Journal of Educational Psychology, 91*(2), 369–378.

Cooper, P. (1993). When stories come to school. *Teachers and Writers, 24*(3), 1–9.

Costa, A. L. & Lowery, L. F. (1989). *Techniques for teaching thinking.* Pacific Grove, CA: Midwest Publications.

Cox, B., Shanahan, T., & Sulzby, E. (1990). Scientific writing courses for pediatric fellows. *Academic Medicine, 65*(10), 652–653.

Cox, B. E., Fang, Z., & Otto, B. W. (1997). Preschoolers' developing ownership of the literate register. *Reading Research Quarterly, 32,* 34–53.

Crafton, L. (1983). Learning from reading: What happens when students generate their own background knowledge. *Journal of Reading, 26,* 586–593.

Craig, K. (1992). Using props to ignite creative thinking. Unpublished manuscript. Renesselaer, IN: St. Joseph College.

Craig, R. R. (1996). Storytelling in the classroom: Some theoretical thoughts. *Storytelling World, 9,* 7–9.

Crawford, L. W. (1993). *Language and literacy learning in multicultural classrooms.* Boston: Allyn & Bacon.

Cullinan, B. (Ed.). (1987). *Children's literature in the reading program.* Newark, DE: International Reading Association.

Cullinan, B. (Ed.). (1992). *Invitation to read: More children's literature in the reading program.* Newark, DE: International Reading Association.

Cullinan, B. & Hickman, J. (1989). *Children's literature in the classroom: Weaving Charlotte's Web.* Needham Heights, MA: Christopher-Gordon.

Cummins, J. (1986). Empowering minority students: A framework for intervention. *Harvard Educational Review, 56*(1), 18–36.

Cunningham, P. (1995). *Reading and writing in elementary classroom: Strategies and observations* (3rd ed.). White Plains, NY: Longman.

Cunningham, P. M. (1995). *Phonics they use: Words for reading and writing* (2nd ed.). New York: HarperCollins.

Cunningham, P. M., Hall, D. P., & Defee, M. (1998). Nonability-grouped, multilevel instruction: Eight years later. *The Reading Teacher, 51*(8), 652–664.

Dahl, K., & Farnan, N. (1998). *Literary studies series: Children's writing—Perspectives from research.* Newark, DE: International Reading Association.

Darlin-Hammond, L. (1991). Measuring schools is not the same as improving them. *Youth Policy, 13*(4–5), 19–43.

Davidson, J. I. (1996). *Emergent literacy and dramatic play in early education.* Albany, NY: Delmar.

De Bono, E. (1970). *Lateral thinking.* New York: Harper & Row.

DeFord, D. E. (1981). Literacy: Reading, writing and other essentials. *Language Arts, 58*(6), 652–658.

De Mille, R. (1981). *Put your mother on the ceiling: Children's imagination games.* Santa Barbara, CA: Ross-Erickson.

Destefano, J. (1973). *Language and the language arts.* Boston: Little, Brown.

De Young, A. & Lawrence, B. (1995). On Hoosiers, Yankees, and Mountaineers. *Phi Delta Kappa, 77*(3), 291–307.

Dewey, J. (1899). *School and society.* Chicago: University of Chicago Press.

Dewey, J. (1938). Experience and education. *Kappa Delta Pi Lecture Series.* New York: Collier Books Edition, 1963.

Dickinson, D. K. & Smith, M. W. (1994). Preschool talk: Patterns of teacher–child interaction in early childhood classroom. *Journal of Research in Child Development, 6,* 20–29.

Diederich, P. (1991). *Writing inservice guide for English language arts and TAAS.* Austin, TX: Texas Education Agency.

Dillon, D. (1988). *The practice of questioning.* New York: Routledge.

Dobervich, C. & Thacker, K. (1996). *Welcoming your non–English-speaking student.* Included as part of Penny Torres' Effective ESL Strategies packet. Fort Worth, TX: Fort Worth Independent School District.

Dodds, D. (1991). Dialing for members. *Currents, 17*(3), 38–40.

Dodge, J. B. (1994). *Constructing curriculum for the primary grades.* Washington, DC: Teaching Strategies.

Dole, J. A. (1991). Moving from the old to the new: Research on reading comprehension instruction. *Review of Educational Research, 61,* 239–264.

Donald, J. L. & Kinzer, C. K. (1995). *Effective literacy instruction* (4th ed.). Upper Saddle River, NJ: Simon & Schuster.

Donogue, P. (1990). Method to teach rationale behind silent consonants. Paper presented at a meeting of the International Reading Association, Atlanta, GA.

Dreeben, R. & Barr, K. (1991). Grouping students for reading instruction. In K. Barr & P. Mosenthal (Eds.), *Handbook of reading research* (pp. 885–911). White Plains, NY: Longman.

Duckworth, E. (1987). *The having of wonderful ideas and other essays on teaching and learning.* New York: Teachers College Press.

Duffelmeyer, F., Kruse, A., Merkley, D., & Fyfe, S. (1994). Further validation and enhancement of the names test. *The Reading Teacher, 48,* 118–128.

Duffy, G. G. & Hoffman, J. V. (1999). In pursuit of an illusion: The flawed search for a perfect method. *The Reading Teacher, 53,* 10–17.

Duffy, G. G. & Rohler, L. R. (1989). *Improving classroom reading instruction: A decision-making approach.* New York: Random House.

Duffy, J. (1991). Business partnerships for a thinking populist. In C. Collins & J. Mangieri (Eds.), *Teaching thinking: An agenda for the twenty-first century.* Hillsdale, NJ: Erlbaum.

Duke, N. (2000). How much time do students spend reading non-fiction in first grade? *Reading Research Quarterly, 35*(5), 566–573.

Duling, M. (1987). *The magic of your mind.* Buffalo, NY: Bearly Limited.

Durkin, D. (1966). *Children who read early.* New York: Teachers College Press.

Durkin, D. (1984). Is there a match between what elementary teachers do and what basal reader manuals recommend? *The Reading Teacher, 38*(8), 734–744.

Durst, R. & Newell, G. (1993). *Exploring texts: The role of discussion and writing in the teaching and learning of literature.* Norwood, MA: Christopher-Gordon.

Duthie, C. (1996). *True stories.* York, ME: Stenhouse.

Dyson, A. H. (1991). On friends and writers in a community of learners. In K. S. Goodman, L. B. Bird, & Y. M. Goodman (Eds.), *The whole language catalog* (pp. 46–47). Santa Rosa, CA: American School Publishers.

Dyson, A. H. (1999). Transforming transfer: Unruly children, contrary texts, and the persistence of the pedagogical order. *Review of Research in Education, 24,* 473–489.

Dyson, A. H. (2000, April). The persistence of contrary pedagogical order. Paper presented at the annual meeting of the American Educational Research Association, New Orleans.

Dyson, A. H. & Genishi, C. (Eds.). (1994). *The need for story.* Urbana, IL: National Council of Teachers of English.

Echevarria, J. (1995). *Instructional conversations in special education settings: Issues and accommodations.* San Diego, CA: National Center for Research on Cultural Diversity and Second Language Learning.

Edelsky, C. (1989). Putting language variation to work for you. In P. Rigg & V. Allen (Eds.), *When they don't all speak English: Integrating the ESL student into the regular classroom* (pp. 96–107). Urbana, IL: National Council of Teachers of English.

Edelsky, C., Altwerger, B., & Flores, B. (1991). *Whole language: What's the difference?* Portsmouth, NH: Heinemann.

Eeds, M. & Peterson, R. (1990). *Grand conversations: Literature groups in action.* New York: Scholastic.

Eeds, M. & Wells, D. (1989). Grand conversations: An exploration of meaning construction in literature study groups. *Research in the Teaching of English, 23,* 4–29.

Eeds, M. & Wells, D. (1991). Talking, thinking, and cooperative learning: Lessons learned from listening to children talk about books. *Social Education, 55,* 134–137.

Ehri, L. C. & Wilce, L. S. (1987). Does learning to spell help beginners learn to read words? *Reading Research Quarterly 22*(1), 47–65.

Elbow, P. (1981, November). Unfocused and focused freewriting. Speech at meeting of the National Council of Teachers of English, Philadelphia, PA.

Elley, W. B. & others. (1976). The role of grammar in a secondary school English curriculum. *Research in the Teaching of English, 10,* 5–21.

English, E. W. (1999). *Gift of literacy for the multiple intelligences classroom.* Arlington Heights, IL: Skylight.

Erickson, J. (1993). Teacher's voices: An interview project. Unpublished master's thesis. Fresno, CA: Fresno Pacific College.

Ericson, L. & Juliebö, M. F. (1998). *The phonological awareness handbook for kindergarten and primary teachers.* Newark, DE: International Reading Association.

Fair, J. & others. (1988). *Kids are consumers, too!: Real-world reading and language arts.* Menlo Park, CA: Addison-Wesley.

Farnan, N., Flood, J., & Lapp, D. (1994). Comprehending through reading and writing: Six research-based instructional strategies. In K. Spangenberg-Urbschat (Ed.), *Kids come in all languages: Reading instruction for ESL students* (pp. 135–157). Newark, DE: International Reading Association.

Farris, P. J. (1993). *Language arts—A process approach.* Madison, WI: Brown & Burchmark.

Fawcett, G. (1998). Curricular innovations in literacy instruction: How students respond to the change. *Journal of Literacy Research, 30*(4), 491–509.

Feitelson, D., Kita, B., & Goldstein, Z. (1986). Effects of listening to series stories on first graders' comprehension and use of language. *Research in the Teaching of English, 20,* 339–356.

Ferreiro, E. & Teberosky, A. (1982). *Literacy before schooling.* Portsmouth, NH: Heinemann Educational Books.

Fiderer, A. (1993). *Teaching writing: A workshop approach.* New York: Scholastic Professional Books.

Fielding, R., Wilson P., & Anderson, R. (1986). A focus on free reading: The role of tradebooks in reading instruction. In T. E. Raphael (Ed.), *The contexts of school-based literacy* (pp. 149–160). New York: Random House.

Fisher, C. W. & Hiebert, E. H. (1990). Characteristics of task in two approaches to literacy instruction. *Elementary School Journal, 91,* 3–18.

Fitzgerald, J. (1993). Literacy and students who are learning English as a second language. *The Reading Teacher, 46*(8), 673–689.

Fitzgerald, J. (1995). English-as-a-second-language reading instruction in the United States. *Journal of Reading Behavior, 27,* 115–152.

Fitzgerald, J. & Markham, L. (1987). Teaching children about revision in writing. *Cognition and Instruction, 4,* 3–24.

Fitzsimmons, R. & Loomer, B. (1978). *Spelling: Learning and instruction.* Des Moines, IA: Iowa State Department of Public Instruction.

Flavell, J. H. (1976). Metacognitive aspects of problem solving. In L. B. Resnick (Ed.), *The nature of intelligence* (pp. 231–235). Hillsdale, NJ: Erlbaum.

Fleckenstein, K. S. (1991, October). Inner sight: Imagery and emotion in writing engagement. *TETYC, 18*(3), 301–310.

Forman, E. A. & Cazden, C. B. (1995). Exploring Vygotskian perspectives in education: The cognitive value of peer interaction. In R. Ruddell & M. Ruddell (Eds.), *Theories and process of literacy* (pp. 155–

179). Newark, DE: International Reading Association.

Fowler, E. D. (1992). Charted response to articles as one method of integrating the language arts. Unpublished manuscript. Austin, TX: University of Texas.

Fox, M. (1988, July). Speech. Teachers College Writing Project. Summer Institute, New York.

Fraser, J. & Skolnick, D. (1994). *On their way: Celebrating second graders as they read and write.* Portsmouth, NH: Heinemann.

Freeman, E. & Person, D. (Eds.). (1992). *Using nonfiction trade books in the elementary classroom.* Urbana, IL: National Council of Teachers of English.

Freeman, Y. S. & Freeman, D. E. (1992). *Whole language for second language learners.* Portsmouth, NH: Heinemann

Freeman, Y. S. & Freeman, D. E. (1994). *Between worlds* (pp. 191–192). Portsmouth, NH: Heinemann.

Freppon, P. A. & Dahl, K. L. (1998). Balanced instruction: Insights and considerations. *Reading Research Quarterly, 33*(2), 240–251.

Freppon, P. S. & Dahl, K. L. (1991). Learning about phonics in a whole language classroom. *Language Arts, 68*(3), 190–198.

Frerichs, L. C. (1996, December). Examining first-graders' construction of knowledge of graphophonemic and orthographic relationships: Reading and writing student-selected continuous text. Paper presented at the 46th annual meeting of the National Reading Conference, Charleston, SC.

Friedman, B. (1978, April). Effects of social context on technology. Paper presented at the annual meeting of the American Educational Research Association, New Orleans, LA.

Friedman, B. (1990, April). An ethnographic investigation of the social context of school computer use. Paper presented at the annual meeting of the American Educational Research Association, Boston, MA.

Fries, C. (1963). *Linguistics and reading.* New York: Holt, Rinehart.

Fry, E. (1998). The most common phonograms. *The Reading Teacher, 51*(7), 620–624.

Fry, E. D., Kress, J. E., & Fountoukidis, D. L. (1993). *The reading teacher's book of*

lists (3rd ed.). Englewood Cliffs, NJ: Prentice Hall.

Fu, D. (1995). *My trouble is my English.* Portsmouth, NH: Heinemann.

Fuchs, D., Fuchs, L. S., Mathes, P. G., & Simmons, D. C. (1997). Peer-assisted learning strategies: Making classrooms more responsive to diversity. *American Educational Research Journal, 34,* 174–206.

Fuhler, C. J. (1990). Let's move toward literature-based reading instruction. *The Reading Teacher, 43*(5), 312.

Gage, N. L. (1978, November). The yield of research on teaching. *Phi Delta Kappan, 60,* 229–235.

Gambrell, L. B. (1986). Reading in the primary grades: How often, how long? In M. R. Sampson (Ed.), *The pursuit of literacy* (pp. 105–107). Dubuque, IA: Kimball/Hunt.

Gambrell, L. B. & Bales, R. J. (1986). Mental imagery and the comprehension monitoring performance of fourth and fifth grade poor readers. *Reading Research Quarterly, XXI*(1), 460–462.

Gambrell, L. B. & Jawitz, P. B. (1993). *Mental imagery, text illustrations and children's story comprehension and recall.* Newark, DE: International Reading Association.

Gambrell, L. B. & Koskinen, P. S. (1982, March). Mental imagery and the reading comprehension of below average. Presented at American Educational Research Association, New York.

Gans, K. D. (1994). *Learning through listening* (2nd ed.). Dubuque, IA: Kendall Hunt.

Garcia, E. E. (1991). The education of linguistically and culturally diverse students: Effective instructional practices. Washington, DC: National Center for Research on Cultural Diversity and Second Language Learning, Center for Applied Linguistics.

Garcia, G. (1993). *Literacy needs of limited English proficient students.* Forty-second yearbook of the National Reading Conference. Chicago: National Reading Conference.

Gardner, H. & Hatch, T. (1989). Multiple intelligences go to school: Educational implications of the theory of multiple intelligences. *Educational Researcher, 18*(8), 4–10.

Gardner, H. & Hatch, T. (1990). When children and adults do not use learning strategies: Toward a theory of settings. *Review of Educational Research, 60,* 517–529.

Garmston, R. & Wellman, B. (1994). Insights from constructivist learning theory. *Educational Leadership, 51*(7), 84–85.

Garner, R. (1987). *Metacognition and reading comprehension.* Norwood, NJ: Ablex.

Gaskins, R. W., Gaskins, J. C., & Gaskins, I. W. (1991). A decoding program for poor readers—and the rest of the class too! *Language Arts, 68*(3), 213–225.

Gay, G. (1995). *At the essence of learning: Multicultural education.* Bloomington, IN: Kappa Delta Pi.

Gee, J. (1992). *The social mind.* New York: Bergin & Gainey.

Genishi, C. (1992). Developing the foundation: Oral language and communicative competence. In C. Seefledt (Ed.), *The early childhood curriculum: Review research* (pp. 85–117). New York: Teachers Press.

Gentry, J. R. (1982, November). An analysis of developmental spelling in GNYS AT WRK. *The Reading Teacher, 36,* 192–200.

Gentry, J. R. (1987). *Spel . . . is a four-letter word.* Portsmouth, NH: Heinemann/Boynton Cook.

Gersten, A. & Dimino, S. (1990). Reading instruction for at-risk students: Implications of current research. *Oregon School Study Council Bulletin, 33*(5).

Gibbs, J., Hewing, R., Hulbert, R., & Ramsey, M. (1985, April). Learning through listening. Paper presented at the annual meeting of the American Educational Research Association, Orlando, FL.

Ginott, Haim. (1972). *Teacher and child.* New York: Macmillan.

Goa, J. P. (1973). Effects of individual goal-setting conferences on achievement, attitudes, and goal-setting behavior. *Journal of Experimental Education, 42,* 22–28.

Godden, R. (1988). Shinning popocatapetl: Poetry for children. *Hornbook Magazine, 64*(3), 305–314.

Godley, A. & Mahiri, J. (1998). Rewriting identity: Social meanings of literacy and "revisions" of self. *Reading Research Quarterly, 33*(4), 424–432.

Golden, J. (1986). Story interpretation as a group process. *English Quarterly, 19,* 254–266.

Goldenberg, C., Saunders, B., & Gallimore, R. (1998). Making the transition from Spanish to English instruction. *CREDE, 6,* 1.

Goldman, R. & Goldman, M. (1988). *Effects of caption vision.* (Research Report No. 316). New York: Center for Visual Acuity.

Gomez, M., Graue, M. E., & Bloch, M. (1991). Reassessing portfoilio assessment: Rhetoric and reality. *Language Arts, 68,* 620.

Good, T. & Grouws, D. (1975). *Process–product relationships in 4th grade mathematics classes.* Doctoral dissertation. Columbia, MO: University of Missouri, College of Education.

Goodman, K. (1967). Reading: A psycholinguistic guessing game. *Journal of the Reading Specialist, 1,* 126–135.

Goodman, K. (1970). Behind the eye: What happens in reading. In K. Goodman & O. Niles (Eds.), *Reading: Process and program* (pp. 3–38). Urbana, IL: National Council of Teachers of English.

Goodman, K. S. (1973). *Miscue analysis: Application to reading instruction.* Urbana, IL: National Council of Teachers of English.

Goodman, K. S. (1986). *What's whole about whole language?* Portsmouth, NH: Heinemann.

Goodman, K. S. (1987). Acquiring literacy is natural. Who skilled Cock Robin? *Theory into Practice, 26,* 368–373.

Goodman, K. S., Goodman, Y., & Hood, W. (1989). *The whole language evaluation book.* Portsmouth, NH: Heinemann.

Goodman, N. (1967). Reading: A psycholinguistic guessing game. *Journal of the Reading Specialist, 6,* 126–135.

Goodman, Y. (1978). Kid watching: An alternative to testing. *National Elementary Principals Journal, 57,* 41–45.

Goodman, Y. (1983) Language, cognitive development and reading behavior. *Claremont reading conference yearbook* (pp. 10–16). Claremont, CA: Claremont Graduate School.

Goodman, Y. (1985). Kidwatching: Observing children in the classroom. In A. Jaggar & M. T. Smith-Burke (Eds.), *Observing the language learner.* Newark, DE: International Reading Association; and Ur-

bana, IL: National Council of Teachers of English.

Gordon, C. & MacGinnis, D. (1993). Using journals as a window on students' thinking in mathematics. *Language Arts, 70,* 37–43.

Gore, D. (1992). Basic word approach and spelling. Unpublished manuscript. Clarksville, TN: Austin Peay State University.

Gough, P. B., Alford, J. A., & Holly-Wilcox, P. (1981). Words and contexts. In O. L. Tzeng & H. Singer (Eds.), *Perception of print: Reading research in experimental psychology.* Hillsdale, NJ: Erlbaum.

Graesser, A. C. & McMahen, M. (1993). Narrative and comprehension. In R. Barr, M. Kamil, P. Mosenthal, & P. D. Pearson (Eds.), *Handbook of reading research, Vol. II* (pp. 171–205). New York: Longman.

Graesser, A. C., Pomeroy, V., Craig, S., & Olde, B. (1999, April). How do adults comprehend the mechanisms of everyday devices: Texts, illustrations, and breakdown scenarios. Paper presented at the meeting of the American Educational Research Association, Montreal, Canada.

Graham, S. & Barker, G. (1990). The downside of help. *Journal of Educational Psychology, 82,* 7–14.

Graham, S. & Block, C. (1993). Elementary students as co-teachers and co-researchers. Paper from a meeting of the National Reading Conference, Charleston, SC: National Reading Conference.

Graves, D. (1999). *Bringing life into learning.* Portsmouth, NH: Heinemann.

Graves, D. H. (1977). Research update: Spelling texts and structural analysis methods. *Language Arts, 45,* 86–90.

Graves, D. H. (1983). *Writing: Teachers and children at work.* Portsmouth, NH: Heinemann.

Graves, D. H. (1990). *Discover your own literacy.* Portsmouth, NH: Heinemann.

Graves, D. H. (1994). *A fresh look at writing.* Portsmouth, NH: Heinemann.

Graves, D. H. & Hansen, J. (1983). The author's chair. *Language Arts, 60,* 176–183.

Graves, M., Graves, B., & Braaten, S. (1996). Scaffolded reading experiences for inclusive classes. *Educational Leadership, 53*(5), 14–18.

Greenlaw, J. M. (1987). Books in the classroom. *Hornbook, 63*(1), 108–110.

Gunning, T. (1995). Word building: A strategic approach to the teaching of phonics. *The Reading Teacher, 48*(6).

Guthrie, J. & others. (1995). Relationships of instruction to amount of reading. *Reading Research Quarterly, 30*(1), 8–25.

Gutierréz, K., Baquedano-Lopez, P., & Turner, M. (1997). Putting language back into language arts: When the radical middle meets the third space. *Language Arts, 74*(5), 368–375.

Haas, T. & Lambert, R. (1995). To establish the bonds of common purpose and mutual enjoyment. *Phi Delta Kappan, 77*(2), 136–140.

Hackney, S. (1995). Who owns history? *Humanities, 16*(1), 6–11.

Hagerty, P. (1992). *Reader's workshop: Real reading.* New York: Scholastic Canada.

Hagerty, P. & Hiebert, E. (1989, March). A comparison of student outcomes in literature-based and conventional classrooms. Presented at a meeting of the American Educational Reading Association, San Francisco.

Hakuta, K. & Gould, L. J. (1987). Synthesis of research on bilingual education. *Educational Leadership, 44*(6), 38–45.

Hall, D. P. & Cunningham, P. M. (1988). Context as a polysyllabic decoding strategy. *Reading Improvement, 25*(4), 261–264.

Hall, M. A. (1981). *Teaching reading as language experience.* Columbus, OH: Merrill.

Hallenbeck, T. (1995, April). Listening actively: A research report. Paper presented at the annual meeting of the American Educational Research Association, Chicago.

Halliday, M. (1993). Some grammatical problems in scientific English. In M. A. K. Halliday & J. R. Martin (Eds.), *Writing science: Literacy & discursive power* (pp. 69–85). London: Falmer.

Halliday, M. A. K. (1982). Relevant models of language. In B. Wade (Ed.), *Language perspectives.* Portsmouth, NH: Heinemann Educational Books.

Hancock, M. (1993). Exploring the meaning-making process, through the content of literature response journals. *Research and Thinking of English, 27*(4), 335–368.

Hanna, P. R. & others. (1966). *Phoneme-grapheme correspondences as cues to spelling improvement.* Washington, DC: U.S. Department of Health, Education, and Welfare.

Hanson, R. A. & Farrell, D. (1995). The long-term effects on high school seniors of learning to read in kindergarten. *Reading Research Quarterly, 30*(4), 908–933.

Harris, V. J. (1993). *Teaching multicultural literature in grades k–8.* Norwood, MA: Christopher-Gordon.

Harste, J., Woodward, V., & Burke, C. (1984). *Language stories and literacy lessons.* Portsmouth, NH: Heinemann.

Harste, J. (1989). *New policy guidelines for reading.* Urbana, IL: National Council of Teachers of English.

Harste, J., Burk, C., & Woodward, V. (1995). *Language stories and literacy lessons* (2nd ed.). Portsmouth, NH: Heinemann.

Harste, J. C., Short, K. G., & Burke, C. (1988). *Creating classrooms for authors: The reading–writing connection.* Portsmouth, NH: Heinemann.

Hartle-Schutte, D. (1993). Literacy development in Navajo home. *Language Arts, 70*(8), 642–654.

Hartley, R. E. & Goldenson, R. M. (1975). *The complete book of children's play.* New York: Cromwell.

Harvey, S. (1998). *Nonfiction matters.* York, ME: Stenhouse.

Hawisher, G. E. (1987). The effects of word processing on the revision strategies. *Research in the Teaching of English, 21,* 145.

Hawkins, J. & Mandl, H. (Eds.). (1996). The Jasper series: A design experiment in complex, mathematical problem-solving. *Design experiments: Integrating technologies into schools.* New York: Cambridge University Press.

Heard, G. (1989). *For the good of the earth and sun: Teaching poetry.* Portsmouth, NH: Heinemann.

Heath, D. H. (1994). *Schools of hope: Developing mind and character in today's youth.* San Francisco: Jossey-Bass.

Heath, S. B. (1983). *Ways with words.* New York: Cambridge University Press.

Heath, S. B. (1986). *Way with words.* New York: Teachers College Press.

Heath, S. B. (1991). The sense of being literate. Historical and cross-cultural features. In R. Barr, M. Kamil, P. Mosenthal, & P. D. Pearson (Eds.), *Handbook of Reading Research,* Vol II (pp. 3–25). White Plains, NY: Longman.

Henderson, E. H. (1990). *Teaching spelling* (2nd ed.). Boston: Houghton Mifflin.

Hepler, S. (1982). Patterns of response to literature. Unpublished dissertation. Columbus: Ohio State University.

Heshusius, L. (1995). Listening to children: "What could we possibly have in common?": From concerns with self to participatory consciousness. *Theory into Practice, 34,* 117–123.

Hess, R. & McDevitt, T. (1984). Some cognitive consequences of matural intervention technics. *Child Development, 55*(6), 2017–2030.

High, J. (1996). *Second language learning through cooperative learning.* New York: Kagan Cooperative Learning.

High, J. (1998, April). Stop stories for ESL students. Paper presented at the annual meeting of the International Reading Association, Orlando, FL.

Hillard, A. (1992). Behaviorial style, culture and teaching and learning. *The Journal of Negro Education, 6,* 370–377.

Hillard, A. G. (1989). Teaching and cultural styles in a pluralistic society. *National Education Association, 7*(6), 65–69.

Hillerich, R. L. (1985). *Teaching children to write, k–8: A complete guide to developing writing skills.* Englewood Cliffs, NJ: Prentice Hall.

Hilliker, J. (1986). Labelling to beginning narrative. In N. Thomas & N. Atwell (Eds.), *Understanding writing.* Portsmouth, NH: Heinemann.

Hillocks, G. (1987). Synthesis of research on teaching writing. *Educational Leadership, 44*(8), 871–882.

Hodges, R. (1991). *Learning to spell.* Urbana, IL: National Council of Teachers of English.

Holdaway, D. (1979). *The foundations of literacy.* Portsmouth, NH: Heinemann.

Holdaway, D. (1990). *Independence in reading.* Portsmouth, NH: Heinemann.

Holmes, C. T. (1989). Grades level retention effects. In L. Shepard & M. Smith (Eds.), *Flunk grades.* London: Falmer Press.

Hong, M. (1995). *To home and back with books.* Newark, DE: International Reading Association.

Hopkins, G. & Bean, T. W. (1998). Vocabulary learning with the verbal–visual word association strategy in a Native-American community. *Journal of Adolescent and Adult Literacy 42*(4), 278.

Horn, T. D. (1947). The effect of the corrected test on learning to spell. *Elementary School Journal, 57,* 233–235, 246.

Hornberger, N. W. (1990). Creating successful learning contexts for bilingual literacy. *Teachers College Record, 92*(2), 212–229.

Howard, K. (1990). Making the writing portfolio real. *The Quarterly of the National Writing Project and the Center for the Study of Writing, 12*(2), 4–6.

Howie, S. M. (1979). A study of the effects of sentence combining and writing ability and reading level of ninth grade students. Unpublished dissertation. Boulder, CO: University of Colorado.

Huck, C. (1992). Literacy and literature. *Language Arts, 69,* 520–526.

Huck, C. S. (1989). No wider than the heart is wide. In J. Hickman & B. E. Cullinan (Eds.), *Children's literature in the classroom: Weaving Charlotte's Web* (pp. 252–262). Needham Heights, MA: Christopher-Gordon.

Hudelson, S. (1989). "Teaching" English through content-area activities. In P. Rigg & V. G. Allen (Eds.), *When they don't all speak English: Integrating the ESL student into the regular classroom.* Urbana, IL: National Council of Teachers of English.

Huizenga, J. (1955). *Homo ludens: A study of the play element in culture.* Boston: Beacon Press.

Hyde, D. (1992). Evaluating student learning in language arts in the primary grades through whole language assessment techniques. Unpublished dissertation. St. Petersburg, FL: Nova University.

Irvin, J. (1989). Reading instruction in middle level schools. *Journal of Reading, 32* (4), 306–311.

Irwin, J. W. (1991). *Teaching reading comprehension processes* (2nd ed.). Englewood Cliffs, NJ: Prentice Hall.

Jacobs, L. (1986). Listening: A skill we can teach. *Early Years, 17,* 109–110.

Jacobson, J. M. (1989). Laptop flannel boards. *The Reading Teacher, 43*(2), 189.

James, C. F. & Stone, S. J. (1999). Collaborative literacy activity in print enriched play centers: Exploring the "Zone" in same-age and multi-age groupings. *Journal of Literacy Research, 31*(2), 109–131.

James, W. (1915). *Talks to teachers.* New York: World Book.

Jensen, E. (1998a). How Julie's brain works. *Educational Leadership: How the Brain Works, 56*(3), 45.

Jensen, E. (1998b). *Teaching with the brain in mind.* Alexandria, VA: Association for Supervision & Curriculum Development.

Jewell, T. A., & Pratt, D. (1999). Literature discussions in the primary grades: Children's thoughtful discourse about books and what teachers can do to make it happen. *The Reading Teacher, 52*(8), 842–850.

Jimenez, R. T., Moll, L., Rodriquez-Brown, F., & Barrera, R. (1999). Conversations: Latina & Latino researchers interact on issues related to literacy learning. *Reading Research Quarterly, 34*(2), 217–230.

Johnson, D. D. & Pearson, P. D. (1984). *Teaching reading vocabulary* (2nd ed.). New York: Holt, Rinehart.

Johnson, D. W. (1993). *Reaching out.* Needham Heights, MA: Allyn & Bacon.

Johnson, K. (1995). Exploring the world with the private eye. *Educational Leadership, 77*(1), 52–57.

Johnson, T. D., Langford, K. G., & Quorn, K. C. (1981). Characteristics of an effective spelling program. *Language Arts, 58,* 581–588.

Johnston, P. (1992). *Constructive evaluation in literacy.* White Plains, NY: Longman.

Johnston, P. H. (1985). Understand reading disability: A case study approach. *Harvard Educational Review, 55,* 153–177.

Johnston, P. H. & Winograd, P. N. (1985). Passive failure in reading. *Journal of Reading Behavior, 17,* 279–301.

Johnston, R., Allinton, R., & Afferbach, P. (1985). The congruence of classroom and remedial reading instruction. *The Elementary School Journal, 85,* 465–477.

Johnstone, F. R. (1998). The text and the task: Learning words in first grade. *The Reading Teacher, 51*(8), 666–675.

Judd, R. (1989). Students self assessment. In N. L. Cecil (Ed.), *Freedom fights: Affective teaching of the language arts.* Salem, WI: Sheffield.

Juel, C. (1990). Effects of reading group assignment on reading development in first and second grade. *Journal of Reading Behavior, 22,* 233–254.

Juel, C. (1991). Cross-age tutoring between students–athletes and at-risk children. *The Reading Teacher, 45,* 178–186.

Kabrin, B. (1998). *Eyeopeners.* New York: Penguin Books.

Kang, Y. (1993). Teacher's strategies and its effect on self-efficacy beliefs of elementary middle school children. Paper presented at the American Educational Research Association, Atlanta, GA.

Karweit, N. (1989c). Time and learning: A review. In R. Slavin, N. Karweit, & N. Madden (Eds.), *Effective programs for students at risk.* Boston: Allyn & Bacon.

Kean, T. H. (1992). Adolescent health: A generation at risk. *Carnegie Quarterly, XXXVII*(4), 7–9.

Keller, H. (1954). *The story of my life.* New York: Doubleday.

Keller, H. (1955). *My life.* New York: World Books.

King, A. (1994, Summer). Guiding knowledge construction in the classroom: Effects of teaching children how to question and how to explain. *American Educational Research Journal, 31*(2), 338–368.

Kletzien, L. (1991). Strategy use by good and poor comprehenders. *Reading Research Quarterly, XXVI*(1), 70–94.

Klimenkov, M. & LaPick, N. (1996). *Writing portfolios in the classroom (policy and practice, promise and peril).* Mahwah, NJ: Lawrence Erlbaum.

Knapp, M. (1998). *Teaching for meaning in high-poverty classroom.* New York: Teachers College Press.

Koskinen, P. (1993). Captioned television improves reading abilities. *The Reading Teacher, 12*(3), 211–219.

Koskinen, P. (Ed.). (1995). The new basals: How are they different? *The Reading Teacher, 49*(1), 17–23.

Koval, C. (1992). *From fact to fantasy—And back again.* Saint Leo, FL: Saint Leo College.

Kozulin, A. (1990). *Vygotsky: A biological perspective.* Cambridge, MA: Harvard University Press.

Krashen, S. & Biber, D. (1988). *On course: Bilingual education's success in California.* Sacramento, CA: California Association of Bilingual Education.

Krashen, S. & Terrell, D. (1983). *The natural approach: Language acquisition in the classroom.* Hayward, CA: Alemany Press.

Kreeft, J. P. & Shuy, R. W. (1985). *Dialogue writing analysis of student–teacher interactive writing in the learning of English as a second language.* (Final report to the National Institute of Education, NIE-G-83-0030). Washington, DC: Center for Applied Linguistics.

Kreiner, D. S. & Gough, P. B. (1990). Two ideas about spelling: Rules and word-specific memory. *Journal of Memory and Language, 29,* 103–118.

Kupfermann, F. (1991, April). Memory: Auditory dependence. Paper presented at the annual meeting of the American Educational Research Association, Boston, MA.

Labov, W. (1972). *Language of the inner city.* Philadelphia, PA: University of Pennsylvania Press.

Ladson P. & Billings, G. (1995). Toward a theory of culturally relevant pedagogy. *American Educational Research Journal, 32*(3), 465–491.

Langer, J. A. (1991). *Literary understanding and literature instruction.* (Report series 2.11). Albany, NY: Center for the Learning and Teaching of Literature.

Langer, J. A. (1992). Rethinking literature instruction. In J. A. Langer (Ed.), *Literature instruction: A focus on student response* (pp. 35–53). Urbana, IL: National Council of Teachers of English.

Langer, J. A. (1994). A response-based approach to reading literature (Report Series 6.7). Albany, NY: National Research Center on Literature Teaching and Learning.

Lansky, B., Broberg, C., & Weiss, E. (Eds.). (1994). *Free stuff for kids.* Deephaven, MN: Meadowbrook Press.

Larrivee, B., Semmel, M. I., & Gerber, M. M. (1997). Case studies of six schools varying in effectiveness for students with learning disabilities. *The Elementary School Journal, 98*(1), 27–50.

Lazear, D. (1994). *Seven pathways of learning.* Tucson, AZ: Zephyr Press.

Lee, C. & Jackson, R. (1992). *Faking it: A look into the mind of a creative learner.* Portsmouth, NH: Heinemann.

Lee, K. & Van Allen, R. (1963). *The language experience approach.* Newwark, DE: International Reading Association.

LeGuin, U. K. (1998). *Steering the craft: Exercises and discussions on story writing for the lone navigator or the mutinous crew.* Denver, CO: Eighth Mountain Press.

Lehr, J. & Harris, H. (1988). *At-risk, low achieving students in the classroom.* Washington, DC: NEA Professional Library.

Lehr, S. (1995). *Battling dragons: Issues and controversy in children's literature.* Portsmouth, NH: Heinemann.

Leibert, R. E. (1991). The dolch list revisted. *Reading Horizons, 31*(3), 217–227.

Lepper, M., Aspinwall, L., Mumme, D., & Chabay, R. (1990). Self-perception and social perception processes in tutoring: Subtle social control strategies of expert tutors. In J. M. Olson & M. P. Zanna (Eds.), *Self-inference process: The Ontario symposium* (pp. 217–237). Hillsdale, NJ: Erlbaum.

Lepper, M. R., Drake, M. F., & O'Donnell-Johnson, T. (1997). Scaffolding techniques of expert human tutors. In M. Pressley & K. Hogan (Eds.), *Advanced in teaching and learning* (pp. 108–144). Cambridge, MA: Brookline Books.

Leseman, P. M. & De Jong, P. F. (1998). Home literacy: Opportunity, instruction, cooperation and social–emotional quality predicting early reading achievement. *Reading Research Quarterly, 33*(3), 294–318.

Lesgold, A. & Resnick, L. (1982). How reading difficulties develop. In J. Das, R. Mulcohey, & A. Wall (Eds.), *Theory and research in learning disabilities* (pp. 155–187). New York: Plenum.

Lesgold, A. (1999). *Beginning a technology of technical training for information age manufacturing* (p. 1). Pittsburgh, PA: University of Pittsburg, Learning Research and Development Center.

Leu, D. J. & Kinzer, C. K. (1995). *Effective literacy instruction* (4th ed.). Upper Saddle River, NJ: Simon & Schuster.

Levi, P. (1990). Assessment and educational vision: Engaging learners and parents. *Language Arts, 67*(3), 269–273.

Levinson, R. (1985). *Watch the stars come out N.Y.E.P.* New York: Dutton.

Lewin, C. (1997). Evaluating talking books? Ascertaining the effectiveness of multiple feedback modes and tutoring techniques. In C. K. Kinzer, K. A. Hinchman, & D. J. Leu (Eds.), *Inquiries in literacy theory and practice* (pp. 360–369). Chicago: National Reading Conference.

Linden, M. J. & Whimbey, A. (1990). *Why Johnny can't write.* Hillsdale: NJ: Lawrence Erlbaum.

Linn, R. L., Baker E. L., & Dunbar, S. B. (1991). Complex, performance-based assessment: Expectations and validation criteria. *Educational Researcher, 20,* 8.

Loban, W. P. (1963). *The language of elementary school children.* Urbana, IL: National Council of Teachers of English.

Lodge, D. (1992). *The art of fiction.* New York: Viking.

Lowe, A. J. (1992). Cautions to consider while preparing whole language materials for the beginning readers. Unpublished manuscript. Tampa, FL: University of South Florida.

Loxterman, J. A., Beck, I. L., & McKeoun, M. G. (1994). The effects of thinking aloud during reading on students' comprehension of more or less coherent text. *Reading Research Quarterly, 29*(4), 353–366.

Lundberg, I. (1987). Phonological awareness facilitates reading and spelling acquisition. In W. Ellis (Ed.), *Intimacy with language: A forgotten basic in teacher education* (pp. 56–63). Baltimore, MD: The Orton Dyslexia Society.

Lundsteen, S. (1979). *Language arts: A problem-solving approach.* New York: Harper & Row.

MacIver, D. J. (1992). Motivating disadvantaged students to reach new heights: Effective evaluations, reward and recognition structures. *CDS Report,* No. 32, Baltimore, MD.

Mackey, M. (1997). Good-enough reading: Momentum and accuracy in the reading of complex fiction. *Research in the Teaching of English, 31*(4), 428–458.

Madaus, G. F. & O'Dwyer, L. M. (1999). A short history of performance assessment lessons learned. *Phi Delta Kappan, 80*(9), 688–695.

Mager, R. (1977). *Behavioral objectives.* New York: Wm. Brown.

Mandler, B. & Johnson, D. (1977). Remembrance of things parsed: Story structure and recall. *Cognitive Psychology, 9,* 111–115.

Mangieri, J. N. & Block, C. C. (1996). *Power thinking for success.* Cambridge, MA: Brookline Books.

Manzo, A. V. (1981). Using proverbs to teach reading and thinking; or come faceva mia nonna (The way my grandmother did it). *The Reading Teacher, 24* (2), 411–416.

Martinez, M., Rosen, N., Worthy, J., Strechen, S., & Gough, P. (1997). Classroom libraries and children's book selections: Redefining "access" in self-selected reading. In C. Kinzer, K. Henchman, & D. Lew (Eds.), *Inquiries in literacy theory and practice* (pp. 121–126). Chicago: National Reading Conference.

Martinez, M., Roser, N. L., & Strecker, S. (1998). I never thought I could be a star: A readers theatre ticket to fluency. *The Reading Teacher, 52*(4), 326.

Marzano, R., Jones, B. F., & Brandt, R. (1988). *Dimensions of thinking.* Alexandria, VA: Association for Supervision and Curriculum.

Mason, J. M. & Au, K. (1990). *Reading instruction for today* (2nd ed.). Glenview, IL: Scott Foresman.

Mason, J. M. & others. (1990). Shared book reading in an early start program for at-risk children. In J. Zuttrell & S. McCormack (Eds.), *Literacy theory and research: Analyses from multiple paradigms.* Chicago: National Reading Conference.

Mastropieri, M. A. & Scruggs, T. E. (1991). Reading comprehension: A synthesis of research in learning diabilities. In T. E. Scruggs & M. A. Mastropieri (Eds.), *Advances in learning and behavioral disabilities.* Greenwich, CT: JAI Press.

Matthews, M. (1992). Gifted students talk about cooperative learning *Educational Leadership, 50*(2), 48–50.

Matute-Bianchi, M. (1986). Ethnic identities and patterns of school success and failure among Mexican descent and Japanese American students in a California high school. *American Journal of Education, 95*(1), 233–255.

Maynor, L. C. (1982). An investigation of the revising practices of college freshmen writers. Doctoral dissertation. Durham, NC: Duke University.

McCaslin, M. & Good, T. (1992). Compliant cognition: The misalliance of management and instructional goals in current school reform. *Educational Researcher, 26* (3) 36–49.

McClelland, J. L. & Rumelhart, D. E. (1986). *Parallel distributed processing, Vol. 2: Psychological and biological models.* Cambridge, MA: MIT Press.

McClure, A. (1995). Fostering talk about poetry. In M. Roser & M. Martinez (Eds.), *Book talk and beyond.* Newark, DE: International Reading Association.

McClure, A., Harrison, P., & Reed, S. (1990). *Sunrises and songs: Reading and writing poetry in an elementary classroom.* Portsmouth, NH: Heinemann.

McClure, J. (1989). *Teaching poetry.* Portsmouth, NH: Heinemann.

McConaughy, S. (1985). Good and poor readers' comprehension of story structure accross different input and output modalities. *Reading Research Quarterly, 20*(27), 219–231.

McGee, L. M. (1998). In practice: Building walls. In S. Neuman & K. Roskos (Eds.), *Children achieving: Best practices in early literacy* (pp. 211–220). Newark, DE: International Reading Association.

McIntyre, E. & Freppan, P. (1995, May). A comparison of childrens' development of alphabetic knowledge in a skills-based and a whole language program. Paper presented at a meeting of the International Reading Association, New Orleans.

McIntyre, J. (1991, April). Phonics: Success in first grade. Speech delivered at Texas Christian University, Fort Worth, TX.

McKenna, M. C. & Kear, D. J. (1990, May). Elementary reading attitude survey. *The Reading Teacher, 42*(7), 628–639.

McKenna, M., Robinson, R., & Miller, J. (1993). Whole language and research. In D. Leu & C. Kinder (Eds.), *Examining central issues in literacy research, theory and practice* (pp. 141–152). Chicago: National Reading Conference.

McKeown, M. G. (1993). Creating effective definitions for young word learners. *Reading Research Quarterly, 28,* 16–31.

McLaughlin, B. (1987). Reading in a second language: Studies with adult and child learners. In S. R. Goldman & H. T. Trueba (Eds.), *Becoming literate in English as a second language* (pp. 57–70). Norwood, NJ: Ablex.

McLaughlin, B. (1995). *Fostering second language development in young children: Principles and practices.* Santa Cruz, CA: University of California, National Center for Research on Cultural Diversity and Second Language Learning.

McMaster J. C. (1998). Doing literature using drama to build literacy. *The Reading Teacher, 51*(7), 582.

McNeil, J. (1987). *Reading comprehension: New direction for classroom practice* (3rd ed.). Glenview, IL: Scott Foresman.

Means, B. & Knapp, M. (1991). Introduction: Rethinking teaching for disadvantaged students. In B. Means, C. Chaiemer, & M. Knapp (Eds.), *Teaching advanced skills to at-risk students.* San Francisco: Jossey-Bass.

Medley, D. M. (1977). *Teacher competence and teacher effectiveness: A review of process–product research.* Washington, DC: American Association of College for Teacher Education.

Meek, M. (1992). The peacekeepers. *Teaching Tolerance, 1*(2), 46–52.

Meichenbaum, D. (1985). *Cognitive behavior modifications: An integrative approach.* New York: Plenum Press.

Meier, T. & Cazden, C. (1982). Research update. *Language Arts, 49*(5), 504–512.

Meltzer, L. & Solomon, B. (1988). *Educational prescriptions for the classroom for students with learning problems.* Cambridge, MA: Educators Publishing Service.

Menke, D. & Pressley, M. (1994). Elaborative interrogation: Using "Why" questions to enhance the learning from text. *Journal of Reading, 37*(8), 642.

Michel, P. A. (1994). *The child's view of reading.* Boston: Allyn & Bacon.

Miller, W. H. (1993). *Complete reading disabilities handbook: Ready-to use techniques for teaching reading disabled students.* West Nyack, NII. The Center for Applied Research in Education.

Miller, W. H. (1997). *Reading and writing remediation kit.* Washington, DC: The Center for Applied Research in Education.

Moffett, J. & Wagner, B. J. (1983). *Student-centered language arts and reading, k–13: A handbook for teachers.* Boston: Houghton Mifflin.

Moll, L. (1990). Social and instructional issues in education disadvantaged students. In M. S. Knapp & P. M. Shields (Eds.), *Better schooling for the children of poverty: Alternative to conventional wisdom: Vol. 2. Commissional papers and literature review.* Washington, DC: Department of

Education, Office of Planning, Budget and Evaluation.

Moll, L. (1999, March). The value of dual-language learning. Paper presented as Green Honors Chair, Texas Christian University, Fort Worth, TX.

Moll, L. C. (1992). Literacy research in community and classroom: A sociocultural approach. In R. Beach, J. P. Green, M. L. Kemil, & T. Shannon (Eds.), *Multidisciplinary perspectives on literacy research* (pp. 211–244). Urbana, IL: National Council of Teachers of English.

Molnar, A. (1999). *Integrating the schoolhouse and the marketplace: A preliminary assessment of the emerging role of electronic technology.* Milwaukee, WI: University of Wisconsin, Center for the Analysis of Commercialism in Education.

Moreno, R. & Mayer, R. E. (1999). Cognitive principles of multimedia learning: The role of modality and contiguity. *Journal of Educational Psychology, 91*(2), 358–368.

Morison, S. H. (1990). A Spanish–English dual language program in New York City. In C. B. Cazden & C. E. Snow (Eds.), *English plus: Issues in bilingual education. The annals of the American Academy of Political and Social Sciences* (pp. 160–169). Newbury Park, CA: Sage.

Morphett, M. V. & Washburne, C. (1931). When should children begin to read? *The Elementary School Journal, 31,* 496–503.

Morrow, K., Tracey, D., Woo, G., & Presley, M. (1999). Characteristics of exemplary first-grade literacy instruction. *The Reading Teacher, 52*(5), 462–476.

Morrow, L. (1990). Small group story readings. *Reading Research and Instruction, 29,* 1–17.

Morrow, L. M. (1992). The impact of a literature-based program on literacy achievement, use of literature, and attitudes of children from minority backgrounds. *Reading Research Quarterly, 27*(3), 250–276.

Morrow, L. M. (1993). The impact of independent reading and writing periods on literacy achievement, use of literature, and attitude. *The Reading Teacher, 47*(3), 160–167.

Morrow, L. M. & Newman, S. B. (1995). Introduction: Family literacy. *The Reading Teacher, 48*(7) 550–551.

Morrow, L. M. & Rand, M. K. (1991). Promoting literacy during play by designing early childhood classroom environments. *The Reading Teacher, 44*(6), 396–406.

Morrow, R. D. (1991). The challenge of Southeast Asian parental involvement. *Principal, 70*(3) 20–22.

Murray, D. (1982). Teaching the other self: The writer's first reader. *College Composition and Communication, 23,* 140–147.

Murray, D. (1984). *Write to learn.* New York: Holt, Rinehart & Winston.

Murray, D. (1989). *Literacy development in the early years.* Englewood Cliffs, NJ: Prentice Hall.

Muter, V. & Snowling, M. (1998). Concurrent and longitudinal predictors of reading: The role of metalinguistic and short-term memory skills. *Reading Research Quarterly, 33*(3), 320–337.

Myers, C. (1992). Overcoming peer pressure: Teaching students to do so. Unpublished manuscript. Fort Worth, TX: Texas Christian University.

Nagy, W. & others. (1989). Morphological families in the internal lexicon. *Reading Research Quarterly, 24*(3), 262–281.

Nagy, W. E. & Herman, P. A. (1984). Incidental vs. instructional approaches to increasing reading vocabulary. *Educational Perspective, 23,* 16–21.

National Assessment of Educational Progress. (1987, June). *Reading objectives 1986 and 1988 assessments.* Princeton, NJ: NAEP, Educational Testing Services.

National Center for Education Statistics. (1993). *Language spoken at home and ability to speak English in United States, regions, and states, 1990.* CPH-L-133. Washington, DC: Author.

National Council of Teachers of English. (1987). *The teaching of formal grammar.* Urbana, IL: National Council of Teachers of English.

National Council of Teachers of English. (1995). *Teaching storytelling.* Urbana, IL: National Council of Teachers of English.

National Council of Teachers of English. (1996). *Standards for the English language arts.* Urbana, IL: National Council of Teachers of English & International Reading Association.

National Council of Teachers of English/ International Reading Association. (1998). *Standards for reading professionals.* Newark, DE: International Reading Association.

National Reading Panel Progress Report. (1999). *Reading progress in America preliminary report.* Washington, DC: National Research Council.

National Society for the Study of Education. (1948). *The forty-seventh yearbook, Part II* (p. 291). Chicago: Author.

Natriello, G., McDill, E. L., & Pallas, A. M. (1990). *Schooling disadvantaged children: Racing against catastrophe.* New York: Teachers College Press.

Neeley, J. (Ed.). (1993, September–October). Tall tales for short listeners. *Quality Time, 7,* 111–120.

Nessel, D. D. & Jones, M. B. (1981). *The language experience approach to reading: A handbook for teachers.* New York: Teachers College Press.

Newell, G. E. & Durst, R. K. (Eds.). (1993). *Exploring texts: The role of discussion and writing in the teaching and learning of literature.* Norwood, MA: Christopher-Gordon.

Newmann, F. M. (1991, February). Linking restructuring to authentic student achievement. *Phi Delta Kappan, 72*(6), 458–464.

Nickerson, R. S. (1995). Can technology help teach for understanding? In D. Perkins (Ed.), *Understanding.* New York: Oxford Press.

Nieto, S. (1999). *The light in their eyes: Creating multicultural learning communities.* New York: Teachers College Press.

Noden, H. R. (1999). *Image grammar: Using grammatical structures to teach writing.* Portsmouth, NH: Boynton/Cook.

Noll, E., Lindahl, C. V., & Salazar, D. (1998). Supporting active and reflective response to multicultural learning. In J. E. Brown & E. C. Stephens (Eds.), *United in diversity* (pp. 98–99). Urbana, IL: National Council of Teachers of English.

Noll, E., Lindahl, C. V., Valencia, C., & Salazar, D. (1998). Supporting active and reflective response to multicultural literature. In E. Noll (Ed.), *United in diversity* (p. 97). Urbana, IL: National Council of Teachers of English.

Norton, D. E. (1993). *The effective teaching of language arts* (4th ed.). New York: Merrill.

Norton, D. M. (1995). *Through the eyes of a child: An introduction to children's literature* (3rd ed.). Columbus, OH: Merrill.

Norwicki, S. & Duke, M. (1994). Why don't some students fit in? *Learning, 22*(8), 18–21.

Noyce, C. (1983). Effects of an integrated approach to grammar instructions on third graders' reading and writing. *Elementary School Journal, 84,* 63–69.

Noyce, R. M. & Christie, J. F. (1989). *Integrating reading and writing instruction in grades k–8.* Boston: Allyn & Bacon.

Nystrand, D. (1989, March). Sharing words: The effects of readers on developing writers. Address to American Educational Research Association, Division C, San Francisco, CA.

Nystrand, M. (1991, April). On the negotiation of understanding between students and teachers: Towards a social-interactive model of school learning. Paper presented at the American Educational Research Association, Chicago, IL.

O'Flahavan, J. (1989, December). Spelling pattern regularities and decoding. Paper presented at the annual meeting of the National Reading Conference, Charleston, SC.

O'Flahavan, J., Stein, R., Wiencek, V., & Marks, R. (1992, December). Decoding pattern recognition and teacher empowerment. Paper presented at the annual meeting of the National Reading Conference, Austin, TX.

O'Hare, F. (1973). *Sentence combining: Improving student writing without formal grammar instruction.* Urbana, IL: National Council of Teachers of English.

O'Keefe, D. (1994). Multiculturalism and cultural literacy. *International Journal of Social Education, 9*(1), 66–80.

O'Neill, S. (1991, September). Some resilient kids. *Educational Leadership, 8,* 626–633.

Oakes, J. (1986) Tracking, inequality, and the rhetoric of school reform. *Journal of Education, 168,* 61–80.

Ogle, D. (1989). The know, want to know, learn strategy. In K. D. Muth (Ed.), *Children's comprehension of text: Research into practice* (pp. 401–420). Newark, DE: International Reading Association.

Ogle, D. (1994). Developing problem-solving through language arts instruction. In C. Collins & J. Mangieri (Eds.), *Thinking development* (pp. 217–230). Hillsdale, NJ: Lawrence Erlbaum.

Olson, D. R. (1977). From utterance to text: The bias of language in speech and writing. *Harvard Educational Review, 47,* 257–281.

Onosko, J. & Newmann, F. (1994). Establishing thoughtful classrooms. In J. Mangieri & C. Collins Block (Eds.), *Advanced educational psychology: Creating effective schools and powerful thinkers* (pp. 231–245). Fort Worth, TX: Harcourt Brace Jovanovich.

Orton, S. J. (1928). Special reading disability strephosymbolia. *Journal of American Medical Association, XC,* 1095–1099.

Osborn, J., Stahl, S., & Stein, M. (1997). *Teachers' guidelines for evaluating commercial phonics packages.* Newark, DE: International Reading Association.

Osburg, B. J. (1989). The student-centered classroom: Speaking and listening in American literature. In P. Phetan (Ed.), *Talking to learn* (pp. 509–530). Urbana, IL: National Council of Teachers of English.

Owens, R. (1984). *Language development.* Columbus, OH: Charles E. Merrill.

Page, W. D. & Pinnell, G. S. (1979). *Teaching reading comprehension.* Urbana, IL: National Council of Teachers of English.

Palinscar, A. S. & Brown, A. L. (1984). Reciprocal teaching of comprehension-fostering and comprehension-monitoring activities. *Cognition and Instruction, 1*(2), 117–175.

Paradis, E. E. & others. (1991). Accountability: Assessing comprehension during literature discussion. *The Reading Teacher, 45*(1), 8–18.

Paris, S. G., Lipson, M. Y., & Wixson, K. K. (1983). Becoming a strategic reader. *Contemporary Educational Psychology, 17,* 293–316.

Parks, J. H. & Parks, J. E. (1992). Combining music instruction with reading instruction. Unpublished manuscript. Topeka, KA: Washburn University.

Paul, R. (1990). *Critical thinking handbook: 4th, 6th grades: A guide for remodeling lesson plans in language arts, social studies, and science.* Rehnert Park, CA: Sonoma State University, Center for Critical Thinking and Moral Critique.

Pearson, D. & Stephens, D. (1995). Learning about literacy. In R. Ruddell & H. Singer (Eds.), *Theoretical models and processes of reading* (pp. 177–199). Newark, DE: International Reading Association.

Pearson, P. D. (1985). Changing the face of reading comprehension instruction. *The Reading Teacher, 38*(8), 724–738.

Peck, M., Askov, E. N., & Fairchild, S. H. (1980). Another decade of research in handwriting: Progress and prospect in the 1970s. *Journal of Educational Research, 73,* 283–298.

Peregoy, S. & Owen, F. (1993). *Reading, writing, and learning in ESL.* New York: Longman.

Perkins, D. (1984). Creativity by design. *Educational Leadership, 47*(1), 18–25.

Perkinson, H. (1991). *The imperfect panacea: American faith in education, 1865–1990.* New York: Random House.

Peterson, R. (1992). *Life in a crowded place: Making a learning community.* Portsmouth, NH: Heinemann.

Petrosky, T. (1977). *The teaching of writing.* Chicago, IL: National Society for the Study of Education.

Pflaum, S. W. (1986). *The development of language and literacy in young children* (3rd ed.). Columbus, OH: Merrill.

Pflomm, P. N. (1986). *Chalk in hand: The draw and tell book.* Metchen, NJ: Scarecrow Press.

Phelan, P., Yu, H. C., & Davidson, A. L. (1994). Navigating the psychosocial pressures of adolescence: The voices and experiences of high school youth. *American Educational Research Journal, 31*(2), 415–447.

Piaget, J. (1963). *The origins of intelligence in children.* New York: W. W. Norton.

Piaget, J. (1969). *The psychology of the child.* New York: Basic Books.

Pierce, K. M. & Gilles, C. J. (1993). *Cycles of meaning.* Portsmouth, NH: Heinemann.

Pierson, C. A. (1992). Letter-writing in kindergarten. Unpublished manuscript. San Marcos, TX: Southwest Texas State University.

Pike, G. (1991). The effects of background, coursework, and involvement on students' grades and satisfaction. *Research in Higher Education, 32*(1), 15–30.

Pils, L. J. (1991). Soon anofc you tout me: Evaluation in a first-grade whole language classroom. *The Reading Teacher, 45*(1), 46–50.

Platt, M. (1994). Grandparents who parent their grandchildren. *Gerontologist, 34*(2), 206–216.

Porter, A. & Brophy, J. (1988). Syntheseis of research on good teaching. *Educational Leadership, 45*(8), 74–85.

Postlethwaite, T. N. & Ross, K. N. (1992). *Effective schools in reading.* The Hague: International Association for the Evaluation of Educational Achievement.

Powell, W. (1992). Goals for the language arts program: Toward a democratic view. *Language Arts, 69*(5), 342–349.

Prater, D. & Terry, C. A. (1985). The effects of a composing model on 5th grade students' reading comprehension. Presented at the 69th annual meeting of the American Educational Research Association, Chicago, IL.

Prawat, R. S. (1991). The value of ideas: The immension. *Educational Researcher, 20*(2), 3–10, 30.

Presseisen, B. (1987). Teaching thinking and at-risk students. *Educational Research and Improvement, 7*(1), 77.

Pressley, M. (1989). Strategies that improve children's memory and comprehension of text. *Elementary School Journal, 90*, 3–32.

Pressley, M. (1991, April). Direct explanation done well: Transactional instruction of reading comprehension strategies. Paper presented at a meeting of the American Educational Research Association, Chicago, IL.

Pressley, M. & Harris, K. (1990). What we really know about strategy instruction. *Educational Leadership, 48*(1), 319–370

Pressley, M., Harris, K., & Guthrie, J. (1995). Mapping the cutting edge in primary level literacy instruction for weak and at-risk readers. In D. Scrubles & M. Mastopieri (Eds.), *Advances in learning and behavioral disabilities* (pp. 399–417). Greenwich, CT: JAI Press.

Pressley, M., Harris, K. R., & Marks, M. B. (1991). But strategy instructors are constructionists!! *Educational Psychologist, 34* (4), 346–378.

Pressley, M., Wharton-McDonald, R., Allington, R., Block, C., & Morrow, L. (2000, December). First grade reading achievement. Paper presented at the annual meeting of the National Reading Conference, Scottsdale, AZ.

Pritchard, F. (1992). Concept spin. Unpublished manuscript. Salisbury, MD: Salisbury State University.   AU: Pg #?

Purcell-Gates, V. (1991). On the outside looking in: A study of remedial readers' meaning-making while reading literature. *Journal of Reading Behavior, XXIII*(2), 235–253.

Purcell-Gates, V. (1999, April). Listening to children's voices. Paper presented at the annual meeting of the American Educational Research Association, San Francisco, CA.

Purcell-Gates, V., Allen, L., & Smith, D. (1995). Literacy at the Hart's and the Larson's: Diversity among poor, inner-city families. *The Reading Teacher, 48*(7) 572–578.

Purcell-Gates, V., McIntyre, E., & Freppon, P. (1995). Learning written storybook languages in school. *American Educational Research Journal, 32*(3), 659–685.

Purnele, K. N. & Solmon, R. T. (1991). The influence of technical illustrations on students' comprehension in geography. *Reading Research Quarterly, XXVI*(3), 277–296.

Putman, J. (1997). *Cooperative learning in diverse classrooms.* Upper Saddle River, NJ: Prentice Hall.

Ramos, F. & Krashen, S. (1998). The impact of one trip to the library: Making books available may be the best incentive for reading. *The Reading Teacher, 51*(7), 614.

Raphael, T. E. (1989). Teaching learners about sources of information for answering comprehension questions. *Journal of Reading, 27*, 303–311.

Raphael, T. E., McMahon, S. I., Goatley, V. J., Bentley, J. L., Boyd, F. B., Pardo, L. S., & Woodman, D. A. (1992). Research directions: Literature and discussion in the reading program. *Language Arts, 69*, 54–61.

Rasinski, T. (1999, March). *Principles of effective vocabulary instruction.* Speech delivered to Dallas Independent School District, Dallas, TX.

Rasinski, T. V. & Gillespie, C. S. (1992). *Sensitive issues: An annotated guide to children's literature k–6.* Phoenix, AZ: Onyx Press.

Rasinski, T. V. & Padak, N. O. (1990). Multicultural learning through children's literature. *Language Arts, 67*, 576–580.

Read, C. (1975). *Children's categorization of speech sounds in English.* Arlington, VA: ERIC Clearinghouse on Languages and Linguistics, ED 112 426.

Reed, A. J. S. (1988). *Comics to classics: A parent's guide to books for teens and preteens.* Newark, DE: International Reading Association.

Reed, P. L. & Roller, C. M. (1991). Moving learners toward independence: The power of scaffolded instruction. *The Reading Teacher, 44*(9), 648–656.

Reyhner, J. & Garcia, R. (1989). Helping minorities read better. *Reading Research and Instruction, 28*(3), 84–91.

Rhodes, L. K. & Shanklin, N. L. (1994). *Windows into literacy: Assessing learners k–8.* Portsmouth, NH: Heinemann.

Richards, J. C. & Gipe, J. P. (1992, February). Activating background knowledge: Strategies for beginning and poor readers. *The Reading Teacher, 45*(6), 551–560.

Richek, M. A. & Glick, L. C. (1991). Coordinating a literacy support program with classroom instruction. *The Reading Teacher, 44*(7), 474–479.

Rigg, P. & Allen, V. (1989). *When they don't all speak English.* Urbana, IL: National Council of Teachers of English.

Robinson, H. & others. (1990). *Reading comprehension instruction 1783–1987.* Newark, DE: International Reading Association.

Rodriques, P. (1983). Brainstorming. Paper presented at a meeting of the International Reading Association, Miami, FL.

Rogers, T. (1991). Students as literacy critics. *Journal of Reading Behavior, 23,* 391–423.

Rose, L. H. (1992). The writing cycle. Unpublished manuscript. Starkville, MS: Mississippi State University.

Rosenblatt, L. M. (1928). *Literature as exploration.* New York: Appleton-Century-Crofts.

Rosenblatt, L. M. (1978). *The reader, the text, the poem: The transactional theory of the literary work.* Carbondale, IL: Southern Illinois University Press.

Rosenblatt, L. M. (1982). The literary transaction: Evocation and response. *Theory into Practice, 21,* 268–277.

Rosenblatt, L. M. (1983). The reading transaction: What for? In R. P. Parker &

F. A. Daves (Eds.), *Developing literacy: Young children's use of language* (pp. 118–135). Newark, DE: International Reading Association.

Rosenblatt, L. M. (1985). Viewpoints: Transactions versus interaction—A terminological rescue operation. *Research in the Teaching of English, 19,* 96–107.

Rosenshine, B. & Furst, N. Research on teacher performance criteria. In B. O. Broudy (Ed.), *Research in teacher education* (pp. 714–737). Englewood Cliffs, NJ: Prentice Hall.

Rosenshine, B. & Stevens, R. (1984). Thinking functions. In M. C. Wittrock (Ed.), *Handbook of research on teaching* (3rd ed., pp. 376–391). New York: MacMillan.

Roskos, K. (1992). Free response with a sketch. Unpublished manuscript. University Heights, OH: John Carroll University.

Ross, R. (1995). Visualizing computer science. In D. Thomas (Ed.), *Scientific visualization in mathematics and science teaching.* Charlottesville, VA. AACE.

Routman, R. (1991). *Invitations: Changing as teachers and learners k–12.* Portsmouth, NH: Heinemann.

Routman, R. (1994). *Invitations.* Portsmouth, NH: Heinemann.

Routman, R. (2000). *Invitations* (2nd ed.). Portsmouth, NH: Heinemann.

Rubin, H. (1988). Morphological knowledge and early writing ability. *Language and Speech, 31,* 337–355.

Ruddell, R. B. (1997). Researching the influential literacy teacher: Characteristics, beliefs, strategies, and new research directions. In C. Kinzer and C. Leu (Ed.), *Inquiries in literacy theory and practice* (pp. 4–22). Chicago: National Reading Conference Yearbook.

Ruddell, R. B. & Haggard, M. R. (1985). Oral and written language acquisition and the reading process. In H. Singer & R. B. Ruddell (Eds.), *Theoretical models and processes of reading* (3rd ed., pp. 63–80). Newark, DE: International Reading Association.

Ruez, L. (1993). *The effect of homogeneous groupings in mathematics.* Washington, DC: Office of Educational Research and Improvement.

Rumelhart, D. E. (1980). Schemata: The building blocks of cognition. In R. J.

Spiro, B. C. Bruce, & W. F. Brewer (Eds.), *Theoretical issues in reading comprehension* (pp. 33–58). Hillsdale, NJ: Erlbaum.

Rupley, W. H. & Blair, T. R. (1989). *Remedial diagnosis and remediation* (3rd ed.). Columbus, OH: Merrill.

Russell, D. (1948–1951). *The ginn basic readers.* Third reader manual II. Boston: Ginn.

Sadoski, M. & others. (1990). Imagination in story reading: The role of imagery, verbal recall, story analysis, and processing levels. *Journal of Reading Behavior, XXII* (1), 55–70.

Sakiey, E. & Fry, E. (1984). *3,000 instant words* (2nd ed.). Providence, RI: Jamestown.

Salinger, T. (1992). Critical thinking and young literacy learners. In C. Collins & J. Mangieri (Eds.), *Teaching thinking.* Hillsdale, NJ: Lawrence Erlbaum.

Salomon, G. & Perkins, D. N. (1998). Individual and social aspects of learning. *Review of Research in Education, 23,* 1–24.

Samuels, S. J. (1988). Decoding and automaticity: Helping poor readers become automatic at word recognition. *The Reading Teacher, 41,* 756–760.

Santa, C. (1992). Finding main idea grid. *The Reading Teacher, 45*(4), 334–335.

Scardamalia, P. & Bereiter, J. (1984). Development of strategies in text processing. In H. P. Mandl, N. L. Stein, & T. Trabasso (Eds.), *Learning and comprehension of text* (pp. 379–406). Hillsdale, NJ: Erlbaum.

Schank, R. (1990, December). Pattern recognition theory. Paper presented at the National Research Conference, San Diego, CA.

Schecter, S. & Parkhurst, S. (1995). *Ideological divergences in a teacher research group* (Revised). Washington, DC: Office of Educational Research and Improvement.

Schiøenz, J. (1998). Early writing stages. Paper presented at the annual meeting of the International Reading Association, Orlando, FL.

Schifini, A. (1994). Language, literacy, and content instruction: Strategies for teachers. In K. Spangenberg-Urbschat (Ed.), *Kids come in all languages: Reading instruction for ESL students* (pp. 158–179). Newark, DE: International Reading Association.

Schmelzer, R. V. (1992). Teaching metacognitive thinking. Unpublished manuscript. Richmond: Eastern Kentucky University.

Schneider, B. & Yongsoak, L. (1991). School and home environment of East Asian students. *Anthropology and Educational Quarterly, 16*(2), 117–128.

Schunk, D. (1991). Self-efficacy and academic motivation. *Educational Psychologist, 26,* 207–231.

Schunk, D. H. & Rice, J. M. (1989). Learning goals and children's reading comprehension. *Journal of Reading Behavior, 21*(3), 279–293.

Scott, L. (1992). Introducing classroom rules in kindergartens. Unpublished manuscript. St. Cloud, MN: St. Cloud State University.

Seidenberg, R. & McClelland, S. (1989). A disturbed, developmental model of word recognition and naming. *Psychological Review, 96,* 523–568.

Sendak, M. (1989). *Imagination.* Videotape from Edwards Film Company, London, England.

Shanahan, T. (1988). The reading–writing relationship: Seven instructional principles. *The Reading Teacher, 41,* 636–647.

Shanahan, T. (1991). New literacy goes to school. Whole language in the classroom. *Educational Horizons, 69*(3) 146–151.

Shanahan T. (1996). Reading–writing relationships, thematic units inquiry learning . . . In pursuit of effective literacy instruction. *The Reading Teacher, 51*(1), 12–19.

Shephard, A. (1991). Negative policies for dealing with diversity: When does assessment and diagnosis turn into sorting and segregation? In E. H. Hiebert (Ed.), *Literacy for a diverse society: Perspectie, practices and policies* (pp. 279–298). New York: Teachers College Press.

Short, K. (Ed.). (1995). *Research and professional resources in children's literature.* Newark, DE: International Reading Association.

Short, K. & Armstrong, J. (1993). Moving toward inquiry. *The New Advocate, 6*(3), 183–197.

Short, K. G. & Pierce, C. (1990). Examining our beliefs and practices through inquiry. *Language Arts, 73*(2), 97–104.

Shuman, R. B. (1991). A portfolio approach to evaluating student writing. *Educational Leadership, 48*(8), 77.

Shuy, R. W. (1987). Research currents: Dialogue as the heart of learning. *Language Arts, 64,* 890–897.

Siegel, R. (1995). *Children's thinking* (2nd ed.). Englewood Cliffs, NJ: Prentice Hall.

Singer, H. & Ruddell, R. (1985b). *Theoretical models and processes of reading* (3rd ed.). Newark, DE: International Reading Association.

Skinner, B. J. (1957). *Verbal behavior.* Boston: Appleton-Century-Crofts.

Skolnick, J. & Frazier, J. (1998, April). A new view of composing. Paper presented at the annual meeting of the American Educational Research Association, New York.

Smey-Richman, B. (1988). *Involvement in learning for low-achieving students.* Philadelphia: Research for Better Schools.

Smith, F. (1971). *Understanding reading.* New York: Holt, Rinehart & Winston.

Smith, F. (1975). *Comprehension and learning.* New York: Holt, Rinehart & Winston.

Smith, F. (1978). *Understanding reading* (2nd ed.). New York: Holt, Rinehart & Winston.

Smith, F. (1982). *Understanding reading* (3rd ed.). New York: Holt, Rinehart & Winston.

Smith, F. (1985). *Reading without nonsense.* New York: Teachers College Press

Smith, F. (1988a). *Insult to intelligence: The bureaucratic invasion of our classrooms.* Portsmouth, NH: Heinemann.

Smith, F. (1988b). *Joining the literacy club.* Portsmouth, NH: Heinemann.

Smith, M. L. (1991). Put to the test: The effects of external testing on teachers. *Educational Researchers, 20,* 8–11.

Smith, R. (1990). *Understanding reading* (4th ed.). New York: Holt, Rinehart & Winston.

Snow, R. & Ninio, C. (1986). Contracts of literacy. In W. Teale & E. Sulzby (Eds.), *Emergent literacy* (pp. 116–138). Norwood, NJ: Ablex.

Sowers, C. (1986). Three responses in the writing conference. In N. Thomas & N. Atwell (Eds.), *Understanding writing* (pp. 221–240). Portsmouth, NH: Heinemann.

Sowers, S. (1985). The story and the "all about" book. In J. Hansen, T. Newkirk, & D. Graves (Eds.), *Breaking ground* (pp. 73–82). Portsmouth, NH: Heinemann.

Spencer, H. (1914). *The principles of psychology.* New York: Appleton.

Spiegel, D. L. (1995). A comparison of traditional remedial programs and reading recovery guidelines for success for all programs. *The Reading Teacher, 49*(2), 86–96.

Spiegel, D. L. (1998). Reader response approaches and the growth of readers. *Language Arts, 76,* 41–47.

Squire, J. R. (1989). For better textbooks. *English Journal, 78*(6), 14–21.

Stahl, S. A., Duffy-Hester, A. M., & Stahl, K. A. D. (1998). Everything you wanted to know about phonics (but were afraid to ask). *Reading Research Quarterly, 33,* 338–355.

Standards & Assessment Development & Implementation. (1995). Council of the State of Colorado.

Stanley, D. (1990). *The conversation club.* New York: Aladdin Books.

Stanovich, K. (1980). Toward an interactive-compensatory model of individual differences in the development of reading fluency. *Reading Research Quarterly, 16,* 32–71.

Stanovich, K. E. & Cunningham, A. E. (1993). Where does knowledge come from? Specific associations between print exposure and information acquisition. *Journal of Educational Psychology, 85,* 211–229.

Staton, J. (1980). Writing and counseling: Using a dialogue journal. *Language Arts, 57,* 514–518.

Staton, J. & others. (1988). *Dialogue journal communication: Classroom linguistic, social, and cognitive views.* Norwood, NJ: Ablex.

Stauffer, R. (1969). *Directed reading and thinking approach.* Urbana, IL: National Council of Teachers of English.

Stauffer, R. (1980, May). DLTA: Directed listening thinking activity. Paper presented at the annual meeting of the International Reading Association, New York.

Steig, J. (1995). *Alpha, beta, chowder.* New York: Trumpet.

Stein, R. & Kirby, W. (1992). The effects of text absent and text present conditions on summarization and recall of text. *Journal of Reading, 24*(2), 217.

Stern, J. (Ed.). (1994). *The condition of education in rural schools.* Washington, DC: Department of Education.

Sternberg, R. & Horvath, J. (1995). A prototype view of expert teaching. *Educational Researcher, 24*(6), 9–16.

Sternberg, R. J. (1985). *Beyond IQ.* New York: Cambridge University Press.

Sternberg, R. J. & Lubant, T. (1991). Creativity reconsidered. *Educational Researcher, 20*(8), 4–14.

Sternberg, R. J. & Lubart, T. I. (1995). *Defying the crowd: Cultivating creativity in a culture of conformity.* New York: Free Press.

Stevens, R. J. & others. (1987). Cooperative integrated reading and composition: Two field experiments. *Reading Research Quarterly, XXII*(4), 433–454.

Stevens, R. J. & Slavin, R. E. (1995). The cooperative elementary school: Effects on students' achievement, attitudes and social relations. *American Educational Research Journal, 32*(2), 321–351.

Sticht, T. & James, J. (1984). Listening and reading. In P. D. Pearson (Ed.), *Handbook of reading research* (pp. 888–920). White Plains, NY: Longman.

Stiggins, R. & Bridgeford, N. (1985). The ecology of classroom assessment. *Journal of Educational Measurement, 22,* 271–286.

Stotsky, S. (1983). Research on reading/writing relationships: A synthesis and suggested directions. *Language Arts, 60*(5), 627–642.

Stotsky, S. L. (1975). Sentence-combining as a curricular activity: Its effects on written language development and reading comprehension. *Research in the Teaching of English, 9,* 30–71.

Stotsky, S. L. (1989). Differences in search process between high school and college seniors, and a comparison with search process of students who have difficulty writing. Paper presented at the American Educational Research Association meeting, New Orleans, LA.

Strickland, D. S. (1998). *Teaching phonics today: A primer for educators.* Newark, DE: International Reading Association.

Strickland, R. (1962, July). The language of elementary school children. *Indiana University Bulletin of School of Education, 38,* 1–131.

Stuart, V. & Graves, D. (1987). *How to teach writing.* Urbana, IL: National Council of Teachers of English.

Sulzby, E. (1994). Computer writing instruction in early literacy. In J. Magieri & C. Collins Block (Eds.), *Advanced educational psychology: Creating effective schools and powerful thinkers* (pp. 421–439). Fort Worth, TX: Harcourt, Brace, Jovanovich.

Sulzby, E., Teale, W. H., & Kamberelis, G. (1989). Emergent writing in the classroom: Home and school connections. In D. S. Strickland & L. M. Morrow (Eds.), *Emergent literacy: Young children learn to read and write* (pp. 231–249). Newark, DE: International Reading Association.

Suzuik, B. H. (1979). Multicultural education: What's it all about? *Integrate Education, 12,* 43–49.

Svotlovskaya, N. (1992, May). Children who do not read well. Paper presented to U.S. Citizen Ambassadors Reading Delegation, University of Moscow.

Sylvester, R. (1995). *A celebration of neurons: An educator's guide to the human brain.* Arlington, VA: Association of Supervision and Curriculum Development.

Sylvester, R. (1998). Art for the brain's sake. *Educational Leadership: How the Brain Learns, 56*(3), 31–35.

Taba, H. (1975). New Social Studies curriculum models. Paper presented at the National Council of Social Studies Teachers, Boston, MA.

Tannen, D. (1985). Relative focus on involvement in oral and written discourse. In D. R. Olson, N. Torrance, & A. Hildyard (Eds.), *Literacy, language and learning: The nature and consequences of reading and writing* (pp. 124–147). Cambridge: Cambridge University Press.

Teale, W. H. (1986) Home background and young children's literacy development. In W. H. Teale & E. Sulzby (Eds.), *Emergent literacy: Writing and reading* (pp. 173–206). Norwood, NJ: Ablex.

Teale, W. H. & Sulzby, E. (1986). *Emergent literacy: Writing and reading.* Norwood, NJ: Ablex.

Temple, C. & others. (1988). *The beginning of writing.* Boston: Allyn & Bacon.

Tenney, Y. J. (1980). Visual factors in spelling. In U. Frith (Ed.), *Cognitive processes in spelling* (pp. 22–39). London: Academic Press.

Texas Education Agency. (1994). Characteristics of at-risk youth. Austin, TX: Texas Education Agency Practitioner's Guide, Series Number One.

Thomson, J. (1987). *Understanding teenagers' reading: Reading processes and the teaching of literature.* New York: Nicols.

Tiedt, P. H. & Tiedt, I. M. (1995). *Multicultural teaching: A handbook of activities, information, and resources* (4th ed.). Boston: Allyn & Bacon.

Tierney, R. (1998). Literacy assessment reform: Shifting beliefs, principled possibilities, and emerging practices. *The Reading Teacher, 51*(5), 374.

Tierney, R., Carter, M., & Desai, L. (1991). *Portfolio assessment in the reading–writing classroom.* Norwood, NJ: Christopher-Gordon.

Tierney, R. J. & Shanahan, T. (1991). Research on the reading–writing relationship: Interactions, transactions, and outcomes. In R. Barr & others (Eds.), *Handbook of reading research* (Vol. 2, pp. 246–280). White Plains, NY: Longman.

Tierney, R. J., Readeance, J. E., & Dishner, E. K. (1990). *Reading strategies and practices, a compendium* (3rd ed.). Boston: Allyn & Bacon.

Tompkins, G. & Hoskisson, K. (1995). *Language arts* (3rd ed.). Des Moines, IA: Prentice Hall.

Travers, P. (1992). The importance of teaching creativity in our schools. Unpublished manuscript. Weatherford: Southwestern Oklahoma State University.

Travers, R. (1982). *Essentials of learning: The new cognitive learning of students in education.* New York: Macmillan.

Tudge, J. (1988). Cooperative problem solving in the classroom: Enhancing young children's cognitive development. *Young Children, 44,* 46–52.

Turner, A. & Paris, S. (1995). How literacy tasks influence children's motivation for literacy. *Reading Teacher, 48*(8), 662–673.

Udall, A. J. & Daniels, J. E. (1991). *Creating the thoughtful classroom: Strategies to promote student thinking.* Tucson, AZ: Zephyr Press.

Unrau, N. & Ruddell, R. (1995). Interpreting texts in classroom context. *Journal of Adolescent and Adult Literacy, 39*(1), 15–27.

Unsworth, L. (1999). Developing critical understanding of the specialized language of school science and history texts: A functional grammatical perspective. *Journal of Adolescent and Adult Literacy, 42*(7), 508–521.

Urzua, C. (1989). I grow for a living. In P. Rigg & V. G. Allen (Eds.), *When they don't all speak English: Integrating the ESL student into the regular classroom* (pp. 104–110). Urbana, IL: National Council of Teachers of English.

Valdés, R. (1996). *Second language development: Principles.* Educational Practice Report, No. 13. Santa Cruz, CA: National Center for Research on Cultural Diversity and Second Language Learning.

Valencia, S. & Pearson, P. D. (1987). Reading and assessment: Time for a change. *The Reading Teacher, 40,* 726–732.

Valencia, S. W. & Lipson, M. Y. (1998). Thematic instruction: A quest for challenging ideas and meaningful learning. In M. Lipson (Ed.), *Literature-based instruction: Reshaping the curriculum* (pp. 61–72). Norwood, MA: Gordon.

Valeri-Gold, M., Olson, J. R., & Deming, M. P. (1991–1992). Portfolios: Collaborative authentic assessment opportunities for college development learners. *Journal of Reading, 35*(4), 298–304.

Van den Bosch, K., Van Bon, W., & Schreuder, R. (1995). Poor readers' decoding skills. *Reading Research Quarterly, 30*(1), 110–125.

Vasquez, O. (1993). A look at language as a resource. In B. Arias & U. Casanova (Eds.), *Bilingual education* (pp. 6–26). Chicago: NSSE.

Vauras, M., Kinnunen, R., & Kuusela, A. (1994). Development of text processing skills in high, average and low achieving primary school children. *Journal of Reading Behavior, 26*(4), 361–389.

Veatch, J. (1991, April). Individualized reading was the beginning of the whole language approach. Paper presented at meeting of the International Reading Association, Las Vegas, NV.

Verhoeven, L. (1987). Literacy in a second language context. *Educational Reading, 39*(3), 245–261.

Villaume, S. (1994). Developing literate voices. *Language Arts, 66*(3), 460–468.

Vygotsky, L. (1962). *Thought and language.* Cambridge, MA: MIT Press.

Vygotsky, L. (1978). *Mind and society.* Cambridge, MA: Harvard University Press.

Vygotsky, L. S. (1979). *Thought and language* (Rev. ed.) A. Kozulin (Trans. & Ed.) Cambridge, MA: MIT Press.

Walker, B. (1992). Guidelines for instruction. In E. Hiebert (Ed.), *Literacy in a diverse society* (pp. 23–39). New York: McGraw-Hill.

Walmsley, S. (1992). State of elementary literature instruction. *Language Arts, 64*(3), 508–514.

Wardhaugh, R. (1971). Theories of language acquisition in relation to beginning reading instruction. In F. B. Davis (Ed.), *The literature of research in reading with emphasis in models* (pp. 337–349). New York: McGraw Hill.

Wasik, B. A. (1998). Volunteer tutoring programs in reading: A review. *Reading Research Quarterly, 33*(3), 266–292.

Wasserstein, P. (1995). How children learn. *Educational Leadership, 71*(1), 39–43.

Watkins, E. (1922). *How to teach silent reading to beginners.* Chicago: Lippincott.

Watson, R. (1979). *Psychology of the child and adolescent.* New York: Macmillan.

Weaver, C. (Ed.). (1998). *Lessons to share: On teaching grammar.* Portsmouth, NH: Boynton/Cook.

Weaver, C. H. & Kintsch, W. (1991). Expository text. In R. Barr & others (Eds.), *Handbook of reading research* (Vol. II, pp. 230–245). New York: Longman.

Webb, N., Newman, K., Chizhik, A., & Sugrue, B. (1998). Equity issues in collaborative group assessment: Group composition and performance. *American Educational Research Journal, 35*(4), 607–657.

Weinberger, N. (1998). The music in our minds. *Educational Leadership: How the Brain Learns, 56*(3), 38.

Weisberg, R. & Balajthy, E. (1991). Transfer effects of prior knowledge and use of graphic organizers on college development readers' summarization and comprehension of expository text. In J. Zutell & S. McCormick (Eds.), *Literacy theory and research: Analysis from multiple paradigms* (pp. 339–346). Chicago: National Reading Conference.

Wells, D. (1995). Leading grand conversations. In N. Roser & M. Martinez (Eds.), *Book talk and beyond* (pp. 263–271). Newark, DE: International Reading Association.

Wells, G. (1986). *The meaning makers: Children learning language and using language to learn.* Portsmouth, NH: Heinemann.

Wells, G. (1993). Text, talk, and inquiry. Paper presented at conference of International Reading Association, Hong Kong.

Wells, R. (1997). *Noisy Nora.* New York: Dial.

Wepner, S. (1992). How to help your child become a better writer. Unpublished manuscript. Wayne: William Paterson College of New Jersey.

Werner, E. (1982). *Vulnerable but invincible: A longitudinal study of resilient children and youth* (2nd ed.). New York: McGraw-Hill.

Werner, J. (1994). *Reaching out to the world.* Austin, TX: Annual Conference of the ACRES.

West, M. (1995). Perceptions of home schools continuity among culturally different parents. Paper presented at American Educational Research Association meeting, San Francisco.

White, R., Sowell, J., & Yanagihare, G. (1989). Teaching elementary students to use word–part clues. *The Reading Teacher, 42,* 302–308.

Whitehurst, G., Zevenbergen, F. L., Crone, C., Schultz, R., Veltiz, M., & Fischel M. (1999). Accelerating language development through picturebook reading. *Journal of Educational Psychology, 93*(5), 501–510.

Whitin, D. J. & Wilde, S. (1992). *Read any good math lately?* Portsmouth, NH: Heinemann.

Wigfield, A., Eccles, J. S., & Rodriguez, D. (1998). The development of children's motivation in school contexts. *Review of Research in Education, 23,* 73–118.

Wiggins, G. (1989). Teaching to the authentic test. *Educational Leadership, 46* (7), 41–47.

Wiggins, G. & McTighe, J. (1998). *Understanding by design.* Alexandria, VA: Association for Supervision and Curriculum Development.

Wilde, S. (1989a). Looking at invented spelling: A kidwatcher's guide to spelling, part 1. In K. Goodman & others (Eds.), *The whole language evaluation book* (pp. 71–84). Portsmouth, NH: Heinemann.

Wilde, S. (1989b). Understanding spelling strategies: A kidwatcher's guide to spelling, part 2. In K. Goodman & others (Eds.), *The whole language evaluation book* (pp. 85–89). Portsmouth, NH: Heinemann.

Wilhem, J. D. (1998). Dramatic encounters: Experiencing multicultural literature. In J. E. Brown & E. C. Stephens (Eds.), *United in diversity* (pp. 22–27, 117). Urbana, IL: National Council of Teachers of English.

Willard, N. (1981). *A visit to William Blake's Inn.* New York: Harcourt Brace.

Williams, J. (1991, April). Phonics: Success in first grade. Speech. Texas Christian University, Fort Worth, TX.

Wilson, L. (1994). *Write me a poem.* Portsmouth, NH: Heinemann.

Witrock, M. C. & Alesandrini, K. (1990). Generation of summaries and analogies and analytic and holistic abilities. *American Research Journal, 27,* 489–502.

Wixon, K., Valencia, S., & Lipson, M. (1994). Issues in literacy assessment: Facing the realities of internal and external assessment. *Journal of Reading Behavior, 26*(3), 315.

Wolf, D. (1991). To use their minds well: Investigating new forms of student assessment. In G. Grant (Ed.), *Review of research in education* (Vol. 17, pp. 31–75). Washington, DC: American Educational Research Association.

Wolf, D. P. (1989). *Reading reconsidered.* New York College Entrance Examination Board.

Wolf, S. (1998). The flight of reading: Shifts in instruction, orchestration, and attitudes through classroom theatre. *Reading Research Quarterly, 33*(4), 409.

Wolf, S. A., Mieras, E. L., & Carey, A. A. (1996). What's after: What's that: Preservice teachers training to ask literacy questions. *Journal of Literacy Research, 28*(4), 361–372.

Wolvin, A. D. & Coakley, C. G. (1979). *Listening instructions (TRIP Booklet).* Urbana, IL: ERIC Clearinghouse on Reading and Communication Association.

Wolvin, A. & Coakley, C. (1985). *Listening* (2nd ed.). Dubuque, IA: Wm. C. Brown.

Wolvin, A. & Coakley, G. (1998). *Listening* (4th ed.). Dubuque, IA: William Brown.

Wong, B. Y. L. (1987). How do the results of metacognitive research impact on the learning disabled individual. *Learning Disability Quarterly, 10,* 189–195.

Wood, J. W. (1993). *Mainstreaming: A practical approach for teachers* (2nd ed.). New York: Merrill/Macmillan.

Worchester, S. (1828). *Primer of the English language.* Boston: J. T. and E. B. Buckingham.

Worthy, J., Moorman, G., & Turner, J. (1999). What Johnny likes to read is hard to find in school. *Reading Research Quarterly, 48*(1), 12–27.

Wrenn, L. C. (1997). "P.S. I love the book!": Using dialogue journals in readers' workshop. *Primary Voices, 3*(1), 17–19.

Wright, J. & Speigel, D. (1983). Biology teachers use of readability concepts when selecting text for students. *Journal of Reading, 27*(1), 28–34.

Wuertenberg, J. (1986). Conferencing with young authors. Paper presented at the Annual Bill Martin Literary Conference, East Texas State University, Commerce, TX.

Wyshynski, R. & Paulsen, D. (1995). Maybe I will do something. *Language Arts, 72*(4), 258–264.

Yao, E. (1991). Adjustment needs of Asian immigrant children. *Elementary School Guidance and Counseling, 19*(1), 222–227.

Yochum, S. (1990). Children's learning informational text: The relationship between prior knowledge and text structure. *Journal of Reading Behavior, XXIII*(1), 87–104.

Yolen, J. (1985). The story between. *Language Arts, 62*(6), 590–592.

Youngblood, C. (1985, April). Language arts developmental stages and principles. Paper presented at the annual meeting of the American Educational Research Association, San Francisco.

Zabrucky, K. & Ratner, N. H. (1989). Effects of reading ability on children's comprehension evaluation and regulation. *Journal of Reading Behavior, 21,* 69–83.

Zane, N., Li-tze Hu, W., & Jung-Hye, K. (1991). Asian-American ascension. *Journal of Counseling Psychology, 38*(1), 63–70.

Zarnowski, M. (1991). An interview with author N. Mohr. *The Reading Teacher, 45*(2), 100–106.

Zarrilla, J. (1991). Theory becomes practice: Aesthetic teaching with literature. *The New Advocate, 4*(4) 221–234.

Zimmerman, B. (1999, April). Strategic transfer. Paper presented at the annual meeting of the American Educational Research Association, New York.

NAME INDEX

SUBJECT INDEX